Application of Various Hydrological Modeling Techniques and Methods in River Basin Management

Application of Various Hydrological Modeling Techniques and Methods in River Basin Management

Guest Editors

Ankur Srivastava
Venkat Sridhar
Nikul Kumari

Basel • Beijing • Wuhan • Barcelona • Belgrade • Novi Sad • Cluj • Manchester

Guest Editors

Ankur Srivastava
Faculty of Science
University of Technology
Sydney
Australia

Venkat Sridhar
Biological Systems
Engineering
Virginia Tech
Blacksburg
United States

Nikul Kumari
Faculty of Science
University of Technology
Sydney
Australia

Editorial Office
MDPI AG
Grosspeteranlage 5
4052 Basel, Switzerland

This is a reprint of the Special Issue, published open access by the journal *Water* (ISSN 2073-4441), freely accessible at: www.mdpi.com/journal/water/special_issues/Hydrological_Modeling_Techniques.

For citation purposes, cite each article independently as indicated on the article page online and using the guide below:

Lastname, A.A.; Lastname, B.B. Article Title. *Journal Name* **Year**, *Volume Number*, Page Range.

ISBN 978-3-7258-3096-1 (Hbk)
ISBN 978-3-7258-3095-4 (PDF)
https://doi.org/10.3390/books978-3-7258-3095-4

Cover image courtesy of Ankur Srivastava

© 2025 by the authors. Articles in this book are Open Access and distributed under the Creative Commons Attribution (CC BY) license. The book as a whole is distributed by MDPI under the terms and conditions of the Creative Commons Attribution-NonCommercial-NoDerivs (CC BY-NC-ND) license (https://creativecommons.org/licenses/by-nc-nd/4.0/).

Contents

About the Editors vii

Preface ix

Ankur Srivastava, Venkataramana Sridhar and Nikul Kumari
Application of Various Hydrological Modeling Techniques and Methods in River Basin Management
Reprinted from: *Water* 2025, 17, 83, https://doi.org/10.3390/w17010083 1

Heng Li, Zhiwei Zhang and Zhen Zhang
Improvement and Evaluation of CLM5 Application in the Songhua River Basin Based on CaMa-Flood
Reprinted from: *Water* 2024, 16, 442, https://doi.org/10.3390/w16030442 7

Liu Zhen and Alina Bărbulescu
Comparative Analysis of Convolutional Neural Network-Long Short-Term Memory, Sparrow Search Algorithm-Backpropagation Neural Network, and Particle Swarm Optimization-Extreme Learning Machine Models for the Water Discharge of the Buzu River, Romania
Reprinted from: *Water* 2024, 16, 289, https://doi.org/10.3390/w16020289 25

Cagri Alperen Inan, Ammar Maoui, Yann Lucas and Joëlle Duplay
Multi-Station Hydrological Modelling to Assess Groundwater Recharge of a Vast Semi-Arid Basin Considering the Problem of Lack of Data: A Case Study in Seybouse Basin, Algeria
Reprinted from: *Water* 2023, 16, 160, https://doi.org/10.3390/w16010160 52

Abhishek Patel, K. V. Ramana Rao, Yogesh A. Rajwade, Chandra Kant Saxena, Karan Singh and Ankur Srivastava
Comparative Analysis of MCDA Techniques for Identifying Erosion-Prone Areas in the Burhanpur Watershed in Central India for the Purposes of Sustainable Watershed Management
Reprinted from: *Water* 2023, 15, 3891, https://doi.org/10.3390/w15223891 71

Oliver Saavedra, Jhonatan Ureña and Moisés Perales
Implementation of HydroBID Model with Satellite-Based Precipitation Products in Guadalquivir Basin, Bolivia
Reprinted from: *Water* 2023, 15, 3250, https://doi.org/10.3390/w15183250 97

Zhaoxin Yue, Huaizhi Liu and Hui Zhou
Monthly Runoff Forecasting Using Particle Swarm Optimization Coupled with Flower Pollination Algorithm-Based Deep Belief Networks: A Case Study in the Yalong River Basin
Reprinted from: *Water* 2023, 15, 2704, https://doi.org/10.3390/w15152704 115

Jeong-Hyeok Ma, Chulsang Yoo, Sung-Uk Song, Wooyoung Na, Eunsaem Cho and Sang-Keun Song et al.
Different Effect of Cloud Seeding on Three Dam Basins, Korea
Reprinted from: *Water* 2023, 15, 2555, https://doi.org/10.3390/w15142555 140

Mohamed Abdelkader, Marouane Temimi and Taha B.M.J. Ouarda
Assessing the National Water Model's Streamflow Estimates Using a Multi-Decade Retrospective Dataset across the Contiguous United States
Reprinted from: *Water* 2023, 15, 2319, https://doi.org/10.3390/w15132319 169

Jhon B. Valencia, Vladimir V. Guryanov, Jeison Mesa-Diez, Jeimar Tapasco and Artyom V. Gusarov
Assessing the Effectiveness of the Use of the InVEST Annual Water Yield Model for the Rivers of Colombia: A Case Study of the Meta River Basin
Reprinted from: *Water* **2023**, *15*, 1617, https://doi.org/10.3390/w15081617 . . . . **194**

Pangam Heramb, K. V. Ramana Rao, A. Subeesh and Ankur Srivastava
Predictive Modelling of Reference Evapotranspiration Using Machine Learning Models Coupled with Grey Wolf Optimizer
Reprinted from: *Water* **2023**, *15*, 856, https://doi.org/10.3390/w15050856 . . . . **211**

Nageswara Reddy Nagireddy, Venkata Reddy Keesara, Venkataramana Sridhar and Raghavan Srinivasan
Streamflow and Sediment Yield Analysis of Two Medium-Sized East-Flowing River Basins of India
Reprinted from: *Water* **2022**, *14*, 2960, https://doi.org/10.3390/w14192960 . . . . **243**

Lixin Ning, Changxiu Cheng, Xu Lu, Shi Shen, Liang Zhang and Shaomin Mu et al.
Improving the Prediction of Soil Organic Matter in Arable Land Using Human Activity Factors
Reprinted from: *Water* **2022**, *14*, 1668, https://doi.org/10.3390/w14101668 . . . . **264**

Megersa Kebede Leta, Tamene Adugna Demissie and Jens Tränckner
Optimal Operation of Nashe Hydropower Reservoir under Land Use Land Cover Change in Blue Nile River Basin
Reprinted from: *Water* **2022**, *14*, 1606, https://doi.org/10.3390/w14101606 . . . . **285**

Anuradha Kumari, Akhilesh Kumar, Manish Kumar and Alban Kuriqi
Modeling Average Grain Velocity for Rectangular Channel Using Soft Computing Techniques
Reprinted from: *Water* **2022**, *14*, 1325, https://doi.org/10.3390/w14091325 . . . . **307**

About the Editors

Ankur Srivastava

Dr. Ankur Srivastava is a hydrologist focusing on critical challenges in sustainable water resource management. His research focuses on understanding ecohydrological processes, such as soil moisture variability, evapotranspiration, and the complex interactions between landforms and vegetation. By applying advanced hydrological models, machine learning techniques, and remote sensing data, he has worked on innovative solutions for water balance assessments, optimizing agricultural water use, and analyzing landscape dynamics.

He contributed to the first-ever modeling study to analyze the effect of coevolving landform–vegetation patterns under orographic precipitation. Dr. Srivastava played a crucial role in improving land surface modeling by changing the vegetation parametrization in the model using high-resolution satellite images. This work gained a high number of citations from top journals, signifying its significant contribution, which is remarkable in hydrology. His international collaborations span the USA, Japan, Argentina, India, and Australia, reflecting the global relevance of his work in fostering ecosystem resilience and bridging the gap between theoretical modeling and practical applications. He has authored over 40 peer-reviewed publications in leading journals that have been recognized with top-cited and top-downloaded article awards. Through his research and international collaborations, Dr. Srivastava continues to advance hydrology and ecohydrology, providing critical insights and tools to address water resource challenges and promote sustainable management practices in the face of a changing climate.

Venkat Sridhar

Venkataramana Sridhar is an Associate Professor in the Department of Biological Systems Engineering at Virginia Tech. Dr. Sridhar earned his PhD in Biosystems Engineering at Oklahoma State University in 2001. He is a hydrologist and conducts modeling research to understand the impact of climate change on hydrology and water resources, water management, drought, and flood modeling. His projects inform improved solutions to avoid water demand conflicts and improve potential yields from agriculture, ensuring a vibrant agricultural industry and enhancing food security. He is a Registered Professional Engineer in Idaho and Nebraska and a member of the American Society of Civil Engineers and the Board-Certified American Academy of Water Resources Engineers.

Nikul Kumari

Dr. Nikul has an extensive academic and research background in the fields of hydrology, water resources management, hydrological modeling, and vegetation modeling. Over the past eight years, Dr. Nikul has worked with exceptional mentors and organizations, significantly advancing her expertise in hydrology, ecohydrology, and remote sensing. During her Master's research at the Indian Institute of Technology, Kharagpur, she contributed to the development of a large-scale Satellite-based Hydrological Model (SHM) as part of the PRACRITI-2 program by the Indian Space Research Organization (ISRO). Her Ph.D. research focused on ecohydrological and ecogeomorphic analyses of semi-arid landscapes, combining remote sensing data with sophisticated landform evolution modeling. Her contributions extend to understanding and examining vegetation greenness at the global level, as well as in some of the critical 'hotspots' in the world (e.g., the Himalayan region).

Her most significant research work highlighted the interactions between climate, vegetation, and landforms, specifically in water-limited ecosystems, at a global scale, leading to substantial advancements in ecohydrology. Dr. Nikul has collaborated with researchers and experts from countries including the United States, Australia, India, Egypt, Turkey, Hong Kong, and China. Furthermore, her approach to research is marked by innovation and interdisciplinarity, as evidenced by her inventive use of remote sensing tools and techniques in the realms of hydrology, water resources, and vegetation monitoring.

Preface

Water is not just a resource—it is the foundation of life, economic prosperity, and ecological sustainability. Yet, as rivers flow through our landscapes, they also carry the consequences of humanity's most pressing challenges: climate change, land-use changes, and increasing demands on finite resources. This Special Issue explores innovative solutions to these challenges through advanced hydrological modeling, aiming to contribute to sustainable water management globally.

The scope of this Special Issue encompasses diverse methodologies, from trusted tools such as the Soil and Water Assessment Tool (SWAT) to cutting-edge machine learning algorithms and hybrid models. The research spans a wide geographical and climatic range, addressing challenges in arid and semi-arid regions of Algeria and India, humid zones of Romania and Korea, and diverse basins in China, Bolivia, Colombia, and the United States. Its purpose is to provide actionable insights into critical issues such as erosion risk, sedimentation management, groundwater recharge, and climate change adaptation, bridging the gap between theoretical research and practical applications.

The motivation for this Special Issue was the urgent need to develop resilient, adaptive management strategies for river basins worldwide. With increasing variability in climate and escalating pressures on water resources, there is a growing demand for integrative approaches that combine traditional models with emerging technologies like Geographic Information Systems (GIS), remote sensing, and optimization algorithms. These studies collectively demonstrate how such innovations can empower policy-makers and water managers with precise, data-rich solutions for sustainable decision-making.

The audience for this Special Issue includes researchers, practitioners, and decision-makers in the fields of hydrology, water resource management, and environmental science. It aims to inspire collaboration among academics, professionals, and stakeholders who are committed to safeguarding the future of global water resources.

This compilation reflects the collaborative efforts of an esteemed group of authors, who have contributed their expertise and creativity to this endeavour. Special acknowledgment is due to the reviewers for their insightful feedback, which significantly enhanced the quality of this Special Issue. We also extend our heartfelt gratitude to the editorial team for their unwavering dedication and support.

As editors, we are honoured to present this collection of work that embodies innovation, collaboration, and scientific excellence. It is our hope that this Special Issue will serve as a valuable resource for advancing hydrological science and addressing water management challenges. With sincere appreciation to all who contributed, we invite you to explore the pages of this Special Issue and join us in fostering sustainable solutions for river basin management.

Ankur Srivastava, Venkat Sridhar, and Nikul Kumari
Guest Editors

Editorial

Application of Various Hydrological Modeling Techniques and Methods in River Basin Management

Ankur Srivastava [1,*], Venkataramana Sridhar [2] and Nikul Kumari [1,*]

1. Faculty of Science, University of Technology Sydney, Sydney 2007, Australia
2. Department of Biological Systems Engineering, Virginia Polytechnic Institute and State University, Blacksburg, VA 24061, USA; vsri@vt.edu
* Correspondence: ankur.srivastava@uts.edu.au (A.S.); nikul.kumari@uts.edu.au (N.K.)

1. Introduction

The techniques of hydrological modeling have greatly improved in the recent past and have been instrumental in the management of river basins. This Special Issue presents state-of-the-art research to cope with the integrated problems of water resource management. The river basins are vital hydrological features that are both vital ecosystems as well as economic assets, and they come up with numerous challenges, including climate change, alteration of land use, and rise in water usage. Such challenges call for new strategies that involve the incorporation of big data, sophisticated computational models, and optimization techniques to assist in the decision-making process.

The research studies in this issue are quite diverse in the methods that have been used, for instance, the application of well-known hydrological models such as the Soil and Water Assessment Tool (SWAT). Some of the advanced machine learning algorithms have been used include Random Forest (RF), Extreme Gradient Boosting (XGB), and deep learning models. The optimization methods, namely the Gray Wolf Optimizer (GWO), have been incorporated with the modeling approaches to enhance the accuracy and the effectiveness of the predictions of patterns as well as sediment transport rates and evapotranspiration. Also, the incorporation of remote sensing data coupled with Geographic Information Systems (GIS) also enhances the spatial and temporal accuracies of these models.

Some of the themes highlighted in these articles include the identification of erosion hotspots and analyzing sediment accumulation in reservoirs as well as optimizing irrigation strategies to improve water use efficiency. In addition, the following studies highlight the need for the prediction of the reactions in the context of climate change and the potential ways of viewing the future impacts and vulnerabilities of the river basin systems. These advancements in the modeling techniques do not only increase the understanding of the phenomenon but also provide factual information that will benefit decision-makers, water resource managers, and other stakeholders. This particular edition stresses the importance of modeling in bridging the gap between the academic knowledge and the application. This research discusses aspects of managing river basins. It assists in developing sustainable and adaptable measures for preventing the deterioration of water sources and impacts caused by people.

2. Main Contributions of This Special Issue

Li et al. (contribution 1) optimized the Community Land Model (CLM5) in the Songhua River Basin (SRB) and incorporated the CaMa-Flood model to enable the utilization of multi-source meteorological data as well as surface characteristics in a detailed manner. This integration made it possible to perform high-resolution simulations of the runoff process over almost two decades with the seasonal variation in the discharge and identification of the flood-prone areas. The model had a coefficient of correlation of 0.65 to 0.80 with the discharge observed, thus making it useful in the understanding of the seasonal variation in hydrology as well as in flood management and prediction under different climate conditions.

Zhen and Bărbulescu (contribution 2) In the Buzău River in Romania, various machine learning models, such as convolutional neural network-long short-term memory (CNN-LSTM), sparrow search algorithm-backpropagation neural network (SSA-BP), and particle swarm optimization-extreme learning machine (PSO-ELM), were compared to predict the flow of the river. The outcomes highlighted the fact that the CNN-LSTM, especially when the model was trained with data collected after the construction of the dam, provided the best results in terms of accuracy and computational time. This type of model comparison not only shows the potential of using hybrid neural network approaches but also shows the importance of such comparisons in the real world for the application and management of river flows, which can then be used as a basis for choosing the most suitable model depending on the given hydrological and infrastructure conditions.

In the Seybouse Basin of Algeria, Inan et al. (contribution 3) used the Soil Water Assessment Tool (SWAT) model to assess the groundwater recharge in a semi-arid region. This model was calibrated with rainfall data and hydrometric station data, and the results were found to be efficient as proven by various performance measures, including Nash–Sutcliffe efficiency and R^2. The study shows that the SWAT can be used to effectively simulate hydrological processes in data-scarce arid regions. It also shows the need to develop accurate methods of estimating groundwater recharge for effective management of water resources in arid and semi-arid regions.

In their study, Patel et al. (contribution 4) proved how hydrological modeling has been useful in identifying the best sequence of measures for soil erosion management within watersheds. In India's Burhanpur watershed, the MCDA approach was coupled with morphometric parameters to rank the sub-watersheds for erosion potential. This analysis employed several approaches, such as the Analytical Hierarchy Process (AHP) and the Technique for Order Preference by Similarity to Ideal Solution (TOPSIS), for ranking the areas in terms of the erosion risk. This kind of prioritization makes it easier to determine which areas need soil conservation measures most and therefore assist in the management of the watersheds that are mainly used for agricultural purposes.

In the contribution by Saavedra et al. (contribution 5), the precipitation data from the satellite-based products were used and incorporated with the HydroBID model in the Guadalquivir Basin in Bolivia to produce high-resolution and distributed inputs for hydrological simulations. This approach showed a high correlation with the observed flow, and it was able to simulate micro-basin flows well with the HydroBID model. This approach using distributed precipitation data have great application in other areas that have scarce hydrometeorological data to produce better water balance, such as using the Yalong Well River for basin flood routing.

In another study by Yue et al. (contribution 6), the hybrid monthly model runoff that forecasting incorporated was particle-enhanced swarm optimization and the flower pollination algorithm with deep belief networks (PSO-FPA-DBN). This model, which was applied in the Yalong River Basin of China, outperformed other traditional models in terms of accuracy, consistency, and computational time, thus proving the potential of data-mining approaches in simulating the variability of monthly runoff. These developments improve the flood and drought forecasting systems, hence facilitating effective water resources management.

In the paper by Ma et al. (contribution 7), the authors demonstrated an effective use of cloud seeding in hydrology and the effect of seeding on water management in three dam basins in Korea and analyzed how the results can be applied to optimize the water management of the basins. The study revealed how the effects of cloud seeding can be different in various reservoirs, and thus, certain reservoirs may need more intense cloud seeding in specific seasons to improve the water supply situation. This study also points out that although the basins are located in the same climatic zone, context-specific approaches are essential to enhance the effectiveness of cloud seeding.

In a large-scale study by Abdelkader et al. (contribution 8) across the United States, the National Water Model (NWM) was assessed for the multi-decade time period, and it was observed that the model produced satisfactory results for the streamflow with and without the presence of regulation structures. The assessments of the model's performance showed better correspondence with the observed flows during winter in the humid regions, while some arid regions needed to be captured better. This analysis highlights how the NWM can be effectively used for large-scale hydrological prediction and where there is still room to enhance the bias correction, especially in the case of regulated flows.

Valencia et al. (contribution 9) demonstrated the innovative use of the InVEST Annual Water Yield model in Colombia's Meta River Basin to assess water yield at a basin scale. Despite the model's limitations, such as low accuracy in certain subbasins, it provided valuable and enlightening insights into hydrological processes in data-scarce regions. The findings from this study contribute to the discourse on the adaptability of models like InVEST in diverse hydrological settings and inform future model enhancements for water management.

Heramb et al. (contribution 10) investigated the application of advanced hydrological modeling techniques to improve river basin management, with a focus on estimating reference evapotranspiration (ET0)—a critical factor in water resource planning. Using machine learning (ML) models such as Random Forest (RF), Extreme Gradient Boosting (XGB), and Light Gradient Boosting (LGB), coupled with the Gray Wolf Optimizer (GWO), the research demonstrates significant improvements in predictive accuracy compared to conventional empirical models. This study applied advanced machine learning (ML) models, including Random Forest (RF), Extreme Gradient Boosting (XGB), and Light Gradient Boosting (LGB), coupled with the Gray Wolf Optimizer (GWO), to estimate reference evapotranspiration (ET0) for improving river basin management [1]. Using 20 years of meteorological data from humid and sub-humid regions of India, hybrid GWO-ML models significantly outperformed empirical and standalone ML methods, achieving a reduced RMSE and increased R^2 values [2]. These findings demonstrate the potential of integrating meta-heuristic algorithms with ML to enhance sustainable water resource management [3,4].

Nagireddy et al. (contribution 11) study is relevant to the focus of this Special Issue as it demonstrates how semi-distributed hydrological models like the Soil and Water Assessment Tool (SWAT) can be utilized for effective management of water resources and sediment yield in medium-sized river basins. The study focuses on two rivers, namely the Nagavali and Vamsadhara river basins in India, which are prone to soil erosion and sedimentation due to steep slopes and huge cultivation activities. Through calibration and sensitivity analysis, some of the major factors that influence the outcome of the model were established, such as the SCS runoff curve number and hydraulic conductivity, in order to produce a realistic simulation of the streamflow and sediment yield. The study revealed that evapotranspiration was the highest water loss process, accounting for the bulk of the annual precipitation, while the sediment yield analysis identified most of both basins as having high erosion rates, hence calling for urgent soil and water conservation measures. By identifying the focus areas of sediment sources, this study demonstrates the capability of hydrological modeling in assisting with the development of sustainable management measures, which is in line with the focus of this Special Issue on how to tackle water resource issues through the use of advanced modeling techniques. The findings of this study will be useful to policymakers and watershed managers to combat erosion and to improve the management of water resources in the vulnerable river basins.

To sum up, these research studies show how hydrological modeling is utilized in a variety of ways for the management of river basins. The incorporation of physical, statistical, and machine learning methods offers a comprehensive approach to forecasting and controlling hydrological conditions, planning of water resources, and issues including erosion, flooding, and reduction in groundwater table. Thus, further development of hydrological modeling methods with their increasing level of integration will allow water resources managers to obtain the necessary tools to support sustainable and flexible management of water resources in river basins under the conditions of climate change and growing water consumption.

3. Conclusions

The research in this Special Issue demonstrates how hydrological modeling techniques can make a huge difference in river basin management and how the findings can help with water resources management, sediment control, and sustainable development. All these studies have been designed and conducted to demonstrate the use of sophisticated models, including the Soil and Water Assessment Tool (SWAT), integrated with machine learning methods and optimization techniques, for the simulation of hydrological and land use change processes in various climatic and geographical conditions. With high-resolution meteorological, land use, soil, and remote sensing data, the studies prove the potential of estimating stream flow, evapotranspiration, and sediment output, which is very useful for the water resource managers.

The results show the potential of these models in determining the potential areas of erosion, enhancing the scheduling of irrigation water, and controlling sedimentation in reservoirs to address challenges in agriculture, flood control, and soil conservation. For instance, the research presented in the studies shows that incorporating the models along with geographical information systems (GIS) and remote sensing data enables quantification and analysis of the condition and changes over time, and, therefore, such tools are invaluable to policymakers and other stakeholders. Also, the research shows how these models can be applied to simulate conditions that would occur under the influence of climate change and provide forecasts for floods and droughts, which are crucial to increasing the basin's resilience.

The outcomes of these studies are quite useful in several sectors. For instance, in the agricultural sector, it is possible to determine the water balance accurately and, therefore, manage the water used for irrigation in a more effective manner with no waste of water and a higher production of crops. In urban planning and infrastructure, information on sedimentation and deposition can be used in preventing the siltation of reservoirs and other water bodies to ensure a constant water supply. In addition, these models assist the environmental protection measures by pinpointing the areas at high risk of soil erosion and assisting in the design of effective measures against it.

Furthermore, the studies identify the limitations and future research directions. The utilization of real-time data and sensor technology can also be enhanced to improve the model's predictive capacity. The application of the ensemble modeling approach, where multiple algorithms are used, can be useful in increasing the prediction capacities for the large and complicated basins. Hence, future work should also focus on the socio-economic effects of model usage to attain just and feasible solutions for all the parties involved. Finally, further development of high-resolution data collection and teamwork between different fields of science will be important for the further implementation of hydrological modeling in river basin management.

Author Contributions: Conceptualization, A.S. and N.K.; investigation, A.S., V.S. and N.K.; writing—original draft preparation, A.S., V.S. and N.K.; writing—review and editing, A.S., N.K. and V.S. All authors have read and agreed to the published version of the manuscript.

Funding: This research received no external funding.

Conflicts of Interest: The authors declare no conflicts of interest.

List of Contributions

1. Li, H.; Zhang, Z.; Zhang, Z. Improvement and Evaluation of CLM5 Application in the Songhua River Basin Based on CaMa-Flood. *Water* **2024**, *16*, 442. https://doi.org/10.3390/w16030442.
2. Zhen, L.; Bărbulescu, A. Comparative Analysis of Convolutional Neural Network-Long Short-Term Memory, Sparrow Search Algorithm-Backpropagation Neural Network, and Particle Swarm Optimization-Extreme Learning Machine Models for the Water Discharge of the Buzău River, Romania. *Water* **2024**, *16*, 289. https://doi.org/10.3390/w16020289.
3. Inan, C.A.; Maoui, A.; Lucas, Y.; Duplay, J. Multi-Station Hydrological Modelling to Assess Groundwater Recharge of a Vast Semi-Arid Basin Considering the Problem of Lack of Data: A Case Study in Seybouse Basin, Algeria. *Water* **2024**, *16*, 160. https://doi.org/10.3390/w16010160.
4. Patel, A.; Ramana Rao, K.V.; Rajwade, Y.A.; Saxena, C.K.; Singh, K.; Srivastava, A. Comparative Analysis of MCDA Techniques for Identifying Erosion-Prone Areas in the Burhanpur Watershed in Central India for the Purposes of Sustainable Watershed Management. *Water* **2023**, *15*, 3891. https://doi.org/10.3390/w15223891.
5. Saavedra, O.; Ureña, J.; Perales, M. Implementation of HydroBID Model with Satellite-Based Precipitation Products in Guadalquivir Basin, Bolivia. *Water* **2023**, *15*, 3250. https://doi.org/10.3390/w15183250.
6. Yue, Z.; Liu, H.; Zhou, H. Monthly Runoff Forecasting Using Particle Swarm Optimization Coupled with Flower Pollination Algorithm-Based Deep Belief Networks: A Case Study in the Yalong River Basin. *Water* **2023**, *15*, 2704. https://doi.org/10.3390/w15152704.
7. Ma, J.-H.; Yoo, C.; Song, S.-U.; Na, W.; Cho, E.; Song, S.-K.; Chang, K.-H. Different Effect of Cloud Seeding on Three Dam Basins, Korea. *Water* **2023**, *15*, 2555. https://doi.org/10.3390/w15142555.
8. Abdelkader, M.; Temimi, M.; Ouarda, T.B.M.J. Assessing the National Water Model's Streamflow Estimates Using a Multi-Decade Retrospective Dataset across the Contiguous United States. *Water* **2023**, *15*, 2319. https://doi.org/10.3390/w15132319.
9. Valencia, J.B.; Guryanov, V.V.; Mesa-Diez, J.; Tapasco, J.; Gusarov, A.V. Assessing the Effectiveness of the Use of the InVEST Annual Water Yield Model for the Rivers of Colombia: A Case Study of the Meta River Basin. *Water* **2023**, *15*, 1617. https://doi.org/10.3390/w15081617.
10. Heramb, P.; Ramana Rao, K.V.; Subeesh, A.; Srivastava, A. Predictive Modelling of Reference Evapotranspiration Using Machine Learning Models Coupled with Grey Wolf Optimizer. *Water* **2023**, *15*, 856. https://doi.org/10.3390/w15050856.
11. Nagireddy, N.R.; Keesara, V.R.; Sridhar, V.; Srinivasan, R. Streamflow and Sediment Yield Analysis of Two Medium-Sized East-Flowing River Basins of India. *Water* **2022**, *14*, 2960. https://doi.org/10.3390/w14192960.

References

1. Yan, K.; Cheng, Z.; Sun, G.; Huang, Z. Hybrid machine learning models for estimating daily reference evapotranspiration with external optimization. *Irrig. Sci.* **2020**, *38*, 631–644.
2. Zhou, J.; Wu, P.; Wang, Y.; Cao, X. Comparative study of different data-driven models for predicting reference evapotranspiration. *Water Resour. Manag.* **2021**, *35*, 857–872.

3. Dong, J.; Zhang, Y.; Liu, J.; Wang, Y. Improving reference evapotranspiration estimation with bio-inspired optimization algorithms coupled with kernel-based models. *Agric. Water Manag.* **2019**, *216*, 122–132.
4. Allen, R.G.; Pereira, L.S.; Raes, D.; Smith, M. *FAO-56 Penman-Monteith Equation for Determining Reference Evapotranspiration*; FAO Irrigation and Drainage Paper No. 56; FAO: Rome, Italy, 1998.

Disclaimer/Publisher's Note: The statements, opinions and data contained in all publications are solely those of the individual author(s) and contributor(s) and not of MDPI and/or the editor(s). MDPI and/or the editor(s) disclaim responsibility for any injury to people or property resulting from any ideas, methods, instructions or products referred to in the content.

Article

Improvement and Evaluation of CLM5 Application in the Songhua River Basin Based on CaMa-Flood

Heng Li *, Zhiwei Zhang and Zhen Zhang

School of Water Conservancy and Civil Engineering, Northeast Agricultural University, Harbin 150038, China; zzw19968023@163.com (Z.Z.); s210101060@neau.edu.cn (Z.Z.)
* Correspondence: neaulih@neau.edu.cn

Abstract: This paper optimized the hydrological postprocessing of CLM5 using CaMa-Flood, combining multi-source meteorological forcing datasets and a dynamically changing surface dataset containing 16 PFTs (plant functional types) to simulate the high-resolution runoff process in the SRB from 1996 to 2014, specifically by integrating discharge with flooded area. Additionally, we evaluated the spatiotemporal variations of precipitation data from meteorological forcing datasets and discharge to validate the accuracy of model improvements. Both the discharge and the flooded area simulated by the coupled model exhibit pronounced seasonality, accurately capturing the discharge increase during the warm season and the river recession process in the cold season, along with corresponding changes in the flooded area. This highlights the model's capability for hydrological process monitoring. The simulated discharge shows a high correlation coefficient (0.65–0.80) with the observed discharge in the SRB, reaching a significance level of 0.01, and the Nash–Sutcliffe efficiency ranges from 0.66 to 0.78. Leveraging the offline coupling of CLM and CaMa-Flood, we present a method with a robust physical mechanism for monitoring and providing a more intuitive representation of hydrological events in the SRB.

Keywords: discharge; land surface model; hydrological model; Songhua River Basin

Citation: Li, H.; Zhang, Z.; Zhang, Z. Improvement and Evaluation of CLM5 Application in the Songhua River Basin Based on CaMa-Flood. *Water* **2024**, *16*, 442. https://doi.org/10.3390/w16030442

Academic Editor: Abasiofiok Mark Ibekwe

Received: 7 January 2024
Revised: 24 January 2024
Accepted: 26 January 2024
Published: 29 January 2024

Copyright: © 2024 by the authors. Licensee MDPI, Basel, Switzerland. This article is an open access article distributed under the terms and conditions of the Creative Commons Attribution (CC BY) license (https:// creativecommons.org/licenses/by/ 4.0/).

1. Introduction

In recent years, in most parts of the globe, storm runoff extremes have systematically approached or exceeded historical precipitation extremes [1], accompanied by large spatial scales and variability on decadal timescales [2], and storm runoff extremes have increased at an approximate Clausius–Clapeyron rate [3]. China has experienced significant warming in recent decades and has already experienced some devastating climate extremes. For example, the Great Flood of 1998 inundated 24×10^4 km^2 of land, destroying 5 million houses, including those in the Yangtze River basin and Songhua River Basin (SRB), and causing more than USD 20 billion in economic losses [4], while studies in the Tibetan Plateau have shown that the risk of flooding is projected to increase with warming temperatures [5]. Northeastern China, where the SRB is located, is one of the most important agricultural regions in the world [6] and home to China's largest plain [4]. Due to socioeconomic development and intensification of agricultural production in the SRB, the demand for water resources has increased rapidly. The SRB is also an area prone to extreme flooding. Many hydraulic structures have been constructed in the SRB, and these infrastructures can prevent flooding during the rainy season and alleviate water scarcity during the dry season [7]. Studying the spatial and temporal variability of runoff throughout the SRB is important for water resource management and for maintaining sustainable socioeconomic and agricultural production.

Discharge is one of the most comprehensive indicators of the overall impact of various factors in basin-scale hydrology [8–10], and accurately modeling discharge is key to understanding the water cycle, water resource management, and climate change. There are various research methods to simulate discharge, such as using the water balance equation combined with precipitation, evapotranspiration, and terrestrial water storage anomaly (TWSA) measured by GRACE Follow-On (GRAFO) to derive the production and sinking process; this method has been validated in the Yangtze River Basin, but the timeliness of the monthly GRAFO for TWSA monitoring is lacking [11,12]. Land surface models (LSMs) driven by meteorological forcing data can simulate discharge at multiple time scales (from monthly to interannual) [13], and LSMs require more meteorologically forcing data than traditional distributed hydrologic models (DHMs), such as precipitation, solar radiation, near-surface air pressure, near-surface wind speed, near-surface air moisture content, and near-surface air temperature data. Weather stations can also measure water fluxes, but the data obtained are at the point scale only, and the scarcity of meteorological stations in developing countries causes the need to seek other more comprehensive and reliable meteorological forcing data to drive models [14]. If the meteorological forcing data are inaccurate, even if the model can handle high-resolution data and has a strong physical mechanism, it will not enhance the accuracy of the model simulation results [15]. Therefore, reliable and accurate meteorological forcing data are essential for LSMs.

The Community Land Model (CLM) is a common and widely used LSM and the land component of the Community Earth System Model 2 (CESM2) [16,17]. We used CLM5, which has been updated from the development of CLM4 [17] and CLM4.5 [18], but the improvements in CLM5 still do not simulate changes in flooded areas on time scales, and most of the previous work on flood characterization has been conducted using runoff data rather than flooded areas [19]. The catchment-based macroscale floodplain model (CaMa-Flood) is a global river hydrodynamic model that can perform high-precision simulations of confluence processes and flooded areas in large basins and has been validated in the Amazon Basin and the Yangtze River Basin [12,20]. In this study, we coupled the model with CLM5 to compensate for the shortcomings of CLM5 in runoff simulation.

The main objective of this study is to improve the hydrological postprocessing of the CLM utilizing CaMa-Flood, and on this basis, we provide a method with a strong physical mechanism for monitoring and presenting a more intuitive representation of hydrological events in the SRB to better understand floods from the perspective of discharge volume combined with flooded area. We enhanced the runoff processing after the land surface process simulation in CLM5 and first selected three sets of meteorologically forcing datasets, namely, CMFD (China Meteorological Forcing Dataset), GSWP3v1 (Global Soil Wetness Project dataset) and CRUv7 (Climatic Research Unit-NCEP forcing data), combined with a high-resolution subsurface dataset of the SRB to simulate the flooding process and obtain high-precision streamflow-producing data. These were then input into the CaMa-Flood to simulate the confluence process to investigate the runoff and flooded area changes. In addition, three representative stations in the SRB, namely, Harbin, Jiamusi and Tonghe, were selected for validation and evaluation. Finally, we present the simulation results for discharge and flooded area obtained from different meteorological forcing dataset-coupled models with simultaneous power downscaling.

2. Materials and Methods
2.1. Study Area

The SRB is in northeastern China, spanning an elevation from 50 to 2700 m above sea level, with a longitude of 119°52′–132°31′ E and a latitude of 41°42′–51°48′ N. Covering an area of approximately 5.568×10^5 km^2, the basin is characterized by mountainous terrain (61%) and plains (24%) [21–23]. Influenced by the high-latitude subpolar westerly winds and the mid-latitude monsoon climate, part of the SRB experiences subfreezing conditions, characterized by cold and lengthy winters and rainy summers. Precipitation varies across regions and seasons. Mountainous areas receive more rainfall than plains. Annual precipitation ranges from 350 to 1000 mm, with a long-term average below 500 mm. Of the yearly precipitation, 70% occurs between July and September. The average temperature in the region ranges from about 3 °C to 5 °C [24]. Due to its high topography in the northwest and southeast, poor drainage in the central area, and the impact of concentrated summer precipitation, the SRB has experienced severe flooding in recent years [25]. Flood occurrences are common in the SRB; however, there is a paucity of robust physical mechanism models for conducting high-resolution runoff process simulations. To enhance flood prevention, reduce economic losses in vulnerable areas, and optimize basin management, a high-resolution discharge simulation study was conducted. This study aimed to reflect the flooding process visually and precisely, facilitating better monitoring and early warning of floods based on discharge volume and flooded area [26]. Given that floods mainly occur in the middle and lower reaches of the basin, Harbin Station, Tonghe Station, and Jiamusi Station were selected for detailed analysis (Figure 1). These three hydrological stations provided daily flow observation data from 1996 to 2014.

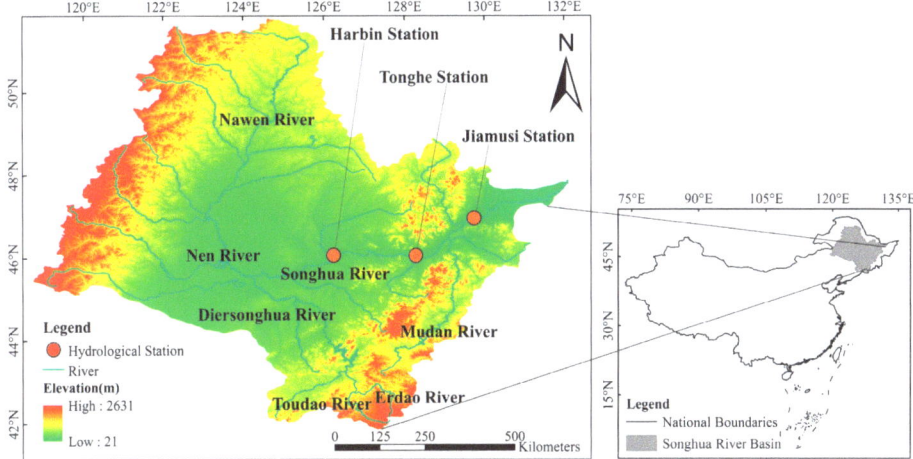

Figure 1. Map of subbasins and river networks within the SRB.

2.2. Data

In this study, temporal resampling was performed to process its temporal resolution to 6 hourly. Three meteorological forcing datasets were used in this study: CMFD, GSWP3 v1, and CRUv7 (refer to Table 1 for details). CMFD is based on internationally available TRMM precipitation data, GEWEX-SRB radiometric data, GLDAS data, and Princeton reanalysis data, combined with the CMA (China Meteorological Administration meteorological observational data), which now covers the period 1979–2018, with a temporal resolution of 3 hourly and a horizontal spatial resolution of $0.1° \times 0.1°$ [27]. GSWP3 is the second version of the reanalysis dataset based on the NCEP model conducted in the 20th century. The raw data are dynamically downscaled by the spectral light-push data assimilation technique using the global spectral model. In addition, GSWP3 is bias-corrected for temperature, precipitation, longwave radiation, and shortwave radiation using the CRU TS v3.21, GPCC v7, and SRB (surface radiation budget) datasets, respectively [28]. GSWP3 v1, used in this, paper has a 6 hourly temporal resolution and a horizontal spatial resolution of $0.5° \times 0.5°$, with a coverage of the period 1901–2014 [29]. CRUv7 [30] is a 6 hourly, $0.5° \times 0.5°$ resolution, globally forced product that combines two existing datasets: CRU TS3.2 and NCEP reanalysis. CRU TS3.2 provides $0.5° \times 0.5°$ resolution monthly data covering 1901–2002, and the NCEP reanalysis provides 6 hourly data at $2.5° \times 2.5°$ resolution covering 1948–2016. In this paper, we used version 7 of its data, which cover the period 1901–2016 and meet the needs of the study. Near-surface barometric pressure, specific humidity, air temperature, wind speed, precipitation, longwave radiation, and shortwave radiation from the dataset were used to force CLM5.

Table 1. General information of the meteorological forcing datasets. "Reanalysis" and "Observations" are corresponding datasets used in producing the atmospheric forcing. A detailed description can be found in Section 2.2.

Datasets	Resolution		Period	Reanalysis	Observations
	Temporal	Spatial			
CMFD	6-hourly	$0.1° \times 0.1°$	1979–2018	Princeton, CMA	TRMM, GEWEX-SRB, GLDAS
GSWP3 v1	6-hourly	$0.5° \times 0.5°$	1901–2014	20CR	CRU TS v3.21, GPCCv7, SRB
CRU v7	6-hourly	$0.5° \times 0.5°$	1901–2016	NCEP	CRU TS3.2

SRB stands for surface radiation budget.

Soil data sources for CLM5 are more complex, with soil thickness data based on ORNL (Oak Ridge National Laboratory) [31] and land cover data from the USGS (U.S. Geological Survey) based on satellite data inversion of the GLCC dataset. Soil texture data were obtained from IGB (The International Geosphere–Biosphere Program) [32]. Soil color determines dry and saturated soil albedo, soil color data were obtained from MODIS, and LAI data were processed from the MODIS LAI dataset based on a range of properties of plant functional types (PFTs) obtained by mapping MODIS LAI monthly average data to different PFTs for each 0.05° grid [33]. LUH2 (Land-Use Harmonization[2]) provided historical and future scenario land use data from 850 to 2100 at 0.25° resolution. The LUH2 data were derived from the 850–2014 History Database of the Global Environment (HYDE version 3.2) and the Integrated Assessment Modeling Team (IAMT) for multiple alternative future scenarios from 2015–2100 [34]. Based on the above data, this study used the CLM land use data tool to generate a surface dataset and a dynamic land use dataset for the SRB at 0.1° resolution from 1996 to 2014 [35]. CaMa-Flood used MERIT Hydro, a global raster hydrographic map with 3 arc seconds resolution, elevation from MERIT DEM, and water body data based on G1 WBM (Global Surface Water Occurrence and OpenStreetMap) [36].

2.3. Hydrological Processes in CLM5

New to the hydrology section of CLM5 are the dry surface layers (DSLs) for representing evapotranspiration processes at the surface, spatially variable soil depths (0.4 to 8.5 m), vertical soil stratification (20 soil layers + 5 bedrock layers), adaptive time-step solving of the Richard equation, and the elimination of unconfined aquifers, with no flux lower boundary conditions. In the river simulation section, the River Transport Model (RTM) used in CLM 4.5 was replaced in CLM 5 by the Model for Scale Adaptive River Transport (MOSART) [37]. The main difference between RTM and MOSART is the way the river flow is calculated. RTM uses a simple linear reservoir approach where the flow transferred from a grid cell upstream of the RTM to an adjacent grid cell downstream of the RTM depends only on the amount of river storage in the upstream grid cell, the average distance between the grid cells, and a globally constant effective streamflow rate such that the RTM only simulates discharge (m^3/s). In MOSART, river flow is calculated explicitly by the physically based kinematic wave method, a common approach in hydrology based on the mass and momentum equations, and in combination with detailed information on the hydrography of the simulation area (i.e., parameters describing river and tributary widths, depths, average slopes, roughness coefficients, and lengths of the main river). MOSART also simulates the flow velocity of the main river channel over time (m/s) and water depth, as well as subgrid surface water flow in hillslopes and tributaries [38].

CLM5 parameterized canopy interception, net precipitation, canopy dripping, snowpack and melt, water transport between snowpack layers, infiltration, evapotranspiration, surface runoff, subsurface drainage, redistribution within the soil column, and groundwater runoff and recharge to simulate changes in canopy water $\Delta W_{can,liq}$, canopy snow water $\Delta W_{can,sno}$, surface water ΔW_{sfc}, snow water ΔW_{sno}, soil water $\Delta W_{liq,i}$, and soil ice $\Delta W_{ice,i}$, as well as changes in water in the unconfined aquifer (all in mm H_2O).

The total water balance equation in this system is as follows [18]:

$$\Delta W_{can,liq} + \Delta W_{can,sno} + \Delta W_{sfc} + \Delta W_{sno} + \sum_{i=1}^{N_{levsoi}} \left(\Delta w_{liq,i} + \Delta w_{ice,i} \right) + \Delta W_a \\ = \\ \left(q_{rain} + q_{sno} - E_v - E_g - q_{over} - q_{h2osfc} - q_{drai} - q_{rgwl} - q_{snwcp,ice} \right) \Delta t \qquad (1)$$

where q_{rain} is liquid precipitation, q_{sno} is solid precipitation, E_v is evapotranspiration from vegetation, E_g is evapotranspiration from soil, q_{over} is surface runoff, q_{h2osfc} is surface water storage runoff, q_{drai} is subsurface runoff, q_{rgwl} and $q_{snwcp,ice}$ are solid and liquid runoff from snow originating in glaciers, lakes, and other surface types, N_{levsoi} denotes the number of soil column layers in CLM5 (the hydrologic section accounts for the $1 - N_{levsoi}$ layer; $(N_{levsoi} + 1) - N_{levgrnd}$ is not currently accounted for in the hydrologic component of the calculation), and Δt is the time step.

The water input at the surface of the grid cell is the sum of precipitation and snowmelt reaching the ground $q_{liq,0}$, and then the water flux is redistributed to surface runoff, terrestrial water storage, and infiltration into the soil. TOPMODEL implements a runoff parameterization, and the key concept in the model is the saturated area fraction, f_{sat}, which is determined by the grid cell's topographic characteristics and soil moisture content. The saturated area directly affected the surface runoff q_{over}, according to the typical hillslope flow production process given by Dunn in 1975, with the following equation [18]:

$$q_{over} = f_{sat} \cdot q_{liq,0}. \qquad (2)$$

The relationship between the saturated area fraction and soil moisture content is as follows [18]:

$$f_{sat} = f_{max} \exp(-0.5 f_{over} z_\nabla), \qquad (3)$$

where f_{max} is the potential or maximum value of f_{sat}, f_{over} is the attenuation factor (m^{-1}), and z_∇ is the depth to the water table (m). z_∇ is determined by finding the first soil layer above the bedrock depth in which the volumetric water content drops below a specified threshold (the default threshold is set to 0.9). The maximum saturation fraction f_{max} is defined as the value of the discrete cumulative distribution function (CDF) of the topographic index when the average water table depth of the grid cell is zero. Thus, f_{max} is the percentage of pixels in a grid cell with a topographic index greater than or equal to the average topographic index of the grid cell and is calculated explicitly at each grid cell at the model-run resolution based on the CDF. An attenuation factor of 0.5 m^{-1} was determined for the global simulation through sensitivity analysis and comparison with observed runoff [39–41].

2.4. CaMa-Flood

To compensate for the shortcomings of CLM5 for land surface process simulation, which can only obtain flow production data (unit: mm), and MOSART for flood simulation, CLM5 was coupled with CaMa-Flood, and the runoff data output from CLM5 was used to drive CaMa-Flood v4.1. The flowchart of the offline coupling model is shown in Figure 2. CaMa-Flood is a distributed global river network confluence model that is mainly used to simulate continental-scale rivers [20].

Based on the local inertia equation, CaMa-Flood calculates the river flow from each unit catchment to the unit catchment downstream by neglecting the second term of the 1-D St. Venant momentum equation Q (m^3/s):

$$\frac{\partial Q}{\partial t} + \frac{\partial}{\partial x}\left[\frac{Q^2}{A}\right] + \frac{gA \partial(h+z)}{\partial x} + \frac{gn^2 Q^2}{R^{4/3} A} = 0. \qquad (4)$$

Moreover, to extract subgrid topographic parameters from the ground elevation data (MERIT DEM) and river network map (MERIT Hydro) of the SRB with 3 arc seconds resolution, the flexible location of waterways (FLOW) method was also used in CaMa-Flood to extract the river channel length (L), river channel width (W), and bank height (B); and the channel storage S_r, floodplain storage S_f, channel water depth D_r, floodplain water depth D_f, and inundation area A_f were calculated from the total storage S (where D_f was obtained by the CDF representing the function between water level and inundation area of a unit's catchment, $D_f = D(A_f)$) [42–44].

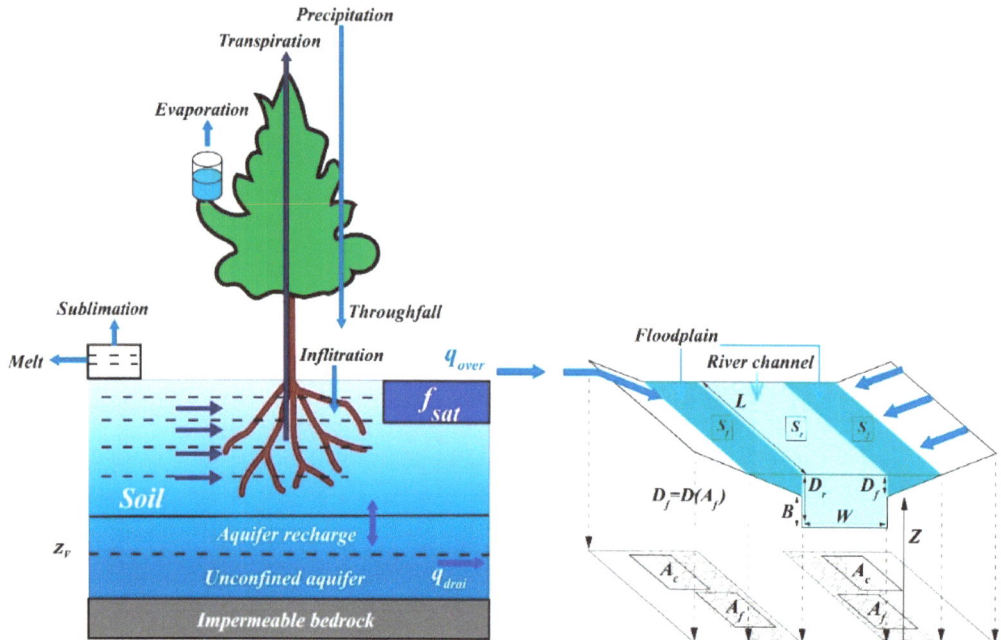

Figure 2. Flowchart of the offline coupling model CLM5 and CaMa-Flood v4.1.

2.5. Methods

The study is divided into two parts: The objective of the first part is to assess the suitability of precipitation data from various observational satellites and reanalysis in a meteorological forcing dataset, then to obtain high-resolution runoff data for the period 1996–2014 by integrating land surface process simulations with a dynamic surface dataset at 0.1° resolution. In the second part, three sets of runoff datasets obtained from the simulation were used to force the hydrological model to obtain the SRB resolution 1' × 1' discharge and flooded area datasets. Finally, the accuracy and applicability of the runoff simulation results were evaluated to determine whether the coupled model was applicable in the SRB.

The comparison of precipitation data from stations and meteorological forcing datasets used two statistical metrics: the correlation coefficient (CC) and root mean squared error (RMSE). Coefficients of variation (CV), correlation coefficient (CC), relative bias (RB), and Nash efficiency coefficients (NSE) were used for the coupled-model runoff simulation results because they are commonly used in runoff uncertainty assessments [8,45,46]. The expressions and specific descriptions of each evaluation metric are shown in Table 2.

Table 2. Evaluation index expressions, ranges, ideal values, and description in the study.

Index and Expression	Range and Ideal Value	Description
(1) $CC = \dfrac{\sum_{i=1}^{n}(Q_{ti} - \overline{Q_t}) \cdot (Q_{pi} - \overline{Q_p})}{\sqrt{\sum_{i=1}^{n}(Q_{ti} - \overline{Q_t})^2 \cdot \sum_{i=1}^{n}(Q_{pi} - \overline{Q_p})^2}}$	$[-1, 1]$, 1	Q_{ti} and Q_{pi} denote the observed and unobserved values at time point i, respectively; $\overline{Q_t}$ and $\overline{Q_p}$ represent the mean of the observed and unobserved values; n denotes the total amount of data; STD denotes the standard deviation; and $\overline{Q}$ denotes the mean value
(2) $NSE = 1 - \dfrac{\sum_{i=1}^{n}(Q_{pi} - Q_{ti})^2}{\sum_{i=1}^{n}(Q_{ti} - \overline{Q_t})^2}$	$(-\infty, 1]$, 1	
(4) $RB = \dfrac{\sum_{i=1}^{n} Q_{pi} - \sum_{i=1}^{n} Q_{ti}}{\sum_{i=1}^{n} Q_{ti}} \times 100\%$	$(-\infty, +\infty)$, 0	
(5) $RMSE = \sqrt{\sum_{i=1}^{n}(Q_{pi} - Q_{ti})^2 / n}$	$[0, +\infty)$, 0	
(6) $CV = \dfrac{STD}{\overline{Q}}$	—	

3. Results

3.1. Evaluation of Precipitation in Meteorological Forcing Data

In this study, we compared the quality of precipitation data in different meteorological forcing data by calculating the average monthly precipitation from 1996 to 2014 in the basin (AMPB) and the average monthly precipitation during the year (AMPY) from three standardized stations in the basin. As shown in Figure 3, CRUv7 underestimated precipitation, which exhibited poor performance, and both CMFD and GSWP3v1 overestimated precipitation. CRUv7 underestimated precipitation for 1996–1998, 2002–2003, 2005–2007, 2009–2010, and 2012–2014; the resolution of CRU v7 is 0.5°, but meteorological stations can represent precipitation only within several kilometers around the observation point, limited in spatial and temporal coverage, because of the large single-point observational errors [9,47]. AMPB underestimated precipitation by an average of 11.2 mm, and AMPY underestimated precipitation by an average of 5.4 mm, the overall precipitation trends differed from the other data. The results suggested that CRUv7 was less applicable in the SRB than in previous study areas [48]. CMFD and GSWP3v1 showed overestimation of precipitation, with a slightly more pronounced overestimation for GSWP3v1. For GSWP3v1, AMPB was overestimated by an average of 6.5 mm, and AMPY was overestimated by an average of 2.4 mm. For CMFD, AMPB was overestimated by an average of 4.6 mm and AMPY by an average of 1.8 mm; while from Table 3, CMFD underestimated precipitation in the cool season and overestimated precipitation in the warm season, which was consistent with previous studies on the Tibetan Plateau [49].

Table 3. Multi-station precipitation comparison across time scales (unit: mm).

Datasets	Day	Jan	Feb	Mar	Apr	May	Jun	Jul	Aug	Sept	Oct	Nov	Dec	Year
OBS	1.46	5.71	4.99	15.25	22.93	55.18	83.05	125.14	118.66	47.61	29.08	16.74	9.59	533.92
CMFD	1.50	6.31	4.90	15.40	23.22	60.26	88.27	127.73	119.28	47.35	28.24	17.08	9.29	547.33
CRUv7	1.37	3.89	4.00	13.15	26.81	52.21	82.95	131.90	107.28	38.36	22.28	10.88	5.96	499.67
GSWP3v1	1.50	6.19	5.60	17.82	28.47	53.04	92.15	130.04	120.03	42.18	27.74	17.31	8.59	549.15

To further understand the data quality of the three datasets under different precipitation intensities (PI, mm/d), the PI was categorized into seven groups ($0 \leq PI < 1$, $1 \leq PI < 5$, $5 \leq PI < 10$, $10 \leq PI < 20$, $20 \leq PI < 30$, $30 \leq PI < 50$, $PI > 50$) in this study. Figure 4 shows the total precipitation for the three datasets from 1996 to 2014 under different PI groups. The analysis results showed that the overestimation of precipitation in CRUv7 was mainly concentrated in the range of PI = 1~10 mm/d, and there was underestimation of precipitation in CRUv7 in the group with PI $\geq$ 10 mm/d. GSWP3v1 and CMFD were closer to the observations (OBS, data from stations) than CRUv7 in all PI groups, but in the low-intensity precipitation (PI = 0~10 mm/d) range, both overestimated precipitation, and in the high-intensity precipitation (PI > 10 mm/d) range, GSWP3v1 and CMFD generally underestimated precipitation. The results of total precipitation in different PI ranges showed only the overestimation and underestimation of precipitation; however, they could not represent the accuracy of precipitation products in detecting actual precipitation. Therefore, in this study, the precipitation products were further grouped according to the PI of OBS, and then the CC and RMSE were calculated for each precipitation dataset with different PI intervals. The results are shown in Table 4. At different PI intervals, Table 4 shows that the correlation between CMFD and OBS was the highest and the RMSE was the smallest, and the most accurate estimation of precipitation was found when $30 \leq PI$, with an RMSE of 5.90 mm, followed by $0 \leq PI < 1$, with an RMSE of 0.22 mm.

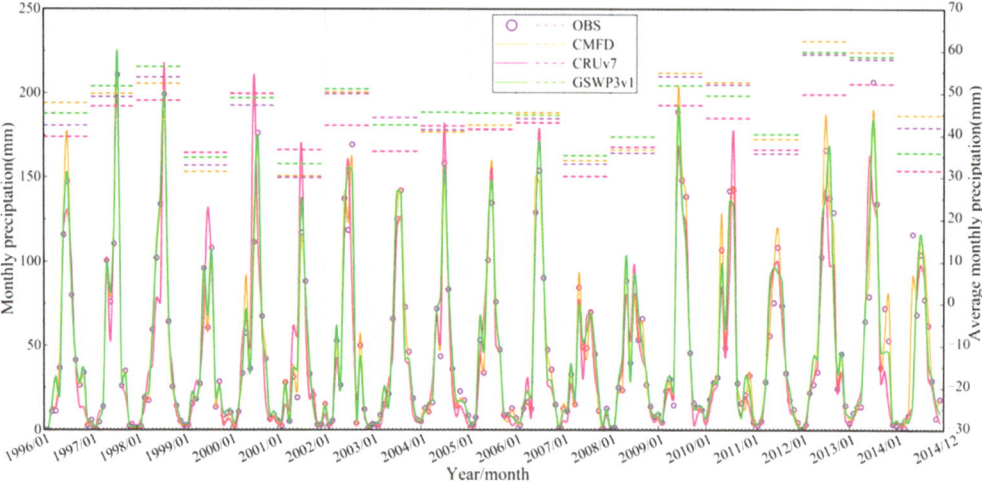

Figure 3. Exploring multi-station perspectives: a comparative study of the average monthly precipitation in the basin (solid lines) and the average monthly precipitation during the year (dashed lines).

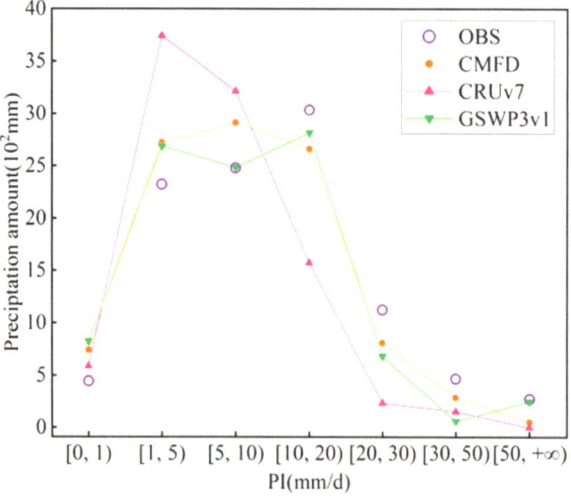

Figure 4. Precipitation in different PI groups from 1996 to 2014.

Table 4. Comparison of different PI groups: statistical overview of multiple precipitation products against OBS.

PI (mm/d)	CMFD		CRUv7		GSWP3v1	
	CC	RMSE	CC	RMSE	CC	RMSE
[0, 1)	0.34	0.22	0.09	0.23	0.03	0.23
[1, 5)	0.37	1.00	0.13	1.13	0.02	1.13
[5, 10)	0.23	1.37	0.02	1.35	0.12	1.42
[10, 20)	0.27	2.71	0.04	2.37	0.11	3.01
[20, 30)	0.06	2.35	−0.12	2.75	0.17	2.81
[30, +∞)	0.48	5.90	−0.59	6.19	−0.08	12.08

3.2. Evaluation of Discharge

In this study, we obtained the average spatial pattern of the SRB for the period 1996–2014 by combining the CaMa-Flood with three datasets of 0.1° × 0.1° runoff obtained from the coupled simulation of CLM5, which represented the dynamic hydrological processes at a high spatial resolution of 1' × 1' and spatially captured the flood flow in autumn and the river recession process in winter in the SRB. Figure 5 shows the seasonal cycle of the simulated discharge during 1996–2014, with a clear ground flood evolution along the SRB from upstream to downstream. The seasonal variation in the simulated flooded area during the period 1996–2014 is illustrated in Figure 6, with a clear exposure to a more severe flood risk during the warm season in the SRB. The performance of the simulated seasonal discharge is demonstrated in Figure 7, which varied depending on the meteorological forcing data, station location, and different rivers in the basin, as shown at the Harbin, Tonghe, and Jiamusi hydrological stations (Figure 2). Comparing the simulated discharge with the OBS at the hydrological stations, in the middle and lower reaches of the SRB, the simulated discharge agreed with the measured discharge in most of the period, and the simulated discharge could override the observed discharge, but during the 1998 and 2013 warm seasons, CMFD, GSWP3v1, and CRUv7 all significantly underestimated the peak discharge, and all three overestimated the discharge in the 2007 and 2008 warm seasons. The interannual variations described by the coefficients of variation (CVs) of the simulated and measured discharge during 1996–2014 are compared in Figure 8. The three datasets of discharge simulations at Harbin, Tonghe, and Jiamusi stations agreed with the CVs of the observed discharge in the cold season, and the simulated discharge significantly underestimated the CVs of the observed discharge in the warm season.

The Taylor plot in Figure 9 summarizes the centered root-mean-square difference (CRMSD), normalized standard deviation (STD), and CC between simulated and OBS daily flows for the period 1996–2014. The CRMSD values consistently exhibit higher magnitudes for Jiamusi station compared to Harbin and Tonghe stations, signifying a relatively diminished accuracy in the simulated discharge outcomes for Jiamusi. No significant difference is observed in the simulated discharge performance between Harbin and Tonghe stations. All simulated discharge STDs were less than 1, with CMFD simulations yielding discharge STDs closest to 1; GSWP3v1 is the next closest, and CRUv7 is the worst. Most of the CC values ranged from 0.65 to 0.80, with the highest correlation between simulated and measured discharge for CMFD at Jiamusi station and GSWP3v1 at Tonghe station, both with CC values of 0.76 ($p < 0.01$), and the poorest fit of simulated discharge to observed discharge for CRUv7 at Harbin station, with a CC value of 0.66 ($p < 0.01$). From the results, the discharge obtained from the CMFD simulation had more points close to the observed data, which was more suitable for the SRB than GSWP3v1 with CRUv7, which was consistent with the results of the analysis and evaluation of precipitation data in Section 3.1.

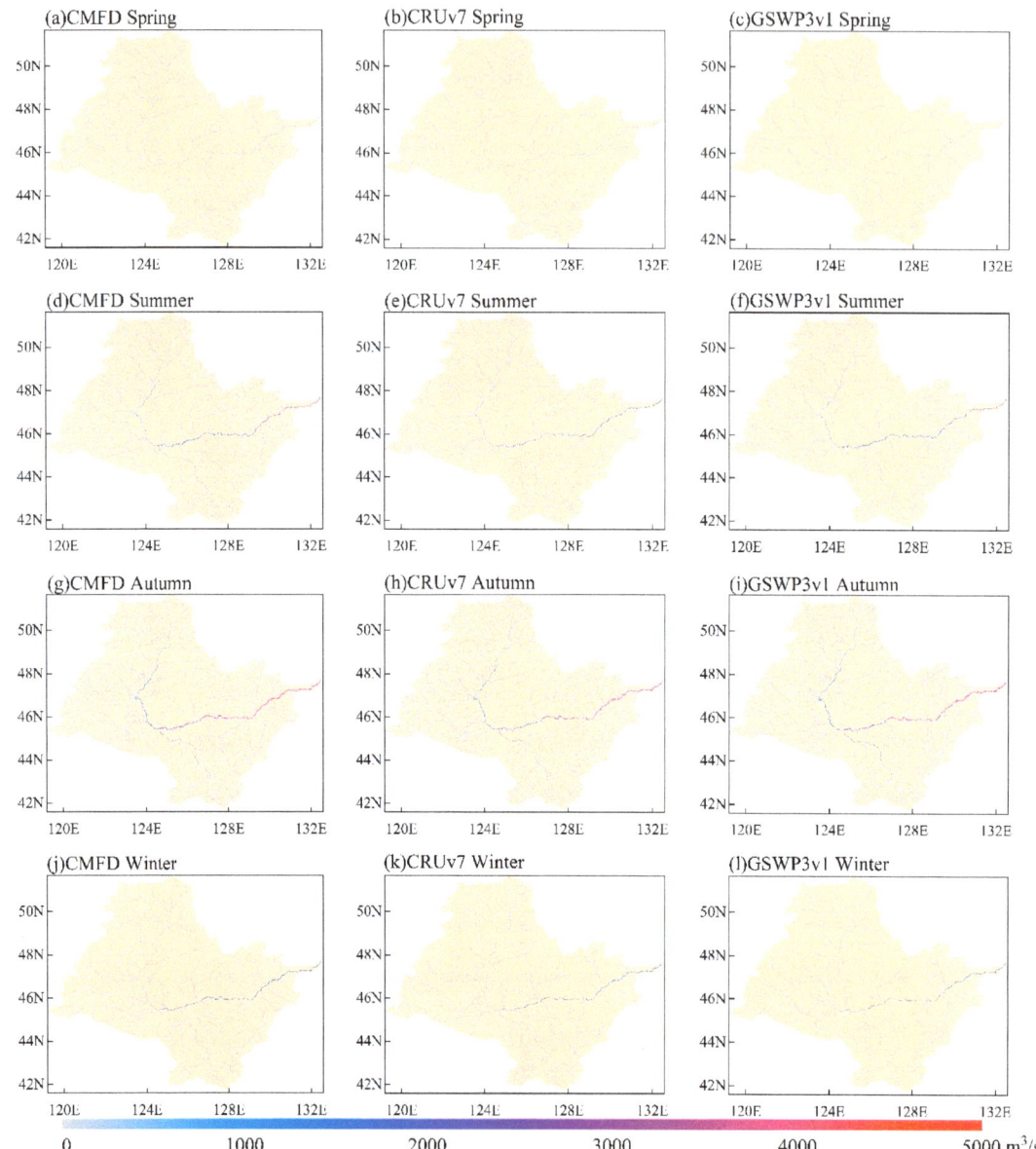

Figure 5. Seasonal spatial distribution of ensemble means of discharge between 1996 and 2014.

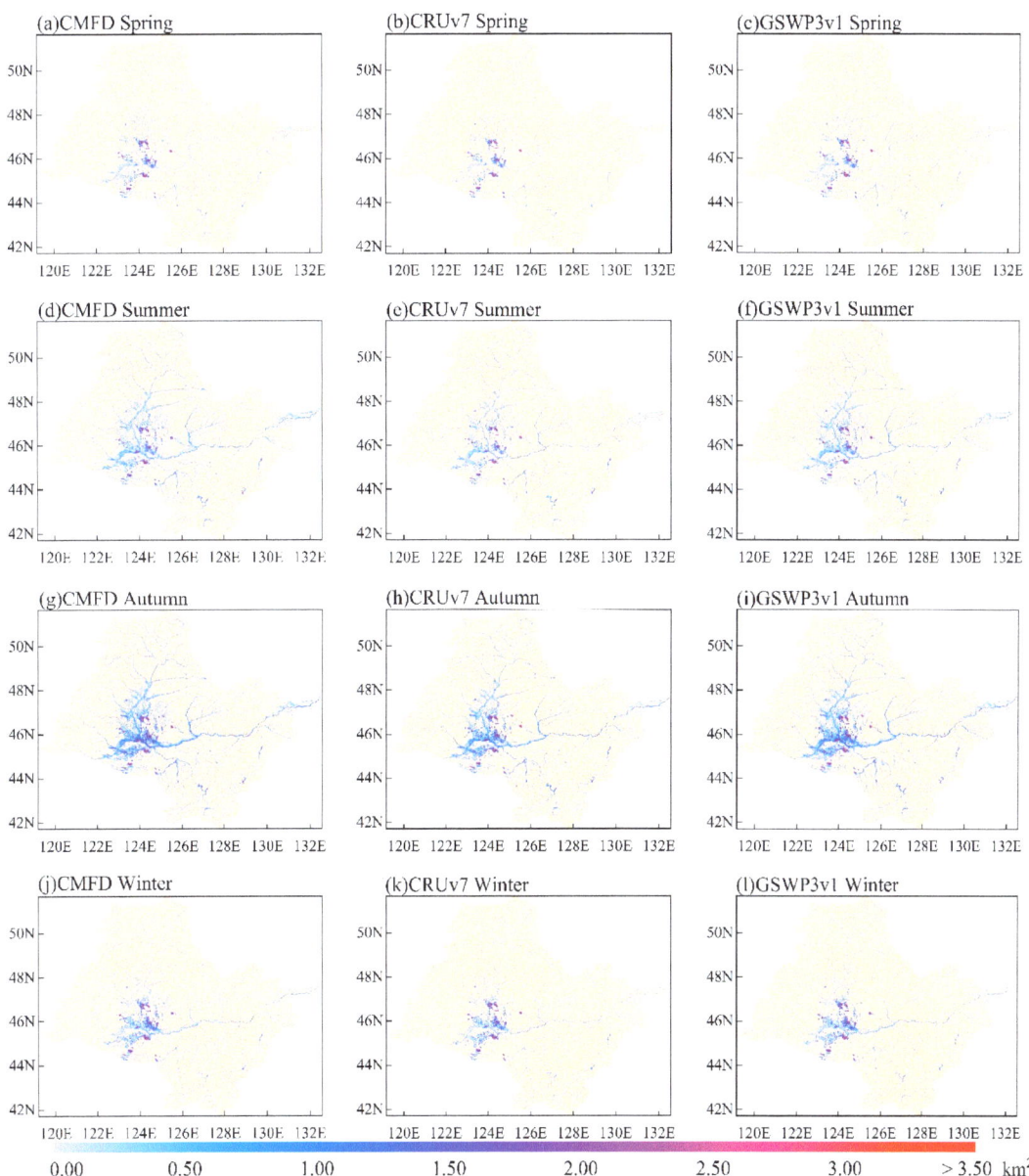

Figure 6. Seasonal spatial distribution of ensemble means of flooded areas between 1996 and 2014.

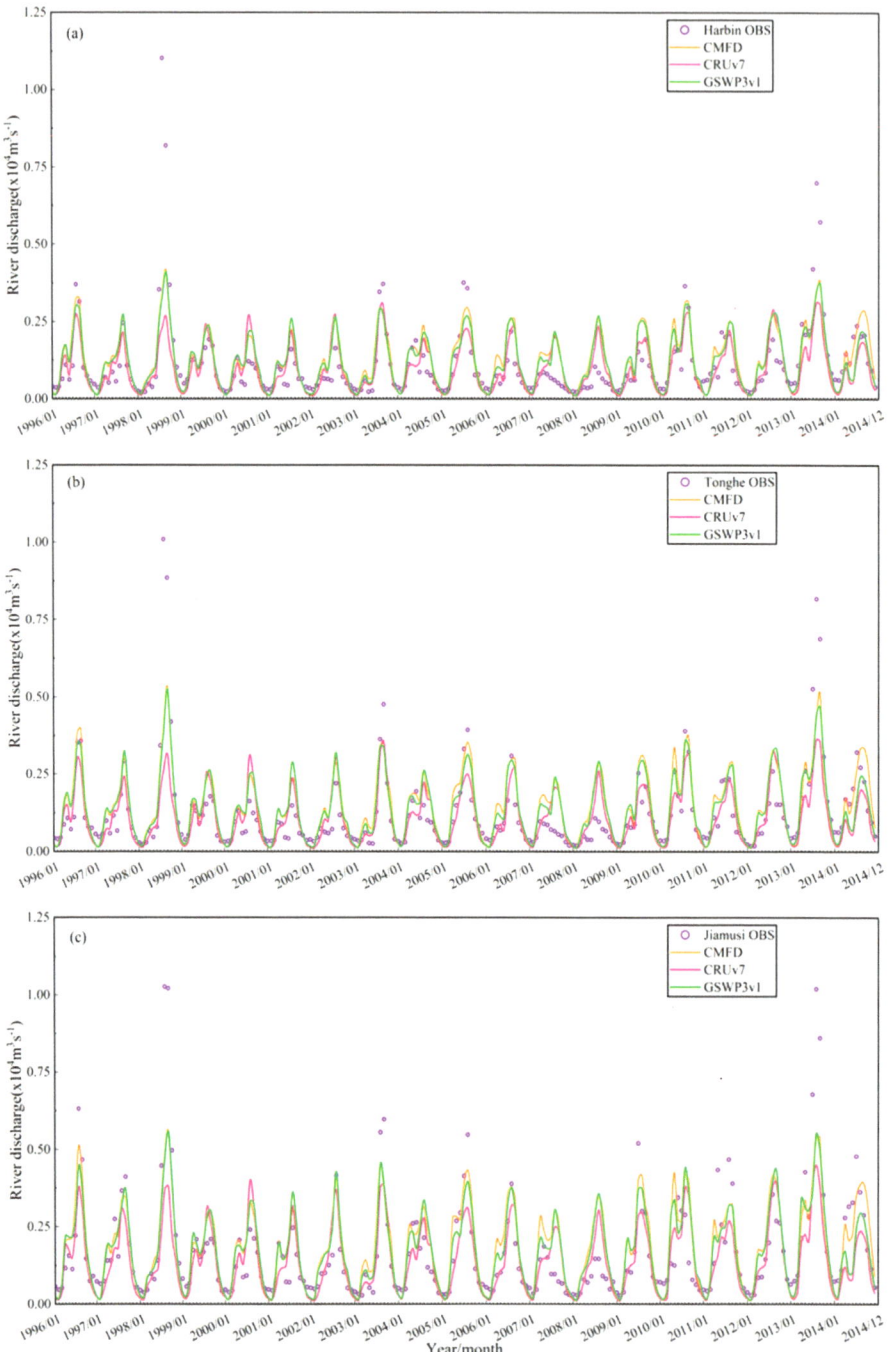

Figure 7. Comparisons of monthly observed and simulated discharge during 1996–2014 at stations (**a**) Harbin, (**b**) Tonghe, and (**c**) Jiamusi in the middle and lower reaches of the SRB.

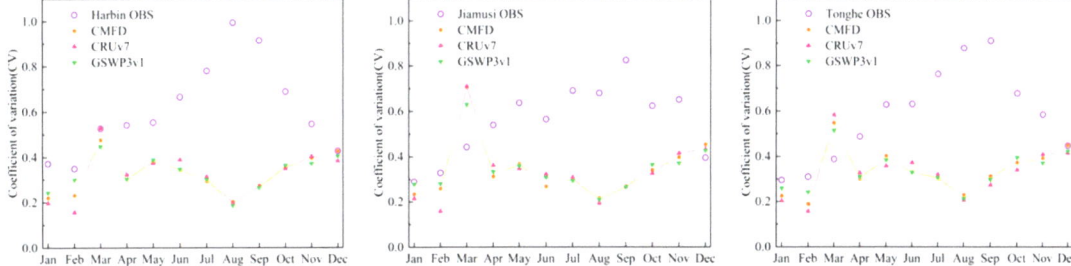

Figure 8. Coefficients of variation (CVs) of monthly discharges during 1996–2014 at three selected hydrological stations in the SRB.

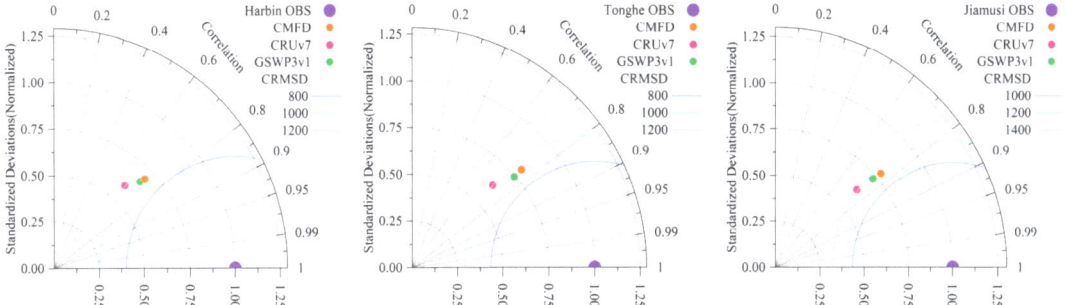

Figure 9. Taylor diagram for monthly discharges at three hydrological stations during 1996–2014, which shows the correlation coefficient (CC), normalized standard deviation (STD), and centered root-mean-square difference (CRMSD).

Figure 10a depicts the NSE of the daily-scale simulated and observed discharges for the period of 1996–2014, and the values of the simulated daily discharges obtained from the three meteorological forcing datasets simulated by the coupled model with the NSE calculated from the measured daily discharges were all greater than 0.6, which implied that the meteorological forcing data combined with CLM5 and CaMa-Flood v4.1 simulated the discharge process better in the SRB. Among them, CMFD performed the best, with the highest NSE value at Jiamusi station (0.78) and the lowest NSE value at Harbin station (0.71), and the mean NSE value of CMFD was 0.74. Similar to CMFD, GSWP3v1 and CRUv7 had the lowest NSE values at Harbin station, which were 0.70 and 0.66, respectively, and the mean NSE values of both were 0.74 (slightly lower than that of CMFD) and 0.70, respectively. In summary, the flow simulation of CMFD was better than that of GSWP3v1 and CRUv7. The difference here may be attributed to the meteorological forcing data uncertainty, model uncertainty, and the interaction between model uncertainty and meteorological forcing data uncertainty. Figure 10b depicts the RBs of the daily-scale simulated and observed discharges for the period 1996–2014. The RBs of the simulated daily discharges obtained by the coupled model simulations at the three hydrological stations by CMFD and GSWP3v1 and the calculated RBs of the measured daily discharges were both greater than 0, and the RBs of CRUv7 were both less than 0, i.e., the discharges in the SRB were overestimated by CMFD and GSWP3v1, and the discharges in the SRBs were underestimated by CRUv7. For discharges, CMFD and GSWP3v1 had the highest uncertainty at Tonghe station, with RB values as high as 20.26% and 14.86%, respectively, and both had the lowest uncertainty at Jiamusi station, with RB values of 10.65% and 4.94%, respectively. CRUv7 was the opposite of the former two, which had the lowest uncertainty at Tonghe station (−9.12%) and the highest at Jiamusi (−16.94%). The mean absolute RB values of CMFD, GSWP3v1, and

CRUv7 were 15.2%, 10.1%, and 12.1%, respectively. GSWP3v1 was closer to the measured discharges than CMFD and CRUv7, but it still had some uncertainty. The underestimation of the discharge by CRUv7 was probably due to its underestimation of the high-intensity precipitation (Figure 4).

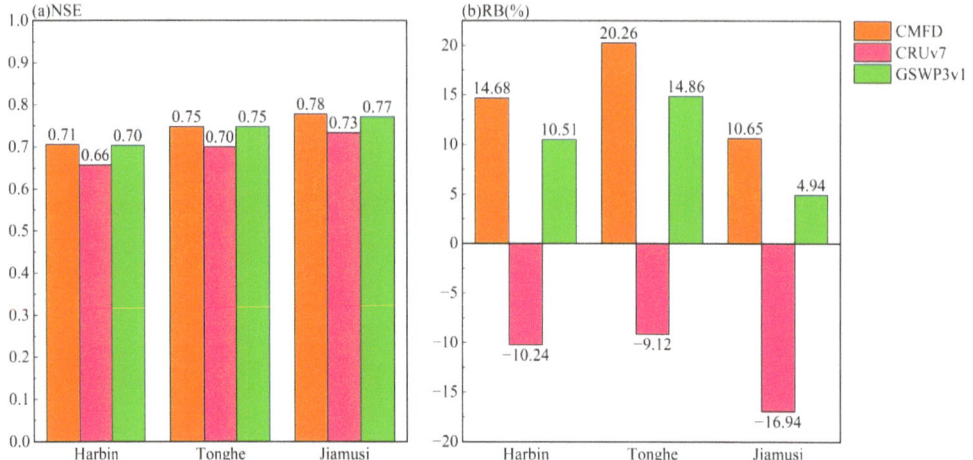

Figure 10. (**a**) Nash–Sutcliffe efficiency coefficient (NSE) and (**b**) relative bias (RB) for daily streamflow at the three hydrological stations during 1996–2014. The names on the x-axis refer to the same stations as in Figure 2.

4. Discussion

4.1. Impact of Precipitation Data on Discharge

In the comparison analysis of each station, we evaluated the accuracy of CMFD, CRUv7, and GSWP3v1 in recording precipitation in the SRB from 1996 to 2014 based on precipitation data obtained from meteorological stations. The results showed that the precipitation trends of the CMFD were the most similar to the trends of OBS at the yearly, monthly, and daily scales. The better performance of CMFD precipitation was attributed to its integration with CMA, in addition to the fact that the spatial resolution of CMFD is higher than that of both CRUv7 and GSWP3v1, which further improves the accuracy of the precipitation data within the SRB. Experiments conducted on the evaluation of meteorological forcing data on the Yunnan-Guizhou Plateau and throughout China also showed that CMFD and GSWP3v1 yielded better results than CRUv7 as forcing data [50]. From Table 4, it can be seen that in the range of medium- to high-intensity precipitation (PI > 10 mm/d), the RSME of CMFD, CRUv7, and GSWP3v1 goes from 2.35 mm/d to 12.08 mm/d, which is much larger than the RMSE (0.22~1.42 mm/d) of low-intensity precipitation ($0 \leq PI < 10$ mm/d), and considering that most of the moderate to heavy precipitation in the SRB occurs in the warm season [24], this result demonstrates that all precipitation data are insufficient to monitor short-term high-intensity precipitation. However, meteorological forcing data contain information at a larger spatial resolution, representing the meteorological conditions in the area covered by the scale, and the observations contain only the real values at this point of the standardized station [51]. This shortcoming is reflected in the discharge simulation results of the model, and the CVs of monthly discharges in Figure 8 show that the simulated discharge fluctuates to a lesser extent than the observed discharge during the cold season in the time period under study, and the value of the CVs is generally in the range of 0.1–0.5. The observed discharge fluctuation in the SRB in the warm season is high throughout the year, and the value of the CVs is generally in the range of 0.6–1.0, while that of the CVs of the simulated discharge is mostly in the range of 0.1–0.4 in the warm season, and the model is not sufficiently accurate to simulate the discharge in the warm season, which makes the simulated discharge differ from the data of the hydrological stations in Harbin, Tonghe, and Jiamusi in the warm seasons of 1996 and 2013—sufficient reason to determine that the meteorological forcing data are deficient in their ability to capture medium- and high-intensity precipitation data in the warm season.

Precipitation is very critical for discharge simulation [51], and the regional discharge simulations performed in this study relied heavily on precipitation data input to CLM5. Precipitation data error is affected by satellites' sensor types and inversion algorithms, and analyzing and evaluating the precipitation data in CMFD, CRUv7, and GSWP3v1 does not provide information on which sensor type and inversion algorithm can be used to improve discharge simulation in the SRB. Therefore, future research could focus on comparing all precipitation products using different sensor types and inversion algorithms with CMFD, CRUv7, and GSWP3v1, which would enhance the discharge simulation capability of CLM5 in the SRB after improving the hydrologic postprocessing routine and provide a basis for higher resolution discharge and flooded area simulations.

4.2. Considerations and Potential Implications for Model Improvement

Studies in arid and semiarid regions have shown that the runoff and river evolution performance of CLM is not satisfactorily improved by parameter calibration [52], so we improved it by introducing physically based runoff and river evolution schemes. From the simulation results of the discharge and flooded areas from 1996 to 2014 (Figures 5 and 6), this study better restored the high-resolution dynamic hydrological processes in the SRB and provided high-resolution discharge datasets and inundation area maps through an offline coupling model with strong physical mechanisms. The NSE of the present simulated daily discharge to station observations ranges from 0.72 ± 0.06, and the RB of daily discharge simulated by GSWP3v1 ranges from 4.94% to 14.86%. Spatially, the higher topography in the southeast and northwest of the SRB results in some areas in the middle and lower reaches of the SRB being permanently flooded, which could be exposed to a greater risk of flooding during the warm season.

The spatial and temporal heterogeneity of surface runoff is driven by a sophisticated mixture of climate change and anthropogenic factors, with multiple drivers overlapping. The consideration of anthropogenic factors in the simulation framework proposed in this study is primarily illustrated by the consideration that the subsurface data in CLM5 is a dynamically varying dataset encompassing a wide number of PFTs, but in a high-latitude SRB with snow and precipitation, we also need to estimate LSMs under the combined influence of different PFTs and reanalysis products, which can be used to model the water fluxes with more accuracy. Based on the rapid development of machine learning and artificial intelligence in the field of climate forecasting and simulation, the accuracy of the meteorological forcing data mass has been substantially enhanced [53,54]. The modeling framework presented in this research can be used as a postprocessing approach to decrease the forecastable bias of the numerical weather prediction, and the high-quality meteorological forcing data provide the foundation of the modified CLM5, which can be applied to the high-resolution discharge modeling and prediction of the SRB.

5. Conclusions

In this study, we quantified the overall performance of SRB discharge estimates obtained from different meteorological forcing datasets simulated by offline coupling CLM5 with CaMa-Flood. Three high-resolution discharge datasets were obtained by inputting three meteorological forcing datasets from 1996–2014, combined with SRB's high-resolution subsurface dataset, into CLM5 for land surface process simulation, followed by offline coupling CaMa-Flood for confluence process simulation of river discharge from 1996 to 2014. The major conclusions of this study are as follows. First, the results of the quantitative assessment of the precipitation data showed that in the SRB, CMFD exhibited the highest quality, followed by GSWP3v1, while CRUv7 performed the least effectively. Notably, all three datasets exhibited limited capability to capture high-intensity precipitation events. Second, both discharge and flooded areas simulated based on the coupled model showed good seasonality, spatially capturing the process of river discharge increase in the warm season and river recession in the cold season. Furthermore, simulating the multi-year average flooded area within the SRB based on runoff showed the ability to monitor flooding. Third, the discharges simulated by the coupled model were validated by comparison with the actual measurements, and the best-performing CMFDs in the Taylor diagrams had higher NSEs at Harbin Station (0.71), Tonghe Station (0.75), and Jiamusi Station (0.78). In addition, the fluctuation range of the simulated discharges generally covers the measured data.

The findings of this study provide a foundation for the application of offline coupling land surface models with hydrological models in flood monitoring and early warning systems. Compared to the flow observation data at the SRB hydrostations, the coupled model simulations exhibit similar spatial patterns. However, due to the inadequate capacity of meteorological datasets to observe short-term intensive precipitation, the discharge during the warm season is largely underestimated [55]. Therefore, prior to application, it is necessary to optimize meteorological data, especially the precipitation component, to achieve reliable simulation results. Furthermore, the low resolution of the subsurface dataset restricts the resolution of the coupled model simulation results. More precise flood risk maps can only be generated by identifying potential flood inundation areas and integrating them with high-intensity rainfall events.

Because the offline coupling model of CLM5 and CaMa-Flood possesses a robust physical mechanism and is relatively insensitive to parameter adjustments [52], its applicability in other regions is assured. This coupled model can be employed to simulate runoff processes in medium and large global basins under varying climate scenarios, aiding in enhancing our understanding of runoff processes under different climate scenarios. The simulation results of inundated areas can serve as a reference for decision-makers in formulating plans to address flooding.

Author Contributions: Conceptualization, H.L. and Z.Z. (Zhiwei Zhang); methodology, Z.Z. (Zhiwei Zhang); validation, H.L., Z.Z. (Zhiwei Zhang) and Z.Z. (Zhen Zhang); formal analysis, Z.Z. (Zhiwei Zhang); investigation, H.L.; resources, Z.Z. (Zhiwei Zhang); data curation, H.L.; writing—original draft preparation, Z.Z. (Zhiwei Zhang); writing—review and editing, Z.Z. (Zhiwei Zhang); visualization, Z.Z. (Zhiwei Zhang); supervision, Z.Z. (Zhiwei Zhang); project administration, Z.Z. (Zhiwei Zhang); funding acquisition, H.L. All authors have read and agreed to the published version of the manuscript.

Funding: This research was supported by Ministry of Agriculture and Rural Affairs of the People's Republic of China Department of Science, Technology and Education (GMO Bio-safety Office), grant number A120201.

Data Availability Statement: The datasets presented in this paper are too large to be retained or publicly archived with available resources. The documentation and methods used to support this study are available from neaulih@neau.edu.cn at Northeast Agricultural University.

Conflicts of Interest: The authors declare no conflict of interest.

References

1. Yin, J.; Gentine, P.; Zhou, S.; Sullivan, S.C.; Wang, R.; Zhang, Y.; Guo, S. Large increase in global storm runoff extremes driven by climate and anthropogenic changes. *Nat. Commun.* **2018**, *9*, 4389. [CrossRef]
2. Miao, Y.; Wang, A. Evaluation of Routed-Runoff from Land Surface Models and Reanalyses Using Observed Streamflow in Chinese River Basins. *J. Meteorol. Res.* **2020**, *34*, 73–87. [CrossRef]
3. Vergara-Temprado, J.; Ban, N.; Schär, C. Extreme Sub-Hourly Precipitation Intensities Scale Close to the Clausius-Clapeyron Rate Over Europe. *Geophys. Res. Lett.* **2021**, *48*, e2020gl089506. [CrossRef]
4. Piao, S.; Ciais, P.; Huang, Y.; Shen, Z.; Peng, S.; Li, J.; Zhou, L.; Liu, H.; Ma, Y.; Ding, Y.; et al. The impacts of climate change on water resources and agriculture in China. *Nature* **2010**, *467*, 43–51. [CrossRef]
5. Cui, T.; Li, Y.; Yang, L.; Nan, Y.; Li, K.; Tudaji, M.; Tian, F. Non-monotonic changes in Asian Water Towers' streamflow at increasing warming levels. *Nat. Commun.* **2023**, *14*, 1176. [CrossRef] [PubMed]

6. Rosa, L.; Chiarelli, D.D.; Rulli, M.C.; Dell'Angelo, J.; D'Odorico, P. Global agricultural economic water scarcity. *Sci. Adv.* **2020**, *6*, eaaz6031. [CrossRef] [PubMed]
7. Qi, W.; Feng, L.; Yang, H.; Zhu, X.; Liu, Y.; Liu, J. Weakening flood, intensifying hydrological drought severity and decreasing drought probability in Northeast China. *J. Hydrol. Reg. Stud.* **2021**, *38*, 100941. [CrossRef]
8. Qi, W.; Liu, J.; Yang, H.; Zhu, X.; Tian, Y.; Jiang, X.; Feng, L. Large Uncertainties in Runoff Estimations of GLDAS Versions 2.0 and 2.1 in China. *Earth Space Sci.* **2020**, *7*, e2019ea000829. [CrossRef]
9. Qi, W.; Zhang, C.; Fu, G.; Zhou, H. Global Land Data Assimilation System data assessment using a distributed biosphere hydrological model. *J. Hydrol.* **2015**, *528*, 652–667. [CrossRef]
10. Zaitchik, B.F.; Rodell, M.; Olivera, F. Evaluation of the Global Land Data Assimilation System using global river discharge data and a source-to-sink routing scheme. *Water Resour. Res.* **2010**, *46*, W06507. [CrossRef]
11. Massoud, E.C.; Bloom, A.A.; Longo, M.; Reager, J.T.; Levine, P.A.; Worden, J.R. Information content of soil hydrology in a west Amazon watershed as informed by GRACE. *Hydrol. Earth Syst. Sci.* **2022**, *26*, 1407–1423. [CrossRef]
12. Xiong, J.; Guo, S.; Yin, J.; Gu, L.; Xiong, F. Using the Global Hydrodynamic Model and GRACE Follow-On Data to Access the 2020 Catastrophic Flood in Yangtze River Basin. *Remote Sens.* **2021**, *13*, 3023. [CrossRef]
13. Zhang, X.-J.; Tang, Q.; Pan, M.; Tang, Y. A Long-Term Land Surface Hydrologic Fluxes and States Dataset for China. *J. Hydrometeorol.* **2014**, *15*, 2067–2084. [CrossRef]
14. Sellers, P.J.; Dickinson, R.E.; Randall, D.A.; Betts, A.K.; Hall, F.G.; Berry, J.A.; Henderson-Sellers, A. Modeling the Exchanges of Energy, Water, and Carbon Between Continents and the Atmosphere. *Science* **1997**, *275*, 502–509. [CrossRef]
15. Mitchell, K.E. The multi-institution North American Land Data Assimilation System (NLDAS): Utilizing multiple GCIP products and partners in a continental distributed hydrological modeling system. *J. Geophys. Res.* **2004**, *109*, D07S90. [CrossRef]
16. Danabasoglu, G.; Lamarque, J.F.; Bacmeister, J.; Bailey, D.A.; DuVivier, A.K.; Edwards, J.; Strand, W.G. The Community Earth System Model Version 2 (CESM2). *J. Adv. Model. Earth Syst.* **2020**, *12*, e2019ms001916. [CrossRef]
17. Lawrence, D.M.; Oleson, K.W.; Flanner, M.G.; Thornton, P.E.; Swenson, S.C.; Lawrence, P.J.; Slater, A.G. Parameterization improvements and functional and structural advances in Version 4 of the Community Land Model. *J. Adv. Model. Earth Syst.* **2011**, *3*, e2011ms000045. [CrossRef]
18. Oleson, K.; Lawrence, D.M.; Bonan, G.B.; Drewniak, B.; Huang, M.; Koven, C.D.; Levis, S.; Li, F.; Riley, W.J.; Subin, Z.M.; et al. *Technical Description of Version 4.5 of the Community Land Model (CLM) (No. NCAR/TN-503+STR)*; National Center for Atmospheric Research: Boulder, CO, USA, 2013. [CrossRef]
19. Berghuijs, W.R.; Harrigan, S.; Molnar, P.; Slater, L.J.; Kirchner, J.W. The Relative Importance of Different Flood-Generating Mechanisms Across Europe. *Water Resour. Res.* **2019**, *55*, 4582–4593. [CrossRef]
20. Yamazaki, D.; Kanae, S.; Kim, H.; Oki, T. A physically based description of floodplain inundation dynamics in a global river routing model. *Water Resour. Res.* **2011**, *47*, W04501. [CrossRef]
21. Faiz, M.A.; Liu, D.; Fu, Q.; Uzair, M.; Khan, M.I.; Baig, F.; Cui, S. Stream flow variability and drought severity in the Songhua River Basin, Northeast China. *Stoch. Environ. Res. Risk Assess.* **2017**, *32*, 1225–1242. [CrossRef]
22. Wang, S.; Wang, Y.; Ran, L.; Su, T. Climatic and anthropogenic impacts on runoff changes in the Songhua River basin over the last 56years (1955–2010), Northeastern China. *Catena* **2015**, *127*, 258–269. [CrossRef]
23. Yu, C.; Shao, H.; Hu, D.; Liu, G.; Dai, X. Merging precipitation scheme design for improving the accuracy of regional precipitation products by machine learning and geographical deviation correction. *J. Hydrol.* **2023**, *620*, 129560. [CrossRef]
24. Chen, J.; Liao, J. Monitoring lake level changes in China using multi-altimeter data (2016–2019). *J. Hydrol.* **2020**, *590*, 125544. [CrossRef]
25. Chen, J.; Fenoglio, L.; Kusche, J.; Liao, J.; Uyanik, H.; Nadzir, Z.A.; Lou, Y. Evaluation of Sentinel-3A altimetry over Songhua river Basin. *J. Hydrol.* **2023**, *618*, 129197. [CrossRef]
26. Wu, Y.; Ju, H.; Qi, P.; Li, Z.; Zhang, G.; Sun, Y. Increasing flood risk under climate change and social development in the Second Songhua River basin in Northeast China. *J. Hydrol. Reg. Stud.* **2023**, *48*, 101459. [CrossRef]
27. He, J.; Yang, K.; Tang, W.; Lu, H.; Qin, J.; Chen, Y.; Li, X. The first high-resolution meteorological forcing dataset for land process studies over China. *Sci. Data* **2020**, *7*, 25. [CrossRef] [PubMed]
28. Peng, J.M.; Liu, S.F.; Dai, Y.J.; Wei, N. Evaluation of Common Land Model Based on International Land Model Benchmarking System. *Clim. Environ. Res.* **2020**, *25*, 649–666. [CrossRef]
29. Kim, H.J. *Global Soil Wetness Project Phase 3 Atmospheric Boundary Couinditions (Experiment 1)*; Data Integration and Analysis System (DIAS): Tokyo, Japan, 2017. [CrossRef]
30. Viovy, N. *CRUNCEP Version 7—Atmospheric Forcing Data for the Community Land Model*; Research Data Archive at the National Center for Atmospheric Research, Computational and Information Systems Lab: Boulder, CO, USA, 2018. [CrossRef]
31. Yu, Z.; Lu, C.; Tian, H.; Canadell, J.G. Largely underestimated carbon emission from land use and land cover change in the conterminous United States. *Glob. Chang. Biol.* **2019**, *25*, 3741–3752. [CrossRef]
32. Loveland, T.R.; Reed, B.C.; Brown, J.F.; Ohlen, D.O.; Zhu, Z.; Yang, L.; Merchant, J.W. Development of a global land cover characteristics database and IGBP DISCover from 1 km AVHRR data. *Int. J. Remote Sens.* **2010**, *21*, 1303–1330. [CrossRef]
33. Lawrence, P.J.; Chase, T.N. Representing a new MODIS consistent land surface in the Community Land Model (CLM 3.0). *J. Geophys. Res.* **2007**, *112*, G01023. [CrossRef]

34. Klein Goldewijk, K.; Beusen, A.; Doelman, J.; Stehfest, E. Anthropogenic land use estimates for the Holocene—HYDE 3.2. *Earth Syst. Sci. Data* **2017**, *9*, 927–953. [CrossRef]
35. Lawrence, D.M.; Hurtt, G.C.; Arneth, A.; Brovkin, V.; Calvin, K.V.; Jones, A.D.; Shevliakova, E. The Land Use Model Intercomparison Project (LUMIP) contribution to CMIP6: Rationale and experimental design. *Geosci. Model Dev.* **2016**, *9*, 2973–2998. [CrossRef]
36. Yamazaki, D.; Ikeshima, D.; Sosa, J.; Bates, P.D.; Allen, G.H.; Pavelsky, T.M. MERIT Hydro: A High-Resolution Global Hydrography Map Based on Latest Topography Dataset. *Water Resour. Res.* **2019**, *55*, 5053–5073. [CrossRef]
37. Wigmosta, M.S.; Li, H.; Wu, H.; Huang, M.; Ke, Y.; Coleman, A.M.; Leung, L.R. A Physically Based Runoff Routing Model for Land Surface and Earth System Models. *J. Hydrometeorol.* **2013**, *14*, 808–828. [CrossRef]
38. Lawrence, D.M.; Fisher, R.A.; Koven, C.D.; Oleson, K.W.; Swenson, S.C.; Bonan, G.; Zeng, X. The Community Land Model Version 5: Description of New Features, Benchmarking, and Impact of Forcing Uncertainty. *J. Adv. Model. Earth Syst.* **2019**, *11*, 4245–4287. [CrossRef]
39. Niu, G.-Y.; Yang, Z.-L.; Dickinson, R.E.; Gulden, L.E. A simple TOPMODEL-based runoff parameterization (SIMTOP) for use in global climate models. *J. Geophys. Res.* **2005**, *110*, D21106. [CrossRef]
40. Tesfa, T.K.; Li, H.Y.; Leung, L.R.; Huang, M.; Ke, Y.; Sun, Y.; Liu, Y. A subbasin-based framework to represent land surface processes in an Earth system model. *Geosci. Model Dev.* **2014**, *7*, 947–963. [CrossRef]
41. Verdin, K.L.; Jenson, S.K. Development of Continental Scale Digital Elevation Models and Extraction of Hydrographic Features. In Proceedings of the Third International Conference/Workshop on Integrating GIS and Environmental Modeling, Sante Fe, NM, USA, 21–25 January 1996; pp. 397–403.
42. Yamazaki, D.; Ikeshima, D.; Tawatari, R.; Yamaguchi, T.; O'Loughlin, F.; Neal, J.C.; Bates, P.D. A high-accuracy map of global terrain elevations. *Geophys. Res. Lett.* **2017**, *44*, 5844–5853. [CrossRef]
43. Yamazaki, D.; Lee, H.; Alsdorf, D.E.; Dutra, E.; Kim, H.; Kanae, S.; Oki, T. Analysis of the water level dynamics simulated by a global river model: A case study in the Amazon River. *Water Resour. Res.* **2012**, *48*, W09508. [CrossRef]
44. Yamazaki, D.; Oki, T.; Kanae, S. Deriving a global river network map and its sub-grid topographic characteristics from a fine-resolution flow direction map. *Hydrol. Earth Syst. Sci.* **2009**, *13*, 2241–2251. [CrossRef]
45. Rojas, M.; Lambert, F.; Ramirez-Villegas, J.; Challinor, A.J. Emergence of robust precipitation changes across crop production areas in the 21st century. *Proc. Natl. Acad. Sci. USA* **2019**, *116*, 6673–6678. [CrossRef] [PubMed]
46. Yang, H.; Zhou, F.; Piao, S.; Huang, M.; Chen, A.; Ciais, P.; Zeng, Z. Regional patterns of future runoff changes from Earth system models constrained by observation. *Geophys. Res. Lett.* **2017**, *44*, 5540–5549. [CrossRef]
47. He, Z.; Hu, H.; Tian, F.; Ni, G.; Hu, Q. Correcting the TRMM rainfall product for hydrological modelling in sparsely-gauged mountainous basins. *Hydrol. Sci. J.* **2016**, *62*, 306–318. [CrossRef]
48. Cao, Y.; Fu, C.; Wang, X.; Dong, L.; Yao, S.; Xue, B.; Wu, H. Decoding the dramatic hundred-year water level variations of a typical great lake in semi-arid region of northeastern Asia. *Sci. Total Environ.* **2021**, *770*, 145353. [CrossRef]
49. Zhang, L.; Gao, L.; Chen, J.; Zhao, L.; Zhao, J.; Qiao, Y.; Shi, J. Comprehensive evaluation of mainstream gridded precipitation datasets in the cold season across the Tibetan Plateau. *J. Hydrol. Reg. Stud.* **2022**, *43*, 101186. [CrossRef]
50. Yu, H.; Wang, L.; Yang, M. Effects of Elevation and Longitude on Precipitation and Drought on the Yunnan–Guizhou Plateau, China. *Pure Appl. Geophys.* **2023**, *180*, 2461–2481. [CrossRef]
51. Bodjrènou, R.; Sintondji, L.O.; Comandan, F. Hydrological modeling with physics-based models in the oueme basin: Issues and perspectives for simulation optimization. *J. Hydrol. Reg. Stud.* **2023**, *48*, 101448. [CrossRef]
52. Sheng, M.; Lei, H.; Jiao, Y.; Yang, D. Evaluation of the Runoff and River Routing Schemes in the Community Land Model of the Yellow River Basin. *J. Adv. Model. Earth Syst.* **2017**, *9*, 2993–3018. [CrossRef]
53. Bi, K.; Xie, L.; Zhang, H.; Chen, X.; Gu, X.; Tian, Q. Accurate medium-range global weather forecasting with 3D neural networks. *Nature* **2023**, *619*, 533–538. [CrossRef]
54. Hu, Y.; Chen, L.; Wang, Z.; Li, H. SwinVRNN: A Data-Driven Ensemble Forecasting Model via Learned Distribution Perturbation. *J. Adv. Model. Earth Syst.* **2023**, *15*, e2022ms003211. [CrossRef]
55. Wang, L.; Zhang, F.; Zhang, H.; Scott, C.A.; Zeng, C.; Shi, X. Intensive precipitation observation greatly improves hydrological modelling of the poorly gauged high mountain Mabengnong catchment in the Tibetan Plateau. *J. Hydrol.* **2018**, *556*, 500–509. [CrossRef]

Disclaimer/Publisher's Note: The statements, opinions and data contained in all publications are solely those of the individual author(s) and contributor(s) and not of MDPI and/or the editor(s). MDPI and/or the editor(s) disclaim responsibility for any injury to people or property resulting from any ideas, methods, instructions or products referred to in the content.

Article

Comparative Analysis of Convolutional Neural Network-Long Short-Term Memory, Sparrow Search Algorithm-Backpropagation Neural Network, and Particle Swarm Optimization-Extreme Learning Machine Models for the Water Discharge of the Buzău River, Romania

Liu Zhen [1,2,3] and Alina Bărbulescu [1,*]

1. Department of Civil Engineering, Transilvania University of Brasov, 5, Turnului Street, 500152 Brasov, Romania; lincoln110@foxmail.com
2. National Key Laboratory of Deep Oil and Gas, China University of Petroleum (East China), Qingdao 266580, China
3. School of Geosciences, China University of Petroleum (East China), Qingdao 266580, China
* Correspondence: alina.barbulescu@unitbv.ro

Citation: Zhen, L.; Bărbulescu, A. Comparative Analysis of Convolutional Neural Network-Long Short-Term Memory, Sparrow Search Algorithm-Backpropagation Neural Network, and Particle Swarm Optimization-Extreme Learning Machine Models for the Water Discharge of the Buzău River, Romania. *Water* **2024**, *16*, 289. https://doi.org/10.3390/w16020289

Academic Editor: Giuseppe Pezzinga

Received: 2 December 2023
Revised: 9 January 2024
Accepted: 11 January 2024
Published: 15 January 2024

Copyright: © 2024 by the authors. Licensee MDPI, Basel, Switzerland. This article is an open access article distributed under the terms and conditions of the Creative Commons Attribution (CC BY) license (https://creativecommons.org/licenses/by/4.0/).

Abstract: Modeling and forecasting the river flow is essential for the management of water resources. In this study, we conduct a comprehensive comparative analysis of different models built for the monthly water discharge of the Buzău River (Romania), measured in the upper part of the river's basin from January 1955 to December 2010. They employ convolutional neural networks (CNNs) coupled with long short-term memory (LSTM) networks, named CNN-LSTM, sparrow search algorithm with backpropagation neural networks (SSA-BP), and particle swarm optimization with extreme learning machines (PSO-ELM). These models are evaluated based on various criteria, including computational efficiency, predictive accuracy, and adaptability to different training sets. The models obtained applying CNN-LSTM stand out as top performers, demonstrating a superior computational efficiency and a high predictive accuracy, especially when built with the training set containing the data series from January 1984 (putting the Siriu Dam in operation) to September 2006 (Model type S2). This research provides valuable guidance for selecting and assessing river flow prediction models, offering practical insights for the scientific community and real-world applications. The findings suggest that Model type S2 is the preferred choice for the discharge forecast predictions due to its high computational speed and accuracy. Model type S (considering the training set recorded from January 1955 to September 2006) is recommended as a secondary option. Model type S1 (with the training period January 1955–December 1983) is suitable when the other models are unavailable. This study advances the field of water discharge prediction by presenting a precise comparative analysis of these models and their respective strengths

Keywords: flow prediction; CNN-LSTM; SSA-BP; PSO-ELM

1. Introduction

From ancient times, rivers are places along which civilizations developed, providing water for consumption, agriculture, transportation, and other activities [1]. Understanding their dynamics is necessary, given their complex role in communities' existence and as a main background for water management policies [2–7]. Studying river discharge in correlation with other environmental variables will lead to a better understanding of climate change [8–11].

Different techniques have been used for modeling the rivers' discharge. Rahayu et al. [12] modeled the Amprong River discharge using an autoregressive integrated moving average (ARIMA) approach. Ghimire [13] applied the same technique in two case studies from the USA, whereas Valipour [14] proposed two alternative models, ARIMA and seasonal ARIMA (SARIMA), for long-term runoff analysis. Yürekli et al. [15] used ARIMA to simulate the monthly discharge of Kelkit Stream.

Conventional flood prediction approaches, often reliant on empirical hydrological and meteorological models, struggle with large-scale and complex data sets. Despite ARIMA models being simple, easy to implement, and flexible, capturing the series components (trend, seasonality, and cycles), they cannot handle nonlinearities, regime changes, or shocks. Moreover, specific hypotheses must be fulfilled using data series and residuals. Since the model's quality may be affected by outliers or missing existence, data preprocessing is necessary before modeling [16]. Therefore, other approaches have been proposed to address these drawbacks. Some of them are artificial intelligence (AI), or machine learning (ML), models that do not consider mathematical relationships, utilizing only sets of input parameters, in contrast with the physical models that utilize mathematical tools to predict hydrological phenomena [17].

AI technology has become a research hotspot in engineering and science fields in recent years due to its significant capabilities in handling big data, pattern recognition, automated decision making, and predictive modeling, as well as enhancing efficiency and accuracy. AI models predict natural disasters, aiding in early preparation and the mitigation of their impacts. Therefore, ML techniques have attracted the attention of scientists working in water resources. For example, Abrahart and See [18] compared the forecasting power of ANN and ARMA models of river flow data for two catchments. Birikundavyi et al. [19] compared the performances of artificial neural networks (ANNs) and autoregressive moving average (ARMA) techniques in predicting the daily streamflow and showed better results obtained by the first approach. Hong and Hong [20] employed ANN to forecast the flooding produced by a river in Malaysia. Kisi and Çobaner [21] employed multi-layer perceptron (MLP) and radial basis (RB) neural networks to model flow series recorded at three stations on Kizilirmak River (Turkey) and study river stage–discharge relationships using different neural network computing techniques. A review of the ANN applications in hydrology can be found in [22]. Valipour et al. [23] compared the forecast of the Dez Dam Reservoir monthly inflow obtained using ARIMA, ARMA, and autoregressive artificial neural networks. They found that the best forecasting model was the dynamic artificial neural network with a sigmoid activation function. Uca et al. [24] compared multiple linear regression (MLRg) and ANN in the discharge prediction of the Jenderam, showing that the first approach had the best performance.

Combined approaches have also been proposed to benefit from the capabilities of various techniques. Li and Yang [25] employed a Bayesian optimized ML seasonally adjusted to model the suspended sediment load. Hayder et al. [26] proposed the use of particle swarm-optimized cascade-forward neural networks on a case study from Malaysia. Xiang et al. [27] introduced an adaptive intelligent dynamic water planning (AIDWRP) model to optimize environmental planning.

During the last period, models combining convolutional neural networks with long short-term memory (CNN-LSTM), the sparrow search algorithm with backpropagation neural networks (SSA-BP), and particle swarm optimization with extreme learning machines (PSO-ELM) provided very good results in various fields.

CNN-LSTM, an innovative deep learning architecture, has achieved breakthrough results in fields such as image and speech recognition and natural language processing. It combines the spatial feature extraction capabilities of CNNs with the sequential data processing strength of long short-term memory (LSTM), effectively handling complex series data. For instance, Essien et al. [28] utilized the CNN-LSTM framework to predict urban traffic flow, achieving higher accuracy and efficiency than traditional methods. Zhang and Li [29] developed a CNN-LSTM model to enhance the accuracy of air quality forecasting. This model outperformed SARIMA.

The SSA-BP method merges the global search capability of the sparrow search algorithm (SSA) with the powerful learning mechanism of backpropagation neural networks

(BP). This approach has shown exceptional performance in power systems, financial market analysis, and bioinformatics. For example, Yan et al. [30] successfully employed an SSA-optimized BP neural network for classifying potential water sources for coal mines. Xin et al. [31] introduced a BP neural network model optimized with the sparrow search algorithm (SSA) to identify pipeline deformation.

PSO-ELM combines the efficient global search capability of particle swarm optimization (PSO) with the rapid learning features of extreme learning machines (ELMs). This combination has demonstrated strong potential in complex problems like predicting the performance of building materials [32].

Zhang et al. [33] developed a CEEMDAN-PSO-ELM approach and applied it to monthly precipitation forecasting. A comparative analysis with LSTM, ELM, and PSO-ELM highlighted its significant benefits in hydrological simulation and prediction.

The hybrid algorithms have shown significant advantages over traditional methods in river flow forecasting. Still, Kratzert et al. [34,35] demonstrated the effectiveness of LSTM in flood forecasting, highlighting its superiority in prediction accuracy and laying the groundwork for applying more complex hybrid methods like CNN-LSTM in flood prediction.

Our search of the scientific literature yielded insignificant results on modeling water discharges based on CNN-LSTM, SSA-BP, or PSO-ELM, despite the proven performances of these approaches.

Our research aims to answer whether the Buzău River discharge is altered after putting the Siriu Dam, one of Romania's most important accumulation lakes in the country, into operation. Two articles [36,37] attempted to answer this question by testing different statistical hypotheses and using indicators of hydrologic alterations (IHA). Two models (regression and generalized regression neural network) [37,38] for the daily river discharge have also been proposed, but neither of them was satisfactory from an accuracy viewpoint. Given the importance of predicting the river discharge (based on correct models) for the Romanian Risk Management Plan, this paper provides three alternative models for the monthly discharge of the Buzău River. The significance of this approach consists of the following.

(1) It provides reliable models for the monthly discharge of the Buzău River for the first time.

(2) It emphasizes that building the Siriu Dam impacted the river flow, confirming the findings of the statistics from [37].

(3) It analyzes and compares the effectiveness of CNN-LSTM, SSA-BP, and PSO-ELM in the river's water discharge forecasting field. From this point of view, these approaches are new in the hydrological series modeling.

Moreover, the potential and advantages of these advanced algorithms in water resources modeling and forecasting are demonstrated, and new perspectives and directions for future research and practice are provided.

2. Materials and Methods

2.1. Study Area and Data Series

Hydrotechnical arrangements, like dams and water accumulations, are built to solve anthropic needs and avoid catastrophic events, diminishing flooding frequencies and intensity. The Siriu Dam, on the Buzău River in Romania, was constructed for such reasons.

The Buzău River is one of the most important rivers in Romania from the viewpoint of the population served for drinking water, agricultural, and industrial uses. The principal floods on the Buzău River were recorded in 1948, 1969, 1971, 1975 (with a peak flow of 2100 m^3/s), 1980, 1984, 1991, and 2005 in May–July. The floods were very frequent, with high intensities, upstream of Nehoiu city, before the Siriu Dam, the second largest embankment dam in Romania, was installed.

The Buzău River's catchment (Figure 1) is located in a temperate–continental climate and covers a surface of 5264 km^2. The river basin's mean elevation is 1043 m. In the natural regimen, the river's flow is between 0.76 m^3/s and 5000 m^3/s.

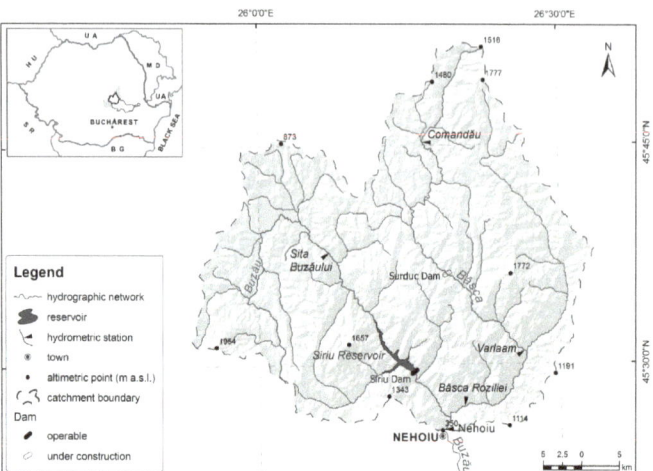

Figure 1. Buzău River basin in Romania [37].

Eighty percent of its annual volume is collected in the upper part, upstream of Nehoiu. The multi-annual and specific mean flow are 25.2 m³/s, and 17 L/s·km², respectively [39]. The Buzău River's complex arrangement includes the Buzau River upper course in the Siriu-Nehoiasu zone and that of its tributary, Bâsca Mare. Siriu Dam started to work on 1 January 1984 on the upper reach of the Buzău River. It has a length of 122 m and a height of 570 m, a maximum storage volume of 125 million m³, and occupies a surface of 420 ha, draining 56.1% of the Buzău River catchment [40].

In the Siriu Dam section, the multiannual flow rate is 9.59 m³/s, the maximum flow with 0.01% insurance is 2900 m³/s, with 0.1% insurance is 1720 m³/s, and with 1% insurance is 980 m³/s. The accumulation must supply drinking and industrial water to settlements and industrial plants downstream with about 2.5 m³/s, and water for irrigation for 50,000 ha [39]. Studies [37–39] showed the change in the river discharge regimen after the dam entered into operation on 1 January 1984.

Taking into account the importance of the Buzău River in the economy of the region, we considered it necessary to conduct a deeper investigation into the results provided using statistical methods and provide more evidence about the river discharge modification after January 1984, using a different approach (modeling, in this study).

The analyzed series consists of the monthly average discharge of the Buzău River recorded at the Nehoiu hydrometric station (45°25′29″ latitude and 26°18′27″ longitude) from January 1955 to December 2010 (Figure 2).

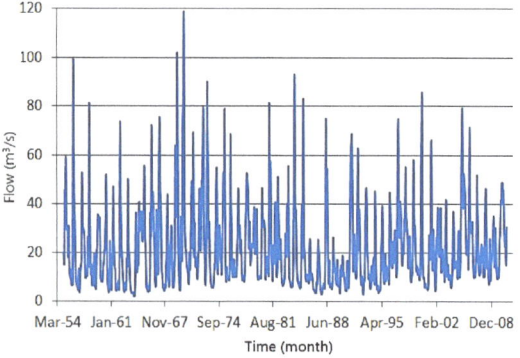

Figure 2. Monthly series of the Buzău River discharge.

The data series was automatically collected twice a day (at 7 a.m. and 7 p.m.) and transmitted to the National Institute of Hydrology and Water Management (INGHA), where they were verified by specialists who built the monthly average flow series from the daily data series. The series contains official data, without gaps, provided to us by INGHA for scientific purposes.

The basic statistics for S, S1, and S2 are presented in Table 1. S1 has the highest mean and variance indicating the highest variability of the river flow, confirmed by the existence of many flooding episodes before 1984. The lowest values of all statistics correspond to S2, showing a more homogenous distribution of the series values around the mean. All distributions are right-skewed and leptokurtic.

Table 1. The basic statistics and the results of the statistical tests (p-values).

	Minimum	Mean	Maximum	Variance	Coefficient of Variation (%)	Skewness	Kurtosis
S	2.18	21.83	117.29	306.82	80.23	1.79	3.93
S1	2.18	23.16	117.29	347.58	80.51	1.76	3.92
S2	2.93	20.41	92.79	259.14	78.87	1.76	3.43

The dataset was divided into a training set and a test set for the purposes of this study. The training set was different for each model: January 1955–September 2006 in Model S, January 1955–December 1983 (before putting the Siriu Dam in operation) in Model S1, and January 1984–September 2006 in Model S2 (after operating the dam). In all cases, the test set consists of data from October 2006 to December 2010.

2.2. Methodology

Classical approaches rely on the assumption of a constant data-generating process. They often fail to provide adequate models due to the nonlinear time series dynamic and the lack of adaptation of the method. Moreover, hydrological series are affected by permanently changing conditions, which are more or less abrupt. These issues make the river flow modeling problem well suited for utilizing ML approaches, which do not make any assumptions on the study process (assumptions generally imposed by other methods, like different regressions or Box–Jenkins methods).

Three alternative techniques are proposed here and described in the following paragraphs.

2.2.1. Convolutional Neural Networks-Long Short-Term Memory (CNN-LSTM)

CNN-LSTM [41] is a deep learning model that combines the characteristics of CNN [42] and LSTM [43,44] networks, designed for processing time-series data, image sequences, videos, and similar data types.

CNN is a deep learning model designed specifically for processing image data. It extracts features from images using convolutional layers and pooling layers. Convolutional layers employ convolution kernels to detect various features within an image while pooling layers reduce the dimensions of the feature maps. The mathematical representation of CNN is as follows:

- Convolution Layer Operation:

$$x^l = f^l\left(x^{(l-1)}\right) = \left(W^l * x^{(l-1)}\right) + b^{(l)}, \tag{1}$$

where $x^{(l-1)}$ is the feature map from the previous layer, W^l is the convolution kernel, $b^{(l)}$ is the bias term, and f^l is the activation function.

- Pooling Layer Operation:

$$x^l = g^{(l)}\left(x^{(l-1)}\right). \tag{2}$$

where $g^{(l)}$ is typically the maximum pooling or average pooling operation.

A CNN typically has three layers: a convolutional layer, a pooling layer, and a fully connected layer. The first layer is responsible for computing the dot product between the kernel (containing the parameters to be learnt) and the matrix containing the features map. The second layer has the role of reducing the representation size by processing individually its slice. The classification is performed in the third layer. It should be understood that "fully connected" expresses the connection between the inputs from one layer and all the nodes from the next layer.

LSTM [43] is a recurrent neural network designed for handling time-series data. It features memory cells that effectively capture long-term time dependencies. The mathematical representation of LSTM is as follows:

Input Gate: $i_t = \sigma(W_i \cdot [h_{t-1}, x_t] + b_i)$,
Forget Gate: $f_t = \sigma\left(W_f \cdot [h_{t-1}, x_t] + b_f\right)$,
Candidate Unit: $\widetilde{C}_t = \tanh(W_C \cdot [h_{t-1}, x_t] + b_C)$,
Update Unit: $C_t = f_t * C_{t-1} + i_t * \widetilde{C}_t$,
Output Gate: $O_t = \sigma(W_o \cdot [h_{t-1}, x_t] + b_o)$,
Hidden State: $h_t = O_t * \tanh(C_t)$,

where t is the time (moment), x_t is the input at time step t, h_t is the hidden state at t, C_t is the cell state at t, i_t, f_t, and O_t are the forget and output gate units at t, W_i, W_f, W_C, W_o and b_i, b_f, b_C, b_o represent the weights and biases, respectively, at the input, forget, candidate, and output gates (Figure 3).

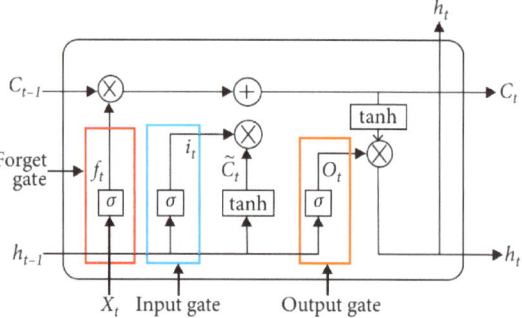

Figure 3. LSTM unit [45].

The LSTM can add or remove information to the cells and controls it by the gates (formed by a sigmoid neural net layer and a multiplication operation, *). The output of the sigmoid layer is zero (nothing will pass through the gate) or one (everything will pass). The Input Gate decides the values to be updated, and then the Candidate Unit builds the new candidates vector's values, $\widetilde{C}_t$, updated in the Update Unit. The last two steps filter the information (in the Output Gate) that will exist in the network after applying a tanh function (to scale the values in the interval $[-1, 1]$) and multiplying by the sigmoid gate's output (in the Hidden state) [46].

In the CNN-LSTM approach (Figure 4), CNN is used to extract spatial features from the sequence data, while LSTM is employed to handle the temporal dependencies of these features.

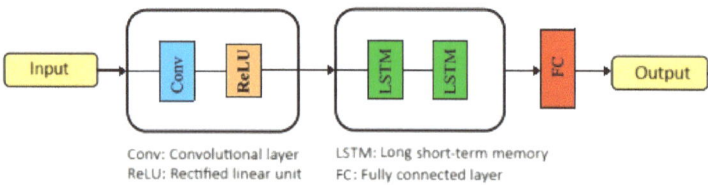

Figure 4. CNN-LSTM model.

The specific steps are as follows:

- CNN Processing: Input sequence data are processed through CNN to extract feature maps for each time step. These feature maps typically contain spatial information from the images.
- Sequence Processing: The feature maps from each time step are the inputs to LSTM. LSTM processes these feature maps and captures their temporal dependencies. The LSTM's hidden state is updated at each time step to capture long-term dependencies in the sequence.
- Output: The output from LSTM is used for time-series prediction.

CNNs are powerful for learning local patterns in data and feature extraction, while LSTMs are effective at capturing long-term dependencies in sequential data.

The benefit of CNN-LSTM is that the model can deal with very long input series, read as sub-series by the CNN and then combined by the LSTM model. Therefore, CNN will capture the data patterns, and LSTM will learn the temporal dependencies and make the final prediction. In such a way, improved performances of the combined model are obtained [47]. The new model can also extract nonlinear features and fluctuating trends [48].

2.2.2. Sparrow Search Algorithm-Backpropagation Neural Network (SSA-BP)

The sparrow search algorithm (SSA) is a novel population-based intelligent optimization algorithm inspired by the sparrows' foraging and anti-predatory behaviors. It was introduced in 2020 [49] and can be abstracted as the "Searcher-Follower" model with the inclusion of surveillance and warning mechanisms. The main actors in this algorithm are sparrows, with each sparrow having a single attribute: its position, representing the direction of discovered food. Sparrow individuals can undergo one of three types of state changes: (1) acting as searchers: leading the population to search for food; (2) becoming followers: following searchers in their food search; or (3) implementing surveillance and warning mechanisms: detecting danger and abandoning the food search.

In SSA, the best individuals within the population are prioritized for obtaining food during the search process. Explorers, as seekers, have a larger foraging search range than followers. During each iteration, the position update rule for explorers is as follows:

$$X_{i,j}^{t+1} = \begin{cases} X_{i,j}^{t+1} \cdot exp\left(\frac{-i}{\alpha \cdot iter_{max}}\right) & if\ R_2 < ST \\ X_{i,j}^{t} + Q \cdot L & if\ R_2 > ST' \end{cases} \quad (3)$$

where $X_{i,j}$ represents the position of a sparrow individual, i is the current iteration number, $iter_{max}$ is the maximum number of iterations, α is a random number in the range [0, 1], $R_2 \in [0, 1]$ and $ST \in [0.5, 1]$ are pre-alert and safety values, Q is a random number drawn from a normal distribution, and L is a $1 \times i$ matrix with all elements equal to 1. When $R_2 < ST$, it signifies that there are no predators nearby, allowing explorers to conduct global searches. If $R_2 \geq ST$, it indicates that some sparrows have detected predators, and all sparrows need to take related actions. As previously mentioned, some followers constantly monitor the explorers during foraging. If explorers find better food, they will immediately leave their current location to compete for the food. If they win the competition, they can obtain the food instantly. The position update rule for followers is as follows:

$$X_{i,j}^{t+1} = \begin{cases} Q \cdot exp\left(\frac{X_{worst}^{t} - X_{i,j}^{t}}{i^2}\right), & i > \frac{n}{2} \\ X_p^{t+1} + \left|X_{i,j}^{t} - X_p^{t+1}\right| \cdot A^+ \cdot L, & otherwise. \end{cases} \quad (4)$$

Here, X_p represents the position of the best explorer, X_{worst} is the current global worst position, and n is the population size. A is a $1 \times d$ matrix with each element randomly taking a value of 1 or -1. A^+ is defined by:

$$A^+ = A^T \left(AA^T\right)^{-1} \quad (5)$$

When $i > n/2$, it means that the fitness of the i-th follower is relatively low, so they need to fly to other places to forage. In the algorithm, it is assumed that 10% to 20% of the individuals in the population become aware of the danger. These individuals' initial positions are randomly generated within the population:

$$X_{i,j}^{t+1} = \begin{cases} X_{best}^t + \beta \cdot \left| X_{i,j}^t - X_{best}^t \right|, & if\ f_i > f_g \\ X_{i,j}^t + K \cdot \left(\frac{\left| X_{i,j}^t - X_{worst}^t \right|}{(f_i - f_w) + \varepsilon} \right), & if\ f_i = f_g \end{cases} \tag{6}$$

where X_{best} represents the current global best position, β is a step size control parameter drawn from a normal distribution with a mean of 0 and a variance of 1, K is a random number in the range $[-1, 1]$, f represents the fitness value, f_g and f_w represent the current best and worst fitness values, and ε is a constant to avoid division by zero.

In summary, $f_i > f_g$ indicates that a sparrow is on the edge of the population, while $f_i = f_{sg}$ signifies that sparrows located in the middle of the population are aware of danger and need to move closer to other sparrows to avoid predation. K represents the direction of sparrow movement and is also a step size control parameter.

The backpropagation neural network (BPNN) is a commonly used supervised learning algorithm for solving classification and regression problems [50]. In the following, we present the detailed principle of the BPNN, including relevant formulas.

(1) Neurons and Activation Functions: The BPNN consists of multiple neurons, including input, hidden, and output layers. Each neuron has weights (w) and a bias (b). The neuron output is computed using an activation function (f), typically a sigmoid or ReLU function.

(2) Feedforward: Input elements from the input future vector X are passed through the input layer to the hidden and output layers, where each layer computes its output values. The output (O_j) of a layer is:

$$O_j = f\left(\sum_i w_{ij} \cdot X_i + b_j \right), \tag{7}$$

where w_{ij} is the weight for the node j for the incoming node i and b_j is the bias for the node j in the same layer.

(3) Training Data: The network is trained using labeled training data.

(4) Loss Function: The loss function measures the error between the model's output and the actual values (Y). Common loss functions include mean squared error (MSE) and cross-entropy loss.

(5) Backpropagation: The BPNN updates weights and biases to minimize the loss function using the backpropagation algorithm. It calculates the error term for the output layer, $E_j = \frac{1}{2}(Y_j - O_j)^2$, and uses the chain rule to compute the error term for the hidden layer, $E_h = f'(O_h) \cdot \sum_j w_{hj} \cdot E_j$. The weights and biases are updated as follows:

$$w_{ij}^{new} = w_{ij}^{old} + \eta \cdot E_j \cdot f'(O_j) \cdot X_i, \tag{8}$$

$$b_j^{new} = b_j^{old} + \eta \cdot E_j \cdot f'(O_j), \tag{9}$$

$$w_{hi}^{new} = w_{hi}^{old} + \eta \cdot E_h \cdot f'(O_h) \cdot X_i, \tag{10}$$

$$b_h^{new} = b_h^{old} + \eta \cdot E_h \cdot f'(O_h), \tag{11}$$

Here, η is the learning rate that controls the step size for weight updates.

(6) Iteration: The feedforward and backpropagation steps are repeated until the loss function converges or reaches a predefined number of iterations.

(7) Output: Once training is completed, the BPNN can be used to predict the output for new input samples.

It is known that BP performance is greatly affected by the random selection of initial weights and thresholds. Due to its capability of exploring the global optimum in different search spaces and avoiding the problem of optimum local, SSA is used in determining the optimal weights and bias in the BP algorithm [51]. SSA-BP results by using SSA to optimize the objective function of BPNN and obtain the best parameters, followed by training and forecasting the series results.

2.2.3. Particle Swarm Optimization-Extreme Learning Machine (PSO-ELM)

Particle swarm optimization (PSO) [52] is an optimization algorithm inspired by collective behavior in birds or fish. The goal of PSO is to find the optimal solution by simulating the movement of individual particles in the solution space. Here is the detailed principle of the PSO algorithm, including relevant formulas:

(1) Initialization: Initialize the size of the particle swarm, N, and the position and velocity of each particle. Typically, each particle has a position vector X_i and a velocity vector V_i, representing the current position and velocity of the particle in the solution space.

(2) Compute Fitness: For each particle i, calculate its fitness value $f(X_i)$. The fitness function is the objective function to be optimized.

(3) Update Individual Best Position: For each particle i, update its individual best position P_i, which is the best known position. When $f(X_i)$ is better than $f(P_i)$, update P_i to X_i.

(4) Update Global Best Position: Select the global best position, P_g, as the best known global position from the individual best positions of all particles.

(5) Update Velocity and Position: For each particle i, update its velocity and position using the following equations:

$$V_i(t+1) = wV_i(t+1) + c_1 r_1 (P_i - X_i) + c_2 r_2 (P_g - X_i) \tag{12}$$

$$X_i(t+1) = X_i(t) + V_i(t+1) \tag{13}$$

where t is the current iteration number, w is the inertia weight that controls the particle's inertia, c_1 and c_2 are learning factors, and r_1 and r_2 are random numbers introduced for randomness.

(6) Iteration: Repeat steps (2) to (5) until termination conditions are met, such as, for example, reaching the maximum number of iterations or finding a solution that meets convergence criteria.

(7) Output: Output the global best position P_g, which represents the discovered optimal solution.

The core idea of PSO is to explore the solution space by simulating the collective behavior of particles. Each particle updates its position and velocity based on its own experience and the global best position. The PSO's performance is influenced by parameters like w, c_1, and c_2, which require appropriate tuning for optimal performance. PSO is commonly used for solving optimization problems, especially in continuous and high-dimensional spaces.

The extreme learning machine (ELM) [53] is a fast neural network training algorithm for supervised learning tasks. Its core principles involve the initialization of a neural network and weight learning. ELM works based on the following principles:

(1) Initialization of the Neural Network:

Input Layer: ELM accepts input feature vectors x, typically represented by $x = [x_1, x_2, \ldots, x_d]$, where d is the feature dimension.

Hidden Layer: ELM initializes a random weight matrix W, usually represented as $W = [w_1, w_2, \ldots, w_M]$, where M is the number of hidden layer neurons. Weights are drawn from random distributions, such as uniform or Gaussian distributions.

(2) Hidden Layer Output: The output of the hidden layer, H, is calculated as $H = g(Wx + b)$, where $g(\cdot)$ is the activation function, typically sigmoid or ReLU, and b is the bias, usually set to zero.

(3) Output Layer Weight Learning: The key to ELM is the weight learning at the output layer, which can be achieved through the least squares method. For classification problems, ELM's output is usually represented as $Y = [y_1, y_2, \ldots, y_C]$, where C is the number of classes. The output layer weight matrix is often denoted by $O = [o_1, o_2, \ldots, o_C]$.

The output layer weight O can be calculated using the following formula: $O = H^+T$, where H^+ is the Moore–Penrose pseudo-inverse of the hidden layer output matrix H, and T is the class label matrix, with each row corresponding to the class label of a sample.

(4) Prediction: Once the output layer weight O is determined, ELM can be used for forecasting new data. For a new input feature vector x_{new}, its predicted output y_{new} can be calculated using the formula:

$$y_{new} = g(W_{new}x_{new} + b)O, \tag{14}$$

where W_{new} represents the weights from the hidden layer to the output layer, specifically $W_{new} = H_{new}^+$. Moreover, H_{new}^+ is the hidden layer output for the new data.

Huang et al. [54] demonstrated the ELM's ability to perform as a universal approximator. It was also shown [55,56] that ELM has a fast learning capability and adequate generalization performance, and combined with other techniques, can enhance its generalization ability [57,58]. However, due to the random initialization of the input weights, ELM may generate non-optimal solutions (affecting algorithm performance) [59,60].

To address this issue, PSO-ELM was applied in the following steps:

(a) Set the training and test set;
(b) Initialize the ELM parameters and set the root mean squared error (RMSE) as the fitness function;
(c) Run PSO for each candidate solution;
(d) Determine the optimal input data for ELM;
(e) ELM Test [32].

According to [32,61,62], PSO-ELM models provided highly reliable solutions to engineering problems. We mention that our scientific literature search did not return results on modeling water discharges using such an approach. Therefore, given that no reliable models for the Buzău River flow were found, we decided to apply this modeling technique.

2.2.4. Data Segmentation

The modality of dividing the data series into the training and testing datasets can also impact training effectiveness. Since the data being used include water flow data with an associated date, the optimal division method is based on the date. Additionally, the proportion of the testing dataset should be considered. Generally, a larger proportion of the training dataset may help the model learn time-series patterns more effectively. However, a smaller testing dataset may lead to inadequate evaluation of the model's performance. In time-series forecasting, a substantial amount of historical data is often necessary to build accurate models. Therefore, increasing the proportion of the training dataset might be beneficial, especially for long-term time-series data, to ensure the model has enough historical information to capture patterns within the time series. However, specific data characteristics and the available data quantity should also be considered. If the data are very limited, allocating more data for training may not be feasible. Furthermore, the size of the testing dataset should be sufficiently large to ensure a comprehensive evaluation of the model's performance. Ultimately, the appropriate ratio depends on experimental requirements and the available data.

Variables were standardized to compare the three models, and the data from January 2006 to December 2010 were designated as the testing dataset. Model S's training dataset encompasses data from January 1955 to December 2005. Model S1's training dataset comprises the period from January 1995 to December 1983. Model S2 is trained using data from January 1984 to December 2005. This approach aligns with the intent of this paper to determine the model with the best predictive performance of the test dataset, and emphasize the existence of a change in the water discharge regimen after 1984.

Table 2 contains the information on data segmentation.

Table 2. Data set segmentation—number of values per series set.

Model	Full Data Range (YYYYMM)	Training Data Range (YYYYMM)	Test Data Range (YYYYMM)	Test Set to Training Set Ratio
S	195501–201012 (672)	195501–200512 (612)	200601–201012 (60)	9.8%
S1	195501–198312 (348)	195501–198312 (348)	200601–201012 (60)	17.2%
S2	198401–201012 (324)	198401–200512 (264)	200601–201012 (60)	22.7%

2.2.5. Description of Algorithmic Running Parameters

This study employed three forecasting algorithms: CNN-LSTM, SSA-BP, and PSO-ELM. We conducted comprehensive parameter tuning and experiments to analyze if they demonstrate good predictive performance in practical applications.

For CNN-LSTM, a series of experiments were conducted to determine the optimal parameter configurations, including parameters for the convolutional layers and settings for the LSTM layers. This experimental process was instrumental in ensuring that CNN-LSTM achieved the best performance in handling flood data and feature extraction.

We applied the same parameter-tuning methodology to SSA-BP and PSO-ELM to ensure fairness in comparative results. The purpose of this consistent approach was to test the performance of these two algorithms under similar conditions, thus enhancing the credibility of the comparison. Through a similar parameter-tuning process, we optimized SSA-BP and PSO-ELM to achieve the best performance on the specific flood forecasting task and dataset.

This consistent parameter-tuning approach helps eliminate performance biases that could be introduced due to different parameter settings. Consequently, each algorithm was tested for performance under thoroughly optimized conditions, and our evaluation results better reflect their actual performance in real-world applications. This procedure ensures our research's scientific rigor and reliability, making our conclusions more compelling. After practical testing, the selected parameters for SSA-BP and PSO-ELM are listed in Table 3.

Table 3. Parameters of SSA-BP and PSO-ELM.

Algorithm	Lower Limit of Value	Upper Limit of Value	Population Size	Maximum Iterations	No. of Hidden Nodes
SSA-BP	−500	500	100	20	100
PSO-ELM	−1	1	100	50	300

The model's structure and parameters' settings of the CNN-LSTM network are as follows:

(1) Input Layer: The model begins with a sequence input layer with an input data structure of [1 1 1], representing input at a single time step.
(2) Sequence Folding Layer: This layer is responsible for serializing the input data for sequence data processing.
(3) Convolutional Layers: The model includes two convolutional layers, named conv_1 and conv_2. Both convolutional layers have a kernel size of [1 1], where conv_1 contains 16 feature maps and conv_2 contains 32 feature maps. These convolutional layers are used to extract features from serialized data, aiding the network in understanding patterns in the input data.
(4) Activation Layers: Following each convolutional layer, a ReLU activation layer (relu_1 and relu_2) is introduced to add non-linearity and enhance feature extraction.

(5) Sequence Unfolding Layer: This layer corresponds to the Sequence Folding Layer and is used for deserializing data for further processing.
(6) Fully Connected Layer: This layer flattens the data from a serialized format for processing by the fully connected layers.
(7) LSTM Layers: The model comprises two LSTM layers, named lstm and lstm2. LSTM (long short-term memory) layers are employed for handling sequence data, with lstm outputting a sequence and lstm2 outputting the result from the last time step.
(8) Fully Connected Layer: This layer (fc) receives the output from the LSTM layers and maps it to a single output node.
(9) Regression Layer: Finally, there is a regression layer responsible for outputting prediction results.

Here are some specific parameter settings:

- MaxEpochs: The maximum number of training epochs is set to 100.
- InitialLearnRate: The initial learning rate is set to 0.01.
- LearnRateSchedule: The learning rate schedule follows a "piecewise" strategy.
- LearnRateDropFactor: The learning rate drop factor is 0.1.
- LearnRateDropPeriod: The learning rate drop period is 80% of the maximum training epochs.
- Shuffle: The dataset is shuffled before each training iteration.
- Plots: Training progress is visualized during the training process.
- Verbose: Detailed information is not displayed during the training process.

The combination of these parameters and network layers is designed for efficient flood forecasting, with the model continually improving its performance over a certain number of training epochs. This model integrates CNN and LSTM networks to effectively handle sequential data, making it well suited for discharge forecasting tasks.

2.2.6. Performance Evaluation Criteria

The performance of the models was assessed using computation time, mean squared error (MSE), mean absolute error (MAE), and coefficient of determination for the training and test set (R^2).

(1) Mean squared error (MSE) measures the average of the squared errors between the model's predictions and the actual observations. A lower MSE indicates a better fit of the model to the observed data. The formula for calculating MSE is

$$\text{MSE} = \sum_{i=1}^{n}(y_i - \hat{y}_i)^2/n, \tag{15}$$

where n is the number of data points, y_i is the actual observation, and $\hat{y}_i$ is the model's prediction.

(2) The mean absolute error (MAE) measures the average of the absolute errors between the model's predictions and the actual observations. Unlike MSE, MAE does not consider the square of errors, making it less sensitive to large errors. The formula for calculating MAE is

$$\text{MAE} = \sum_{i=1}^{n}|y_i - \hat{y}_i|/n. \tag{16}$$

(3) The coefficient of determination for the training set (R^2) represents the goodness of fit of the model to the training set data. Its value ranges from 0 to 1, with a higher value indicating a better fit of the model to the training data. The computation formula is

$$R^2 = 1 - SSR/SST, \tag{17}$$

where SSR is the sum of squared residuals, and SST is the total sum of squares.

(4) The coefficient of determination for the test set is similar to R^2 for the training set, and it is used to assess the model's fit to independent test data. It provides a performance metric for the model on new data.

In summary, computation time is used to evaluate the computational efficiency of the model. MSE and MAE are used to measure the model's prediction errors, while R^2 for both the training and test sets is used to assess the model's fit to the data. In general, all these metrics help evaluate the model's performance, ensuring that it accurately fits the training data and performs well on new data.

2.2.7. Computational Setup

The computations in this study were conducted on a workstation equipped with an AMD Ryzen 9 5900X 12-Core Processor CPU (3.70 GHz, 12 cores, 24 threads), 64 GB of RAM, and an NVIDIA GeForce RTX 3090 GPU. The operating system used was Windows 11, and the programming environment included Matlab R2023a. All training was carried out on the CPU, and there was no need for the GPU to be involved in the computation.

2.2.8. Comparison of Hybrid Models with Other Models Used in Hydrological Modeling

For comparisons, two different types of models have been used, ARIMA and MLP. Brief information on the mentioned approaches is presented in the following paragraphs. We do not insist on them since they do not fall under the main goal of the article.

An ARIMA(p,d,q) model for a time series $\{x_t\}$ has the equation

$$\left(1 - \varphi_1 B - \ldots - \varphi_p B^p\right)\nabla^d x_t = \left(1 - \theta_1 B - \ldots - \theta_q B^q\right)\varepsilon_t, \ \varphi_p \neq 0, \ \theta_q \neq 0, \tag{18}$$

where

$$\nabla^d = (1 - B)^d, \tag{19}$$

p is the autoregressive order, q is the moving average order, d is the differentiation degree, and $\{\varepsilon_t\}$ is a white noise with zero mean and a constant variance [63].

The autoregressive moving average model of the orders p and q, denoted by ARMA(p, q) is an ARIMA(p, 0, q). If $p = d = 0$, the model is called moving average MA(q).

The best model is that with the lowest value of the Akaike criterion.

Multilayer perceptron (MLP) neural network [64] is a feedforward ANN formed by fully connected neurons organized in minimum three layer. In this article, we used four layers, two of which are hidden. In the actual MLP, an logistic activation function was used for both hidden and output layer. The classical and still preferred training algorithm for neural networks is called stochastic gradient descent. Network size evaluation was performed using a 20% hold-back procedure.

3. Results and Discussion

3.1. Modeling Results

Following the described methodology, we first modeled the data series, and then conducted a comprehensive performance comparison of three prediction approaches (CNN-LSTM, SSA-BP, and PSO-ELM) and the related models (S, S1, and S2) on the river discharge data series.

In the realm of computational modeling, particularly with algorithms that incorporate elements of randomness or stochastic processes, the role of the random seed is pivotal in determining the outcome of each run. In our study, we employed models which inherently involve random search methods in their optimization or learning processes. The random seed in these algorithms influences the initialization of weights, the selection of subsets of data, and the trajectory of the search process in the solution space.

Acknowledging the influence of random seeds, our methodology incorporated measures to ensure a fair and unbiased comparison across all iterations. To mitigate the variability introduced by random seeds, we adopted the following approaches:

- Multiple runs with different seeds: Each model was run 20 times with a range of different random seeds. This approach averages out the anomalies that might arise from any particular initialization, providing a more generalizable and reliable estimate of each model's performance.

- Consistent seeds across models: For each iteration, the same set of random seeds was used across all models. This consistency ensures that each model is subjected to the same degree of randomness in their respective processes, allowing for a fairer comparison of their capabilities.

Through these methodological choices and analytical approaches, we aimed to ensure that our comparison of the CNN-LSTM, SSA-BP, and PSO-ELM models was as fair and unbiased as possible. This rigorous approach allowed us to draw more reliable conclusions about the relative strengths and applicability of these models in the context of water discharge forecasting.

Figure 5 presents the visualization of the CNN-LSTM S, S1, and S2 models.

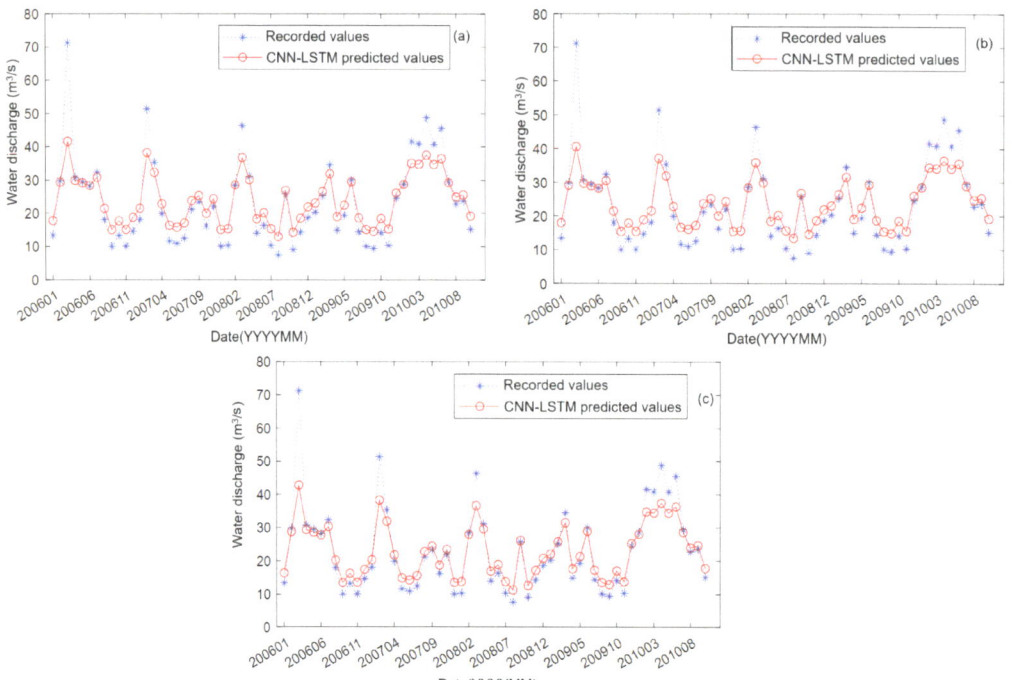

Figure 5. CNN-LSTM models on the test set when the training set was (**a**) S, (**b**) S1, and (**c**) S2.

The analysis of the three charts indicates that all models follow the shapes of the recorded data series. A higher bias of the computed values from the recorded ones is noticed for the extremes (for example, during the periods May–July 2007, September 2009, and March–June 2006) in S1 (Figure 5b) compared to S and S2 (Figure 5a,c). The lowest biases are noticed in Figure 5c—Model 2. Still, the differences are insignificant, and reflected in the goodness of fit indicators that will be discussed later in this section.

The output of the SSA-BP is displayed in Figure 6. Whereas the series formed by the computed values in the models S and S1 have similar shapes as the recorded series, with some higher biases between the recorded and computed values in S1 compared to S2, especially for the values from August and October 2008, and February–June 2010, the shape of the series in Model S2 is quite different. It is worth noting the mismatches between the recorded and forecasted values after February 2009, March and August 2008, etc., leading to the lowest performance of S2 compared with the S and S1 SSA-BP models.

The PSO-ELM output is represented in Figure 7. Similar to the previous approaches, the worst fitted are the highest values. For the values recorded in March 2006 (over 70 m^3/s),

March 2007 (about 50 m³/s), and March 2008 (46 m³/s), and those after February 2010, the best estimations are provided by Model S2 (Figure 7c).

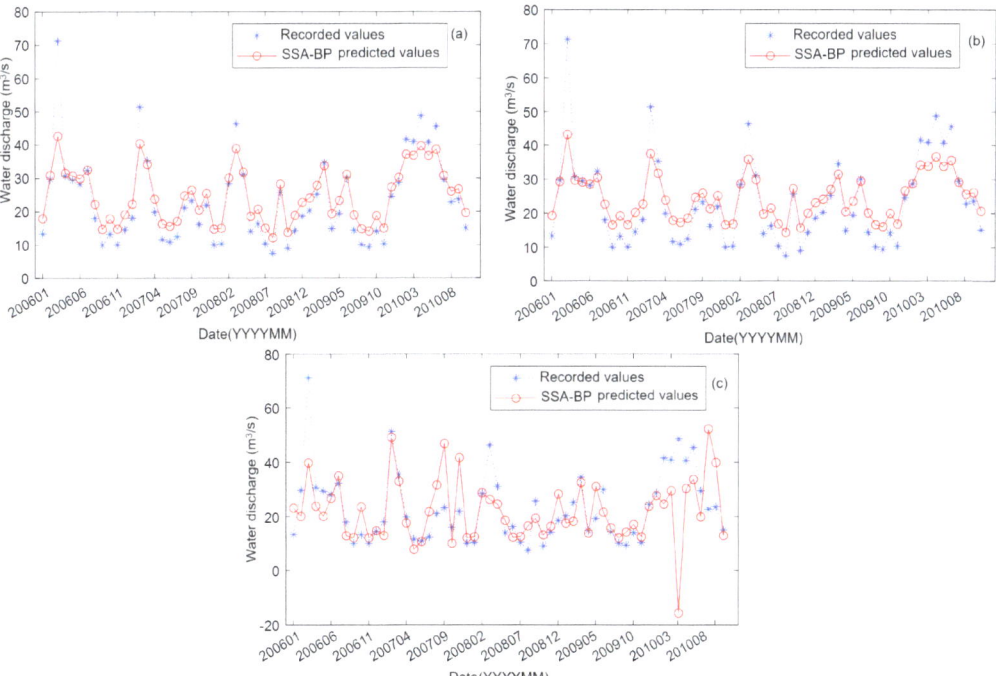

Figure 6. SSA-BP models on the test set when the training set was (**a**) S, (**b**) S1, and (**c**) S2.

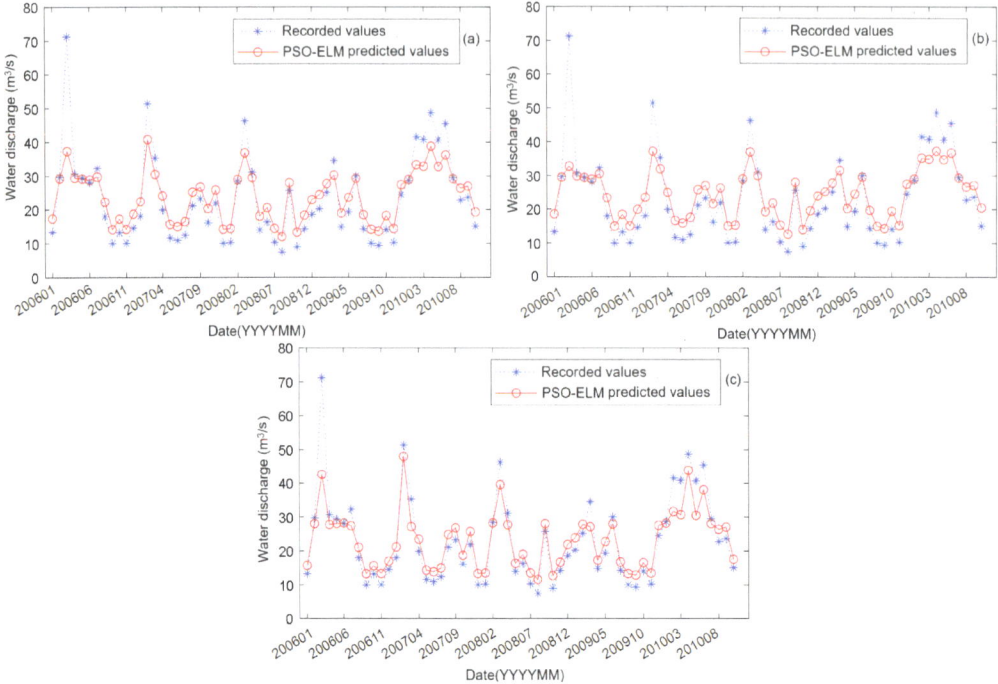

Figure 7. PSO-ELM models on the test set when the training set was (**a**) S, (**b**) S1, and (**c**) S2.

The same is true for the lowest recorded values, meaning that Model S2 better captures the extreme compared to S and S1.

A comparison of Figures 5c and 7c shows that the values provided by the CNN-LSTM-S2 model for the highest records are smaller than those issued from the PSO-ELM-S2 model, indicating smaller errors in the second case. Still, correct conclusions on the models' performances can be drawn only after observing the goodness-of-fit indicators.

MSE is a key indicator for assessing predictive accuracy. The study computed MSE for both the training and test sets (Table 4—rows 3–5).

Table 4. Values of the goodness-of-fit indicators for the training and test sets in the models.

Indicator	Model	Training Set			Test Set		
		S	S1	S2	S	S1	S2
MSE	CNN-LSTM	93.8144	115.0937	62.0042	36.0007	39.9782	29.8323
	SSA-BP	91.2629	105.403	132.454	32.4993	44.6227	168.5962
	PSO-ELM	98.125	126.5485	70.7001	41.2751	52.1818	30.9637
MAE	CNN-LSTM	6.0307	6.5177	4.7433	4.2351	4.4784	3.5245
	SSA-BP	5.7250	6.9987	7.7131	4.2882	5.2037	8.0949
	PSO-ELM	6.0070	6.7809	5.0355	4.6031	5.1284	3.9898
R^2	CNN-LSTM	0.8945	0.8839	0.9301	0.9458	0.9426	0.9504
	SSA-BP	0.8397	0.9276	0.5311	0.9297	0.9612	0.1976
	PSO-ELM	0.8305	0.7596	0.7966	0.8868	0.8335	0.8994

The analysis reveals that the training set MSE ranges from 62.0042 (for CNN-LSTM-S2) to 132.454 (for SSA-BP-S2), whereas the corresponding test set MSE ranges from 29.8323 (for CNN-LSTM-S2) to 168.5962 (for SSA-BP-S2).

Among the models, the lowest test set MSE occurs when using CNN-LSTM, particularly in Model S2, with a value of 29.8323, corresponding to the lowest training set MSE (62.0042). This finding suggests that CNN-LSTM exhibits low error rates and fits the actual observations excellently. In contrast, SSA-BP in Model S2 shows the highest MSE, indicating comparatively poorer predictive performance, emphasizing the significant variation in predictive accuracy among different models. Overall, the training set MSE is significantly higher than the test set MSE in all models but SSA-BP-S2, which might be attributed to the larger volume of training data.

Generally, the MAEs for the test set remain lower than for the training sets. MAE, known for its robustness, is less sensitive to outliers, as it solely considers the absolute value of errors. The training set's lowest MAE corresponds to the CNN-LSTM-S2 model (4.7433) and the highest to the SSA-BP-S2 model. In the case of the test sets, the lowest MAE was computed in the CNN-LSTM-S2 model (3.5245) and the highest in the SSA-BP S2 (8.0949). For SSA-BP-S2, the MAE's ranking on the test set is similar to the MSE's ranking on the same set. These results highlight the superior predictive performance of CNN-LSTM in terms of MAE. However, the poorest predictive performance is still unexpectedly observed in SSA-BP-S2, given that both test and training sets belong to the period after putting the Siriu Dam in operation.

Regarding R^2 on the training set (Table 4, rows 9–11), all three models but SSA-BP-S2 consistently exhibited relatively high R^2 values, showing their ability to effectively explain variance in the test data. On the test set, R^2 recorded values over 0.8335 for all but the SSA-BP models. CNN-LSTM achieved the highest R^2 in Model S2 on both the training and test sets.

Compared to its competitors, PSO-ELM displayed the lowest R^2 values on Models S and S1, whereas CNN-LSTM and SSA-BP consistently demonstrated higher R^2 values, over 0.8397 on the same models. The R^2 values of the SSA-BP on Model S2 were very low on the test and the training sets, rendering it practically unusable.

These results reflect the predictive accuracy of the CNN-LSTM and PSO-ELM models on the training dataset while revealing their adaptability to different datasets.

The following should be noted, given each training set's significance and relating it to the algorithms' prediction accuracy.

- Before running the algorithms, it was expected to obtain the best results for the S2 models because the training and test sets were recorded after operating the Siriu Dam. However, the second algorithm performed differently than expected, providing the worst S2 model compared to S and S1.
- It was also expected that the S models better fit the data compared to S1 given that the training set includes data from both periods (before and after January 1984), so with different flow regimens. This happened in terms of MAE and MSE for all models. In terms of R^2, the assertion is true for CNN-LSTM and PSO-ELM models.
- It was also expected that S1 has the worst performance because the training and test sets came from different periods. But SSA-BP S1 is the best in terms of R^2, compared to SSA-BP S and SSA S1.

The residuals' analysis rejects the autocorrelation hypothesis. Figure 8 shows the residuals' correlograms in CNN-LSTM S2, SSA-BP S2, and PSO-ELM S2 (with 95% confidence limits). The normality hypothesis was tested using the Anderson–Darling test [65]. Table 5 contains the associated p-values. At the significance level of 5%, the residuals' normality was rejected in all models. At a significance level of 1%, the normality hypothesis cannot be rejected in the CNN-LSTM models (because the p-values are higher than 0.01).

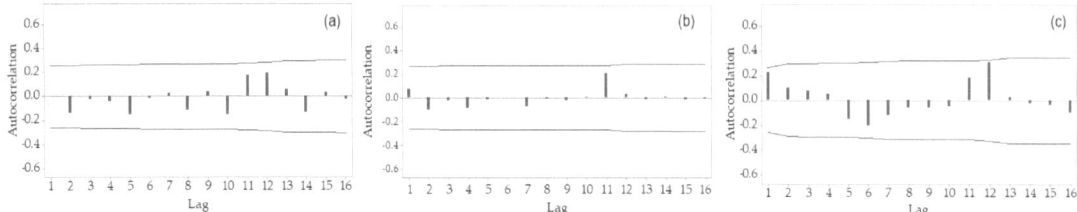

Figure 8. The correlograms of residuals in (**a**) CNN-LSTM S2, (**b**) SSA-BP S2, and (**c**) PSO-ELM S2. The vertical bars represent the values of the autocorrelation function, and the red lines are the limits of the confidence interval with 95% confidence limits.

Table 5. Analysis of residuals' normality in the models.

Model	CNN-LSTM		SSA-BP		PSO-ELM	
	p-Value	Normality Reached	p-Value	Normality Reached	p-Value	Normality Reached
S	0.018	Box–Cox: $\lambda = 1.22$	<0.005	no	<0.005	no
S1	0.017	Box–Cox: $\lambda = 1.23$	<0.005	no	<0.005	no
S2	0.031	Box–Cox: $\lambda = 1.15$	<0.005	no	<0.005	no

Normality was reached by Box–Cox transformations [66], with the parameters 1.22 (1.23 and 1.15) for the residual series in the CNN-LSTM S (S1 and S2) models.

Considering the MSE, MAE, R^2, and the residuals' analysis, CNN-LSTM has the best performance. Its robustness, even in the presence of outliers, suggests a consistent predictive reliability. Additionally, the model's higher determination coefficient (R^2) values, both in the training and testing phases, indicate its enhanced capability to explain the variance in the dataset.

The complexity of hydrological patterns post Siriu Dam construction (including altered flow regimes and seasonal variations) are effectively captured by the CNN-LSTM model due to its architecture, which combines convolutional layers (for spatial feature recognition) and LSTM layers (for temporal dependencies), particularly adequate at modeling non-linearity and non-stationarity. The robustness of CNN-LSTM in variable hydrological conditions is attributable to the LSTM component's ability to remember long-term dependencies and disregard irrelevant data. Moreover, the hierarchical patch-based convolution operations performed by CNNs reduce the computational effort, and the input is abstracted on different feature levels, diminishing the network's parameter number. Also, convolution layers consider the context in the local neighborhood of the input data and construct features from that neighborhood.

The performance of SSA-BP is relatively less impressive than those of other models. This behavior might be related to SSA's large randomness issue, easily falling into the local optimum. Moreover, the poor communication mechanism between the participants (that communicate only with the best discoverers) can result in missing the best solutions, affecting fitting quality [67].

ELM has good generalization and learning capacity (thousands of times faster than learning algorithms for feed-forward NN) [53]. PSO has a strong global exploration ability. It approaches the optimum solution by self- and social learning, continuously updating the global and historical optimal solutions. Therefore, the PSO-ELM will benefit from these characteristics and improve the PSO convergence rate.

3.2. Sensitivity Analysis

First, we have to mention that the models were built in scenarios S–S2 (described in Table 2) in order to determine if there is an alteration of the Buzău River flow after building the dam. Since sensitivity analysis is a very complex task for the complex ML algorithms used here, we decided to perform an extended analysis in another article.

But here we used the rolling origin evaluation technique according to which the forecasting origin is updated successively and the forecasts are produced from each origin [68]. In the case of ML techniques, this involves changing the ratio between the training and test sets.

Performing this analysis for all network types resulted in the highest sensitivity of the SSA-BP model, for which R^2 drastically decreased, whereas MSE increased, especially when the ratio test/training test is over 35%. For example, for a ratio of 38% (68%), MSE = 1020.7045 (2472.2555) on the training set and 2010.9544 (4291.441) on the test set. The corresponding R^2 decreased at values under 0.05 in the same cases, whereas for ratios under 22%, it remained around 0.828 on the training and 0.928 on the test set.

PSO-ELM had comparative performances with S1-S3 models on the training set in terms of all goodness-of-fit parameters, whereas on the test set, MSE and MAE slightly increased.

CNN-LSTM had almost the same values of R^2 as in the S–S2 scenarios. A moderate increase of MSE and a slight increase of MAE (in the range of 4.60 and 5.50) on the test sets were also noticed. Overall, the least sensitive model was CNN-LSTM.

3.3. Computational Time Complexity

The time needed to run the algorithms is also a crucial factor. It is presented in Figure 9 for each model as a function of the data volume on the training set. In our comprehensive analysis of computational time for the CNN-LSTM, SSA-BP, and PSO-ELM models in water discharge forecasting, distinct patterns emerged, highlighting the varying efficiencies of these models in handling datasets of different sizes.

The PSO-ELM model demonstrated a significant reduction in computational time as the data volume was diminished from 612 to 264, with a notable decrease by approximately a third when transitioning from Model S (612 data points) to Model S1 (348 data points). This augmentation of the computational burden with larger datasets indicates that PSO-ELM may not be optimally suited for scenarios involving extensive data, owing to its intrinsic algorithmic complexity that scales unfavorably with increased data dimensions and search space.

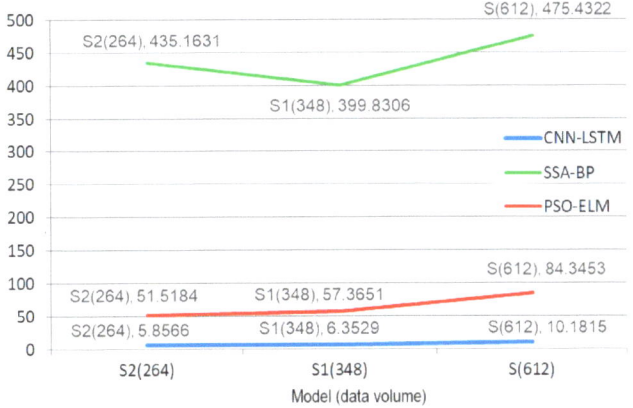

Figure 9. Computational time function of the number of values.

The CNN-LSTM model exhibited a near-linear relationship between data volume and computational time. This scalability, presumably a result of the parallelizable nature of CNNs for spatial feature processing and the linear time complexity of LSTMs with respect to sequence length, suggests its suitability for larger, more complex time-series datasets. Such a characteristic is particularly advantageous in real-time or near-real-time forecasting systems where handling extensive hydrological data efficiently is crucial.

The SSA-BP model, however, did not show a clear correlation between data volume and computational time, indicating that other factors than data volume, such as algorithmic structure, initialization parameters, and convergence criteria, play a more significant role in influencing its computational efficiency. This observation underscores the need for meticulous parameter optimization and algorithmic adjustments to harness the full potential of SSA-BP in specific hydrological forecasting scenarios.

Despite SSA's known fast convergence capacity, the very slow convergence of the BPNN impacted the total computational time of the SSA-BP algorithm [67,69].

Our comprehensive analysis reveals that the CNN-LSTM model exhibits exceptional performance, outshining its counterparts, SSA-BP and PSO-ELM, in several critical aspects. Firstly, the CNN-LSTM model demonstrates a marked efficiency in computational time, leveraging GPU acceleration to process extensive datasets rapidly, as evidenced by its remarkable processing time of only 5.8566 s in Model S2. This efficiency is crucial when dealing with decade-spanning hydrological data, as in our study.

- *CNN-LSTM time complexity.*

The convolutional layer complexity time in CNN is $O\left(\sum_{l=1}^{k} n_{l-1} s_l^2 n_l m_l^2 \right)$ [70], where k is the number of convolutional layers (two in our case), n_l is the number of filters in the l-th layer, n_{l-1} is the number of input channels of the l-th layer, s_l is the spatial size of the filter, and m_l is the spatial size of the output feature map [71]. Hochreiter and Schmidhuber proved [43] that the LSTM is local in space and time, so the time complexity per weight for each time step is O (1). Therefore, the overall complexity of an LSTM per time step is equal to O (w), where w is the number of weights. Therefore the CNN-LSTM complexity per time step is $O\left(\sum_{l=1}^{k} n_{l-1} s_l^2 n_l m_l^2 + w\right)$, and for the entire training process is $O\left(\left(\sum_{l=1}^{k} n_{l-1} s_l^2 n_l m_l^2 + w\right) NM\right)$, where N is the input volume and M is the number of iterations [72].

- *PSO-ELM time complexity:*

In a PSO:

(1) If N particles are initialized and the solution space has the dimension d, the time complexity is O(Nd).
(2) The time complexity for the fitness function is O(d). The time complexity of the fitness computation for all the n particles is O(Nd).
(3) The time complexity in an iterative operation for updating and computing the extremum for each particle is O(N).
(4) The time complexity for the global extremum computation in an iterative operation is O(N).
(5) The time complexity in an iterative operation to update the velocity and position vectors of the particles is O(Nd).
(6) The time complexity of completing the computation after an iterative step, according to the termination condition, is O(1).

Summing up the time complexities in (2)–(6) results in O($2Nd + 2N + 1$), so the time measure level is O(Nd) [73]. If the algorithm runs M times, the complexity is O($2MNd + 2NM + M$), and the entire time complexity is O($2MNd + Nd + 2NM + M$), so the measure level is O(MNd).

In an ELM that transforms the input feature matrix with the dimension $d \times N$ to a hidden layer of h neurons, the following complexities for each computational step are determined:

(a) Linear transform to ELM-space-O(hdN).
(b) Application of activation function, assuming ReLU-O(Nh).
(c) Calculating the output weight matrix-O(N^3).

Adding up the values from (a)–(c) results in the ELM time complexity being O($hdN + Nh + N^3$), so the measure level is O(N^3) [74].

Based on the above, the PSO-ELM algorithm's time complexity is $O(2MNd + Nd + 2NM + M + hdN + Nh + N^3)$, so the measure level is $O(MNd + N^3)$.

- *SSA-BP time complexity*

The time complexity of the BPNN is influenced by the maximum number of iterations M, the sample size N, and the spatial dimension d, and its time complexity is $O(M Nd^2)$. After using the SSA algorithm with BPNN, the complexity increases by $O(MNd)$. Thus, the time complexity of the SSA-BP algorithm is $O(Mnd^2 + Mnd)$ [75].

When the spatial dimension d is high, $O(MNd^2)$ and $O(MNd)$ are approximated by $O(d^2)$, so, in such a case, SSA-BP has the complexity in the same measure level, $O(d^2)$.

These insights into the models' computational time complexities have profound implications for their application in practical scenarios. While PSO-ELM may be more suited for smaller datasets or situations where longer computation times are acceptable, CNN-LSTM, with its excellent scalability and linear computational time relationship, emerges as a more viable option for applications demanding the rapid processing of large-scale data sets, such as dynamic hydrological models or real-time prediction systems. The SSA-BP model, requiring careful tuning and optimization, could be effectively employed in specific scenarios, provided that its parameters are optimally adjusted to the unique demands of the task at hand. This analysis not only aids in selecting the most appropriate model for a given hydrological forecasting application but also contributes to the broader understanding of leveraging advanced computational methods in environmental science research.

3.4. Discussion

Among the most used techniques for modeling river discharge, ARIMA and ANN are the most well known. Therefore, to compare the output of the hybrid models proposed in this article with the results from the literature, we built ARIMA-type models, denoted S_A, S1_A, and S2_A, with the series used for training the models S, S1, and S2 in the hybrid algorithm. Based on each model, the forecast was performed for the next 60 months and compared to the test set from the hybrid models. The types and the coefficients of the best ARIMA models are presented in Table 6.

Table 6. The coefficients (and standard errors—s.e.), MSE, MAE, and R^2 in the ARMA and MA models.

Model	Type	ar1 (s.e.)	ar2 (s.e.)	ar3 (s.e.)	ma1 (s.e.)	ma2 (s.e.)	Mean (s.e.)	MSE	MAE	R^2
S_A	ARMA(3, 1)	1.0310 (0.1106)	−0.1852 (0.0804)	−0.1500 (0.0416)	−0.5562 0.1066		21.6297 0.9047	234.7931	10.9039	0.2680
S1_A	ARMA(3, 1)	0.9942 (0.1166)	−0.1272 (0.0917)	−0.2089 0.0544	−0.5803 0.1108		23.1170 1.0657	260.6423	11.4934	0.2501
S2_A	MA(2)				0.4375 0.0572	0.2935 0.0606	23.1397 1.8383	299.0880	12.3642	0.4882

First, the portmanteau tests (Box–Ljung and Box–Pierce tests) [63] applied to the models' residuals rejected the autocorrelation of the residuals. The MSEs and MAEs (R^2) in the ARMA and MA models are generally much higher (lower) than those on the hybrid models, indicating an inferior output accuracy.

The forecast based on S_A, S1_A, and S2_A is shown in Figure 10, compared with the recorded series values. The forecast series becomes linear after a short period. Thus, the models fail to capture the nonlinearities in the recorded series. By comparison, the MLP models' fits in similar scenarios are better than the ARIMA ones, given their capacity to capture the abrupt changes in the series behavior. Figure 11 presents the modeling results using MLP in the first scenario for exemplification.

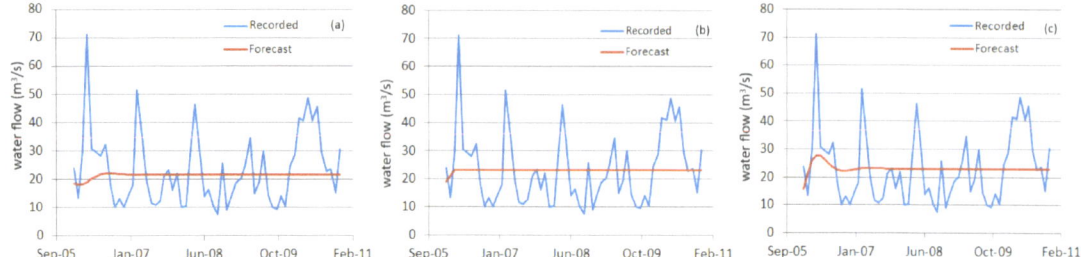

Figure 10. Recorded values and forecast by the (**a**) S_A, (**b**) S1_A, and (**c**) S2_A models.

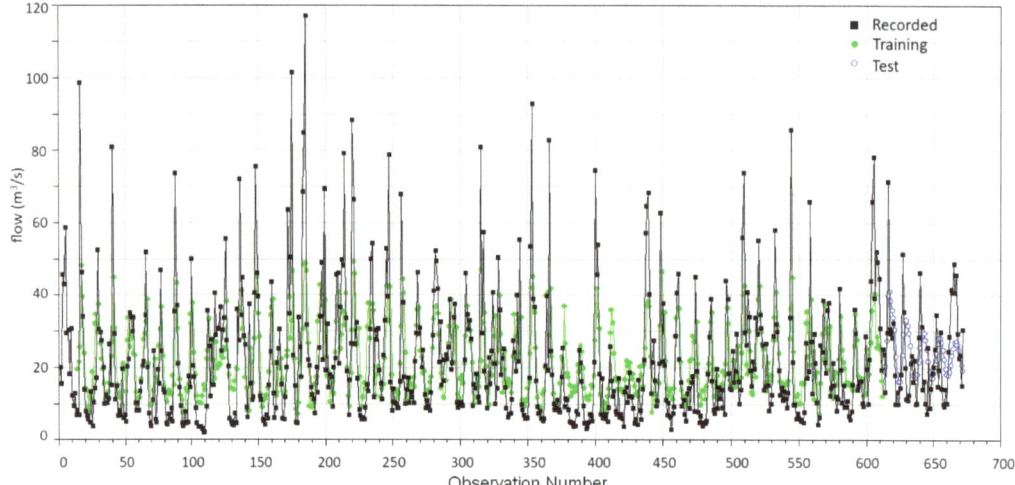

Figure 11. MLP models in S_A.

The forecast values on the test series (the points in blue) better follow the pattern of the recorded ones (the black dots).

The results of our ARIMA models are not in concordance with the findings of Yürekli et al. [15], whose simulations describe the recorded series well. They do not confirm the similar forecasting power of ANN and ARMA found by Abrahart and See [18] in a case study from Turkey. Our study output is in concordance with the findings from [17,76,77] that emphasized the better performances of the neural networks against ARIMA, given the better ability to learn of the neural network and less sensitivity to the abrupt changes in the time series.

The variation intervals for the goodness-of-fit indicators in the MLP models are as follows:

- On the training set: MSE—181.6991 (S2)–252.1943 (S1), MAE—9.2589 (S2)–11.4146, (S1), and R^2—0.2744 (S1)–0.3693 (S2);
- On the test set: MSE—135.7250 (S1)–158.1449 (S2), MAE—8.8535 (S1)–10.1030 (S2) and R^2—0.0969 (S)–0.1618 (S1).

So, MLP S1 performed the worst on the training set (it has the lowest R^2), and the highest and the best on the test one was S1. Still, the low R^2 indicates the necessity of running many optimization scenarios to overcome MLP's known drawback which is the difficult parameters' optimization [78]. Since the goal of this article is not modeling with MLP, we leave it for a further deeper research.

The performances of the MLP algorithm in all scenarios are worse than those of the hybrid models. The results regarding the predictive performance of both MLP and

CNN-LSTM concord with those from [45,79,80]. They were somehow expected, given the advantages of CNN (smaller weights, shared, easy to train, going deeper, sparsely connected layers) over MLP, which are shared by the CNN-LSTM network. Moreover, the high forecast accuracy of CNN-LSTM, emphasized by this study, confirms its high performance in the case of long data series [81]. The results are also in concordance with those of Liu et al. [82] and Anupan and Pani [83], who indicated the considerable accuracy of the PSO-ELM network in terms of MSE and MAE, even when forecasting is carried out for a long period (60 months, in this case).

4. Conclusions

Against the backdrop of rapid technological advancement, hybrid computational methods have emerged as key tools for solving complex problems. These methods, integrating the strengths of various algorithms, offer more efficient and precise solutions for specific challenges. This paper rigorously examined the efficacy of three such hybrid models—CNN-LSTM, SSA-BP, and PSO-ELM—in the context of water discharge forecasting for the Buzău River, particularly in the wake of environmental changes induced by the Siriu Dam's operationalization in 1984.

Through a comprehensive analysis of runtime, MSE, and R^2, it can be concluded that CNN-LSTM and PSO-ELM can be used with good results on various cases (training sets) from flow forecast. CNN-LSTM stands out due to its computational efficiency and high predictive accuracy, especially in the case of Model S2. Its robustness extended to MAE, emphasizing CNN-LSTM's consistency, even in the presence of outliers.

We found that computational time was a crucial consideration, with CNN-LSTM demonstrating a significant advantage due to its efficient GPU utilization. It excelled in Model S2, requiring only 5.8566 s for processing, while SSA-BP and PSO-ELM, running on CPUs, consumed considerably more time. Therefore, for practical flood prediction, Model S2 is recommended as the primary choice due to its short runtime, low MSE, reasonable MAE, and test and training set R^2 values exceeding 0.92, indicating excellent fit without overfitting.

Regarding the determination coefficient (R^2), CNN-LSTM and SSA-BP consistently showed higher values, indicating their better ability to explain the variance in test data. In contrast, PSO-ELM exhibited relatively lower R^2 values, hovering around 0.83 to 0.9, suggesting its diminished performance under certain circumstances. The training set R^2 mirrored these trends, with CNN-LSTM achieving the highest values in Model S2 and SSA-BP the lowest in Model S1. It should be noted that SSA-BP S1 performed best on both training and test sets in terms of R^2.

The results of the study confirm the existence of a different behavior in the monthly river discharge of the Buzău River, emphasized by the lowest performances of the models built using as training and test sets the series before, and after January 1984, respectively, i.e., Model S1.

In conclusion, the CNN-LSTM model's advanced architectural design, coupled with its ability to efficiently process large datasets and adapt to significant environmental changes, positions it as a highly effective tool for water discharge prediction in altered river systems. This study not only underscores the model's potential for widespread application in hydrological research but also offers invaluable insights for the scientific community and policymakers in enhancing our understanding and management of global water resources in an era marked by rapid environmental transformations.

Author Contributions: Conceptualization, L.Z. and A.B.; methodology, L.Z. and A.B.; software, L.Z.; validation, L.Z. and A.B.; formal analysis, L.Z. and A.B.; investigation, L.Z. and A.B.; resources, A.B.; data curation, A.B.; writing—original draft preparation, L.Z. and A.B.; writing—review and editing, A.B.; visualization, L.Z.; supervision, A.B.; project administration, A.B.; funding acquisition, A.B. All authors have read and agreed to the published version of the manuscript.

Funding: The APC was funded in part by Transilvania University of Brașov, Romania.

Data Availability Statement: Data will be available on request from the authors.

Conflicts of Interest: The present research work carries no conflicts of interest.

References

1. Naiman, R.J.; Decamps, H.; Pollock, M. The role of riparian corridors in maintaining regional biodiversity. *Ecol. Appl.* **1993**, *3*, 209–212. [CrossRef]
2. Magilligan, F.J.; Nislow, K.H. Changes in hydrologic regime by dams. *Geomorphology* **2005**, *71*, 61–78. [CrossRef]
3. Popescu, C.; Bărbulescu, A. On the Flash Flood Susceptibility and Accessibility in the Vărbilău Catchment (Romania). *Rom. J. Phys.* **2022**, *67*, 811.
4. Dumitriu, C.S.; Bărbulescu, A.; Maftei, C. IrrigTool—A New Tool for Determining the Irrigation Rate Based on Evapotranspiration Estimated by the Thornthwaite Equation. *Water* **2022**, *14*, 2399. [CrossRef]
5. Bărbulescu, A.; Maftei, C. Statistical approach of the behavior of Hamcearca River (Romania). *Rom. Rep. Phys.* **2021**, *73*, 703.
6. Bucurica, I.-A.; Dulama, I.-D.; Radulescu, C.; Banica, A.L. Surface Water Quality Assessment Using Electroanalytical Methods and Inductively Coupled Plasma Mass Spectrometry (ICP-MS). *Rom. J. Phys.* **2022**, *67*, 802.
7. Chilian, A.; Tanase, N.-M.; Popescu, I.V.; Radulescu, C.; Bancuta, O.-R.; Bancuta, I. Long-Term Monitoring of the Heavy Metals Content (Cu, Ni, Zn, Cd, Pb) in Wastewater Before and after the Treatment Process by Spectrometric Methods of Atomic Absorption (FAAS and ETAAS). *Rom. J. Phys.* **2022**, *67*, 804.
8. Bhowmik, R.D.; Sankarasubramanian, A.; Sinha, T.; Patskoski, J.; Mahinthakumar, G.; Kunkel, K.E. Multivariate downscaling approach preserving cross correlations across climate variables for projecting hydrologic fluxes. *J. Hydrometeorol.* **2017**, *18*, 2187–2205. [CrossRef]
9. Vrac, M.; Thao, S.; Yiou, P. Changes in temperature–precipitation correlations over Europe: Are climate models reliable? *Clim. Dyn.* **2023**, *60*, 2713–2733. [CrossRef]
10. Dekens, L.; Parey, S.; Grandjacques, M.; Dacunha-Castelle, D. Multivariate distribution correction of climate model outputs: A generalization of quantile mapping approaches. *Environmetrics* **2017**, *28*, e2454. [CrossRef]
11. Bărbulescu, A.; Dumitriu, C.S.; Maftei, C. On the Probable Maximum Precipitation Method. *Rom. J. Phys.* **2022**, *67*, 801.
12. Rahayu, W.S.; Juwono, P.T.; Soetopo, W. Discharge prediction of Amprong river using the ARIMA (autoregressive integrated moving average) model. *IOP Conf. Ser. Earth Environ. Sci.* **2020**, *437*, 012032. [CrossRef]
13. Ghimire, B.N. Application of ARIMA Model for River Discharges Analysis. *J. Nepal Phys. Soc.* **2017**, *4*, 27–32. [CrossRef]
14. Valipour, M. Long-term runoff study using SARIMA and ARIMA models in the United States. *Meteorol. Appl.* **2015**, *22*, 592–598. [CrossRef]
15. Yürekli, K.; Kurunc, A.; Ozturk, F. Application of Linear Stochastic Models to Monthly Flow Data of Kelkit Stream. *Ecol. Model.* **2005**, *183*, 67–75. [CrossRef]
16. MA Models for Forecasting: Pros, Cons, and Examples. Available online: https://www.linkedin.com/advice/0/what-advantages-disadvantages-using-arima (accessed on 4 January 2024).
17. Zhou, J.; Wang, D.; Band, S.S.; Jun, C.; Bateni, S.M.; Moslehpour, M.; Pai, H.-T.; Hsu, C.-C.; Ameri, R. Monthly River Discharge Forecasting Using Hybrid Models Based on Extreme Gradient Boosting Coupled with Wavelet Theory and Lévy–Jaya Optimization Algorithm. *Water Resour. Manag.* **2023**, *37*, 3953–3972. [CrossRef]
18. Abrahart, R.J.; See, L. Comparing Neural Network and Autoregressive Moving Average Techniques for the Provision of Continuous River Flow Forecasts in Two Contrasting Catchments. *Hydrol. Process.* **2000**, *14*, 2157–2172. [CrossRef]
19. Birikundavyi, S.; Labib, R.; Trung, H.T.; Rousselle, J. Performance of Neural Networks in Daily Streamflow Forecasting. *J. Hydrol. Eng.* **2002**, *7*, 392. [CrossRef]
20. Hong, J.L.; Hong, K. Flood Forecasting for Klang River at Kuala Lumpur using Artificial Neural Networks. *Int. J. Hybrid Inf. Technol.* **2016**, *9*, 39–60. [CrossRef]
21. Kisi, Ö.; Cobaner, M. Modeling River Stage-Discharge Relationships Using Different Neural Network Computing Techniques. *Clean* **2009**, *37*, 160–169. [CrossRef]
22. Tanty, R.; Desmukh, T.S. Application of Artificial Neural Network in Hydrology—A Review. *Int. J. Eng. Resear. Techn.* **2015**, *4*, 184–188.
23. Valipour, M.; Banihabib, M.E.; Behbahani, S.M.R. Comparison of the ARMA, ARIMA, and the autoregressive artificial neural network models in forecasting the monthly inflow of Dez dam reservoir. *J. Hydrol.* **2013**, *476*, 433–441. [CrossRef]
24. Uca; Toriman, E.; Jaafar, O.; Maru, R.; Arfan, A.; Ahmar, A.S. Daily Suspended Sediment Discharge Prediction Using Multiple Linear Regression and Artificial Neural Network. *J. Phys. Conf. Ser.* **2018**, *954*, 012030. [CrossRef]
25. Li, S.; Yang, J. Modelling of suspended sediment load by Bayesian optimized machine learning methods with seasonal adjustment. *Eng. Appl. Comput. Fluid Mech.* **2022**, *16*, 1883–1901. [CrossRef]
26. Hayder, G.; Solihin, M.I.; Mustafa, H.M. Modelling of River Flow Using Particle Swarm Optimized Cascade-Forward Neural Networks: A Case Study of Kelantan River in Malaysia. *Appl. Sci.* **2020**, *10*, 8670. [CrossRef]
27. Xiang, X.J.; Li, Q.; Khan, S.; Khalaf, O.I. Urban water resource management for sustainable environment planning using artificial intelligence techniques. *Environ. Impact Assess. Rev.* **2021**, *86*, 106515. [CrossRef]

28. Essien, A.E.; Chukwukelu, G.; Giannetti, C. A Scalable Deep Convolutional LSTM Neural Network for Large-Scale Urban Traffic Flow Prediction using Recurrence Plots. In Proceedings of the 2019 IEEE Africon, Accra, Ghana, 25–27 September 2019; pp. 1–7.
29. Zhang, J.X.; Li, S.Y. Air quality index forecast in Beijing based on CNN-LSTM multi-mode. *Chemosphere* **2022**, *308*, 136180. [CrossRef]
30. Yan, P.; Shang, S.; Zhang, C.; Yin, N.; Zhang, X.; Yang, G.; Zhang, Z.; Sun, Q. Research on the Processing of Coal Mine Water Source Data by Optimizing BP Neural Network Algorithm with Sparrow Search Algorithm. *IEEE Access* **2021**, *9*, 108718–108730. [CrossRef]
31. Xin, J.X.; Chen, J.Z.; Li, C.Y.; Lu, R.K.; Li, X.L.; Wang, C.X.; Zhu, H.W.; He, R.Y. Deformation characterization of oil and gas pipeline by ACM technique based on SSA-BP neural network model. *Measurement* **2022**, *189*, 110654. [CrossRef]
32. Kaloop, M.R.; Kumar, D.; Samui, P.; Gabr, A.R.; Hu, J.W.; Jin, X.; Roy, B. Particle Swarm Optimization Algorithm-Extreme Learning Machine (PSO-ELM) Model for Predicting Resilient Modulus of Stabilized Aggregate Bases. *Appl. Sci.* **2019**, *9*, 3221. [CrossRef]
33. Zhang, X.Q.; Zhao, D.; Wang, T.; Wu, X.L.; Duan, B.S. A novel rainfall prediction model based on CEEMDAN-PSO-ELM coupled model. *Water Supply* **2023**, *22*, 4531–4543. [CrossRef]
34. Kratzert, F.; Klotz, D.; Brenner, C.; Schulz, K.; Herrnegger, M. Rainfall–runoff modelling using Long Short-Term Memory (LSTM) networks. *Hydrol. Earth Sys. Sci.* **2018**, *22*, 6005–6022. [CrossRef]
35. Kratzert, F.; Klotz, D.; Herrnegger, M.; Sampson, A.K.; Hochreiter, S.; Nearing, G.S. Towards Improved Predictions in Ungauged Basins: LSTM Networks for Rainfall-Runoff Modeling. *Water Resour. Res.* **2019**, *55*, 11344–11354. [CrossRef]
36. Mocanu-Vargancsik, C.A.; Bărbulescu, A. On the variability of a river water flow, under seasonal conditions. Case study. *IOP Conf. Ser. Earth Environ. Sci.* **2019**, *344*, 012028. [CrossRef]
37. Minea, G.; Bărbulescu, A. Statistical assessing of hydrological alteration of Buzău River induced by Siriu dam (Romania). *Forum Geogr.* **2014**, *13*, 50–58. [CrossRef]
38. Bărbulescu, A. Statistical Assessment and Model for a River Flow under Variable Conditions. Available online: https://cest2017.gnest.org/sites/default/files/presentation_file_list/cest2017_00715_poster_paper.pdf (accessed on 28 December 2023).
39. The Arrangement of the Buzău River. Available online: https://www.hidroconstructia.com/dyn/2pub/proiecte_det.php?id=110&pg=1 (accessed on 17 October 2023). (In Romanian)
40. Chendeș, V. *Water Resources in Curvature Subcarpathians. Geospatial Assessments*; Editura Academiei Române: Bucureşti, Romania, 2011. (In Romanian with English Abstract)
41. Yao, H.; Tang, X.; Wei, H.; Zheng, G.; Li, Z. Revisiting spatial-temporal similarity: A deep learning framework for traffic prediction. *Proc. AAAI Conf. Artif. Intell.* **2019**, *33*, 5668–5675. [CrossRef]
42. Goodfellow, I.; Bengio, Y.; Courville, A. *Deep Learning*; MIT Press: Cambridge, MA, USA, 2006.
43. Hochreiter, S.; Schmidhuber, J. Long Short-Term Memory. *Neural Comput.* **1997**, *9*, 1735–1780. [CrossRef]
44. Gers, F. Long Short-Term Memory in Recurrent Neural Networks. Ph.D. Thesis, Ecole Polytechnique Federale de Lausanne, Lausanne, Switzerland, 2001. Available online: http://www.felixgers.de/papers/phd.pdf (accessed on 29 November 2023).
45. Lu, W.; Li, J.; Li, Y.; Sun, A.; Wang, J. A CNN-LSTM-Based Model to Forecast Stock Prices 2020. *Complexity* **2020**, *2020*, 6622927. [CrossRef]
46. Colah's Blog. Understanding LSTM Networks. 2015. Available online: https://colah.github.io/posts/2015-08-Understanding-LSTMs/ (accessed on 29 November 2023).
47. Aksan, F.; Li, Y.; Suresh, V.; Janik, P. CNN-LSTM vs. LSTM-CNN to Predict Power Flow Direction: A Case Study of the High-Voltage Subnet of Northeast Germany. *Sensors* **2023**, *23*, 901. [CrossRef]
48. Zhang, F.; Deng, S.; Wang, S.; Sun, H. Convolutional neural network long short-term memory deep learning model for sonic well log generation for brittleness evaluation. *Interpretation* **2022**, *10*, T367–T378. [CrossRef]
49. Xue, J.; Shen, B. A novel swarm intelligence optimization approach: Sparrow search algorithm. *Syst. Sci. Control Eng.* **2020**, *8*, 22–34. [CrossRef]
50. Rumelhart, D.; Hinton, G.; Williams, R. Learning representations by back-propagating errors. *Nature* **1986**, *323*, 533–536. [CrossRef]
51. Wang, X.; Liu, J.; Hou, T.; Pan, C. The SSA-BP-based potential threat prediction for aerial target considering commander emotion. *Defen. Techn.* **2022**, *18*, 2097–2106. [CrossRef]
52. Poli, R.; Kennedy, J.; Blackwell, T. Particle swarm optimization. *Swarm Intell* **2007**, *1*, 33–57. [CrossRef]
53. Huang, G.-B.; Zhu, Q.-Y.; Siew, C.-K. Extreme learning machine: Theory and applications. *Neurocomputing* **2006**, *70*, 489–501. [CrossRef]
54. Huang, G.-B.; Chen, L.; Siew, C.K. Universal approximation using incremental constructive feedforward networks with random hidden nodes. *IEEE Trans. Neural Netw.* **2006**, *17*, 879–892. [CrossRef]
55. Karami, H.; Karimi, S.; Bonakdari, H.; Shamshirband, S. Predicting discharge coefficient of triangular labyrinth weir using extreme learning machine, artificial neural network and genetic programming. *Neural Comput. Appl.* **2018**, *29*, 983–989. [CrossRef]
56. Cui, D.; Bin Huang, G.; Liu, T. ELM based smile detection using Distance Vector. *Pattern Recognit.* **2018**, *79*, 356–369. [CrossRef]
57. Zhu, B.; Feng, Y.; Gong, D.; Jiang, S.; Zhao, L.; Cui, L. Hybrid particle swarm optimization with extreme learning machine for daily reference evapotranspiration prediction from limited climatic data. *Comput. Electron. Agric.* **2020**, *173*, 105430. [CrossRef]

58. Zhu, H.; Tsang, E.C.C.; Zhu, J. Training an extreme learning machine by localized generalization error model. *Soft Comput.* **2018**, *22*, 3477–3485. [CrossRef]
59. Cao, J.; Lin, Z.; Huang, G.B. Self-adaptive evolutionary extreme learning machine. *Neural Process. Lett.* **2012**, *36*, 285–305. [CrossRef]
60. Mohapatra, P.; Chakravarty, S.; Dash, P.K. An improved cuckoo search based extreme learning machine for medical data classification. *Swarm Evol. Comput.* **2015**, *24*, 25–49. [CrossRef]
61. Chen, S.; Shang, Y.; Wu, M. Application of PSO-ELM in electronic system fault diagnosis. In Proceedings of the 2016 IEEE International Conference on Prognostics and Health Management (ICPHM), Ottawa, ON, Canada, 20–22 June 2016.
62. Liu, D.; Li, G.; Fu, Q.; Li, M.; Liu, C.; Faiz, M.A.; Khan, M.I.; Li, T.; Cui, S. Application of particle swarm optimization and extreme learning machine forecasting models for regional groundwater depth using nonlinear prediction models as preprocessor. *J. Hydrol. Eng.* **2018**, *23*, 04018052. [CrossRef]
63. Brockwell, P.; Davies, R. *Introduction to Time Series*; Springer: New York, NY, USA, 2002.
64. Brownlee, J. Crash Course on Multi-Layer Perceptron Neural Networks. 2022. Available online: https://machinelearningmastery.com/neural-networks-crash-course/ (accessed on 7 January 2024).
65. Anderson, T.W.; Darling, D.A. A Test of Goodness-of-Fit. *J. Am. Stat. Assoc.* **1954**, *49*, 765–769. [CrossRef]
66. LibreTexts Statistics. 16.4. Box-Cox Transformations. Available online: https://stats.libretexts.org/Bookshelves/Introductory_Statistics/Introductory_Statistics_(Lane)/16%3A_Transformations/16.04%3A_Box-Cox_Transformations (accessed on 7 January 2024).
67. Yan, S.; Liu, W.; Li, X.; Yang, P.; Wu, F.; Yan, Z. Comparative Study and Improvement Analysis of Sparrow Search Algorithm. *Wirel. Comm. Mobile Comput.* **2022**, *2022*, 4882521. [CrossRef]
68. Svetunkov, I. Rolling Origin. 2003. Available online: https://cran.r-project.org/web/packages/greybox/vignettes/ro.html#:~:text=Rolling%20origin%20is%20an%20evaluation,of%20how%20the%20models%20perform (accessed on 7 January 2024).
69. AL-Allaf, O.N.A. Improving the Performance of Backpropagation Neural Network Algorithm for Image Compression/Decompression System. *J. Comp. Sci.* **2010**, *6*, 1347–1354.
70. He, K.; Sun, J. Convolutional neural networks at constrained time cost. In Proceedings of the IEEE Conference on Computer Vision and Pattern Recognition, Boston, MA, USA, 7–12 June 2015; pp. 5353–5360.
71. Chellapilla, K.; Puri, S.; Simard, P. High performance convolutional neural networks for document processing. In Proceedings of the Tenth International Workshop on Frontiers in Handwriting Recognition, La Baule, France, 1 October 2006. Available online: https://inria.hal.science/inria-00112631/document (accessed on 6 January 2024).
72. Tsironi, E.; Barros, P.; Weber, C.; Wermter, S. An analysis of Convolutional Long Short-Term Memory Recurrent Neural Networks for gesture recognition. *Neurocomputing* **2017**, *268*, 76–86. [CrossRef]
73. Xu, L.; Zhang, Z.; Yao, Y.; Yu, Z. Improved Particle Swarm Optimization-Based BP Neural Networks for Aero-Optical Imaging Deviation Prediction. *IEEE Access* **2022**, *10*, 26769–26777. [CrossRef]
74. Karlsson, V.; Rosvall, E. Extreme Kernel Machine. Available online: https://www.diva-portal.org/smash/get/diva2:1130092/FULLTEXT01.pdf (accessed on 6 January 2024).
75. Zhang, R.; Pan, Z.; Yin, Y.; Cai, Z. A Model of Network Security Situation Assessment Based on BPNN Optimized by SAA-SSA. *Int. J. Digital Crime Forens.* **2022**, *14*, 1–18. [CrossRef]
76. Fashae, O.; Olusola, A.; Ndubuisi, I.; Udomboso, C. Comparing ANN and ARIMA model in predictingthe discharge of River Opeki from 2010 to 2020. *River. Res. Appl.* **2019**, *35*, 169–177. [CrossRef]
77. Musarat, M.A.; Alaloul, W.S.; Rabbani, M.B.; Ali, M.; Altaf, M.; Fediuk, R.; Vatin, N.; Klyuev, S.; Bukhari, H.; Sadiq, A.; et al. Kabul river flow prediction using automated ARIMA forecasting: A machine learning approach. *Sustainability* **2021**, *13*, 10720. [CrossRef]
78. Senthil Kumar, A.; Sudheer, K.; Jain, S.; Agarwal, P. Rainfall-runoff modelling using artificial neural networks: Comparison of network types. *Hydrol. Process. Int. J.* **2005**, *19*, 1277–1291. [CrossRef]
79. Lilhore, U.K.; Dalal, S.; Faujdar, N.; Margala, M.; Chakrabarti, P.; Chakrabarti, T.; Simaiya, S.; Kumar, P.; Thangaraju, P.; Velmurugan, H. Hybrid CNN-LSTM model with efficient hyperparameter tuning for prediction of Parkinson's disease. *Sci. Rep.* **2023**, *13*, 14605. [CrossRef] [PubMed]
80. Ehteram, M.; Ahmed, A.N.; Khozani, Z.H.; El-Shafie, A. Graph convolutional network—Long short term memory neural network-multi layer perceptron—Gaussian progress regression model: A new deep learning model for predicting ozone concentration. *Atmos. Poll. Res.* **2023**, *14*, 101766. [CrossRef]
81. Wibawa, A.P.; Utama, A.B.P.; Elmunsyah, H.; Pujianto, U.; Dwiyanto, F.A.; Hernandez, L. Time-series analysis with smoothed Convolutional Neural Network. *J. Big. Data* **2022**, *9*, 44. [CrossRef] [PubMed]
82. Liu, T.; Ding, Y.; Cai, X.; Zhu, Y.; Zhang, X. Extreme learning machine based on particle swarm optimization for estimation of reference evapotranspiration. In Proceedings of the 2017 36th Chinese Control Conference (CCC), Dalian, China, 26–28 July 2017; pp. 4567–4572.
83. Anupam, S.; Pani, P. Flood forecasting using a hybrid extreme learning machine-particle swarm optimization algorithm (ELM-PSO) model. *Model. Earth Syst. Environ.* **2020**, *6*, 341–347. [CrossRef]

Disclaimer/Publisher's Note: The statements, opinions and data contained in all publications are solely those of the individual author(s) and contributor(s) and not of MDPI and/or the editor(s). MDPI and/or the editor(s) disclaim responsibility for any injury to people or property resulting from any ideas, methods, instructions or products referred to in the content.

Article

Multi-Station Hydrological Modelling to Assess Groundwater Recharge of a Vast Semi-Arid Basin Considering the Problem of Lack of Data: A Case Study in Seybouse Basin, Algeria

Cagri Alperen Inan [1,*], Ammar Maoui [2], Yann Lucas [1,*] and Joëlle Duplay [1]

1. Institute of Earth and Environment of Strasbourg, University of Strasbourg, 67084 Strasbourg, France; jduplay@unistra.fr
2. Laboratory of Civil Engineering and Hydraulic, University of 8 May 1945, Guelma 24000, Algeria; maoui_ammar@yahoo.fr
* Correspondence: cagrialpereninan@gmail.com (C.A.I.); ylucas@unistra.fr (Y.L.)

Citation: Inan, C.A.; Maoui, A.; Lucas, Y.; Duplay, J. Multi-Station Hydrological Modelling to Assess Groundwater Recharge of a Vast Semi-Arid Basin Considering the Problem of Lack of Data: A Case Study in Seybouse Basin, Algeria. *Water* 2024, *16*, 160. https://doi.org/10.3390/w16010160

Academic Editor: YongJiang Zhang

Received: 30 November 2023
Revised: 27 December 2023
Accepted: 28 December 2023
Published: 31 December 2023

Copyright: © 2023 by the authors. Licensee MDPI, Basel, Switzerland. This article is an open access article distributed under the terms and conditions of the Creative Commons Attribution (CC BY) license (https://creativecommons.org/licenses/by/4.0/).

Abstract: Water resource management scenarios have become more crucial for arid to semi-arid regions. Their application prerequisites rigorous hydrological modelling approaches since data are usually exposed to uncertainties and inaccuracies. In this work, Soil Water Assessment Tool (SWAT), an open source semi-distributed, continuous-time, process-based physical hydrological model is used to model hydrological processes and eventually calculate groundwater recharge estimations in Seybouse basin, Northeast Algeria. The model uses estimated rainfall to calibrate the model with observed discharge from hydrometric stations. Model calibration and validation are performed over four hydrometric stations located in the basin. Uncertainty analysis and sensitivity analysis supported the calibration period. SUFI-2 algorithm is used for uncertainty estimations along with a global sensitivity analysis prior to calibration simulations. Simulated flood hydrographs showed generally good accuracy with few misfits on the peaks. The model obtained satisfactory and consistent calibration and validation results for which the Nash score varied from 0.5 to 0.7 for calibration and from −0.1 to 0.6 for validation and R^2 from 0.6 to 0.7 for calibration and 0.03 to 0.8 for validation. Moreover, estimated water budget values show strong similarities with the observed values found in the literature. The present work shows that the rigorously calibrated and validated SWAT model can simulate hydrological processes as well as major high and low flows using estimated rainfall data.

Keywords: hydrology; SWAT; Seybouse basin; SUFI-2; multi-station modelling; semi-arid regions; groundwater recharge

1. Introduction

In semi-arid zones, the problem of water scarcity is exacerbated, posing a threat to food cultivation, ecosystems, and public health. A swift expansion of semi-arid regions in the Mediterranean, Africa, as well as North and South America is projected [1]. Mediterranean semi-arid regions have been exposed to an increase in population due to industrial, economic, and touristic developments since the late 70s. Water stress in those regions today has become more critical under ongoing increases in temperature in subtropical zones.

Considering these socio-economical and hydro-climatological conditions, water resources management measures need more scientific attention. Modelling surface and ground waters and their interactions can be preliminary actions in terms of water resource management in Mediterranean semi-arid regions. To secure the availability and sustainability of water in many regions, various methods of artificial groundwater recharge are used to replenish underground aquifers [2–6]. Wastewater treatment and reuse, artificial recharge, and water storage in aquifers for drought emergencies with respect to current or future climate change conditions have been considered to be sustainable solutions. Understanding general water fluxes through surface waters and groundwaters in hydro systems and their interactions are very important for further applications of water resource management scenarios [7]. For the TRUST project supported by the PRIMA 2020 program, we are interested in estimating aquifer recharge and studying artificial recharge scenarios. In this preliminary work, we aim to create a model that can estimate groundwater recharge with hydrological models.

Hydro(geo)logical models provide extensive modelling approaches for simulating water resource management measures and scenarios to the regional or national stakeholders and authorities. There are two major schools in hydrological modelling: physical and statistical (black box) models. While physical models represent the hydro system via physical equations, statistical models aim to characterize the system in the mathematical form [8]. Different advantages and inconveniences exist for both approaches. One can address related literature for further lectures [8–11].

In this study, a process-based physical hydrological model, SWAT, is preferred for hydrological modelling purposes thanks to its wide use and efficiency in recent years on different types and sizes of basins. The aim of this study is mainly modelling hydrological processes in a semi-arid Mediterranean basin, Seybouse, in Northeast Algeria within the scope of the TRUST project: management of industrial treated wastewater reuse as mitigation measures to water scarcity in the context of in two Mediterranean regions. This preliminary modelling approach will provide hydrological simulations through a calibrated and validated model and water budget. These results will be used as input data in a hydrodynamic groundwater model. Therefore, modelling hydrological processes and estimating hydrological entities, especially those related to river and groundwater interactions such as groundwater recharge is an important focus for this study.

2. Materials and Methods

2.1. Study Area

The study area is the semi-arid Seybouse basin located in the northeastern part of Algeria. It covers 6775 km². The elevation in the basin ranges from 0 to 1600 m.a.s.l. (Figure 1).

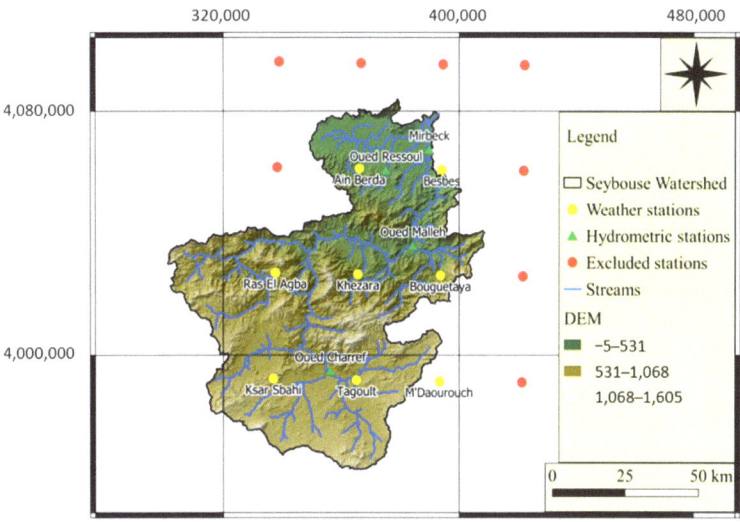

Figure 1. Digital elevation map of the Seybouse basin and the locations of the hydro meteorological stations.

It is bounded in the North by the Mediterranean Sea, to the East and West by the Constantinois coastline, and to the South by the Kébir-Rhumel, Constantinois and Medjerda high plateaus. The Seybouse river recharges to the Mediterranean Sea at Sidi Salem towards the South of the city of Annaba. The Seybouse basin rises in the semi-arid high plains on the southern slope of the Atlas Tellien, flowing from South to North. According to the Natural Waer Resource Agency, the Seybouse basin is divided into five sub-basins [12]. However, in this study, the basin is divided into 62 sub basins to better represent and model the real-world hydrological processes.

2.1.1. Hydro-Climatology

The upper Seybouse is a mountainous area with a typically Mediterranean climate, with hot summers and relatively mild winters; the annual amplitude characterizes the degree of continental climate in the southern part of the Seybouse basin. In the middle of Seybouse, the hot season runs from May to October, with an average temperature of 25 °C, peaking in August, and corresponding to the dry season, with an absence of precipitation. The wet season runs from October to April, with average temperatures below 15 °C. The maximum temperature recorded in the lower Seybouse is around 46 °C and the minimum is around 23 °C [13]. The mean annual temperature in the entire basin is recorded as approximately 20 °C.

The spatial distribution of rainfall fields in the region is subject to three influences; that of altitude, topographical conditions of longitude and finally that of distance from the sea. The rainfall intensity increases with altitude and from West to East but is higher on slopes exposed to wet winds than on leeward slopes. It decreases moving away from the coast [13]. The mean annual rainfall in the entire basin varies from 500 mm to 1100 mm approximately which proves a heterogenous rainfall distribution in the study area.

2.1.2. Hydrology and Hydrogeology

The Seybouse basin is characterized by a heterogeneous, compartmentalized relief (plains, mountains, valleys, hills, slopes, etc.). The basin drains a series of highly heterogeneous regions. The high plains, with their simple relief and low or even non-existent runoff, are followed by the rugged Atlas Tellien, with its highly complex structure. The wadis have irregular flows. The longitudinal profile allows rapid drainage. The Seybouse basin has a hydrographic network of over 3000 km, with forty-two wadis over 10 km long. It is made up of highly heterogeneous natural units, e.g., mountains, depressions, and plateaus resulting in different modes of feeding and runoff. The existence of depressions containing alluvial aquifers through which the Seybouse flows regulates the seasonal flow and results in low to zero river flows in summer despite the high proportion of winter rainfall received by this mountain range.

2.1.3. Database

The Seybouse basin contains 17 rain gauges, and 4 hydrometric stations. However, the database has data gap issues in different scales (i.e., monthly, or annually). For instance, the hydrometric station that is closest to the basin outlet, chosen as the station to calibrate the model with, has discharge data available from 1968 to 1991. Rain gauges have rainfall data in different measurement time steps (annual mean, monthly mean or daily and daily or monthly maximum). Due to the rainfall measurements possessing significant data gaps, Climate Forecast System Reanalysis (CFSR) of The National Centers for Environmental Prediction (NCEP) weather estimates are used. The CFRS system includes daily precipitation, wind, relative humidity, and solar radiation data from 1979 to 2014. The CFSR was designed and executed as a global, high resolution, coupled atmosphere-ocean-land surface-sea ice system to provide the best estimate of the state of these coupled domains over this period. In situ rain gauge data and CFRS data showed good correlations for the periods where both databases had available data. Therefore, databases were used for model calibration and validation for the period of 1979–1991. Calibration and validation periods were divided into two parts after excluding two years of warming up (training period) to avoid initial condition-related uncertainty issues.

2.2. SWAT Modelling

The Soil and Water Assessment Tool (SWAT) is a semi-distributed, continuous-time, process-based, physical hydrological model. It is meant to assess the impacts of water resource management alternatives in large river basins [14]. The spatial distribution of model parameters is controlled by subbasins having distinct spatial positions and hydrological response units (HRUs) which are lumped within subbasins with respect to distinct combinations of land use, soil, and slope characteristics. The SWAT model requires a wide range of parameters using manual or automated calibration processes such as shuffled complex evolution method SCE-UA [15–17], semi-automated SUFI-2 method providing sensitivity and uncertainty analysis [18–20] and GLUE [21,22]. SUFI-2 conducts a comprehensive optimization and uncertainty analysis via employing a global search approach, enabling it to handle a considerable quantity of parameters.

SWAT embedded in geographic information system platforms, e.g., QGis and ArcGis, works via a graphical user interface and allows users to design hydrological models. Model design is supported by digital elevation topographical map (DEM), river networks, land use, soil, and slope maps in order first to create subbasins and then hydrological units.

2.2.1. Model Inputs

The basic data set required for a SWAT model includes: a DEM of the basin, climate data, land use/land cover and soil data. The DEM used for this study was of 30 m resolution from NASA's Shuttle Radar Topography Mission (SRTM). The soil map is obtained from FAO and related soil textures and soil hydraulic groups are written in SWAT database (Table 1).

Table 1. Soil classes in the basin with associated soil textures and hydraulic groups.

Soil Group Numbers	Soil Textures	Hydraulic Group
1	CLAY	D
2	CLAY	C
3	CLAY_LOAM	D
4	LOAM	D
5	LOAM	D
6	SANDY_CLAY_LOAM	C
7	LOAM	D

Climate data include daily precipitation, temperature, solar radiation, relative humidity, and wind data from the CFRS dataset which is compatible with SWAT. Eight weather stations from the CFRS system were considered as weather data out of sixteen stations. Discharge data from 4 hydrometric stations is used during calibration for rainfall-runoff modelling (Figure 1).

The land use data is obtained from ESA's Global land use GlobCover, 2009 data (Table 2). Global land use GlobCover data is adapted to the SWAT codes and a new land use database is created to be read by SWAT model easily.

Table 2. Global Land Use GlobCover with related SWAT land use classes.

GlobCover Code	GlobCover Definition	SWAT Code	SWAT Definition
AGIR	Post-flooding or irrigated crops	AGRL	Agricultural land
AGRF	Rainfed croplands	AGRL	Agricultural land
AGMX	Cropland (50–70%)/grassland, shrubland, forest (20–50%)	AGRL	Agricultural land
CRGR	Grassland, shrubland, forest (50–70%)/cropland (20–50%)	CRGR	Cropland/grassland

Table 2. Cont.

GlobCover Code	GlobCover Definition	SWAT Code	SWAT Definition
FRSE	Broadleaved evergreen	FRST	Forest-evergreen
FRSD	Broadleaved deciduous forest	FRSD	Forest-deciduous
PINE	Needle-leaved evergreen forest	PINE	Pine
FRST	Mixed broadleaved and needle-leaved forest	FRST	Forest-mixed
RNG1	Mosaic forest or shrubland (50–70%)/grassland (20–50%)	RNGB	Range-brush
RNE1	Mosaic grassland (50–70%)/forest or shrubland (20–50%)	RNGE	Range-grasses
FRST	Closed to open (>15%) evergreen or deciduous, shrubland (<5 m)	FRST	Forest-mixed
RNGB	Sparse (<15%) vegetation	RNGB	Range-brush
URBN	Artificial surfaces and associated areas (urban areas >50%)	URMD	Residential
BSVG	Bare areas	BSVG	Barren or sparsely vegetated
WATB	Water bodies	WATR	Water bodies

2.2.2. Model Design

The hydrologic cycle in the SWAT model is based on the water balance equation:

$$SW_t = SW_0 + \sum_{i=1}^{t} \left(R_{day} - Q_{surf} - W_{seep} - E_a - Q_{gw} \right) \tag{1}$$

where SW_t is the humidity of the soil (mm), SW_0 is the base humidity of the soil (mm), t is time (days), R_{day} is rainfall volume (mm), Q_{surf} is the value of surface runoff, W_{seep} is the value of seepage of water from the soil into deeper layers, E_a is the value of evapotranspiration (mm), and Q_{gw} is the value of underground runoff (mm).

Subbasin and stream calculations are performed with the automatic delineation tool incorporated in QSWAT 3 version 1.6.3. Land use map, soil classification map and slope map are created for the Seybouse basin and introduced to the database concerning the global land use and user soil options in the QSWAT 3 1.6.3.

2.2.3. Hydrologic Response Unit (HRU)

HRUs are specified subunits within each subbasin. They are lumped land areas with overlapping unique combination of land use, soil, and slope classes. Each subbasin contains at least one HRU and one main tributary.

HRUs are created using physically based data, i.e., land use data, soil type and soil properties and digital elevation model for slope calculation (Figures 2–4). HRUs are created by splitting individual subbasins apart, resulting in distinct combinations of land use, slope, and soil classes within each subbasin that can represent a different number of HRUs. These HRUs, found across subbasins, share comprehensive attributes like soil type, land use, and slope. Calculations related to physical processes performed separately on these HRUs are aggregated by summation through the outlet point for each corresponding subbasin. While creating the HRUs, a threshold is used by defining the land use, soil, and slope classes percentage in a subbasin. The first threshold is applied to land uses by its percentage in a subbasin area that eliminates small land covers in each subbasin. Secondly, a percentage of soil classes relative to land use area after first threshold eliminates the unimportant (in size) soil occupations. The final threshold is the elimination of slope classes relative to the soil area by another percentage to eliminate minor slope classes [23]. The threshold information can be addressed in Table 3.

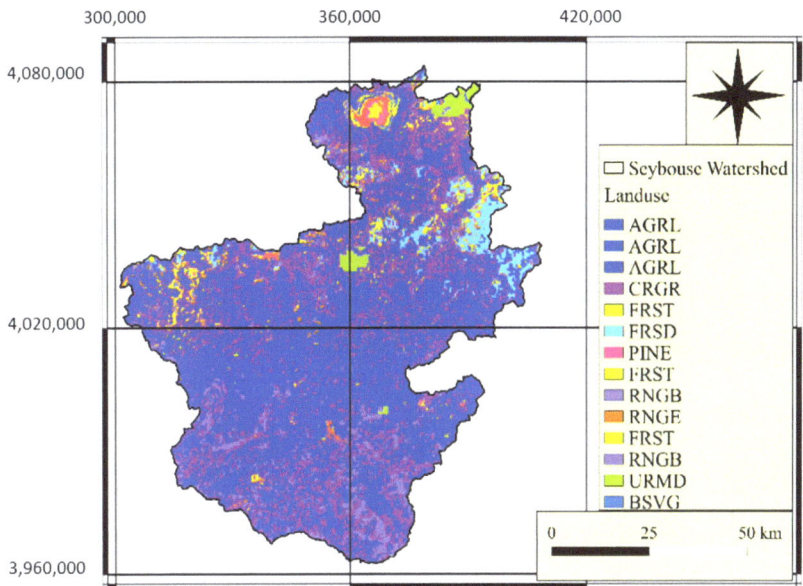

Figure 2. Land use map.

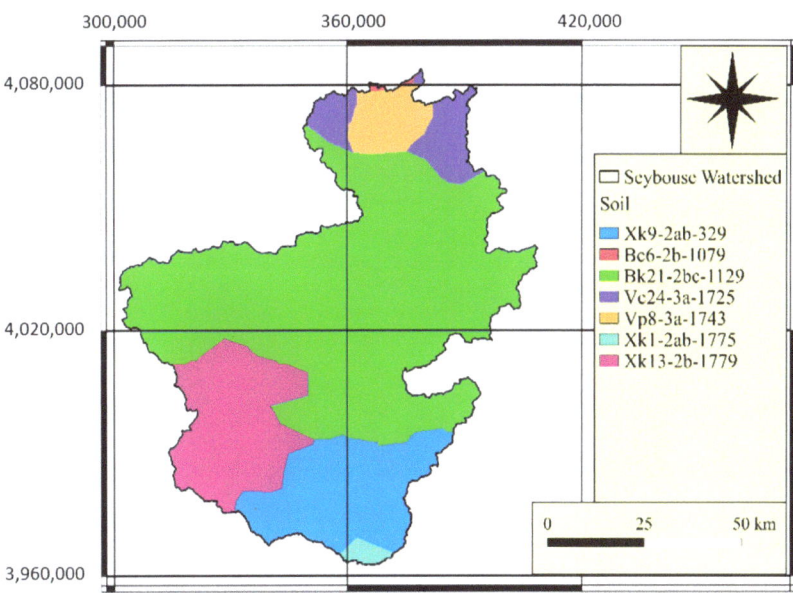

Figure 3. Soil classification map.

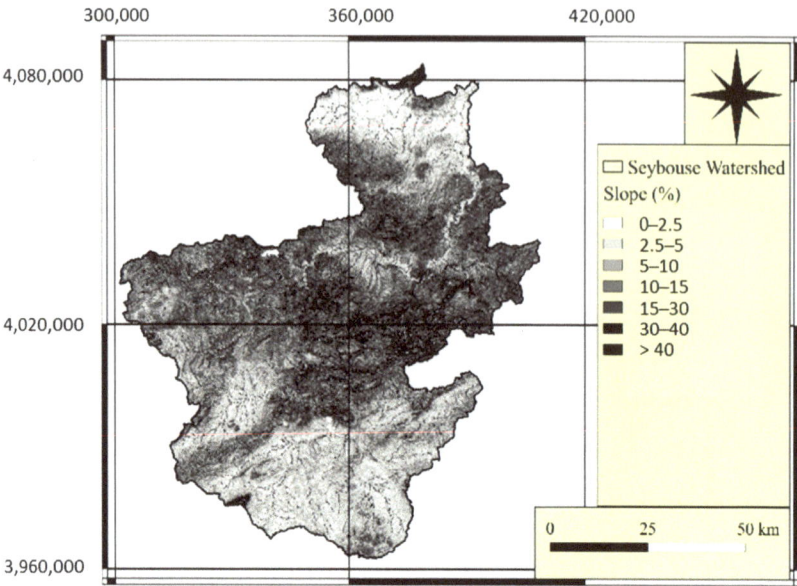

Figure 4. Slope classification map.

Table 3. Threshold definitions for land use, soil and slope classes used in formation of HRUs.

HRU Threshold	Minimum % of Land Area
Land use by subbasin area	0
Soil class by land use area after 1st threshold	10
Slope class by soil class area after 2nd threshold	15

2.2.4. Swat Model Simulations

The main objective of the simulations is to calibrate and validate the model with respect to existing discharge observations from ground stations to finally obtain a value of groundwater recharge from the validated model. Therefore, meteorological data was used as input and the only output variable was the river discharge. SWAT provides two methods for surface runoff estimation: the Soil Conservation Service (SCS) curve number and the Green-Ampt infiltration method. In the present study, the SCS curve number method is preferred. The SCS method uses the following formula for runoff computation to estimate runoff under varying land use and soil types [24]:

$$Q_{surf} = \frac{(R_{day} - I_a)^2}{(R_{day} - I_a + S)} \qquad (2)$$

$$S = 25.4 \left(\frac{1000}{CN} - 10 \right) \qquad (3)$$

where Q_{surf} is accumulated runoff (mm), R_{day} is daily rainfall depth, I_a is the initial abstractions (mm), S is the retention parameter (mm) and CN is the curve number.

After model simulation, the model is checked via SWAT Error Checker for possible inconveniences in hydrological cycle prior to calibration period. Model calibration can accomodate these inconveniences, if any.

For instance, surface runoff is found to be too low during the pre-calibration period to be used as an index in the calibration period. This could be due to high evaporation and transpiration present in the region or underestimation of surface runoff during simulation. In any case, it seems that model design is meaningful, and calibration can be functional at this point.

2.2.5. Calibration, Sensitivity, and Validation

Hydrological models face different levels of inaccuracies coming from different sources of uncertainty. Major uncertainty sources are input forcings, model parameters, and model structure. Processes-based distributed hydrological models provide a large variety of parameters so that models can better represent the real-world hydrological systems. However, it is known that the more parameters a model is run with, the more uncertainty its simulations would possess. Therefore, rigorous calibration, validation, and uncertainty and sensitivity analyses steps are required.

The SWAT Calibration and Uncertainty Program (SWAT-CUP), a computer-based software is widely used for calibration, validation, and sensitivity analysis purposes for SWAT models [25]. The program provides uncertainty and sensitivity analyses for multi-site calibration through different calibration algorithms such as the Sequential Uncertainty Fitting version-2 (SUFI-2), Particle Swarm Optimization (PSO), Generalized Likelihood Uncertainty Estimation (GLUE), Parameter Solution (ParaSol), Markov Chain Monte Carlo (MCMC), that can be used for analyzing SWAT outputs based on different cost functions. In this study, the SUFI-2 algorithm is used to calibrate the SWAT model. The calibration algorithm, SUFI-2 is an iterative algorithm and projects all the model uncertainties to a certain parameter range. The total uncertainty is determined by the 95% predictive uncertainty (95PPU) calculated at the 2.5% and 97.5% levels of the cumulative distribution of an output variable which disallows 5% of very inaccurate simulations. SUFI-2 assumes, at first, a large parameter uncertainty. Therefore, the measured data initially falls within the 95PPU. Then, the model decreases this uncertainty step by step while monitoring the p-factor and the r-factor. In each step, previous parameter ranges are updated by calculating the sensitivity matrix (i.e., Jacobian matrix), and equivalent of a Hessian matrix, which is then followed by the covariance matrix calculation, 95% confidence intervals, and correlation matrix. Parameters are later updated in such a way that the new ranges are always smaller than the previous ranges and are centered on the best simulation.

Hydrological modelling of a basin does not occur in a unique way. It is always possible to calibrate a model with different parameter sets which is explained by the equifinality phenomenon in hydrology [26,27]. Therefore, acknowledging which parameters really represent and affect the physical processes in a basin is essential. This can be done through sensitivity analysis. Sensitivity analysis is the process of determining the change in model output based on the changes in parameters space. Global sensitivity analysis is where the uncertainty in outputs to the uncertainty in each input factor is examined over their entire range of interest. It is considered to be global when all the input variables are modified simultaneously [28]. A multiple regression analysis called the *t*-test is used for sensitivity analysis in the SUFI-2 algorithm. T-stat is the ratio of the coefficient of a parameter to its standard error. If the coefficient is higher than its standard error, then the parameter is likely to be sensitive [29]. The *p*-value in *t*-tests is more decisive to understand if the parameter is sensitive. A low *p*-value (<0.05) generally indicates the model response changes related to the changes in parameter. A large *p*-value is associated with non-sensitive parameters.

The SUFI-2 algorithm provides two statistical terms to quantify the fitness between the observation and the simulation, which is expressed as 95PPU. These are called p-factor and r-factor. p-factor is the percentage of the measured data covered by the 95 PPU simulation results while r-factor is the width of the cover. The aim is to cover the maximum of the observed data in 95PPU and decrease the width of the 95PPU band. In general, >70% of p-factor and r-factor around 1 is considered as a good threshold for discharge data [18,19].

Validation data should be completely different from the calibration data for a rigorous and robust hydrological modelling practice. Therefore, data from four discharge observation stations were divided into two parts for the calibration and validation steps. All the stations are used for both calibration and validation steps with respect to different time periods (Table 4).

Table 4. Names and locations of the discharge observation stations used for model calibration and validation.

Discharge Observation Station	UTM Easting	UTM Northing
Mirbeck	389,563.39	4,066,965.44
Oued Ressoul	374,818.87	4,060,178.06
Oued Malleh	383,958.91	4,035,417.7
Oued Charref	355,941.82	3,994,372.54

In this way, the model is validated, with the parameter set decided during the calibration, with data from different periods which are unknown to the model, i.e., as we would have to do in a prediction case.

2.2.6. Cost Functions

- Nash—Sutcliffe (NS); is one of the most preferred evaluation criteria in literature. It takes its maximum value (i.e., 1) when the ratio of the error variance of model estimation to the variance of observed time series is zero [30].

$$NS = 1 - \frac{\sum_{k=1}^{k=n}(s(k) - q(k))^2}{\sum_{k=1}^{k=n}(q(k) - \bar{q})^2} \qquad (4)$$

where $s(k)$ is estimated output, $q(k)$ is observed output, $\bar{q}$ is mean observed output, n is total number of time steps of variables, and k is discrete time.

- Coefficient of determination (R^2); is defined as the proportion of the variation in the dependent variable that is modelled from the independent variables. It measures how well the simulated variable represents the observed variable.

$$R^2 = \frac{\sum_{k=1}^{k=n}((q(k) - \bar{q})(s(k) - \bar{s}))^2}{\sum_{k=1}^{k=n}((q(k) - \bar{q}))^2 \sum_{k=1}^{k=n}((s(k) - \bar{s}))^2} \qquad (5)$$

where $s(k)$ is estimated output, $q(k)$ is observed output, $\bar{q}$ is mean observed output, $\bar{s}$ is mean simulated output, n is total number of time steps of variables, and k is discrete time.

- Percentage bias ($PBIAS$); is a measure of the difference between the amount of produced water by the basin and the amount of estimated water by the model. This criterion considers water volume transfers explicitly. A lower value indicates a better simulation. Positive values indicate that the model underestimates the observations while negative values indicate the inverse.

$$PBIAS = \frac{\sum_{k=1}^{k=n}(q(k) - s(k))}{\sum_{k=1}^{k=n} q(k)} \qquad (6)$$

where $s(k)$ is estimated output, $q(k)$ is observed output, $\bar{q}$ is mean observed output, $\bar{s}$ is mean simulated output, n total number of time steps of variables, and k is discrete time.

- Kling–Gupta efficiency criteria (KGE); is a measure of the linear regression coefficient between observed and simulated variables.

$$KGE = 1 - \sqrt{(r-1)^2 + (\alpha - 1)^2 + (\beta - 1)^2} \qquad (7)$$

where $a = \frac{\sigma_s}{\sigma_q}$, and $\beta = \frac{\mu_s}{\mu_q}$ and r is the linear regression coefficient between observed and simulated variables, σ_s and σ_q are standard deviation, and μ_s and μ_q are means of simulated and observed variables [31].

3. Results

3.1. Calibration and Validation Results

The SWAT model is calibrated with the database concerning the years between 1979 and 1986. The first two years are used for model training. Therefore, calibration results cover the years from 1981 to 1986. Validation period was between 1987 and 1991. Two years of training were also adapted for validation as in calibration but for the period between 1985 and 1986. Calibration with the SUFI-2 algorithm is an iterative approach. Each calibration run is composed of 1000 iterations. The more parameters that the model is calibrated with, the more iterations the model would require. In the case of the present study, 1000 iterations were needed to obtain a global sensitivity analysis. A global sensitivity analysis is performed following a run in SWAT-CUP model to understand the relative influence of the change in all parameters on the change of model output.

Sensitivity analysis results present the least and most sensitive parameters to the changes applied to the model parameters. Global sensitivity analysis and evaluation are repeated several times, since after each run sensitivity analysis could give different results. Final sensitivity analysis results of model parameters are given (Table 5). The six most sensitive parameters were the ones with p-value equal to or lower than 0.05.

Table 5. Sensitivity analysis results.

Parameter Name	t−Stat	p-Value
r__SOL_K(2).sol__C	−0.08	0.93
v__SURLAG.bsn	0.10	0.92
v__SOL_ALB(1).sol__C	−0.17	0.85
v__SOL_ALB(1).sol__D	0.19	0.85
v__REVAPMN.gw	−0.21	0.83
v__CH_K2.rte	−0.26	0.79
v__EPCO.hru	0.24	0.81
r__SOL_AWC(2).sol__D	0.41	0.68
v__CH_N2.sub	0.43	0.67
v__ALPHA__BF.gw	0.43	0.67
r__PLAPS.sub	−0.60	0.55
v__GW_REVAP.gw	−0.63	0.53
v__SOL_BD().sol__C	0.67	0.66
r__SOL_K(2).sol__D	−0.71	0.48
v__ALPHA_BNK.rte	0.63	0.53
r__SOL_AWC(2).sol__C	1.2	0.23
r__OV_N__.hru	−1.23	0.22
r__SOL_AWC(1).sol__C	−1.32	0.18
v__ESCO.hru	1.56	0.12
v__CH_N1.sub	−1.65	0.098
v__GWQMN.gw	−1.85	0.065
v__ GW_DELAY.gw	−1.88	0.06
r__SOL_AWC(1).sol__D	1.97	0.05
r__SOL_K(1).sol__D	−2.2	0.02
r__SOL_K(1).sol__C	2.6	0.009
v__CH_K1.sub	4.97	0.000001
v__SOL_BD().sol__D	−7.04	0
v__RCHRG_DP.gw	−9.9	0
r__CN2.mgt	−42.7	0

These parameters are SCS curve number (CN2.mgt) deep aquifer percolation fraction (RCHRG_DP.gw), soil bulk density for soil hydraulic group D (SOL_BD__D), effective hydraulic conductivity in tributary channel alluvium (CH_K1.sub), saturated hydraulic conductivity of the first soil layer for soil hydraulic group C (SOL_K(1)__C), and saturated hydraulic conductivity of the first soil layer for soil hydraulic group D (SOL_K(1)__D). Although there were parameters with low sensitivity for each iteration, the model is still calibrated with these parameters not to exclude the minor effects on the calibration and the validation.

Some of the parameters are calibrated with respect to certain soil layers, indicated as (1) for first soil layer and (2) for second soil layer; or soil hydraulic groups, indicated as "__D" for soil hydraulic group D and "__C" for soil hydraulic group C, to better represent the spatial variability of these parameters. Other parameters, e.g., groundwater parameters, are run for whole HRUs. Different groundwater, soil and surface related parameters are used in calibration periods following the sensitivity analysis. The calibrated parameters are presented in Table 6.

Table 6. Final limit ranges and the fitted parameter values of the calibrated model.

Name	Definition	Min	Max	Fit
v__SOL_ALB(1).sol__D	Moist soil albedo of the first soil layer	0	0.4	0.01
v__SOL_ALB(1).sol__C	Moist soil albedo of the first soil layer	0	0.4	0.01
v__GWQMN.gw	Threshold water depth in the shallow aquifer for return flow (mm H_2O)	0	5700	5020
v__GW_REVAP.gw	Groundwater "revap" coefficient	0.01	0.5	0.24
v__GW_DELAY.gw	Groundwater delay time (days)	0	100	92
v__REVAPMN.gw	Threshold water depth of shallow aquifer for "Revap" or percolation (mm H_2O/)	300	400	343
v__ESCO.bsn	Soil evaporation compensation factor	0.1	1	1
v__EPCO.bsn	Plant uptake compensation factor	0.1	1	0.86
r__SOL_AWC(1).sol__D	Available water capacity (mm H_2O/mm)	0	8	1.55
r__SOL_AWC(2).sol__D	Available water capacity (mm H_2O/mm)	0	8	1.03
r__SOL_AWC(1).sol__C	Available water capacity (mm H_2O/mm)	0	8	1.6
r__SOL_AWC(2).sol__C	Available water capacity (mm H_2O/mm)	0	8	4.5
r__SOL_K(1).sol__D	Saturated hydraulic conductivity (mm/h)	0.1	2000	0.001
r__SOL_K(2).sol__D	Saturated hydraulic conductivity (mm/h)	0.1	2000	5.9
r__SOL_K(1).sol__C	Saturated hydraulic conductivity (mm/h)	0.1	2000	0.6
r__SOL_K(2).sol__C	Saturated hydraulic conductivity (mm/h)	0.1	2000	8.1
r__OV_N.hru	Manning's "n" value for overland flow	−0.3	0.3	−0.03
r__CN2.mgt	Initial SCS runoff curve number	−0.99	0.99	−0.94
v__ALPHA_BF.gw	Baseflow alpha factor (days)	0	0.1	0.08
v__ALPHA_BNK.rte	Baseflow alpha factor for bank storage (days)	0	1	0.92
v__SURLAG.bsn	Surface runoff lag coefficient	0.05	24	7.8
v__CH_K1.sub	Effective hydraulic conductivity in tributary channel alluvium (mm/h)	0	500	183
v__CH_K2.rte	Effective hydraulic conductivity in main channel alluvium (mm/h)	0	500	339
v__CH_N1.sub	Manning's "n" value for the tributary channels	0.1	10	1.6

Table 6. Cont.

Name	Definition	Min	Max	Fit
v__CH_N2.rte	Manning's "n" value for the main channel	0.1	10	0.05
v__RCHRG_DP.gw	Deep aquifer percolation fraction	0	1	0.001
v__SOL_BD.sol__C	Moist bulk density (mg/m^3 or g/cm^3)	0.8	2.5	2.2
v__SOL_BD.sol__D	Moist bulk density (mg/m^3 or g/cm^3)	0.8	2.5	0.81
r__PLAPS.sub	Precipitation lapse rate (mm H$_2$O/km)	−1000	1000	−0.05

Model calibration is performed with two iterative approaches: by replacing the parameter calibration ranges directly (indicated with v__parameter.name) and multiplying the ranges with new range +1 (indicated by r__parameter.name). The latter is usually suggested for the parameters where the spatial distribution of the parameter is important, and calibration should be done considering spatial variations in the basin. For instance, groundwater parameters are replaced with new ranges at each iteration (i.e., v__parameter.name.gw) such as groundwater evaporation factor, v_GW_REVAP.gw, and deep aquifer percolation fraction, v__RCHRG_DP.gw, while surface runoff parameter ranges are multiplied with "new ranges +1" such as r__CN2.mgt and r__OV_N.hru (Table 6).

Some of the parameters are calibrated with respect to certain soil layers, indicated as (1) for first soil layer and (2) for second soil layer; or soil hydraulic groups, indicated as "__D" for soil hydraulic group D and "__C" for soil hydraulic group C, to represent better the spatial variability of these parameters. Other parameters, e.g., groundwater parameters, are run for whole HRUs. Different underground, soil and surface related parameters are calibrated following the sensitivity analysis (Table 6).

It is important to note that for a rigorous result evaluation, one should consider using the calibrated parameter ranges rather than the final fit. The range indicates the uncertainty levels on those variable estimations by giving an envelope of possible values of the parameter. On the other hand, fitted parameter lacks the uncertainty information related to that parameter.

3.2. Model Performance Evaluation

Model calibration and validation results are evaluated graphically and statistically as explained in Section 2.2.6. For the calibration period, the model successfully managed to reproduce overall discharge trends and simulated the flood peaks well, especially for the Mirbeck station (Figure 5).

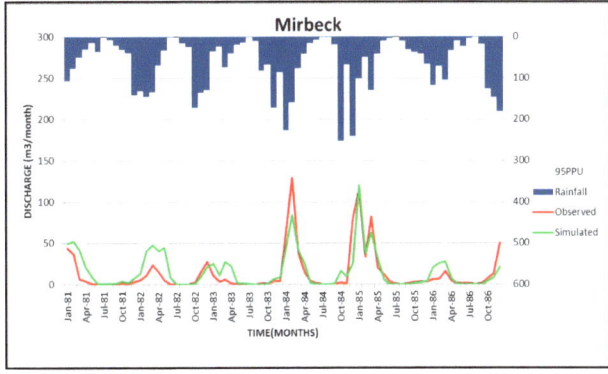

Figure 5. The simulated versus observed discharge for the calibration at Mirbeck station.

Simulation results are relatively less efficient at the Malleh and Ressoul stations with more underestimation of the main flood event recorded in 1984 winter (Figures 6 and 7). However, the model perfectly reproduced most of the other discharge anomalies. However, for the most upstream station, (i.e., Charref) the model performed good simulations with an underestimation for only one flood episode (Figure 8).

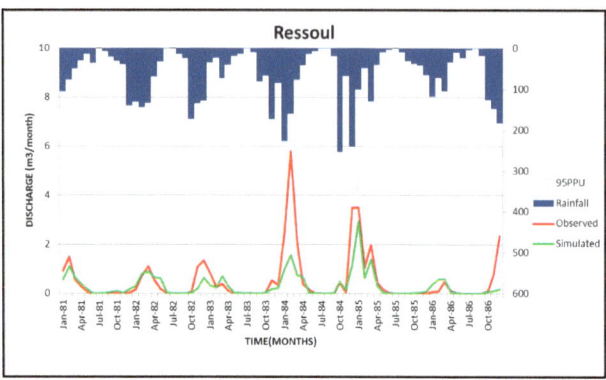

Figure 6. The simulated versus observed discharge for the calibration at Ressoul station.

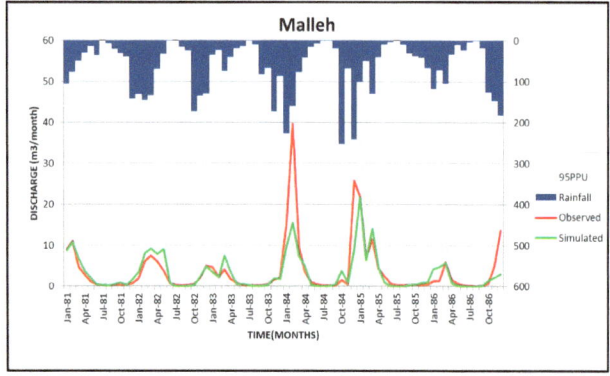

Figure 7. The simulated versus observed discharge for the calibration at Malleh station.

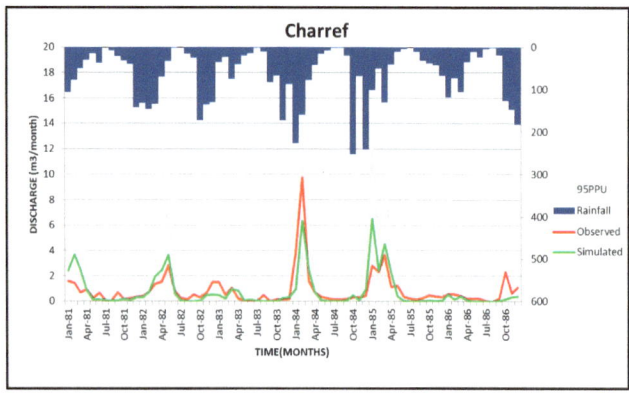

Figure 8. The simulated versus observed discharge for the calibration at Charref station.

We can observe that the model underestimates the flood peaks more in the validation period than in the calibration period (Figures 9–12). However, the model generally performs reliable simulations for the validation period.

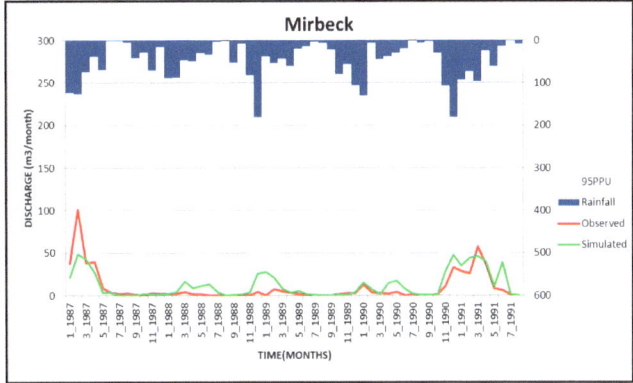

Figure 9. The simulated versus observed discharge for the validation at Mirbeck station.

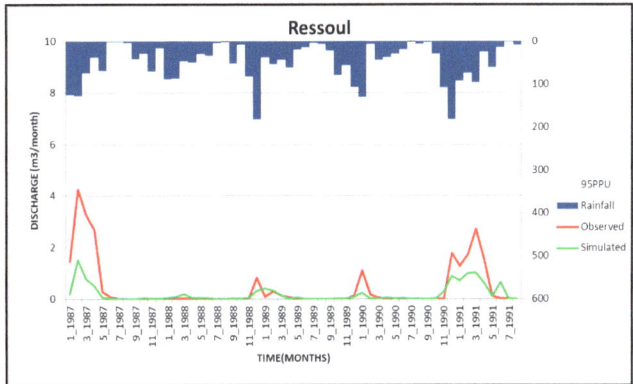

Figure 10. The simulated versus observed discharge for the validation at Ressoul station.

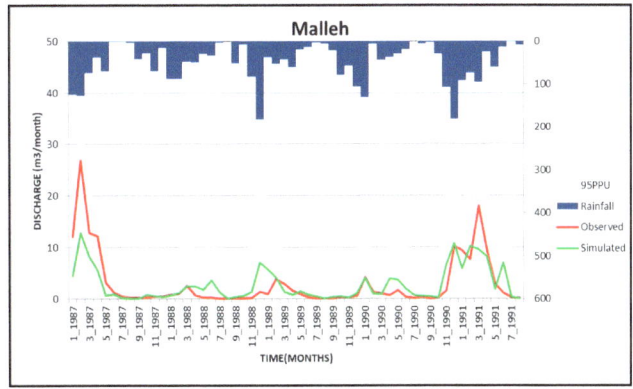

Figure 11. The simulated versus observed discharge for the validation at Malleh station.

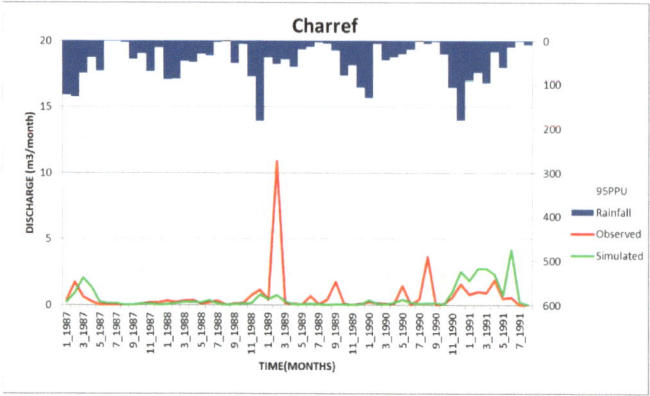

Figure 12. The simulated versus observed discharge for the validation at Charref station.

The statistical results of model calibration and validation are given in Table 7 for four hydrometric stations. The results showed reliable results overall varying mostly from satisfactory to very good results for the calibration according to Table 8 [32,33]. For the validation period, there were less satisfactory results at several stations.

Table 7. Statistical results of the model calibration and validation for four discharge stations.

Station	Calibration				Validation			
	R^2	NS	PBIAS	KGE	R^2	NS	PBIAS	KGE
Mirbeck	0.7	0.7	20	0.7	0.6	0.6	30.7	0.6
Ressoul	0.6	0.5	37	0.3	0.8	0.4	53.5	0.15
Malleh	0.7	0.6	12	0.6	0.6	0.6	5.0	0.6
Charref	0.6	0.5	8	0.8	0.03	−0.12	17.3	0.07

Table 8. Evaluation ranges for calibration and validation results.

Criteria	Very Good	Good	Satisfactory	Unsatisfactory
R^2	$0.75 \leq R^2 \leq 1$	$0.65 \leq R^2 < 0.75$	$0.50 \leq R^2 < 0.65$	$R^2 < 0.5$
NS	$0.75 \leq NS \leq 1$	$0.65 \leq NS < 0.75$	$0.50 \leq NS < 0.65$	$NS < 0.5$
KGE	$0.9 \leq KGE < 1$	$0.75 \leq KGE < 0.9$	$0.5 \leq KGE < 0.65$	$KGE < 0.5$
PBIAS	$|PBIAS| < 10$	$10 \leq |PBIAS| < 15$	$15 \leq |PBIAS| < 25$	$25 \leq |PBIAS|$

The model simulated discharges with satisfactory to good statistical results at Mirbeck station both for calibration and validation. That is an indicator for good representation of water balance in the watershed during low or high flows. Only the PBIAS score degraded significantly and showed unsatisfactory results for validation. Calibration results obtained at the other stations (e.g., Malleh, Ressoul, and Charref) are also reliable for the rest of the watershed apart from relatively lower performance at the Ressoul station with unsatisfactory scores for KGE and PBIAS (Table 7). Both calibration and validation scores were satisfactory for Malleh stations and likewise for Mirbeck. However, it can be noted that simulation performances decreased for the validation period for Ressoul and Charref stations. For Ressoul station, the performance scores were unsatisfactory except for R^2. For Charref station, the performance scores were unsatisfactory except PBIAS.

Once the model calibration and validation are performed, the SWAT model is rerun for the whole period with the calibrated parameters to calculate the amount of total aquifer recharge and deep aquifer recharge. The results show that annual average total and deep aquifer recharge values are 345 mm and 38 mm. Re-evaporation from shallow aquifer by the soil and plants is 292.3 mm while aquifer discharge to the river through return flow is 37 mm annually (Table 9). Net annual average infiltration is approximately 150 mm which is equivalent to 15% of the net annual average rainfall. Whereas the evapotranspiration is 61% and the river flow is 12% of the net annual average, which is consistent with the findings of other studies in the same basin [13,34,35].

Table 9. Water balance results with the validated model.

Basin Values	Annual Averages (mm)
Precipitation	1037.1
Snowfall	6.61
Snowmelt	6.59
Surface runoff	9.21
Lateral soil flow	74.2
Groundwater discharge	36.7
Percolation out of soil	347.7
Total aquifer recharge	345
Deep aquifer recharge	38
Re-evaporation	392.3
Evapotranspiration	627

The results demonstrated that a modest amount of rainfall becomes surface runoff. Moreover, the groundwaters feed the rivers only with an amount equal to 3.5% of annual rainfall. On the other hand, evapotranspiration and re-evapotranspiration from shallow aquifers is quite dominant in the water budget of the watershed. Moreover, only 38 mm of water infiltrates deeper aquifers.

4. Discussion

Calibrating the model with discharge data obtained from four hydrometric stations corresponding to four sub basins was a challenging task (i.e., subbasins 2, 8, 51, and 60). Since the different hydrological responses are created at different stations, the model had to reproduce different discharge regimes with the same rainfall data recorded in physical stations in different parts of such a vast watershed. For instance, high flows and low flows were observed in different downstream tributaries (e.g., Mirbeck and Oued Ressoul, respectively) during the same period of the year.

Statistically speaking, performance evaluation scores were accumulated mostly in the reliable limits, varying from satisfactory to good results. Even though the model validation performance is less than that of calibration, the deviation was affordable. Considering that the model is calibrated with some of the most extreme events recorded in the region, model validation performance was acceptable in simulating mostly moderate to low flows with fewer significant high flow episodes.

Simulated hydrographs showed that the calibrated model could reproduce the observed discharge trends. This is the case for most of the low flows and peaks. Moreover, average volume bias error remained at satisfactory levels. This is an important indicator for process-based semi distributed models for satisfactory calibration especially when the model is calibrated and validated for multiple hydrometric stations in the same watershed.

Model calibration for Mirbeck station was more crucial since it is the closest station to the basin outlet. The best calibration results are obtained at this station which shows that the model could represent the hydrological cycle in the watershed and reproduce the discharge observed in the main channel despite the existence of extreme events.

Simulations were performed using estimated long-term rainfalls from a weather forecast system and observed in-situ discharge data. When the simulation accuracies in calibration and validation steps are considered, it is a significant output that model was capable of reproducing observed output data with estimated input data for four stations at once. Moreover, observed rainfalls in the basin showed good correlation with estimated ones, confirming that CFRS estimated rainfalls can represent the real rainfall fields well in the Seybouse basin. This can be an insight for future studies to use rainfall estimates for hydrological or hydrogeological studies. Moreover, the model is calibrated and validated with discharge data covering the period between 1979 and 1991. Unfortunately, there was no available discharge data beyond 1991. Other studies also mentioned the data unavailability and used periods of data for model calibration for different stations [36]. In this work, on the other hand, the model is calibrated with the same period of data for all stations.

Several studies suggested increase and shifts in average annual rainfalls after the 90s and drought conditions focused only on the central part of the basin [37]. Even though the data used in this study do not cover recent warmer decades with relatively higher evaporation losses [36,38], the process-based model based on rigorous calibration and validation practices is considered capable of performing accurate simulations also with more recent data. The model's relatively good performance over the 1979–1991 period provides the basis for a new data collection campaign to test the model against climatic conditions impacted by global warming in more recent years.

Proposing a reliable water balance model would allow future works to compute river discharge or groundwater recharge to feed groundwater hydrodynamic models for water resource management alternatives for nearby residences, agricultural lands, and industry. Water balance calculations obtained by the calibrated model shows consistent results. Water balance, annual rainfall and evapotranspiration values correspond to the values found in the literature [34,35]. Moreover, estimated water uptake from shallow aquifers and percolation to deeper aquifer present reasonable amounts. Therefore, the estimated water amount infiltrating into the aquifers can be used to feed the hydrodynamic model to assess the groundwater fluctuations as mentioned earlier as an objective of the project.

5. Conclusions

This work presents an example of hydrological modelling practices with an open-source tool, i.e., SWAT, in a semi-arid southern Mediterranean, Seybouse, basin. Seybouse basin is marked with inaccurate and scarce hydro-meteorological data. Despite the data availability issues, water scarcity underscores the importance of water resource management applications and rigorous hydrological modelling practices. The objective of this study is to calibrate the model with different hydrometric stations to simulate different discharge trends in different locations of the basin to eventually obtain groundwater recharge estimation. The estimated groundwater recharge is an important result to feed future groundwater models as an input variable to apply groundwater resource management scenarios.

To provide a rigorously calibrated and validated hydrological model, estimated long-term rainfall data, considering the data unavailability, are used to calibrate observed discharge data for four hydrometric stations in SWAT model. Provided hydrographs and statistical results showed that the model could produce reliable simulations for all the hydrometric stations. Model calibration results show that model could simulate discharge with NS $\geq$ 0.5, $R^2 \geq$ 0.6, KGE $\geq$ 0.6 in average and PBIAS < 37 which represent overall satisfactory to good results. Although the validation results are relatively less accurate, they still represent satisfactory results for at least two out of four stations (Tables 8 and 9). Therefore, model calibration and validation results are overall satisfactory to assure water budget calculation accuracy which provides estimated groundwater recharge. This could be used to feed a hydrodynamic model of the basin which will be the next step in this project.

Data unavailability issues and the model's relatively good performance suggest that further data acquisition campaigns would be necessary to test model simulation accuracy under the ongoing global warming changes. Further applications could include performing hydrological simulations with different hydrological model types such as statistic-based hydrological models e.g., neural networks, to compare with the process-based hydrological models.

Author Contributions: Conceptualization, C.A.I. and A.M.; methodology, C.A.I.; software, C.A.I.; validation, Y.L., A.M. and J.D.; formal analysis, C.A.I.; investigation, C.A.I. and A.M.; resources, Y.L.; data curation, C.A.I.; writing—original draft preparation, C.A.I.; writing—review and editing, Y.L. and A.M.; visualization, C.A.I.; supervision, Y.L. and A.M.; project administration, Y.L.; funding acquisition, J.D. All authors have read and agreed to the published version of the manuscript.

Funding: This work is supported by the PRIMA 2020 program under grant agreement No. 2024–TRUST project (The PRIMA program is supported by the European Union).

Data Availability Statement: The data presented in this study are available on request from the corresponding author. The data are not publicly available due to third party regulations of the data providers.

Acknowledgments: No support given which is not covered by the author contribution or funding sections.

Conflicts of Interest: The authors declare no conflict of interest. The funders had no role in the design of the study; in the collection, analyses, or interpretation of data; in the writing of the manuscript; or in the decision to publish the results.

References

1. Morante-Carballo, F.; Montalván-Burbano, N.; Quiñonez-Barzola, X.; Jaya-Montalvo, M.; Carrión-Mero, P. What Do We Know about Water Scarcity in Semi-Arid Zones? A Global Analysis and Research Trends. *Water* **2022**, *14*, 2685. [CrossRef]
2. Lu, Y.; Liu, Y.; Huang, J.; Yang, X.; Yin, H. Numerical modeling of groundwater recharge in a coastal city with multi-layered aquifer systems. *Water Sci. Eng.* **2019**, *12*, 293–301. [CrossRef]
3. Dillon, P.; Pavelic, P.; Page, D.; Vanderzalm, J.L.; Pavelic, V. Global overview of managed aquifer recharge: Regional applications, success stories, and future prospects. *Hydrogeol. J.* **2018**, *26*, 395–420.
4. Aladenola, O.O.; Durowoju, O.S.; Adedeji, O.H. Potential impacts of rainwater harvesting on groundwater recharge in a typical basement complex region. *J. Afr. Earth Sci.* **2016**, *114*, 53–60. [CrossRef]
5. Elliott, D.; Singh, R.; Dillon, P. Performance evaluation of permeable reactive barriers for groundwater recharge. *J. Hydrol.* **2016**, *538*, 842–853. [CrossRef]
6. Kurtulus, B.; Yaylım, T.N.; Avşar, O.; Kulac, H.F.; Razack, M. The Well Efficiency Criteria Revisited—Development of a General Well Efficiency Criteria (GWEC) Based on Rorabaugh's Model. *Water* **2019**, *11*, 1784. [CrossRef]
7. Kilic, D.; Rivière, A.; Gallois, N.; Ducharne, A.; Wang, S.; Peylin, P.; Flipo, N. Assessing water and energy fluxes in a regional hydrosystem: Case study of the Seine basin. *Comptes Rendus. Géosci.* **2023**, *355*, 1–21. [CrossRef]
8. Chow, V.T.; Maidment, D.R.; Mays, L.W. *Applied Hydrology*; McGraw-Hill: New York, NY, USA, 1988.
9. Beven, K.J. *Rainfall-Runoff Modelling: The Primer*; John Wiley & Sons: Hoboken, NJ, USA, 2011.
10. Jajarmizadeh, M.; Harun, S.; Salarpour, M. A review on theoretical consideration and types of models in hydrology. *J. Environ. Sci. Technol.* **2012**, *5*, 249–261. [CrossRef]
11. Devi, G.K.; Ganasri, B.P.; Dwarakish, G.S. A review on hydrological models. *Aquat. Procedia* **2015**, *4*, 1001–1007. [CrossRef]
12. Louamri, A. Le bassin-versant de la Seybouse (Algérie orientale): Hydrologie et aménagement des eaux. *Constantine* **2013**, *1*, 315.
13. Hebal, A. Analyse Hydrologique de Quelques Bassins Versants du Nord Algérien: Eaux Superficielles, Crues et Aménagement. Ph.D. Thesis, Blida University, Ouled Yaïch, Algeria, 2013.
14. Arnold, J.G.; Moriasi, D.N.; Gassman, P.W.; Abbaspour, K.C.; White, M.J.; Srinivasan, R.; Jha, M.K. SWAT: Model use, calibration, and validation. *Trans. ASABE* **2012**, *55*, 1491–1508. [CrossRef]
15. Duan, Q.; Sorooshian, S.; Gupta, V. Effective and efficient global optimization for conceptual rainfall-runoff models. *Water Resour. Res.* **1992**, *28*, 1015–1031. [CrossRef]
16. Duan, Q.Y.; Gupta, V.K.; Sorooshian, S. Shuffled complex evolution approach for effective and efficient global minimization. *J. Optim. Theory Appl.* **1993**, *76*, 501–521. [CrossRef]
17. Duan, Q.; Sorooshian, S.; Gupta, V.K. Optimal use of the SCE-UA global optimization method for calibrating watershed models. *J. Hydrol.* **1994**, *158*, 265–284. [CrossRef]
18. Abbaspour, K.C.; Johnson, C.A.; Van Genuchten, M.T. Estimating uncertain flow and transport parameters using a sequential uncertainty fitting procedure. *Vadose Zone J.* **2004**, *3*, 1340–1352. [CrossRef]
19. Abbaspour, K.C.; Yang, J.; Maximov, I.; Siber, R.; Bogner, K.; Mieleitner, J.; Zobrist, J.; Srinivasan, R. Modelling hydrology and water quality in the pre-alpine/alpine Thur watershed using SWAT. *J. Hydrol.* **2007**, *333*, 413–430. [CrossRef]
20. Abbaspour, K.C.; Vaghefi, S.A.; Srinivasan, R. A Guideline for Successful Calibration and Uncertainty Analysis for Soil and Water Assessment: A Review of Papers from the 2016 International SWAT Conference. *Water* **2018**, *10*, 6. [CrossRef]
21. Beven, K.J. *Interflow, Unsaturated Flow in Hydrologic Modelling*; Morel-Seytoux, H.J., Ed.; D. Reidel: Norwell, MA, USA, 1989; pp. 191–219.
22. Freer, J.; Beven, K.; Ambroise, B. Bayesian Estimation of Uncertainty in Runoff Prediction and the Value of Data: An Application of the GLUE Approach. *Water Resour. Res.* **1996**, *32*, 2161–2173. [CrossRef]

23. Her, Y.; Frankenberger, J.; Chaubey, I.; Srinivasan, R. Threshold effects in HRU definition of the soil and water assessment tool. *Trans. ASABE* **2015**, *58*, 367–378.
24. Soil Conservation Service. Section 4: Hydrology. In *National Engineering Handbook*; SCS: Sunderland, UK, 1972.
25. Abbaspour, K.C.; Rouholahnejad, E.; Vaghefi Srinivasan, R.; Yang, H.; Kløve, B. A continental-scale hydrology and water quality model for Europe: Calibration and uncertainty of a high-resolution large-scale SWAT model. *J. Hydrol.* **2015**, *524*, 733–752. [CrossRef]
26. Beven, K. A manifesto for the equifinality thesis. *J. Hydrol.* **2006**, *320*, 18–36. [CrossRef]
27. Her, Y.; Seong, C. Responses of hydrological model equifinality, uncertainty, and performance to multi-objective parameter calibration. *J. Hydroinform.* **2018**, *20*, 864–885. [CrossRef]
28. Zhou, X.; Lin, H.; Lin, H. Global Sensitivity Analysis. In *Encyclopedia of GIS*; Shekhar, S., Xiong, H., Eds.; Springer: Boston, MA, USA, 2008. [CrossRef]
29. Abbaspour, K.C. *SWAT-CUP: SWAT Calibration and Uncertainty Programs—A User Manual*; Eawag: Dübendorf, Switzerland, 2015; pp. 16–70.
30. Nash, J.; Sutcliffe, J. River Flow Forecasting through Conceptual Models, part I—A Discussion of Principles. *J. Hydrol.* **1970**, *10*, 282–290. [CrossRef]
31. Gupta, H.V.; Kling, H.; Yilmaz, K.K.; Martinez, G.F. Decomposition of the mean squared error and NSE performance criteria: Implications for improving hydrological modelling. *J. Hydrol.* **2009**, *377*, 80–91. [CrossRef]
32. Kouchi, D.H.; Esmaili, K.; Faridhosseini, A.; Sanaeinejad, S.H.; Khalili, D.; Abbaspour, K.C. Sensitivity of Calibrated parameters and Water Resource Estimates on Different Objective Functions and Optimization Algorithms. *Water* **2017**, *9*, 384. [CrossRef]
33. Thiemig, V.; Rojas, R.; Zambrano-Bigiarini, M.A. Hydrological Evaluation of Satellite-based Rainfall Estimates Over the Volta and Baro-Akobo Basin. *J. Hydrol.* **2013**, *499*, 324–338. [CrossRef]
34. Aichouri, I. Contribution à la Mise en Evidence de L'intrusion Marine Dans la Plaine d'Annaba. Master's Thesis, Mémoire de Magister, Université d'Annaba, Annaba, Algérie, 2009.
35. Aichouri, I.; Hani, A.; Bougherira, N.; Djabri, L.; Chaffai, H.; Lallahem, S. River flow model using artificial neural networks. *Energy Procedia* **2015**, *74*, 1007–1014. [CrossRef]
36. Aoulmi, Y.; Marouf, N.; Amireche, M. The assessment of artificial neural network rainfall-runoff models under different input meteorological parameters Case study: Seybouse basin, Northeast Algeria. *J. Water Land Dev.* **2021**, *50*, 38–47. [CrossRef]
37. Khezazna, A.; Amarchi, H.; Derdous, O.; Bousakhria, F. Drought monitoring in the Seybouse basin (Algeria) over the last decades. *J. Water Land Dev.* **2017**, *33*, 79. [CrossRef]
38. Zettam, A.; Sauvage, S.; Taleb, A.; Nouria, B.E.; Sanchez-Perez, J.M. Hydrology, nitrate, and sediment fluxes towards the Mediterranean Sea: Case of the main North Africa catchments. 20 July 2022, PREPRINT (Version 1) available at Research Square. 2022. [CrossRef]

Disclaimer/Publisher's Note: The statements, opinions and data contained in all publications are solely those of the individual author(s) and contributor(s) and not of MDPI and/or the editor(s). MDPI and/or the editor(s) disclaim responsibility for any injury to people or property resulting from any ideas, methods, instructions or products referred to in the content.

Article

Comparative Analysis of MCDA Techniques for Identifying Erosion-Prone Areas in the Burhanpur Watershed in Central India for the Purposes of Sustainable Watershed Management

Abhishek Patel [1,2,*], K. V. Ramana Rao [2], Yogesh A. Rajwade [2], Chandra Kant Saxena [2], Karan Singh [2] and Ankur Srivastava [3,*]

[1] ICAR-Central Arid Zone Research Institute, Regional Research Station, Bhuj 370105, India
[2] ICAR-Central Institute of Agricultural Engineering, Bhopal 462038, India; kondapalli.rao@icar.gov.in (K.V.R.R.); yogesh.rajwade@icar.gov.in (Y.A.R.); chandra.saxena@icar.gov.in (C.K.S.); karan.singh1@icar.gov.in (K.S.)
[3] School of Life Sciences, Faculty of Science, University of Technology Sydney (UTS), Ultimo, NSW 2007, Australia
* Correspondence: abhishek.patel@icar.gov.in (A.P.); ankur.srivastava@uts.edu.au (A.S.)

Citation: Patel, A.; Ramana Rao, K.V.; Rajwade, Y.A.; Saxena, C.K.; Singh, K.; Srivastava, A. Comparative Analysis of MCDA Techniques for Identifying Erosion-Prone Areas in the Burhanpur Watershed in Central India for the Purposes of Sustainable Watershed Management. *Water* **2023**, *15*, 3891. https://doi.org/10.3390/w15223891

Academic Editor: Tammo Steenhuis

Received: 13 October 2023
Revised: 1 November 2023
Accepted: 2 November 2023
Published: 8 November 2023

Copyright: © 2023 by the authors. Licensee MDPI, Basel, Switzerland. This article is an open access article distributed under the terms and conditions of the Creative Commons Attribution (CC BY) license (https:// creativecommons.org/licenses/by/ 4.0/).

Abstract: The degradation of land and increasing water scarcity are existing challenges for agricultural sustainability, necessitating the implementation of improved soil-conservation practices at the watershed scale. The identification and selection of critical/prone areas based on erosion-governing criteria is essential and helps in the execution of the management process for determining priority. This study prioritizes erosion-prone sub-watersheds (alternatives) based on morphometric parameters (multiple criteria) via five Multi-Criteria Decision Analysis (MCDA) approaches, i.e., AHP: Analytical Hierarchy Process; TOPSIS: Technique for Order of Preference by Similarity to Ideal Solution; VIKOR: VIseKriterijumska Optimizacija I Kompromisno Resenje; SAW: Simple Additive Weighting; and CF: Compound Factor. Based on their priority score, 19 sub-watersheds were classified into four priority classes: low priority (0–0.25), moderate priority (0.25–0.50), high priority (0.50–0.75), and very high priority (0.75–1). The results revealed that about 8.34–30.15% area of the Burhanpur watershed is critically prone to erosion, followed by 23.38–52.05% area classed as high priority, 7.47–49.99% area classed as moderate priority, and 10.33–18.28% area classed as low priority. Additionally, four indices—percentage of changes (ΔP), intensity of changes (ΔI), the Spearman rank correlation coefficient test (SCCT), and the Kendall tau correlation coefficient test (KTCCT)—were employed to compare the models. This study confirms the efficacy of morphometric parameters for prioritizing sub-watersheds to preserve soil and the environment, particularly in areas for which limited information is available.

Keywords: AHP; erosion; TOPSIS; SAW; VIKOR; Tapi Basin

1. Introduction

Land and water are not only valuable natural resources, but also critical for sustaining life and agricultural production. The ongoing degradation of land, coupled with increasing water scarcity, is a major concern for achieving sustainability in agriculture [1,2]. Globally, it has been reported that approximately 15% of ice-free land surface is under degradation, and in India, this figure is as high as 45% of the country's geographical area [3,4]. Additionally, India is losing its valuable soil at a rate of approximately 16.4 tons/ha per year due to erosion, deforestation, and other destructive agents [5]. Soil erosion is a serious environmental hazard that contributes to land degradation [6,7]. Given that soil formation is a slow process that can take up to 300 years to produce a 1 cm layer of soil [8], it is necessary to conserve soil resources through better management practices in erosion-prone areas, with a focus on watershed-scale management measures [9] to mitigate soil erosion and conserve land and soil resources.

Watersheds are natural drainage units that respond to rainfall, depending on factors such as climate, land use, hydrogeology, and morphology, to generate runoff [10]. As such, watersheds represent an ideal unit for both land and water resources management. Watershed-level management strategies have a positive impact on resource productivity [11–13]. The drainage morphometry and parameters of watersheds are responsible for runoff, and thereby erosion phenomena and their characteristics occurring within watersheds [14–16]. Morphometric parameters are quantitative representations of watershed geometry and topography [17,18], and they help in understanding a watershed's linear drainage system, its areal pattern, and its relief behavior for the purposes of hydrological engineering [19,20]. These parameters, which include linear, areal, and relief aspects of the watershed, are derived during morphometric analysis of watershed topography [21–24]. Several studies have demonstrated the potential of Remote Sensing (RS) and Geographical Information Systems (GIS) for conducting morphometric analysis [25–29] and providing valuable information for watershed management and planning. Moreover, remote sensing-based Digital Elevation Models (DEMs) have been widely used for topography-based studies [30–32].

Understanding watershed morphometry assists watershed management, in an efficient and integrated manner, to increase productivity with optimum use of resources. Moreover, it helps in planning degradation neutrality strategies through sub-watersheds prioritization [12,33]. Recently, researchers have successfully implemented morphometric parameters as criteria in the prioritization of sub-watersheds by applying Multi Criteria Decision Analysis (MCDA) techniques [19,34–37]. MCDA techniques were used for complex decision making while considering a set of criteria to improve decision accuracy [8,38–41]. Several MCDA techniques, such as Analytical Hierarchy Process (AHP) [42], Technique for Order of Preference by Similarity to Ideal Solution (TOPSIS) [43], VIseKriterijumska Optimizacija I Kompromisno Resenje (VIKOR) [44], Simple Additive Weighting (SAW), compound factor (CF) analysis, etc., have been successfully used by several researchers for accurate decision making [5,10,19,34,35,45–50]. Hembram and Saha [45] prioritized sub-watersheds of the Chota Nagpur Plateau in Jharkhand using fuzzy AHP and the compound factor (CF) approach. The results obtained from both analyses highlight sub-watersheds 6 and 13 as very highly erosion-prone areas. The study demonstrated the effectiveness of morphometric indices in assessing erodibility priority at the sub-basin scale. The authors of [51] applied the analytical network process and fuzzy logic theory when considering the interrelationship of environmental and geomorphic factors in the watershed of the Araz River basin of Iran. A criteria-based decision framework was developed for the calculation of the watershed health scores (WHS) and to prioritize watersheds. The study recommended the potential of such frameworks for the identification of highly critical zones, especially in data-scarce areas.

A number of studies have been undertaken in recent years to map erosion-prone areas using individual MCDA on GIS- and DEM-derived morphometric data. However, there have been few studies that apply multiple MCDA techniques simultaneously and compare them to determine the optimal model. Thus, in the present study, a number of MCDA approaches (AHP, TOPSIS, VIKOR, SAW, and CF) were applied to prioritize erosion-prone sites in the Burhanpur watershed, and their performance was evaluated. Using GIS and RS techniques, this study analyzes fourteen morphometric parameters to effectively prioritize the nineteen sub-watersheds, providing valuable information for the development of improved decision support and a comprehensive land degradation management plan in the Burhanpur watershed in Central India.

2. Materials and Methods

2.1. Study Area and Data

The Burhanpur is situated in the Upper Tapi river basin in Central India. The geographic boundaries of the watershed encompass a longitude range of 75°55′ E to 78°18′14″ E and a latitude range of 21°1′51″ N to 22°1′52″ N (Figure 1). Within this area, the watershed spans approximately 10,585 km². The elevation in the region ranges from 188 to 1171 m above mean sea level, while the average annual rainfall is around 900 mm. The study area primarily consists of clayey to loamy clayey soils [52], with land use types including agriculture, range lands, water bodies, barren land, built-up areas, and forests. The geomorphometric parameters of the Burhanpur watershed were quantified using Remote Sensing (RS) data and Geographic Information System (GIS) techniques. The Shuttle Radar Topography Mission (SRTM) 1 arc-second Digital Elevation Model (DEM) from the USGS Earth Resources Observation and Science (EROS) Center archive was utilized to obtain elevation and topographic information for the study area (source: https://www.usgs.gov/ accessed on 25 August 2023).

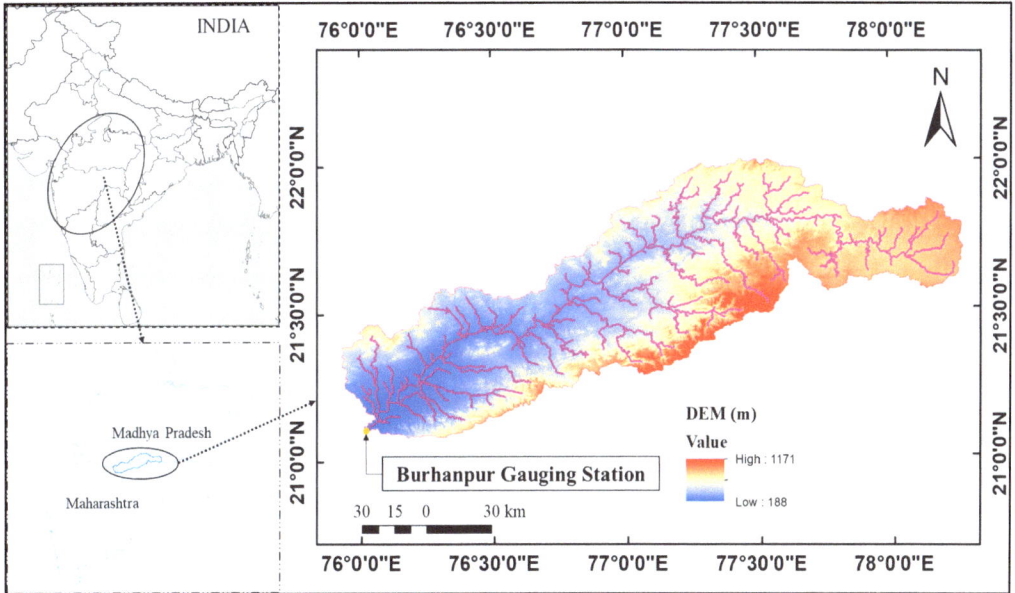

Figure 1. Study area with DEM map and river reaches.

2.2. Sub-Watershed Mapping and Morphometric Analysis

For the delineation of the sub-watersheds, SRTM DEM data were obtained and imported into the GIS environment. A delineation procedure involving steps such as 'fill sinks", "flow direction", "flow accumulation", etc., was performed and the nineteen sub-watersheds were delineated. Further morphometric parameters, related to linear, areal, and relief aspects (mean bifurcation ratio (R_{bfm}), drainage density (D_d), stream frequency ($S_{f\mu}$), form factor (F_f), shape factor (F_s), circulatory ratio (R_c), elongation ratio (R_e), constant of channel maintenance (C), infiltration number (I_f), length of overland flow (L_g), texture ratio (T), basin relief (H), relief ratio (R_r), and slope (S)) were computed as per the methods outlined in Table 1 [53–56]. These sub-watersheds and parameters were subsequently employed as alternatives and criteria, respectively, for prioritizing the sub-watersheds.

Table 1. Computation and relation of morphometric parameters with erosion sensitivity.

Parameters	Quantification	Relation with Erosion Sensitivity	References
Mean bifurcation ratio (R_{bfm})	Mean of R_b	DP	[57]
Drainage density (D_d)	$D_d = \Sigma L_u / A$	DP	[58]
Stream frequency ($S_{f\mu}$)	$F_s = \Sigma N_u / A$	DP	[58]

Table 1. Cont.

Parameters	Quantification	Relation with Erosion Sensitivity	References
Form factor (F_f)	$F_f = A/L_b^2$	IP	[58,59]
Shape factor (F_s)	$F_s = L_b^2/A$	IP	[59]
Circulatory ratio (R_c)	$R_c = 4\pi A/P^2$	IP	[18,60]
Elongation ratio (R_e)	$R_e = 1.128\sqrt{A/L_b}$	IP	[57]
Constant of channel maintenance (C)	$C = 1/D_d$	DP	[57]
Infiltration number (I_f)	$I_f = D \times F_s$	IP	[61]
Length of overland flow (L_g)	$L_g = 1/2D_d$	DP	[58]
Texture ratio (T)	$T = \Sigma N_u/P$	DP	[62]
Basin relief (H)	$H = H_{max} - H_{min}$	DP	[63]
Relief ratio (R_r)	$R_r = H/L$	DP	[57]
Slope (S)	Mean of slope	DP	[23]

Note: DP: directly proportional (higher the parameter value, higher the erosion sensitivity), IP: inversely proportional (higher the parameter value, lower the erosion sensitivity).

2.3. MCDA-Based Sub-Watersheds Prioritization

The morphometric parameters of watersheds play a crucial role in describing various surface phenomena, such as soil erosion, which depend on the hydrology, climate, geology, and geomorphology of the watershed [15]. The erosion sensitivity of the watershed is directly or inversely proportional to these morphometric parameters, which means that higher parameter values correspond to either higher or lower erosion sensitivity. The MCDA techniques involve considering a set of criteria with their relative weights to prioritize alternatives [64,65]. In this study, 14 morphometric parameters (listed in Table 1) were used as criteria to evaluate and prioritize the 19 sub-watersheds using five different MCDA techniques (AHP, TOPSIS, VIKOR, SAW, and CF). These techniques utilize criteria weights and normalized values for the morphometric parameters to calculate the rankings of the sub-watersheds. The flowchart in Figure 2 summarizes the overall methodology employed in this study. The following sections provide a brief overview of the MCDA techniques used.

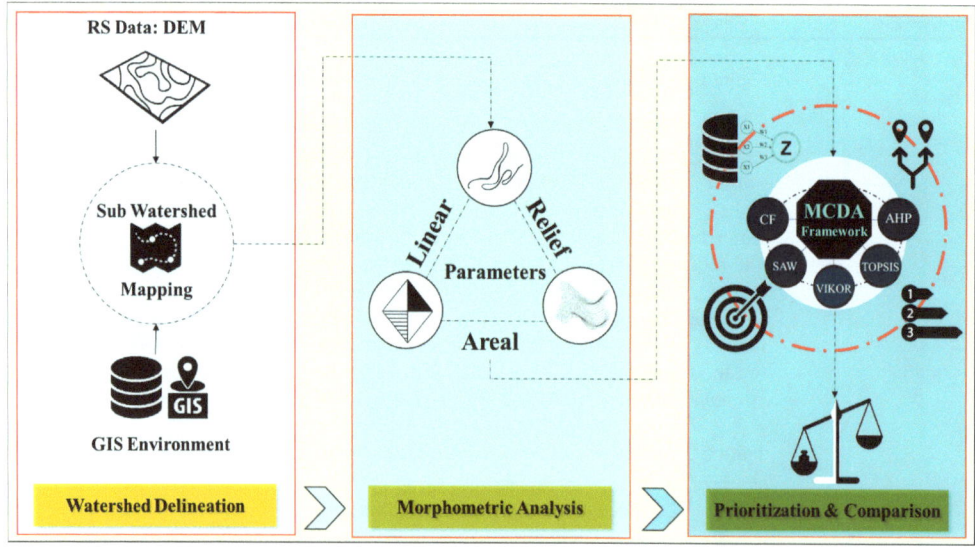

Figure 2. Depiction of overall methodology employed in this study.

2.3.1. Criteria Weightage for MCDA

The weightage for the different criteria was determined using pairwise comparisons, following the method proposed by Thomas L. Saaty [66]. In this approach, a parameter with a higher impact on erosion sensitivity was given greater preference in the comparison matrix. As mentioned earlier, the pairwise comparisons matrix was constructed using the 14 morphometric parameters as criteria. Subsequently, the weight matrix $[W]_{Q \times 1}$ was calculated, representing the weight of the j-th criterion as w_j (an element of the weight matrix). It is important to note that consistency in pairwise comparisons is essential to derive meaningful weights [67]. Therefore, a consistency check procedure, as described in [68], was followed to ensure consistency. Typically, a consistency ratio below 0.1 indicates consistency in the comparisons, and the weights are considered acceptable [67].

2.3.2. Analytical Hierarchy Process Technique

The AHP technique introduced by T.L. Saaty [42] is one of the most popular and easiest MCDA methods [41]. AHP breaks down the complex problem into hierarchically structured sub-problems to find a solution from among alternatives [42,69]. It involves generation of a decision matrix based on alternatives and criteria followed by normalization of the decision matrix. A further weighted normalized decision matrix is generated [70,71], and priority scores are calculated [72]. The higher the value of the score the higher the priority in the case of AHP. The general steps involved in the AHP process are presented in Appendix A.1.

2.3.3. Technique for Order of Preference by Similarity to Ideal Solution (TOPSIS)

Ching-Lai Hwang and Kwangsun Yoon introduced TOPSIS, which is based on the distance of alternatives from the negative ideal option (NIO) and the positive ideal option (PIO) [43]. It picks the best alternative, which is the one that is found to be nearest to the IPO and farthest from the INO, based on a closeness coefficient [73]. In TOPSIS, a decision matrix based on alternatives and criteria is formulated. This decision matrix is normalized to generate a weighted normalized decision matrix [70,71]. Then, the PIO and the NIO are calculated [34]. Finally, the direct distance and the closeness index are measured to calculate the priority scores [72]. TOPSIS has been widely adopted for prioritization and decision making [46–48,50,74]. The general steps involved in the TOPSIS process are presented in Appendix A.2.

2.3.4. VIseKriterijumska Optimizacija I Kompromisno Resenje Technique (VIKOR)

The VIKOR method is a reference-based, well-known MCDA technique introduced by Opricovic and Tzeng which emphasizes the ordering of alternatives based on conflicting parameters (utility vs. regret) [44]. This technique ranks the options on the basis of "distance to optimal solution" [70]. Then, from a normalized weighted matrix, the best and worst values are calculated to generate a boundary-values utility index (S_i) and regret index (R_i). Finally, these indices are used to generate the final measure (Q_i) [75]. The general steps involved in the VIKOR process are presented in Appendix A.3.

2.3.5. Simple Additive Weighting (SAW)

In the SAW technique, each alternative is scored by multiplying the alternative value by criterion weight for all criteria and then summing them to rate the alternative accordingly [34]. The SAW prioritization technique involves generation of a decision matrix based on alternatives and criteria followed by normalization of the decision matrix. A further weighted normalized decision matrix is generated [70,71], and priority scores for alternatives are calculated [72]. The general steps involved in the SAW process are presented in Appendix A.4.

2.3.6. Compound Factor (CF) Technique

The compound factor, also referred to as the combination factor, is a scientifically driven MCDA technique that utilizes scientific knowledge and data [76]. This technique quantitatively estimates the qualitative relationship between parameters (criteria) and the goal of the problem (prioritizing erosion-prone areas in this study), based on scientific knowledge. In this study, equal importance was assigned to all criteria [77]. Thus, the mean of the rating values was calculated as the compound factor, representing the integrated impact of all the parameters. The relationship between different morphometric parameters and erosion sensitivity (sub-watershed prioritization) is provided in Table 1. The general steps involved in the compound factor process are presented in Appendix A.5 [78,79].

2.4. Model Synthesis and Final Priority Ranking

The initial priority scores obtained from different MCDA methods exhibited variation. To ensure comparability, these scores were transformed into final priority values on a uniform scale ranging from 0 to 1 using Equations (1) and (2). Subsequently, the entire range of values was divided into four classes: low priority (0–0.25), moderate priority (0.25–0.50), high priority (0.50–0.75), and very high priority (0.75–1) [34]. Consequently, all 19 sub-watersheds were categorized into these four priority classes.

$$1 - \frac{PV_{max} - PV_i}{PV_{max} - PV_{min}} \quad for\ AHP, TOPSIS, SAW \tag{1}$$

$$\frac{PV_{max} - PV_i}{PV_{max} - PV_{min}} \quad for\ VIKOR, CF \tag{2}$$

2.5. MCDA Model Comparison

This study employed two change indices, namely the percentage of changes (ΔP, see Equation (3)) and the intensity of changes (ΔI, see Equation (4)), and two non-parametric statistical tests, namely the Spearman rank correlation coefficient test (SCCT) and the Kendall tau correlation coefficient test (KTCCT), to assess and compare the outcomes of the models in a comparative manner [34,80,81].

$$\Delta P = \frac{N - N_{constant}}{N} \times 100 \tag{3}$$

$$\Delta I = \frac{\sum_{i=1}^{N} \frac{rank\ i(r1)}{rank\ i(r2)}}{N} \tag{4}$$

The equations involved parameters such as N—representing the total number of alternatives; $N_{constant}$—representing the number of alternatives with the same rank; $i(r1)$—denoting the rank of an alternative in the first method; and $i(r2)$—representing the rank of the same alternative in the second method.

Non-parametric statistical tests determine the measure of association between ranks obtained by different MCDA techniques [82]. In the SCCT test, Equation (5) is used if two compared models have no similar ranks, and Equation (6) is applied if one of the compared models has similar ranks.

$$\rho = 1 - \frac{6\sum_{i=1}^{N} D_i^2}{N(N^2 - 1)} \tag{5}$$

$$\rho = \frac{\sum_{i=1}^{N}(x_i - \bar{x})(y_i - \bar{y})}{\sqrt[2]{\sum_{i=1}^{N}(x_i - \bar{x})^2 \sum_{i=1}^{N}(y_i - y)^2}} \tag{6}$$

where D_i is the difference between the ranks of the MCDA methods for the i-th alternative, and $\bar{x}$ and $\bar{y}$ are the mean of the x and y method models, respectively.

The KTCCT is calculated using Equation (7) when the two compared models do not have any similar ranks. By contrast, Equation (8) is used when one of the compared models has the same ranks.

$$\tau = \frac{C - D}{N(N-1)/2} \tag{7}$$

$$\tau = \frac{C - D}{\sqrt[2]{\left(\frac{N(N-1)}{2} - T\right)\left(\frac{N(N-1)}{2} - U\right)}} \tag{8}$$

where C and D are the numbers of agreeing (concordant) and disagreeing (discordant) pairs, respectively. T and U are the numbers of pairs with similarities in each pair of compared MCDA methods.

3. Results
3.1. Sub-Watershed Mapping and Morphometric Analysis

The SRTM 1 arc-DEM data were introduced into a GIS environment using UTM projection WGS-84. The gauging station in the Burhanpur district on the Tapi river was considered as an outlet for the Burhanpur watershed, and 19 sub-watersheds (SW) were delineated using GIS features (Figure 3). The area of the sub-watersheds ranges from 146 km² to 1670 km² attributed to the smallest (SW_7) and the largest (SW_0) watershed, respectively. The total number of first order, second order, third order, and fourth order streams in the watershed were found to be 132, 63, 22, and 62, respectively. All these basic parameters are very useful in analyzing the watershed morphometry [83]. Further, the different morphometric parameters were extracted for the corresponding sub-watersheds and are listed in Table 2. Table 2 shows that the highest standard deviation was recorded for basin relief (171.1 m) followed by slope (4.67%) and relief ratio (4.39 m/m), whereas the lowest value was reported for infiltration number. A similar pattern was observed with range, being highest for basin relief and lowest for infiltration number. Table 3 depicts the effect of individual parameters on the erosivity of a watershed according to their relationship with erosion sensitivity.

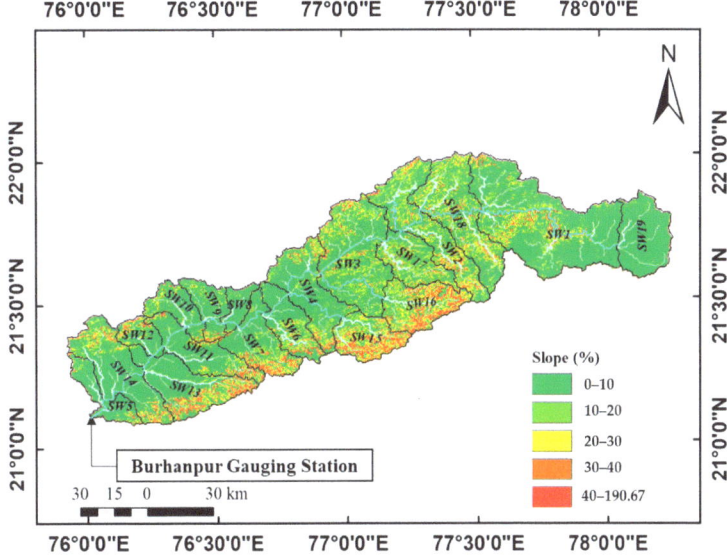

Figure 3. Map of Burhanpur watershed showing delineated sub-watersheds and slopes.

Table 2. Sub-watershed-wise quantification of morphometric parameters of Burhanpur watershed—the decision matrix.

SW	H	S	R_r	R_{bfm}	C	S_f	L_g	R_c	R_e	T	F_f	D_d	$S_{f\mu}$	I_f
1	429	9.37	4.83	4.67	4.94	4.72	2.47	0.28	0.52	0.16	0.21	0.20	0.03	0.005
2	812	14.02	14.40	2.31	4.83	4.24	2.42	0.15	0.55	0.07	0.24	0.21	0.02	0.005
3	418	10.93	6.31	3.94	5.41	4.40	2.71	0.33	0.54	0.13	0.23	0.18	0.03	0.005
4	548	9.28	10.60	1.61	5.43	4.15	2.71	0.23	0.55	0.09	0.24	0.18	0.03	0.005
5	383	6.69	12.27	1.67	5.43	3.68	2.72	0.16	0.59	0.08	0.27	0.18	0.04	0.008
6	592	10.54	15.13	2.00	4.53	3.88	2.27	0.26	0.57	0.09	0.26	0.22	0.03	0.007
7	593	12.39	13.54	2.50	5.93	3.99	2.96	0.26	0.56	0.07	0.25	0.17	0.02	0.004
8	278	5.98	12.50	3.00	4.13	3.39	2.07	0.29	0.61	0.09	0.29	0.24	0.05	0.012
9	382	8.39	12.21	2.00	4.79	3.68	2.40	0.31	0.59	0.09	0.27	0.21	0.03	0.007
10	453	8.81	14.12	2.50	4.35	3.70	2.17	0.30	0.59	0.10	0.27	0.23	0.04	0.009
11	655	9.86	15.08	3.00	4.93	3.98	2.46	0.21	0.57	0.08	0.25	0.20	0.03	0.006
12	485	11.33	18.85	3.00	4.97	3.51	2.48	0.38	0.60	0.09	0.28	0.20	0.04	0.007
13	716	12.40	13.82	1.33	4.34	4.15	2.17	0.24	0.55	0.09	0.24	0.23	0.03	0.006
14	493	9.23	9.12	1.80	4.04	4.19	2.02	0.28	0.55	0.10	0.24	0.25	0.03	0.007
15	814	22.59	20.93	2.33	5.09	3.88	2.54	0.46	0.57	0.09	0.26	0.20	0.02	0.005
16	780	22.42	17.58	3.67	4.88	4.00	2.44	0.35	0.56	0.11	0.25	0.20	0.03	0.006
17	741	13.83	18.40	2.00	4.20	3.91	2.10	0.27	0.57	0.07	0.26	0.24	0.02	0.005
18	654	13.60	10.97	2.25	4.01	4.29	2.01	0.23	0.54	0.09	0.23	0.25	0.02	0.006
19	290	4.90	6.06	2.33	5.76	4.07	2.88	0.41	0.56	0.07	0.25	0.17	0.02	0.003
SD	171.1	4.67	4.39	0.85	0.58	0.32	0.29	0.08	0.02	0.02	0.02	0.02	0.01	0.002
Mean	553.5	11.40	12.99	2.52	4.84	3.99	2.42	0.28	0.57	0.09	0.25	0.21	0.03	0.006
Min	278	4.90	4.83	1.33	4.01	3.39	2.01	0.15	0.52	0.07	0.21	0.17	0.02	0.003
Max	814	22.59	20.93	4.67	5.93	4.72	2.96	0.46	0.61	0.16	0.29	0.25	0.05	0.012
Range	536.0	17.70	16.10	3.34	1.91	1.33	0.96	0.30	0.09	0.09	0.08	0.08	0.03	0.009

Note(s): sub-watershed (SW), basin relief (H), slope (S), relief ratio (Rr), mean bifurcation ratio (R_{bfm}), constant of channel maintenance (C), shape factor (S_f), length of overland flow (L_g), circularity ratio (R_c), elongation ratio (R_e), texture (T), form factor (F_f), drainage density (D_d), stream frequency ($S_{f\mu}$), infiltration number (I_f), standard deviation (SD).

Table 3. Sensitivity of the sub-watersheds to erosion based on relation with parameters.

No.	Parameter	Relation with Erosion Sensitivity	Min (SW ID)	Max (SW ID)	WS with Erosion Sensitivity	
					Lowest	Highest
1	Basin relief (H)	DP	278 (8)	814 (15)	8	15
2	Slope (S)	DP	4.90 (19)	22.59 (15)	19	15
3	Relief ratio (R_r)	DP	4.83 (1)	20.93 (15)	1	15
4	Mean bifurcation ratio (R_{bfm})	DP	1.33 (13)	4.67 (1)	13	1
5	Constant of channel maintenance (C)	DP	4.01 (18)	5.93 (7)	18	7
6	Shape Factor (S_f)	IP	3.39 (8)	4.72 (1)	1	8
7	Length of overland flow (L_g)	DP	2.01 (18)	2.96 (7)	18	7
8	Circularity Ratio (R_c)	IP	0.15 (2)	0.46 (15)	15	2
9	Elongation ratio (R_e)	IP	0.52 (1)	0.61 (8)	8	1
10	Texture (T)	DP	0.07 (17)	0.16 (1)	17	1
11	Form factor (F_f)	IP	0.21 (1)	0.29 (8)	8	1
12	Drainage density (D_d)	DP	0.17 (7)	0.25 (18)	7	18
13	Stream frequency ($S_{f\mu}$)	DP	0.02 (19)	0.05 (8)	19	8
14	Infiltration number (I_f)	IP	0.003 (19)	0.012 (8)	8	19

Notes: DP: directly proportional (the higher the parameter value, the higher the erosion sensitivity), IP: inversely proportional (the higher the parameter value, the lower the erosion sensitivity).

As the watershed's morphometric parameters are able to describe soil erosion phenomena occurring in the watershed [15], Table 3 summarizes the erosion sensitivity of the delineated watersheds on the basis of individual morphometric parameters. It was observed that the parameters, when considered individually, indicate those sub-watersheds that should be given lowest and highest priority for soil erosion, conservation, and management. For example, when considering basin relief, the parameter indicated that SW_8 and SW_15 must be given the lowest and highest priority, respectively, whereas, when mean bifurcation ratio was considered, this parameter indicated that SW_13 and SW_1 must be given the lowest and highest priority, respectively—and so on. However, this standalone parameter approach resulted in ambiguity in the decision making and did not lead to a specific prioritization, as some of the SWs were recognized as having the lowest priority by one parameter and the highest priority by another parameter. Hence, these 14 morphometric parameters were investigated as criteria in relation with erosion sensitivity to explicitly prioritize 19 sub-watersheds (considered as alternatives) using five different MCDA techniques (AHP, TOPSIS, VIKOR, SWA, and CF).

3.2. Criterion Weightage for MCDA

To investigate the relation between the criteria and erosion sensitivity, the relative significance scale suggested by the authors of [42] was adopted to construct Saaty's pairwise comparison matrix [66]. Table 4 represents this comparison matrix among all 14 criteria, which was used to estimate the relative weights of criteria. In this approach, a parameter with a higher impact on erosion sensitivity was given greater preference in the comparison matrix. The majority of areal parameters exhibited low to medium values, while the linear parameters showed similar trends (Table 2). However, the relief parameters recorded a significant increase in their values, with considerable variation among the studied sub-watersheds, highlighting the pronounced influence of these parameters on erosion sensitivity. Consequently, the relief parameters were assigned higher weights in the analysis, taking into account their substantial impact while also acknowledging the significance of the other parameters [19]. Figure 4 depicts the relative weights, and it was observed that basin relief was assigned the highest weight value of 0.308, followed by slope (0.154) and relief ratio (0.103). The lowest weight value of 0.022 was observed to be that of the infiltration number criterion. In a further step, to assess the consistency of the decision and the relative weights, a consistency check was performed. The estimated weights were found to be acceptable, as the consistency ratio (0.008) falls below 0.1 in this study of the Burhanpur watershed [67].

Table 4. Saaty's pairwise comparison matrix for criteria weight estimation.

	H	S	R_r	R_{bfm}	C	S_f	L_g	R_c	R_e	T	F_f	D_d	$S_{f\mu}$	I_f
H	1	2	3	4	5	6	7	8	9	10	11	12	13	14
S	0.50	1	1.5	2	2.5	3	3.5	4	4.5	5	5.5	6	6.5	7
R_r	0.33	0.67	1	1.33	1.67	2	2.33	2.67	3	3.33	3.67	4	4.33	4.67
R_{bfm}	0.25	0.50	0.75	1	1.25	1.5	1.75	2	2.25	2.5	2.75	3	3.25	3.5
C	0.20	0.40	0.60	0.80	1	1.2	1.4	1.6	1.8	2	2.2	2.4	2.6	2.8
S_f	0.17	0.33	0.50	0.67	0.83	1	1.17	1.33	1.5	1.67	1.83	2	2.17	2.33
L_g	0.14	0.29	0.43	0.57	0.71	0.86	1	1.14	1.29	1.43	1.57	1.71	1.86	2
R_c	0.13	0.25	0.38	0.50	0.63	0.75	0.88	1	1.125	1.25	1.375	1.5	1.625	1.75
R_e	0.11	0.22	0.33	0.44	0.56	0.67	0.78	0.89	1	1.11	1.22	1.33	1.44	1.56
T	0.10	0.20	0.30	0.40	0.50	0.60	0.70	0.80	0.90	1	1.1	1.2	1.3	1.4
F_f	0.09	0.18	0.27	0.36	0.45	0.55	0.64	0.73	0.82	0.91	1	1.09	1.18	1.27
D_d	0.08	0.17	0.25	0.33	0.42	0.50	0.58	0.67	0.75	0.83	0.92	1	1.08	1.17
$S_{f\mu}$	0.08	0.15	0.23	0.31	0.38	0.46	0.54	0.62	0.69	0.77	0.85	0.92	1	1.08
I_f	0.07	0.14	0.21	0.29	0.36	0.43	0.50	0.57	0.64	0.71	0.79	0.86	0.93	1

Note: Notations are the same as those provided in Table 2.

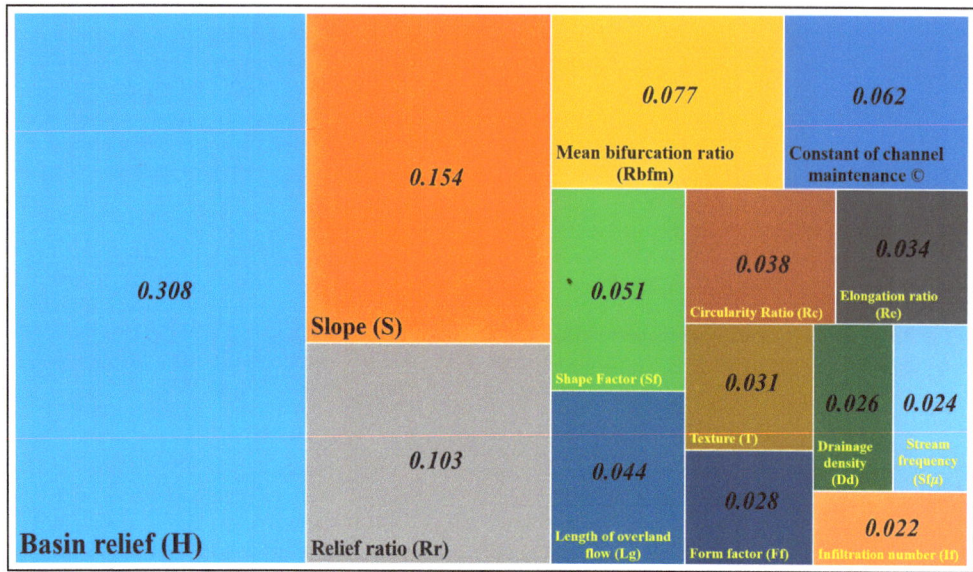

Figure 4. The weight of each of the criteria (parameters).

3.3. Sub-Watershed Prioritization Using Different MCDA Techniques

3.3.1. Watershed Prioritization Using AHP

In Analytic Hierarchy Process technique [42] of SWs prioritization the decision matrix was formulated from Table 2. The results of the AHP model, presented in Table 5, show that SWs 15 and 16 are ranked first and second, respectively, indicating that they are highly prone to erosion and classified as very high priority sub-watersheds (8.34% area). Similarly, five SWs (23.38% area), seven SWs (49.99% area) and five SWs (18.28% area) are classified as high priority, moderate priority, and low priority, respectively (Figure 5). The spatial distribution of the AHP-based SW prioritization is depicted in Figure 6.

Table 5. Prioritization ranking and class of sub-watersheds using different MCDA techniques.

SW	AHP		TOPSIS		VIKOR		SAW		CF	
	Rank	Class	Rank	Class	Rank	Class	Rank	Class	Rank	Class
1	13	MP	14	MP	14	MP	13	MP	7	HP
2	3	HP	3	HP	3	VHP	3	VHP	2	VHP
3	12	MP	15	MP	15	MP	15	MP	9	HP
4	14	MP	11	MP	10	MP	11	MP	15	MP
5	17	LP	17	LP	17	LP	17	LP	18	LP
6	10	MP	9	MP	8	HP	9	HP	8	HP
7	9	MP	8	HP	9	HP	8	HP	13	HP
8	18	LP	18	LP	18	LP	18	LP	16	MP
9	16	LP	16	LP	16	LP	16	LP	17	LP
10	11	MP	13	MP	13	MP	12	MP	12	HP
11	6	HP	7	HP	7	HP	6	HP	4	VHP
12	7	HP	10	MP	11	MP	10	HP	14	HP
13	5	HP	5	HP	5	HP	5	HP	5	VHP
14	15	LP	12	MP	12	MP	14	MP	11	HP
15	1	VHP	2	VHP	2	VHP	2	VHP	6	HP
16	2	VHP	1	VHP	1	VHP	1	VHP	1	VHP
17	4	HP	4	HP	4	VHP	4	VHP	9	HP
18	8	MP	6	HP	6	HP	7	HP	3	VHP
19	19	LP	19	LP	19	LP	19	LP	19	LP

Note: LP: low priority, MP: moderate priority, HP: high priority, and VHP: very high priority.

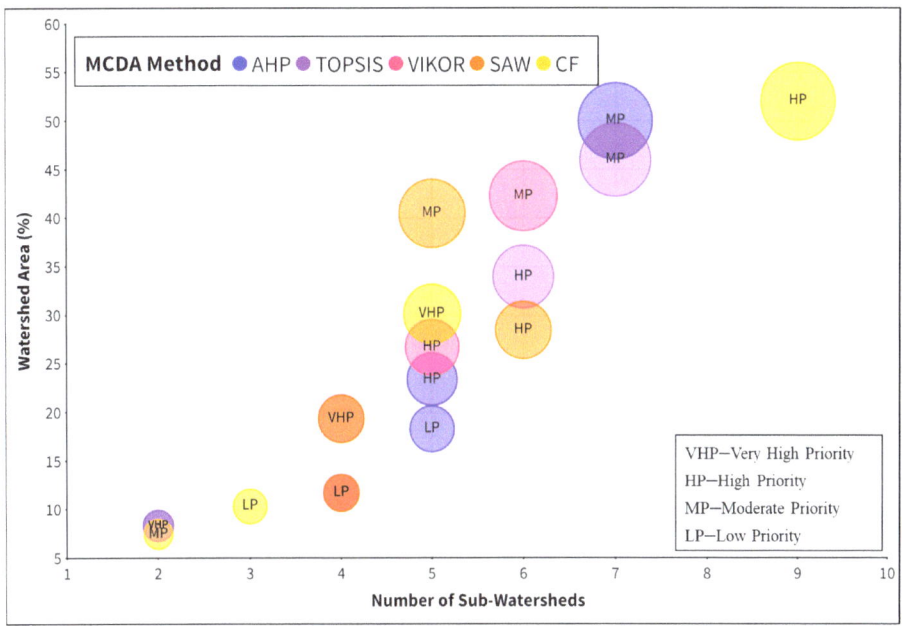

Figure 5. Sub-watersheds classified into different classes by different MCDA methods.

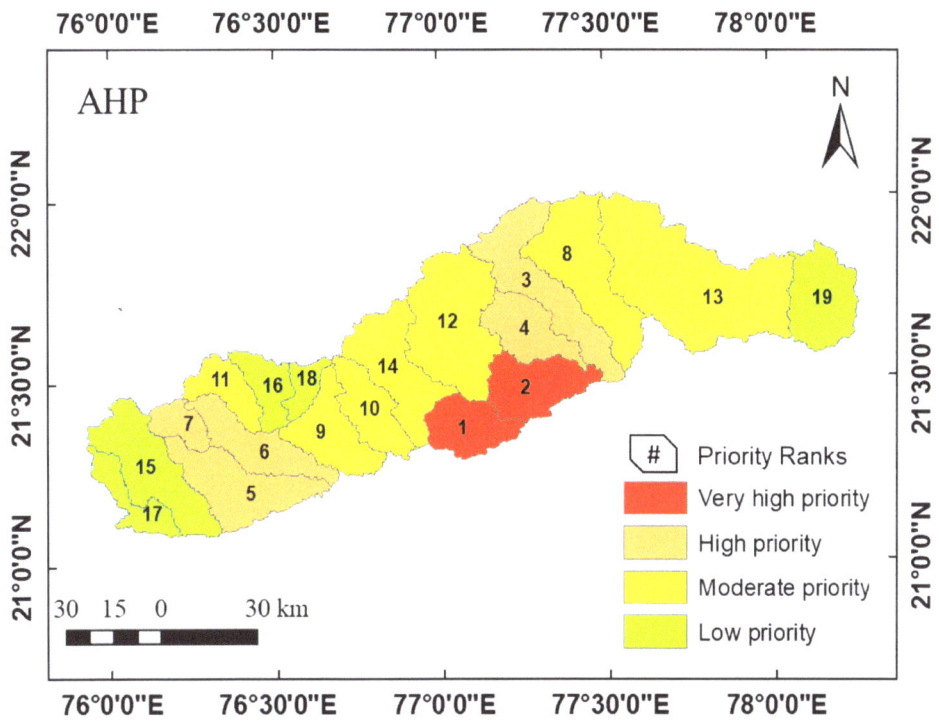

Figure 6. Spatial distribution of SW prioritization using AHP.

3.3.2. Watershed Prioritization Using TOPSIS

TOPSIS calculates the distances of alternatives from the NIO and the PIO [43] and picks the best alternative, which is the one found to be nearest to the IPO and farthest from the INO, based on a closeness coefficient [73]. The results of the TOPSIS model, presented in Table 5, show that SWs 16 and 15 are ranked first and second, respectively, indicating that they are highly prone to erosion and classified as very high priority sub-watersheds. Similarly, six SWs (33.96% area), seven SWs (45.99% area), and four SWs (11.71% area) are classified as high priority, moderate priority, and low priority, respectively (Figure 5). The spatial distribution of the TOPSIS-based SW prioritization is depicted in Figure 7.

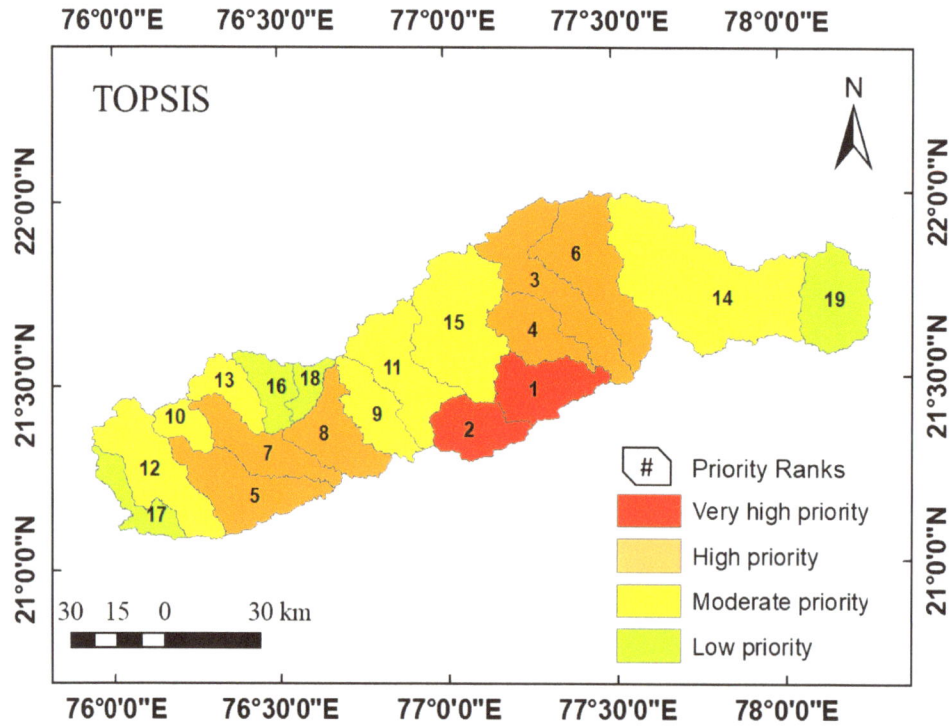

Figure 7. Spatial distribution of SW prioritization using TOPSIS.

3.3.3. Watershed Prioritization Using VIKOR

VIKOR emphasizes the ordering of alternatives based on conflicting parameters [44] and ranks the alternatives based on "distance to optimal solution" [70]. The results of the VIKOR model, presented in Table 5, show that four SWs, i.e., SW 16, SW 15, SW 2, and SW 17 are ranked first, second, third, and fourth, respectively, indicating that they are highly prone to erosion and classified as very high priority sub-watersheds. Similarly, five SWs (26.68% area), six SWs (42.26% area), and four SWs (11.71% area) are classified as high priority, moderate priority, and low priority, respectively (Figure 5). The spatial distribution of the VICOR-based SW prioritization is depicted in Figure 8.

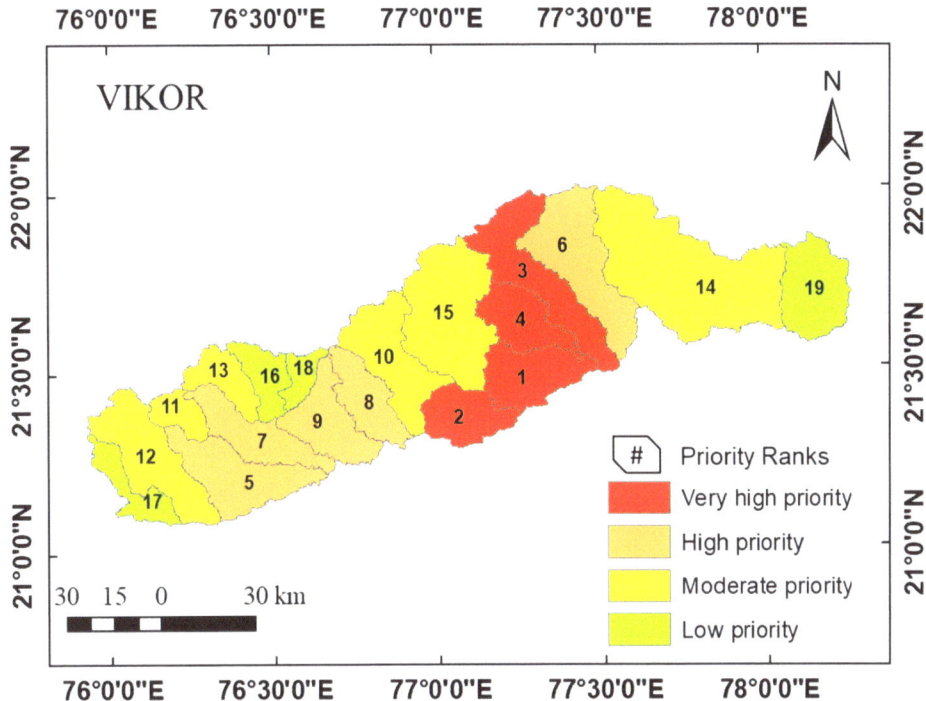

Figure 8. Spatial distribution of SW prioritization using VIKOR.

3.3.4. Watershed Prioritization Using SAW

In the SAW technique, each alternative is scored by multiplying the alternative value by criterion weight for all criteria and then summing them to rate the alternative accordingly [34]. The results of the SAW model, presented in Table 5, show that four SWs, i.e., SW 16, SW 15, SW 2, and SW 17 are ranked first, second, third, and fourth, respectively, indicating that they are highly prone to erosion and classified as very high priority sub-watersheds. Similarly, six SWs (28.46% area), five SWs (40.48% area), and four SWs (11.71% area) were classified as high priority, moderate priority, and low priority, respectively (Figure 5). The spatial distribution of SAW-based SW prioritization is depicted in Figure 9.

3.3.5. Watershed Prioritization Using Compound Factor (CF)

The Compound Factor (CF) MCDA technique is utilized to estimate the relationship between criteria and the goal [76], giving equal importance to all criteria [77]. The results of the CF model, presented in Table 5, show that out of the total of 19 SWs, five SWs (16, 2, 18, 11, and 13) are found to be highly prone to erosion and classified with very high priority. Likewise, nine SWs (52.05% area), two SWs (7.47% area), and three SWs (10.33% area) are classified as high priority, moderate priority, and low priority, respectively (Figure 5). The spatial distribution of CF-based SW prioritization is depicted in Figure 10.

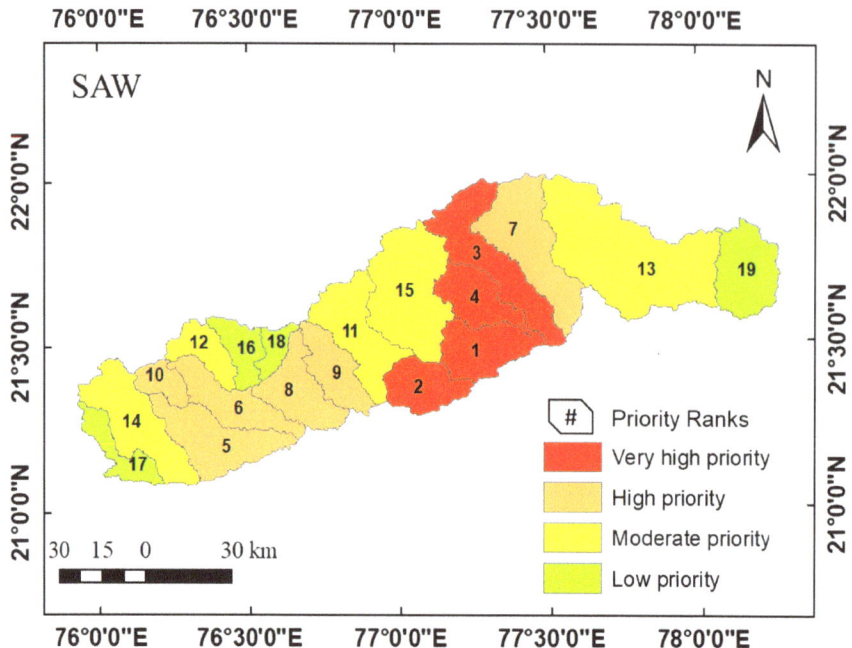

Figure 9. Spatial distribution of SW prioritization using SAW.

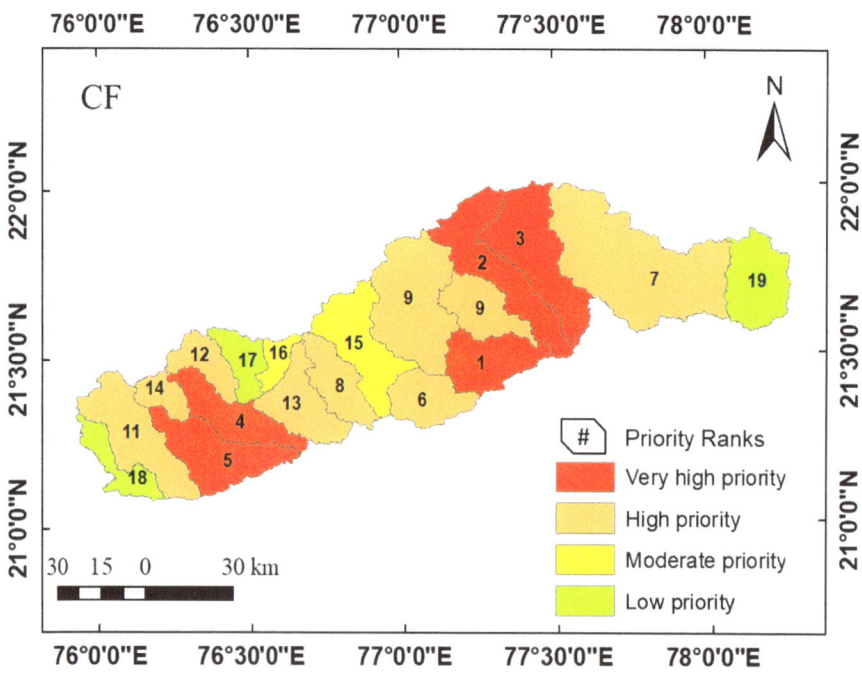

Figure 10. Spatial distribution of SW prioritization using CF.

3.4. MCDA Model Comparison

The variations in the rankings of watersheds as obtained using different multiple criteria decision making (MCDA) techniques can be attributed to the specific characteristics of each method and the values assigned to the utilized criteria [84]. The performance of the models in terms of prioritization was evaluated using two change indices (ΔP and ΔI) and two non-parametric statistical tests (SCCT and KTCCT) using Equations (3)–(8) [34,80–82]. Table 6 demonstrates that the CF technique exhibited the highest percentage change of ranks compared to other methods, with a value of 66.32%. This technique is followed by AHP, VIKOR/SAW, and TOPSIS, with percentages of changes of about 52.63%, 41.05%, and 38.95%, respectively. Again, CF demonstrated the highest intensity of change—with a value of 1.098—among all five MCDA techniques, whereas AHP and TOPSIS/VIKOR/SAW exhibited intensities of changes of about 1.055 and 1.03, respectively. The results from the non-parametric correlation tests are represented in Figure 11, revealing that AHP, TOPSIS, VIKOR, and SAW had an average correlation coefficient greater than 0.84 for the KTCCT and greater than 0.93 for the SCCT at $p = 0.01$. However, CF led to the lowest values for the average correlation coefficient, namely 0.70 and 0.85 for the KTCCT and the SCCT, respectively, compared with the other MCDA methods.

Table 6. Percentage change and change of intensity of MCDA techniques.

	Percentage Change					Change of Intensity				
	AHP	TOPSIS	VIKOR	SAW	CF	AHP	TOPSIS	VIKOR	SAW	CF
AHP	0	63.16	57.89	52.63	89.47	1	1.038	1.042	1.034	1.165
TOPSIS	63.16	0	21.05	26.32	84.21	1.038	1	1.001	1.002	1.109
VIKOR	57.89	21.05	0	47.37	78.95	1.042	1.001	1	1.003	1.107
SAW	52.63	26.32	47.37	0	78.95	1.034	1.002	1.003	1	1.111
CF	89.47	84.21	78.95	78.95	0	1.165	1.109	1.107	1.111	1
Average	52.63	38.95	41.05	41.05	66.32	1.055	1.030	1.030	1.030	1.098

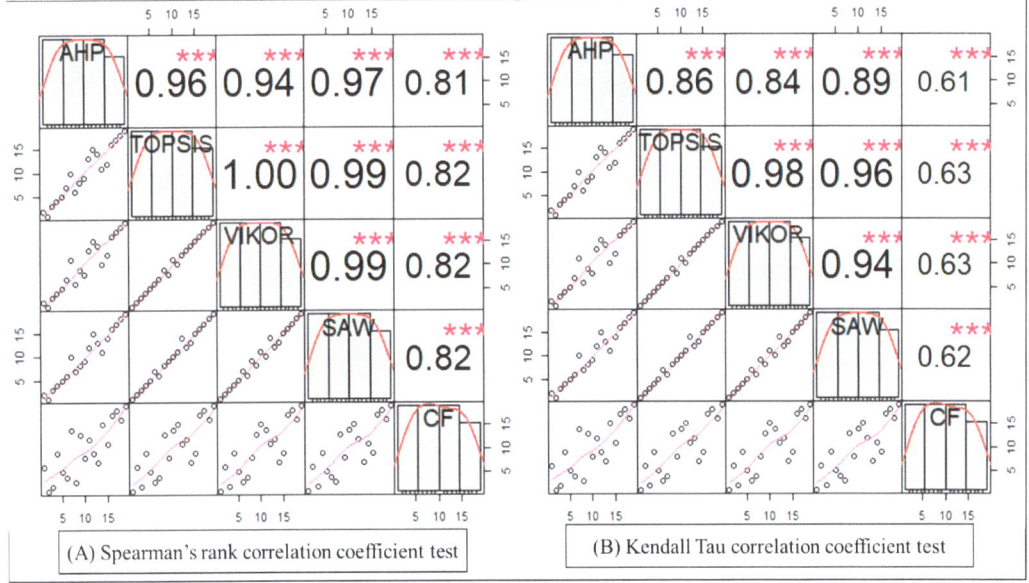

Figure 11. Results for correlation among MCDA methods using non-parametric statistical tests (*** indicates the significance of the correlation test at $p = 0.01$ and red lines depict the correlation function between the methods).

4. Discussion
4.1. Morphometric Analysis

The Burhanpur watershed was delineated into 19 sub-watersheds using SRTM DEM data in a GIS environment. These sub-watersheds were analyzed for their morphometric properties derived from the topography, including linear, areal, and relief characteristics, to assess the impact of these characteristics on erosion susceptibility. The assessment of soil erosion vulnerability requires information about the drainage and relief parameters, which significantly influence the hydrological behavior of the watershed, such as runoff and infiltration [45]. The derived morphometric parameters offer a more convenient, accurate, and quantitative approach to understanding the watershed's variations. Consequently, using the results of morphometric analysis (as shown in Tables 2 and 3), the erosion sensitivity of the SWs can be anticipated.

Basin relief significantly affects hydrological behavior of a basin [85] and in turn directly influences the intensity of erosion forces, thus, putting SW 8 and SW 15 into the highest and lowest erosion susceptibility categories, respectively. Similarly, the steepest average slope is observed for SW 15, placing it under the highest risk of erosion. The relief ratio, being a direct function of slope, affects the erosion process in direct proportion, with an increased risk of erosion forces. As regards the relief ratio, SW 15 is found to have the highest relief ratio, reflecting the fact that it is in the highest erosion susceptibility category. The mean bifurcation ratio (R_{bfm}) signifies an inverse relation between basin infiltration and flooding. A high R_{bfm} value corresponds to the peak of the initial hydrograph, indicating increased soil degradation during flooding [8]. The presence of high R_{bfm} values (ranging from 1.33 to 4.67) suggests a complex structure and low infiltration rates. This indicates a higher susceptibility to degradation during flood events. The constant of channel maintenance for the SWs varies in the range of 4.01–5.93 (lowest for SW 18 and highest for SW 7), indicating that SW7 is the most erodible watershed, as it reflects infiltration and control of flow to the outlet [60]. The form factor and elongation ratio exhibit a similar behavior, showing an inverse relationship with soil erosion susceptibility. This analogous effect resulted in SW 1 having the highest erosion susceptibility, while SW 8 exhibited the lowest susceptibility. The smaller value of the elongation ratio suggests a steep slope with high relief, making the area more prone to erosion. Conversely, the smaller value of the form factor indicates a relatively elongated watershed, leading to flatter peak flows over an extended period. Thus, this characteristic makes the peak flows easier to manage compared to circular sub-watersheds. The circularity ratio is a measure of the shape of SWs, i.e., where basin shape approaches a circle, the circulatory ratio approaches unity. For the Burhanpur SWs the circularity ratios are low, indicating their elongated shape; however the highest value for the circularity ratio belongs to SW 15, making it prone to erosion.

Considering these parameters individually, sub-watersheds were identified as having the lowest and highest erosion sensitivity. However, this approach did not lead to a clear decision-making state, as some sub-watersheds were classified as low priority by one parameter and high priority by another. This may be attributed to the fact that the linear and landscape parameters directly contribute to erosion, while shape parameters exhibit an inverse relationship, in which a lower value indicates higher sensitivity to erosion [19,86,87]. Hence, to address this, an MCDA approach was adopted, using morphometric parameters as criteria to prioritize the 19 sub-watersheds for erosion susceptibility.

4.2. Prioritization by MCDA Models

Due to variations in morphometric characteristics, watersheds exhibit different behaviors in terms of erosion. Therefore, it is crucial to identify/prioritize critical areas for effective management and planning [88]. In this study, a pairwise comparisons method was used to determine the weights of each criteria [66] (Figure 4) and was found to be consistent, i.e., below 0.1 [67]. The resultant weights demonstrate that relief parameters (basin relief, slope, and relief ratio) with higher weights have the greatest effect on the erosion process, because relief aspects significantly affect the hydrological behavior of a basin and in turn directly influence the intensity of erosion forces [85]. Accordingly, the parameters with lower weights have a comparatively lesser impact on the erosion process. These results are in line with the results of the studies in [89] and [90].

The AHP model demonstrated about 8.34%, 23.38%, 49.99%, and 18.28% of the area to be classified as VHP, HP, MP, and LP, respectively. The TOPSIS model revealed that about 8.34% of the area is classed as VHP, followed by 33.96% (HP), 45.99% (MP), and 11.71% (LP). Similarly, the VIKOR, SAW, and CF approaches classified 19.35%, 19.35%, and 30.15% area as being in the very high priority (HP) class, respectively (Figure 5). The areas classified as VHP and HP can attribute their classification to higher values for relief and linear aspects imposing a higher likelihood and intensity of erosion in these areas. Further, the variations in the amount of area classified under different classes by different MCDA techniques can be attributed to the specific characteristics of each method and the values assigned to the utilized criteria [84]. However, the overall analysis revealed that in the Burhanpur watershed 8.34–30.15% of the area is in a critically-erosion-prone zone, and about 23.38–52.05% of the area is in the high priority class. Thus, these erosion-prone areas of the watershed must be the subject of soil conservation measures within the scientific approach of catchment development.

4.3. Comparative Analysis

The ranks generated for the SWs from the five MCDA methods were compared between themselves using change indices and non-parametric correlation tests. It was observed that the rankings of sub-watersheds obtained using SAW, VIKOR, TOPSIS, and AHP had a higher correlation (0.84–0.99 at $p = 0.01$) and a lesser change in both percentage and intensity than the CF method. This is because the AHP, TOPSIS, VIKOR, and SAW methods utilize the same relative weights as derived from the comparison matrix, while the CF technique gives equal weight to all criteria, irrespective of their relative importance. The small variation in the correlation coefficients among AHP, TOPSIS, VIKOR, and SAW can be attributed to their inherent characteristics [84]. Further, the models that use weights that take into account the relative importance of criteria are able to provide more accurate information for taking confident decisions. Here, these models had higher correlation among the priority ranks and lower changes in percentage and intensity. Hence, the SAW, TOPSIS, VIKOR, and AHP models were superior to the CF model and were found to be more accurate, with higher confidence. Similar results have also been reported by others [34,91].

4.4. Application and Role of Prioritization in Soil Conservation Approach

Erosion can lead to the loss of topsoil, reduced agricultural productivity, and environmental degradation. Soil and water conservation measures play a crucial role in mitigating these effects. Implementation of effective conservation measures is vital to ensure the sustainability of soil and water resources. In erosion management, one key aspect is the prioritization of critical areas. Prioritization allows for targeted allocation of resources and efforts. This is where morphometric analysis, combined with MCDA techniques, proves to be invaluable and helps in the following:

- Targeted approach: Prioritization directs resources to high-risk and vulnerable areas, maximizing the impact of soil conservation measures for effective outcomes.
- Resource optimization: Prioritization optimizes the use of limited resources (time, manpower, and funding), ensuring that they are allocated to areas where they can have the greatest impact in implementing soil conservation measures.
- Prevention of further degradation: Prioritization aids in timely intervention and prevention of soil degradation and erosion in high-priority areas, resulting in stabilized soils, reduced erosion rates, and preservation of valuable topsoil and nutrients.
- Long-term sustainability: By addressing the most vulnerable areas first, the overall health and productivity of the watershed is enhanced. This supports sustainable

land-use practices, preserves ecosystem integrity, secures fertile soils, and promotes long-term sustainability for future generations.
- Stakeholder engagement and support: Prioritization facilitates stakeholder (communities, farmers, landowners, and relevant authorities) engagement and collaboration. This can enhance the acceptance of, participation in, and support for soil conservation measures, leading to their successful implementation and long-term maintenance.

4.5. Challenges with MCDA Techniques

MCDA techniques used in prioritization processes often focus on a specific set of factors or data classes, such as morphometric, land use, hydrological, or soil texture [92]. These results are subjective to expert opinions and may vary in terms of accuracy [83,93]. Furthermore, these methods may not adequately address the associated uncertainties in the model's output [94]. A key limitation in applying these methods is the requirement for expertise in watershed knowledge [95], posing a significant challenge for sub-watershed prioritization using MCDA. Each prioritization technique has its own strengths and weaknesses, depending on its complexity [96]. However, detailed quantitative assessment of erosion often requires extensive and high-quality field data, which is often challenging to obtain in many locations. In such circumstances, a comparative assessment of sub-watersheds based on governing factors can provide insights into erosion-prone areas [91].

5. Conclusions

The present study employed GIS tools and remote sensing data, specifically digital elevation models (DEMs), to delineate and analyze morphometric parameters in the Burhanpur watershed of Central India. Fourteen parameters were considered as criteria for prioritizing nineteen sub-watersheds, with weights assigned based on their relative importance in erosion processes. The most important findings of the study were highlighted as follows:

- Morphometric parameters: The study emphasized the higher significance of relief parameters compared to linear and areal parameters in prioritization, based on their relative importance in the erosion process.
- MCDA techniques: The study successfully prioritized sub-watersheds using five MCDA techniques (AHP, TOPSIS, VIKOR, SAW, and CF) and found these techniques suitable for providing valuable insights into the relative priority of sub-watersheds in terms of their erosion susceptibility.
- Sub-watershed prioritization: The results indicated that the amount of area in each of the priority classes varied across the models. The area classed as very high-priority was recorded in the range of 8.34% to 30.15%. Further, the area classed as high, moderate, and low priority was found to be in the range of 23.38–52.05%, 7.47–49.99%, and 10.33–18.28%, respectively.
- Comparative Performance: The performance of the models was compared using four indices (percentage of changes, intensity of changes, the Spearman rank correlation coefficient test, and the Kendall tau correlation coefficient test), and it was found that the SAW, TOPSIS, VIKOR, and AHP models had higher correlation (0.84–0.99 at $p = 0.01$) and lesser percentage change and change intensity than the CF technique. Overall, the SAW, TOPSIS, VIKOR, and AHP models performed better than the CF model, with higher confidence.

The study also highlighted the applicability and role of morphometric analysis-based prioritization for targeted approaches, resource optimization, stakeholder engagement, and long-term sustainability in soil conservation efforts. However, it acknowledged the challenges associated with the use of MCDA techniques in watershed prioritization. Despite these challenges, the study confirmed the effectiveness of using morphometric parameters and MCDA approaches to identify critical areas and improve decision-making support to preserve soil and the environment, particularly in data-limited regions.

Author Contributions: Conceptualization, A.P.; methodology, A.P., K.V.R.R., Y.A.R. and C.K.S.; software A.P. and K.S.; resources, A.P., K.V.R.R., Y.A.R., C.K.S., K.S. and A.S.; data curation, A.P. and K.V.R.R.; writing—original draft preparation, A.P.; writing—review and editing, K.V.R.R., Y.A.R., C.K.S. and A.S.; visualization, A.P.; supervision, K.V.R.R., Y.A.R. and C.K.S. All authors have read and agreed to the published version of the manuscript.

Funding: This research received no external funding.

Data Availability Statement: Data are contained within the article.

Conflicts of Interest: The authors declare that they have no known competing financial interests or personal relationships that could have appeared to influence the work reported in this paper.

Appendix A

Appendix A.1. Analytical Hierarchy Process Technique

The AHP technique introduced by Saaty [42] is one of the most popular and easiest MCDA methods [41]. AHP breaks down the complex problem into hierarchically structured sub-problems to find a solution from among alternatives [42,69]. The general steps involved in the AHP process are as follows:

I. Generation of decision matrix (D) of dimension $m \times n$ with respect to the alternatives and the criteria, respectively:

$$D = \begin{bmatrix} x_{11} & x_{12} & \cdots & x_{1n} \\ x_{21} & x_{22} & \cdots & x_{2n} \\ \cdot & \cdot & & \cdot \\ \cdot & \cdot & & \cdot \\ x_{m1} & x_{m2} & \cdots & x_{mn} \end{bmatrix} \quad (A1)$$

The decision matrix is a matrix containing all the criteria values relative to all the alternatives and is used in several MCDA techniques to evaluate and rank the alternatives. Where $i = 1, 2, \ldots, m$ (number of alternatives), $j = 1, 2, \ldots, n$ (number of criteria).

II. Normalizing the decision matrix (N)

$$n_{ij} = \frac{x_{ij}}{\sum_{i=1}^{m} x_{ij}} \quad (A2)$$

where n_{ij} is the element of the normalized decision matrix for the i-th alternative in the j-th criterion.

III. Deriving a weighted normalized decision matrix (V) by multiplying the normalized matrix with the weight matrix (w_q) [70,71]:

$$v_{ij} = n_{ij} \times w_j \quad (A3)$$

where v_{ij} is the element of the weighted normalized decision matrix for the i-th alternative in the j-th criterion.

IV. Calculating score (initial priority value) for alternatives [72]:

$$A_i = \sum_{j=1}^{n} v_{ij} \quad (A4)$$

These A_i scores are the initial priority values obtained using AHP. A higher A_i value is of higher priority in the case of AHP.

Appendix A.2. Technique for Order of Preference by Similarity to Ideal Solution (TOPSIS)

Ching-Lai Hwang and Kwangsun Yoon introduced TOPSIS, which is based on the on distance of alternatives from the negative ideal option (NIO) and the positive ideal option (PIO) [43]. It picks the best alternative, which is the one that is found to be nearest to the IPO and farthest from the INO, based on a closeness coefficient [73]. TOPSIS has been widely adopted for prioritization and decision making [46–48,50,74]. The general steps involved in the TOPSIS process are as follows:

I. Generation of decision matrix (D) as described in Equation (A1).
II. Normalizing the decision matrix (N),

$$n_{ij} = \frac{x_{ij}}{\sqrt{\sum_{i=1}^{m} x_{ij}^2}} \quad (A5)$$

where n_{ij} is the element of normalized decision matrix for the i-th alternative in the j-th criterion.

III. Derive weighted normalized decision matrix (V) by multiplying the normalized matrix with the weight matrix (w_q) [70,71],

$$v_{ij} = n_{ij} \times w_j \quad (A6)$$

where v_{ij} is the element of weighted normalized decision matrix for the i-th alternative in the j-th criterion

IV. Finding PIO (A^+) and NIO (A^-) [34]:

$$A^+ = \left\{ \left(v_{ij}^{max} \middle| \text{for DP criterion} \right), \left(v_{ij}^{min} \middle| \text{for IP criteria} \right) \right\} \\ = \left\{ V_1^+, V_2^+, \ldots, V_j^+, \ldots, V_n^+ \right\} \quad (A7)$$

$$A^- = \left\{ \left(v_{ij}^{min} \middle| \text{for DP criterion} \right), \left(v_{ij}^{max} \middle| \text{for IP criterion} \right) \right\} \\ = \left\{ V_1^-, V_2^-, \ldots, V_j^-, \ldots, V_n^- \right\} \quad (A8)$$

V. Estimation of direct distance to A^+ and A^-:

$$d_{i+} = \sqrt{\sum_{j=1}^{n} \left(v_{ij} - V_j^+ \right)^2}, i = 1, 2, 3, \ldots, m \quad (A9)$$

$$d_{i-} = \sqrt{\sum_{j=1}^{n} \left(v_{ij} - V_j^- \right)^2}, i = 1, 2, 3, \ldots, m \quad (A10)$$

VI. Extraction of closeness index (CI) as initial priority values:

$$CI_i = \frac{d_{i-}}{d_{i+} + d_{i-}}; 0 \leq CI_i \leq 1; i = 1, 2, 3 \ldots m \quad (A11)$$

These CI values are the initial priority values obtained using TOPSIS. A higher CI value is of higher priority in the case of TOPSIS.

Appendix A.3. VIseKriterijumska Optimizacija I Kompromisno Resenje Technique (VIKOR) Technique

The VIKOR method is a reference-based, well-known MCDA introduced by Opricovic and Tzeng which emphasizes the ordering of alternatives based on conflicting parameters (utility vs. regret) [44]. This technique ranks the options on the basis of "distance to optimal solution" [70]. The general steps involved in the VIKOR process are as follows:

I. Generation of decision matrix (D) as described in Equation (A1).
II. Normalizing the decision matrix (N), where n_{pq} is the element of matrix

$$n_{ij} = \frac{d_{ij}}{\sqrt{\sum_{i=1}^{m} d_{ij}^2}} \quad (A12)$$

and n_{ij} is the element of normalized decision matrix for the i-th alternative in the j-th criterion.

III. Derive a weighted normalized decision matrix (V) by multiplying the normalized matrix with the weight matrix (w_q) [70,71]:

$$v_{ij} = n_{ij} \times w_j \tag{A13}$$

where v_{ij} is the element of weighted normalized decision matrix for the *i*-th alternative in the *j*-th criterion.

IV. Retrieving the best (v_j^{*+}) and the worst (v_j^{*-}) value:

$$v_j^{*+} = \left(v_{ij}^{max}\middle| for\ DP\ criteria\right); j = 1, 2, \ldots, n \tag{A14}$$

$$v_j^{*-} = \left(v_{ij}^{min}\middle| for\ DP\ croteria\right); j = 1, 2, \ldots, n \tag{A15}$$

V. Calculating boundary values utility index (S_i) and regret index (R_i):

$$S_i = L_{1,i} = \sum_{i=1}^{m} w_j \frac{\left(V_j^{*+} - v_{ij}\right)}{\left(V_j^{*+} - V_j^{*-}\right)}; j = 1, 2, \ldots, n \tag{A16}$$

$$R_i = L_{\infty,i} = max\left[\sum_{i=1}^{m} w_j \frac{\left(V_j^{*+} - v_{ij}\right)}{\left(V_j^{*+} - V_j^{*-}\right)}\right]; j = 1, 2, \ldots, n \tag{A17}$$

VI. Calculating the final measure (Q_i) [75]:

$$Q_i = \mu \frac{\left(S_i - S_i^-\right)}{\left(S_i^+ - S_i^-\right)} + (1 - \mu)\frac{\left(R_i - R_i^-\right)}{\left(R_i^+ - R_i^-\right)} \tag{A18}$$

where S_i^+, S_i^-, R_i^+, and R_i^- are $maxS_i$, $minS_i$, $maxR_i$, and $minR_i$, respectively, and μ is the balance weight between S_i and R_i. Here, $\mu = 0.5$.
The option with minimum values for all three parameters (S, R, and Q) is the best option. These Q_i values are the initial priority values obtained using the VIKOR technique. A lower Q_i value is of higher priority in the case of VIKOR.

Appendix A.4. Simple Additive Weighting (SAW)

In the SAW technique, each alternative is scored by multiplying the alternative value by criterion weight for all criteria and then summing them to rate the alternative accordingly [34]. The general steps involved in the SAW process are as follows:

I. Generation of decision matrix (D) as described in Equation (A1).
II. Determination of values d_{ij} as d_{ij}^{max} or d_{ij}^{min}; if the *j*-th criterion is directly proportional (DP) or indirectly proportional (IP) with the goal, respectively.
III. Normalizing the decision matrix (N), where n_{pq} is the element of matrix,

$$n_{ij} = \frac{d_{ij}}{d_{ij}^{max}}; for\ DP\ criterion \tag{A19}$$

or

$$n_{ij} = \frac{d_{ij}^{min}}{d_{ij}}; for\ IP\ criterion \tag{A20}$$

where n_{ij} is element of normalized decision matrix for *i*-th alternative in *j*-th criterion

IV. Derive the weighted normalized matrix (V) by multiplying the normalized matrix with the weight matrix (w_q) [70,71],

$$v_{ij} = n_{ij} \times w_j \tag{A21}$$

where v_{ij} is the element of weighted normalized decision matrix for the i-th alternative in the j-th criterion

V. Calculating score (initial priority value) for alternatives [72]:

$$A_i = \sum_{j=1}^{n} v_{ij} \tag{A22}$$

These A_i scores are the initial priority values obtained using SAW. A higher A_i value is of higher priority in the case of SAW.

Appendix A.5. Compound Factor (CF) Technique

The compound factor, also referred to as the Combination Factor, is a scientifically driven MCDA technique that utilizes scientific knowledge and data [76]. This technique quantitatively estimates the qualitative relationship between parameters (criteria) and the goal of the problem (prioritizing erosion-prone areas in this study) based on scientific knowledge. In this study, equal importance was assigned to all criteria [77]. Thus, the mean of the rating values was calculated as the compound factor, representing the integrated impact of all the parameters. The relationship between different morphometric parameters and erosion sensitivity (sub-watershed prioritization) is shown in Table 1. The general steps involved in the compound factor process are as follows [78,79]:

I. Generation of decision matrix (D) as described in Equation (A1).
II. Generation of rating matrix:
If the criterion is directly proportional to the goal (erosion sensitivity), ascending ordering must be completed, i.e., the alternative (sub-watershed) having the highest value for a criterion must be rated as first rank, the sub-watershed with the second-highest value must be rated as second rank, and so on.
If the criterion is inversely proportional to the goal (erosion sensitivity), descending ordering must be completed, i.e., the alternative (sub-watershed) having the lowest value for a criterion must be rated first, the sub-watershed with the second-lowest value must be rated second, and so on.
III. Calculating the compound values:

$$CF_i = \frac{1}{n}\sum_{j=1}^{n} R_i; \; i = 1, 2, \ldots, m \tag{A23}$$

where CF_i is the compound factor value (initial priority value) for the i-th alternative, R_i is the rating of alternatives, and n is the number of criteria. A lower CF_i value is of higher priority in the case of CF.

References

1. Machiwal, D.; Patel, A.; Kumar, S.; Naorem, A. Status and Challenges of Monitoring Soil Erosion in Croplands of Arid Regions. In *Soil Health and Environmental Sustainability: Application of Geospatial Technology*; Shit, P.K., Adhikary, P.P., Bhunia, G.S., Sengupta, D., Eds.; Environmental Science and Engineering; Springer International Publishing: Cham, Switzerland, 2022; pp. 163–192. ISBN 978-3-031-09270-1.
2. Patel, A.; Kushwaha, N.L.; Rajput, J.; Gautam, P.V. Advances in Micro-Irrigation Practices for Improving Water Use Efficiency in Dryland Agriculture. In *Enhancing Resilience of Dryland Agriculture under Changing Climate: Interdisciplinary and Convergence Approaches*; Naorem, A., Machiwal, D., Eds.; Springer Nature: Singapore, 2023; pp. 157–176. ISBN 978-981-19915-9-2.
3. Manivannan, S.; Thilagam, V.K.; Khola, O.P.S. Soil and Water Conservation in India: Strategies and Research Challenges. *J. Soil Water Conserv.* **2017**, *16*, 312. [CrossRef]
4. Patel, A.; Kethavath, A.; Kumar, M.; Rao, K.; Srinivasrao, C. Sustainable Land and Water Management for Reducing Soil Erosion in Tropical India. In *Agricultural Research, Technology and Policy: Innovations and Advances*; Srinivasrao, C., Balakrishnan, M., Krishnan, P., Sumanthkumar, V., Eds.; National Academy of Agricultural Research Management: Hyderabad, India, 2021; pp. 333–347. ISBN 978-93-5526-149-6.
5. Meshram, S.G.; Alvandi, E.; Meshram, C.; Kahya, E.; Fadhil Al-Quraishi, A.M. Application of SAW and TOPSIS in Prioritizing Watersheds. *Water Resour. Manag.* **2020**, *34*, 715–732. [CrossRef]
6. Weldu Woldemariam, G.; Edo Harka, A. Effect of Land Use and Land Cover Change on Soil Erosion in Erer Sub-Basin, Northeast Wabi Shebelle Basin, Ethiopia. *Land* **2020**, *9*, 111. [CrossRef]

7. Patel, A.; Kethavath, A.; Kushwaha, N.L.; Naorem, A.; Jagadale, M.; Sheetal, K.R.; Renjith, P.S. Review of Artificial Intelligence and Internet of Things Technologies in Land and Water Management Research during 1991–2021: A Bibliometric Analysis. *Eng. Appl. Artif. Intell.* **2023**, *123*, 106335. [CrossRef]
8. Arabameri, A.; Tiefenbacher, J.P.; Blaschke, T.; Pradhan, B.; Tien Bui, D. Morphometric Analysis for Soil Erosion Susceptibility Mapping Using Novel GIS-Based Ensemble Model. *Remote Sens.* **2020**, *12*, 874. [CrossRef]
9. Alexakis, D.D.; Hadjimitsis, D.G.; Agapiou, A. Integrated Use of Remote Sensing, GIS and Precipitation Data for the Assessment of Soil Erosion Rate in the Catchment Area of "Yialias" in Cyprus. *Atmos. Res.* **2013**, *131*, 108–124. [CrossRef]
10. Chopra, R.; Dhiman, R.D.; Sharma, P.K. Morphometric Analysis of Sub-Watersheds in Gurdaspur District, Punjab Using Remote Sensing and GIS Techniques. *J. Indian Soc. Remote Sens.* **2005**, *33*, 531–539. [CrossRef]
11. Wang, G.; Mang, S.; Cai, H.; Liu, S.; Zhang, Z.; Wang, L.; Innes, J.L. Integrated Watershed Management: Evolution, Development and Emerging Trends. *J. For. Res.* **2016**, *27*, 967–994. [CrossRef]
12. Wani, S.P.; Pathak, P.; Sreedevi, T.K.; Singh, H.P.; Singh, P. Efficient Management of Rainwater for Increased Crop Productivity and Groundwater Recharge in Asia. In *Water Productivity in Agriculture: Limits and Opportunities for Improvement*; Kijne, J.W., Barker, R., Molden, D.J., Eds.; CABI Publishing: Wallingford, UK, 2003; pp. 199–215.
13. Rezaei-Moghaddam, K.; Fatemi, M. The Network Analysis of Organizations in Watershed Management toward Sustainability in Northern Iran. *Front. Environ. Sci.* **2023**, *11*, 1078007. [CrossRef]
14. Malik, M.I.; Bhat, M.S.; Kuchay, N.A. Watershed Based Drainage Morphometric Analysis of Lidder Catchment in Kashmir Valley Using Geographical Information System. *Recent Res. Sci. Technol.* **2011**, *3*, 118–126.
15. Paul, I.I.; Bayode, E.N. Watershed Characteristics and Their Implication for Hydrologic Response in the Upper Sokoto Basin, Nigeria. *J. Geogr. Geol.* **2012**, *4*, 147. [CrossRef]
16. Rodrigo Comino, J.; Iserloh, T.; Lassu, T.; Cerdà, A.; Keestra, S.D.; Prosdocimi, M.; Brings, C.; Marzen, M.; Ramos, M.C.; Senciales, J.M.; et al. Quantitative Comparison of Initial Soil Erosion Processes and Runoff Generation in Spanish and German Vineyards. *Sci. Total Environ.* **2016**, *565*, 1165–1174. [CrossRef] [PubMed]
17. Sarkar, P.; Kumar, P.; Vishwakarma, D.K.; Ashok, A.; Elbeltagi, A.; Gupta, S.; Kuriqi, A. Watershed Prioritization Using Morphometric Analysis by MCDM Approaches. *Ecol. Inform.* **2022**, *70*, 101763. [CrossRef]
18. Strahler, A. Quantitative Geomorphology of Drainage Basins and Channel Networks. In *Handbook of Applied Hydrology*; Chow, V.T., Ed.; McGraw Hill: New York, NY, USA, 1964; pp. 439–476.
19. Faisal, R.M. GIS and MCDMA Prioritization Based Modeling for Sub-Watershed in Bastora River Basin. *Geocarto Int.* **2021**, *37*, 6826–6847. [CrossRef]
20. Yadav, S.K.; Dubey, A.; Szilard, S.; Singh, S.K. Prioritisation of Sub-Watersheds Based on Earth Observation Data of Agricultural Dominated Northern River Basin of India. *Geocarto Int.* **2018**, *33*, 339–356. [CrossRef]
21. Ahmed, R.; Sajjad, H.; Husain, I. Morphometric Parameters-Based Prioritization of Sub-Watersheds Using Fuzzy Analytical Hierarchy Process: A Case Study of Lower Barpani Watershed, India. *Nat. Resour. Res.* **2018**, *27*, 67–75. [CrossRef]
22. Bogale, A. Morphometric Analysis of a Drainage Basin Using Geographical Information System in Gilgel Abay Watershed, Lake Tana Basin, Upper Blue Nile Basin, Ethiopia. *Appl. Water Sci.* **2021**, *11*, 122. [CrossRef]
23. Nautiyal, M.D. Morphometric Analysis of a Drainage Basin Using Aerial Photographs: A Case Study of Khairkuli Basin, District Dehradun, U.P. *J. Indian Soc. Remote Sens.* **1994**, *22*, 251–261. [CrossRef]
24. Patel, A.; Ajaykumar, K.; Dhaloiya, A.; Rao, K.V.R.; Rajwade, Y.; Saxena, C.K. Application of Remote Sensing and Gis for Morphometric Analysis: A Case Study of Burhanpur Watershed. In *Surface and Groundwater Resources Development and Management in Semi-arid Region*; Pande, C.B., Kumar, M., Kushwaha, N.L., Eds.; Springer International Publishing: Cham, Switzerland, 2023; pp. 21–37. ISBN 978-3-031-29393-1.
25. Chatterjee, S.; Krishna, A.P.; Sharma, A.P. Geospatial Assessment of Soil Erosion Vulnerability at Watershed Level in Some Sections of the Upper Subarnarekha River Basin, Jharkhand, India. *Environ. Earth Sci.* **2014**, *71*, 357–374. [CrossRef]
26. Kushwaha, N.L.; Elbeltagi, A.; Patel, A.; Zakwan, M.; Rajput, J.; Sharma, P. Chapter 6—Assessment of Water Resources Using Remote Sensing and GIS Techniques. In *Current Directions in Water Scarcity Research*; Zakwan, M., Wahid, A., Niazkar, M., Chatterjee, U., Eds.; Water Resource Modeling and Computational Technologies; Elsevier: Amsterdam, The Netherlands, 2022; Volume 7, pp. 85–98.
27. Okumura, M.; Araujo, A.G.M. Long-Term Cultural Stability in Hunter–Gatherers: A Case Study Using Traditional and Geometric Morphometric Analysis of Lithic Stemmed Bifacial Points from Southern Brazil. *J. Archaeol. Sci.* **2014**, *45*, 59–71. [CrossRef]
28. Shekar, P.R.; Mathew, A. Evaluation of Morphometric and Hypsometric Analysis of the Bagh River Basin Using Remote Sensing and Geographic Information System Techniques. *Energy Nexus* **2022**, *7*, 100104. [CrossRef]
29. Khan, M.Y.A.; ElKashouty, M.; Subyani, A.M.; Tian, F. Morphometric Determination and Digital Geological Mapping by Rs and Gis Techniques in Aseer–Jazan Contact, Southwest Saudi Arabia. *Water* **2023**, *15*, 2438. [CrossRef]
30. Patel, A.; Jena, P.P.; Khatun, A.; Chatterjee, C. Improved Cartosat-1 Based DEM for Flood Inundation Modeling in the Delta Region of Mahanadi River Basin, India. *J. Indian Soc. Remote Sens.* **2022**, *50*, 1227–1241. [CrossRef]
31. Shaikh, M.; Yadav, S.; Manekar, V. Accuracy Assessment of Different Open-Source Digital Elevation Model through Morphometric Analysis for a Semi-Arid River Basin in the Western Part of India. *J. Geovisualization Spat. Anal.* **2021**, *5*, 23. [CrossRef]
32. Sharma, S.; Mahajan, A.K. GIS-Based Sub-Watershed Prioritization through Morphometric Analysis in the Outer Himalayan Region of India. *Appl. Water Sci.* **2020**, *10*, 163. [CrossRef]

33. Sakthivel, R.; Jawahar Raj, N.; Sivasankar, V.; Akhila, P.; Omine, K. Geo-Spatial Technique-Based Approach on Drainage Morphometric Analysis at Kalrayan Hills, Tamil Nadu, India. *Appl. Water Sci.* **2019**, *9*, 24. [CrossRef]
34. Ameri, A.A.; Pourghasemi, H.R.; Cerda, A. Erodibility Prioritization of Sub-Watersheds Using Morphometric Parameters Analysis and Its Mapping: A Comparison among TOPSIS, VIKOR, SAW, and CF Multi-Criteria Decision Making Models. *Sci. Total Environ.* **2018**, *613–614*, 1385–1400. [CrossRef]
35. Rahmati, O.; Samadi, M.; Shahabi, H.; Azareh, A.; Rafiei-Sardooi, E.; Alilou, H.; Melesse, A.M.; Pradhan, B.; Chapi, K.; Shirzadi, A. SWPT: An Automated GIS-Based Tool for Prioritization of Sub-Watersheds Based on Morphometric and Topo-Hydrological Factors. *Geosci. Front.* **2019**, *10*, 2167–2175. [CrossRef]
36. Meshram, S.G.; Tirivarombo, S.; Meshram, C.; Alvandi, E. Prioritization of Soil Erosion-Prone Sub-Watersheds Using Fuzzy-Based Multi-Criteria Decision-Making Methods in Narmada Basin Watershed, India. *Int. J. Environ. Sci. Technol.* **2023**, *20*, 1741–1752. [CrossRef]
37. Mahmoodi, E.; Azari, M.; Dastorani, M.T. Comparison of Different Objective Weighting Methods in a Multi-criteria Model for Watershed Prioritization for Flood Risk Assessment Using Morphometric Analysis. *J. Flood Risk Manag.* **2023**, *16*, e12894. [CrossRef]
38. Georgiou, D.; Mohammed, E.S.; Rozakis, S. Multi-Criteria Decision Making on the Energy Supply Configuration of Autonomous Desalination Units. *Renew. Energy* **2015**, *75*, 459–467. [CrossRef]
39. Govindan, K.; Jepsen, M.B. ELECTRE: A Comprehensive Literature Review on Methodologies and Applications. *Eur. J. Oper. Res.* **2016**, *250*, 1–29. [CrossRef]
40. Mulliner, E.; Malys, N.; Maliene, V. Comparative Analysis of MCDM Methods for the Assessment of Sustainable Housing Affordability. *Omega* **2016**, *59*, 146–156. [CrossRef]
41. Opricovic, S. Fuzzy VIKOR with an Application to Water Resources Planning. *Expert Syst. Appl.* **2011**, *38*, 12983–12990. [CrossRef]
42. Saaty, T.L. *The Analytic Hierarchy Process*; McGraw-Hill: New York, NY, USA, 1980.
43. Hwang, C.-L.; Yoon, K. Methods for Multiple Attribute Decision Making. In *Multiple Attribute Decision Making: Methods and Applications a State-of-the-Art Survey*; Hwang, C.-L., Yoon, K., Eds.; Lecture Notes in Economics and Mathematical Systems; Springer: Berlin/Heidelberg, Germany, 1981; pp. 58–191. ISBN 978-3-642-48318-9.
44. Opricovic, S.; Tzeng, G.-H. Compromise Solution by MCDM Methods: A Comparative Analysis of VIKOR and TOPSIS. *Eur. J. Oper. Res.* **2004**, *156*, 445–455. [CrossRef]
45. Hembram, T.K.; Saha, S. Prioritization of Sub-Watersheds for Soil Erosion Based on Morphometric Attributes Using Fuzzy AHP and Compound Factor in Jainti River Basin, Jharkhand, Eastern India. *Environ. Dev. Sustain.* **2020**, *22*, 1241–1268. [CrossRef]
46. Darji, K.; Patel, D.; Vakharia, V.; Panchal, J.; Dubey, A.K.; Gupta, P.; Singh, R.P. Watershed Prioritization and Decision-Making Based on Weighted Sum Analysis, Feature Ranking, and Machine Learning Techniques. *Arab. J. Geosci.* **2023**, *16*, 71. [CrossRef]
47. Raha, A.; Biswas, M.; Mukherjee, S. Application of TOPSIS Model in Active Tectonic Prioritization: Madeira Watershed, South America. *J. S. Am. Earth Sci.* **2023**, *129*, 104502. [CrossRef]
48. Ikram, R.M.A.; Meshram, S.G.; Hasan, M.A.; Cao, X.; Alvandi, E.; Meshram, C.; Islam, S. The Application of Multi-Attribute Decision Making Methods in Integrated Watershed Management. *Stoch. Environ. Res. Risk Assess.* **2023**. [CrossRef]
49. Biswas, B.; Ghosh, A.; Sailo, B.L. Spring Water Suitable and Vulnerable Watershed Demarcation Using AHP-TOPSIS and AHP-VIKOR Models: Study on Aizawl District of North-Eastern Hilly State of Mizoram, India. *Environ. Earth Sci.* **2023**, *82*, 80. [CrossRef]
50. Sarkar, P.; Sarma, U.S.; Gayen, S.K. Prioritization of Sub-Watersheds of Teesta River According to Soil Erosion Susceptibility Using Multi-Criteria Decision-Making in Sikkim and West Bengal. *Arab. J. Geosci.* **2023**, *16*, 398. [CrossRef]
51. Alilou, H.; Rahmati, O.; Singh, V.P.; Choubin, B.; Pradhan, B.; Keesstra, S.; Ghiasi, S.S.; Sadeghi, S.H. Evaluation of Watershed Health Using Fuzzy-ANP Approach Considering Geo-Environmental and Topo-Hydrological Criteria. *J. Environ. Manag.* **2019**, *232*, 22–36. [CrossRef] [PubMed]
52. Chandra, P.; Patel, P.L.; Porey, P.D. Prediction of Sediment Erosion Pattern in Upper Tapi Basin, India. *Curr. Sci.* **2016**, *110*, 1038–1049. [CrossRef]
53. Tukura, N.G.; Akalu, M.M.; Hussein, M.; Befekadu, A. Morphometric Analysis and Sub-Watershed Prioritization of Welmal Watershed, Ganale-Dawa River Basin, Ethiopia: Implications for Sediment Erosion. *J. Sediment. Environ.* **2021**, *6*, 121–130. [CrossRef]
54. Bharath, A.; Kumar, K.K.; Maddamsetty, R.; Manjunatha, M.; Tangadagi, R.B.; Preethi, S. Drainage Morphometry Based Sub-Watershed Prioritization of Kalinadi Basin Using Geospatial Technology. *Environ. Chall.* **2021**, *5*, 100277. [CrossRef]
55. Dali, N.; Ziouch, O.R.; Dali, H.; Daifallah, T.; Cherifa, B.; Sara, H. Remote Sensing, and (Gis) Approach, for Morphometric Assessment and Sub-Watershed Prioritization According to Soil Erosion and Groundwater Potential in an Endorheic Semi-Arid Area of Algeria. *Arab. J. Geosci.* **2023**, *16*, 95. [CrossRef]
56. Shelar, R.S.; Shinde, S.P.; Pande, C.B.; Moharir, K.N.; Orimoloye, I.R.; Mishra, A.P.; Varade, A.M. Sub-Watershed Prioritization of Koyna River Basin in India Using Multi Criteria Analytical Hierarchical Process, Remote Sensing and GIS Techniques. *Phys. Chem. Earth Parts ABC* **2022**, *128*, 103219. [CrossRef]
57. Schumm, S.A. Evaluation of Drainage System and Slopes in Badlands at Perth Amboy, New Jersey. *GSA Bull.* **1956**, *67*, 597–646. [CrossRef]

58. Horton, R.E. Erosional Development of Streams and Their Drainage Basins Hydrophysical Approach to Quantitative Morphology. *GSA Bull.* **1945**, *56*, 275–370. [CrossRef]
59. Horton, R.E. Drainage-Basin Characteristics. *Eos Trans. Am. Geophys. Union* **1932**, *13*, 350–361. [CrossRef]
60. Miller, V.C. *A Quantitative Geomorphic Study of Drainage Basin Characteristics in the Clinch Mountain Area, Virginia and Tennessee*; Department of Geology, Columbia University: New York, NY, USA, 1953; pp. 389–402.
61. Faniran, A. The Index of Drainage Intensity: A Provisional New Drainage Factor. *Aust J Sci* **1968**, *31*, 326–330.
62. Smith, K.G. Standards for Grading Texture of Erosional Topography. *Am. J. Sci.* **1950**, *248*, 655–668. [CrossRef]
63. Hadley, R.F.; Schumm, S.A. *Sediment Sources and Drainage Basin Characteristics in Upper Cheyenne River Basin*; US Geological Survey Water-Supply Paper 1531; US Geological Survey Water: Washingaton, DC, USA, 1961; 198p.
64. Chakrabortty, R.; Pal, S.C.; Chowdhuri, I.; Malik, S.; Das, B. Assessing the Importance of Static and Dynamic Causative Factors on Erosion Potentiality Using SWAT, EBF with Uncertainty and Plausibility, Logistic Regression and Novel Ensemble Model in a Sub-Tropical Environment. *J. Indian Soc. Remote Sens.* **2020**, *48*, 765–789. [CrossRef]
65. Patel, D.P.; Gajjar, C.A.; Srivastava, P.K. Prioritization of Malesari Mini-Watersheds through Morphometric Analysis: A Remote Sensing and GIS Perspective. *Environ. Earth Sci.* **2013**, *69*, 2643–2656. [CrossRef]
66. Saaty, T.L. How to Make a Decision: The Analytic Hierarchy Process. *Eur. J. Oper. Res.* **1990**, *48*, 9–26. [CrossRef]
67. Triantaphyllou, E.; Mann, S. Using the Analytic Hierarchy Process for Decision Making in Engineering Applications: Some Challenges. *Int. J. Ind. Eng. Appl. Pract.* **1995**, *2*, 35–44.
68. Yadav, B.; Malav, L.C.; Jiménez-Ballesta, R.; Kumawat, C.; Patra, A.; Patel, A.; Jangir, A.; Nogiya, M.; Meena, R.L.; Moharana, P.C.; et al. Modeling and Assessment of Land Degradation Vulnerability in Arid Ecosystem of Rajasthan Using Analytical Hierarchy Process and Geospatial Techniques. *Land* **2022**, *12*, 106. [CrossRef]
69. Aoki, K.; Uehara, M.; Kato, C.; Hirahara, H. Evaluation of Rugby Players' Psychological-Competitive Ability by Utilizing the Analytic Hierarchy Process. *Open J. Soc. Sci.* **2016**, *4*, 103–117. [CrossRef]
70. Huang, J.-J.; Tzeng, G.-H.; Liu, H.-H. A Revised VIKOR Model for Multiple Criteria Decision Making—The Perspective of Regret Theory. In Proceedings of the Cutting-Edge Research Topics on Multiple Criteria Decision Making; Shi, Y., Wang, S., Peng, Y., Li, J., Zeng, Y., Eds.; Springer: Berlin/Heidelberg, Germany, 2009; pp. 761–768.
71. Sanayei, A.; Farid Mousavi, S.; Yazdankhah, A. Group Decision Making Process for Supplier Selection with VIKOR under Fuzzy Environment. *Expert Syst. Appl.* **2010**, *37*, 24–30. [CrossRef]
72. Ma, J.; Fan, Z.-P.; Huang, L.-H. A Subjective and Objective Integrated Approach to Determine Attribute Weights. *Eur. J. Oper. Res.* **1999**, *112*, 397–404. [CrossRef]
73. Liou, T.-S.; Wang, M.-J.J. Ranking Fuzzy Numbers with Integral Value. *Fuzzy Sets Syst.* **1992**, *50*, 247–255. [CrossRef]
74. Wenye, L.; Jinpeng, Y.; Xiaoping, G.; Yachao, L.; Dongming, X.; Guoqi, L.; Fan, Y.; Wei, Z.; Qingmin, G. Effects of Ecological Restoration Modes on Runoff and Erosion Reduction and Vegetation Restoration of Waste Dump Slopes in Lingwu. *J. Resour. Ecol.* **2023**, *14*, 822–832. [CrossRef]
75. El-Santawy, M.F. A VIKOR Method for Solving Personnel Training Selection Problem. *Int. J. Comput. Sci.* **2012**, *1*, 9–12.
76. Todorovski, L.; Džeroski, S. Integrating Knowledge-Driven and Data-Driven Approaches to Modeling. *Ecol. Model.* **2006**, *194*, 3–13. [CrossRef]
77. Farhan, Y. Morphometric Assessment of Wadi Wala Watershed, Southern Jordan Using ASTER (DEM) and GIS. *J. Geogr. Inf. Syst.* **2017**, *9*, 158–190. [CrossRef]
78. Abdeta, G.C.; Tesemma, A.B.; Tura, A.L.; Atlabachew, G.H. Morphometric Analysis for Prioritizing Sub-Watersheds and Management Planning and Practices in Gidabo Basin, Southern Rift Valley of Ethiopia. *Appl. Water Sci.* **2020**, *10*, 158. [CrossRef]
79. Altaf, S.; Meraj, G.; Romshoo, S.A. Morphometry and Land Cover Based Multi-Criteria Analysis for Assessing the Soil Erosion Susceptibility of the Western Himalayan Watershed. *Environ. Monit. Assess.* **2014**, *186*, 8391–8412. [CrossRef]
80. Athawale, V.M.; Chakraborty, S. A Comparative Study on the Ranking Performance of Some Multi-Criteria Decision-Making Methods for Industrial Robot Selection. *Int. J. Ind. Eng. Comput.* **2011**, *2*, 831–850. [CrossRef]
81. Raju, K.S.; Duckstein, L.; Arondel, C. Multicriterion Analysis for Sustainable Water Resources Planning: A Case Study in Spain. *Water Resour. Manag.* **2000**, *14*, 435–456. [CrossRef]
82. Gibbons, J.D.; Chakraborti, S. *Nonparametric Statistical Inference: Revised and Expanded*, 4th ed.; CRC Press: Boca Raton, FL, USA, 2003; ISBN 978-0-203-91156-3.
83. Balasubramanian, A.; Duraisamy, K.; Thirumalaisamy, S.; Krishnaraj, S.; Yatheendradasan, R.K. Prioritization of Subwatersheds Based on Quantitative Morphometric Analysis in Lower Bhavani Basin, Tamil Nadu, India Using DEM and GIS Techniques. *Arab. J. Geosci.* **2017**, *10*, 552. [CrossRef]
84. Thor, J.; Ding, S.-H.; Kamaruddin, S. Comparison of Multi Criteria Decision Making Methods from the Maintenance Alternative Selection Perspective. *Int. J. Eng. Sci.* **2013**, *2*, 27–34.
85. Pimentel, D.; Burgess, M. Soil Erosion Threatens Food Production. *Agriculture* **2013**, *3*, 443–463. [CrossRef]
86. Gajbhiye, S.; Mishra, S.K.; Pandey, A. Prioritizing Erosion-Prone Area through Morphometric Analysis: An RS and GIS Perspective. *Appl. Water Sci.* **2014**, *4*, 51–61. [CrossRef]
87. Nooka Ratnam, K.; Srivastava, Y.K.; Venkateswara Rao, V.; Amminedu, E.; Murthy, K.S.R. Check Dam Positioning by Prioritization of Micro-Watersheds Using SYI Model and Morphometric Analysis—Remote Sensing and GIS Perspective. *J. Indian Soc. Remote Sens.* **2005**, *33*, 25–38. [CrossRef]

88. Aher, P.D.; Adinarayana, J.; Gorantiwar, S.D.; Sawant, S.A. Information System for Integrated Watershed Management Using Remote Sensing and GIS. In *Remote Sensing Applications in Environmental Research*; Srivastava, P.K., Mukherjee, S., Gupta, M., Islam, T., Eds.; Society of Earth Scientists Series; Springer International Publishing: Cham, Switzerland, 2014; pp. 17–34. ISBN 978-3-319-05906-8.
89. Farhan, Y.; Anaba, O. A Remote Sensing and GIS Approach for Prioritization of Wadi Shueib Mini-Watersheds (Central Jordan) Based on Morphometric and Soil Erosion Susceptibility Analysis. *J. Geogr. Inf. Syst.* **2016**, *8*, 1–19. [CrossRef]
90. Rahaman, S.A.; Ajeez, S.A.; Aruchamy, S.; Jegankumar, R. Prioritization of Sub Watershed Based on Morphometric Characteristics Using Fuzzy Analytical Hierarchy Process and Geographical Information System—A Study of Kallar Watershed, Tamil Nadu. *Aquat. Procedia* **2015**, *4*, 1322–1330. [CrossRef]
91. Pourghasemi, H.R.; Honarmandnejad, F.; Rezaei, M.; Tarazkar, M.H.; Sadhasivam, N. Prioritization of Water Erosion–Prone Sub-Watersheds Using Three Ensemble Methods in Qareaghaj Catchment, Southern Iran. *Environ. Sci. Pollut. Res.* **2021**, *28*, 37894–37917. [CrossRef]
92. Adhami, M.; Sadeghi, S.H. Sub-Watershed Prioritization Based on Sediment Yield Using Game Theory. *J. Hydrol.* **2016**, *541*, 977–987. [CrossRef]
93. Mendoza, G.A.; Martins, H. Multi-Criteria Decision Analysis in Natural Resource Management: A Critical Review of Methods and New Modelling Paradigms. *For. Ecol. Manag.* **2006**, *230*, 1–22. [CrossRef]
94. Janssen, J.A.E.B.; Krol, M.S.; Schielen, R.M.J.; Hoekstra, A.Y.; de Kok, J.-L. Assessment of Uncertainties in Expert Knowledge, Illustrated in Fuzzy Rule-Based Models. *Ecol. Model.* **2010**, *221*, 1245–1251. [CrossRef]
95. Jhariya, D.C.; Kumar, T.; Pandey, H.K. Watershed Prioritization Based on Soil and Water Hazard Model Using Remote Sensing, Geographical Information System and Multi-Criteria Decision Analysis Approach. *Geocarto Int.* **2020**, *35*, 188–208. [CrossRef]
96. Şengül, Ü.; Eren, M.; Eslamian Shiraz, S.; Gezder, V.; Şengül, A.B. Fuzzy TOPSIS Method for Ranking Renewable Energy Supply Systems in Turkey. *Renew. Energy* **2015**, *75*, 617–625. [CrossRef]

Disclaimer/Publisher's Note: The statements, opinions and data contained in all publications are solely those of the individual author(s) and contributor(s) and not of MDPI and/or the editor(s). MDPI and/or the editor(s) disclaim responsibility for any injury to people or property resulting from any ideas, methods, instructions or products referred to in the content.

Article

Implementation of HydroBID Model with Satellite-Based Precipitation Products in Guadalquivir Basin, Bolivia

Oliver Saavedra [1,*], Jhonatan Ureña [1] and Moisés Perales [2]

1. Centro de Investigaciones en Ingeniería Civil y Ambiental, Universidad Privada Boliviana (UPB), Cochabamba 3967, Bolivia; jhonatanurena@upb.edu
2. Centro de Investigación del Agua, Universidad Autónoma Juan Misael Saracho, Tarija 0000, Bolivia; moisesperales@uajms.edu.bo
* Correspondence: oliversaavedra@upb.edu

Abstract: The use of distributed precipitation data in hydrological models is critically important to simulate processes at a micro-basin scale. However, aerial precipitation at a high resolution is required to run these models. This study aimed to set up the HydroBID tool in the Guadalquivir River basin using satellite-based precipitation products. The employed products included GSMaP gauge version 6, interpolated rain gauges using Kriging, the combined GS product for Bolivia, and the proposed combined product for the Guadalquivir basin. The GS Guadalquivir was generated by combining the satellite-based product GSMaP gauge version 6 with the local rain gauge network. The main difference with GS Bolivia is the improvement of the resolution from 5 km to 250 m. An iteration scheme using 230 micro-basins was employed, reaching a correlation of 0.98 compared to the control dataset. By using the hydrological model with the precipitation products, the daily river discharge was obtained, showing a high correlation of 0.99 and efficiency of 0.96 in relation to observed data between 2000 and 2016 at Obrajes station. Simulated flows with Kriging and GS Guadalquivir products presented similarly high correlations compared to the observed flows. In the case of GSMaP and GS Bolivia, these products showed general underestimations of the simulated flows, reaching correlations between 0.28 and 0.91, respectively. Moreover, annual volumes were analyzed, where the overestimation of GSMaP, Kriging, and GS Guadalquivir showed similar characteristics concerning the distribution of specific river discharges and volumes. Therefore, HydroBID appeared to be a feasible tool with enough adaptability to use distributed precipitation and simulate flows at a micro-basin scale. Therefore, we recommend applying this scheme to other basins to carry out analysis of events, water balance, and floods and similar studies.

Keywords: Guadalquivir basin; HydroBID; rain gauge; distributed precipitation; Bolivia

Citation: Saavedra, O.; Ureña, J.; Perales, M. Implementation of HydroBID Model with Satellite-Based Precipitation Products in Guadalquivir Basin, Bolivia. *Water* **2023**, *15*, 3250. https://doi.org/10.3390/w15183250

Academic Editors: Momcilo Markus, Venkat Sridhar, Ankur Srivastava and Nikul Kumari

Received: 31 May 2023
Revised: 17 August 2023
Accepted: 4 September 2023
Published: 13 September 2023

Copyright: © 2023 by the authors. Licensee MDPI, Basel, Switzerland. This article is an open access article distributed under the terms and conditions of the Creative Commons Attribution (CC BY) license (https://creativecommons.org/licenses/by/4.0/).

1. Introduction

Hydrological modeling analyzes the water sources contributing to a hydrological unit within a specified period while simplifying the physical characteristics of the hydrological unit. Depending on how the data are input and the spatial characteristics being considered, models can be categorized as lumped, semi-distributed, and distributed [1].

Lumped models offer advantages in studies with limited information. The mathematical equations governing these scenarios are not linked to the physical characteristics of the catchment watershed; rather, they are solely functions of time. Lumped models exhibit higher performance efficiency based on the available data. Some lumped models include the Sacramento Soil Moisture Accounting (SAC-SMA) model, the McMaster University-Hydrologiska Byråns Vattenbalansavdelning (MAC-HBV) model, SMARG, the *modèle du Génie Rural à 4 paramètres Journalier* (GR4J), and the Hydrologic Engineering Center Hydrologic Modeling System (HEC-HMS) [2].

Distributed models consider the spatial heterogeneity of precipitation data. Semi-distributed models view hydrological units as arrangements of discretized sub-units that are internally homogeneous within a given hydrological unit [3]. These models find application in various studies, including climate change analysis with an improved three-parameter hydrological model in Zhejiang Province, China [1], the implementation of the Xinanjiang model to analyze flood frequency [4], and analysis of hydrological forecasting to predict climate change effects in the Naryn River basin [5].

Several studies have reported on hydrological model applications in Bolivia. the two significant works are the editions of *Balance Hídrico Superfical de Bolivia (BHSB)* published in 2016 and 2018. The *BHSB 2016* looked at the period from 1998 to 2011, using precipitation data from the National Meteorological and Hydrological Service (SENAMHI) and the Tropical Rainfall Measuring Mission (TRMM) and employing the Témez hydrological model [6]. The *BHSB 2018* considered a longer and updated period, 1980–2016. It also included the Climate Hazards Group InfraRed Precipitation with Station (CHIRPS) data and used the Water Evaluation and Planning System (WEAP) tool developed by the Stockholm Environment Institute (SEI) [7]. The use of numerical hydrological models has become increasingly popular in Bolivia.

The Guadalquivir basin, located in the southern part of Bolivia, has been prioritized by the Environment and Water Ministry (MMAyA, *Ministerio de Medio Ambiente y Agua* in Spanish) as a key basin within its master plan for hydrological analysis and water balance. Consequently, the Guadalquivir basin was analyzed with studies that employ different hydrological models. In 2016, a water balance was developed that considers a climate change analysis with the WEAP model [8]. In 2018, the Swiss Cooperation Office in Bolivia, in collaboration with the departmental government of Tarija, developed a study to design water maps indicating water use and availability and employing a multiple linear regression model [9]. These maps form part of the master plan of the Guadalquivir basin of 2022 where the WEAP tool was updated [10].

So far in Bolivia, WEAP and HEC-HMS are the most popular software packages for hydrological modeling. WEAP is a modeling and planning tool for water distribution whose parameters include the types of land use, soil types, climate data (precipitation and temperature), wind, and demands on water supply [11]. Other parameters are appropriate for other study themes, such as water supply and demand, rules of operation, usage rights, and water quality in terms of organic contamination [12]. Particularly in Bolivia, WEAP has been used for analysis of hydroelectric sources, national hydro-ecological monitoring [13], analysis of climate change in the Katari basin [14], policy development for water-resource management in the Rocha River basin [12], and socioeconomic analysis for crop optimization in the Bolivian Andes [15].

The Hydrologic Engineering Center (HEC) developed different simulation models. The HEC-HMS mentioned earlier and the River Analysis System (RAS) are analysis-oriented models for continuous precipitation and storm scenarios, respectively. Like other hydrological models, the HEC-HMS requires data, such as information about climate, land use, soil type, and so on, and utilizes different methodologies to process them. For example, in the case of land use, the Soil Conservation Service Curve Number (SCS-CN), Soil Moisture Accounting (SMA), Green and Ampt (GA), and Deficit and Constant (D.C.) are alternatives [16]. These applications include the analysis of digital elevation models based on the management of the Colorado River [17], flood and landslide analysis in Cochabamba, [18] and the employment of HEC-RAS and the analysis of satellite precipitation products and combined products [19] and hourly continuous modeling analysis [20] using HEC-HMS in the Rocha River basin.

The *Banco Interamericano de Desarrollo* (BID), within its Latin America and Caribbean water resources and climate change program, sponsored the development of the Hydro-BID tool [21]. This tool allows hydrological and climate change analysis to estimate the availability of fresh water. This modeling system is based on runoff by the Generalized Watershed Loading Functions (GWLFs). In contrast to the WEAP and HEC hydrological models, HydroBID integrates a database of land use and soil type, hydrological units, and river courses at the Latin America and Caribbean level. Moreover, HydroBID uses an analysis of the sources of precipitation and temperature, allowing, through an inverse distance weighted (IDW) interpolation, the assignment of a unique value to each of the hydrological units that make up the study basin.

The applications of the HydroBID tool have led to a limited number of studies in Latin America. These showed how HydroBID was applied at different sizes of basins, including climate change scenarios, in order to assess potential changes in precipitation and temperature. First, the management of water resources in the Rio Grande basin, Argentina, was carried out. The overestimation of flow peaks was noticed, but there was an underestimation of baseflow [22,23]. Second, in the Peru Piura River basin advantage was taken of a historical dataset to calibrate the model [24]. Third, also in Peru, at the Chancay-Lambayeque basin, potential impacts of El Niño events on sediment loading were assessed [25]. Fourth, in northern Argentina, the Bermejo River basin was modeled [26]. Fifth, in Ecuador, at the Chalpi basin, water investments considering climate change were performed with the aid of HydroBID [27]. Another case study is the Guali River basin in Colombia. In this one, HydroBID was employed as a tool that enabled fundamental hydrological modeling, which was subsequently used in other models such as WEAP. For this purpose, rainfall stations around the study basin were utilized [28]. Most of them focused on climate change scenarios analysis, but none of them explored the merit of the precipitation pattern utilizing satellite-based products. Additionally, the simulation periods in this study, 2000–2016, were more updated than previous reported applications of HydroBID, and, particularly, an application of HydroBID in Bolivia was not reported yet.

HydroBID can be categorized as a semi-distributed model, with precipitation being considered the most important hydrological variable. In the case of Bolivia, the presence of the rain gauge is found closer to capital cities. Moreover, the database provided by these stations may be affected by periods without records or equipment malfunctions that impact their functioning [29]. However, satellite-based precipitation (SBP) measurement products are an alternative for developing studies of ungauged areas. However, despite presenting comprehensive databases, they only allow for an estimation of the actual precipitation value. For example, GSMaP in Bolivia exhibits a daily precipitation correlation of 0.59 and an efficiency of 0.8 with the local rain gauge network. Then, another alternative was considered, the usage of a combination of the rain gauge database with an SBP product. The results present a considerable improvement compared to initial SBP products with further potential in the development of hydrological studies [30]. However, the spatial resolution of this study can be a constraint for micro-basin analysis. Normally, micro-basins are considered with watershed areas of less than 100 km^2 where most of the decision making is required.

The objective of this study is to explore the capabilities of the HydroBID model when combined with satellite-based precipitation products at a micro-basin scale to better understand hydrological processes and support decision making.

2. Materials and Method

2.1. Study Area

The Guadalquivir River basin is located in the department of Tarija, in southern Bolivia. The basin has an area of 3342 km^2, equivalent to 9% of the area of the whole department. The basin has a population of 294,000, encompassing the 51% departmental population. The Guadalquivir basin has elevations between 1600 and 4600 m above sea level [10], presenting two of the national ecological steps, highlands and valleys, with the latter predominating, as can be seen in Figure 1. The basin was divided into 230 micro-basins obtained from the HydroBID database.

In terms of climatic conditions, the basin shows precipitation between 580 and 840 mm/year, with the highest values occurring at the south of the basin. The average temperatures are between 9 °C and 19 °C, with the highest values in the central part of the basin. These data came from the BHSB database [7]. In Figure 2, the precipitation and temperature distribution maps for the study area can be seen.

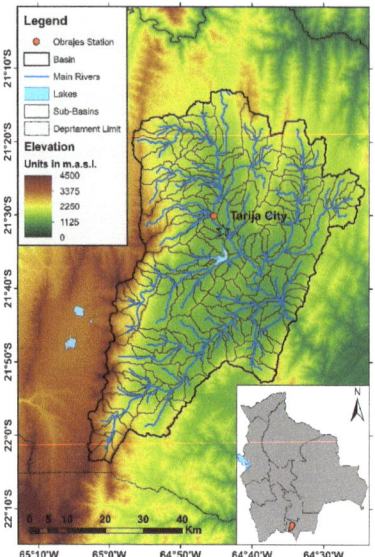

Figure 1. Location map of Tarija city within Guadalquivir River basin, in southern Bolivia.

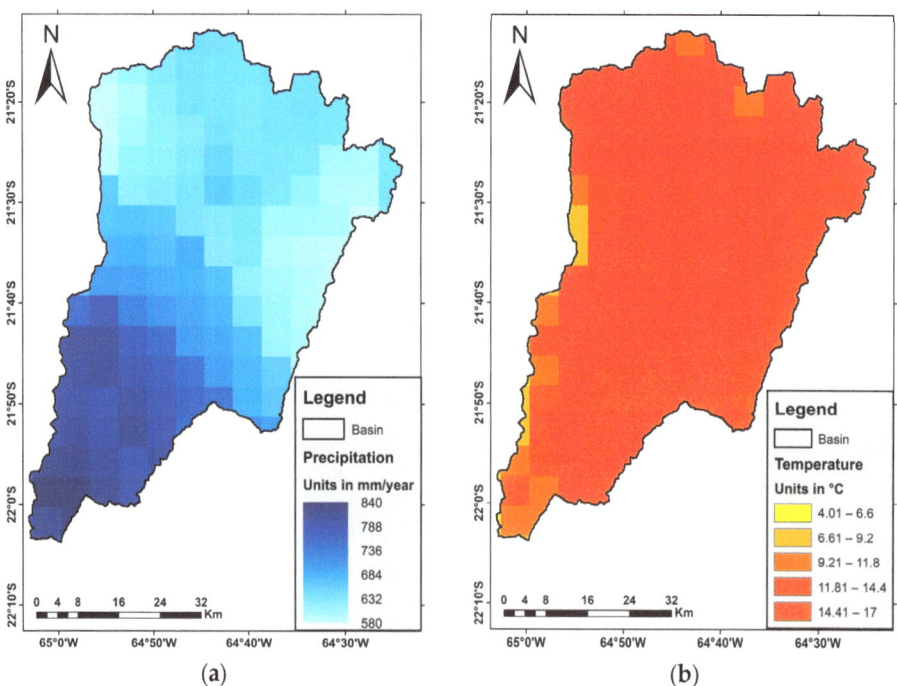

Figure 2. Average annual meteorological maps for the period 2001–2016 in Guadalquivir basin for (**a**) precipitation and (**b**) temperature, with rain gauge data interpolation.

Challenges to the basin include water supply, climate change, and pollution. Tarija city, the capital of the department, is located within the basin. Twenty-five percent of the population within the basin experience water-shortage problems. Shortages can equate to

70% of water need. Pollution is the result of the urban and industrial activities of different communities and the city located in the watershed [10]. Finally, heavy metal has been found to be present in a few streams. Lead, iron, and manganese are consequences of mineralogical activity, which has also led to desertification in some zones of the basin [31]. However, studies have been conducted to evaluate treatment methods for the heavy metals, for example, the implementation of reverse osmosis [32].

2.2. Methodology

2.2.1. HydroBID Model

HydroBID model employs the GWLF runoff model. This model uses a micro-basin system and considers land use and soil type for an individual unit analysis. With the HydroBID model, the flow is generated for each micro-basin in the analysis.

This model already has a database prepared for different hydrological variables such as land use, soil types and curve number. Another database included in HydroBID is the Analytical Hydrological Database (AHD), which includes delineated micro-basins and a hydrological network for Latin America and the Caribbean.

Because of this, the model mainly requires the introduction of climatological variables and observed flow data to perform the calibration and validation of the parameters [21]. Figure 3 shows the methodology used by HydroBID in order to generate flows using the precipitation products.

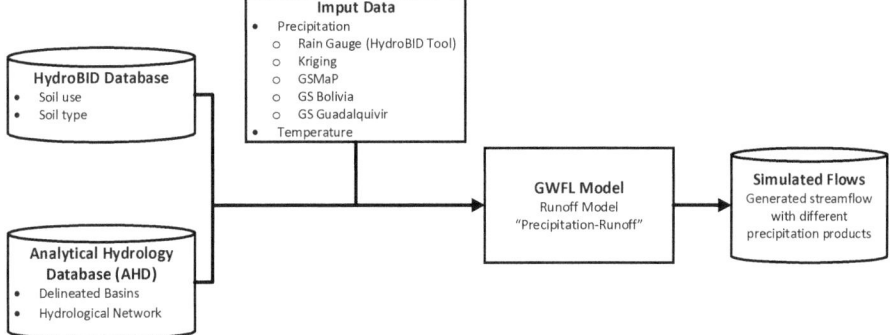

Figure 3. HydroBID flowchart for hydrological modelling using different precipitation inputs.

The flow simulation can be slightly adjusted by the management of four parameters. The Curve Number (CN) allows characterizing the type of land use and representing the hydrology in the soil. A CN value is assigned at each micro-basin. This parameter within the HydroBID can be changed by including a multiplier. The default multiplier value of this parameter is 0.8. The Available Water Content (AWC) indicates the beginning of the percolation process and estimates the amount of water that can be stored in the soil to be used by plants, affecting the infiltration directed to groundwater. Like the previous parameter, the modification of this parameter can be performed using a multiplier. The default value is 1. The Recession Coefficient "r" characterizes the contribution of groundwater near the surface to river flows after a flood event and controls the rate of groundwater flow in the saturated zone. This parameter needs to be entered numerically. The default value is 0.008. Finally, the Percolation Coefficient "s" controls the rate of percolation into the deep groundwater aquifer. The default value is 0.005.

The generated streamflow was evaluated at Obrajes station located at the outlet of the Alta del Guadalquivir basin, see red spot in Figure 4a. Then, the adjusted parameters were used as representative for the whole basin.

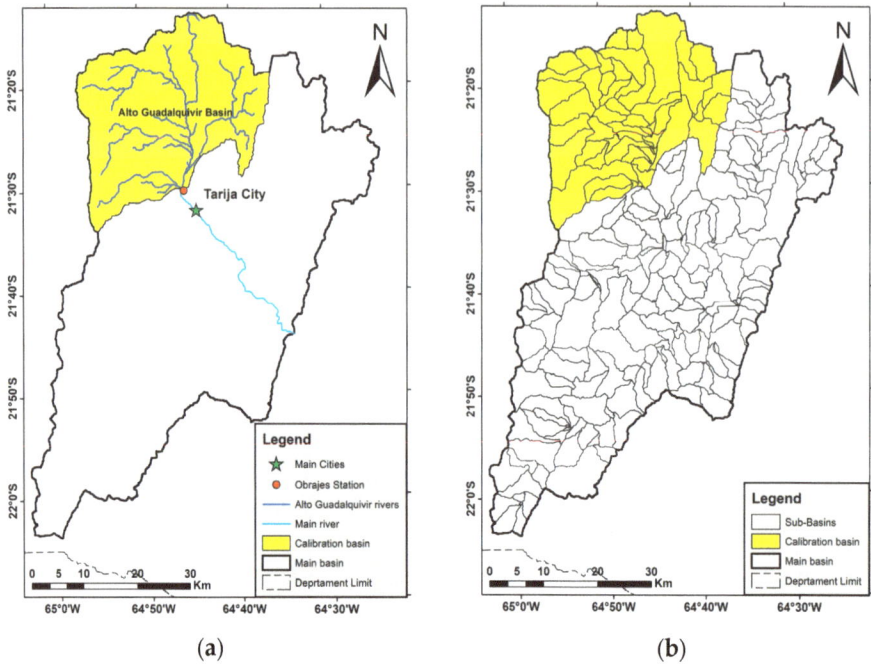

Figure 4. (**a**) Alto Guadalquivir basin, Obrajes station and Tarija city; (**b**) Micro-basins with average of 15 km² in Guadalquivir River basin.

In this study, the calibration period was set as between 1/1/1980 and 12/31/1999 and a validation period was set as between 1/1/2000 and 12/31/2014. Figure 4 shows the area of contribution to the Alto Guadalquivir basin with reference to the whole basin, and in Figure 4b the micro-basins are depicted.

The calibration process was carried out with trial and error. Actually, the sensitivity of parameters was analyzed. In this sense, the maximum and minimum values of the different parameters were used (see the left columns in Table 1). Initially, only one parameter was changed at a time, while keeping the default value for the rest. Moreover, statistical indicators, such as Nash and Sutcliffe efficiency and variance in relation to observed data, were included to analyze the simulated streamflow. Then, another parameter's value was tried. The parameter that displays the greatest sensitivity in efficiency is the curve number, affecting the peak flows, which define infiltration rates. The parameter that generates the highest statistical variability compared to the observed data is the Available Water Content, impacting the base flow and exhibiting errors ranging from −55.9% to 43.3%.

Table 1. HydroBID's parameter ranges for the contributing area down to Obrajes station.

Parameter	Values		Nash and Sutcliffe Efficiency		Variance (%)	
	Min	Max	Min	Max	Min	Max
Curve Number (CN)	0.1	1	0.1	−3.5	−23.8	12.6
Available Water Content (AWC)	0.1	2	−0.5	−0.8	43.3	−55.9
Recession Coefficient	0.0001	0.01	−1.3	−0.5	−13.3	−14.9
Percolation Coefficient	0.0001	0.01	−0.7	−0.5	22.1	−40.7

Within the sensitivity analysis, various combinations were tested to obtain simulated flows against the observed ones. As a result of the calibration process, the selected parameter values are compared to the default values (see Table 2).

Table 2. Default and calibrated parameters for Obrajes basin.

Parameters	Default	Calibrated
Curve Number (CN)	0.8	0.46
Available Water Content (AWC)	1	0.1
Recession Coefficient	0.008	0.006
Percolation Coefficient	0.005	0.008

Based on these parameters, the hydrological modeling of the basin was carried out, obtaining the following hydrographs for calibration (Figure 5a) and validation (Figure 5b) for the periods 1980–1999 and 2000–2014, respectively.

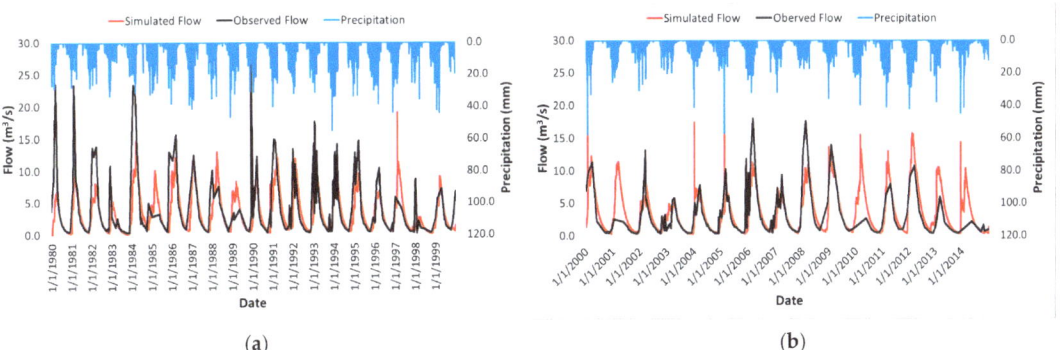

Figure 5. Hydrographs for (a) calibration and (b) validation in the Obrajes station.

With these simulation values, we proceeded to obtain statistical indicators to determine the proximity between the simulated and observed values. These values are presented in Table 3. Correlation coefficients of 0.709 and 0.744 were obtained for the calibration and validation stages, respectively. The efficiency values were found to be between 0.474 and 0.481, indicating an acceptable approximation in relation to individual observed flows in the station.

Table 3. Statistic indicators for calibration and validation process in Alto Guadalquivir basin.

Statistic Indicators	Calibration	Validation
Determination Coefficient (R2)	0.503	0.554
Correlation Coefficient (R)	0.709	0.744
Mean Absolute Error (MAE)	1.846	1.447
Root Mean Square Error (RMSE)	3.230	2.428
Nash and Sutcliffe Efficiency (NSE)	0.474	0.481
Variation (%)	−14.21	13.5

2.2.2. Precipitation Data

In the Guadalquivir basin, there are a total of 77 rain gauges. However, the database of these rain gauges presents discontinuous records for 55 stations, meaning that only 22 stations showed complete records. Due to this limitation, the satellite-based precipitation products were used as an alternative in this study.

The management of climatological data is one of the most important aspects of HydroBID. The model allows for the introduction of climatological data in a timely manner through an interpolation method. Specifically, the IDW method is used to obtain a representative value for each sub-basin of the database. To achieve this, a variable allows for the consideration of the number of stations to carry out the IDW interpolation. In the case of the Guadalquivir basin, three stations were used for each micro-basin. The precipitation and temperature values employed in this interpolation process correspond to the values used in the available rain gauge network from *BSHB 2018* [7].

However, in the event of a lack of rain gauges, satellite-based products can be used to keep the precipitation pattern. Since these products have different spatial resolutions, a treatment prior to its inclusion in the HydroBID model is needed.

First, the IDW interpolation method, used by HydroBID as the default approach for generating climatological data for micro-basins, was compared with the Kriging method, which was employed in other studies for precipitation data analysis [33]. This product has a daily temporal resolution and a spatial resolution of 0.0025° (approx. 250 m).

The satellite product GSMaP.v6_Gauge was selected as the distributed precipitation product to be used. This product was developed by the Japan Aerospace Exploration Agency (JAXA). The product employs micro-wave and infrared sensors to capture information. This product presents a database from March of 2000 to the current date. GSMaP presents different temporal resolutions: hourly, daily, and monthly. In the case of spatial resolution, the product presents a grid of 0.1° (approx. 10 km). For the case of this study, the product with an hourly temporal resolution was selected, and then it was aggregated daily based on the time difference between Bolivia and the initial data capture zone.

Additionally, the combined precipitation product GS Bolivia was selected to be included in the study. According to Saavedra and Ureña (2022), GS was generated using an iterative methodology that applied the relative error to combined rain gauge and GSMaP data. The product has a daily temporal resolution and spatial temporal resolution of 0.05° (approx. 5 km).

When comparing the GSMaP and GS Bolivia products in the La Plata basin, correlations of 0.33 and 0.98 were observed, respectively. This indicates a significant improvement compared to the original satellite product [30].

However, the spatial resolution of GS Bolivia is 5 km, causing a loss of precision based on the information at the Guadalquivir basin. To improve this limitation, a new version of the GS product was created, adjusting to the defined 230 micro-basins and a spatial resolution of 250 m. The combination methodology proposed by Saavedra and Ureña (2022) was used, consisting of a combination of daily rain gauge data and a satellite-based precipitation measurement product through an iterative generation methodology. This method uses a correction coefficient based on the relative error at each micro-basin. In the case of the Guadalquivir basin, five iterations were needed to reach convergence. Figure 6 shows the average daily precipitation of the four mentioned products.

The default rain gauge precipitation data generated by HydroBID presents a great resemblance to the precipitation data generated with Kriging interpolation. In Figure 7, the precipitation data obtained using Kriging shows a slight difference at the high values compared to the precipitation data interpolated by IDW from HydroBID.

In the case of satellite-based precipitation products, GSMaP presents a general underestimation in the period 2000–2014. However, during the periods from 09/2002 to 12/2003 and from 03/2015 to 06/2016, it shows several overestimations. In contrast, the GS Bolivia data displays a general underestimation throughout the study period. As for GS Guadalquivir, the precipitation closely resembles the IDW interpolation by HydroBID. These patterns can be seen in Figure 8.

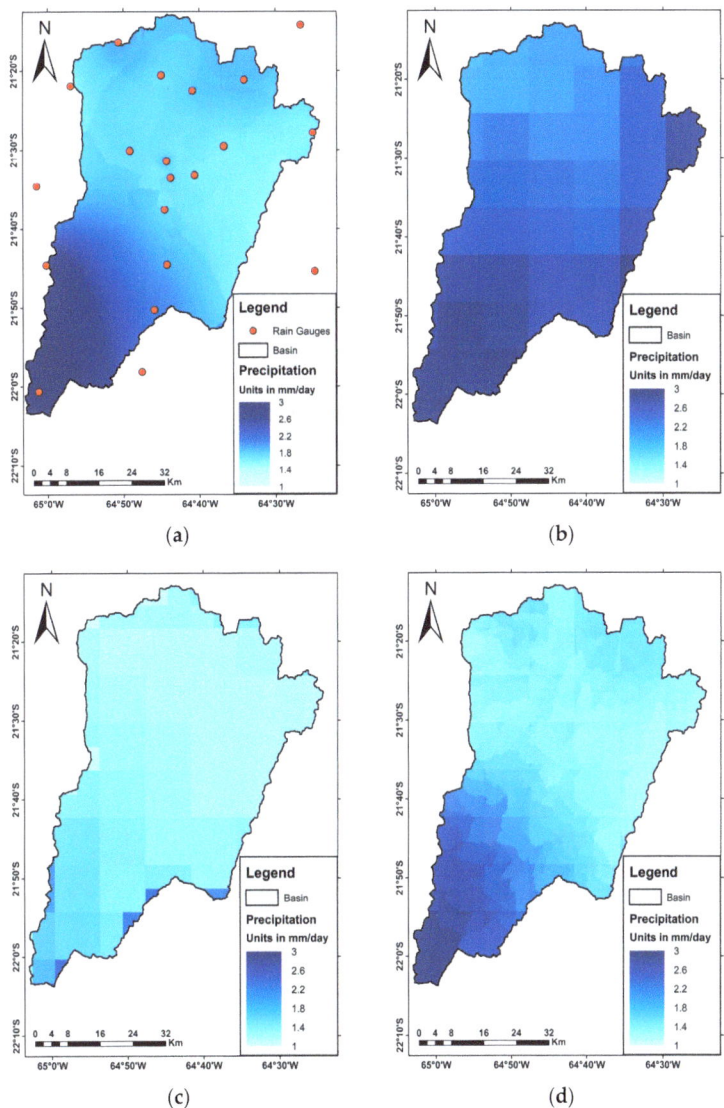

Figure 6. Guadalquivir precipitation daily map for the period 2001–2015: (**a**) Kriging interpolation, (**b**) GSMaP.v6_Gauge, (**c**) GS Bolivia, and (**d**) GS Guadalquivir.

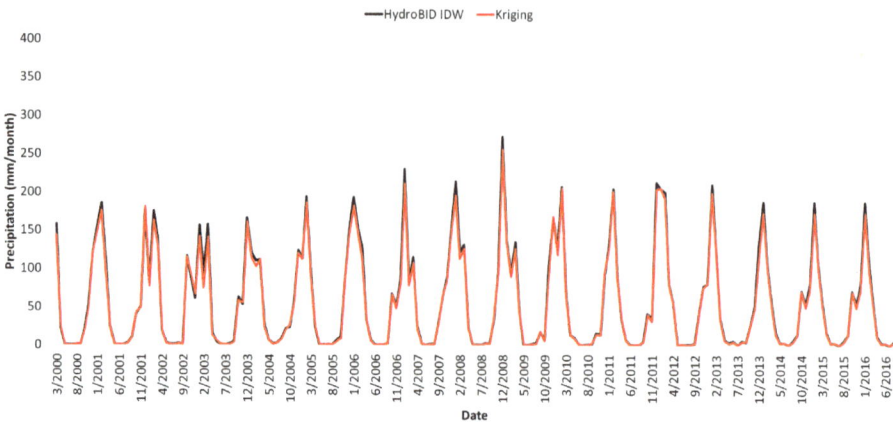

Figure 7. Time series of monthly precipitation from interpolated rain gauge products for the period 2000–2016.

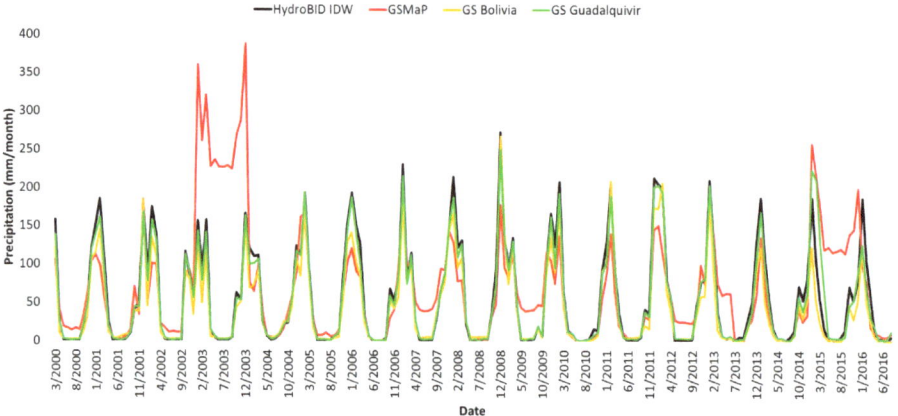

Figure 8. Time series of monthly precipitation for rain satellite-based products for the period 2000–2016.

Moreover, a statistical analysis was carried out for the study area. It was observed that GS Bolivia correlations of 0.54 and 0.78 were obtained in Guadalquivir basin. However, using the GS Guadalquivir product found a correlation of 0.98. The efficiency of the Nash and Sutcliffe product increases slightly depending on the size of the study area. The comparative indicators are summarized in Table 4.

Table 4. Statistic indicators for satellite and combined precipitation.

Statistic Indicators	GSMaP	GS Bolivia	GS Guadalquivir
Determination Coefficient (R^2)	0.30	0.62	0.95
Correlation Coefficient (R)	0.54	0.78	0.98
Mean Absolute Error (MAE)	1.82	0.74	0.17
Root Mean Square Error (RMSE)	3.34	1.63	0.70
Nash and Sutcliffe Efficiency (NSE)	0.25	0.82	0.97

3. Results

3.1. Flow Analysis

For the generation of flows through the HydroBID tool, the distributed precipitation data were used. The method of introducing these was adjusted from distributed maps to representative values per hydrological unit of the model.

As a result, in Figure 9, the data iterated through the Kriging method show simulated flows very similar to those observed through the IDW method. The Kriging flows present a drastic reduction in the maximum values registered in January 2004 and 2014 within the study period. This is due to the way the Kriging method generates the data, where the maximum and minimum values of the input data are reduced by the logic of the interpolation model.

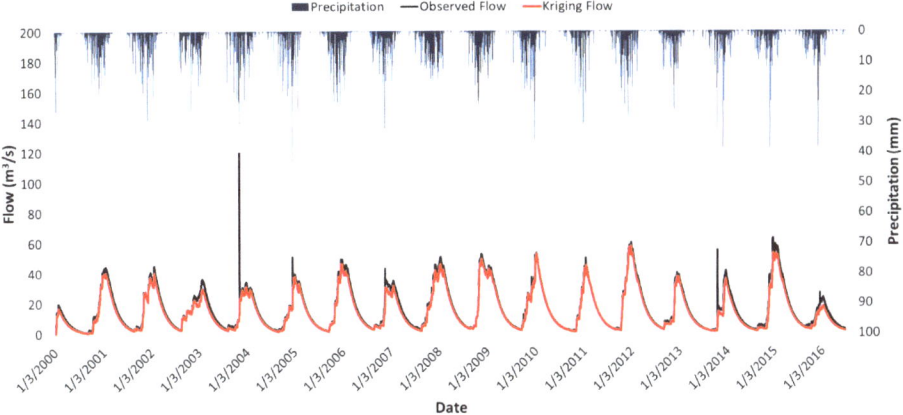

Figure 9. Simulated and observed hydrographs using interpolated rain gauge with Kriging method.

Figure 10 shows a comparison of the simulated flows using the products derived from satellites: GSMaP, GS Bolivia, and GS Guadalquivir. In the case of GSMaP precipitation, the simulated flows presented a general underestimation throughout the assessed period. However, during the periods 2003–2004 and 2015–2016, there are cases of persistent overestimations.

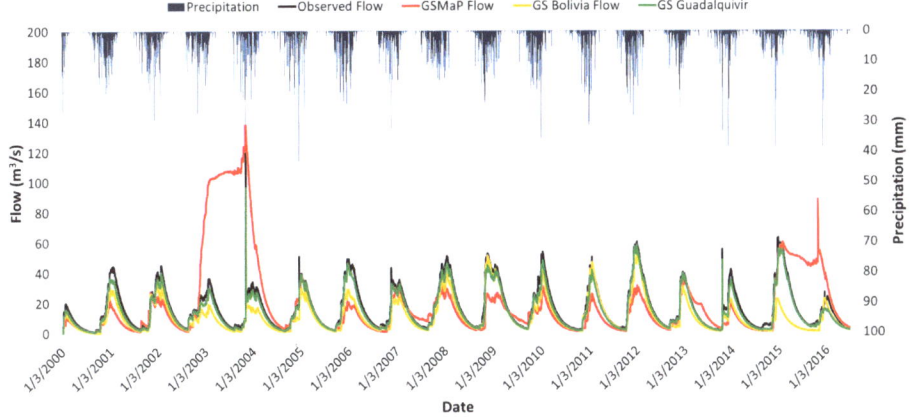

Figure 10. Simulated and observed hydrographs using satellite and combined precipitation.

However, the simulated flows using GS products show closer agreement to the overserved flow. Actually, the GS Guadalquivir product exhibits the highest similarity to the observed values, even simulating the peak flows recorded in 2004 and 2014.

Statistically analyzing the flows, the GSMaP product presents the lowest indicators in relation to the other products, as seen in Table 5. With a correlation of 0.28 and a negative efficiency, the flows generated by this satellite product present an overestimation flow. However, the other products present correlations greater than 0.9 and present a positive efficiency, with the Kriging and GS version for Guadalquivir products being the ones with the best indicators.

Table 5. Statistic indicators of simulated streamflow using satellite and combined products.

Statistic Indicators	Kriging	GSMaP	GS Bolivia	GS Guadalquivir
Determination Coefficient (R2)	0.98	0.08	0.83	0.99
Correlation Coefficient (R)	0.99	0.28	0.91	0.99
Mean Absolute Error (MAE)	1.64	13.58	5.47	2.02
Root Mean Square Error (RMSE)	2.64	25.82	8.21	2.82
Nash and Sutcliffe Efficiency (NSE)	0.96	−2.47	0.65	0.96

Moreover, the specific river discharge at each micro-basin was estimated in the Guadalquivir basin. This variable makes possible the comparison of the amount of streamflow that can be generated per unit of area. Three main regions within the basin were classified based on elevation: highlands, valleys, and lowlands, as seen in Figure 11.

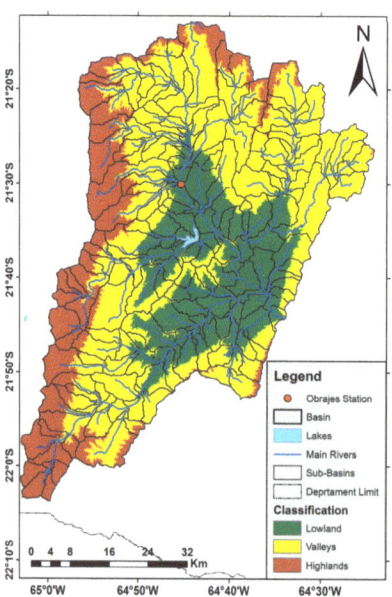

Figure 11. Three main regions within Guadalquivir basin.

As expected, the specific river discharge at lowlands showed higher values due to the flow accumulation downstream. Using the GS Guadalquivir product, values of 0.039, 0.095, and 4.892 $m^3/s/km^2$ were obtained in the highlands, valleys, and lowlands, respectively. The complete values for four products can be seen in Table 6.

Table 6. Specific river discharge in Guadalquivir basin.

Streamflow (m^3/s/km^2)	Highlands	Valleys	Lowlands
Rain Gauge (HydroBID)	0.044	0.107	5.689
Kriging Interpolation	0.029	0.094	5.176
GSMaP	0.038	0.128	6.962
GS Bolivia	0.023	0.073	3.917
GS Guadalquivir	0.039	0.095	4.892

Then, a specific river discharge using the GS Guadalquivir product was generated showing the differences among micro-basins, as seen in Figure 12. Four main contributions to the main river in the direction to the outlet can be seen. Particularly, there were higher values in the southwestern part where the Sama Biological protected area is located. This finding is consistent with the higher precipitation pattern in this southwestern zone.

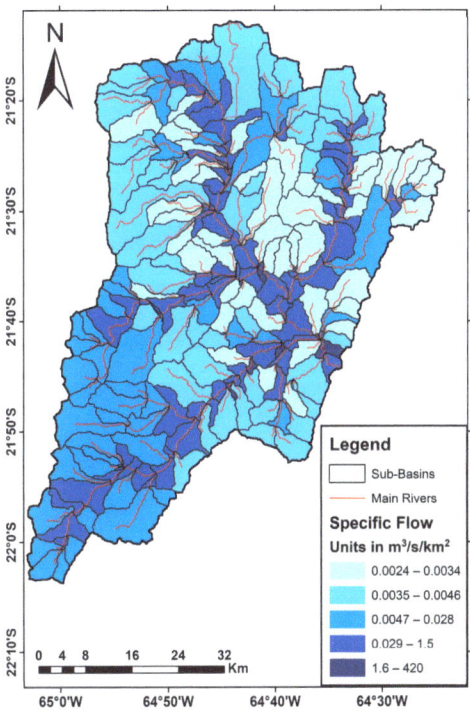

Figure 12. Distribution of specific river discharge using GS Guadalquivir product.

3.2. Volume Analysis

Further analysis is presented of the annual volumes resulting from the flows generated. Figure 13 shows the different volumes obtained from the streamflow modeling of the different products. Using Kriging and GS Guadalquivir, simulated volumes with HydroBID were plotted against observed volumes. However, during the period 2008–2011, GS Guadalquivir presents an underestimation that is not appreciated in Kriging. The GS Bolivia product showed cases of underestimations throughout the modeling period.

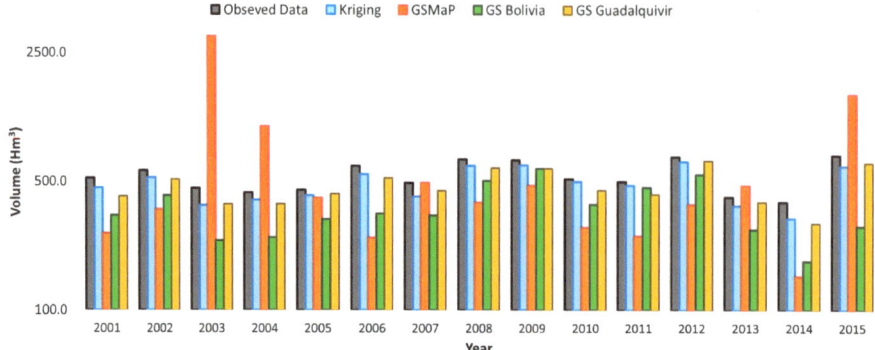

Figure 13. Annual simulated volume using four simulated flows against observed streamflow.

Based on these data, statistical indicators were generated that allowed us to analyze the behavior of the volumes and corroborate the observations. According to the data in Table 7, the precipitation generated using Kriging presents a correlation of 0.98, close to the default values generated by HydroBID, and, thanks to the efficiency of Nash and Sutcliffe, a minimum variance can be determined. A similar case can be observed with the GS Guadalquivir product, which presents a correlation of 0.97 and an efficiency of 0.98.

Table 7. Statistic indicators for satellite and combined volume.

Statistic Indicators	Kriging	GSMaP	GS Bolivia	GS Guadalquivir
Determination Coefficient (R2)	0.95	0.00	0.50	0.95
Correlation Coefficient (R)	0.98	0.06	0.70	0.97
Mean Absolute Error (MAE)	50.7	426	174	62.7
Root Mean Square Error (RMSE)	55.0	748	194	67.1
Nash and Sutcliffe Efficiency (NSE)	0.99	−1.00	0.87	0.98

The difference lies in the database, where, through the mean absolute error (MAE) and the root mean square error (RMSE), a slight difference is observed where Kriging presents a better tendency in relation to GS Guadalquivir. However, the GSMaP product presents a correlation of 0.06 and a negative efficiency, indicating its lack of similarity with the observed volumes.

4. Discussion

4.1. Precipitation Data

The meteorological introduction data tool of HydroBID employs by default the IDW interpolation to generate the value per hydrological unit. This study analyzed the possibility of distributed precipitation values. Subsequently, an aerial precipitation was calculated for each hydrological unit. Kriging interpolation rain gauge data, GSMaP_Gauge.v6, and GS Bolivia [30] were tested. Only the Kriging data presented a similar correlation to that generated with the IDW method. The product GS Bolivia showed a correlation in the La Plata basin of 0.98. In the analysis for the Guadalquivir basin, the correlation was reduced to 0.8. For this reason, a new version of this product was developed for the basin, increasing the spatial resolution to 250 m.

The iterative method to generate the combined precipitation product was found very useful to fulfill the required spatial resolution of 230 micro-basins. Five iterations were found to be enough to reach convergence.

4.2. HydroBID as a Hydrological Model

The model employed for the Guadalquivir basin was set up without further inconvenience. The inclusion of a soil type database and its assignment to each of the micro-basins comprising the AHD allows HydroBID users to have support when collecting and formatting other required variables (such as precipitation and temperature). Moreover, the soil type is based on the Global Land Cover Characterization (GLCC) of 1993 [21]. To present more accurate results, it is possible to develop interpretation and management skills to update the HydroBID database at a smaller scale. However, addressing this issue is beyond the scope of their study.

The calibration and validation of the model parameters were carried out smoothly with trial-and-error analysis checking both visual and statistical indicators. Since there are only four parameters to calibrate, the job becomes feasible in terms of computation cost. Actually, CN and AWC use multipliers, which narrows the spectrum of options. The multipliers are applied at each micro-basin.

The Guadalquivir HydroBID model was run with different precipitation products. The raw GSMaP product highlighted the need to analyze satellite-based precipitation data before using it in modeling. Due to the overestimation cases observed, it is plausible that a similar error may occur when using other satellite products.

Another significant aspect in handling satellite products is the spatial resolution. TRMM, with a spatial resolution of 25 km, offers lower precision when using its data. In the present study of the Guadalquivir basin, products with resolutions of 10, 5, and 0.25 km were employed, with Kriging interpolation and the GS Guadalquivir product presenting the smallest resolution and yielding better results.

4.3. Applications of HydroBID Model

Regarding the volume analysis, at recent studies in hydrological models of this basin, values of 436, 514, and 647 Hm^3 were reported [8–10]. In the present study, the simulated average values were 536, 485, 647, 362 and 474 Hm^3 using rain gauges, Kriging interpolation, GSMaP, GS Bolivia and GS Guadalquivir, respectively. In the case of Kriging and GS Guadalquivir precipitations products, the variance in relation to previous reported data is between 9 and 11%, with a tendency to underestimate values. Then, the estimates using GS Guadalquivir are recommended to be employed.

These volumes in future studies can be used to encourage sustainable development considering water consumption per capita, hectares to be irrigated, storage volumes required for hydroelectric power generation and environmental flow.

Finally, since Guadalquivir basin is located in a semi-arid region, and the specific river discharge was already estimated, a sediment transport analysis is feasible to be performed using the module within HydroBID platform.

5. Conclusions

In this study, a hydrological model of the Guadalquivir basin has been set up using the HydroBID tool and combined precipitation products. The results showed considerable adaptability when used with these products. During the calibration of the model parameters, the Curve Number (CN) showed control over the simulation of peak flows. However, the Available Water Content (AWC) generally controls the baseflow. The calibration and validation of the model depicted correlation coefficients of 0.709 and 0.744, respectively.

After the generation of the GS precipitation product version for Guadalquivir (GS Guadalquivir), this product obtained a correlation of 0.98 and an efficiency of 0.97. These results are much better than those obtained with GS Bolivia, which presented a correlation of 0.78 and an efficiency 0.82. The transition from a spatial resolution of 5 km to 250 m showed an improvement in the precipitation data.

In the modeling process with the generated precipitation data, it was observed that the data management with Kriging and the GS Guadalquivir product presented high correlations in relation to the simulated flows with HydroBID (0.99 for both products).

However, the GS product presents a better visual approach to the modeled flows, even simulating extreme flows with slight underestimations. In the case of GSMaP and GS Bolivia, these products present general underestimations of the flows simulated by the model, reaching correlations between 0.28 and 0.91, respectively.

In the case of GSMaP, it is possible to observe overestimated flows in the periods 2003–2004 and 2015–2016 that could not be detected with the precipitation analysis. In the case of GS Bolivia, this product presented an MAE of 5.47 and an RMSE of 8.21, double and quadruple the values of its exclusive version of the basin.

Analyzing the annual volumes in the basin, we observed firstly the overestimation of values presented by GSMaP, which reached 4 times the maximum value registered by the original simulated products. Kriging and GS Guadalquivir presented similar characteristics with respect to the distribution of volumes, emphasizing a greater number of underestimations by the GS product. This is validated with the MAE and RMSE values presented by these products (50.7 and 62.7 for MAE and 62.7 and 67.1 in the case of RMSE).

Furthermore, when analyzing the output volumes at the end of the basin, it can be observed that the products using IDW and Kriging precipitation show a slight difference, strengthening the usage of interpolated rain gauges with the HydroBID model. In the case of GS Guadalquivir, the volume presents a similar behavior to Kriging, and this product presents better values than GSMaP.

In summary, three main achievements are reported in this study: (1) the generation of a GS Guadalquivir satellite-based precipitation product with 230 micro-basins; (2) the usage of the HydroBID tool to convert precipitation products into simulated flows, specific river discharge, and volumes within micro-basins; (3) the ground validation of satellite-based precipitation products at two stages, against local rain gauges and the observed streamflow.

The use of HydroBID In other basins is therefore recommended as a support tool not only for flow forecasts but also for water resources management.

Author Contributions: Conceptualization, J.U. and O.S.; methodology, O.S. and J.U.; software, J.U.; validation, J.U., O.S. and M.P.; formal analysis, O.S.; investigation, J.U.; resources, J.U., O.S. and M.P.; data curation, J.U. and M.P.; writing—original draft preparation, O.S. and J.U.; writing—review and editing, O.S. and M.P.; visualization, O.S.; supervision, O.S. and M.P.; project administration, O.S. All authors have read and agreed to the published version of the manuscript.

Funding: This research received no external funding.

Data Availability Statement: Publicly available data sets were analyzed in this study. The combined precipitation product GS data can be found here: https://drive.google.com/drive/folders/1tkXsnLO3HO4joEIb7DE6NuLMDOYc1V7Y?usp=sharing.

Acknowledgments: This research has been supported by the 3rd Research Announcement on the Earth Observations of the Japan Aerospace Exploration Agency (JAXA) for data sharing of GSMaP_Gauge v6. Moreover, we would like to thank engineer Mario Gamarra, researcher at Universidad Autónoma Juan Misael Saracho, for his insightful comments to this study.

Conflicts of Interest: The authors declare no conflict of interest.

References

1. Chen, H.; Huang, S.; Xu, Y.-P.; Teegavarapu, R.S.V.; Guo, Y.; Xie, J.; Nie, H. Quantitative Assessment of Impact of Climate Change and Human Activities on Streamflow Changes Using an Improved Three-Parameter Monthly Water Balance Model. *Remote Sens.* **2022**, *14*, 4411. [CrossRef]
2. Darbandsari, P.; Coulibaly, P. Inter-Comparison of Lumped Hydrological Models in Data-Scarce Watersheds Using Different Precipitation Forcing Data Sets: Case Study of Northern Ontario, Canada. *J. Hydrol. Reg. Stud.* **2020**, *31*, 100730. [CrossRef]
3. Paul, P.K.; Zhang, Y.; Mishra, A.; Panigrahy, N.; Singh, R. Comparative Study of Two State-of-the-Art Semi-Distributed Hydrological Models. *Water* **2019**, *11*, 871. [CrossRef]
4. Jiang, S.; Ding, Y.; Liu, R.; Wei, L.; Liu, Y.; Ren, M.; Ren, L. Assessing the Potential of IMERG and TMPA Satellite Precipitation Products for Flood Simulations and Frequency Analyses over a Typical Humid Basin in South China. *Remote Sens.* **2022**, *14*, 4406. [CrossRef]

5. Pamirbek kyzy, M.; Chen, X.; Liu, T.; Duulatov, E.; Gafurov, A.; Omorova, E.; Gafurov, A. Hydrological Forecasting under Climate Variability Using Modeling and Earth Observations in the Naryn River Basin, Kyrgyzstan. *Water* **2022**, *14*, 2733. [CrossRef]
6. Ministerio de Medio Ambiente y Agua. *Balance Hídrico Superficial de Bolivia: Documento de Difusión*; Ministerio de Medio Ambiente y Agua: La Paz, Bolivia, 2016; ISBN 978-99954-774-8-6.
7. Ministerio de Medio Ambiente y Agua. *Balance Hídrico Superficial de Bolivia (1980–2016): Documento de Difusión*; Ministerio de Medio Ambiente y Agua: La Paz, Bolivia, 2018.
8. Espejo, A. *Balance Hídrico Integral Para La Cuenca Del Río Guadalquivir*; Ministerio de Medio Ambiente y Agua: Tarija, Bolivia, 2016.
9. Caba, J. *Mapeo Temático de La Oferta, Uso Actual y Disponibilidad Delos Recursos Hídricos Del Valle Central de Tarija, En El Marco Del Sistema de Información Hídrica Del Valle Central de Traija-SIHITA*; Gobierno Autónomo Departamental de Tarija: Tarija, Bolivia, 2018.
10. Plataforma Interinstitucional de la Cuenca Guadalquivir. *Plan Director de La Cuenca Del Río Guadalquivir Programa Plurianual 2021–2025*; Ministerio de Medio Ambiente y Agua: Tarija, Bolivia, 2022.
11. Sieber, J.; Purkey, D. *WEAP Water Evaluation and Planning System—User Guide*; Stockholm Environmental Institute, U.S. Center: Somerville, MA, USA, 2015.
12. Lima-Quispe, N.; Coleoni, C.; Rincón, W.; Gutierrez, Z.; Zubieta, F.; Nuñez, S.; Iriarte, J.; Saldías, C.; Purkey, D.; Escobar, M.; et al. Delving into the Divisive Waters of River Basin Planning in Bolivia: A Case Study in the Cochabamba Valley. *Water* **2021**, *13*, 190. [CrossRef]
13. Zarate, S.; Villazon, M.; Navia, M.; Balderrama Subieta, S.L.; Quoilin, S. *Modeling Hydropower to Assess Its Contribution to Flexibility Services in the Bolivian Power System*; SWEDES: Dubrovnik, Croatia, 2021.
14. Fernandez, J.; Wickel, B.A.; Escobar, M. *Hydro-Ecological Monitoring of High-Elevation Wetlands in the Katari Watershed, Bolivia*; Stockholm Environment Institute: Stockholm, Sweden, 2021.
15. Mautner, M.R.L.; Coleoni, C.; Forni, L. Socioeconomic Modeling for Water Resource Planning: Optimizing Crop Distribution in the Bolivian Andes under Hydrologic and Social Constraints. In Proceedings of the American Geophysical Union Fall Meeting, Chicago, IL, USA, 12–16 December 2022. [CrossRef]
16. Sahu, M.K.; Shwetha, H.R.; Dwarakish, G.S. State-of-the-Art Hydrological Models and Application of the HEC-HMS Model: A Review. *Model. Earth Syst. Environ.* **2023**, *9*, 3029–3051. [CrossRef]
17. Li, J.; Zhao, Y.; Bates, P.; Neal, J.; Tooth, S.; Hawker, L.; Maffei, C. Digital Elevation Models for Topographic Characterisation and Flood Flow Modelling along Low-Gradient, Terminal Dryland Rivers: A Comparison of Spaceborne Datasets for the Río Colorado, Bolivia. *J. Hydrol.* **2020**, *591*, 125617. [CrossRef]
18. García, W.; Delfín, M.; Ledezma, M.; Arévalo, B. Integrando Métodos de Evaluación de Riesgos de Deslizamientos e Inundaciones En Cuencas Del Tunari y Zona de Alto Cochabamba. *Acta Nova* **2021**, *10*, 61–95.
19. Achá, N.A.; Saavedra, O.C.; Ureña, J.E. Modelación Hidrológica en la Cuenca del Río Rocha Incorporando Lineamientos de Caudal Ecológico. *Rev. Investig. Desarro.* **2022**, *22*, 49–62. [CrossRef]
20. Villazon, M.; Maldonado Zegarra, I. *Hourly Continuous Hydrologic Modelling of the Rocha River Basin*; XIX Congreso Internacional Región II de Ingeniería Sanitaria y Ambiental AIGIS: La Paz, Bolivia, 2022.
21. Moreda, F.; Miralles-Wilhelm, F.; Muñoz, R. *Hydro-BID: An Integrated System for Modeling Impacts of Climate Change on Water Resources. Part 2*; Inter-American Development Bank: New York, NY, USA, 2014.
22. Miralles-Wilhelm, F.; Brantly, E. Water Resources Management and Climate Adaptation in the Río Grande Basin, Argentina: A Case Study Introducing the Hydro-BID Modelling System. In *Water and Cities in Latin America: Challenges for Sustainable Development*; Earthscan Studies in Water Resource Management; Routledge, Taylor & Francis Group: London, UK; New York, NY, USA, 2015; ISBN 978-0-415-73097-6.
23. Wyatt, A.; Moreda, F.; Brantly, E.; Miralles-Wilhelm, F.; Muñoz Castillo, R. *Caso de Estudio de Hydro-BID No 1: Modelo de Gestión Del Recurso Hídrico En La Cuenca Del Río Grande En Argentina*; Inter-American Development Bank: New York, NY, USA, 2014.
24. Moreda, F.; Miralles-Wilhelm, F.; Muñoz Castillo, R.; Coli Valdes Daussa, P. *Hydro-BID Case Study No 2: Modeling the Impact of Climate Change on Flows of the Rio Piura Using Hydro-BID*; Inter-American Development Bank: New York, NY, USA, 2014.
25. Escurra, J.; Moreda, F.; Brantly, E.; Coli Valdes Daussa, P. *Hydro-BID Case Study No. 3: Impact of El Niño Events on Sediment Loading in the Chancay-Lambayeque Basin, Peru*; Inter-American Development Bank: New York, NY, USA, 2016.
26. Moreda, F.; Lord, B.; Coli Valdes Daussa, P.; Corrales, J.C. *Hydro-BID Case Study No. 4: Application of Hydro-BID in Bermejo River Basin to Quantify Sediment Loads, Argentina*; Inter-American Development Bank: New York, NY, USA, 2016.
27. Moreda, F.; Coli Valdes Daussa, P.; Brantly, E.; Serago, J.; Escurra, J. *Hydro-BID Case Study No. 5: Impact of Climate Change on Proposed Water Investments in Chalpi Basin, Ecuador*; Inter-American Development Bank: New York, NY, USA, 2017.
28. Mena, D.; Solera, A.; Restrepo, L.; Pimiento, M.; Cañón, M.; Duarte, F. An Analysis of Unmet Water Demand under Climate Change Scenarios in the Gualí River Basin, Colombia, through the Implementation of Hydro-BID and WEAP Hydrological Modeling Tools. *J. Water Clim. Chang.* **2021**, *12*, 185–200. [CrossRef]
29. Ureña, J.; Saavedra, O.; Kubota, T. The Development of a Combined Satellite-Based Precipitation Dataset across Bolivia from 2000 to 2015. *Remote Sens.* **2021**, *13*, 2931. [CrossRef]
30. Saavedra, O.; Ureña, J. Generation of Combined Daily Satellite-Based Precipitation Products over Bolivia. *Remote Sens.* **2022**, *14*, 4195. [CrossRef]

31. Alvizuri-Tintaya, P.A.; Villena-Martínez, E.M.; Avendaño-Acosta, N.; Lo-Iacono-Ferreira, V.G.; Torregrosa-López, J.I.; Lora-García, J. Contamination of Water Supply Sources by Heavy Metals: The Price of Development in Bolivia, a Latin American Reality. *Water* **2022**, *14*, 3470. [CrossRef]
32. Villena-Martínez, E.M.; Alvizuri-Tintaya, P.A.; Lora-García, J.; Torregrosa-López, J.I.; Lo-Iacono-Ferreira, V.G. Reverse Osmosis Modeling Study of Lead and Arsenic Removal from Drinking Water in Tarija and La Paz, Bolivia. *Processes* **2022**, *10*, 1889. [CrossRef]
33. Ureña, J.; Saavedra, O. Evaluation of Satellite Based Precipitation Products at Key Basins in Bolivia. *Asia-Pac. J. Atmos. Sci.* **2020**, *56*, 641–655. [CrossRef]

Disclaimer/Publisher's Note: The statements, opinions and data contained in all publications are solely those of the individual author(s) and contributor(s) and not of MDPI and/or the editor(s). MDPI and/or the editor(s) disclaim responsibility for any injury to people or property resulting from any ideas, methods, instructions or products referred to in the content.

Article

Monthly Runoff Forecasting Using Particle Swarm Optimization Coupled with Flower Pollination Algorithm-Based Deep Belief Networks: A Case Study in the Yalong River Basin

Zhaoxin Yue [1,2,3], Huaizhi Liu [4] and Hui Zhou [1,*]

1 School of Computer and Software, Nanjing Vocational University of Industry Technology, Nanjing 210023, China; yzx10000@163.com
2 Key Laboratory of River Basin Digital Twinning of Ministry of Water Resources, China Institute of Water Resources and Hydropower Research, Beijing 100038, China
3 Industrial Perception and Intelligent Manufacturing Equipment Engineering Research Center of Jiangsu Province, Nanjing Vocational University of Industry Technology, Nanjing 210023, China
4 CSIC PRIDe (Nanjing) Atmospheric & Oceanic Information System Co., Ltd., Nanjing 211106, China; liuhz1985@126.com
* Correspondence: kokohhu@126.com

Citation: Yue, Z.; Liu, H.; Zhou, H. Monthly Runoff Forecasting Using Particle Swarm Optimization Coupled with Flower Pollination Algorithm-Based Deep Belief Networks: A Case Study in the Yalong River Basin. *Water* **2023**, *15*, 2704. https://doi.org/10.3390/w15152704

Academic Editors: Venkat Sridhar, Ankur Srivastava and Nikul Kumari

Received: 25 June 2023
Revised: 21 July 2023
Accepted: 25 July 2023
Published: 27 July 2023

Copyright: © 2023 by the authors. Licensee MDPI, Basel, Switzerland. This article is an open access article distributed under the terms and conditions of the Creative Commons Attribution (CC BY) license (https://creativecommons.org/licenses/by/4.0/).

Abstract: Accuracy in monthly runoff forecasting is of great significance in the full utilization of flood and drought control and of water resources. Data-driven models have been proposed to improve monthly runoff forecasting in recent years. To effectively promote the prediction effect of monthly runoff, a novel hybrid data-driven model using particle swarm optimization coupled with flower pollination algorithm-based deep belief networks (PSO-FPA-DBNs) was proposed, which selected the optimal network depth via PSO and searched for the optimum hyper parameters (the number of neurons in the hidden layer and the learning rate of the RBMs) in the DBN using FPA. The methodology was divided into three steps: (i) the Comprehensive Basin Response (COM) was constructed and calculated to characterize the hydrological state of the basin, (ii) the information entropy algorithm was adopted to select the key factors, and (iii) the novel model was proposed for monthly runoff forecasting. We systematically compared the PSO-FPA-DBN model with the traditional prediction models (i.e., the backpropagation neural network (BPNN), support vector machines (SVM), deep belief networks (DBN)), and other improved models (DBN-PLSR, PSO-GA-DBN, and PSO-ACO-DBN) for monthly runoff forecasting by using an original dataset. Experimental results demonstrated that our PSO-FPA-DBN model outperformed the peer models, with a mean absolute percentage error (MAPE) of 18.23%, root mean squared error (RMSE) of 230.45 m^3/s, coefficient of determination (DC) of 0.9389, and qualified rate (QR) of 64.2% for the data from the Yalong River Basin. Also, the stability of our PSO-FPA-DBN model was evaluated. The proposed model might adapt effectively to the nonlinear characteristics of monthly runoff forecasting; therefore, it could obtain accurate and reliable runoff forecasting results.

Keywords: data-driven models; information entropy; monthly runoff forecasting; PSO-FPA-DBN model

1. Introduction

Accuracy in monthly runoff forecasting is of great significance in the full utilization of flood and drought control and water resources [1–3]. At present, monthly runoff forecasting is in the stage of exploration and development. Moreover, the prediction accuracy cannot satisfy the actual needs of various production departments. Therefore, it is of high scientific significance and practical value to develop a precise and robust runoff prediction model to significantly promote the prediction effect of monthly runoff. However, runoff series are susceptible to many uncertainties and exhibit highly nonlinear characteristics. This hinders hydrology departments from predicting runoff [4–6].

The identification of key factors plays an important role in monthly runoff forecasting. However, it is difficult to determine key influencing factors closely related to runoff variation because of the highly nonlinear characteristics of the process of runoff changes, which seriously affects the accuracy and reliability of runoff forecasting [7]. In recent years, the antecedent runoff, rainfall, vegetation index, and other meteorological parameters, such as air pressure, wind speed, etc., have been found to be closely related to the runoff forecasting [8]. In addition, many teleconnection climate factors influencing runoff variation [9,10] have been considered as alternative candidate predictive factors, including the East Asian Trough Intensity Index, ENSO Modoki Index, and other indexes. The approaches used in key factor selection are principally the prior knowledge method [11], correlation coefficient method [12,13], principal component analysis (PCA) [14,15], mutual information (MI) [16], and partial mutual information (*PMI*) [17]. Among the various factor-selection methods, the prior knowledge method relies mainly on artificial experience, which is subjective and has certain limitations. The correlation coefficient method and PCA are generally linear methods that are difficult to adapt to the complex nonlinear characteristics of the monthly runoff process and have a certain scope of application. Information entropy methods, particularly the MI method, omit the distribution of variables and are suitable for linear and nonlinear correlations between alternative factors. The *PMI* method is an improvement over the MI method. It can effectively prevent the influence of selected factors and reduce redundant variables and computational complexity in monthly runoff prediction.

The selection of the prediction model is critical for monthly runoff forecasting [18–21]. Currently, the commonly used prediction methods are divided into two categories: process- and data-driven model methods. Process-driven models refer to the improvement in the structure of the conceptual rainfall–runoff model based on the hydrological theory, to predict runoff, such as the Tank [22] and Xin'anjiang model [23]. The process-driven models are widely used and have many achievements. However, many problems also need to be addressed. For example, the physical causes affecting long-term variations in the runoff sequence are complex, which hinders the determination of model parameters. Moreover, runoff variation processes with complex nonlinear characteristics limit the application of process-driven models. On the contrary, data-driven models omit the physical mechanisms of hydrological processes, demand less data, and can offer satisfactory forecast results. These alternatively utilize the relationship between the input and output patterns and have been widely used in monthly runoff forecasting. These include the backpropagation neural network (BPNN) [1], support vector machine (SVM) [24], extreme learning machine (ELM) [25,26], multilayer perceptron model for stochastic synthesis (MLPS) [27], and multiple combination models [28,29]. However, these shallow data-driven models have many problems (such as a relatively complex model structure and parameters that need to be initialized, optimized constantly, and adjusted in the training process) with relatively low efficiency. At present, deep-learning-based prediction models have attracted an increasing number of hydrologists [30,31]. In contrast to shallow networks, deep neural networks include multiple layers with nonlinear operational units, and the output of the upper layer serves as the input for the next layer. Through layer-by-layer transmission, the feature data in the higher layer can be distinguished from the original data in the lower layer to acquire better object representation. The advantages of deep learning can compensate for the shortcomings of existing monthly runoff forecasting methods and improve the forecasting speed, accuracy, and generalization capability [32,33]. For example, Ren et al. [34] adopted the RNN, LSTM, and GRU models for mid- to long-term runoff prediction and obtained good effects. Wang et al. [35] proposed the SMD-SE-WPD-LSTM hybrid forecasting model for annual runoff and achieved higher accuracy and consistency.

Despite these data-driven models performing well in runoff prediction, it should be noted that the prediction effect of data-driven models largely relies on the hyperparameters and model parameters [36]. Nevertheless, these parameters must be tuned in the training stage for better application of data-driven models. In general, the parameter optimization algorithms are principally the grid search and gradient decent-based algorithms. However, due to the complexity of the hyperparameters, the acquired trained models occasionally exhibit poor performance [37]. In addition, these parameter-optimization algorithms can introduce too much computation and lead to entrapment in the local optimum. In contrast, bio-inspired algorithms are more conducive to solving global optimization problems. As a result, integrating data-driven models with bio-inspired optimization algorithms may raise the computational speed, accuracy, and robustness of the models and thereby have been widely applied in hydrology, such as particle swarm optimization [38] (PSO), a genetic algorithm (GA) [39], an artificial bee colony (ABC) [40], a flower pollination algorithm (FPA) [41], and a firefly algorithm (FFA) [42]. For instance, Yaseen et al. [43] proposed a hybrid ANFIS-FFA model for monthly streamflow forecasting, and the proposed model performed better than the original ANFIS model. Yue et al. [3] developed a novel IPSO-ELM for mid-long-term runoff and found the hybrid IPSO-ELM model was superior to the BPNN, SVM, ELM, PSO-ELM, and other bio-inspired algorithm-based models. Although bio-inspired algorithms have been recently used to search for the optimal parameters of the data-driven models for monthly runoff forecasting, they mainly depend on traditional bio-inspired algorithms (e.g., GA and PSO) rather than current state-of-the-art algorithms, such as FPA. Therefore, this study intended to evaluate the runoff prediction accuracy based on the deep belief networks (DBNs) model optimized using PSO coupled with FPA: (i) selecting the optimal network depth of the DBN via PSO; (ii) searching for the optimum hyperparameters of the DBN using FPA.

In summary, data-driven models, especially the Deep Belief Networks, have rarely been integrated with PSO and FPA methods for monthly runoff forecasting. Therefore, to further promote the prediction effect of monthly runoff, a novel hybrid PSO-FPA-DBN model was developed in this paper. The objectives of this study were as follows: first, a Comprehensive Basin Response (COM) was constructed and calculated to characterize the hydrological state of the basin. Second, the information entropy algorithm was adopted to select key factors by calculating the correlation between the candidate factors and the COM for the inputs of the prediction model. Finally, a novel hybrid PSO-FPA-DBN model was proposed for monthly runoff forecasting using the deep belief networks (DBNs) optimized using PSO and FPA. With these effective components, our model achieved good runoff forecasting results. It outperformed state-of-the-art data-driven models. The main contributions of this study were as follows:

(1) The COM was constructed to characterize the hydrological state of the entire basin.
(2) Partial mutual information was applied to select the key factors and reduce redundant variables and the computational complexity.
(3) The PSO-FPA-DBN model was proposed for monthly runoff forecasting. Highly accurate and reliable results were obtained.

2. Methodology

The methodology is divided into five parts: Comprehensive Basin Response, factor reduction using information entropy, PSO, FPA, and DBN. These aspects are discussed in detail in the following sections. The flowchart of the proposed methodology is presented in Figure 1.

2.1. Comprehensive Basin Response

The important factors affecting runoff over watersheds include rainfall, climate, vegetation conditions, and human activities. In this study, the lagged predictive factors of runoff, rainfall, and climate from the current time-step t until the previous 12 time-steps (one month) were considered in our method. Moreover, the corresponding data were collected at hydrological stations with a monthly temporal scale. To describe the weighted response and then characterize the hydrological state of the basin, we constructed the Comprehensive Basin Response. The following are its details.

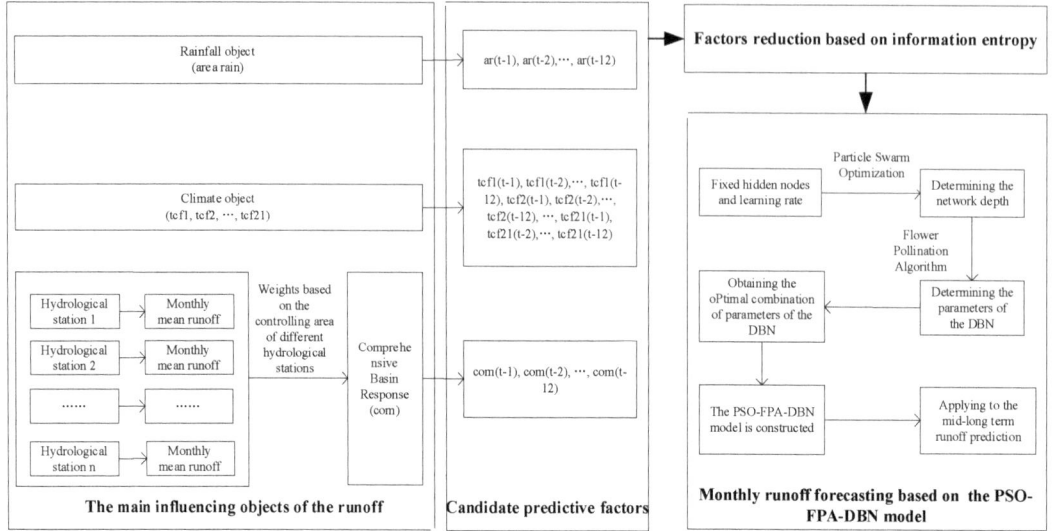

Figure 1. The flowchart of the proposed methodology (ar: rainfall factors; tcf: climate factors; com: comprehensive basin response; DBN: deep belief networks; PSO: particle swarm optimization; FPA: flower pollination algorithm).

As mentioned above, the weight of the ith hydrological station is defined as follows:

$$W_i = \frac{1/S_i}{\sum_{i=1}^{n} 1/S_i} \tag{1}$$

where n is the number of hydrological stations and S_i is the controlling area of the ith hydrological station.

Consequently, the Comprehensive Basin Response for the jth month is obtained by

$$C_j = \sum_{i=1}^{n} W_i C_{ij} \tag{2}$$

where C_{ij} denotes the monthly average runoff at the ith hydrological station in the jth month.

2.2. Factor Reduction Using Information Entropy

In recent years, factor selection methods based on information entropy, particularly MI methods, have been widely applied in hydrology. MI can calculate the linear and nonlinear correlations between predictive objects and measure the amount of information contained in a variable [44,45]. Thus, a few researchers have selected MI to reduce the candidate predictive factors influencing runoff variation. However, this strategy is controlled by the correlation between the input variables, which causes redundancy in the factors. To solve this problem, R.J. May [46,47] proposed the *PMI* method to remove the correlation between variables. It can raise the speed and accuracy of variable selection.

Assuming that the number of discrete samples is N, the *PMI* is defined in the following discrete form:

$$PMI = \frac{1}{N} \sum_{i=1}^{N} \ln \frac{f_{X',Y'}(x_i', y_i')}{f_{X'}(x_i') f_{Y'}(y_i')} \tag{3}$$

To present Equation (3) in a simple form, the *PMI* is calculated using the kernel density. It is a nonparametric probability density-estimation method with high accuracy. The sample probability density function is defined as follows:

$$\hat{f}_X(x_i) = \frac{1}{N}\sum_{j=1}^{N}\frac{1}{(2\pi)^{d/2}\lambda^d \det(S)^{1/2}}\exp\left(-\frac{(x_i-x_j)^T S^{-1}(x_i-x_j)}{2\lambda^2}\right) \quad (4)$$

where $\hat{f}_X(x_i)$ represents the estimated density function of the variable at x_i, d represents the dimension, S represents the covariance matrix, and λ represents the window width [48]:

$$\lambda = \left(\frac{1}{d+2}\right)^{1/(d+4)} N^{(-1/(d+4))} \quad (5)$$

2.3. Particle Swarm Optimization

Among evolutionary computation methods, PSO is widespread [49]. Assuming that N represents the dimension of the searching domain, the ith swarm particle at the time-step k is denoted with an N-dimensional vector $x_i^k = \{x_{i1}^k, x_{i2}^k, \ldots, x_{iN}^k\}^T$. The particle velocity at the time-step k is denoted with the vector $v_i^k = \{v_{i1}^k, v_{i2}^k, \ldots, v_{iN}^k\}^T$. The previously best-visited position of the ith particle at the time-step k is denoted with $p_i^k = \{p_{i1}^k, p_{i2}^k, \ldots, p_{iN}^k\}^T$. g denotes the exponent of the optimum particle during the evolution process. The new velocity and position of the ith particle are calculated by Equations (6) and (7), respectively:

$$v_{id}^{(k+1)} = v_{id}^k + c_1 r_1 (p_{id}^k - x_{id}^k) + c_2 r_2 (p_{gd}^k - x_{id}^k) \quad (6)$$

$$x_{id}^{(k+1)} = x_{id}^k + v_{id}^{(k+1)} \quad (7)$$

where the vector dimension of the particle is denoted by $d = 1, 2, \ldots, N$. The particle exponent is denoted by $i = 1, 2, \ldots, N_s$. N_s is the number of the swarm. c_1 and c_2 are the acceleration factors. r_1 and r_2 are uniformly distributed random numbers that vary within the range [0, 1].

2.4. Flower Pollination Algorithm

This paper introduces the FPA. It is inspired by the pollination characteristics of flowering plants. For the FPA, the global search results are obtained by

$$x_i^{t+1} = x_i^t + \gamma L(\lambda)(g_{best} - x_i^t) \quad (8)$$

where γ denotes the scaling parameter. $L(\lambda)$ denotes the random number vector of a Lévy distribution with the scaling parameter λ. g_{best} is the optimum result provided by the selection mechanism. The x_i^t at the current time step is modified by varying the step sizes. The local search result is obtained by

$$x_i^{t+1} = x_i^t + \varepsilon(x_j^t - x_k^t) \quad (9)$$

Here, ε is the uniformly distributed random number. x_j^t and x_k^t are the solution representations given by flower patches.

2.5. Deep Belief Networks

In recent years, deep learning has yielded performance improvements in several studies. For example, DBN, convolutional neural networks (CNNs), and stacked autoencoders (SSAEs) have achieved significant success. In 2006, Hinton [50] proposed the DBN model, including many restricted Boltzmann machines (RBMs), BP neural networks, and softmax classifiers. A CNN [51] has a multilayer network structure that analyzes the spatial correlation of data and reduces the number of training parameters. These exhibit remarkable robustness and are widely used in face recognition, speech recognition, and many other fields. The SSAE is composed of many sparse auto-encoders and softmax classifiers [52]. These methods pre-train the network layer-by-layer to initialize the parameters of the SSAE in the unsupervised learning stage. Supervised learning is used after the pretraining.

2.5.1. Restricted Boltzmann Machine (RBM)

The RBM is an energy-based model that combines all the input parameters with energy functions to obtain the dependence between the input parameters. The probability of various combinations of parameters is inversely proportional to the energy. The corresponding energy value is minimized through continuous training and learning, as shown in Figure 2.

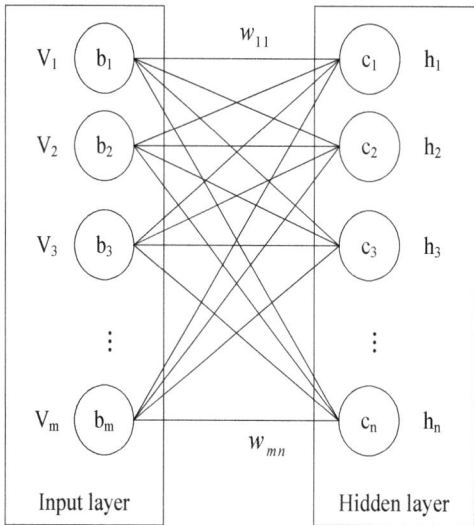

Figure 2. The architecture of RBM (RBM: restricted boltzmann machine; v and h represent the state of elements in the input and hidden layers, respectively; m is the number of neurons in the input layer; n is the number of neurons in the hidden layer; b and c represent the biases of the input and hidden layers, respectively; w represents the connection weight between the input and hidden layers of the RBM model).

Assuming that the variable is v, the probability distribution can be expressed as

$$p(v) = \frac{e^{-E(v)}}{z} \qquad (10)$$

In Equation (10), z is the normalization factor. It can be expressed as

$$z = \sum_v e^{-E(v)} \qquad (11)$$

The RBM contains an input layer and a hidden layer. Herein, the number of neurons in the input layer is equal to the vector dimension of the training sample features. The dependence between each dimension of the input sample features is extracted by the hidden layer. The two layers are connected by undirected edges. Assuming that the weight is w_{ij}, the bias values of the input and hidden layers are b_j and c_i, respectively. The internal neurons of the input or hidden layer are not connected by edges such that the internal neurons of each layer are independent of each other.

For a convenient calculation, the values of the hidden and input layers are limited to binary zero or one. After inputting the samples, a probability of zero or one can be determined for each hidden layer, and the expectation of the hidden layer is the feature output. The energy function of the RBM is defined as follows:

$$E(v,h) = -bv - ch - hWv \quad (12)$$

In Equation (12), W represents the connection weight between the input and hidden layers of the RBM model; b and c represent the biases of the input and hidden layers; and v and h represent the state of elements in the input and hidden layers, respectively. According to the energy function, the joint probability distribution (v, h) can be defined as follows:

$$p(v,h) = \frac{e^{-E(v,h)}}{z} \quad (13)$$

In Equation (13), $z = \sum_{v,h} e^{-E(v)}$.

Because the elements within each layer of RBM are not connected,

$$p(h|v) = \prod_{i}^{n} p(h_i|v) \quad (14)$$

$$p(v|h) = \prod_{j}^{m} p(v_j|h) \quad (15)$$

When the state of the input elements is given, the activation probability of a point in the jth hidden layer is

$$p(h_i = 1|v) = \sigma(c_i + W_i v) \quad (16)$$

In Equation (16), σ is the activation function, $\sigma(x) = \frac{1}{1+e^{-x}}$.

The activation probability of a unit in the input layer can be defined as

$$p(v_j = 1|h) = \sigma\left(b_j + W'_j h\right) \quad (17)$$

The training process of the RBM is generally realized using a gradient descent algorithm or Gibbs sampling. However, these methods are inefficient when addressing high-dimensional data. The contrastive divergence algorithm of the RBM has the following advantages:

(1) Training sample initialization, denoted as v_0.
(2) Calculating the state values h of the elements in all the hidden layers employing Formula (16).
(3) Calculating the state values v of the elements in the input layer and reconstructing these.
(4) The weights are updated according to the error of the real and reconstructed values.

Thus, the updating algorithms of the model parameters b_j, c_i, and W_{ij} are as follows:

$$\Delta W_{ij} = \varepsilon(\langle v_j h_i \rangle_{data} - \langle v_j h_i \rangle_{recon}) \quad (18)$$

$$\Delta b_j = \varepsilon(\langle v_j \rangle_{data} - \langle v_j \rangle_{recon}) \quad (19)$$

$$\Delta c_i = \varepsilon(\langle h_i \rangle_{data} - \langle h_i \rangle_{recon}) \quad (20)$$

where ε is the learning rate, $\langle \cdot \rangle_{data}$ is the input sample for RBM, and $\langle \cdot \rangle_{recon}$ represents the reconstructed data.

2.5.2. The Architecture of the DBN

The typical architecture of the DBN is shown in Figure 3.

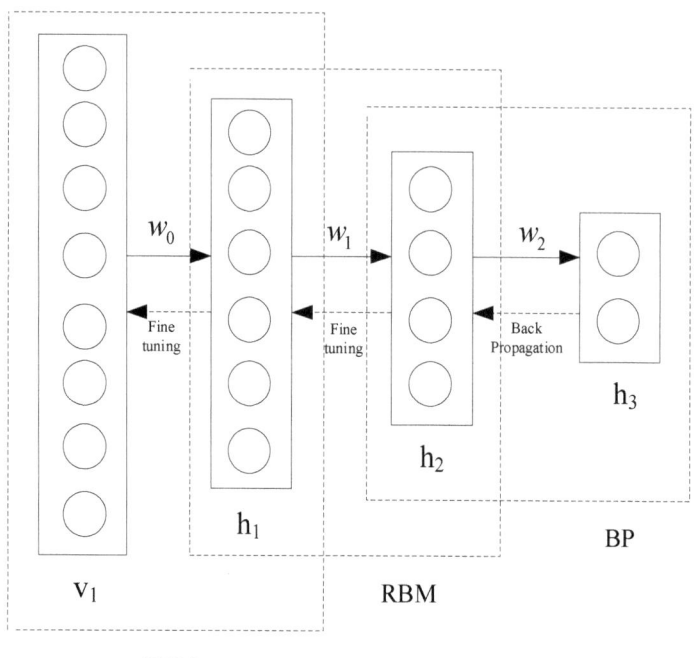

Figure 3. The architecture of the DBN.

From Figure 3, the input layer formed the first RBM with the first hidden layer of the DBN. The data features extracted by the first RBM are inputted into the second RBM through the hidden layer of the first RBM. At this time, the hidden layer of the first RBM functions as the input layer of the second RBM. Meanwhile, the hidden layer of the second RBM is the second hidden layer of the DBN, which constitutes the DBN model with multiple RBMs.

Conventional supervised learning has an excessive number of hidden layers. This results in problems, such as long training times and low convergence speeds. However, this approach is not suitable for DBN. Hinton proposed a level-by-level unsupervised greedy training algorithm that has been widely used because of its unsupervised learning, fast parameter determination, and accurate feature extraction. Therefore, this algorithm was adopted in this study to train the DBN model. The algorithm includes two stages: (i) RBM pretraining (feature extraction from training samples and initialization parameters of the model) and (ii) fine-tuning (the BP algorithm is used for fine-tuning the model parameters to further optimize the DBN). The training process is shown in Figure 4. The specific training steps are as follows:

(1) Based on the contrastive divergence algorithm, the input samples (original data) are trained in the first RBM.
(2) The output of the hidden layers in the first RBM is regarded as the input of the second RBM, and the second RBM is trained with a contrastive divergence algorithm.
(3) Training is continued according to the above method until all the RBMs are trained.
(4) After training all the RBMs to obtain the appropriate model parameters through the above steps, supervised training with the BP algorithm is used for fine-tuning all the DBN parameters in the output layer at the end of the DBN. At this point, the BP

algorithm should only search for the weights of the network in a local space. Thus, compared with the common BP algorithm, the training speed is improved significantly, the parameters converge more straightforwardly, and it is not straightforward to fall into the dilemma of a local extremum.

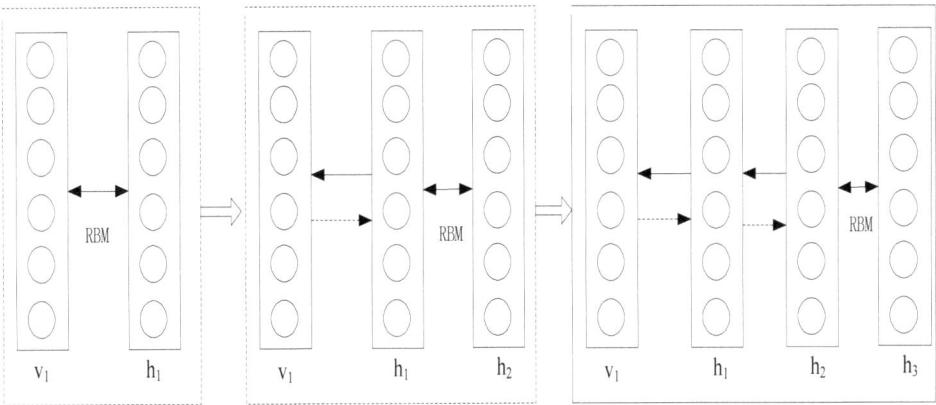

Figure 4. The training process of the DBN.

To overcome the shortage of local extrema caused by the random generation of initial weights of the model, the DBN is divided into multiple single RBMs for training layer-by-layer with a contrastive divergence algorithm. It optimizes the initial weights of the DBN and reduces the complexity. The above structure and training methods enable the DBN to outperform conventional shallow learning network models, such as BPNN and SVM.

2.6. Normalization of the Original Experimental Data

To improve the accuracy and reliability and avoid overfitting for monthly runoff forecasting, the min-max normalization method [53,54] was selected for standardization and normalization before the machine learning model development.

2.7. Evaluation Criteria

Five evaluation indicators, namely the mean absolute percentage error (*MAPE*), root mean squared error (*RMSE*), coefficient of determination (*DC*) [55], relative error (*RE*), and qualified rate (*QR*), were employed to verify the monthly runoff prediction effect of the data-driven models. Generally, the smaller *MAPE*, *RMSE*, and *RE* are and the higher the *DC* and *QR* are, the better the model performance [19].

The calculation formulas for each evaluation index are as follows:

$$MAPE = \frac{1}{n}\sum_{t=1}^{n}\left|\frac{(y_a^t - y_p^t)}{y_a^t}\right| \qquad (21)$$

$$RMSE = \sqrt{\frac{1}{n}\sum_{t=1}^{n}(y_a^t - y_p^t)^2} \qquad (22)$$

In Equations (21) and (22), y_a^t denotes the actual value at the time-step t, and y_p^t denotes the predicted value at the time-step t. n is the number of sampled data. *RMSE* was used to evaluate the degree of variation in the data.

$$QR = \frac{m}{n_{QR}} \times 100\% \qquad (23)$$

In Formula (23), m represents the number of qualified predictions, and n_{QR} represents the total prediction time.

$$DC = 1 - \frac{\sum_{t=1}^{n}(y_a^t - y_p^t)^2}{\sum_{t=1}^{n}(y_a^t - \overline{y_a^t})^2} \quad (24)$$

$$RE = \left|\frac{(y_a^t - y_p^t)}{y_a^t}\right| \times 100\% \quad (25)$$

In Formula (24), $\overline{y_a^t}$ represents the average of the actual values, and the range of the DC variation is $[0,1]$. The closer DC is to one, the higher is the precision of the model. The RE was used to evaluate the reliability of the prediction model.

3. The Proposed PSO-FPA-DBN Model for Monthly Runoff Forecasting

Currently, hydrologists have performed research on runoff forecasting. The methods can be classified into four: cause analysis, statistical methods, intelligent-computing-based forecasting, and numerical-weather-forecast-based forecasting.

Runoff production is influenced by complex factors. The main influencing factors differ across regions, thereby exhibiting complex non-linear characteristics. To obtain highly accurate and reliable runoff prediction results, an improved DBN model (PSO-FPA-DBN) was developed for runoff prediction using a DBN optimized by PSO and the FPA. The network architecture, learning algorithms, and parameter optimization methods of the model were analyzed in detail.

3.1. Network Architecture

In this study, the hybrid PSO-FPA-DBN model was proposed for monthly runoff forecasting (Figure 5). The prediction model is divided into $(L+2)$ layers. The training of the prediction model included the following two stages:

(1) Pre-training stage. Unsupervised learning was used to extract samples step-by-step. The specific steps included inputting and obtaining the parameters of RBM1 using a contrastive divergence algorithm. We then obtained the output of RBM1 by training it for the initial extraction of the feature vectors of the impact factors influencing monthly runoff. Similarly, after completing the training process of RBM2, RBM $(L-1)$, and RBML, the training process of the entire model for monthly runoff forecasting was completed.

(2) Parameter fine-tuning stage. The parameters of the model were fine-tuned using supervised learning with the BP algorithm so that the model had a better fitting effect. When the prediction error was less than a given threshold, the training process was considered complete.

3.2. Learning Algorithms

The hybrid PSO-FPA-DBN model was divided into the following steps.

Step 1: Network initialization. Each layer of neurons in the RBM was randomly initialized as zero or one. The connection weight W_{ij} between the different layers was set to a value in the range $[0,1]$.

Step 2: Steps 2.1 and 2.4 were repeated until the energy function $E(v,h)$ yielded the convergence state. The threshold value α was set to determine whether the energy function $E(v,h)$ converged.

$$E(v,h) = -\sum_{i=1}^{n} b_i v_i - \sum_{j=1}^{m} b_j h_j - \sum_{i=1}^{n}\sum_{j=1}^{m} v_i h_j w_{ij} \quad (26)$$

where v_i was the binary state of input samples X and b_i was the bias of the input samples. h_j was the binary state of the input sample features j, and b_j was the bias of the input sample features. The energy function converged as

$$\left| A'(v,h) - A(v,h) \right| < \alpha \tag{27}$$

$$A(v,h) = \sum_{a=k}^{K+k} \frac{E_a(v,h)}{K} \tag{28}$$

$$A\prime(v,h) = \sum_{b=k-K}^{k-1} \frac{E_b(v,h)}{K} \tag{29}$$

where α was the defined threshold, k was the iteration number, and K was a constant used to represent the number of variables influencing the monthly runoff forecasting in the basin.

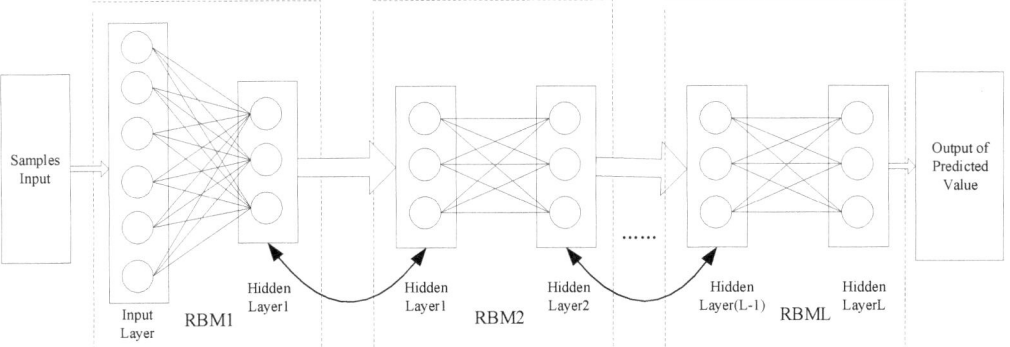

Figure 5. The hybrid PSO-FPA-DBN model for monthly runoff forecasting (L is the number of RBMs).

Step 2.1 Assuming that the probability expectation of hidden layer h_j was one.

$$p_j = \frac{1}{1 + e^{-\Delta E_j}} \tag{30}$$

$$\Delta E_j = \sum_{i=1}^{n} w_{ij} v_i + b_j \tag{31}$$

where b_j was the bias of the hidden layer element h_j, $j = 1, 2, \ldots, m$.

Step 2.2 Assuming that the probability expectation of the input layer v_i was one.

$$p_i = \frac{1}{1 + e^{-\Delta E_i}} \tag{32}$$

$$\Delta E_i = \sum_{j=1}^{m} w_{ij} h_j + b_i \tag{33}$$

where b_i was the bias of hidden layer element v_i, $i = 1, 2, \ldots, n$.

Step 2.3 Calculating the expected value and reconstruction value of the RBM.

$$p_{ij} = \langle v_i h_j \rangle_{data} \tag{34}$$

$$p'_{ij} = \langle v_j h_i \rangle_{recon} \tag{35}$$

Step 2.4 Updating the weights W_{ij}.

$$\Delta W_{ij} = \varepsilon(p_{ij} - p_{ij}') \tag{36}$$

where ε represented the learning rate, and $0 < \varepsilon < 1$.

Step 3: Considering the hidden layer of RBM1 as the input layer of RBM2, repeating steps 1 and 2. Similarly, considering the hidden layer of RBM2 as the input layer of RBM3, ..., RBML, repeating steps 1 and 2.

Step 4: After training, the output of RBML was the preliminary predicted value $X(d)$.

Step 5: Calculating the mean square error (MSE) of $X(d)$ and the sample-labeled data $\hat{X}(d)$. In addition, fine-tuning the parameters of the PSO-FPA-DBN model with the BP algorithm so that the model had a better prediction effect.

Step 6: If the MSE was less than a predefined threshold, the training of the model was completed, and the convergence formula was defined as follows:

$$\frac{MSE(N-1) - MSE(N)}{MSE(N-1)} < \beta \tag{37}$$

where β represented a pre-given threshold and N represented the number of cycles for fine-tuning with the BP algorithm.

Step 7: After the training, a prediction model was constructed to predict the variation in monthly runoff in the basin.

These steps were the main learning algorithms for monthly runoff forecasting based on the PSO-FPA-DBN model. The parameters of the model obtained from the training of multiple RBMs were well-fitted to the optimal solution. This was followed by the adoption of supervised learning with a BPNN to fine-tune the parameters and finally achieve all the training rapidly. This helped the model extract features conveniently from massive, high-dimensional, and multi-factor data.

3.3. Determining the Network Depth of the Proposed Model Based on Particle Swarm Optimization

To construct the PSO-FPA-DBN model, the optimal network depth of the DBN was first solved. An ineffective network depth significantly affected the prediction model accuracy. At present, there are several methods for selecting the network depth, such as trial-and-error and parameter-optimization methods. Trial-and-error methods are used to search for the optimal network depth through many experiments. These increase the computational complexity. Thus, in this study, the PSO algorithm was selected to acquire the optimal network depth based on the network error reconstruction algorithm (Figure 6). The network error reconstruction was defined as

$$RE = \sum_{i=1}^{n} (X - S_i)^2 \tag{38}$$

where X denoted the ith batch matrix, S_i denoted the reconstruction results of the ith batch matrix, and RE denoted the reconstruction error.

3.4. Parameter Optimization Based on the Flower Pollination Algorithm

Conventional methods, such as the trial-and-error method, can identify better model parameters through repeated trial-and-error. However, these require many experiments and comparisons and have low generalization capability. To solve this problem, this study adopted a dynamic optimization algorithm based on the FPA to improve the accuracy and reliability of monthly runoff using a DBN. The FPA could prevent a local extremum by searching for optimization over a large range and ensured a global optimal solution. This increased the convergence speed of the network and improved the generalization capability of the model.

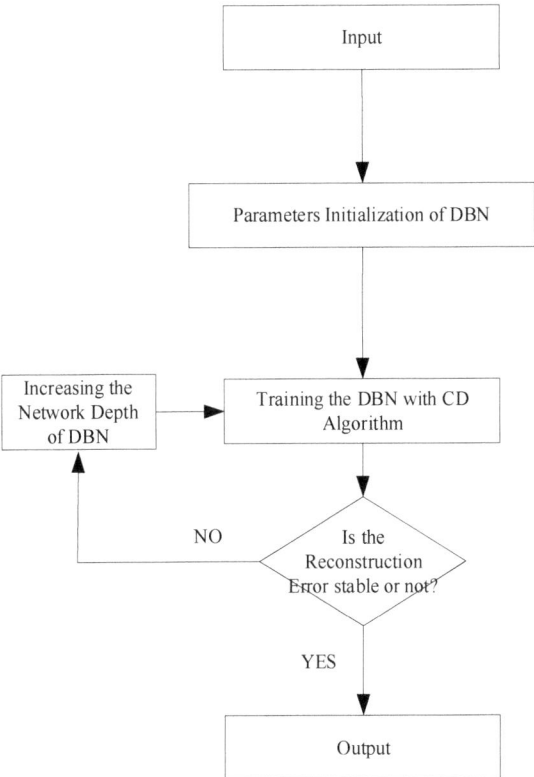

Figure 6. The flow of network error reconstruction (CD: contrastive divergence).

According to the training sample data, the FPA algorithm was used to dynamically determine the number of neurons in the hidden layer and the learning rate of the RBMs. Therefore, a group of optimal parameter combinations was constructed as a pollen position for iterative updating to solve the global optimization problems (Figure 7).

Assuming that M represented the number of neurons in the hidden layers, L represented the number of RBMs, ε_1 represented the learning rate of RBM1, ε_2 represented that of RBM2, and ε_L represented that of RBML. In this study, we considered an $(L + 1)$-dimensional vector particle $y(m, \varepsilon_1, \varepsilon_2, \ldots, \varepsilon_L)$, $m = 1, 2, \ldots, M$, $\varepsilon_1, \varepsilon_2, \ldots, \varepsilon_L \in (0, 1)$. The algorithm was divided into the following steps:

Step 1: Parameter initialization

Assuming that $[x_i, y_i]$ represented the given training samples, $x_i \in R_n$, R_n represented the sample space with n-dimensional feature vectors, $i = 1, 2, \cdots, Q$, and Q represented the number of training samples. The population size was set to P, and the maximum number of iterations was set to I.

Step 2: Fitness function selection

Using the root mean square error ($RMSE$) for model fitting.

Step 3: Iteration and updating

According to step 2, the fitness values were calculated and individuals were updated.

Step 4: Obtaining an optimal parameter combination for the PSO-FPA-DBN model.

Therefore, it was necessary to determine whether the termination condition had been attained. When the termination condition was attained, the optimal parameter combination for the PSO-FPA-DBN model was obtained. Otherwise, return to step 3.

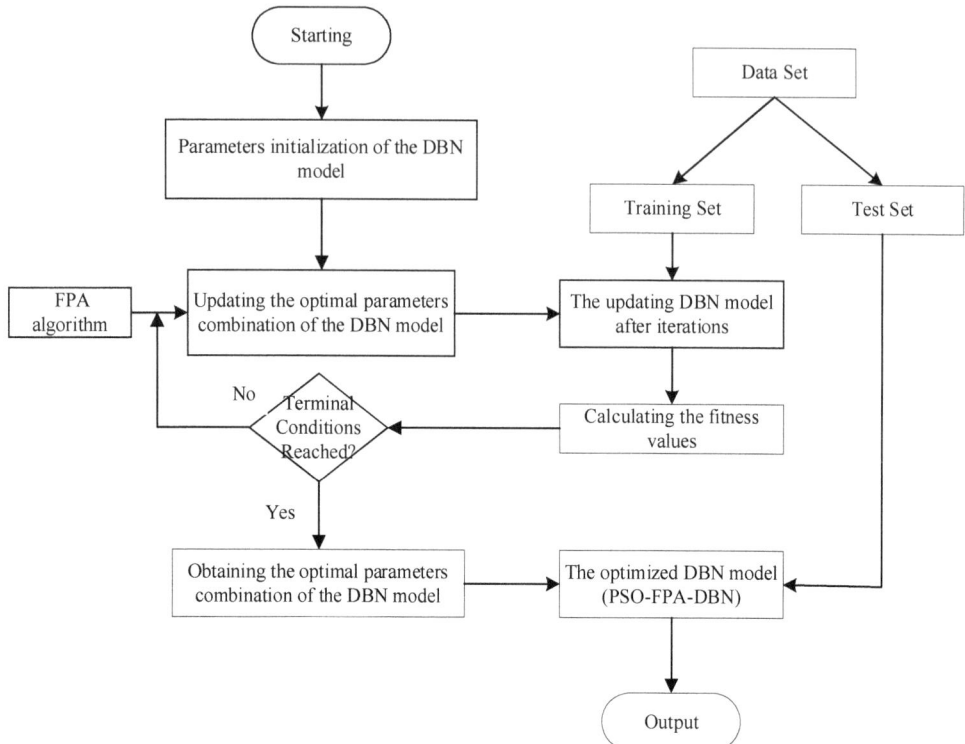

Figure 7. Flow chart of parameter optimization based on FPA algorithm.

4. Study Area and Data

The Yalong River (25°12–34°9 N, 96°47–102°42 E) is the largest tributary of the Jinsha River in the southern region of the Tibetan Plateau. It runs from the northwest to the southeast. Therefore, the research on monthly runoff forecasting is of high scientific significance and practical value. The geography of the Yalong River is shown in Figure 8.

In this study, the dataset was from the period from January 1960 to December 2011. It included the monthly mean runoff, rainfall, and climatic factors. The data from January 1960 to December 2001 were used for training, and those from January 2002 to December 2011 were used for validation. The original monthly runoff series in Lianghekou, Jinping, Guandi, and Ertan hydrological stations are shown in Figure 9. The runoff data were provided by the Hydrological Bureau of Changjiang Water Resources Commission of The Ministry of Water Resources, China (http://www.cjh.com.cn/ (accessed on 20 January 2023)). The atmospheric circulation factors and meteorological data were provided by the National Climate Center of China (http://data.cma.cn/ (accessed on 20 January 2023)).

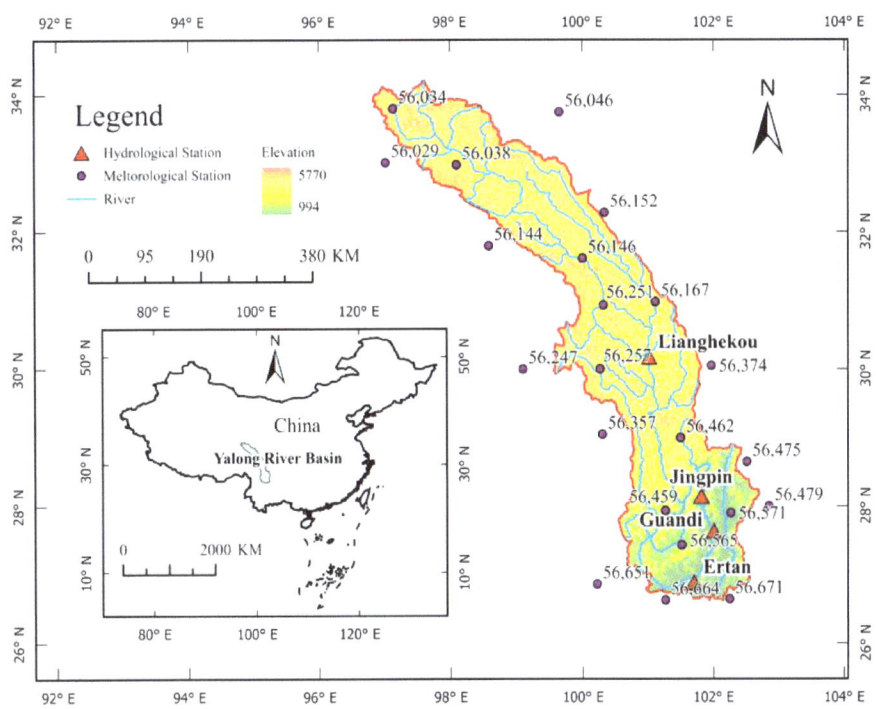

Figure 8. The Yalong River Basin.

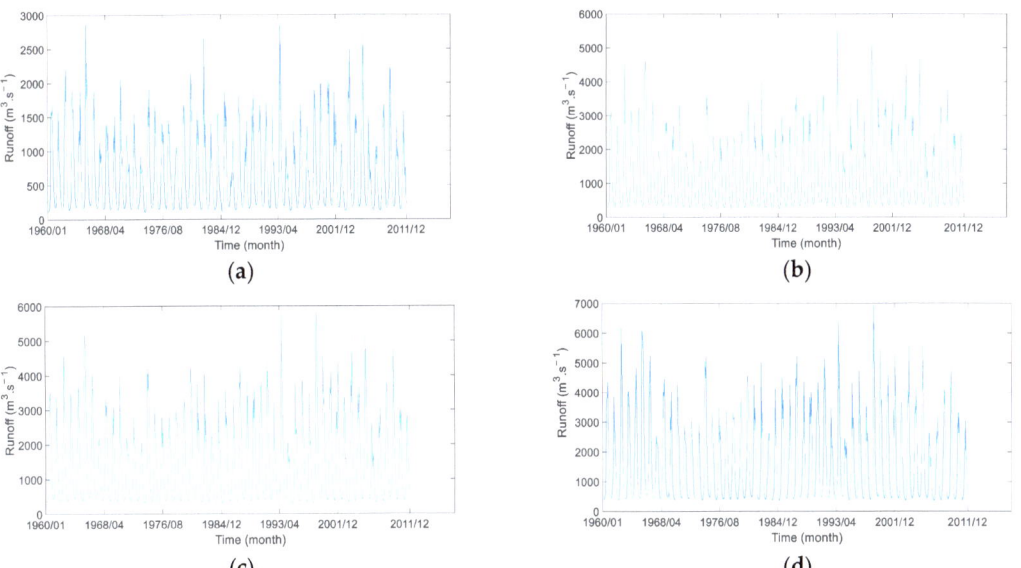

Figure 9. Original monthly runoff series: (**a**) Lianghekou, (**b**) Jinping, (**c**) Guandi, (**d**) Ertan.

5. Results

This section includes the COM selection results, factor selection results, and proposed PSO-FPA-DBN model. Moreover, the proposed PSO-FPA-DBN model was compared with the traditional prediction methods (namely, BPNN and SVM) and other improved DBN models to demonstrate its superiority according to the evaluation criteria in the Yalong River Basin.

5.1. COM Selection Results

According to Section 2.1, the COM was constructed by Lianghekou, Jinping, Guandi, and Ertan hydrological stations, and the weight calculation results are shown in Table 1.

Table 1. The weight calculation results.

Station	Lianghekou	Jinping	Guandi	Ertan
Percentage of the controlled area	51%	81%	89%	97%
Weight normalization	0.37	0.23	0.21	0.19

5.2. Factor Selection Results

According to Section 2.2, this study selected the *PMI* method for factor selection from the measured COM, rainfall, and climatic factors to effectively promote the prediction effect of monthly runoff.

In terms of predictive variable selection, the predictive factors of the dataset included the measured values of 23 variables from the previous 12 months. Consequently, the candidate factors include COM (com(t-1), com(t-2), ..., com(t-12)), area rainfall (ar(t-1), ar(t-2), ..., ar(t-12)), and 21 climatic factors (tcf1(tcf1(t-1), tcf1(t-2), ..., tcf1(t-12)), tcf2(tcf2(t-1), tcf2(t-2), ..., tcf2(t-12)), ..., tcf21(tcf21(t-1), tcf21(t-2), ..., tcf21(t-12))). The total number of factors is 276.

As described in Section 2.2, the *PMI* method was employed to determine key influencing factors closely related to runoff variation according to the AIC criterion. The selection procedure was as follows:

(1) The top 20 candidate variables are listed in Table 2.
(2) The key variable factors were selected from the above results and a new factor selection result was formed. As a result, the reduced factors were 13 in number, as shown in Table 3.

Table 2. The importance ranking of candidate factors in the top 20.

Importance Ranking	The Candidate Factors	Importance Ranking	The Candidate Factors
1	ar(t-1), 253th	2	com(t-12), 276th
3	ar(t-7), 259th	4	tcf1(t-1), 1st
5	ar(t-12), 264th	6	com(t-1), 265th
7	com(t-11), 275th	8	com(t-2), 266th
9	tcf15(t-6), 174th	10	tcf3(t-7), 31th
11	tcf13(t-8), 152th	12	tcf16(t-1), 181th
13	tcf16(t-5), 185th	14	com(t-3), 267th
15	tcf5(t-9), 57th	16	tcf21(t-5), 245th
17	tcf3(t-3), 27th	18	tcf4(t-7), 43th
19	tcf14(t-8), 164th	20	tcf7(t-4), 76th

Table 3. Factor selection results.

Influencing Factors	Selected Factors
COM	com(t-1), com(t-2), com(t-3), com(t-11), com(t-12)
Rainfall Factors	ar(t-1), ar(t-7), ar(t-12)
Climate Factors	tcf1(t-1), tcf3(t-7), tcf15(t-6), tcf13(t-8), tcf16(t-1)

5.3. Monthly Runoff Forecasting Based on PSO-FPA-DBN Model

5.3.1. Network Depth of the Proposed Model

As described in Section 3.3, the DBN was set as follows: 13 input elements, 1 output element, a learning rate of 0.01, and 800 iterations. The optimal network depth of the proposed model was selected from two to six based on the PSO algorithm. The selection process is shown in Figure 10.

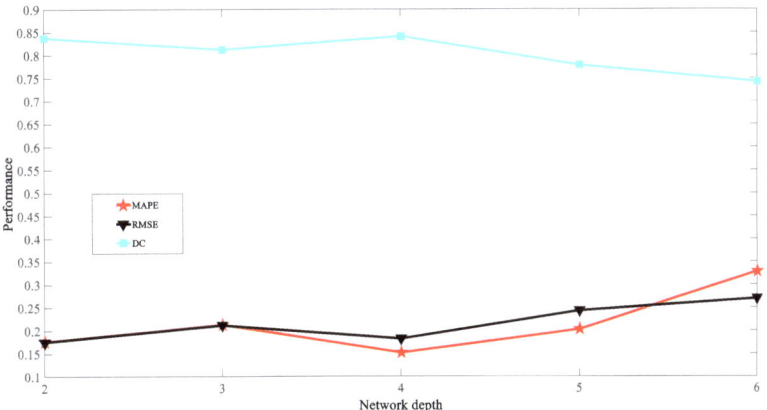

Figure 10. Network depth selection (MAPE: mean absolute percentage error; RMSE: root mean squared error; DC: coefficient of determination).

As shown in Figure 10, when the network depth of the PSO-FPA-DBN model was four, the COM prediction results were the best. Thus, the optimal network depth of the PSO-FPA-DBN model was four layers.

5.3.2. Parameter Optimization of the Proposed Model

The PSO-FPA-DBN model was trained using 504 sets of sample data collected between January 1960 and December 2001. With the RMSE as the objective, the PSO-FPA-DBN model was used to determine the optimal combination of the number of neurons in the hidden layer and the learning rate of the RBMs. The parameters of the PSO-FPA-DBN model were set as follows:

(1) The number of elements in the input layer was 13, the number of hidden layers was three, the learning rate for fine-tuning the BP algorithm was 0.01, and the number of training iterations was 600.
(2) FPA: The population size was 90, the maximum number of iterations was 600, the transition probability was 0.8, the scaling parameter was one, the scaling parameter γ was one, and the λ was 1.5.

After iteration and updating, when the number of hidden layer neurons was 12, the learning rates of RBM1, RBM2, and RBM3 were 0.2, 0.4, and 0.5, respectively. The RMSE was minimal, and the model performance was optimal. Thus, the optimal parameter combination for the PSO-FPA-DBN model was obtained.

5.3.3. Comparison Models

This study used the MATLAB R2016a software modeling tools as the working platform on a personal computer (Windows 11 operation system; CPU: 12th Gen Intel (R) Core (TM) i5-12400F @ 2.50 GHz; RAM: 16 GB). The parameters of comparison models are set in Table 4.

Table 4. Parameter setting of comparison models.

Models	Parameter Setting
BPNN	The hidden nodes = 12; the training function = "tansig", learning function = "logsig"; the maximum training time = 600, learning rate = 0.1, momentum factor = 0.9, and expected error = 0.001; selecting the LM algorithm as the training algorithm.
SVM	The kernel function = "sigmoid", and the parameters of SVM were optimized via the grid-search algorithm with cross-validation.
DBN-PLSR	The number of iterations of every RBM = 300, the enhancement coefficient of the learning rate = 1.4, the decrease coefficient of the learning rate = 0.7, and the limited value = 0.02.
PSO-GA-DBN	PSO: the population size = 90, the maximum number of iterations = 600, the learning rate = 0.1, and the expected error = 0.001. GA: the population size = 90, the maximum number of iterations = 600, the mutation probability rate = 0.01, and the crossover ratio = 0.7.
PSO-ACO-DBN	PSO: the population size = 90, the maximum number of iterations = 600, the learning rate = 0.1, and the expected error = 0.001. ACO: the ant colony size = 90, the maximum number of iterations = 600, the important factor of pheromone = 1, the importance factor of the heuristic function = 5, and the pheromone factor = 0.1.

Note: BPNN: backpropagation neural network; SVM: support vector machines; PLSR: partial least square regression; GA: genetic algorithm; ACO: artificial bee colony.

5.3.4. Runoff Forecasting

To sufficiently demonstrate the highly accurate and reliable runoff prediction results of the proposed PSO-FPA-DBN model, the BPNN, SVM, DBN, DBN-PLSR, PSO-GA-DBN, and PSO-ACO-DBN were selected for a comparison. The monthly runoff forecasting results are shown in Figure 11. The calibrations of the models are shown in Figure 12. The relative percent error based on the seven data-driven models are shown in Figure 13.

As shown in Figures 11–13, we can see that the proposed novel PSO-FPA-DBN hybrid model may adapt effectively to the nonlinear characteristics of monthly runoff forecasting and obtain accurate and reliable runoff forecasting results. The monthly runoff forecasting effect of all data-driven models is relatively ideal, and the predicted and observed runoff are highly consistent. In addition, the forecasting effect of the data-driven models coupled with bio-inspired optimization algorithms (i.e., PSO-FPA-DBN, DBN-PLSR, PSO-GA-DBN, and PSO-ACO-DBN) are much better than other models.

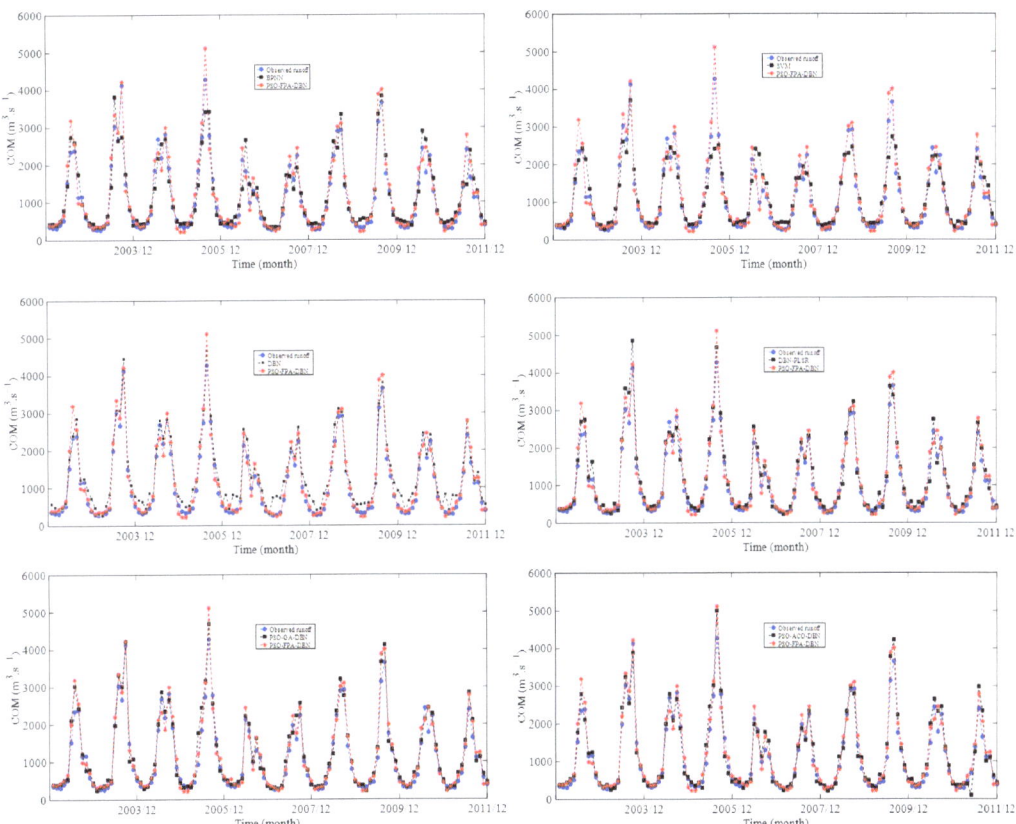

Figure 11. Monthly runoff forecasting results obtained using the PSO-FPA-DBN model compared with those obtained using other models.

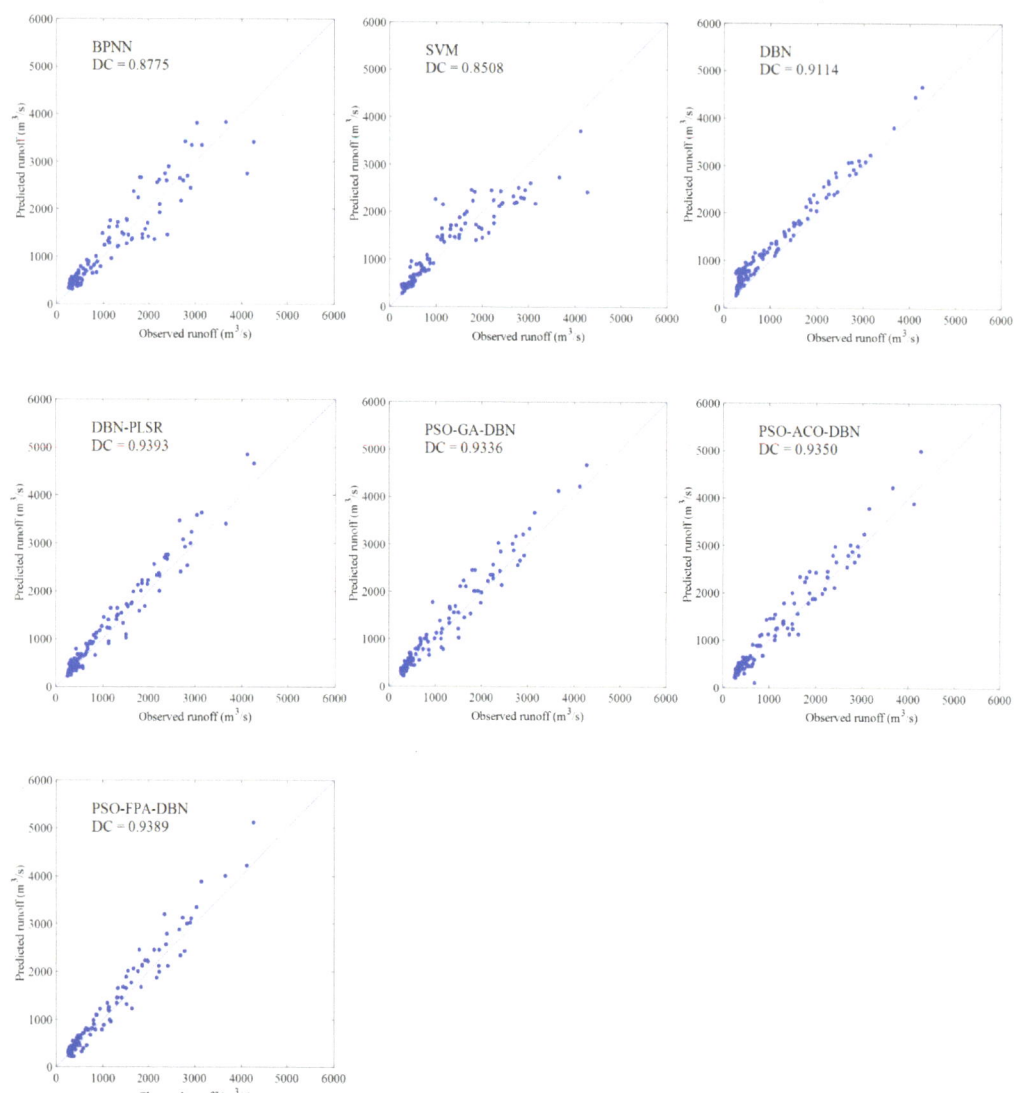

Figure 12. Predicted and observed runoff obtained using the PSO-FPA-DBN model compared with those obtained using other models.

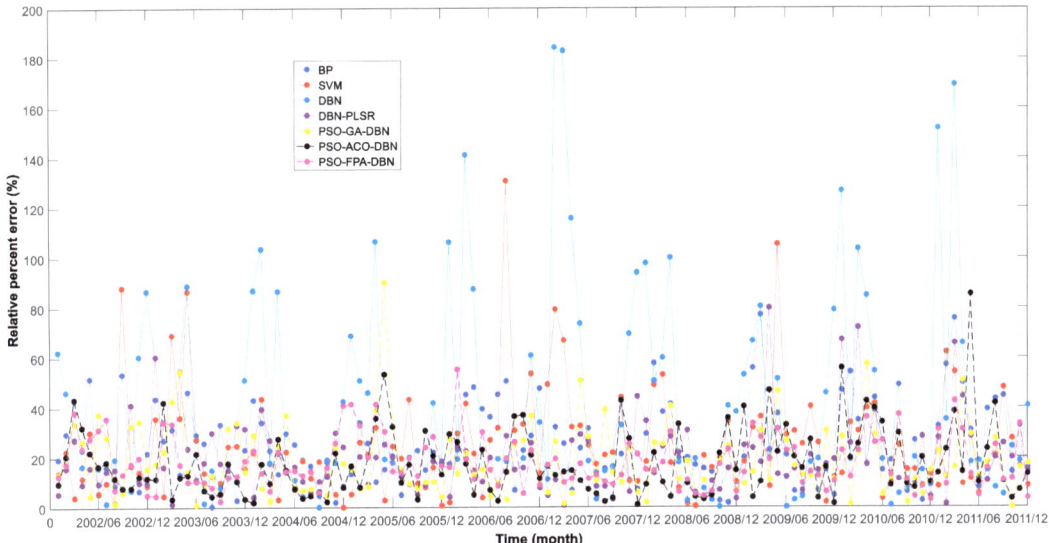

Figure 13. Relative percent error obtained using the PSO-FPA-DBN model compared with those obtained using other models.

6. Discussion

To effectively promote the prediction effect of monthly runoff, we proposed a novel PSO-FPA-DBN hybrid model, which selected the optimal network depth via PSO and searched for the optimum hyperparameters in the DBN using FPA. We also selected six data-driven models (i.e., BPNN, SVM, DBN, and other improved models (DBN-PLSR, PSO-GA-DBN, and PSO-ACO-DBN)) as benchmarks to investigate the performance comparison for monthly runoff prediction. In addition, the MAPE, RMSE, DC, RE, and QR were employed as evaluation indicators of point prediction results to evaluate the prediction accuracy of the above data-driven models. The performance comparison based on the seven data-driven models are shown in Table 5.

Table 5. Performance comparison between the PSO-FPA-DBN model and other models.

Model	MAPE (%)	RMSE ($m^3 \cdot s^{-1}$)	DC	QR (%)
BPNN	24.75	326.29	0.8775	45.8
SVM	24.64	360.02	0.8508	51.7
DBN	41.00	277.50	0.9114	55.8
DBN-PLSR	19.98	229.70	0.9393	61.7
PSO-GA-DBN	18.77	240.20	0.9336	62.5
PSO-ACO-DBN	17.85	237.63	0.9350	63.3
PSO-FPA-DBN	18.23	230.45	0.9389	64.2

Note: QR: qualified rate.

As shown in Table 5, the proposed PSO-FPA-DBN model was better than the traditional prediction methods, i.e., BPNN and SVM, and other improved DBN models (DBN-PLSR, PSO-GA-DBN, and PSO-ACO-DBN). Moreover, it could adapt well to the highly nonlinear characteristics of monthly runoff forecasting. For the MAPE index, PSO-ACO-DBN, PSO-FPA-DBN, and PSO-GA-DBN models were better than other models (17.85%, 18.23%, and 18.77%, respectively). These indicated a marginal error via the prediction models based on the bio-inspired algorithms. For the RMSE index, the DBN-PLSR and PSO-FPA-DBN models were the best (229.70 m^3/s and 230.45 m^3/s, respectively), and the SVM model was the worst. In terms of the DC index, the improved DBN models were better than the other data-driven models (DBN-PLSR model: 0.9393, PSO-FPA-DBN model: 0.9389, PSO-ACO-DBN model: 0.9350, and PSO-GA-DBN model: 0.9336). This revealed that the improved DBN models were in good agreement with the related experimental data. For the QR index, the PSO-FPA-DBN model was the best (64.2%). The BPNN model had a lower score for this index.

To summarize, the methodology presented in this study consists of Comprehensive Basin Response, factor reduction using information entropy, DBN, PSO, and the FPA. Among these, the COM and *PMI* methods were selected to reduce the factors influencing runoff prediction. The PSO-FPA-DBN method was developed to acquire good runoff prediction results. In a case study of the Yalong River Basin, the comprehensive performance of the PSO-FPA-DBN model was better than those of the BPNN, SVM, and other improved DBN models in terms of the evaluation indicators. Also, the forecasting effect of the data-driven models coupled with bio-inspired optimization algorithms (i.e., PSO-FPA-DBN, DBN-PLSR, PSO-GA-DBN, and PSO-ACO-DBN) were much better than other models, because bio-inspired optimization algorithms could deduct the optimal solutions for the optimization problem and increasing the computational speed.

7. Conclusions

In general, it is difficult to characterize runoff trends and realize accurate and reliable monthly runoff forecasts. To overcome the drawbacks of other conventional data-driven models, a hybrid model using particle swarm optimization coupled with flower pollination algorithm-based deep belief networks (PSO-FPA-DBNs) was proposed. In contrast, the optimization-parameter-selection algorithms of the DBN were studied to obtain highly accurate and reliable results. The novelty of our proposed methodology lied in the Comprehensive Basin Response, PMI-based factor selection, and PSO-FPA-DBN model. Finally, we systematically compared the PSO-FPA-DBN model with the traditional prediction methods for monthly runoff forecasting (i.e., BPNN, SVM, DBN, and other improved models (DBN-PLSR, PSO-GA-DBN, and PSO-ACO-DBN)) using an original dataset containing monthly runoff series measured at the Lianghekou, Jinping, Guandi, and Ertan hydrological stations; rainfall data; and climate data from January 1960 to December 2011, in the Yalong River Basin, China. The experimental results demonstrated that the proposed PSO-FPA-DBN model could adapt effectively to the highly nonlinear characteristics of monthly runoff forecasting. Therefore, it could obtain highly accurate and reliable runoff prediction results.

We acknowledge that certain factors were not considered in this study, such as vegetation data and human activities. Moreover, because of the limit of conditions, more recent data were not included in the study. In the future, we would investigate more underlying surface conditions, human activities, and recent data that would be considered in runoff prediction. In addition, future work would also include investigations of additional data-driven models and their parameter-optimization algorithms. Firstly, some state-of-the-art data-driven models would be developed for monthly runoff forecasting, including a Convolutional Neural Network (CNN), Reinforcement Learning (RL), Long-Short Term Memory network (LSTM), machine learning-based hybrid models, or ensemble approaches integrating physics-based models with deep learning algorithms. Secondly, the development of more efficient multi-parameter optimization methods is based on bio-inspired algorithms for determining the optimal parameters of the data-driven models.

Author Contributions: Conceptualization, Z.Y.; Data curation, H.L.; Formal analysis, H.L.; Methodology, Z.Y.; Software, Z.Y. and H.L.; Validation, H.L. and H.Z.; Writing—original draft, Z.Y.; Writing—review & editing, H.Z. All authors have read and agreed to the published version of the manuscript.

Funding: This research was funded by 'the school research fund of Nanjing Vocational University of Industry Technology' (Grant No. YK21-05-05), 'the Open Research Fund of Key Laboratory of River Basin Digital Twinning of Ministry of Water Resources, (Grant No. Z0202042022)', 'the Open Foundation of Industrial Perception and Intelligent Manufacturing Equipment Engineering Research Center of Jiangsu Province (Grant No. ZK22-05-13)', and 'the vocational undergraduate education research fund of Nanjing Vocational University of Industry Technology' (Grant No. ZBYB22-07).

Data Availability Statement: Hydrological data used to support the findings of this study were supplied by the Hydrology Bureau of Yangtze River Water Conservancy Commission of China and the National Climate Center of China (https://data.cma.cn/).

Conflicts of Interest: The authors declare no conflict of interest.

References

1. Tan, Q.-F.; Lei, X.-H.; Wang, X.; Wang, H.; Wen, X.; Ji, Y.; Kang, A.-Q. An adaptive middle and long-term runoff forecast model using EEMD-ANN hybrid approach. *J. Hydrol.* **2018**, *567*, 767–780. [CrossRef]
2. Yue, Z.; Ai, P.; Xiong, C.; Hong, M.; Song, Y. Mid- to long-term runoff prediction by combining the deep belief network and partial least-squares regression. *J. Hydroinform.* **2020**, *22*, 1283–1305. [CrossRef]
3. Yue, Z.; Ai, P.; Yuan, D.; Xiong, C. Ensemble approach for mid-long term runoff forecasting using hybrid algorithms. *J. Ambient. Intell. Humaniz. Comput.* **2020**, *13*, 5103–5122. [CrossRef]
4. Mohammadi, B. A review on the applications of machine learning for runoff modeling. *Sustain. Water Resour. Manag.* **2021**, *7*, 98. [CrossRef]
5. Wang, W.-C.; Cheng, Q.; Chau, K.-W.; Hu, H.; Zang, H.-F.; Xu, D.-M. An enhanced monthly runoff time series prediction using extreme learning machine optimized by salp swarm algorithm based on time varying filtering based empirical mode decomposition. *J. Hydrol.* **2023**, *620*, 129460. [CrossRef]
6. Han, D.; Liu, P.; Xie, K.; Li, H.; Xia, Q.; Cheng, Q.; Wang, Y.; Yang, Z.; Zhang, Y.; Xia, J. An attention-based LSTM model for long-term runoff forecasting and factor recognition. *Environ. Res. Lett.* **2023**, *18*, 024004. [CrossRef]
7. Cheng, Q.; Zuo, X.; Zhong, F.; Gao, L.; Xiao, S. Runoff variation characteristics, association with large-scale circulation and dominant causes in the Heihe River Basin, Northwest China. *Sci. Total Environ.* **2019**, *688*, 361–379. [CrossRef]
8. Zhang, Y.; Wang, M.; Chen, J.; Zhong, P.-A.; Wu, X.; Wu, S. Multiscale attribution analysis for assessing effects of changing environment on runoff: Case study of the Upstream Yangtze River in China. *J. Water Clim. Chang.* **2021**, *12*, 627–646. [CrossRef]
9. Mosavi, A.; Ozturk, P.; Chau, K.-W. Flood Prediction Using Machine Learning Models: Literature Review. *Water* **2018**, *10*, 1536. [CrossRef]
10. Li, X.; Zhang, L.; Zeng, S.; Tang, Z.; Liu, L.; Zhang, Q.; Tang, Z.; Hua, X. Predicting Monthly Runoff of the Upper Yangtze River Based on Multiple Machine Learning Models. *Sustainability* **2022**, *14*, 11149. [CrossRef]
11. Bojang, P.O.; Yang, T.-C.; Pham, Q.B.; Yu, P.-S. Linking singular spectrum analysis and machine learning for monthly rainfall forecasting. *Appl. Sci.* **2020**, *10*, 3224. [CrossRef]
12. Liang, Z.; Li, Y.; Hu, Y.; Li, B.; Wang, J. A data-driven SVR model for long-term runoff prediction and uncertainty analysis based on the Bayesian framework. *Theor. Appl. Clim.* **2018**, *133*, 137–149. [CrossRef]
13. Meng, J.; Dong, Z.; Shao, Y.; Zhu, S.; Wu, S. Monthly Runoff Forecasting Based on Interval Sliding Window and Ensemble Learning. *Sustainability* **2022**, *15*, 100. [CrossRef]
14. Ai, P.; Song, Y.; Xiong, C.; Chen, B.; Yue, Z. A novel medium- and long-term runoff combined forecasting model based on different lag periods. *J. Hydroinform.* **2022**, *24*, 367–387. [CrossRef]
15. Zhang, J.; Chen, X.; Khan, A.; Zhang, Y.-K.; Kuang, X.; Liang, X.; Taccari, M.L.; Nuttall, J. Daily runoff forecasting by deep recursive neural network. *J. Hydrol.* **2021**, *596*, 126067. [CrossRef]
16. Fernando, T.; Maier, H.; Dandy, G. Selection of input variables for data driven models: An average shifted histogram partial mutual information estimator approach. *J. Hydrol.* **2009**, *367*, 165–176. [CrossRef]
17. Tao, L.; He, X.; Li, J.; Yang, D. A multiscale long short-term memory model with attention mechanism for improving monthly precipitation prediction. *J. Hydrol.* **2021**, *602*, 126815. [CrossRef]
18. Li, B.-J.; Sun, G.-L.; Liu, Y.; Wang, W.-C.; Huang, X.-D. Monthly runoff forecasting using variational mode decomposition coupled with gray wolf optimizer-based long short-term memory neural networks. *Water Resour. Manag.* **2022**, *36*, 2095–2115. [CrossRef]
19. Li, B.J.; Sun, G.L.; Li, Y.P.; Zhang, X.L.; Huang, X.D. A hybrid variational mode decomposition and sparrow search algorithm-based least square support vector machine model for monthly runoff forecasting. *Water Supply* **2022**, *22*, 5698–5715. [CrossRef]
20. Zhang, F.; Kang, Y.; Cheng, X.; Chen, P.; Song, S. A Hybrid Model Integrating Elman Neural Network with Variational Mode Decomposition and Box–Cox Transformation for Monthly Runoff Time Series Prediction. *Water Resour. Manag.* **2022**, *36*, 3673–3697. [CrossRef]
21. Ai, P.; Xiong, C.; Li, K.; Song, Y.; Gong, S.; Yue, Z. Effect of Data Characteristics Inconsistency on Medium and Long-Term Runoff Forecasting by Machine Learning. *IEEE Access* **2023**, *11*, 11601–11612. [CrossRef]
22. SugaWara, M. Automatic calibration of the tank model/L'étalonnage automatique d'un modèle à cisterne. *Hydrol. Sci. J.* **1979**, *24*, 375–388. [CrossRef]

23. Zhao, R.J.; Liu, X.R. The Xinanjiang Model. In *Computer Models of Watershed Hydrology*; Singh, V.P., Ed.; Water Resources Publications: Colorado, CO, USA, 1995; pp. 215–232.
24. Samantaray, S.; Das, S.S.; Sahoo, A.; Satapathy, D.P. Monthly runoff prediction at Baitarani river basin by support vector machine based on Salp swarm algorithm. *Ain Shams Eng. J.* **2022**, *13*, 101732. [CrossRef]
25. Yaseen, Z.M.; Jaafar, O.; Deo, R.C.; Kisi, O.; Adamowski, J.; Quilty, J.; El-Shafie, A. Stream-flow forecasting using extreme learning machines: A case study in a semi-arid region in Iraq. *J. Hydrol.* **2016**, *542*, 603–614. [CrossRef]
26. Yaseen, Z.M.; Sulaiman, S.O.; Deo, R.C.; Chau, K.-W. An enhanced extreme learning machine model for river flow fore-casting: State-of-the-art, practical applications in water resource engineering area and future research direction. *J. Hydrol.* **2018**, *569*, 387–408. [CrossRef]
27. Rozos, E.; Dimitriadis, P.; Mazi, K.; Koussis, A.D. A Multilayer Perceptron Model for Stochastic Synthesis. *Hydrology* **2021**, *8*, 67. [CrossRef]
28. Chen, S.; Ren, M.; Sun, W. Combining two-stage decomposition based machine learning methods for annual runoff forecasting. *J. Hydrol.* **2021**, *603*, 126945. [CrossRef]
29. Yang, M.; Yang, Q.; Shao, J.; Wang, G.; Zhang, W. A new few-shot learning model for runoff prediction: Demonstration in two data scarce regions. *Environ. Model. Softw.* **2023**, *162*, 105659. [CrossRef]
30. Sit, M.; Demiray, B.Z.; Xiang, Z.; Ewing, G.J.; Sermet, Y.; Demir, I. A comprehensive review of deep learning applications in hydrology and water resources. *Water Sci. Technol.* **2020**, *82*, 2635–2670. [CrossRef]
31. Wei, M.; You, X.-Y. Monthly rainfall forecasting by a hybrid neural network of discrete wavelet transformation and deep learning. *Water Resour. Manag.* **2022**, *36*, 4003–4018. [CrossRef]
32. LeCun, Y.; Bengio, Y.; Hinton, G. Deep learning. *Nature* **2015**, *521*, 436–444. [CrossRef] [PubMed]
33. Shrestha, A.; Mahmood, A. Review of Deep Learning Algorithms and Architectures. *IEEE Access* **2019**, *7*, 53040–53065. [CrossRef]
34. Ren, Y.; Zeng, S.; Liu, J.; Tang, Z.; Hua, X.; Li, Z.; Song, J.; Xia, J. Mid- to Long-Term Runoff Prediction Based on Deep Learning at Different Time Scales in the Upper Yangtze River Basin. *Water* **2022**, *14*, 1692. [CrossRef]
35. Wang, W.C.; Du, Y.J.; Chau, K.W.; Xu, D.M.; Liu, C.J.; Ma, Q. An ensemble hy-brid forecasting model for annual runoff based on sample entropy, secondary decomposi-tion, and long short-term memory neural network. *Water Resour. Manag.* **2021**, *35*, 4695–4726. [CrossRef]
36. Wu, L.; Zhou, H.; Ma, X.; Fan, J.; Zhang, F. Daily reference evapotranspiration prediction based on hybridized extreme learning machine model with bio-inspired optimization algorithms: Application in contrasting climates of China. *J. Hydrol.* **2019**, *577*, 123960. [CrossRef]
37. Olatomiwa, L.; Mekhilef, S.; Shamshirband, S.; Mohammadi, K.; Petković, D.; Sudheer, C. A support vector machine–firefly algorithm-based model for global solar radiation prediction. *Sol. Energy* **2015**, *115*, 632–644. [CrossRef]
38. Petković, D.; Gocic, M.; Shamshirband, S.; Qasem, S.N.; Trajkovic, S. Particle swarm optimization-based radial basis function network for estimation of reference evapotranspiration. *Theor. Appl. Clim.* **2016**, *125*, 555–563. [CrossRef]
39. Yin, Z.; Wen, X.; Feng, Q.; He, Z.; Zou, S.; Yang, L. Integrating genetic algorithm and support vector machine for modeling daily reference evapotranspiration in a semi-arid mountain area. *Hydrol. Res.* **2017**, *48*, 1177–1191. [CrossRef]
40. Ozkan, C.; Kisi, O.; Akay, B. Neural networks with artificial bee colony algorithm for modeling daily reference evapotranspi-ration. *Irrig. Sci.* **2011**, *29*, 431–441. [CrossRef]
41. Abdel-Basset, M.; Shawky, L.A. Flower pollination algorithm: A comprehensive review. *Artif. Intell. Rev.* **2019**, *52*, 2533–2557. [CrossRef]
42. Tao, H.; Diop, L.; Bodian, A.; Djaman, K.; Ndiaye, P.M.; Yaseen, Z.M. Reference evapotranspiration prediction using hybridized fuzzy model with firefly algorithm: Regional case study in Burkina Faso. *Agric. Water Manag.* **2018**, *208*, 140–151. [CrossRef]
43. Yaseen, Z.M.; Ebtehaj, I.; Bonakdari, H.; Deo, R.C.; Mehr, A.D.; Mohtar, W.H.M.W.; Diop, L.; El-Shafie, A.; Singh, V.P. Novel approach for streamflow forecasting using a hybrid ANFIS-FFA model. *J. Hydrol.* **2017**, *554*, 263–276. [CrossRef]
44. Bennasar, M.; Hicks, Y.; Setchi, R. Feature selection using joint mutual information maximisation. *Expert Syst. Appl.* **2015**, *42*, 8520–8532. [CrossRef]
45. Qian, W.; Shu, W. Mutual information criterion for feature selection from incomplete data. *Neurocomputing* **2015**, *168*, 210–220. [CrossRef]
46. May, R.J.; Dandy, G.C.; Maier, H.R.; Nixon, J.B. Application of partial mutual information variable selection to ANN forecasting of water quality in water distribution systems. *Environ. Model. Softw.* **2008**, *23*, 1289–1299. [CrossRef]
47. May, R.J.; Maier, H.R.; Dandy, G.C.; Fernando, T.G. Non-linear variable selection for artificial neural networks using partial mutual information. *Environ. Model. Softw.* **2008**, *23*, 1312–1326. [CrossRef]
48. Scott, D.W. *Multivariate Density Estimation: Theory, Practice, and Visualization*; John Wiley & Sons: Hoboken, NJ, USA, 1992.
49. Poli, R.; Kennedy, J.; Blackwell, T. 2007 Particle swarm optimization. *Swarm Intell.* **2015**, *1*, 33–57. [CrossRef]
50. Hinton, G.E. Training Products of Experts by Minimizing Contrastive Divergence. *Neural Comput.* **2002**, *14*, 1771–1800. [CrossRef]
51. Gu, J.; Wang, Z.; Kuen, J.; Ma, L.; Shahroudy, A.; Shuai, B.; Liu, T.; Wang, X.; Wang, G.; Cai, J.; et al. Recent advances in convolutional neural networks. *Pattern Recognit.* **2018**, *77*, 354–377. [CrossRef]
52. Qi, Y.; Shen, C.; Wang, D.; Shi, J.; Jiang, X.; Zhu, Z. Stacked Sparse Autoencoder-Based Deep Network for Fault Diagnosis of Rotating Machinery. *IEEE Access* **2017**, *5*, 15066–15079. [CrossRef]

53. Yang, X.; Zhang, X.; Xie, J.; Zhang, X.; Liu, S. Monthly Runoff Interval Prediction Based on Fuzzy Information Granulation and Improved Neural Network. *Water* **2022**, *14*, 3683. [CrossRef]
54. Yuan, X.; Chen, C.; Lei, X.; Yuan, Y.; Muhammad Adnan, R. Monthly runoff forecasting based on LSTM–ALO model. *Stoch. Environ. Res. Risk Assess.* **2018**, *32*, 2199–2212. [CrossRef]
55. Bai, Y.; Chen, Z.; Xie, J.; Li, C. Daily reservoir inflow forecasting using multiscale deep feature learning with hybrid models. *J. Hydrol.* **2016**, *532*, 193–206. [CrossRef]

Disclaimer/Publisher's Note: The statements, opinions and data contained in all publications are solely those of the individual author(s) and contributor(s) and not of MDPI and/or the editor(s). MDPI and/or the editor(s) disclaim responsibility for any injury to people or property resulting from any ideas, methods, instructions or products referred to in the content.

Article

Different Effect of Cloud Seeding on Three Dam Basins, Korea

Jeong-Hyeok Ma [1], Chulsang Yoo [1,*], Sung-Uk Song [1], Wooyoung Na [2], Eunsaem Cho [3], Sang-Keun Song [4] and Ki-Ho Chang [5]

[1] School of Civil, Environmental and Architectural Engineering, Korea University, Seoul 02841, Republic of Korea; 2022020510@korea.ac.kr (J.-H.M.); ssu0103@korea.ac.kr (S.-U.S.)
[2] Department of Civil Engineering, Dong-A University, Busan 49315, Republic of Korea; wna92@dau.ac.kr
[3] Department of Civil and Environmental Engineering, FAMU-FSU College of Engineering, Florida State University, Tallahassee, FL 32310, USA; ec22ba@fsu.edu
[4] Department of Earth and Marine Sciences, Jeju National University, Jeju 63243, Republic of Korea; songsk@jejunu.ac.kr
[5] Convergence Meteorological Research Department, National Institute of Meteorological Sciences, Jeju 63568, Republic of Korea; khchang@korea.kr
* Correspondence: envchul@korea.ac.kr; Tel.: +82-2-3290-3912

Citation: Ma, J.-H.; Yoo, C.; Song, S.-U.; Na, W.; Cho, E.; Song, S.-K.; Chang, K.-H. Different Effect of Cloud Seeding on Three Dam Basins, Korea. *Water* **2023**, *15*, 2555. https://doi.org/10.3390/w15142555

Academic Editor: Ankur Srivastava

Received: 28 May 2023
Revised: 7 July 2023
Accepted: 10 July 2023
Published: 12 July 2023

Copyright: © 2023 by the authors. Licensee MDPI, Basel, Switzerland. This article is an open access article distributed under the terms and conditions of the Creative Commons Attribution (CC BY) license (https:// creativecommons.org/licenses/by/ 4.0/).

Abstract: This study shows that cloud seeding should be planned by considering the dam reservoir characteristics as well as the dam basin characteristics. First, the collection efficiency of increased rainfall by cloud seeding is compared for three dam basins (Boryeong Dam, Yongdam Dam, and Namgang Dam basins) located in the western part of the Korean Peninsula. Second, the additional runoff volumes in those three basins from cloud seeding are compared with each other. Finally, the change in water supply capacity is evaluated by considering the dam reservoir operation and planned water supply. In this study, cloud seeding is simulated using the WRF−ARW model, and, additionally, four different rainfall data generated by considering the scenarios of a rainfall increase of 5, 10, 15, and 20% are used for more practical evaluation. The results in this study show that the situation in Boryeong Dam basin is better than in the other two dam basins. More active cloud seeding is necessary in the Yongdam Dam and Namgang Dam basins. However, it has also been found that cloud seeding alone cannot solve the water supply problems in those two dam basins. The above findings also indicate that cloud seeding should be carefully planned. It can vary dam-by-dam. Cloud seeding might be effective every season in one dam, but only in Spring in another dam basin, while in other dams, summer or fall season might be the best option. The target increase of rainfall is also an important issue. Just a mild increase could be better in one dam, but it can be important to secure much more rainfall in other dams. Even though the three dams considered in this study are located in practically the same climatic zone, the conditions required for cloud seeding differ completely.

Keywords: cloud seeding; rainfall–runoff analysis; water securement; water supply

1. Introduction

Climate change due to global warming leads to significant change in the rainfall pattern, as well as the increase of mean temperature. Higher rainfall intensity and localization are the typical patterns of rainfall under the climate change condition. In contrast, a longer drought period in a wider region is also expected [1]. In the future, this ironic situation will become worse and worse [2]. Simply put, water-related disasters are expected to increase, while the security and management of water resources is also becoming a very difficult task. These interesting phenomena are also fully explainable; in simple terms, the increase of mean temperature increases the capacity of water content in the atmosphere, but it is also true that rainfall occurrence by the cooling process can be more difficult. As a result, if it rains, more severe rainfall can occur, but the period without rain must be longer than that in the past [3]. It is reported that the rainfall duration has shortened [4] and localized [5]. This changed rainfall pattern can increase the runoff in small and urban basins, but decrease the runoff in large basins, regardless of the increase of total rainfall amount.

Recently, droughts have become more frequent in Korea. The frequency of droughts in the 2010s is much higher than in previous decades. According to the National Drought Informational Portal (https://www.drought.go.kr, accessed on 10 January 2023), the rainfall amount in the eastern part of the Korean Peninsula in 2012 was just 32% of the average level, and as a result, the dam water storage level was also recorded as lower than 30%. This drought was expanded the following year to the entire Korean Peninsula. The annual rainfall in the middle of the Korean Peninsula was about 50% of the average level, and for the entire Korean Peninsula, just 60%. Especially, in the Boryeong Dam basin located in the western part of the Korean Peninsula, the dam storage recorded a historic low of 18.9% in 2013. In the same year, the annual rainfall in the Han River basin was also the lowest in history and the second lowest in the Geum River basin [6,7]. Rather small droughts have also continued sporadically over the Korean Peninsula. The spring drought was severe in 2017 in the middle of the Korean Peninsula, and in the same year, the drought moved to the Kangwon Province in the eastern part of the Korean Peninsula. In 2022, both flood in the middle and drought in the southern parts of the Korean Peninsula occurred at the same time [8,9].

Decrease in the total runoff has also been observed in major river basins. As a result, drying streams and the invasion of vegetation into channels have been widely reported. Based on Lee et al. (2020) [10], the minimum flow in a channel has decreased by about 10% since 1980. Lowered groundwater level, increased vegetation density, and increased evapotranspiration amount were the major reasons mentioned in the study. Kim and Kim (2019) [11] also analyzed aerial photographs to evaluate the increase of vegetation area within river section, and reported that during the last 10 years, the vegetation area in Seom River, Chungmi Stream, and Naesung Stream has increased by 2 to 17 times. This change must be fundamentally due to global warming and related climate change.

As a countermeasure to this problem, cloud seeding is considered. This cloud seeding is especially important to alleviate the impact from drought. Cloud seeding is a method of artificially increasing rainfall [12]. It can help to moisten the soil, vitalize the vegetation, and secure additional water resources [13]. Seeding material is sprayed to enhance vapor condensation to make water droplets and to increase rainfall occurrence [14]. Cloud seeding has been considered as a means of securing additional water resources in the 1950s and 1960s in several countries, like Thailand and Israel [15,16], and also in the 1990s in countries like the United States and Australia [17–19]. In Korea, cloud seeding experiments started in 1963. During the droughts in the 1990s and 2000s, several experiments were also conducted as a possible countermeasure to drought [20]. In the 2010s, cloud seeding research was expanded to include theoretical study, numerical modeling, field experiment with aircraft, and intensive ground observation for validation [21]. In 2017, a new aircraft for cloud seeding was also introduced to support the practical application of weather modification techniques [22].

The effect of cloud seeding has been proven in many countries. It must be dependent on the region of cloud seeding experiment, period, and applied techniques, but the overall increase of rainfall was reported to range 5–20%. In experiments in Wyoming, North Dakota, and California, an increase in rainfall of about 5–15% was reported [18,23–27]. In the regions of Adelaide, Tasmania, and New England in Australia, an increase in rainfall of about 5–30% was also reported [28–30]. It was about 10–20% in Israel, about 20% in Jianxi Province, China, and about 27% in Karnataka, India [27,31–33]. Runoff increase due to cloud seeding was also evaluated by Yoo et al. (2022) [13]. Their result was very positive that most of the increased rainfall contributed to increased runoff. This was mainly because the soil was already wet or saturated by the antecedent rainfall before the cloud seeding experiment. The optimal cloud seeding time was selected as the time when there was some antecedent rainfall, or when the soil moisture was very high. As a result, the loss of rainfall could be minimized in the rainfall–runoff analysis.

However, there are also many other issues like benefit–cost, environmental impact, societal responses, etc. [12,34]. More fundamentally, it is also true that the water use or water supply is a somewhat different issue from the increase of rainfall or runoff. This is because the water is generally collected by dam basins. The usefulness of secured water resources by cloud seeding can differ depending on the size of dam basin area and volume of the dam reservoir. It is also important to consider that the water resources in a dam reservoir are distributed by a given rule that differs widely dam-by-dam. A small dam with small dam basin area can be effective if the increased rainfall can be collected fully by the dam basin. If the spatial variability is high, a rather large dam basin area can be positive for cloud seeding. If the planned water supply is small, just a small increase of rainfall could be enough. Depending on these various characteristics of dam basin area, dam reservoir, dam operation, planned water supply, etc., the effectiveness of cloud seeding can vary widely.

This study aims to show that the effectiveness of cloud seeding is highly dependent on the dam and dam basin characteristics. This study selects three dam basins located in the western part of the Korean Peninsula to evaluate cloud seeding from the point of view of water supply. To achieve this study objective, the following three evaluations are carried out. First, the collection efficiency of increased rainfall in those three dam basins is compared. That is, how much rainfall can additionally be received is evaluated. Second, additional runoff volumes by cloud seeding are compared. Depending on the basin characteristics, like the soil, land use, and vegetation, the runoff volume can vary. In particular, if the evapotranspiration amount is large, the basin is disadvantageous for securing addition water resources. Finally, by considering the dam reservoir operation and planned water supply, the change in water supply is evaluated. Cloud seeding can be a huge contribution in one dam, but just small in other dams. The results derived in this study emphasize that cloud seeding should be planned to consider every possible aspect from collection to distribution of the additional water resources.

2. Three Dam Basins in Korea

Three dam basins located in the western part of the Korean Peninsula were considered in this study (Figure 1). These are the Boryeong Dam, Yongdam Dam, and Namgang Dam basins. The Boryeong Dam basin is the most northerly of these three dam basins. Boryeong City is also located within the Boryeong Dam basin. The basin area of the Boryeong Dam is just 163.6 km^2, rather smaller than other multi-purpose dams in Korea. The water resources secured by Boryeong Dam are also small, thus making it vulnerable to drought. In particular, in 2015, the water reserve rate in the Boryeong Dam reservoir receded to an historic low level of just 18.9%. This water storage was far less than the 50% of a normal year [35]. As a counter measure to the drought, an emergency waterway was introduced to supply water to this dam from the nearby Geum River. This waterway can cover about 50% of the water supply capacity from the Boryeong Dam [36].

Yongdam Dam is located in the upstream part of the Geum River. Its basin area is 930.0 km^2, much larger than that of the Boryeong Dam basin. In the same year, 2015, the water storage of Yongdam Dam also receded to be just 25.4%, due to the small annual rainfall of 877.6 mm in the basin. This amount of rainfall was just 67.5% of the normal year's rainfall of about 1300 mm [37]. Namgang Dam is located on the Nam River, the largest tributary of the Nakdong River. Of the three dams, Namgang Dam is located in the southernmost part of the Korean Peninsula. The basin area of the Namgang Dam is 2285 km^2, which is very large, covering 9.6% of the entire Nakdong River basin. In particular, Namgang Dam basin is frequently affected by monsoons and typhoons, and its annual rainfall, a bit higher than 1400 mm, is also the highest of the three dam basins. However, in 2022, the rainfall amount until July 17 was recorded as just 325.4 mm (about 23% of the annual rainfall), then the water storage in the Namgang Dam receded to be just 21.9% [38].

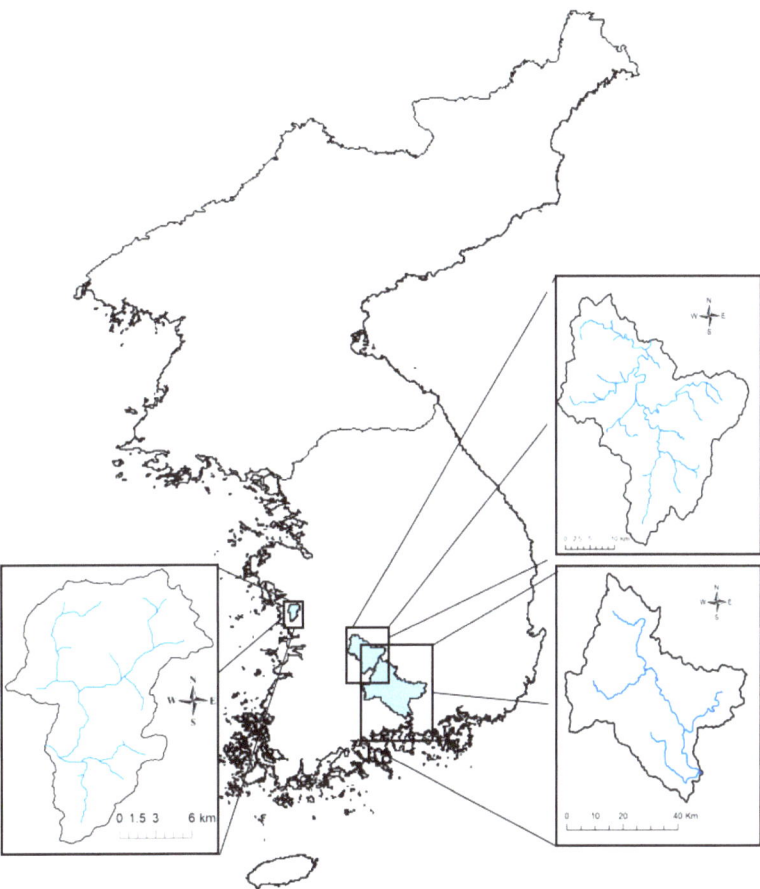

Figure 1. Location of three dam basins considered in this study (clockwise from left, Boryeong Dam, Yongdam Dam, and Namgang Dam basins).

Figure 2 compares the daily rainfall time series for those three dam basins from 2018 to 2020. This figure shows that the overall patterns of rainfall are similar to each other. However, the annual rainfall amounts differ somewhat. Boryeong Dam basin in the northernmost location of the three dam basins shows the smallest annual rainfall, while Namgang Dam basin in the southernmost location shows the highest. The annual rainfall in Yongdam Dam basin lies between the two. However, in 2018 and 2019, the annual rainfall in Yongdam Dam basin was closer to that in Boryeong Dam basin, and in 2020 and 2021, it was closer to that in the Namgang Dam basin. In those four years, the annual rainfall in the Boryeong Dam basin was around 1000 mm, but was 1400 mm in the Yongdam Dam basin and 1600 mm in the Namgang Dam basin. In all three basins, the variation of annual rainfall was found to be very high, with standard deviations of 200 mm or more. Even though there was high variation of annual rainfall, their order was not reversed.

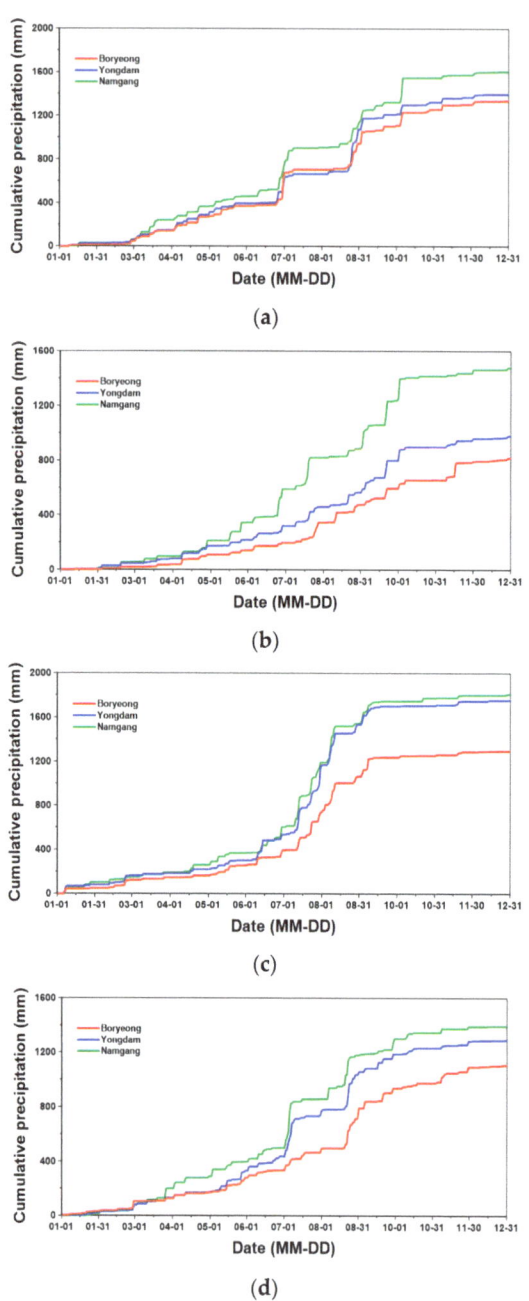

Figure 2. Comparisons of the daily rainfall time series from 2018 to 2020 for the three dam basins considered in this study. (**a**) 2018; (**b**) 2019; (**c**) 2020; (**d**) 2021.

Figure 3 shows the overall characteristics of the three basins. Yongdam Dam basin is located in a high land area, but Boryeong Dam and Namgang Dam basins are located in low land areas near the sea. All three dam basins are mostly covered in forest, along with some farmland, paddy fields, and small urban areas. As most dam basins in Korea are strictly protected to secure clean water, it is not easy to develop an urban area within a dam basin. The soil composition in all three dam basins is also similar. The portion of loam (brownish brown in the figure) is much higher than that of sand (brown) or silt (light brown). Some rock area is also noticeable in the Yongdam Dam basin.

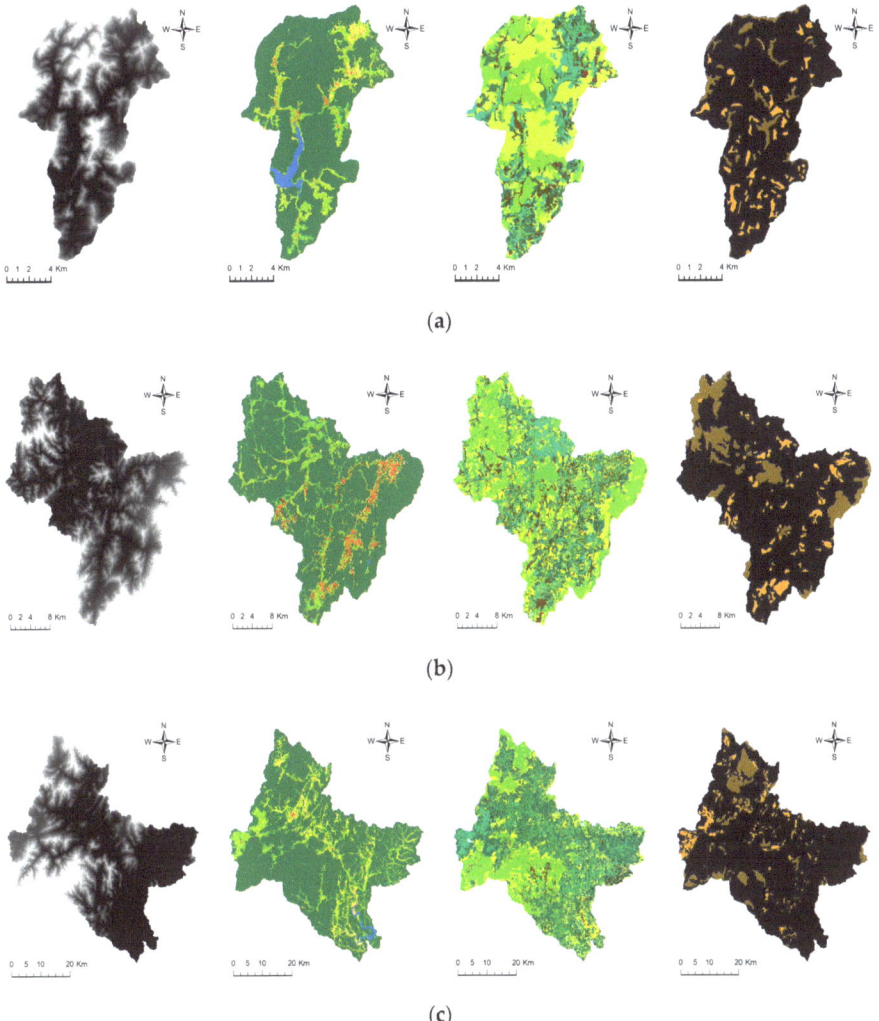

Figure 3. Basic characteristics of the three basins (from left, geomorphology, land use, vegetation and soil). (**a**) Boryeong Dam basin; (**b**) Yongdam Dam basin; (**c**) Namgang Dam basin.

Table 1 summarizes the characteristics of those three dam basins and their land use. As can be seen in this table, the basin area is very different from each other. The Boryeong Dam basin is the smallest, and the Namgang Dam basin is the largest. However, other characteristics are similar. Their basin slopes and shape factor are similar. Also, their land use pattern is similar. About 80% of the dam basin is forest, and paddies and farms cover 15 to 20%. The percentage of urban land use is relatively small in a dam basin, as the urban development is strictly controlled to secure the clean water in Korea.

Table 1. Characteristics of three basins considered in this study.

Basin	Area (km^2)	Slope (Degree)	Shape Factor	Land Use (%)
Boryeong Dam	163.6	16.20	0.279	Forest (77.5)
				Paddy (11.6)
				Farm (5.8)
				Urban (1.0)
				Others (4.1)
Yongdam Dam	930.0	16.21	0.317	Forest (80.0)
				Paddy (9.0)
				Farm (5.4)
				Urban (2.9)
				Others (2.7)
Namgang Dam	2285.5	15.63	0.279	Forest (78.2)
				Paddy (12.4)
				Farm (8.3)
				Urban (0.3)
				Others (0.8)

As mentioned in the previous paragraphs, the three dam basins are mostly covered by forest. Coniferous trees, like pitch pine (colored turquoise in the vegetation map of Figure 3) and nut pine (greenish brown), are quite common, along with deciduous trees like oak (light green). It is also found that mixed forest (bright light green) is significant in the Boryeong Dam basin. These differences in the types of trees and their composition affect the evapotranspiration in each basin. In particular, in Boryeong Dam and Yongdam Dam basins, the portion of needle leaf trees, like pitch pine, nut pine, and larch, is higher than that in Namgang Dam basin [39]. In fact, these three trees are known to have high transpiration rates [40]. As a result, it can be expected that the evapotranspiration amounts in Boryeong Dam and Yongdam Dam basins must be higher than that in Namgang Dam basin.

Table 2 summarizes the specifications of each dam. First, Boryeong Dam was built to provide domestic and industrial water. The construction was started in 1991 and ended in 2000. As Boryeong Dam was built mostly for water supply, its flood control ability is small, with flood control capacity of just 10.0 × 106 m^3 [41]. Construction of Yongdam Dam was begun in 1990, and completed in 2001. The dam reservoir capacities of the Yongdam dam are known to be comparable to other multi-purpose dams in Korea, considering the basin area [42,43].

Table 2. Specifications of the three dams considered in this study.

Dam	Height (m)	Length (m)	Basin Area (km^2)	Total Storage (10^6 m^3)	Effective Storage (10^6 m^3)	Flood Control Volume (10^6 m^3)	Annual Water Supply (10^6 m^3)
Boryeong Dam	50.0	291.0	163.6	116.9	108.7	10.0	106.6
Yongdam Dam	70.0	498.0	930.0	815.0	672.5	137.0	1143.2
Namgang Dam	34.0	1126.0	2285.0	309.2	299.7	269.8	573.3

Namgang Dam has a long history. Construction of this dam was started in 1936, but was interrupted by the Second World War. Its construction was resumed in 1962 and ended in 1969. The size of this dam was increased by reinforcement work during the 10-year period of 1989−1999. However, the total storage capacity and effective storage capacity of the dam are still not large at just 309.2 and 299.7 × 106 m^3, respectively. On the one hand, if considering the basin area, these capacities are particularly small. On the other hand, the planned annual water supply of Namgang Dam is rather high at 573.3 × 106 m^3; also, the flood control capacity is high at 269.8 × 106 m^3. To secure this flood control capacity, the flood water level is reduced by 5 m during the summer rainy season. This new flood water level during the flood season is called the restrictive water level in Korea [44].

3. Cloud Seeding Simulation
3.1. Model Setting

This study used the Weather Research and Forecasting Model—Advanced Research WRF Version 3.8 Model (WRF−ARW model) for cloud seeding simulation. The WRF model was developed by the National Center of Atmospheric Research (NCAR) and National Centers for Environmental Prediction (NCEP) in the United States (http://www.mmm.ucar.edu/wrf/users, accessed on 20 March 2023). This model is a medium-range atmospheric modeling and forecasting system that is used worldwide [45]. It is also designed to be used for both meteorological research and operational forecast.

The WRF model contains two main cores, the Non-hydrostatic Mesoscale Model (NMM) core and the ARW core. The NMM core was developed by NCEP, which is mainly designed for the U.S. region, and is used for operational work. The ARW core was also developed by NCAR, and is available for rather general use [46]. The WRF−ARW is known to be effective for parallel calculations; it also contains physical terms for numerical simulation using the latest technology. It can be used both for ideal simulation and for various research purposes, such as data assimilation and weather forecast.

The numerical simulation area of the WRF−ARW in this study was set to be one domain (200 km × 160 km) centered on the Boryeong Dam (Figure 4), based on the Lambert conformal projection (LCP) coordinate system. To reflect the storm characteristics in this region, which are developed over the West Sea approaching inland and showing high precipitation, the West Sea was included in the domain of the model. The simulation domain consists of grids with a horizontal resolution of 1 km × 1 km and 40 layers in the vertical direction. High-resolution (30 m × 30 m) land cover maps of Korea and Advanced Space-borne Thermal Emission and Reflection Radiometer (ASTER) DEM (also with a resolution of 30 m × 30 m) were used to reflect the geographical and topographical characteristics of the target area around Boryeong Dam. In addition, the sea surface temperature data with a resolution of 0.25° × 0.25° (i.e., 2750 m × 2750 m) from the Fleet Numerical Meteorology and Oceanography Center (FNMOC) were used to account for atmosphere–ocean interactions to improve the model prediction accuracy. Noah Land Surface Model (Noah LSM) was applied to consider changes in surface physical states, such as soil temperature, soil moisture, and partial snowfall. Also, in this simulation, the meteorological data from Unified Model Local Data Assimilation and Prediction System (UM LDAPS) of the Korea Meteorological Administration were applied as a boundary condition, and the simulations were produced for a horizontal grid of 1.5 km × 1.5 km at the integral time interval of 30 s.

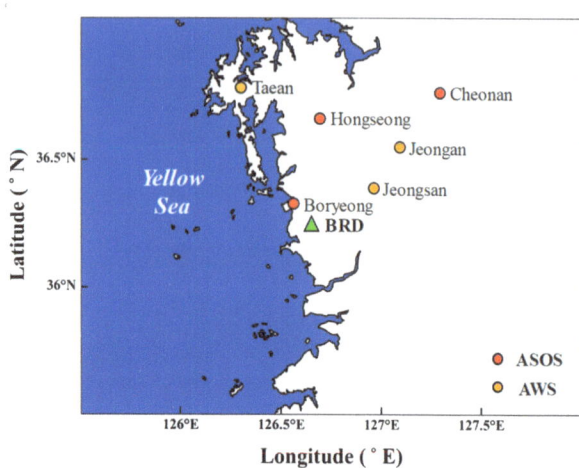

Figure 4. Domain for cloud seeding simulation, where BRD represents the location of the Boryeong Dam, and the red and yellow circles show the weather stations considered in this study for the verification of the rainfall simulation (Adapted with permission from [47]. 2023, Korean Society for Atmospheric Environment).

3.2. Seeding Results

The seeding material ($CaCl_2$) was sprayed into clouds at a time when there was a high possibility of precipitation increase in the target area. The seeding rate was on average 2000 g/h. One the one hand, the seeding was simulated very passively for 2018 and 2019. The seeding was simulated whenever the daily rainfall was 10 mm or more. The seeding location was also fixed to be in the Yellow Sea just in front of the Boryeong Dam basin. This practice is somewhat different from the standard practice for cloud seeding [12,34]. On the other hand, for 2020 and 2021, the cloud seeding was simulated rather actively. The cloud seeding experiment was conducted whenever the minimum liquid water content (LWC) was 0.05 g/m^2 or more. Also, to find the optimal timing and location of seeding, a reverse trajectory tracking method was applied to the horizontal wind field. That is, the seeding location and height was determined as that with the highest LWC. The determined seeding height was about 1~3 km. As a result, the number of seeding flights in the years of 2020 and 2021 was a bit more than the number of rainfall events (about 50 times). It was, however, just one half of the number of rainfall events in the years of 2018 and 2019. In those two years, the simulation was used to find the optimal condition and strategy for cloud seeding. The overall increase rate of annual rainfall in these two years was thus small.

For reference, the effect of El Niño/La Niña was found not so significant in Korea during this period of cloud seeding experiment. The ONI (Oceanic Niño Index), an ENSO index from the NWS Weather Prediction Center (https://origin.cpc.ncep.noaa.gov/products/analysis_monitoring/ensostuff/ONI_v5.php, accessed on 1 July 2023), shows that the years 2018 and 2019 were in the El Niño period (a weak El Niño) and that the La Niña period began from July 2020. The ONI fluctuated from +0.5 and −1.2 in 2020 and remained within the range of −0.5 and −1.0 in 2021 (a weak La Niña). Even though the EOI showed a bit higher fluctuation than the normal level (−0.5 to +0.5) in the years of 2020 and 2021, its effect on the rainfall over the Korean Peninsula was found not to be significant. In the yearbooks from 2019 to 2021 published by the Korea Meteorological Administration (KMA), no significant comments were found on the effect of El Niño/La Niña (https://www.kma.go.kr/kma/archive/pub.jsp?field1=grp&text1=yearbook, accessed on 1 July 2023).

Cloud seeding simulation by the WRF−ARW model was repeated twice for both the unseeded condition (UNSD) and seeded condition (SEED). Simply put, the UNSD is the case where the seeding material was not sprayed, while the SEED is the case where the seeding material was sprayed. The UNSD was used in this study to validate the accuracy of WRF–ARW model performance. The simulation data have a structure of a three-dimensional array with respect to time, latitude, and longitude.

Figure 5 shows an example of the seeding process and the corresponding results of cloud seeding simulation. This example was the cloud seeding simulation experiment performed in the spring of 2021. In this case, the seeding height was 2970 m. Based on the spatial distribution of $CaCl_2$ in this simulation, the effect of cloud seeding could easily be found, especially along the path of the seeding material. The average accumulated precipitation amount in the UNSD was just 2.0, 2.28, and 3.14 mm, respectively, for 60, 120, and 180 min after the completion of seeding. However, the average accumulated precipitation in the SEED was found to be increased to be 2.04, 2.57, and 3.59 mm, respectively. These increases correspond to 1.6, 13.1, and 14.4%, respectively.

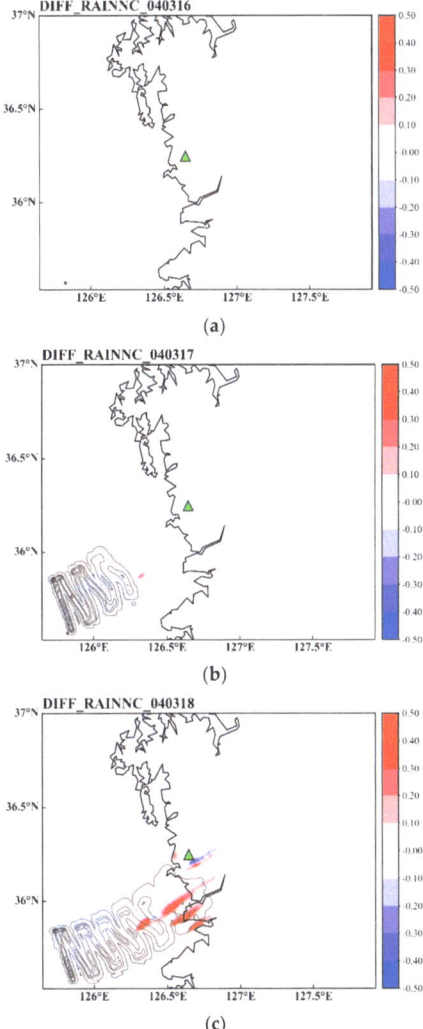

Figure 5. *Cont.*

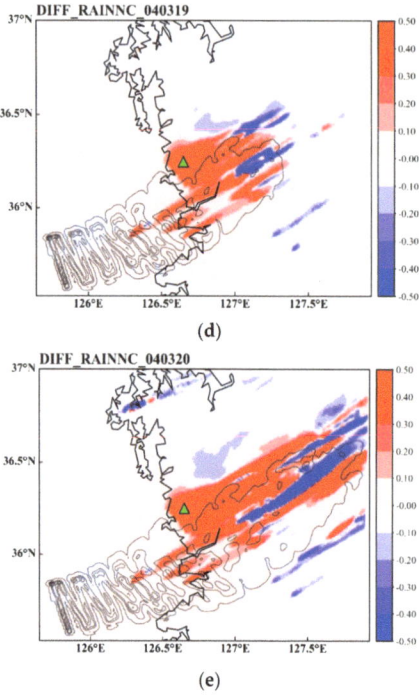

Figure 5. Results of cloud seeding experiment on 3 April 2021 (00UTC~18UTC). The green triangle at the center of the domain is the location of the Boryeong Dam (Adapted with permission from [47]. 2023, Korean Society for Atmospheric Environment). (**a**) Seeding started; (**b**) Seeding ended; (**c**) 60 min after seeding; (**d**) 120 min after seeding; (**e**) 180 min after seeding.

4. Increase Rate of Rainfall in the Three Basins

4.1. Basin Location in the Cloud Seeding Simulation

Cloud seeding was simulated for the domain in Figure 4. The center of the domain is located at the site of Boryeong Dam. Additionally, in this study, the other two dams, Yongdam Dam and Namgang Dam, were also assumed to be located at the domain center. This assumption was introduced to compare the rainfall collection efficiency depending on the size and shape of the dam basin. Figure 6 shows the three basins located at the center of the simulation domain by the WRF model.

4.2. Evaluation of Rainfall Collection Efficiency

This study first evaluated the rainfall collection efficiency of the three dam basins using the increased rate of rainfall. With different dam basin sizes and shapes, the areal mean rainfall amount was estimated differently. Obviously, wind direction and velocity much affected the spatio-temporal variability of each rain field, and the different spatio-temporal distribution of a rain field affected the resulting increase rate of rainfall over the given dam basin. The result in this part of the study was summarized annually to compare the cases with and without cloud seeding (i.e., the seeded case (SEED) and unseeded case (UNSD), respectively). Table 3 shows the result derived for each dam basin from 2018 to 2021. The difference between UNSD and SEED was very small in 2018 and 2019, but somewhat larger in 2020 and 2021. As explained in the previous chapter, the cloud seeding experiment was conservative in the first two years but rather active in the final two years. In particular, the number of cloud seeding experiments was smaller in the first two years, and thus the resulting rainfall increase was also smaller.

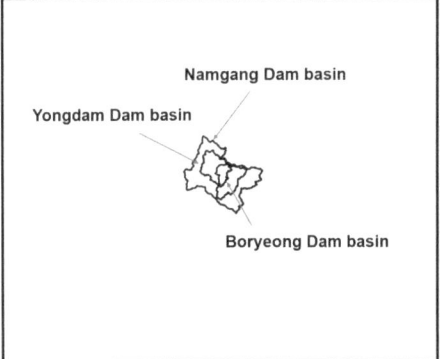

Figure 6. Comparison of three dam basins located at the center of the cloud seeding simulation domain.

Table 3. Increase rate of annual rainfall due to cloud seeding at three dam basin from 2018 to 2021.

Year	UNSD (Annual Rainfall, Entire Domain)	SEED (Annual Rainfall and Increase Rate)			
		Boryeong Dam	Yongdam Dam	Namgang Dam	Entire Domain
2018	1337.2 mm	1338.8 mm (+0.12%)	1338.6 mm (+0.10%)	1338.0 mm (+0.06%)	1339.1 mm (+0.14%)
2019	821.9 mm	825.1 mm (+0.39%)	826.2 mm (+0.52%)	824.6 mm (+0.33%)	827.3 mm (+0.66%)
2020	1301.8 mm	1327.0 mm (+1.94%)	1333.6 mm (+2.44%)	1321.2 mm (+1.52%)	1338.9 mm (+2.84%)
2021	1092.1 mm	1142.9 mm (+4.65%)	1133.1 mm (+3.75%)	1124.7 mm (+2.99%)	1111.6 mm (+1.79%)

An interesting point to notice in Table 3 is that the increase rate is different for each dam basin. In the year 2018, the increase rate was 0.12% in the Boryeong Dam basin, but was somewhat smaller at 0.10% in the Yongdam Dam basin, and 0.07% in the Namgang Dam basin. A similar tendency was also found in 2019 and 2020. Even though the cloud seeding experiment was focused on the domain center, that is, the three dam basins in this study, a very high concentration of increased rainfall was not expected, due to the spatial and temporal variability of the rain field. However, the targeted cloud seeding was still assumed successful, as the rainfall increase rate was somewhat higher in the small dam basins, the Boryeong Dam and Yongdam Dam basins, rather than the large Namgang Dam basin. The cloud seeding experiment in 2021 was also found to be quite successful, and the highest rainfall increase rate was observed in the Yongdam Dam basin.

The rainfall increase rate is important, but the total amount of increased rainfall over the dam basin is also important, especially in terms of water resources. The total amount of increased rainfall in a dam basin is simply calculated by multiplying the dam basin area by the increased rainfall. As can be seen in Figure 7, even though the rainfall increase rate was small in the Namgang Dam basin, the total amount of increased rainfall was larger than that of the other two basins. That is, in 2021, the rainfall increase rate was just 2.99% in the Namgang Dam basin, compared to 4.65 and 3.75% in the Boryeong Dam and Yongdam Dam basins, respectively, while the total amount of increased water resources secured by the cloud seeding was 73.7×10^6 m^3, much higher than the 8.3 and 37.3×10^6 m^3 in the Boryeong Dam and Yongdam Dam basins, respectively. This result indicates that cloud seeding can be more effective in a large basin. This must be limited to the situation where several dam basins are available for cloud seeding, Also, this result must be dependent on the spatial coverage of cloud seeding, as well as the climate in the target region. However, it is not easy to deny that a larger basin area provides an important advantage for securing additional water resources.

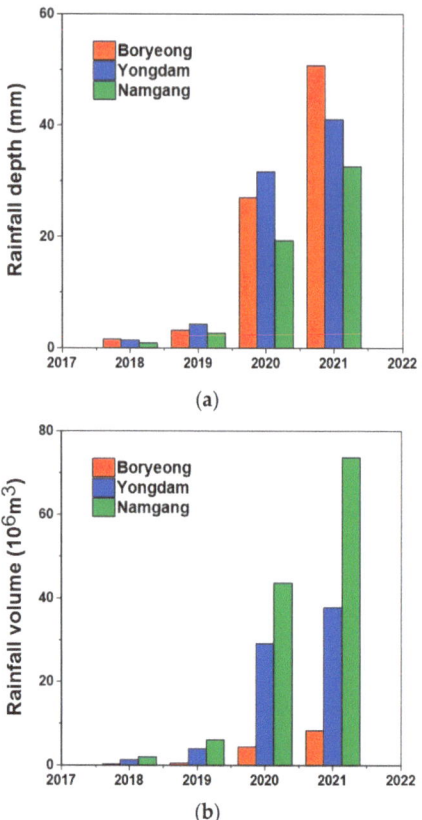

Figure 7. Comparison of increased annual rainfall depth (**a**) and increased annual rainfall volume (**b**) in the three dam basins. The increased rainfall depth is the areal average one over the dam basin, and the increased rainfall volume is calculated by multiplying the increased rainfall depth by the basin area. (**a**) Increased rainfall depth; (**b**) Increased rainfall volume.

5. Contribution of Cloud Seeding to Securing Additional Water Resources

5.1. Rainfall–Runoff Analysis Using the PRMS Model

The rainfall–runoff model used in this study is the Precipitation Runoff Modeling System (PRMS) model. The PRMS model is a long-term runoff model developed by the United States Geological Survey (USGS) [48]. With this model, it is possible to simulate various components of the hydrologic process, such as interception, infiltration, effective rainfall, direct runoff, subsurface runoff, and groundwater runoff.

Runoff simulation is performed by dividing a basin into hydrological response units (HRU), with each unit being an area with homogeneous topographic characteristics, such as slope, elevation, vegetation distribution, and soil type. By dividing the basin into HRUs, the hydrologic process for each sub-basin can be evaluated separately. The runoff simulation result for the entire basin is derived by combining the runoff simulation results performed by each HRU.

The major input data to the PRMS model include the meteorological data, like precipitation, maximum and minimum temperatures, solar radiation, and evaporation. Daily precipitation is corrected by the precipitation correction factor for each HRU, and the correction factor is determined by considering the characteristic of precipitation. In the case of the maximum and minimum temperature data, the spatially interpolated value is used according to the elevation difference between the weather station and the HRU. Solar radiation can be calculated directly from the model using information such as latitude, longitude, and temperature. Temperature and solar radiation are used to simulate processes such as evaporation, transpiration, sublimation, and snowmelt.

The three dam basins, the Boryeong Dam, Yongdam Dam, and Namgang Dam basins, considered in this study have different basin areas. Thus, sub-basin division was also performed differently by considering the basin area and channel network. In Korea, 250 km^2 is generally considered as the criteria for sub-basin division [49]. First, due to its small size, the Boryeong Dam basin was considered as a single basin. The Yongdam Dam basin, with its basin area of 930.0 km^2, was divided into four sub-basins. Finally, the Namgang Dam basin, which has the largest basin area of 2285.0 km^2, was divided into a total of 10 sub-basins. Each sub-basin was assumed to represent each HRU in this study.

Parameters of the PRMS model are determined by analyzing the topographical, soil, land use, and vegetation data of the basin. The PRMS model contains two types of parameters: easy-to-estimate parameters (EEPs), and difficult-to-estimate parameters (DEPs). The EEPs are mostly related to interception, surface runoff, and the behavior of water within the soil. These are determined rather easily using the available basin characteristics. In contrast, the DEPs are related to evapotranspiration, surface runoff, behavior of water in soil, and behavior of groundwater. Generally, the DEPs are difficult to estimate directly using the available data. These parameters are generally determined empirically, or by applying the concept of optimization. For the initial values of these parameters, it is possible to use the suggested values by the PRMS model, or it is also possible to consider other parameters determined in other basins with similar basin characteristics.

In this study, the EEPs were determined directly with the available data of basin characteristics. Also, the initial estimates of DEPs were determined by considering existing study in Korea, the Hydrological Survey Report of Geum River Basin [50]. The Rosenbrock technique was applied in the optimization procedure, which is a built-in method of the PRMS model. The dada observed in 2017 were used for parameter estimation, while the data collected from 2018 to 2019 were used for parameter validation. Figure 8 compares the observed and simulated runoff by the PRMS model with the parameters having finally been determined. These results are also found in line with previous studies [51]. Also, Table 4 summarizes this comparison between simulated and observed runoff hydrographs.

Table 4. Comparison of simulated and observed runoff data from 2018 to 2019.

Basin	Mean (m^3/s)		Stdv (m^3/s)		Max (m^3/s)		RMSE (m^3/s)
	Obs	Est	Obs	Est	Obs	Est	
Boryeong Dam	3.6	3.5	11.4	12.1	186.9	226.8	8.0
Yongdam Dam	21.0	22.7	64.2	80.1	1226.8	1252.1	44.9
Namgang Dam	70.3	72.1	225.1	246.9	2905.5	2901.8	93.8

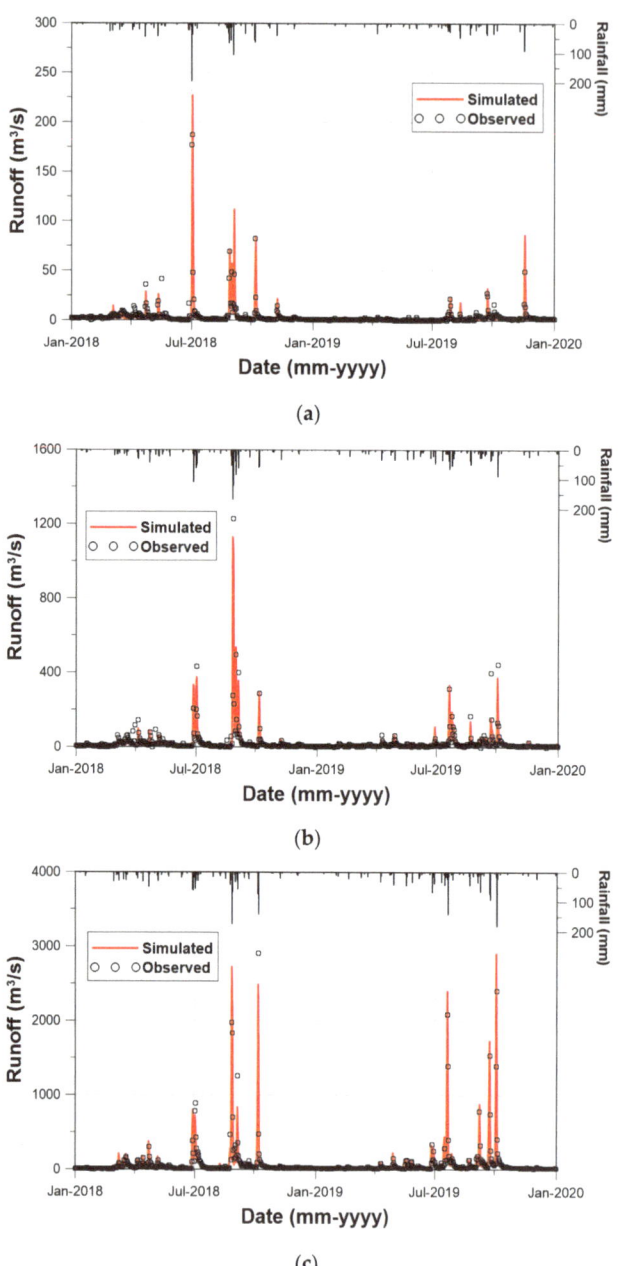

Figure 8. Comparison of simulated and observed runoff hydrographs in 2018 and 2019 in the three dam basins considered in this study. The rainfall data are the areal average one over the basin, and the runoff hydrograph was derived by the PRMS model. (**a**) Boryeong Dam; (**b**) Yongdam Dam; (**c**) Namgang Dam.

As can be seen in Table 4, the rainfall–runoff analysis for the three basins was conducted properly. In the case of Boryeong Dam basin, the observed and simulated mean runoffs are 3.6 and 3.5 m^3/s, respectively. The difference in other statistics was the same to be within 10%. Generally, less than 10% difference is proof of an acceptable simulation result [46]. Even in the cases of the Yongdam Dam and Namgang Dam basins, the differences between the simulated and observed statistics were all found to be within 10%. However, the RMSEs for all three dam basins were still high at 8.0, 44.9, and 93.8 m^3/s, respectively. These high RMSEs were mostly from the difference in the rainy season, when the variation of runoff was very high.

5.2. Analysis of Increased Runoff

5.2.1. Application of Simulated Rainfall by the WRF−ARW

The rainfall–runoff analysis with the PRMS model was performed for the years 2018−2021 in all three dam basins. First, the observed rainfall and temperature data were used as input, and the resulting runoff was compared with the observed data at the exit of the basin. Additionally, the cloud seeding result (i.e., increased portion of rain rate) was considered in the same rainfall–runoff analysis, and a new runoff result derived. These two runoff results were then compared as the unseeded case (UNSD) and seeded case (SEED). As the simulated rainfall of both SEED and UNSD cases is distributed over the dam basin, the rain gauge density did not give any effect on the simulation result. Also, the simulated rainfall data were averaged over the basin or sub-basin to be used as input to the PRMS model. Thus, their spatial variability within the basin or sub-basin did not give any significant effect on the runoff result.

Table 5 shows various runoff components, i.e., baseflow, interflow, direct runoff, and total runoff, simulated for those years 2018−2021, respectively. Here, the baseflow indicates the flow from the groundwater and the interflow the flow from the three soil layers in the PRMS model. The direct runoff indicates the runoff due to effective rainfall [45]. The first thing to notice in this table is that the runoff increase rate is higher than the rainfall increase rate. In the Yongdam Dam and Namgang Dam basins, the runoff increase rate was about two times or more than the rainfall increase rate. A similar result was also found in Yoo et al. (2022) [12], who mentioned that this result was mainly due to the far smaller loss rate. As the cloud seeding was generally performed when the soil was wet with antecedent rainfall, most of the increased rainfall could directly contribute to the runoff increase. This is one important reason why the cloud seeding is effective for securing additional water resources.

It is also noticeable that cloud seeding has significantly increased interflow. In particular, when the increase rate of rainfall was small, rather than the direct runoff and baseflow, the increase rate of interflow was higher. Increased rainfall due to cloud seeding might be high enough to increase the infiltration, but too small to increase the groundwater level. In particular, in the Yongdam Dam and Namgang Dam basins, the increase rate of interflow was highest in all years of simulation. On the other hand, the increase rates of direct runoff and baseflow were found to be dependent on the increase rate of rainfall. With the large increase rate of rainfall, the increase rates of baseflow and direct runoff became large enough to be similar to the increase rate of interflow, such as in the Yongdam Dam and Namgang Dam basins in the years 2020 and 2021. But, in the small Boryeong Dam basin, the increase rate of baseflow was found to be always smaller than the interflow and direct runoff, in all cases.

Simulated runoff becomes the inflow to the dam reservoir. Additional inflow to the dam reservoir increases the storage, whose contribution is relative to the total storage capacity, effective storage capacity, and planned annual water supply. Table 6 shows the relative amount of cloud seeding to these dam capacities. This information shows that the effect of cloud seeding can differ, depending on the dam basin and dam reservoir characteristics. First, in the Boryeong Dam and Yongdam Dam basins, the increase rate of total storage was found to be smaller than that of the total runoff. This is mainly due to the large total storage capacity, compared to the size of dam basin area. This imbalance is somewhat more serious in the Yongdam Dam basin, where the increase rate of total storage was found to be less than that of the total runoff. On the other hand, a totally opposite result was derived from the Namgang Dam. The increase rate of total storage was found to be more than three times the total runoff. In fact, this is an exceptional result, due to the very small storage capacity, compared to the dam basin area. A similar result was also found in the comparison of the increase rate of effective rainfall. As the effective storage capacity is smaller than the total storage capacity, it is normal that the increase rate of effective storage is higher than that of the total storage.

Table 5. Volume change in runoff components due to cloud seeding from 2018 to 2021.

Basin	Component (Unit)	2018		2019		2020		2021	
		UNSD	SEED	UNSD	SEED	UNSD	SEED	UNSD	SEED
Boryeong Dam	Total rainfall (mm)	1337.2	1338.8 (+0.1%)	821.9	825.1 (+0.4%)	1301.8	1327.0 (+1.9%)	1092.1	1142.9 (+4.7%)
	Baseflow (mm)	304.7	304.7 (+0.0%)	297.6	297.8 (+0.1%)	303.4	303.7 (+0.1%)	299.4	299.5 (0.1%)
	Interflow (mm)	49.7	49.7 (+0.1%)	28.0	28.1 (+0.6%)	46.5	47.6 (+2.3%)	38.6	40.4 (4.7%)
	Direct runoff (mm)	540.7	542.3 (+0.3%)	127.7	129.3 (+1.2%)	504.2	518.3 (+2.8%)	343.9	366.4 (6.5%)
	Total runoff (mm)	894.1	895.7 (+0.2%)	453.2	455.1 (+0.4%)	854.1	869.7 (+1.8%)	681.9	706.4 (3.6%)
Yongdam Dam	Total rainfall (mm)	1337.2	1338.6 (+0.1%)	821.9	826.2 (+0.5%)	1301.8	1333.6 (+2.4%)	1066.4	1133.1 (+6.3%)
	Baseflow (mm)	190.7	191.1 (+0.3%)	79.3	80.2 (+1.2%)	179.9	184.1 (+2.3%)	110.5	125.3 (+13.4%)
	Interflow (mm)	459.5	460.7 (+0.3%)	90.3	91.8 (+1.7%)	443.6	466.9 (+5.3%)	260.2	286.5 (+10.1%)
	Direct runoff (mm)	52.2	52.3 (+0.18%)	23.8	24.0 (+0.8%)	42.6	43.9 (+3.2%)	33.1	35.7 (+8.0%)
	Total runoff (mm)	702.3	704.1 (+0.3%)	193.3	195.9 (+1.3%)	666.1	695.0 (+4.3%)	403.8	447.4 (+10.8%)
Namgang Dam	Total rainfall (mm)	1337.2	1338.0 (+0.1%)	821.9	824.6 (+0.3%)	1301.8	1321.2 (+1.5%)	1018.5	1124.7 (+10.4%)
	Baseflow (mm)	257.6	257.8 (+0.1%)	145.0	145.9 (+0.7%)	262.4	266.0 (+1.4%)	155.1	180.2 (+16.2%)
	Interflow (mm)	436.7	437.4 (+0.2%)	118.1	119.3 (+1.01%)	448.7	461.2 (+2.8%)	266.9	313.9 (+17.6%)
	Direct runoff (mm)	137.2	137.3 (+0.1%)	49.4	49.6 (+0.5%)	97.8	99.6 (+1.9%)	69.8	79.9 (+14.5%)
	Total runoff (mm)	831.3	832.4 (+0.1%)	312.4	314.8 (+0.8%)	809.0	826.9 (+2.2%)	492.1	573.9 (+16.6%)

Table 6. Relative volume of runoff increase due to cloud seeding from 2018 to 2021 at Boryeong Dam (B), Yongdam Dam (Y), and Namgang Dam (N).

Year	Increase Rate of Runoff Volume (%)			Increased Runoff Volume/Total Storage (%)			Increased Runoff Volume/Effective Storage (%)			Increased Runoff Volume/Planned Annual Water Supply (%)		
	B	Y	N	B	Y	N	B	Y	N	B	Y	N
2018	0.2	0.3	0.1	0.2	0.2	0.7	0.2	0.2	0.8	0.2	0.1	0.4
2019	0.4	1.3	0.8	0.3	0.3	1.7	0.3	0.4	1.8	0.3	0.2	0.9
2020	1.8	4.3	2.2	2.2	3.3	13.1	2.3	4.0	13.5	2.4	2.3	7.1
2021	3.6	10.8	16.6	3.4	4.9	59.9	3.7	6.0	61.8	3.8	3.5	32.3

The relative amount of the increased total runoff to the planned annual water supply (i.e., the increase rate of water supply) has another meaning, as it can be directly linked to the end user. In the Boryeong Dam basin, the increase rate of water supply was almost the same as that of total runoff. However, in the Yongdam Dam basin, this increase rate of annual water supply was found to be smaller than a half of the runoff increase rate. This result indicates that the planned annual water supply in the Yongdam Dam basin is too high. Finally, in the Namgang Dam basin, even though the increase rate of annual water supply is smaller than the increase of total storage, it is still more than twice the increase rate of total runoff. This result indicates that the effect of cloud seeding on the water supply could be higher in the Namgang Dam basin. This must depend on the fact that the increased total runoff can be supplied to the end users without any loss.

The above consideration shows that the relative role of cloud seeding differs, depending on the dam reservoir characteristics. In one dam, the increase rate of total storage might be remarkable, while in other dams, the increase of annual water supply might be significant. However, as the final goal of cloud seeding in this study is to increase the water supply, the increase rate of annual water supply must have a higher weight. In that sense, the contribution of cloud seeding may be higher in the Namgang Dam basin than in the other two dam basins. That is, assuming that the practical expectation of rainfall increase by cloud seeding may not be that high, the cloud seeding can be more advantageous in a dam basin with large basin area compared to small effective storage capacity (or small planned annual water supply).

5.2.2. Application of Scenario-Based Rainfall

In this part of the study, the rainfall data generated by considering the given increase scenario were considered in the same evaluation of cloud seeding. As explained in the previous chapter, four different increase scenarios, i.e., 5, 10, 15, and 20% increase, were considered in the rainfall data generation. The rainfall data observed in 2021 were considered as the base scenario. Rainfall has been increased by the given percentage at the same date when the cloud seeding was applied in the WRF−ARW simulation. Finally, the four different rainfall data generated by considering the four different increase scenarios along with the based data were applied to the same PRMS model for rainfall–runoff analysis. Table 7 summarizes the relative change in the runoff components, like the baseflow, interflow, and direct runoff.

As can be found in Table 7, the relative changes of the runoff components, like the baseflow, interflow, and direct runoff, are dependent on the rainfall increase rate, but also differ basin-by-basin. Different from the application of the simulated rainfall by WRF−ARW in the previous section, the increase of interflow and direct runoff were found dominant in all three basins. The increase of baseflow was found to be smaller than that of the interflow and the direct runoff. This result seems to be due to the rather large increase of rainfall. As the soil was already wet before the cloud seeding, the increased rainfall might contribute much to the direct runoff and interflow. As the groundwater is charged by the percolation process, it must have some limitation, even under the condition of large rainfall increase.

Additionally, it is also noticeable that the increase rate of total runoff seems to be proportional to the basin area. The increase rate of total runoff was smaller in the Bo-ryeong Dam basin, but quite high in the Yongdam Dam and Namgamg Dam basins. As a result, the increase rate of the total runoff in the Boryeong Dam basin was 21.9% when the increase rate of rainfall was 20%. It was much higher at 34.8% in the Yongdam Dam basin and at 33.0% in the Namgang Dam basin. In the latter two basins, the increase of interflow was a highly significant cause of the increase of total runoff. On the other hand, in the Boryeong Dam basin, the increase of total runoff was mostly from the increase of direct runoff.

Table 7 also confirms that the increase rate of runoff was higher than that of rainfall. That is, in the Boryeong Dam basin, the increase rate of runoff was 1.1 times higher than that of the rainfall, which in the Namgang Dam basin was much higher at 1.5 times. However, it should also be remembered that the increase amount of runoff is still smaller than that of the rainfall. The increased amount of runoff was found to be just 70% of the increased amount of rainfall in the Boryeong Dam and Yongdam Dam basins, while it was 80% in the Namgang Dam basin. This higher ratio in the Namgang Dam basin was mainly due to the smaller evapotranspiration amount with somewhat different vegetation types. Regardless of whether it is 70 or 80%, this ratio is an extremely high runoff ratio, if considering the normal runoff ratio in a basin in Korea. In these three dam basins, the normal runoff ratio is around 50%. It reduces to below 40% under extreme drought condition, just like in 2015 [52].

The runoff ratio of 70 to 80% should be assumed to be a significant level, especially under the water shortage situation.

Table 7. Volume change in runoff components depending on the rainfall increase scenarios for the year of 2021.

Basin	Component (Unit)	UNSD	SEED			
			5%	10%	15%	20%
Boryeong Dam	Total rainfall (mm)	1092.1	1144.9	1197.7	1250.5	1303.4
	Baseflow (mm)	299.4	299.4 (+0.0%)	299.7 (+0.1%)	300.1 (+0.2%)	300.4 (+0.3%)
	Interflow (mm)	38.4	40.6 (+5.6%)	42.8 (+11.3%)	44.9 (16.8%)	47.1 (+22.4%)
	Direct runoff (mm)	363.7	399.3 (+9.8%)	435.9 (+19.9%)	472.0 (+29.8%)	507.3 (+39.5%)
	Total runoff (mm)	700.4	738.3 (+5.4%)	777.3 (+11.0%)	816.0 (+16.5%)	853.8 (+21.9%)
Yongdam Dam	Total rainfall (mm)	1066.4	1118.1	1169.8	1221.6	1273.3
	Baseflow (mm)	120.9	126.0 (+4.2%)	130.5 (+7.9%)	134.2 (+11.1%)	138.0 (+14.2%)
	Interflow (mm)	281.3	310.7 (+10.4%)	341.2 (+21.3%)	374.2 (+33.0%)	406.6 (+44.5%)
	Direct runoff (mm)	33.5	35.7 (+6.5%)	37.9 (+13.3%)	40.3 (+20.2%)	42.7 (+27.5%)
	Total runoff (mm)	435.6	472.2 (+8.4%)	509.6 (+17.0%)	548.6 (+25.9%)	587.2 (+34.8%)
Namgang Dam	Total rainfall (mm)	1018.5	1068.1	1117.7	1167.4	1217.0
	Baseflow (mm)	163.6	169.2 (+3.4%)	173.8 (+6.2%)	178.7 (+9.3%)	184.0 (+12.5%)
	Interflow (mm)	265.7	295.0 (+11.0%)	324.9 (+22.3%)	354.8 (+33.6%)	384.4 (+44.7%)
	Direct runoff (mm)	69.7	75.5 (+8.3%)	81.7 (+17.1%)	88.2 (+26.5%)	95.2 (+36.5%)
	Total runoff (mm)	498.9	539.6 (+8.2%)	580.3 (+16.3%)	621.7 (+24.6%)	663.5 (+33.0%)

6. Relative Contribution to Water Supply According to Different Reservoir Operation Method

6.1. Reservoir Operation Methods

Increase of runoff in a basin indicates the increase of water resources. In simple terms, the increase of water resources is dependent upon the basin area and the rainfall increase. However, the usefulness of water resources is more dependent upon the characteristics of dam reservoirs, as well as the dam operation method. For example, Boryeong Dam is a small dam with a small reservoir; its basin area is also small. On the other hand, Yongdam Dam is big with a large reservoir; its basin area is also large. Interestingly, while Namgang Dam is much smaller than Yongdam Dam, its basin area is much larger. These characteristics highly affect the usefulness of the increased water resources by cloud seeding, which has been reviewed in previous sections. Additionally, it should be considered that the reservoir operation method can completely change the usefulness of the additional water resources. Simply put, the additional water resources secured in the dam reservoir may not be used effectively if the given dam reservoir and reservoir operation method cannot accept it.

The reservoir operation method (ROM) may be divided into the following five categories: the automatic ROM (Auto ROM), spillway rule curve ROM (SRC ROM), rigid ROM, technical ROM, and scheduled release discharge ROM (SRD ROM) [53]. First, the Auto ROM is a simple method whereby the discharge from a dam occurs when the reservoir stage is higher than the given target stage. The dam discharge is determined by the spillway discharge rating curve. The SRC ROM is an empirical method to control the water gate to decrease the downstream peak flow, in which the downstream flood control is achieved by following the predetermined spillway rule curve. This method is known to be effective when the inflow is similar to the design flood. However, if the inflow is much higher than the design flood, the downstream flood damage could be worse.

The rigid ROM may be the most popular ROM in Korea. This ROM is also called the constant rate–constant magnitude method. That is, until the peak inflow, a constant rate is applied to the inflow to determine the discharge. After the peak inflow, a constant magnitude is discharged. This constant discharge is generally determined by the discharge determined at the time of peak inflow, i.e., simply by multiplying the peak inflow by the constant rate. The constant rate is thus important in the Rigid ROM. This constant rate is determined by trial-and-error method to satisfy the condition that the flood control capacity is filled with the inflow flood. The technical ROM is the method of determining the discharge by considering the predicted inflow hydrograph. This method is known to be very effective under the condition that the predicted inflow hydrograph is accurate, and it can then fully use the flood control volume. Finally, the SRD ROM considers past experience in the determination of discharge. Even though it is a primeval method, the SRD ROM is frequently used to test the change in reservoir stage before and after a flood.

Among the three dams considered in this study, Boryeong Dam and Yongdam Dam adopt the rigid ROM for their reservoir operation. However, Namgang Dam operates the reservoir rather empirically, as the size of dam reservoir is very small compared to the basin area [54]. During the rainy season, to secure the flood control capacity, the flood water level is reduced by 5 m. That is, the restrictive water level is applied during the rainy season. Table 8 summarizes the basic information of reservoir operation for those three dams in this study.

Table 8. Basic information of three dams considered in this study.

Dam	Flood Water Level (EL. m)	Restricted Water Level (EL. m)	Low Water Level (EL. m)	Planned Annual Water Supply (10^6 m^3)	Effective Storage (10^6 m^3)/ Flood Control Storage (10^6 m^3)	Reservoir Operation Method (Constant Rate)
Boryeong Dam	75.50	74.00	50.00	106.60	10.9	Rigid ROM (0.586)
Yongdam Dam	265.50	261.50	228.50	1143.20	4.9	Rigid ROM (0.560)
Namgang Dam	46.00	41.00	32.00	573.30	1.1	Empirical Method

6.2. Reservoir Operation with Simulated Rainfall by the WRF−ARW

This study first considered the runoff data simulated by the PRMS model with the rainfall input generated by the WRF−ARW model from 2018 to 2021. The runoff data simulated with the observed rainfall data without considering the cloud seeding were also used for the comparison. The temporal resolution of this runoff simulation was one day, which is generally accepted for the evaluation of water supply from a dam [55,56]. Thus, the reservoir operation was performed on a daily basis, and as results, the daily reservoir storage and daily water supply could be derived. Figure 9 shows the daily variation of reservoir storage. The solid line is the UNSD case, while the red circle indicates the SEED case. These two cases move between the low water level (dotted line) and the high water level (alternated long and short dash line). From this figure, it is also possible to conjecture the normal water supply and water shortage. That is, if the remaining reservoir storage is smaller than the planned daily water supply, then a shortage of water supply occurs. However, the reservoir stage cannot be lower than the low water level. In the reservoir operation in this study, evaporation from the dam reservoir was not considered.

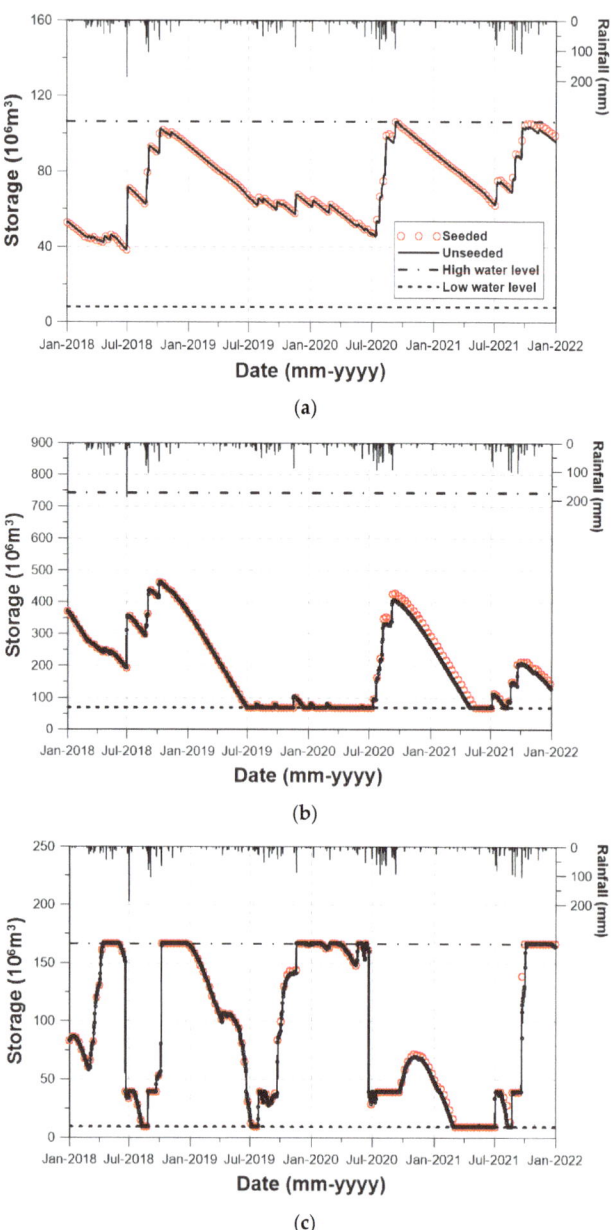

Figure 9. Change in dam water storage in three dam reservoirs due to cloud seeding from 2018 to 2021. (**a**) Boryeong Dam; (**b**) Yongdam Dam; (**c**) Namgang Dam.

Figure 9 clearly shows the difference of dam situations. Even though they are all located within similar climatic regions, their reservoir operation results are totally different. The Boryeong Dam seems to have no serious problem, at least during the simulation period from 2018 to 2021. Its storage moved from about 40 to 100%, with its mean around 75%. A similar variation pattern of dam storage could be found in the Yongdam Dam. However, the mean storage was just 25%, moving from 0 to 50%. The behavior of dam storage in the Namgang Dam was more dramatic, moving from 0 to 100%, with its mean around 50%. As explained earlier, this totally different behavior is due to the different conditions of the dam basin, dam reservoir, and operation rule.

As can be seen in Figure 9, the effect of cloud seeding was not that obvious. This trend was the same in all three dams, which was mainly due to the rather small increase of rainfall by cloud seeding. In 2020 and 2021, when the rainfall increase was rather high, it was possible to clearly find the difference. After 2020, the difference was rather high in the Yongdam Dam reservoir.

During the four years of simulation, the water level in Boryeong Dam was higher than the low water level. That is, during this simulation period, no water shortage occurred in Boryeong Dam. However, in the Yongdam Dam basin, the water level stayed around the low water level for almost one year from July 2019. A severe water shortage problem continued in this dam, but the cloud seeding somewhat alleviated the problem. Even though the water level became higher due to cloud seeding, this effect was not that vivid in this figure. The situation in the Namgang Dam was also similar to that in the Yongdam Dam. Due to the small increase rate of rainfall, the effect of cloud seeding could not be clearly detected. Also, during the wet summer season, frequent release from the dam reservoir to secure the flood control volume kept the Namgang Dam from securing the additional water resource by cloud seeding. This was the fundamental limitation of the Namgang Dam, with its large basin area but very small storage capacity.

Table 9 summarizes the number of water shortage days during this four-year simulation period. As mentioned in the previous paragraph, in Boryeong Dam, there was no water shortage. On the other hand, in Yongdam Dam, the number of water shortage days was 351 (about 88 days annually) under the UNSD condition. This corresponds to about 25% of the year. The cloud seeding decreased the number of water shortage days by 16 days. This decrease was concentrated in 2021, when the rainfall increase was rather large. Similar change could also be found in Namgang Dam, where the number of water shortage days was decreased from 171 to 154 (from about 43 to 38 days annually). The decrease in Namgang Dam was also concentrated in 2020 and 2021, when the rainfall increase was rather large. This change must be significant, especially considering the rainfall increase was not that large. However, this amount of rainfall increase by cloud seeding cannot solve the water shortage problem. More rainfall increase must be secured; also, it should consider the characteristics of the dam reservoir and the reservoir operation method.

Table 9. Change in water shortage days due to cloud seeding from 2018 to 2021.

Year	Number of Water Shortage (Days)					
	Boryeong Dam		Yongdam Dam		Namgang Dam	
	UNSD	SEED	UNSD	SEED	UNSD	SEED
2018	0	0	0	0	17	17
2019	0	0	124	121	19	19
2020	0	0	164	164	0	0
2021	0	0	63	50	135	117
Sum	0	0	351	335	171	154

6.3. Reservoir Operation with Scenario-Based Rainfall

A similar analysis and evaluation to that in Section 6.2 is repeated in this section, but with the scenario-based rainfall data. As explained earlier, the four different scenario-based rainfall data were prepared by considering a 5, 10, 15, and 20% increase to the rainfall data in 2021. The runoff data simulated by the PRMS model were applied to the corresponding dam. The initial water stage in each dam was assumed to be the same as that at the end of 2020. Figure 10 shows the change in water level, just as in the previous Figure 9. In the figure, the solid line indicates the UNSD case, the red circle indicates the 5% increase, the blue diamond indicates the 10% increase, the green triangle indicates the 15% increase, and finally, the blue cross indicates the 20% increase. They all lie between the low water level and the high water level.

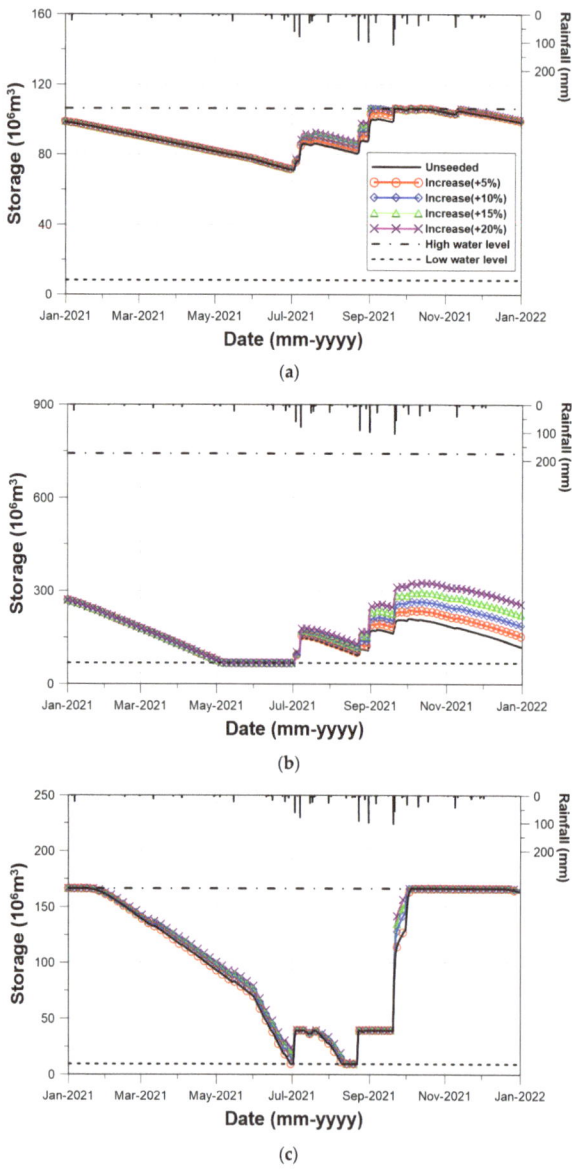

Figure 10. Change in dam water storage in three dam reservoirs based on the rainfall increase scenarios in 2021 (initial condition of the simulation was set to be the observed dam storage on January 1). (**a**) Boryeong Dam; (**b**) Yongdam Dam; (**c**) Namgang Dam.

In Boryeong Dam, as the initial dam storage was high, no water shortage occurred. It was the same for all four scenarios of rainfall increase. However, the situations in Yongdam Dam and Namgang Dam basins were different. The role of rainfall increase was clear in both dams. In Yongdam Dam, as the initial dam storage was small, it was impossible to avoid a water shortage problem. However, the increased rainfall worked significantly to alleviate the problem. A more serious problem in the Yongdam Dam was that the dam storage was simulated to be even smaller at the end of the year. This was mainly due to the rather small rainfall during the wet summer season in 2021. More active cloud seeding should have been considered during, and just after, the wet summer season. As a result, it seems almost impossible to avoid a very severe water shortage problem in the following year without any large rainfall in the Spring.

Namgang Dam revealed its structural problem. Even though the initial dam storage was large, the water shortage problem could not be avoided. This was simply because the planned water supply was too much compared to the effective storage capacity. As a result, without sufficient dam inflow, the water shortage problem could not be avoided. Additionally, it is noticeable that the water shortage problem also occurred in the wet summer season. This problem shows how difficult it is to handle both flood control and water supply problems successfully at the same time. This worse problem in the Namgang Dam is simply due to it having a large basin area but very small dam reservoir. Even though the dam reservoir could be easily filled in the fall, just after the rainy summer season, any successful water supply the following year cannot be guaranteed. They should expect to have enough rainfall the next spring.

Table 10 summarizes the number of water shortage days. As mentioned earlier, no water shortage occurred in Boryeong Dam. However, in Yongdam Dam, the number of water shortage days was 58 days under the UNSD situation, but became 57, even under the scenario of 20% increase. The water shortage days simply remained unchanged. This was because most of the water shortage occurred during the dry spring season. In simple terms, the effect of cloud seeding was very limited and could not decrease the water shortage problem. These results indicate that cloud seeding should be considered during the wet summer season, as well as in the early fall. This is the only way to make the Yongdam Dam work normally. Finally, in the Namgang Dam basin, the effect of cloud seeding was found to be more direct than that in the Yongdam Dam basin. That is, the increase of rainfall decreased the water shortage days. The number of water shortage days decreased from 16 days under the UNSD situation to 11 days under the scenario of 10% increase, and 8 days under the scenario of 20% increase.

Table 10. Change in water shortage days depending on the rainfall increase scenarios for the year of 2021 (with two initial conditions of dam storage, one the observed dam storage at January 1, 2021, and the other, the 50% of effective storage).

Initial Condition	Rainfall Increase (%)	Number of Water Shortage (Days)					
		Boryeong Dam		Yongdam Dam		Namgang Dam	
		UNSD	SEED	UNSD	SEED	UNSD	SEED
1 January 2021	+5%	0	0	58	58	16	16
	+10%		0		58		11
	+15%		0		58		9
	+20%		0		57		8
50% of effective storage	+5%	0	0	0	0	66	66
	+10%		0		0		58
	+15%		0		0		51
	+20%		0		0		46

Additionally, the above simulation and evaluation were repeated, but with the initial condition of dam storage, simply 50% of effective storage capacity (Figure 11). This 50% is a normal level in Boryeong Dam and Yongdam Dam, but is somewhat lower in Namgang Dam [57]. First, no water shortage occurred in Boryeong Dam, just as in the previous case.

At the end of the simulation year, the dam storage was about 50%. With the rainfall increase by cloud seeding, the dam storage at the end of year could be increased to be around 80% under the 20% rainfall increase scenario. This result shows that in the Boryeong Dam basin, cloud seeding could be very effective. However, in the Yongdam Dam basin, the situation was different. Even though water shortage did not occur in 2021, the dam storage at the end of the year was far less than 50%. Even under the 20% increase scenario, the dam storage could not reach the 50% level. A severe water supply problem could not be avoided the following year. A more active approach to secure additional water resources should be prepared.

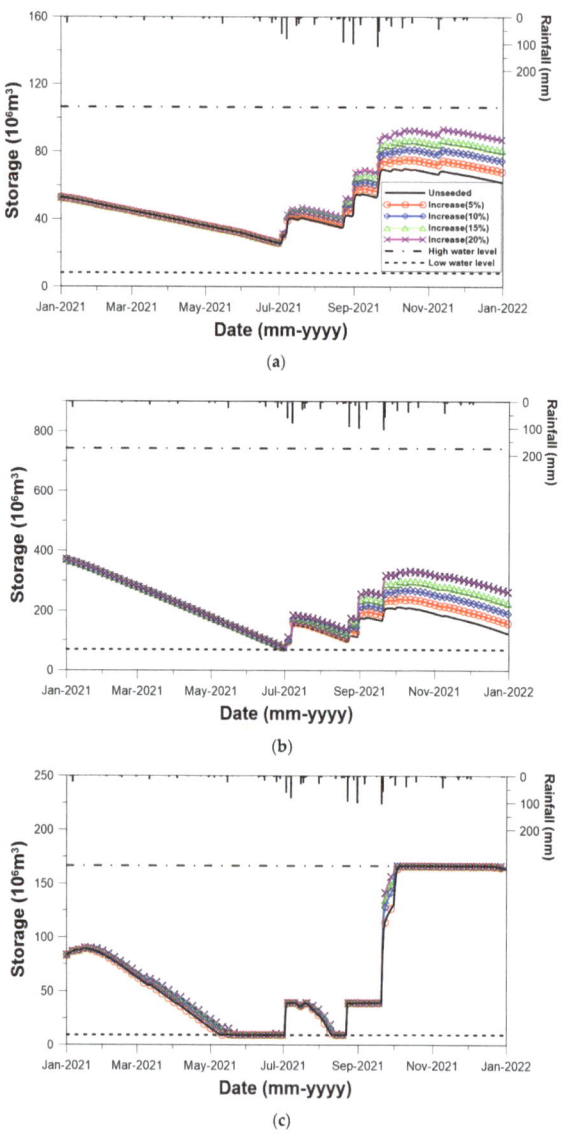

Figure 11. Same as Figure 10, but the initial condition of the simulation was set to be 50% of the dam effective storage. (**a**) Boryeong Dam; (**b**) Yongdam Dam; (**c**) Namgang Dam.

The simulation results for the Namgang Dam look to be more difficult. During the Spring season, it is almost impossible to avoid the water shortage problem. Even though the cloud seeding effect can be expected to help a little, it seemed to not be sufficient. The increased rainfall and resulting runoff were still not enough to fill the planned water supply. The number of water shortage days was found to be 66 under the UNSD condition but decreased to 58 and 46 under the 10 and 20% increase scenarios, respectively (Table 10). Simply put, while the large basin area of the Namgang Dam is advantageous, the small effective storage capacity is an obstacle that prevents saving the additional water resources by cloud seeding. Additionally, as the flood control volume is increased during the wet Summer season, it is not favorable to consider more active cloud seeding. The only option available is to fill the dam reservoir during the Fall season. Additionally, more active cloud seeding is important in the Spring season.

7. Conclusions

This study showed that the usefulness of cloud seeding is highly dependent on the dam and dam basin characteristics. First, the collection efficiency of increased rainfall by cloud seeding was compared for three dam basins, Boryeong Dam, Yongdam Dam, and Namgang Dam basins, located in the western part of the Korean Peninsula. Additionally, how much rainfall could be collected by the dam basin was evaluated. Second, the additional runoff volumes in those three basins by cloud seeding were compared with each other. The runoff volume can change, depending on the basin characteristics, like the soil, land use, and vegetation. Finally, by considering the dam reservoir operation and planned water supply, the change in water supply capacity was evaluated. The cloud seeding can contribute much in one dam, but only a little in other dams. In this study, the cloud seeding was simulated using the WRF−ARW model. Also, four different rainfall data generated by considering the scenarios of rainfall increase (i.e., 5, 10, 15, and 20%) were used for more practical evaluation.

The results may be summarized as follows: First, the increase rates over the three dam basins were compared to evaluate the collection efficiency of the dam basins. As the rainfall increase rate was found to be somewhat higher in a small dam basin (i.e., the Boryeong Dam basin), the cloud seeding might be assumed to be successful. However, the total amount of increased rainfall was larger in the dam with the larger basin area (i.e., the Namgang Dam basin). Even though the rainfall increase rate was just 2.99% in the Namgang Dam basin (in year 2021), compared to 4.65 and 3.75% in the Boryeong Dam and Yongdam Dam basins, respectively, the total amount of increased water resources secured by the cloud seeding was 73.7×10^6 m^3, which is much higher than the 8.3 and 37.3×10^6 m^3 in the Boryeong Dam and Yongdam Dam basins, respectively. Simply put, the larger basin area is an important advantage for securing additional water resources.

Second, the runoff increase rate was found to be higher than the rainfall increase rate. In fact, the runoff increase rate was about two times or more than the rainfall increase rate in all three dam basins considered in this study. Also, the increase of total runoff was mostly due to the increase of interflow and direct runoff. In particular, the increase of interflow was noticeable in all three basins. This result shows the advantage of cloud seeding to secure additional water resources, as the cloud seeding is generally conducted when the soil is wet with antecedent rainfall. As a result, most of the increased rainfall can directly contribute to the runoff increase.

Third, even though the additional inflow to the dam reservoir increases the storage, its contribution was found to be highly relative, depending on the storage capacity and planned annual water supply from a dam. For example, in the Yongdam Dam and Boryeong Dam basins, the increase rate of total storage was found to be less than that of the total runoff. On the other hand, in the Namgang Dam basin, it was found to be more than three times that of the total runoff. Because of the small total storage capacity of the Namgang Dam, this was an exceptional result, even though its basin area was the largest among the three dams. The increase of annual water supply was also different from dam to dam. In

Boryeong Dam, the increase rate of water supply was almost the same as that of the total runoff. In the Yongdam Dam, it was less than half of the runoff increase rate. However, in the Namgang Dam basin, it was more than twice the increase rate of the total runoff. This result indicates that in the Namgang Dam basin, the effect of cloud seeding on the water supply can be higher.

Finally, the results of reservoir operation revealed another practical aspect of those three dams. Basically, the situation in the Boryeong Dam was found to be better. More active cloud seeding was found necessary in the Yongdam Dam basin. This was also the same situation in the Namgang Dam basin. However, it was also found that cloud seeding cannot solve the water supply problems in those dams. In particular, the situation in the Namgang Dam basin looks very serious. Regardless of the significant help of cloud seeding, the water shortage problem in the Spring season was found to be unavoidable. In simple terms, the large basin area of the Namgang Dam is advantageous, but the small dam storage capacity is a major obstacle to prevent saving the additional water resources by cloud seeding.

The above results show that cloud seeding should be carefully planned and might well vary dam-by-dam. Cloud seeding can be effective every season in one dam, but only in Spring in another dam. In other dams, the Summer or Fall seasons can be the best option. The target increase of rainfall is also an important issue. Just a mild increase could be better in one dam, but it can be important to secure much more rainfall in others. It is interesting to note that, even though the three dams considered in this study are located in practically the same climatic zone, the conditions required for cloud seeding are totally different.

This study tried to show that there are many other factors to consider in the cloud seeding. Basically, the basin characteristics are very important. Basin characteristics, including the soil, geology, etc., control the runoff ratio. Increased rainfall may not directly result in the increased runoff if the soil is very permeable or the evapotranspiration is very high. Other socioeconomic factors are assumed to be considered in the planned amount of water supply. Depending on the size of population or industry, the amount of water supply can be larger even though the size of dam reservoir is small. Those three dams considered in this study are also very different in their basin area, size of dam reservoir, and the amount of planned water supply. Depending on these characteristics, the effect of cloud seeding can be so different. However, relative roles of these characteristics to the efficiency of cloud seeding could not be quantified in this study. This issue may be solved based on the sensitivity analysis. Consideration of more dam basins with different characteristics would also be helpful to derive a more significant result.

Author Contributions: Data curation, J.-H.M., S.-U.S. and W.N.; formal analysis, J.-H.M. and W.N.; methodology, W.N., E.C. and C.Y.; Supervision, K.-H.C., S.-K.S. and C.Y.; visualization, J.-H.M.; writing—original draft, J.-H.M. and C.Y.; writing—review and editing, C.Y. All authors have read and agreed to the published version of the manuscript.

Funding: This work was supported by the National Research Foundation of Korea (NRF) grant funded by the Korean government (MSIT) (No. NRF-2021R1A5A1032433) and the National Institute of Meteorological Sciences (NIMS) through Research on Weather Modification and Cloud Physics (KMA2018-00224).

Institutional Review Board Statement: Not applicable.

Data Availability Statement: Not applicable.

Conflicts of Interest: The authors declare no conflict of interest.

References

1. Sharma, A.; Wasko, C.; Lettenmaier, D.P. If precipitation extremes are increasing, why aren't floods? *Water Resour. Res.* **2018**, *54*, 8545–8551. [CrossRef]
2. Hettiarachchi, S.; Wasko, C.; Sharma, A. Do longer dry spells associated with warmer years compound the stress on global water resources? *Earth's Future* **2022**, *10*, e2021EF002392. [CrossRef]

3. Wasko, C.; Sharma, A. Steeper temporal distribution of rain intensity at higher temperatures within Australian storms. *Nat. Geosci.* **2015**, *8*, 527–529. [CrossRef]
4. Emmanuel, I.; Andrieu, H.; Leblois, E.; Flahaut, B. Temporal and spatial variability of rainfall at the urban hydrological scale. *J. Hydrol.* **2012**, *430*, 162–172. [CrossRef]
5. Prein, A.F.; Liu, C.; Ikeda, K.; Trier, S.B.; Rasmussen, R.M.; Holland, G.J.; Clark, M.P. Increased rainfall volume from future convective storms in the US. *Nat. Clim. Chang.* **2017**, *7*, 880–884. [CrossRef]
6. Mun, J.W.; Lee, D.R. Analysis of 2014–2015 drought conditions by multipurpose dam using water supply capacity index. *Mag. Korea Water Resour. Assoc. Water Future* **2015**, *48*, 51–57.
7. Lee, J.W.; Jang, S.S.; Ahn, S.R.; Park, K.W.; Kim, S.J. Evaluation of the relationship between meteorological, agricultural and in-situ big data droughts. *J. Korean Assoc. Geogr. Inf. Stud.* **2016**, *19*, 64–79. [CrossRef]
8. Korea Water Resources Association (KWRA). *Drought Characteristics and Countermeasures in the Yeongsan River Basin Seomjin River Basin*; KWRA: Seoul, Republic of Korea, 2022.
9. Korea Water Resources Association (KWRA). *Flooding Occurrence and Response in Chungcheong Province in 2022 Korea*; KWRA: Seoul, Republic of Korea, 2022.
10. Lee, Y.G.; Jung, C.G.; Kim, W.J.; Kim, S.J. Analysis of national stream drying phenomena using DrySAT-WFT Model: Focusing on inflow of dam and weir watersheds in 5 river basins. *J. Korean Assoc. Geogr. Inf. Stud.* **2020**, *23*, 53–69.
11. Kim, W.; Kim, S. Analysis of the riparian vegetation expansion in middle size rivers in Korea. *J. Korea Water Resour. Assoc.* **2019**, *52*, 875–885.
12. Czys, R.R.; DeFelice, T.P.; Griffith, D.A. *Guidelines for Cloud Seeding to Augment Precipitation*; ASCE Manuals and Reports on Engineering Practice No. 81; ASCE: Reston, VA, USA, 2006.
13. Yoo, C.; Na, W.; Cho, E.; Chang, K.H.; Yum, S.S.; Jung, W. Evaluation of cloud seeding on the securement of additional water resources in the Boryeong Dam basin, Korea. *J. Hydrol.* **2022**, *613*, 128480. [CrossRef]
14. Neyman, J.; Scott, E.L. Planning an Experiment with Cloud Seeding. In *Volume 5 Weather Modification Experiments*; University of California Press: Oakland, CA, USA, 1967.
15. Silverman, B.A.; Sukarnjanaset, W. Results of the Thailand warm-cloud hygroscopic particle seeding experiment. *J. Appl. Meteorol.* **2000**, *39*, 1160–1175. [CrossRef]
16. Maryadi, A.; Tomine, K.; Nishiyama, K. Some aspects of a numerical glaciogenic artificial cloud seeding experiment using liquid carbon dioxide over Kupang, Indonesia. *J. Agric. Meteorol.* **2015**, *71*, 1–14. [CrossRef]
17. Ryan, B.F.; King, W.D. A critical review of the Australian experience in cloud seeding. *Bull. Am. Meteorol. Soc.* **1997**, *78*, 239–254. [CrossRef]
18. Acharya, A.; Piechota, T.C.; Stephen, H.; Tootle, G. Modeled streamflow response under cloud seeding in the North Platte River watershed. *J. Hydrol.* **2011**, *409*, 305–314. [CrossRef]
19. Pokharel, B.; Wang, S.Y.S.; Gu, H.; LaPlante, M.D.; Serago, J.; Gillies, R.; Meyer, J.; Beall, S.; Ikeda, K. A modeling examination of cloud seeding conditions under the warmer climate in Utah, USA. *Atmos. Res.* **2021**, *248*, 105239. [CrossRef]
20. Oh, S. Meteorological disasters in Korea and the development of cloud seeding technique. *Mag. Korean Soc. Hazard Mitig.* **2005**, *5*, 57–65.
21. National Institute of Meteorological Sciences (NIMS). *Research on the Cloud Seeding in Japan*; NIMS: Seoquipo, Republic of Korea, 2016.
22. National Institute of Meteorological Sciences (NIMS). *The Principle and Application Technique of Cloud Seeding*; NIMS: Seoquipo, Republic of Korea, 2018.
23. Solak, M.E.; Henderson, T.J.; Allan, R.B.; Duckering, D.W. Winter orographic cloud seeding over the Kern River Basin in California. *J. Weather Modif.* **1987**, *19*, 36–40.
24. Weather Modification Association (WMA). *Weather Modification Association Capability Statement*; WMA: Huntsville, UT, USA, 2005.
25. Griffith, D.A.; Solak, M.E.; Yorty, D.P.; Brinkman, B. A level II weather modification feasibility study for winter snowpack augmentation in the Salt River and Wyoming ranges in Wyoming. *J. Weather Modif.* **2007**, *39*, 76–83.
26. Wyoming Water Development Commission (WWDC). *Wyoming Weather Modification Pilot Project*; WWDC: Cheyenne, WY, USA, 2010.
27. Kulkarni, J.R.; Morwal, S.B.; Deshpande, N.R. Rainfall enhancement in Karnataka state cloud seeding program "Varshadhare" 2017. *Atmos. Res.* **2019**, *219*, 65–76. [CrossRef]
28. Chambers, L.E.; Long, A.B. *Precipitation Enhancement Feasibility Study in Aid of Cotton Irrigation*; NSW Department of Primary Industries: Narrabri, NSW, Australia, 1992.
29. Morrison, A.E.; Siems, S.T.; Manton, M.J.; Nazarov, A. On the analysis of a cloud seeding dataset over Tasmania. *J. Appl. Meteorol. Climatol.* **2009**, *48*, 1267–1280. [CrossRef]
30. Beare, S.; Chambers, R.; Peak, S. Statistical modeling of rainfall enhancement. *J. Weather Modif.* **2010**, *42*, 13–32.
31. Gagin, A.; Neumann, J. The second Israeli randomized cloud seeding experiment: Evaluation of the results. *J. Appl. Meteorol. Climatol.* **1981**, *20*, 1301–1311. [CrossRef]
32. Ben, Z. Springflow enhancement in Northern Israel due to cloud seeding. *Isr. J. Earth Sci.* **1990**, *39*, 103–117.
33. Wang, N.; Quesada, B.; Xia, L.; Butterbach-Bahl, K.; Goodale, C.L.; Kiese, R. Effects of climate warming on carbon fluxes in grasslands—A global meta-analysis. *Glob. Chang. Biol.* **2019**, *25*, 1839–1851. [CrossRef] [PubMed]

34. DeFelice, T.P. (Ed.) *ASCE Standard Practice for the Design, Conduct and Evaluation of Operational Precipitation Enhancement Projects*; ASCE Standard ANSI/ASCE/EWRI 42-17; ASCE: Reston, VA, USA, 2017.
35. ChungNam Institute (CNI). *A Study on Water Supply Capacity Evaluation and Drought Response Plan of Boryeong Dam*; CNI: Gongju, Republic of Korea, 2016.
36. Choi, Y. *Analysis of Boryeong Dam Diversion Tunnel*; Ajou University Press: Seoul, Republic of Korea, 2017.
37. Son, K.; Oh, S. *Drought and Water Resources in 2015*; Korea River Association: Seoul, Republic of Korea, 2015.
38. Ministry of Environment (ME). *Austerity Operation of the Namgang Dam Due to Rainfall Shortage in the Western Part of Kyungnam Province*; ME: Seoul, Republic of Korea, 2022.
39. National Institute of Forest Science (NIFS). *Development of Long-Term Monitoring and Management Technology for Forest Water Resources*; NIFS: Seoul, Republic of Korea, 2016.
40. Korea Forest Service (KFS). *Time Series Analysis and Climate Change Adaptation Management Techniques for Temperate Northern Forest*; KFS: Seoul, Republic of Korea, 2016.
41. Kim, S. Current status of dams in Korea. *Mag. Korea Water Resour. Assoc. Water Future* **1988**, *21*, 4–8.
42. Mun, T.W. Yongdam multipurpose dam construction project. *Mag. Korea Water Resour. Assoc. Water Future* **1997**, *30*, 137–145.
43. Yoo, C.; Shin, H.; Lee, J. Evaluation of the Storage Effect Considering Possible Redevelopment Options of the Peace Dam in South Korea. *Water* **2020**, *12*, 1674. [CrossRef]
44. Kang, T.; Lee, S.; Kang, S. A study for flood control of a dam using flood guide curves and release determination method in accordance with reservoir water level. *J. Korean Soc. Hazard Mitig.* **2015**, *15*, 129–136. [CrossRef]
45. Skamarock, W.C.; Klemp, J.B.; Dudhia, J.; Gill, D.O.; Barker, D.M.; Duda, M.G.; Huang, X.; Wang, W.; Powers, J.G. *A Description of the Advanced Research WRF Version 3*; National Center for Atmospheric Research: Boulder, CO, USA, 2008.
46. Bernardet, L.; Wolff, J.; Nance, L.; Loughe, A.; Weatherhead, B.; Gilleland, E.; Brown, B. Comparison between WRF-ARW and WRF-NMM Objective Forecast Verification Scores. In Proceedings of the 23rd Conference on Weather Analysis and Forecasting/19th Conference on Numerical Weather Prediction, Denver, CO, USA, 1–5 June 2009.
47. Kang, C.Y.; Song, S.K.; Moon, S.H.; Lim, Y.K.; Chang, K.H.; Chae, S. Effect of cloud seeding using hygroscopic aerosol particles on artificial rainfall enhancement and Its sensitivity analysis in spring 2021. *J. Korean Soc. Atmos. Environ.* **2023**, *39*, 335–350. [CrossRef]
48. Leavesley, G.H.; Lichty, R.W.; Troutman, B.M.; Saindon, L.G. *Precipitation-Runoff Modeling System: User's Manual. U.S. Geological Survey*; Water Resources Division: Denver, CO, USA, 1983.
49. Ministry of Environment (MOE). *A General Guideline for Flood Estimation*; MOE: Seoul, Republic of Korea, 2019.
50. Ministry of Construction and Transportation (MOCT). *Hydrologic Survey Report of Geumgang River Basin*; MOCT: Seoul, Republic of Korea, 2006.
51. Bae, D.; Jung, I.; Chang, H. Long-term trend of precipitation and runoff in Korean river basins. *Hydrol. Process.* **2008**, *22*, 2644–2656. [CrossRef]
52. Kim, H.S.; Kim, H.S.; Jeon, G.I.; Gang, S.U. Evaluation of drought from 2014 to 2015. *Mag. Korea Water Resour. Assoc. Water Future* **2016**, *49*, 61–75. [CrossRef]
53. Korea Institute of Civil Engineering and Building Technology (KICT). *Dam Operation Status and Improvement Direction in Dry Season and Flood Season: Focusing on the Soyang River Multipurpose Dam in the Han River Basin*; KICT: Goyang, Republic of Korea, 1996.
54. Nakdong River Flood Control Office (NRFCO). *Improvement of Nakdong River Flood Forecasting and Warning System According to Construction of Hapcheon Dam and Imha Dam*; NRFCO: Busan, Republic of Korea, 1994.
55. Asian Development Bank (ADB). Evaluation of Water Supply Projects: An Economic Framework. 1990. Available online: https://www.adb.org/publications/ (accessed on 7 July 2023).
56. FEMA. Water Supply Systems and Evaluation Methods Volume I: Water Supply System Concepts. 2008. Available online: https://www.usfa.fema.gov/downloads/pdf/publications/ (accessed on 7 July 2023).
57. Yoo, C.; Jun, C.; Zhu, J.H.; Na, W. Evaluation of dam water supply capacity in Korea using water shortage index. *Water* **2021**, *13*, 956. [CrossRef]

Disclaimer/Publisher's Note: The statements, opinions and data contained in all publications are solely those of the individual author(s) and contributor(s) and not of MDPI and/or the editor(s). MDPI and/or the editor(s) disclaim responsibility for any injury to people or property resulting from any ideas, methods, instructions or products referred to in the content.

Article

Assessing the National Water Model's Streamflow Estimates Using a Multi-Decade Retrospective Dataset across the Contiguous United States

Mohamed Abdelkader [1,*], Marouane Temimi [1] and Taha B.M.J. Ouarda [2]

1. Department of Civil, Environmental and Ocean Engineering (CEOE), Stevens Institute of Technology, Hoboken, NJ 07030, USA; mtemimi@stevens.edu
2. Institut National de la Recherche Scientifique, Centre Eau Terre Environnement, INRS-ETE, 490 De la Couronne, Québec City, QC G1K 9A9, Canada; taha.ouarda@inrs.ca
* Correspondence: mabdelka@stevens.edu

Citation: Abdelkader, M.; Temimi, M.; Ouarda, T.B.M.J. Assessing the National Water Model's Streamflow Estimates Using a Multi-Decade Retrospective Dataset across the Contiguous United States. *Water* 2023, *15*, 2319. https://doi.org/10.3390/w15132319

Academic Editors: Venkat Sridhar, Ankur Srivastava and Nikul Kumari

Received: 9 May 2023
Revised: 18 June 2023
Accepted: 18 June 2023
Published: 21 June 2023

Copyright: © 2023 by the authors. Licensee MDPI, Basel, Switzerland. This article is an open access article distributed under the terms and conditions of the Creative Commons Attribution (CC BY) license (https://creativecommons.org/licenses/by/4.0/).

Abstract: The goal of this study is to evaluate the performance of the National Water Model (NWM) in time and space across the contiguous United States. Retrospective streamflow simulations were compared to records from 3260 USGS gauging stations, considering both regulated and natural flow conditions. Statistical metrics, including Kling–Gupta efficiency, Percent Bias, Pearson Correlation Coefficient, Root Mean Squared Error, and Normalized Root Mean Squared Error, were employed to assess the agreement between observed and simulated streamflow. A comparison of historical trends in daily flow data between the model and observed streamflow provided additional insight into the utility of retrospective NWM datasets. Our findings demonstrate a superior agreement between the simulated and observed streamflow for natural flow in comparison to regulated flow. The most favorable agreement between the NWM estimates and observed data was achieved in humid regions during the winter season, whereas a reduced degree of agreement was observed in the Great Plains region. Enhancements to model performance for regulated flow are necessary, and bias correction is crucial for utilizing the NWM retrospective streamflow dataset. The study concludes that the model-agnostic NextGen NWM framework, which accounts for regional performance of the utilized model, could be more suitable for continental-scale hydrologic prediction.

Keywords: continental-scale hydrological model; simulated streamflow; NWM; model performance; natural flow; regulated flow

1. Introduction

The estimation of streamflow plays a pivotal role in water resource management. It facilitates the forecasting of forthcoming flood events and contributes to the optimization of water demand processes, thereby serving as an indispensable component of effective and sustainable water system management [1–4]. The ability to forecast streamflow accurately can assist water resource managers in making informed decisions regarding the release of water from reservoirs, irrigation, and other water uses [5–7]. The effectiveness of streamflow forecasting in water management has been demonstrated through the use of hydrological models to optimize the operation of reservoir systems to meet the demands of irrigation and hydropower generation [8]. Streamflow forecasts are also utilized to issue flood warnings and aid emergency managers in preparing for, and responding to, flooding events. Furthermore, the accuracy and quality of hydrological forecasts play a vital role improving the efficiency of hydropower generation by allowing power companies to better align their generation schedules with available water resources [9,10].

Simulating streamflow is complex due to the intricate nature of the hydrologic system [11]. A number of factors, encompassing precipitation, evaporation, groundwater recharge, and land use, changes impact streamflow estimation. The scarcity of precise and reliable data further exacerbates the difficulty in accurately estimating streamflow [12]. Additionally, quantifying and modeling these factors is a challenging task [13,14]. Moreover, it is often challenging to obtain long-term streamflow data for model calibration, particularly in ungauged or inadequately gauged catchments. Therefore, developing accurate prediction models, particularly for ungauged catchments, is a daunting task. Furthermore, estimating streamflow entails increased uncertainty due to the combined impacts of land use development and climate change [15–17].

The estimation of streamflow is further complicated by the nonlinearity and nonstationary of the hydrological system. Due to its nonlinearity, even small variations in input can lead to substantial changes in output. Previous studies have demonstrated how alterations in precipitation can have significant impacts on streamflow estimation [18–21]. Moreover, the hydrological modeling process uncertainty raises concerns from the simplified or incorrect representation of the hydrological system. Therefore, the lack of a full comprehension of the underlying mechanisms that govern streamflow exacerbates the challenge of creating accurate forecasting models [3,22]. A variety of modeling approaches are used to issue these forecasts, including empirical models and process-oriented models. Process-oriented models use mathematical equations to simulate the physical processes operating in the watershed and estimated streamflow. Several types of process-oriented hydrological models, such as conceptual models and physically based models, which rely on a high degree of spatial discretization, are employed for operational streamflow forecasting [22].

The estimation of streamflow can be issued using hydrological models at various scales, including watersheds, regions, and even the continental scale. Several hydrological models have been developed to estimate streamflow on large scales, including the continental and global scale. Some notable examples of large-scale hydrological models include the Variable Infiltration Capacity (VIC) model [23], the Land Dynamics (LaD) Model [24], and, more recently, the GEOGloWS ECMWF Streamflow service [25]. The models have been employed to simulate streamflow, furnishing valuable insights for water resource managers, thereby enabling them to make well-informed decisions.

In the Unites States, the National Weather Service (NWS) Advanced Hydrologic Prediction Service (AHPS) supplies streamflow forecasts and warnings for more than 3600 locations across the country [26,27]. However, those forecasts are specific to NWS River Forecast Centers (RFC). The system leverages streamflow forecasts, precipitation observations, and river-gauge measurements to issue flood and flash flood warnings. These alerts are communicated to the public through various channels, encompassing the NWS website, social media platforms, and emergency management agencies. Nonetheless, the National Research Council identified a discrepancy between the state-of-the-art modeling capabilities currently considered cutting edge and those utilized in the AHPS [27]. This observation underscores the necessity to integrate more advanced hydrologic models. In 2016, the National Water Model (NWM), a group of physics-based, hydrodynamic, and hydrologic models, was implemented by NOAA's Office of Water Prediction (OWP). The NWM is based on the Weather Research and Forecasting Model Hydrological modeling system (WRF–Hydro) framework [28] and generates streamflow forecasts for over 2.7-million locations across the CONUS [29].

Streamflow estimation is a key component of flood-risk mitigation. Thus, it is imperative to evaluate hydrological models' performance. It is essential to compare the model's predictions to observed data to validate the model and determine its capacity to reproduce in-land processes. Moreover, assessing the performance of hydrological models can help identify areas for improvement, including addressing model biases, improving the representation of key processes, and incorporating new data and observational capabilities. Additionally, continental-scale models are commonly used to support water management decisions and facilitate decision-making [30]. Thus, evaluating the performance of continental scale models can assist in communicating the model's capabilities and limitations to stakeholders, which can build trust in the model and its predictions.

The evaluation of continental-scale hydrological models is critical in ensuring their accuracy and reliability for various applications, such as water-resource management and flood forecasting. A key component of model evaluation involves comparing model estimates to observed data and assessing the model's ability to reproduce historical streamflow patterns. Retrospective simulations are a valuable tool in assessing the performance of continental-scale hydrological models. This approach involves running the model using historical data and comparing its output with observed data from the same period. The retrospective analysis serves to evaluate the model's ability to accurately simulate past hydrological conditions, identify sources of bias or error, and improve its performance. This analysis enables the identification of areas for model improvement, thereby increasing confidence in its predictions. Thus, the evaluation of retrospective simulations plays a crucial role in the continual improvement and refinement of continental-scale hydrological models.

This study aims to evaluate the performance of the NWM V2.1 through the analysis of the results of multi-decadal retrospective simulations across the contiguous United States (CONUS). The study identifies the limitations of the NWM as reported by the retrospective runs, which could be indicative of the necessary areas of improvement to enhance the operational runs. The study investigates the spatial and temporal variability of streamflow bias, with the objective of identifying instances and locations where the model underestimates or overestimates streamflow. Understanding the factors underlying the variations in the model's performance is essential in this regard. Eventually, recommendations could be made to enhance the modeling of hydrologic processes across the US based on the determined biases.

2. Materials and Methods

2.1. NWM Retrospective Dataset

The National Water Model is a parallelized distributed hydrologic modeling framework based on the WRF–Hydro hydrologic model architecture [28]. In a one-way modeling framework, the model can be forced using precipitation and atmospheric surface data, or in a coupled framework by using the Weather Research and Forecasting (WRF-ARW) atmospheric model. With an hourly modeling cycle, the NWM simulates streamflow for 2.7'million river reaches across the CONUS (Figure 1). In the NWM, hydrologic processes and routing components have been sourced from the community WRF–Hydro modeling system developed at the National Center for Atmospheric Research (NCAR). In the NWM system, land surface processes are represented by the Noah Multi-Parameterization (Noah–MP) land surface model (LSM) [31], while water routing is represented by separate flow routing modules. Based on a 1-km grid, the LSM simulates the vertical exchange of water and energy between the Earth's surface and the atmosphere. The routing modules include diffusive wave surface routing and saturated subsurface routing, utilizing a 250-m grid, and Muskingum–Cunge channel routing utilizing vectorized NHDPlusV2 stream units. In order to improve the model's forecasting cycles' initial states, a nudging data assimilation (DA) scheme was implemented. However, it should be noted that streamflow observations are not incorporated into the retrospective simulations. Currently, there are three versions of the NWM reanalysis dataset available. The NWM versions 1.2 and 2.0 incorporate a 25- and 26-year retrospective simulation, respectively, while Version 2.1 includes an extended retrospective simulation spanning 42 years, from February 1979 to December 2020. A retrospective simulation of NWM V2.1 was used in this study in order to evaluate the performance of the model. All model output and forcing input fields are available in the NetCDF format. Furthermore, all model output fields, as well as the precipitation forcing field, are accessible in the Zarr format. Our study utilized the Zarr format, a cloud-friendly format, to obtain streamflow data. The data were downloaded based on the NWM forecast point reference number and processed locally [32]. The data retrieval process from Zarr files is well-documented in the Amazon Web Services (AWS) portal, where the data is stored [33].

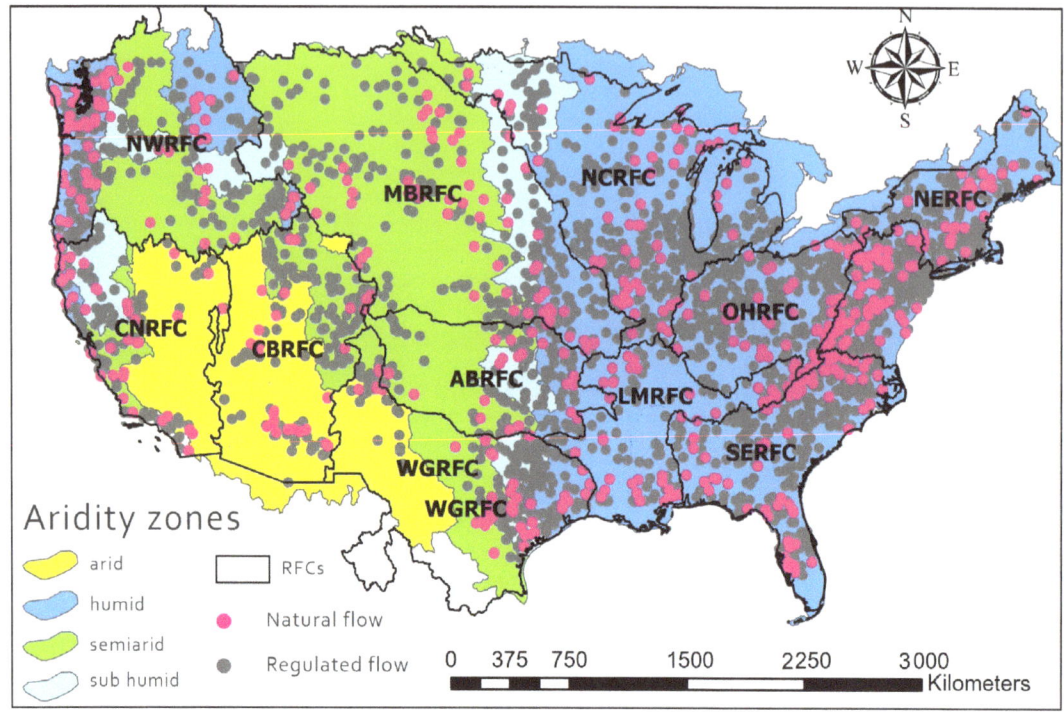

Figure 1. Geographical location of USGS streamflow gaging stations collocated with NWM forecast points.

2.2. In-Situ Streamflow Data

In this study, the Geospatial Attributes of Gages for Evaluating Streamflow, Version II (GAGES-2) database, maintained by the United States Geological Survey (USGS), was utilized to obtain stream gage locations. The GAGES-2 dataset comprises daily streamflow data for over 9000 stream gages located throughout the United States and its territories, as well as metadata describing the stream gages and the data, including both natural flow and regulated flow sites. Notably, the GAGES-2 dataset was employed solely for the purpose of identifying watersheds, which have natural flow conditions. In the GAGES-2 dataset, stream gages, which at some point in their history had periods which represented natural flow, are identified as USGS hydro-Climatic Data Network (HCDN) [34]. It should be noted that the original composition of the HCDN dataset incorporated a total of 743 distinct sites. The flow type (natural or regulated) was further investigated through the NHDPlus version 2.1 dataset [35]. Subsequently, streamflow data were obtained from the USGS National Water Information System (NWIS) portal [36].

In this study, streamflow data were obtained from the USGS stream gage network. These gages are instruments that measure the water level of a stream or river, and the data are subsequently quality controlled and processed by USGS scientists and technicians to ensure its accuracy and reliability. The USGS stream gage network offers a comprehensive dataset of streamflow records with hourly or sub-hourly intervals, which enables the development of a continental-scale performance evaluation of simulated streamflow. The streamflow records were obtained by converting measured water levels into discharge using established rating curves, which were developed by the USGS through periodic measurement of the stage–discharge relationship, particularly during low- and high-flow events. It is important to note that the accuracy of the USGS rating curves was assumed in the analysis, and their uncertainty was not considered.

In this study, streamflow data from the USGS gauging stations were temporally and spatially matched with forecast points from the NWM to ensure alignment with the modeled domain. The integrity and continuity of the data are of utmost importance as we evaluate the temporal evolution of streamflow, comparing outputs from the NWM simulations with USGS station records. In line with widely accepted standards for hydroclimatic research, we uphold the need for a minimum of 30 years of records to ensure a reliable long-term analysis. Furthermore, our stringent data completeness criteria stipulate less than 10% missing data, with no consecutive gaps exceeding 24 months [37–40]. Thus, the used dataset was refined by retaining stations meeting the requisite recording period and excluding those with more than 10% missing data. This ensures the findings of this study are based on a robust and reliable data foundation.

Furthermore, we identified certain locations in the NWM's output where the model was unable to accurately simulate streamflow, resulting in either a constant value or zero for the entirety of the simulation period. These situations, which we refer to as "simulation failures," introduced potential inaccuracies into the analysis. As such, stations corresponding to these forecast points exhibiting simulation failures were judiciously excluded from our study. This ensured the reliability of our assessment by focusing solely on locations where the model effectively represented the streamflow temporal variability. The final list of streamflow gauging stations used in this study consisted of 3260 stations, with 548 stations located in catchments with natural flow and 2712 located in regulated catchments (Figure 1, Table 1).

Table 1. Description of gauging stations, drainage basins, and dominant climate in the studied RFCs.

River Forecast Center	No. of Streamflow Gauging Stations		Median Drainage Basin Area (km^2)		Dominant Climate Class
	NF	RF	NF	RF	
Missouri Basin (MBRFC)	58	269	760.1	3467.9	Semi-arid
Colorado Basin (CBRFC)	26	165	203.3	1362.3	Arid
Arkansas–Red Basin (ABRFC)	22	125	485.6	2395.7	Semi-humid
California–Nevada (CNRFC)	37	147	189.1	924.6	Arid
Lower Mississippi (LMRFC)	38	111	786.1	1279.4	Humid
Middle Atlantic (MARFC)	60	282	264.2	323.7	Humid
North Central (NCRFC)	55	362	916.8	1414.1	Humid
Northeast (NERFC)	32	183	225.3	489.5	Humid
Northwest (NWRFC)	69	271	401.43	1491.8	Semi-humid
Ohio (OHRFC)	42	263	374.2	1090.4	Humid
Southeast (SERFC)	67	295	323.7	981.6	Humid
West Gulf (WGRFC)	42	236	463.6	1102	Arid & Semi-arid

Note: NF: Natural flow gauging stations; RF: Regulated flow gauging stations.

2.3. Ancillary Data

In this study, the Aridity Index (AI) was computed to investigate the NWM model performance for the different climate types. AI was calculated as a function of the Mean Annual Precipitation (MAP) and Mean Annual Potential Evapotranspiration (MAE) as suggested by United Nations Environment Program [41]:

$$AI = \frac{MAP}{MAE}, \tag{1}$$

Total precipitation and potential evapotranspiration data for the period spanning from January 1979 to December 2020 were obtained from the North American Land Data Assimilation System (NLDAS) and aggregated over the Hydrological Unit Code 8 (HUC8) basins. The annual precipitation and potential evapotranspiration time series were processed using the BASINS 4.5 software in accordance with prior investigations that appraised NLDAS products over the CONUS [42,43]. HUC-8 basins were classified into different climate types based on the calculated AI values, which were determined using the UNEP generalized climate classification [41]. The classification was performed based on the AI values, and the resulting categories were Arid (0.03 < AI < 0.2), Semi-Arid (0.2 < AI < 0.5), Sub-Humid (0.5 < AI < 0.65), and Humid (AI > 0.65) (Figure 1). It is important to mention that the data used for climate zones classification is subject to climate change signal and to the effects of teleconnections and climate variability (impact of different low frequency climate oscillation indices with different phases), and this topic is important.

2.4. Model Evaluation Metrics

In this study, the accuracy of the NWM streamflow simulations was assessed by comparing time series from the model forecast point to in-situ streamflow observations from USGS stations network. Five statistics were used, including the modified Kling–Gupta efficiency metric (KGE), Percent Bias (PB), Pearson Correlation Coefficient (CC), the Root Mean Squared Error (RMSE), and the Normalized Root Mean Squared Error (NRMSE). It is important to mention that the acceptance threshold for the evaluation metrics used in our study was inferred from commonly used practices in hydrological studies [19,44–49].

The NWM performance at the hourly time scale was evaluated using the KGE metric. The Kling–Gupta efficiency (KGE) metric is used to evaluate the performance of hydrological models in terms of their ability to reproduce the temporal and spatial patterns of observed streamflow. It is a statistical measure that compares the correlation, bias, and variability of simulated streamflow to those of the observed streamflow. A KGE value of 1 indicates perfect agreement between the observed and simulated streamflow, while a value less than 1 indicates that the model is not performing as well. The KGE metric is widely used in the hydrological community to evaluate model performance and to identify areas where model improvement is needed [50]. The assessment of hydrological dynamics in the KGE metric is defined by three components: the temporal error through correlation (CC), bias errors (β), and variability errors (γ) expressed as follows:

$$KGE = 1 - \sqrt{(CC-1)^2 + (\beta-1)^2 + (\gamma-1)^2}, \qquad (2)$$

$$CC = \frac{\sum_{i=1}^{N}(o_i - \mu_o)(s_i - \mu_s)}{\sqrt{\sum_{i=1}^{N}(o_i - \mu_o)^2 \sum_{i=1}^{N}(s_i - \mu_s)^2}}, \qquad (3)$$

$$\beta = \frac{\mu_s}{\mu_o}, \qquad (4)$$

$$\gamma = \frac{\sigma_s/\mu_s}{\sigma_o/\mu_o}, \qquad (5)$$

where N is the total number of observations i at each station, the streamflow observations are denoted by (o), and simulations obtained from the NWM are denoted by (s). The mean and standard deviation of the streamflow are defined by μ and σ, respectively.

The root mean square error (RMSE) constitutes a prevalent metric employed for assessing the performance of numerical models in simulating hydrological processes. As a measure of deviation between predicted and observed values, RMSE is computed by obtaining the square root of the mean of squared differences between these values. This particular metric proves advantageous in hydrological applications, as it furnishes a quantitative method for comparing model performance across distinct temporal and spatial scales and delivers a singular, comprehensive metric encapsulating the overall model accuracy. In general, lower RMSE values signify superior model performance, with a value of zero denoting an impeccable correspondence between predicted and observed values. The RMSE for each forecast point was calculated as follows:

$$\text{RMSE} = \sqrt{\frac{\sum_{i=1}^{N}(s_i - o_i)2}{N}}, \quad (6)$$

It is imperative to highlight that the root mean square error (RMSE) is inherently sensitive to the magnitude and frequency of deviations between simulated and observed values. In the realm of hydrological modeling, the primary objective is to accurately represent the temporal and spatial variability of hydrological processes, with a particular focus on peak streamflow values, as these significantly influence the overall model precision. Owing to the computation of RMSE as the square root of the mean of squared discrepancies, substantial deviations in peak values may disproportionately affect the composite RMSE value. For example, in cases where a model persistently underestimates peak flow values, the resultant RMSE will be considerably inflated, even if the model demonstrates adequate performance in simulating the majority of flow values. This inherent limitation of RMSE as a performance metric stems from its inability to discern between errors in simulating peak and low-flow events. Consequently, additional metrics, including normalized root mean square error, correlation coefficient, and percent bias, are incorporated into this study to furnish a comprehensive assessment of model performance.

In order to evaluate the performance of the NWM relative to in-situ observations, the NRMSE was computed. The utilization of NRMSE is particularly advantageous in scenarios where the range of observed values exhibits considerable variability or spans a wide spectrum, as it accounts for the inherent fluctuations within the observed data and furnishes a more robust and equitable comparison of model performance. Additionally, NRMSE was employed primarily to probe the spatial performance of the model across the continental United States. Given the broad spatial scale of our model's application, it is fundamental to understand how its relative performance varies spatially when compared to the observed dataset. The NRMSE was calculated as follows:

$$\text{NRMSE} = \frac{\text{RMSE}}{\mu_o}, \quad (7)$$

In conjunction with the aforementioned evaluation metrics, the percent bias metric was computed to estimate the error and uncertainty associated with the National Water Model (NWM) streamflow simulations. PB serves as a metric employed in the assessment of hydrological model performance by quantifying the disparity between predicted and observed values, expressed as a percentage of the observed values. PB is beneficial in hydrological model evaluation, as it offers a measure of the overall bias inherent in a model's predictions. A PB value of zero signifies an unbiased model, where the predicted values, on average, correspond to the observed values. Positive PB values denote an overestimation of observed values by the model, while negative PB values imply model underestimation of the observed values. In this study, the PB was calculated as follows:

$$\text{PB} = \frac{\sum_{i=1}^{N}(s_i - o_i)}{\sum_{i=1}^{N} o_i} \times 100, \quad (8)$$

Further analysis of streamflow time series for monotonic trends (one direction, either increasing or decreasing) was performed using the non-parametric Modified Mann–Kendall trend test.

2.5. Modified Mann–Kendall Trend Test

In the present study, the spatiotemporal evaluation of NWM streamflow estimates was partially investigated by performing streamflow trend analysis utilizing the Modified Mann–Kendall (MMK) trend test [51]. The non-parametric MMK test, which is widely employed [39,52–54], was selected for this investigation due to its lack of requirements for data to adhere to a specific distribution, reduced sensitivity to abrupt shifts resulting from non-homogeneity in the data, and its ability to account for autocorrelation in streamflow time series. Within this context, we analyze trend outcomes for observed and simulated streamflow series, comparing the spatial variation of the trend results. Consequently, the congruence between trends derived from the NWM streamflow series and observed series is scrutinized to evaluate the model's capacity to replicate historical streamflow patterns. It is crucial to note that the trend analysis test was applied exclusively to natural flow series.

3. Results

The accuracy of the NWM streamflow simulation was assessed by comparing with in-situ data using five evaluation statistics, namely KGE, PB, RMSE, NRMSE, and CC. The hourly streamflow data acquired from in-situ and retrospective simulations from February 1979 to December 2020 were used to analyze the Spatiotemporal Variability of the model accuracy. The basin drainage area and RFCs differences were considered.

3.1. Spatial Analysis

The findings derived from the evaluation metrics assessing the NWM streamflow simulations' performance are illustrated in Figure 2. The acquired results demonstrate that 57% of natural flow forecast points exhibit KGE values exceeding 0.5 (Figure 2a), while 43% of forecast points associated with regulated flow present KGE values surpassing 0.5 (Figure 2b). The outcomes reveal suboptimal model performance for forecast points situated within the MBRFC, ABRFC, and WGRFC. Conversely, the model exhibits a commendable performance in estimating streamflow within the NERFC, MARFC, and NWRFC. It is crucial to note that KGE values represent an overall estimation of the concordance between observed and simulated streamflow. In essence, KGE values may be influenced by errors related to correlation, variability, bias, or a combination of these metric components.

The variation in bias error across the different River Forecast Centers (RFCs) was investigated utilizing the percent bias (PB) metric. For natural flow, a satisfactory agreement between observed and simulated streamflow was achieved for 50% of the forecast points, with PB values ranging between −10% and 10%. PB values did not exhibit a discernible spatial distribution of bias error. However, a tendency for the model to underestimate streamflow values was observed in the eastern and northwestern portions of the contiguous United States, specifically within the NERFC, MARFC, SERFC, and NWRFC. Conversely, the model exhibited a propensity to overestimate streamflow in the central and western regions of the CONUS, predominantly over the MBRFC, ABRFC, and WGRFC (Figure 2c).

The findings are also applicable to regulated flow forecast points, where the model tends to underestimate streamflow values in eastern RFCs and overestimate streamflow in central and western RFCs. The results revealed that 36% of regulated flow estimates demonstrated low bias error with PB values between −10% and 10%. Low PB values (close to zero) were primarily observed in the NERFC, MARFC, SERFC, NCRFC, and NWRFC (Figure 2d). It is vital to note that RFCs where the NWM displays low PB values are characterized by high annual precipitation rates (reference). In contrast, high PB values were observed in regions with low annual precipitation rates. The results suggest that the NWM configuration is well-suited for regions dominated by high precipitation. In other words, the model structure and calibration parameters accurately represent surface runoff processes.

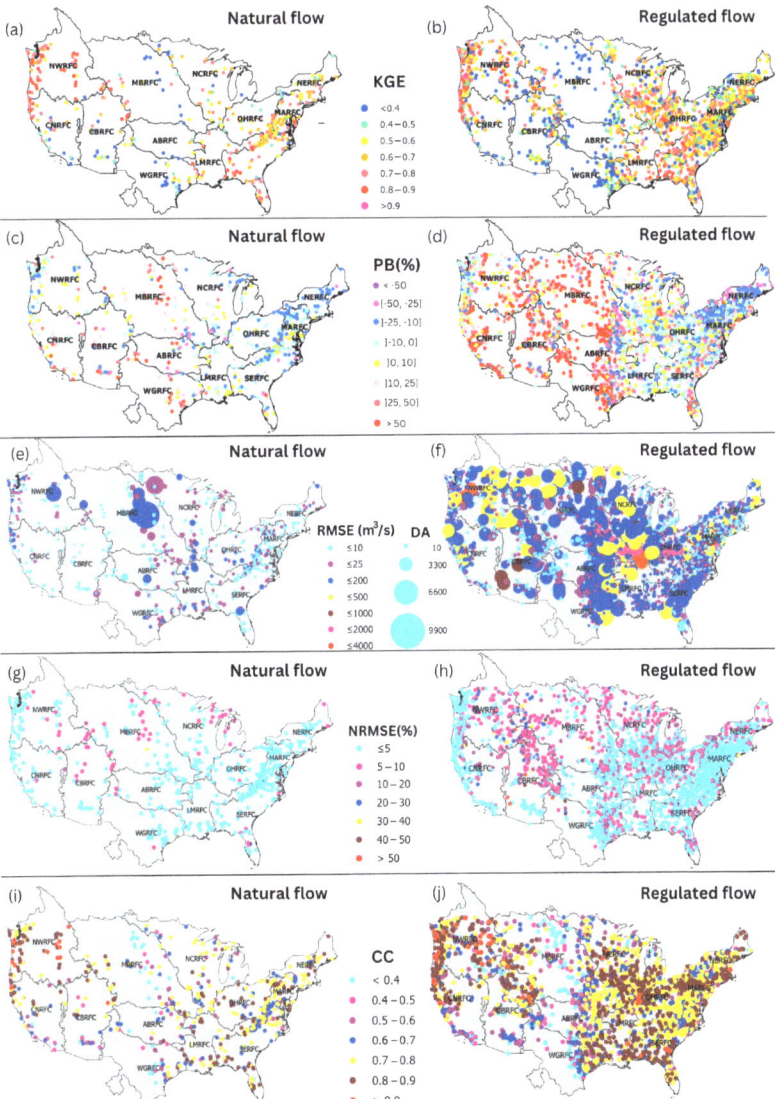

Figure 2. Spatial variation of evaluation metrics results for the NWM hourly streamflow series against observed natural and regulated streamflow series. PB, RMSE, NRMSE, and CC results for natural flow sites are presented in subfigures (**a**,**c**,**e**,**g**,**i**), respectively. PB, RMSE, NRMSE, and CC results for regulated flow are presented in subfigures (**b**,**d**,**f**,**h**,**j**), respectively.

Natural streamflow estimates exhibited low RMSE values in the eastern and western RFCs of the CONUS, irrespective of drainage basin area (Figure 2e). High RMSE values were observed for natural streamflow estimates in the central and eastern regions of the United States. In terms of drainage area, the highest RMSE values were associated with drainage basins encompassing an area exceeding 3000 km². Both RMSE and normalized NRMSE demonstrated optimal results for NWM streamflow estimates in the eastern and western RFCs. The NWM natural streamflow data displayed elevated NRMSE results in the central region, particularly in the MBRFC and portions of the CBRFC. Regulated flow data exhibited inferior performance compared to natural flow, as indicated by higher RMSE and NRMSE values (Figure 2g,h) across the various RFCs within the CONUS. Regulated streamflow estimates yielded the most favorable outcomes in terms of RMSE and NRMSE values in the northeastern region, primarily for forecast points with a drainage area of less than 1000 km^2. NRMSE values below 5% were obtained for 86% of natural forecast points and 63% of regulated forecast points, respectively.

Overall, the model error outcomes in terms of RMSE and NRMSE indicate enhanced performance of the NWM in estimating natural streamflow. The obtained results can be attributed to the fact that regulated flow watersheds exhibit altered hydrological regimes due to the presence of water control structures, such as dams, weirs, and other hydraulic structures. These structures can significantly alter the timing and magnitude of downstream discharge. Consequently, it is challenging to capture the effects of these alterations on a continental-scale hydrological system. In essence, the NWM configuration may not be capable of simulating the intricate interactions between hydraulic structures and the hydrological system. Furthermore, regulated flow basins are often subject to human interventions, which can further complicate the hydrological regime, rendering it challenging for the NWM to accurately simulate streamflow.

Natural streamflow estimates demonstrated optimal results in terms of CC values (CC > 0.50) within the eastern and western RFC. The natural streamflow estimates exhibited the weakest correlation with in situ streamflow observations in the central region, particularly for the MBRFC and WGRFC (Figure 2i). Overall, 89% of the natural flow forecast points had CC values exceeding 0.5. Conversely, 88% of the regulated flow forecast points had CC values greater than 0.5 (Figure 2j). Forecast points with CC values larger than 0.8 represented 30% and 31% of the natural flow and regulated flow forecast points, respectively. The observed results indicated a favorable agreement between observed and estimated streamflow values for regulated flow across the majority of the RFCs. However, the model performance deteriorated for regulated flow forecast points situated within the MBRFC, ABRFC, and WGRFC. The results revealed that the NWM is proficient in capturing the temporal evolution of streamflow for both natural and regulated flow. It is crucial to note that the inferior performance of the NWM in terms of CC is observed in regions with low annual precipitation rates. The findings suggest that the total error associated with streamflow estimates in terms of KGE predominantly originates from the bias error when compared to RMSE, NRMSE, and CC values. Consequently, further model accuracy analysis in the present study will be conducted based on percent bias results.

Overall, the spatial analysis demonstrated a superior agreement between the NWM streamflow estimates and natural flow observations compared to regulated flow observations. The NWM's performance was suboptimal in the Missouri Basin, Arkansas–Red Basin, and West Gulf River Forecast Centers. However, a more favorable agreement was attained in RFCs situated along the east and northwest coasts of the CONUS. Notably, a commendable model performance (KGE > 0.5) was generally observed in humid regions characterized by substantial precipitation rates, suggesting that the NWM accurately represents the rainfall-runoff process. Conversely, the model's poor performance in drier regions may be attributed to its limitations in capturing the seasonal variability of the hydrological system in arid and semi-arid regions. The NWM may be incapable of capturing these types of variations in the natural system, resulting in a weak agreement between observed and estimated streamflow in regions where precipitation contribution to streamflow generation is limited.

The performance of NWM streamflow estimates across different RFCs CONUS as a function of drainage areas was investigated. The watershed classification based on drainage area was derived from the classification scheme proposed by Singh (1994) [55]. Figure 3 depicts the PB variation for distinct watershed classes across the CONUS. The results indicated a superior performance of the model in estimating streamflow for natural flow compared to regulated flow. Overall, the model exhibited a propensity for underestimating streamflow for Milli-watersheds (1000–10,000 ha) and sub-watersheds

(10,000–50,000 ha) in natural flow estimates, with median PB values of −3.90% and −3.60%, respectively. Conversely, for the watershed class (>50,000 ha), the results demonstrated a lower median PB value of −1.51%, with the model tending to overestimate streamflow. In contrast, regulated flow outcomes displayed a suboptimal model performance with a broader spread in PB values. However, the model's behavior was more stable for sub-watersheds, exhibiting a median PB value of −0.49% and a limited spread of obtained results (Q1 = −13.60, and Q3 = 19.06%). It is vital to note that the findings did not reveal any large-scale systematic bias in the model's performance as a function of watershed drainage area. Consequently, to better characterize the model bias on a regional scale, the PB values for each RFC were extracted and analyzed individually.

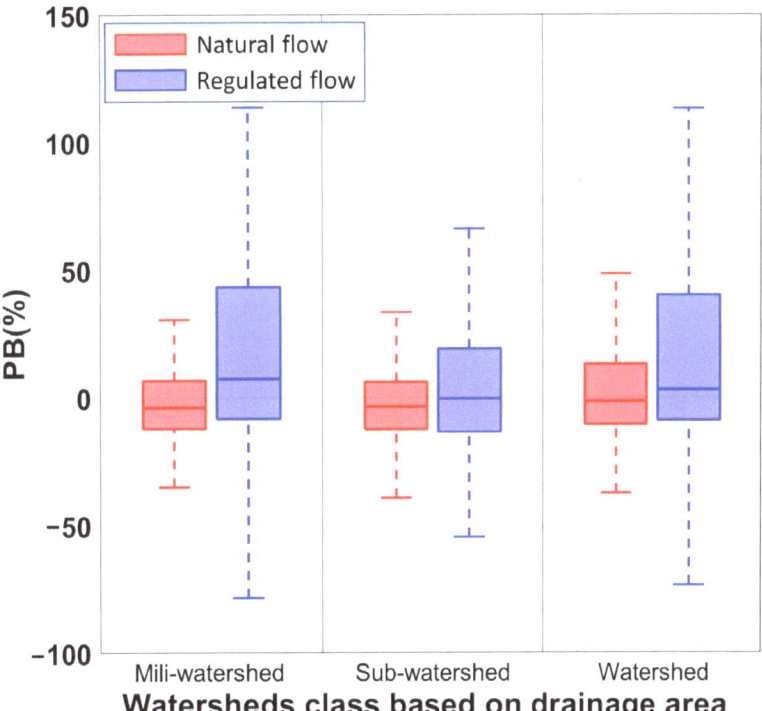

Figure 3. Boxplot showing PB variation as a function drainage area for natural and regulated flow. Boxes indicate the interquartile range (IQR) of the data. Within each box, horizontal lines indicate the median PB value; the first (Q1) and third (Q3) quantiles are marked by boxes, and whiskers extend to 1.5 interquartile ranges.

PB results for each RFC as a function of drainage area are delineated in Tables 2 and 3 for natural flow and regulated flow, respectively. The findings revealed that the model tends to underestimate natural flow in Milli-watersheds within the MARFC, NERFC, NWRFC, OHRFC, and SERFC. Conversely, the model exhibits a propensity to overestimate natural flow in Milli-watersheds situated in the MBRFC and CNRFC. For sub-watershed and watershed drainage basins, the model demonstrates a tendency to underestimate natural flow in the MARFC, NERFC, NCRFC, and OHRFC while overestimating natural flow in the MBRFC and CNRFC. The analysis suggests that NWM natural streamflow estimates are predominantly underestimated in eastern RFCs and overestimated in central RFCs, particularly for forecast points draining Milli-watersheds and sub-watersheds.

Table 2. Comparison of natural flow PB results for the different RFC as a function of watershed drainage area.

RFC	Milli-Watershed			Sub-Watershed			Watershed		
	Q1	Median	Q3	Q1	Median	Q3	Q1	Median	Q3
Missouri Basin (MBRFC)	2.66	4.46	12.53	−5.61	5.93	20.52	−9.24	11.02	32.78
Colorado Basin (CBRFC)	−6.90	−3.52	6.87	−16.02	2.91	27.74	−17.76	−13.58	65.53
Arkansas–Red Basin (ABRFC)	N/A	N/A	N/A	−27.75	1.55	15.35	−12.46	2.24	57.36
California–Nevada (CNRFC)	−6.53	12.98	28.84	4.42	10.78	31.22	5.82	13.44	18.52
Lower Mississippi (LMRFC)	N/A	N/A	N/A	1.54	5.20	6.33	−5.81	−1.75	3.66
Middle Atlantic (MARFC)	−12.91	−4.25	0.53	−10.48	−4.63	3.52	−13.36	−10.88	3.49
North Central (NCRFC)	N/A	N/A	N/A	−20.21	−10.15	2.19	−9.09	−3.08	6.62
Northeast (NERFC)	−12.81	−9.06	−5.57	−21.76	−18.64	−12.07	−23.71	−23.02	−19.25
Northwest (NWRFC)	−4.46	−2.10	1.18	−12.04	−4.77	0.60	−6.64	0.73	5.68
Ohio (OHRFC)	−6.75	−4.98	−0.10	−12.10	−6.41	−2.36	−11.33	−8.87	−4.07
Southeast (SERFC)	−15.87	−12.50	−9.35	−10.23	−4.60	1.95	−9.81	−1.83	10.35
West Gulf (WGRFC)	N/A	N/A	N/A	−20.08	7.73	22.74	6.52	21.74	58.78

Note: N/A: No forecast points representing this class, or limited number of forecast points.

Table 3. Comparison of regulated flow PB results for the different RFC as a function of watershed drainage area.

RFC	Milli-Watershed			Sub-Watershed			Watershed		
	Q1	Median	Q3	Q1	Median	Q3	Q1	Median	Q3
Missouri Basin (MBRFC)	−6.59	3.56	18.82	0.74	18.89	30.77	2.65	49.38	95.14
Colorado Basin (CBRFC)	−9.92	3.19	34.40	−15.22	−1.84	25.87	16.65	56.06	102.26
Arkansas–Red Basin (ABRFC)	N/A	N/A	N/A	−6.11	7.17	17.49	−10.69	11.03	83.97
California–Nevada (CNRFC)	−6.66	25.98	74.61	11.22	36.04	85.69	16.07	80.43	175.08
Lower Mississippi (LMRFC)	N/A	N/A	N/A	−10.29	−4.50	1.54	−9.99	−4.42	2.27
Middle Atlantic (MARFC)	−12.55	0.16	14.92	−12.52	−2.88	7.85	−13.78	−8.24	2.89
North Central (NCRFC)	15.08	47.14	78.24	−11.15	0.99	23.45	−6.86	2.21	13.65
Northeast (NERFC)	−11.07	2.47	35.84	−19.74	−12.67	−2.62	−25.40	−19.48	−12.88
Northwest (NWRFC)	−2.23	1.76	26.49	−11.34	−2.51	19.45	−3.73	6.75	39.54
Ohio (OHRFC)	−5.16	−2.33	14.04	−15.44	−5.20	6.67	−13.74	−6.35	−1.67
Southeast (SERFC)	−9.20	26.35	63.87	−10.09	−1.47	16.16	−8.47	−2.67	8.39
West Gulf (WGRFC)	15.42	59.55	84.37	−7.42	19.38	53.09	12.96	48.02	127.11

Note: N/A: No forecast points representing this class, or limited number of forecast points.

For regulated flow, the PB results exhibited less uniformity in bias distribution across various RFCs and drainage basin sizes. The outcomes indicated a propensity for the model to underestimate regulated flow over sub-watersheds and watersheds situated in the MARFC, NERFC, and OHRFC. Additionally, the results demonstrated a clear overestimation of streamflow in the MBRFC and CNRFC for different drainage basin sizes. The findings imply a random bias associated with streamflow estimates in regulated channels (Table 3). These results can be attributed to both natural and anthropogenic alterations in the drainage basin environment that may not be accurately captured by the model due to static inputs such as land use/cover and catchment topography. Consequently, such changes may be more pronounced for smaller drainage basins where less consistency in the model behavior was observed.

A crucial aspect of the NWM's performance lies in streamflow estimates as a function of stream order. In the present study, PB values corresponding to forecast points for different stream orders were analyzed. As depicted in Figure 4, the PB values for natural flow estimates exhibit an approximately normal distribution, displaying a symmetrical distribution around the median and a relatively small interquartile range. It is also noteworthy that the PB values for natural flow series do not demonstrate significant skewness in any direction. Conversely, boxplots for the regulated flow outcomes indicate that PB values vary considerably as a function of stream order, exhibiting a substantial spread in IQR. The results also reveal high bias streamflow estimates obtained from first- and second-order regulated streams, suggesting a persistent bias associated with low-order regulated streams. The observed results can be attributed to the inherent assumptions related to channel properties in the NWM river network, including the adoption of trapezoidal channel geometry, uniform flow, and constant channel roughness that only varies depending on the stream order (up to 10 orders). These assumptions may influence flow routing and potentially introduce uncertainties in streamflow estimation that are order dependent. Additionally, the NWM employs the Noah–MP land surface model to simulate atmospheric exchanges with the surface and vertical fluxes within the soil moisture column at a 1-km grid resolution. Consequently, the model is anticipated to exhibit greater error generation in low order streams (small catchment), where the representation of channel infiltration may be insufficiently captured [56]. This limitation underscores the need for further refinements in the model's representation of channel properties and soil moisture distribution to improve streamflow predictions, particularly in small-scale drainage systems.

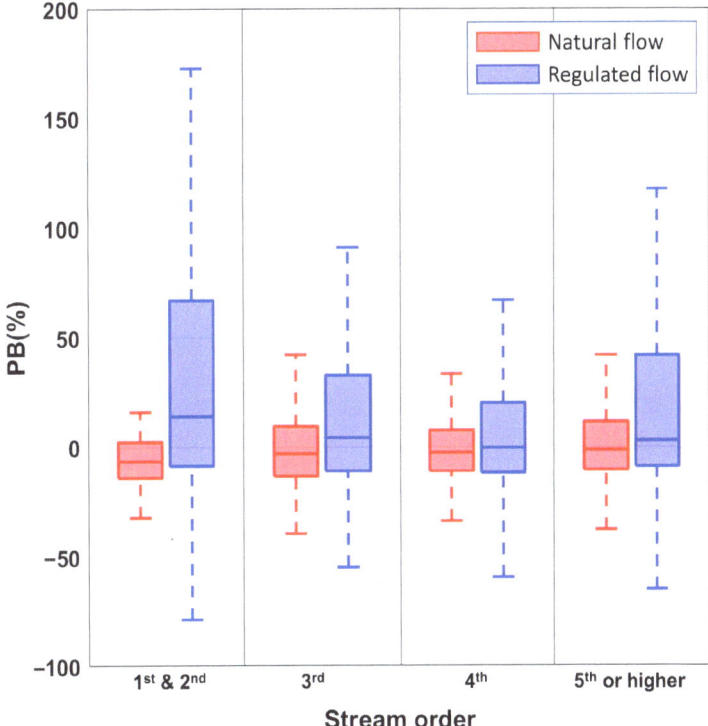

Figure 4. Boxplot showing PB variation as a function stream order for natural and regulated flow.

3.2. Temporal Analysis

The PB results were calculated for the NWM's natural and regulated flow estimates in comparison with in-situ streamflow data. As shown in Figure 5, a more favorable agreement between the estimated and observed streamflow data is achieved for natural flow across all 12 months of the year. For natural flow estimates, the results indicate that the model has a tendency to overestimate streamflow during the period between August and January, with median PB values greater than zero and a relatively positive skew in PB data. Natural flow estimates are predominantly underestimated during the period between March and June, with negative Q1 and median PB values, and Q3 values closer to 0. Higher negative PB values were obtained during March and April when seasonal transitions in streamflow regimes occur in most of the CONUS. The transition season coincides with snowmelt periods, which could be attributed to the NWM tendency to underestimate snow water equivalent (SWE). Conversely, the model's positive bias during the wet season could be attributed to errors in precipitation inputs that trigger the generation of excess runoff.

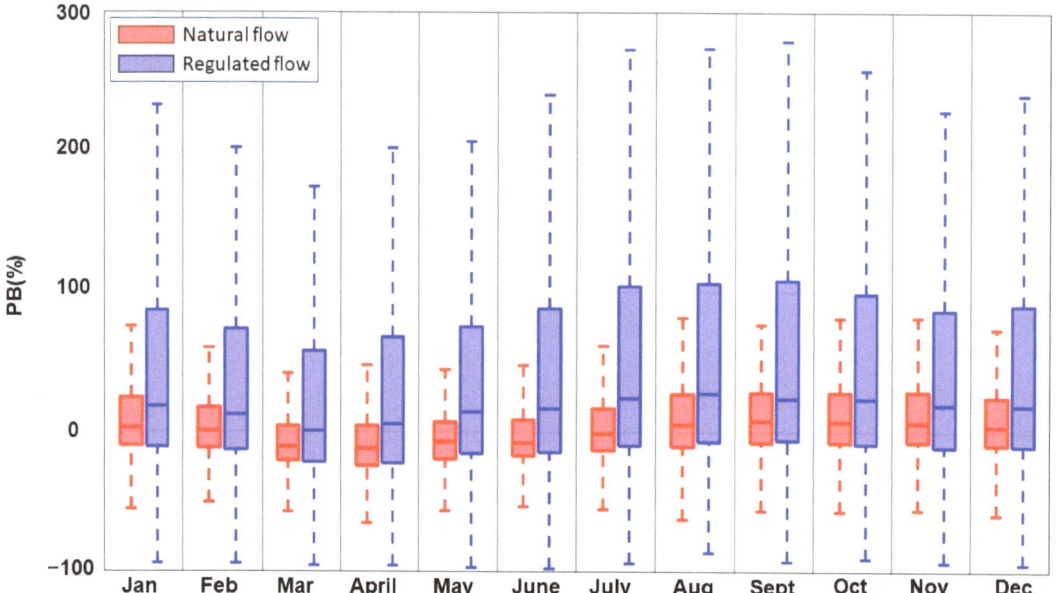

Figure 5. Boxplot showing monthly PB variation for natural flow and regulated flow hourly data.

The monthly variation of PB for regulated flow was assessed in this analysis. The PB for NWM estimates exhibited positive median values for all months, indicating a general propensity for the model to overestimate regulated flow (Figure 5). The regulated flow estimates displayed enhanced performance during February and March, with median PB values closer to 0 and a relatively smaller IQR spread. Conversely, the results revealed the poorest PB values in July, August, and September, with median PB values of 23.90%, 27.37%, and 23.59%, respectively, and a large IQR spread, showcasing a tendency to overestimate streamflow. The larger PB values can be attributed to the fact that the NWM does not incorporate reservoir management practices. In other words, water retention in reservoirs is not represented in the model, which explains the substantial positive PB values.

3.3. Temporal–Spatial Analysis

The hourly streamflow data derived from the NWM retrospective simulation were contrasted with hourly in-situ streamflow data on a seasonal basis, taking into account the various climate zones encompassing the CONUS. It is crucial to acknowledge that the data utilized for the classification of climate zones could be influenced by the signal of climate change, as well as the impacts of teleconnections and climate variability, including the implications of diverse low-frequency climate oscillation indices at varying phases. This topic warrants substantial attention. However, the primary objective of the present research is to offer a preliminary delineation of the spatial distribution of aridity zones.

Regardless, the methodologies derived for climate zone classification align well with both regional and global studies that have explored the spatial variation of the Aridity Index [57,58]. Additionally, the findings of the current study correspond closely with those of Heidari et al. (2020) [58]. Heidari et al. (2020) evaluated shifts in regional hydroclimatic conditions across the contiguous United States, in response to climate change throughout the 21st century. He generated Aridity Index maps for the period from 1989–2015, which exhibited patterns remarkably similar to those discerned in the present study [58].

Figure 6 illustrates the spatiotemporal variation in the accuracy of the NWM natural flow estimates in terms of PB. In arid regions, the results revealed that the model generally overestimates streamflow values across all seasons, with median PB values of 7.85%, 18.80%, 19.54%, and 11.89% for fall, winter, spring, and summer estimates, respectively. These findings imply that the model exhibits enhanced performance during the summer and fall seasons in arid regions, while the performance deteriorates during the winter and spring seasons.

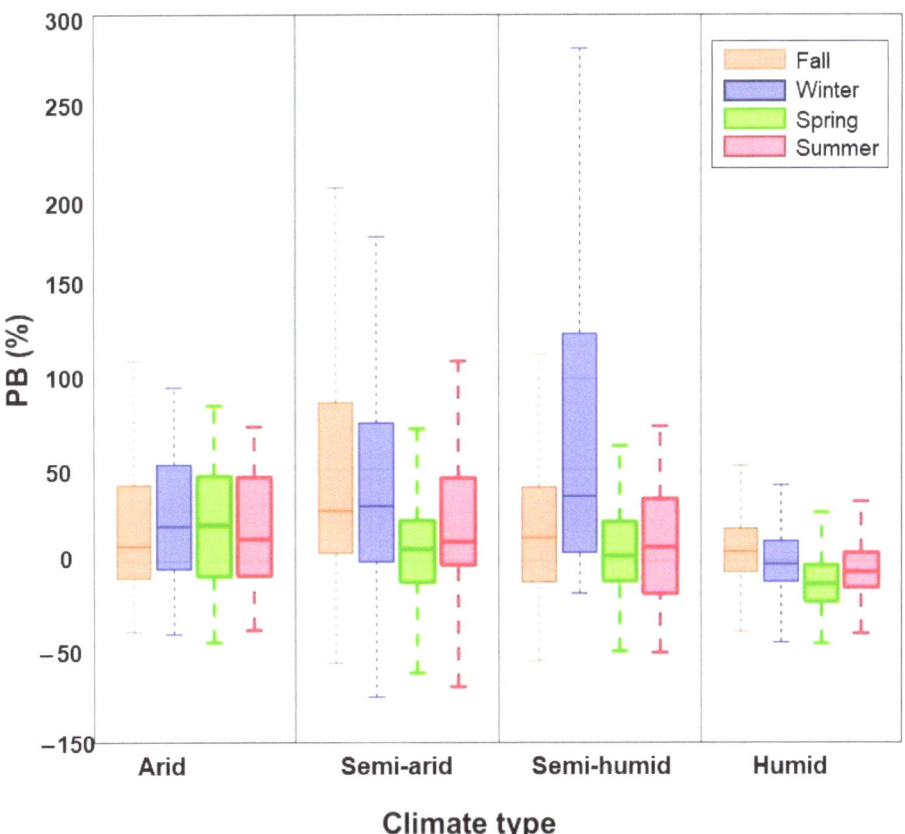

Figure 6. Box plot showing seasonal PB variation for natural flow as a function of climate type.

In semi-arid regions, the results indicated a favorable agreement between the model estimates and observed streamflow data during the spring season. In the remaining seasons, the model exhibited a tendency to overestimate streamflow, with median PB values exceeding zero and an IQR heavily skewed towards positive PB values. Streamflow estimates in semi-humid regions demonstrated a good correspondence with in-situ measurements, exhibiting a median PB value of 2.53%. The model displayed a clear inclination to overestimate streamflow during the winter season in the same region. Although the NWM streamflow estimates did not exhibit any systematic bias, the PB values were skewed in a positive direction.

The most favorable agreement between the NWM estimates and observed data was obtained for simulations conducted in humid regions. The results revealed low-bias error values with median PB values close to zero. The model's best performance was observed during the winter season, potentially reflecting the model's capability to generate accurate runoff during wet periods. It is worth noting that the model tends to underestimate streamflow during the spring season, which could be attributed to the model's limitations in snowmelt-dominated regions.

Based on the results, it can be concluded that the accuracy of the NWM streamflow estimates is significantly influenced by seasonal streamflow variation. In semi-arid and sub-humid climate zones, the NWM streamflow estimates displayed good agreement with in-situ observations for spring season results. In humid regions, streamflow estimates were more accurate during fall and winter. For arid regions, the model demonstrated better agreement with in-situ observations during the fall season.

Figure 7 shows that, compared to natural flow, the NWM streamflow estimates for regulated flow exhibit lower accuracy in terms of PB for the different climate regions except humid areas. For instance, the median PB values for all seasons over the arid, semi-arid, and semi-humid regions obtained for natural flow simulations (Figure 6) were remarkably lower than those obtained for the regulated flow simulations (Figure 7). The NWM-regulated flow estimates yielded the poorest PB results, predominantly during the fall season, across most of the studied climate zones. The NWM regulated flow estimates demonstrated the most favorable agreement with in-situ measurements in humid regions, exhibiting low PB values throughout the various seasons. Conversely, the model performance deteriorated in arid regions, with a tendency to overestimate streamflow, as evidenced by positive Q1 and median PB values across different seasons. It is crucial to emphasize that, in semi-arid and sub-humid regions, the model error in terms of PB during the spring season was comparatively lower than in other seasons. The categorization of model PB results as a function of climate types across different seasons revealed a more distinct pattern in the spatial and temporal distribution of model error. For both natural and regulated flow simulations, the model exhibited commendable performance in streamflow estimation for humid and sub-humid regions. However, a diminished agreement between the simulated and observed streamflow was observed in arid and semi-arid regions.

The obtained results shown in Figure 8 unveiled analogous streamflow trend patterns for the observed and simulated streamflow data from the years 1979 to 2020. The results showed a prevailing increasing trend in NERFC, MARFC, NCRFC, MBRFC, and MRRFC. Conversely, a dominant decreasing trend was observed in the western and southern portions of the CONUS, particularly for stations situated in the NWRFC, CNRFC, CBRFC, and WGRFC. However, this analysis primarily aims to compare results obtained from USGS streamflow records with NWM streamflow simulations. In the case of the NERFC, a significant discrepancy was observed between the MMK results for the in-situ observation series and the simulated series. The MMK outcomes for the NWM streamflow series exhibited a predominance of decreasing trends in the region, with 40% of the forecast point series revealing an opposing trend direction (decreasing trend) in comparison to the in-situ measurement trend direction (increasing trend). It is important to note that the NWM underestimated streamflow values for those simulations (negative PB values).

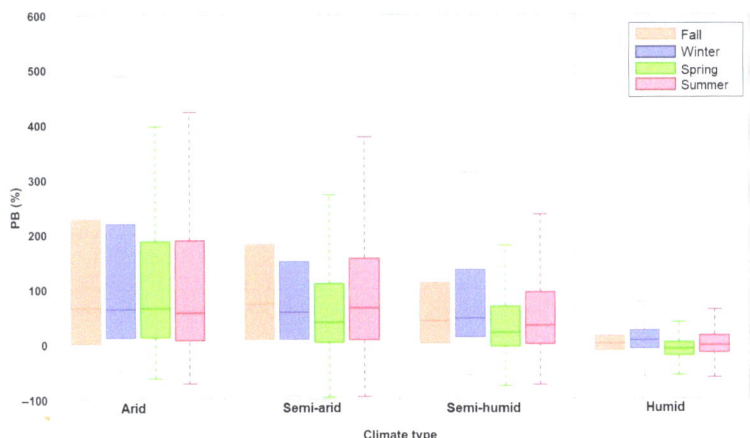

Figure 7. Box plot showing seasonal PB variation for regulated flow as a function of climate type.

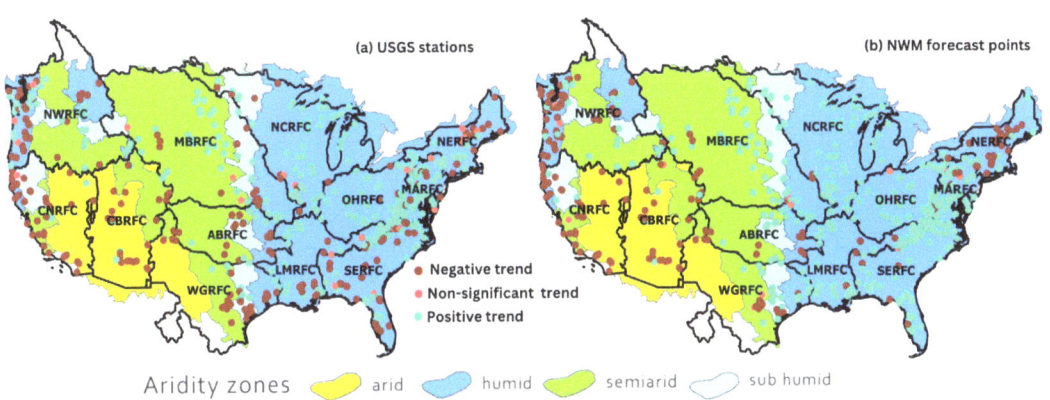

Figure 8. Spatial distribution of Z-MMK results for natural flow stations applied to in-situ observations and NWM retrospective data.

The opposite case was observed in parts of the SERFC, where in-situ observations disclosed a prevailing decreasing trend, while the NWM simulation displayed a dominant increasing trend. In those locations, PB results indicated a tendency of the model to overestimate streamflow. It is also pertinent to mention that distinct trend results for the NERFC and SERFC cases were discovered in forecast points within channels with a stream order of three or higher. The obtained results align with the findings presented in Figure 4, where forecast points with higher stream order exhibited larger PB results, leading to an inadequate representation of the temporal evolution of streamflow in high-order streams.

For other RFCs where streamflow values were overestimated, such as the MBRFC, ABRFC, and WGRFC, trend results obtained from the NWM series demonstrated a dominant increasing trend in those regions. However, in-situ measurement results revealed a prevailing decreasing trend in the ABRFC and WGRFC. The obtained results could be elucidated by the positive PB and low correlation for forecast points located in these regions (Figure 2c,i). Overall, the MMK test results disclosed a satisfactory agreement between the temporal evolution of the observed and simulated natural streamflow series for 74% of the studied dataset.

Regions exhibiting dominant negative streamflow trends and negative PB values pose significant concerns for products generated from the retrospective data, such as annual exceedance probability threshold values at forecast points, which are utilized to trigger flood inundation mapping in the operational NWM. To investigate this issue, we selected two representative stations with negative trends and negative PB values, characterized by close Z-MMK values, to retrieve the annual peak series and flood return periods. Initially, we extracted annual peak discharge from the daily streamflow time series and temporally matched these values with the corresponding values from the NWM simulations. It is crucial to note that the annual peak discharge values from the NWM simulation occurred within a 3-day time window of the USGS measurements, accounting for potential discrepancies in runoff generation lag time representation. In other words, within the same year, the NWM simulation could present a higher value than the selected value, which we consider a biased estimation of streamflow that could be attributed to biases in the forcing data.

As illustrated in Figure 9, the annual peak series and flood return period demonstrate that, although the NWM simulation captures the trend of annual peak discharge values, there is a significant concern regarding the model's representation of flood return periods. The 15-year return period flood value, which is used to trigger flood mapping in the operational model, is underestimated by the NWM simulation, as shown in Figure 9b,d. This finding highlights the issue of the NWM underestimating peak flood values, necessitating bias correction of the NWM retrospective data. Several factors can contribute to the NWM model's underestimation of peak discharge values. In addition to input data inaccuracies, model parameterization plays a substantial role in generating negative biases. Initial investigations into the source of the bias should primarily focus on land use and land cover data. The impact of updating the land use and land cover data while generating the retrospective dataset remains uncertain. Inaccurate land use and land cover data can lead to the misrepresentation of a catchment's response to precipitation events, thereby causing an underestimation of peak discharge values. Furthermore, an incorrect representation of channel routing and floodplain storage can significantly impact the model's ability to accurately simulate peak discharge values.

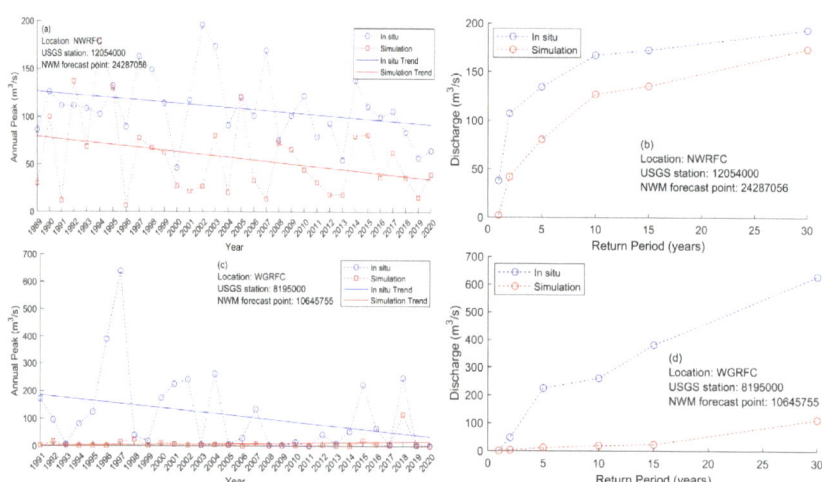

Figure 9. Annual peak series and flood return period series (up to 30 years) for selected stations from the NWRFC and WGRFC. Annual peak series (**a**,**c**) were used to estimate the 1, 2, 5, 10, 15, and 30-year return period discharge values, marked as dots in (**b**,**d**).

4. Discussion

In this study, the evaluation of the National Water Model retrospective data concentrated on the model's streamflow estimation performance across the regional and temporal variations in the contiguous United States. The model bias and bias variation were scrutinized using multiple metrics, emphasizing percent bias (PB) variation for distinct climate classes. This approach facilitated a more standardized portrayal of the model's performance across diverse climate regions.

In this section, we delve into the sources of uncertainty associated with the NWM streamflow simulation, encompassing input and output data, model structure, and model parameters. In the present study, the spatial analysis facilitated the delineation of underperforming catchments, predominantly situated along the high plains and desert southwest. The analysis of the spatial dispersion of model bias shows that regions characterized by elevated non-seasonal streamflow variability and frequent precipitation occurrences, such as the Southeast River Forecast Center and Northwest River Forecast Center, exhibited low variability errors. In contrast, arid and semi-arid regions demonstrated heightened variability errors. Catchments dominated by snowpack, including those within the Missouri Basin River Forecast Center, and areas with a more distinct seasonal cycle, such as the California–Nevada River Forecast Center, also revealed substantial variability errors.

It is widely acknowledged that hydrological models are susceptible to errors in hydrometeorological input data [59]. Consequently, biases in forcing variables, particularly precipitation and near-surface air temperature, yield corresponding biases in model output. Lahmers et al. (2019) demonstrated that refining forcing data by integrating modeled atmospheric forcing with gauge-based precipitation measurements mitigated evapotranspiration biases and augmented the simulation of streamflow behavior [60]. In a separate study, Viterbo et al. (2020) conducted an event-based model assessment and deduced that the NWM streamflow bias is influenced by both model errors and input errors [61]. Furthermore, Garousi–Nejad and Tarboton (2022) identified a prevalent tendency for the NWM to underestimate Snow Water Equivalent (SWE) as a result of hydrologic process representation and hydrometeorological input errors [62]. Their investigation revealed that the incorporation of observed precipitation and bias-corrected air temperature data ameliorated the general downward bias in NWM–SWE estimations. The model is also certainly sensitive to potential biases in soil moisture especially in watersheds with natural flow. The advent of satellite missions like the NASA SMAP that hold a potential to enhance streamflow forecast through data assimilation. This requires an exhaustive calibration and validation of the sensor's estimates through various field campaigns [63,64].

For the NWM V2.1 retrospective simulations, the Analysis of Period of Record for Calibration (AORC) dataset was employed as forcing data. Although the blended product has high temporal and spatial resolutions and contains over a dozen individual rainfall datasets, there is need to evaluate the product performance over the CONUS while taking into account the seasonal variation of the product accuracy. For instance, Kim and Villarini (2022) assessed the AORC rainfall across Louisiana while focusing on the precipitation accuracy associated with Tropical Cyclone (TC) and non-TC conditions [65]. The study showed that AORC performs better for the TC period compared to the non-TC ones. Thus, for regions with dominant small precipitation amounts, it is expected that the bias in AORC data would affect the soil condition and infiltration rates in the model simulation, as well as impact the water storage and the baseflow estimations. Hong et al. (2022) analyzed the AORC performance over the Great Lakes basin, and the analysis showed compared to 632 gauge stations, the product tends to overestimate daily precipitation and underestimate heavy rains with a notable larger bias value in cold months [66]. The study also showed that the interannual change in AORC precipitation has divergent years while compared to other gridded precipitation products. To our knowledge, there are no continental scale assessments of AORC forcing hourly data, including precipitation, air temperature, specific humidity, surface pressure, radiation, and near-surface wind, which may have significant impact on accurately simulating evapotranspiration, snowmelt, and runoff generation processes. A better understanding of the NWM bias inherited from the forcing data would include the assessment of the AORC forcing.

The NWM performance is contingent upon the quality and accuracy of the static input data, which fundamentally represent catchment characteristics and significantly influence runoff generation, flow direction, and the configuration of the stream network. For instance, land use and land-cover data are crucial for determining the spatial distribution of vegetation, urban areas, and other surface types within a catchment, thereby directly impacting parameters associated with infiltration, evapotranspiration, and surface runoff generation. In the case of the NWM retrospective simulation, it is unclear which land cover dataset was used. However, the usage of static datasets similar to the retrospective runs of Versions 2.0 and 2.1 may result in biased simulations for periods when the used land cover layer does not match with the land cover of the simulation period. Similarly, using static soil data for a long-term simulation, encompassing properties such as texture, depth, and hydraulic conductivity, play a pivotal role in shaping infiltration capacity, water retention, and groundwater recharge processes throughout the catchment. Lastly, the accurate representation of river network and geometry, including parameters such as river width, depth, and slope, is indispensable for modeling flow routing and overland flow processes. For example, Ghanghas et al. (2022) assessed the reliability of Synthetic Rating Curves (SRC) across the CONUS by comparing them with the rating curves from USGS gauges [67]. The identified errors in the SRC were attributed to topographical factors and inherent assumptions, such as employing reach-averaged channel properties, constant channel roughness, and uniform flow. These assumptions are consistent with those utilized in the NWM river network (NHDPlus). It is imperative to note that the NWM retrospective simulations serve as a basis for obtaining the 15-year return period flood discharge values across the CONUS. Subsequently, these discharge values are employed to initiate the flood inundation mapping process within the operational NWM framework. Consequently, inaccuracies in flood maps generated during forecasting may stem from errors in the estimated 15-year return period discharge values and/or the underlying SRC, emphasizing the importance of refining these components for improved flood prediction and mapping.

The uncertainty inherent in model streamflow simulations may also stem from errors in the in-situ measurements employed for model calibration and output assessment. While the gathered USGS streamflow data is verified through statistical and deterministic methods, such as flagging extreme discharge values, correlating independent observations, and conducting continuity tests, inherent errors in streamflow records may arise from alterations in stage–discharge relationships, backwater effects due to ice or debris, or equipment malfunctions. Thus, the correction of ice-affected streamflow is critical for evaluating models' simulations in cold regions [68]. Nevertheless, it is important to note that with advancements in estimating data uncertainty, the impact of such errors may be negligible. Conversely, it is imperative to emphasize that the NWM retrospective simulations scrutinized in this study do not incorporate streamflow observation nudging. As a result, the performance of the operational model version may be superior in localized areas where USGS observations are available. Despite this, the reported performance remains pertinent in identifying limitations in model parameterization and underlining the necessity for further refinement.

In this study, several key findings and recommendations emerge from the analysis of the model's performance. First, it is evident that incorporating soil moisture data assimilation in humid regions, where frequent precipitation events are common, is essential to improve the model's accuracy, as soil moisture dynamics play a crucial role in partitioning precipitation into runoff and infiltration, thereby directly impacting streamflow estimates. We would like to emphasize that the NWM's soil moisture estimates are grid-based with a spatial resolution of 1 km. Consequently, a faithful representation of soil moisture within these grid cells would contribute substantially to a more accurate estimation of streamflow in such regions. In addition, it is also important to note that the operational version of the NWM actively nudging streamflow data from USGS stations. This nudging process is critical in updating the streamflow estimates within the model, but it does not affect the other hydrological components. Consequently, continuous and accurate soil moisture data assimilation would not only maintain the up-to-date status of soil moisture but also significantly enhance the model's streamflow estimates, especially in predicting and managing flood events. These collective measures, in effect, would amplify the overall reliability and accuracy of the NWM's streamflow estimates. Second, in cold regions, the assimilation of river ice data is necessary to better capture the effects of ice processes, such as freeze-up and break-up events, on streamflow dynamics, ultimately leading to more accurate predictions in these areas. Third, the uncertainty associated with the lack of knowledge regarding reservoir operation rules has been identified as a potential source of error in the model's performance.

The challenges posed by river systems in the context of hydrological modeling necessitate a more sophisticated and adaptive approach. To tackle these complexities, we advocate for the exploration and integration of advanced computational methods, such as physics-informed machine learning and data mining, into the operational procedures of the NWM. Physics-informed machine-learning algorithms, which couple the power of data-driven models with the underlying physical principles governing the system, can provide insightful and reliable representations of reservoir operation rules. In this context, these techniques can help leverage the existing wealth of observational and operational data, enabling the extraction of complex relationships and patterns that traditional methods may struggle to discern. Moreover, enhancing the NWM's capabilities through data-assimilation techniques could also significantly improve the simulation of streamflow estimates in regulated systems. Data assimilation, which blends model predictions with observed data to improve forecast accuracy and reduce uncertainty, has emerged as a powerful tool in hydrological modeling. Incorporating these inferred operation rules into the NWM would allow for a more faithful representation of the regulated systems, thereby significantly improving the accuracy of the model's streamflow estimates. In this way, these advanced techniques could serve as catalysts in boosting the model's overall performance, while simultaneously offering a more nuanced understanding of the hydrological processes at play in these regulated systems. These proposed recommendations, while demanding in terms of computational resources and methodological implementation, are projected to considerably enhance the capacity of the NWM to provide more reliable and accurate hydrological forecasts, ultimately benefiting a range of stakeholders in water resources management, flood prediction, and environmental conservation.

On the other hand, as we move towards the implementation of the Next Generation Modeling System (NextGen) for the National Water Model, opportunities for enhanced streamflow estimation, particularly in regions exhibiting poor performance with the current NWM, are anticipated [69]. The NextGen framework, inherently model agnostic, offers immense flexibility, permitting the application of disparate methods or models to simulate specific hydrological fluxes. These simulations can be adjusted for diverse temporal and spatial scales, thereby accommodating unique hydrological characteristics across regions. The collaborative ethos embedded in the open-source philosophy of the NextGen framework augments methodological development within the scientific community. This atmosphere of collective engagement accelerates advancements in hydrological modeling techniques, promoting knowledge exchange and bolstering scientific growth. Moreover, this open-source approach empowers agencies to integrate proven models effectively within the NextGen framework, a feature that is notably advantageous for regions wherein certain models have demonstrated exceptional performance [69]. Overall, the evolution towards the NextGen framework heralds a promising era for the NWM, offering pathways to surmount current limitations in streamflow estimation and substantially enhance the accuracy and reliability of hydrological predictions across the Continental United States. This transition signifies a noteworthy advancement in our ongoing journey towards comprehensive and adaptable hydrological modeling.

5. Conclusions

This study aimed to assess the NWM streamflow estimates using a multi-decade retrospective dataset across the contiguous United States. The performance of the models was found to vary regionally, with the primary factors influencing this variation being aridity and precipitation alternation and chaotic dynamics, snowmelt contribution, and runoff seasonality. Model static input data, such as river network and land cover data, were also identified as potential sources of bias. Our findings revealed that 57% of natural flow forecast points exhibited KGE values greater than 0.5, while 43% of regulated flow forecast points surpassed a KGE value of 0.5. The model performance was notably poor in the Great Plains region, while it demonstrated better performance in estimating streamflow in the Northeastern and Northwestern regions. Ultimately, the model bias was found to be governed by both the representation of hydrologic processes and the presence of forcing errors. Our findings revealed that the accuracy of the NWM streamflow estimates is significantly influenced by seasonal streamflow variation. In semi-arid and sub-humid climate zones, the NWM streamflow estimates displayed good agreement with in-situ observations for spring season results. In humid regions, streamflow estimates were more accurate during fall and winter, while for arid regions, the model demonstrated better agreement with in-situ observations during the fall season. These insights can inform future model improvements and contribute to more accurate and reliable hydrologic predictions across the contiguous United States. Future work will focus on leveraging the outcomes of the assessment of the performance of the NWM in this study to guide the evaluation of the streamflow of the operational NWM. In addition, future work will involve the bias correction of streamflow from the retrospective simulation and its frequency analysis to better estimate the annual exceedance probability threshold values at the forecast points, which are used to trigger flood inundation mapping, anticipated in late 2023, using the NWM V3.0. On the other hand, the transition towards the NextGen modeling system holds promising prospects for improved streamflow estimations, particularly in areas of suboptimal current performance of the NWM. Its model-agnostic structure and open-source philosophy foster innovation and integration of proven models. This transformative shift signifies a critical advancement towards a more robust and adaptable hydrological modeling system.

Author Contributions: Conceptualization, M.A., M.T. and T.B.M.J.O.; Methodology, M.A., M.T. and T.B.M.J.O.; Software, M.A.; Formal analysis, M.A.; Investigation, M.A., M.T. and T.B.M.J.O.; Resources, M.A. and M.T.; Data curation, M.A.; Writing—original draft, M.A. and M.T.; Supervision, M.T. and T.B.M.J.O. All authors have read and agreed to the published version of the manuscript.

Funding: This research received no external funding.

Data Availability Statement: The data for the National Water Model (NWM) streamflow retrospective simulations are openly available in the following website: https://registry.opendata.aws/nwm-archive/ (accessed on 17 June 2023). The in-situ streamflow data from the United States Geological Survey (USGS) are openly available in the following website: https://waterdata.usgs.gov/nwis/sw (accessed on 17 June 2023). Codes developed for this study are publicly available in the following HydroShare repository: Abdelkader, M., J. H. Bravo Mendez (2023). NWM version 2.1 model output data retrieval, HydroShare, https://doi.org/10.4211/hs.c4c9f0950c7a42d298ca25e4f6ba5542 (accessed on 17 June 2023).

Acknowledgments: The authors would like to thank the editor and the anonymous reviewers for their comments that improved the quality of the manuscript. The authors acknowledge the partial support of the Cooperative Institute for Research to Operations in Hydrology (CIROH) that is under Federal Award Number: NA22NWS4320003, Subaward Number: A22-0305-S003.

Conflicts of Interest: The authors declare no conflict of interest.

References

1. Makwana, J.J.; Tiwari, M.K. Intermittent Streamflow Forecasting and Extreme Event Modelling Using Wavelet Based Artificial Neural Networks. *Water Resour. Manag.* **2014**, *28*, 4857–4873. [CrossRef]
2. Bai, T.; Chang, J.; Chang, F.J.; Huang, Q.; Wang, Y.; Chen, G. Synergistic Gains from the Multi-Objective Optimal Operation of Cascade Reservoirs in the Upper Yellow River Basin. *J. Hydrol.* **2015**, *523*, 758–767. [CrossRef]
3. Pagano, T.C.; Wood, A.W.; Ramos, M.-H.; Cloke, H.L.; Pappenberger, F.; Clark, M.P.; Cranston, M.; Kavetski, D.; Mathevet, T.; Sorooshian, S.; et al. Challenges of Operational River Forecasting. *J. Hydrometeorol.* **2014**, *15*, 1692–1707. [CrossRef]
4. Li, J.; Wang, Z.; Wu, X.; Xu, C.Y.; Guo, S.; Chen, X. Toward Monitoring Short-Term Droughts using a Novel Daily Scale, Standardized Antecedent Precipitation Evapotranspiration Index. *J. Hydrometeorol.* **2020**, *21*, 891–908. [CrossRef]
5. Chiew, F.H.S.; Zhou, S.L.; McMahon, T.A. Use of Seasonal Streamflow Forecasts in Water Resources Management. *J. Hydrol.* **2003**, *270*, 135–144. [CrossRef]
6. Li, X.; Rankin, C.; Gangrade, S.; Zhao, G.; Lander, K.; Voisin, N.; Shao, M.; Morales-Hernández, M.; Kao, S.C.; Gao, H. Evaluating Precipitation, Streamflow, and Inundation Forecasting Skills during Extreme Weather Events: A Case Study for an Urban Watershed. *J. Hydrol.* **2021**, *603*, 127126. [CrossRef]
7. Sushanth, K.; Mishra, A.; Mukhopadhyay, P.; Singh, R. Real-Time Streamflow Forecasting in a Reservoir-Regulated River Basin using Explainable Machine Learning and Conceptual Reservoir Module. *Sci. Total Environ.* **2023**, *861*, 160680. [CrossRef]
8. Anghileri, D.; Voisin, N.; Castelletti, A.; Pianosi, F.; Nijssen, B.; Lettenmaier, D.P. Value of Long-Term Streamflow Forecasts to Reservoir Operations for Water Supply in Snow-Dominated River Catchments. *Water Resour. Res.* **2016**, *52*, 4209–4225. [CrossRef]
9. Cassagnole, M.; Ramos, M.H.; Zalachori, I.; Thirel, G.; Garçon, R.; Gailhard, J.; Ouillon, T. Impact of the Quality of Hydrological Forecasts on the Management and Revenue of Hydroelectric Reservoirs—A Conceptual Approach. *Hydrol. Earth Syst. Sci.* **2021**, *25*, 1033–1052. [CrossRef]
10. Kao, S.C.; Sale, M.J.; Ashfaq, M.; Uria Martinez, R.; Kaiser, D.P.; Wei, Y.; Diffenbaugh, N.S. Projecting Changes in Annual Hydropower Generation using Regional Runoff Data: An Assessment of the United States Federal Hydropower Plants. *Energy* **2015**, *80*, 239–250. [CrossRef]
11. Sivakumar, B. Nonlinear Dynamics and Chaos in Hydrologic Systems: Latest Developments and a Look Forward. *Stoch. Environ. Res. Risk Assess.* **2009**, *23*, 1027–1036. [CrossRef]
12. Perrin, C.; Oudin, L.; Andreassian, V.; Rojas-Serna, C.; Michel, C.; Mathevet, T. Impact of Limited Streamflow Data on the Efficiency and the Parameters of Rainfall-Runoff Models. *Hydrol. Sci. J.* **2007**, *52*, 131–151. [CrossRef]
13. Butts, M.B.; Payne, J.T.; Kristensen, M.; Madsen, H. An Evaluation of the Impact of Model Structure on Hydrological Modelling Uncertainty for Streamflow Simulation. *J. Hydrol.* **2004**, *298*, 242–266. [CrossRef]
14. Orth, R.; Staudinger, M.; Seneviratne, S.I.; Seibert, J.; Zappa, M. Does Model Performance Improve with Complexity? A Case Study with Three Hydrological Models. *J. Hydrol.* **2015**, *523*, 147–159. [CrossRef]
15. Hung, C.L.J.; James, L.A.; Carbone, G.J.; Williams, J.M. Impacts of Combined Land-Use and Climate Change on Streamflow in Two Nested Catchments in the Southeastern United States. *Ecol. Eng.* **2020**, *143*, 105665. [CrossRef]
16. Sunde, M.G.; He, H.S.; Hubbart, J.A.; Urban, M.A. An Integrated Modeling Approach for Estimating Hydrologic Responses to Future Urbanization and Climate Changes in a Mixed-Use Midwestern Watershed. *J. Environ. Manag.* **2018**, *220*, 149–162. [CrossRef] [PubMed]
17. Zhou, Q.; Leng, G.; Su, J.; Ren, Y. Comparison of Urbanization and Climate Change Impacts on Urban Flood Volumes: Importance of Urban Planning and Drainage Adaptation. *Sci. Total Environ.* **2019**, *658*, 24–33. [CrossRef] [PubMed]
18. Abbas, S.A.; Xuan, Y. Impact of Precipitation Pre-Processing Methods on Hydrological Model Performance using High-Resolution Gridded Dataset. *Water* **2020**, *12*, 840. [CrossRef]
19. Shafqat Mehboob, M.; Kim, Y.; Lee, J.; Eidhammer, T. Quantifying the Sources of Uncertainty for Hydrological Predictions with WRF-Hydro over the Snow-Covered Region in the Upper Indus Basin, Pakistan. *J. Hydrol.* **2022**, *614*, 128500. [CrossRef]
20. Segond, M.L.; Wheater, H.S.; Onof, C. The Significance of Spatial Rainfall Representation for Flood Runoff Estimation: A Numerical Evaluation Based on the Lee Catchment, UK. *J. Hydrol.* **2007**, *347*, 116–131. [CrossRef]
21. Gu, P.; Wang, G.; Liu, G.; Wu, Y.; Liu, H.; Jiang, X.; Liu, T. Evaluation of Multisource Precipitation Input for Hydrological Modeling in an Alpine Basin: A Case Study from the Yellow River Source Region (China). *Hydrol. Res.* **2022**, *53*, 314–335. [CrossRef]
22. Bourdin, D.R.; Fleming, S.W.; Stull, R.B. Streamflow Modelling: A Primer on Applications, Approaches and Challenges. *Atmos. Ocean* **2012**, *50*, 507–536. [CrossRef]
23. Nijssen, B.; Schnur, R.; Lettenmaier, D.P. Global Retrospective Estimation of Soil Moisture using the Variable Infiltration Capacity Land Surface Modl, 1980–93. *J. Clim.* **2001**, *14*, 1790–1808. [CrossRef]
24. Milly, P.C.D.; Shmakin, A.B. Global Modeling of Land Water and Energy Balances. Part II: Land-Characteristic Contributions to Spatial Variability. *J. Hydrometeorol.* **2002**, *3*, 301–310. [CrossRef]
25. Hales, R.C.; Nelson, E.J.; Souffront, M.; Gutierrez, A.L.; Prudhomme, C.; Kopp, S.; Ames, D.P.; Williams, G.P.; Jones, N.L. Advancing Global Hydrologic Modeling with the GEOGloWS ECMWF Streamflow Service. *J. Flood Risk Manag.* **2022**, *16*, 12859. [CrossRef]
26. McEnery, J.; Ingram, J.; Duan, Q.; Adams, T.; Anderson, L. NOAA'S advanced hydrologic prediction service: Building pathways for better science in water forecasting. *Bull. Am. Meteorol. Soc.* **2005**, *86*, 375–386. [CrossRef]

27. National Research Council. *Toward a New Advanced Hydrologic Prediction Service (AHPS)*; The National Academies Press: Washington, DC, USA, 2006; ISBN 0309101441. [CrossRef]
28. Gochis, D.J.; Barlage, M.; Dugger, A.; Fitzgerald, K.; Karsten, L.; Mcallister, M.; Mccreight, J.; Mills, J.; Rafieeinasab, A.; Read, L.; et al. *The WRF-Hydro Modeling System Technical Description, Version 5.0*; NCAR Technical Note; UCAR: Boulder, CO, USA, 2018.
29. Office of Water Prediction. Available online: https://water.noaa.gov/about/nwm (accessed on 6 May 2023).
30. Wagener, T.; Sivapalan, M.; Troch, P.A.; McGlynn, B.L.; Harman, C.J.; Gupta, H.V.; Kumar, P.; Rao, P.S.C.; Basu, N.B.; Wilson, J.S. The Future of Hydrology: An Evolving Science for a Changing World. *Water Resour. Res.* **2010**, *46*, W05301. [CrossRef]
31. Niu, G.Y.; Yang, Z.L.; Mitchell, K.E.; Chen, F.; Ek, M.B.; Barlage, M.; Kumar, A.; Manning, K.; Niyogi, D.; Rosero, E.; et al. The Community Noah Land Surface Model with Multiparameterization Options (Noah-MP): 1. Model Description and Evaluation with Local-Scale Measurements. *J. Geophys. Res. Atmos.* **2011**, *116*, 1–19. [CrossRef]
32. Abdelkader, M.; Bravo Mendez, J.H. NWM Version 2.1 Model Output Data Retrieval. *HydroShare*. 2023. Available online: https://www.hydroshare.org/resource/c4c9f0950c7a42d298ca25e4f6ba5542/ (accessed on 17 June 2023).
33. NOAA National Water Model CONUS Retrospective Dataset—Registry of Open Data on AWS. Available online: https://registry.opendata.aws/nwm-archive/ (accessed on 6 May 2023).
34. USGS Water Mission Area NSDI Node. Available online: https://water.usgs.gov/GIS/metadata/usgswrd/XML/gagesII_Sept2011.xml (accessed on 6 May 2023).
35. Database of Modified Routing for NHDPlus, Version 2.1; Flowlines: ENHDPlusV2_us—ScienceBase-Catalog. Available online: https://www.sciencebase.gov/catalog/item/5b92790be4b0702d0e809fe5 (accessed on 6 May 2023).
36. USGS Surface—Water Data for the Nation. Available online: https://waterdata.usgs.gov/nwis/sw (accessed on 6 May 2023).
37. Hamilton, A.S.; Moore, R.D. Quantifying Uncertainty in Streamflow Records. *Can. Water Resour. J.* **2012**, *37*, 3–21. [CrossRef]
38. Giuntoli, I.; Renard, B.; Vidal, J.P.; Bard, A. Low Flows in France and Their Relationship to Large-Scale Climate Indices. *J. Hydrol.* **2013**, *482*, 105–118. [CrossRef]
39. Yerdelen, C.; Abdelkader, M. Hydrological Data Trend Analysis with Wavelet Transform. *Comptes Rendus L'Academie Bulg. Sci.* **2021**, *74*, 1194–1202. [CrossRef]
40. Abdelkader, M.; Yerdelen, C. Hydrological Drought Variability and Its Teleconnections with Climate Indices. *J. Hydrol.* **2022**, *605*, 127290. [CrossRef]
41. World Atlas of Desertification: Second Edition. Available online: https://wedocs.unep.org/20.500.11822/30300 (accessed on 6 May 2023).
42. Xu, T.; Guo, Z.; Xia, Y.; Ferreira, V.G.; Liu, S.; Wang, K.; Yao, Y.; Zhang, X.; Zhao, C. Evaluation of Twelve Evapotranspiration Products from Machine Learning, Remote Sensing and Land Surface Models over Conterminous United States. *J. Hydrol.* **2019**, *578*, 124105. [CrossRef]
43. Zhang, B.; Xia, Y.; Long, B.; Hobbins, M.; Zhao, X.; Hain, C.; Li, Y.; Anderson, M.C. Evaluation and Comparison of Multiple Evapotranspiration Data Models over the Contiguous United States: Implications for the next Phase of NLDAS (NLDAS-Testbed) Development. *Agric. For. Meteorol.* **2020**, *280*, 107810. [CrossRef]
44. Knoben, W.J.M.; Freer, J.E.; Woods, R.A. Technical Note: Inherent Benchmark or Not? Comparing Nash-Sutcliffe and Kling-Gupta Efficiency Scores. *Hydrol. Earth Syst. Sci.* **2019**, *23*, 4323–4331. [CrossRef]
45. Waseem, M.; Mani, N.; Andiego, G.; Usman, M. A Review of Criteria of Fit for Hydrological Models. *Int. Res. J. Eng. Technol.* **2008**, *9001*, 1765.
46. Liu, D. A Rational Performance Criterion for Hydrological Model. *J. Hydrol.* **2020**, *590*, 125488. [CrossRef]
47. Lamontagne, J.R.; Barber, C.A.; Vogel, R.M. Improved Estimators of Model Performance Efficiency for Skewed Hydrologic Data. *Water Resour. Res.* **2020**, *56*, e2020WR027101. [CrossRef]
48. Yuemei, H.; Xiaoqin, Z.; Jianguo, S.; Jina, N. Conduction between Left Superior Pulmonary Vein and Left Atria and Atria Fibrillation under Cervical Vagal Trunk Stimulation. *Colomb. Med.* **2008**, *39*, 227–234.
49. de Salis, H.H.C.; da Costa, A.M.; Vianna, J.H.M.; Schuler, M.A.; Künne, A.; Fernandes, L.F.S.; Pacheco, F.A.L. Hydrologic Modeling for Sustainable Water Resources Management in Urbanized Karst Areas. *Int. J. Environ. Res. Public Health* **2019**, *16*, 2542. [CrossRef]
50. Gupta, H.V.; Kling, H.; Yilmaz, K.K.; Martinez, G.F. Decomposition of the Mean Squared Error and NSE Performance Criteria: Implications for Improving Hydrological Modelling. *J. Hydrol.* **2009**, *377*, 80–91. [CrossRef]
51. Hamed, K.H.; Ramachandra Rao, A. A Modified Mann-Kendall Trend Test for Autocorrelated Data. *J. Hydrol.* **1998**, *204*, 182–196. [CrossRef]
52. Naizghi, M.S.; Ouarda, T.B.M.J. Teleconnections and Analysis of Long-Term Wind Speed Variability in the UAE. *Int. J. Clim.* **2017**, *37*, 230–248. [CrossRef]
53. Vazifehkhah, S.; Kahya, E. Hydrological and Agricultural Droughts Assessment in a Semi-Arid Basin: Inspecting the Teleconnections of Climate Indices on a Catchment Scale. *Agric. Water Manag.* **2019**, *217*, 413–425. [CrossRef]
54. Yerdelen, C.; Tastan, M.; Abdelkader, M. Assessment of Trend Analysis Methods for Annual Streamflow. *Environ. Eng. Manag. J.* **2022**, *21*, 569–577.
55. Singh, V.P. *Elementary Hydrology*; Pearson: Londen, UK, 1992; 973p.

56. Lahmers, T.M.; Hazenberg, P.; Gupta, H.; Castro, C.; Gochis, D.; Dugger, A.; Yates, D.; Read, L.; Karsten, L.; Wang, Y.H. Evaluation of NOAA National Water Model Parameter Calibration in Semiarid Environments Prone to Channel Infiltration. *J. Hydrometeorol.* **2021**, *22*, 2939–2969. [CrossRef]
57. Srivastava, A.; Rodriguez, J.F.; Saco, P.M.; Kumari, N.; Yetemen, O. Global Analysis of Atmospheric Transmissivity using Cloud Cover, Aridity and Flux Network Datasets. *Remote Sens.* **2021**, *13*, 1716. [CrossRef]
58. Heidari, H.; Arabi, M.; Warziniack, T.; Kao, S.C. Assessing Shifts in Regional Hydroclimatic Conditions of U.S. River Basins in Response to Climate Change over the 21st Century. *Earth's Futur.* **2020**, *8*, e2020EF001657. [CrossRef]
59. Wu, X.; Guo, S.; Qian, S.; Wang, Z.; Lai, C.; Li, J.; Liu, P. Long-Range Precipitation Forecast Based on Multipole and Preceding Fluctuations of Sea Surface Temperature. *Int. J. Clim.* **2022**, *42*, 8024–8039. [CrossRef]
60. Lahmers, T.M.; Gupta, H.; Castro, C.L.; Gochis, D.J.; Yates, D.; Dugger, A.; Goodrich, D.; Hazenberg, P. Enhancing the Structure of the WRF-Hydro Hydrologic Model for Semiarid Environments. *J. Hydrometeorol.* **2019**, *20*, 691–714. [CrossRef]
61. Viterbo, F.; Mahoney, K.; Read, L.; Salas, F.; Bates, B.; Elliott, J.; Cosgrove, B.; Dugger, A.; Gochis, D.; Cifelli, R. A Multiscale, Hydrometeorological Forecast Evaluation of National Water Model Forecasts of the May 2018 Ellicott City, Maryland, Flood. *J. Hydrometeorol.* **2020**, *21*, 475–499. [CrossRef]
62. Garousi-Nejad, I.; Tarboton, D.G. A Comparison of National Water Model Retrospective Analysis Snow Outputs at Snow Telemetry Sites across the Western United States. *Hydrol. Process.* **2022**, *36*, e14469. [CrossRef]
63. Karamouz, M.; Alipour, R.S.; Roohinia, M.; Fereshtehpour, M. A Remote Sensing Driven Soil Moisture Estimator: Uncertain Downscaling with Geostatistically Based Use of Ancillary Data. *Water Resour. Res.* **2022**, *58*, e2022WR031946. [CrossRef]
64. Abdelkader, M.; Temimi, M.; Colliander, A.; Cosh, M.H.; Kelly, V.R.; Lakhankar, T.; Fares, A. Assessing the Spatiotemporal Variability of SMAP Soil Moisture Accuracy in a Deciduous Forest Region. *Remote Sens.* **2022**, *14*, 3329. [CrossRef]
65. Kim, H.; Villarini, G. Evaluation of the Analysis of Record for Calibration (AORC) Rainfall across Louisiana. *Remote Sens.* **2022**, *14*, 3284. [CrossRef]
66. Hong, Y.; Xuan Do, H.; Kessler, J.; Fry, L.; Read, L.; Rafieei Nasab, A.; Gronewold, A.D.; Mason, L.; Anderson, E.J. Evaluation of Gridded Precipitation Datasets over International Basins and Large Lakes. *J. Hydrol.* **2022**, *607*, 127507. [CrossRef]
67. Ghanghas, A.; Dey, S.; Merwade, V. Evaluating the Reliability of Synthetic Rating Curves for Continental Scale Flood Mapping. *J. Hydrol.* **2022**, *606*, 127470. [CrossRef]
68. Chaouch, N.; Temimi, M.; Romanov, P.; Cabrera, R.; Mckillop, G.; Khanbilvardi, R. An Automated Algorithm for River Ice Monitoring over the Susquehanna River using the MODIS Data. *Hydrol. Process.* **2014**, *28*, 62–73. [CrossRef]
69. Next Gen Water Modeling Framework Prototype. Available online: https://github.com/NOAA-OWP/ngen (accessed on 17 June 2023).

Disclaimer/Publisher's Note: The statements, opinions and data contained in all publications are solely those of the individual author(s) and contributor(s) and not of MDPI and/or the editor(s). MDPI and/or the editor(s) disclaim responsibility for any injury to people or property resulting from any ideas, methods, instructions or products referred to in the content.

Article

Assessing the Effectiveness of the Use of the InVEST Annual Water Yield Model for the Rivers of Colombia: A Case Study of the Meta River Basin

Jhon B. Valencia [1], Vladimir V. Guryanov [1], Jeison Mesa-Diez [2], Jeimar Tapasco [3] and Artyom V. Gusarov [4,*]

[1] Institute of Environmental Sciences, Kazan Federal University, 420008 Kazan, Russia; jbrayanvalenciag@gmail.com (J.B.V.); vladimir.guryanov@kpfu.ru (V.V.G.)
[2] Escuela de Estadística, Universidad del Valle, Calle 13 No. 100-00—Edificio E43, Santiago de Cali 760042, Colombia; jeison.mesa@correounivalle.edu.co
[3] Climate Action, Alliance of Bioversity International and the International Center for Tropical Agriculture (CIAT), Palmira 763537, Colombia; j.tapasco@cgiar.org
[4] Institute of Geology and Petroleum Technologies, Kazan Federal University, 420008 Kazan, Russia
* Correspondence: avgusarov@mail.ru

Citation: Valencia, J.B.; Guryanov, V.V.; Mesa-Diez, J.; Tapasco, J.; Gusarov, A.V. Assessing the Effectiveness of the Use of the InVEST Annual Water Yield Model for the Rivers of Colombia: A Case Study of the Meta River Basin. *Water* 2023, *15*, 1617. https://doi.org/10.3390/w15081617

Academic Editor: Ankur Srivastava

Received: 15 March 2023
Revised: 11 April 2023
Accepted: 19 April 2023
Published: 21 April 2023

Copyright: © 2023 by the authors. Licensee MDPI, Basel, Switzerland. This article is an open access article distributed under the terms and conditions of the Creative Commons Attribution (CC BY) license (https:// creativecommons.org/licenses/by/ 4.0/).

Abstract: This paper presents the results of one of the hydrological models, the InVEST "Annual Water Yield" (InVEST–AWY), applied to the Meta River basin in Colombia, which covers an area of 113,981 km^2. The study evaluates the performance of the model in different subbasins of the Meta River basin. The model's accuracy was assessed using different statistical measures, including Nash–Sutcliffe Efficiency (NSE) coefficient, Root Mean Square Error (RMSE), correlation coefficients for the calibration (r_{cal}) and validation (r_{val}) periods. The overall performance of the model in the Meta River basin is relatively poor as indicated by the low NSE value of 0.07 and high RMSE value of 1071.61. In addition, the model explains only a 7% of the variance in the observed data. The sensitivity analysis revealed that a 30% reduction in crop coefficient (Kc) values would result in a 10.7% decrease in water yield. The model estimated, for example, the annual average water yield of the river in 2018 as 1.98×10^{11} m^3/year or 6273.4 m^3/s, which is 1.3% lower than the reported value. The upper Meta River subbasin shows the highest NSE value (0.49), indicating a good result between observed and simulated water discharge. In contrast, the South Cravo River subbasin shows a negative NSE value of −1.29, indicating poor model performance. The Yucao River subbasin and the upper Casanare River subbasin also show lower NSE values compared to the upper Meta River subbasin, indicating less accurate model performance in these subbasins. The correlation coefficients in calibration (r_{cal}) and validation (r_{val}) for the upper Meta River, Yucao River, South Cravo River, and upper Casanare River subbasins were 0.79 and 0.83, 0.4 and 0.22, 0.5 and −0.25, and 0 and 0.18, respectively. These results provide useful insights into the limitations for the proper use of the InVEST–AWY model in Colombia. This study is the first to use the InVEST–AWY model on a large scale in the territory of Colombia, allowing to evaluate its effectiveness in hydrological modeling for water management.

Keywords: watershed; water balance; land cover; runoff; water discharge; Orinoco River

1. Introduction

Water is vital for human activities. This resource provides ecosystem services such as water provision, purification, and regulation, which are crucial for the health and productivity of natural ecosystems, as well as for human well-being. However, as the world's population continues to grow and the effects of climate change become more noticeable, the demand for water resources is increasing, and the availability of clean water is becoming increasingly scarce [1–3].

Effective planning and management of water resources require the use models to predict water yield and to understand the complex interactions between different water sources and uses [4]. However, some of the challenges in hydrology modeling are the low availability of information in remote environments, as well as the lack of knowledge of ecosystems as providers of water [5].

The Meta River basin in Colombia has an approximate area of 99,500 to 105,000 km^2 [6]. The river has a length of 1002 km from Guamal (upstream) to the mouth in the Orinoco River [7]. This river basin has a large percentage of areas suitable for agricultural activities [8], suggesting higher pressure on the water resources of this region in the future.

In Colombia, some studies have quantified water resources at the basin-scale level [9–17]. Among the limitations for water modeling in Colombia is access to hydro-climatological data in its eastern regions due to low station coverage [18].

Modeling hydrological services requires significant implementation effort and data requirements, which may not always be available [19]. For example, [16] performed one of the largest scale hydrological modeling projects in the Magdalena River basin in Colombia, which obtained good results using global and in-situ hydrometeorological information as input for multiple hydrological models.

When selecting a hydrological model, it is important to consider its capability to represent the hydrological characteristics of the region. For instance, [20] used selection scores to choose a model for the Kangsabati River basin, where they compared five conceptual models (AWBM, GR4J, HBV-light, SRM, and Sacramento) and five semi-distributed models (HEC–HMS, VIC, HFAM, HSPF, and TOPMODEL). They selected the GR4J and VIC models because they had the best performance criteria for their research zone.

Although hydrological models have different approaches to simulate the hydrological cycle, they all require input data such as rainfall, runoff, wind speed, relative humidity, soil type, catchment properties, hydrogeology, and other properties in a daily scale [20,21]. However, there are also differences between the models. The InVEST "Annual Water Yield" (InVEST–AWY) model is easy to use and requires minimum input data but may not perform well for large watersheds with low data. Nonetheless, the model can be calibrated using the Soil and Water Assessment Tool (SWAT) model outputs [22]. On the other hand, HEC-HMS is a powerful model that can handle large watersheds but requires a significant amount of input data and expertise to use effectively [23].

Furthermore, some models like Sacramento and GR4J use a lumped approach, while others like HEC-HMS and VIC use a distributed approach [20,24]. The lumped approach models are easier to use and require less input data, but they may not be suitable for large watersheds. The distributed approach models, on the other hand, are more complex and require more input data, but they can handle large watersheds and provide more accurate results [25].

Some models may require long-term series of observed hydrological and meteorological data to calibrate the model parameters, which can be difficult to obtain [24]. Models like SWAT, VIC, and GR4J may require a significant amount of input data and expertise to use effectively [23,26,27]. In areas where a reliable weather monitoring system is absent, utilizing satellite information for hydrological modeling can be a viable solution [28]. Nonetheless, the overestimation of weather variables, such as precipitation, remains a concern [28].

One of the most used models in catchment scale is the Soil and Water Assessment Tool (SWAT) [29]. However, it requires a vast amount of daily hydroclimatic information and can only be applicable in zones with good weather station data coverage. [17] used SWAT to determine water yield in northeastern Colombia, in an area with a high density of weather stations, and established the relationship between water availability, land-use change, and climate change.

Due to the high demand for information in some hydrological models [30] and the lack of hydroclimatic information in remote zones, it is necessary to explore models that require less information and computational effort but can still provide a good approximation of hydrological services assessment [31]. One such tool is the Integrated Valuation of Ecosystem Services and Tradeoffs (InVEST) [32], a model developed in 2007 by Stanford University, the World Wildlife Fund (WWF), and the Nature Conservancy (TCN). It contains several sub-models to assess ecosystem services [33], including a model for estimating water yield.

Hydrological models are often limited by their requirements for extensive daily data and the high computational expense associated with watershed modeling [34]. However, the InVEST–AWY model, which simplifies parameters in a spatial format, offers a fast and convenient approach to accessing relevant information with a relatively lower computational burden compared to more complex models such as SWAT [35]. The InVEST–AWY model has several advantages, including its requirement for fewer inputs and ease of setup, which makes it accessible to a broader range of users [35]. In addition, the InVEST–AWY model provides estimates at a finer spatial resolution, making it suitable for assessments at different scales. The model can also estimate annual water yield using remotely-sensed data, which are especially useful in areas where ground-based data is unavailable or scarce. For example, a study conducted by [36] used the InVEST–AWY model to estimate the impact of climate change on water resources in the Shule River basin (China), where the model provided accurate estimates of annual water yield with an R^2 of 0.986 and RMSE of 3, comparable to those obtained from more complex models such as SWAT.

The Orinoco region (Región de la Orinoquía) in Colombia faces limitations in weather station coverage, which can affect the accuracy of hydrological modeling [37]. The Orinoco River is one of the world's longest rivers, ranking third in terms of annual average water discharge [38]. However, the sources of water that feed it have not been studied in detail [39]. The Orinoco River basin is a key and strategic conservation area, with over 200,000 km^2 of natural savannas [18]. Nevertheless, significant plans for agro-industrial expansion in the Orinoco region may seriously affect water availability [18].

Hydrological models, such as SWAT, VIC, GR4J, InVEST-AWY, and HEC-HMS, are commonly used for hydrological simulations. However, in areas with a low density of weather stations, these models may have key uncertainties in accurately estimating water yield [40]. For example, a study that used the SWAT model for three U.S. watersheds found that the model's ability to simulate evapotranspiration was affected by parameter equifinality, energy-related weather input uncertainty, and limited process representation [41]. To address this uncertainty, the study proposed a remote sensing-based solution that assimilates remotely-sensed potential evapotranspiration [41].

Another key uncertainty in hydrological models is related to their ability to accurately simulate extreme hydrological events, such as floods and droughts. A study that used the Variable Infiltration Capacity (VIC) land surface model found that uncertainties in model structure, parameter identifiability, and meteorological forcings limit the reliability of model predictions [42]. To address these challenges, the study used a Bayesian statistical inference framework for parameter uncertainty modeling of the VIC model [42].

The InVEST–AWY model is based on the Budyko framework and has been shown to provide similar estimates of the spatial distribution of water yield as SWAT in some cases [43]. However, the InVEST–AWY model may not accurately estimate the spatial distribution of water yield in some areas with poor evapotranspiration estimation, such as the upper Upatoi Creek watershed in Georgia, USA [43].

The InVEST is gaining interest in the ecosystem services community [44]. This model has reached popularity and has had good results in China in recent years [45–50]. Its sub-model "Annual Water Yield" does not require a high level of expertise or extensive data analysis. It is based on the Budyko curve [51] and estimates annual average runoff at the pixel level, using subbasin-level and basin-level inputs such as precipitation, reference evapotranspiration, land use/cover, soil depth, and available water content for plants. This model can produce accurate results; however, it is important to consider an exhaustive sensitivity and calibration analysis due to the high uncertainty that can be introduced by climatic data, the heterogeneous non-spatiality, subsequently affecting the spatial estimation of water yield [52].

The InVEST–AWY model has some flaws and uncertainties, especially in areas with few weather stations and in-situ data [44,53]. The model's sensitivity to eco-hydrological parameters and the effect of extrapolating a lumped theory to a fully distributed model are some of the uncertainties associated with the model [44]. The effect of climate input errors, especially annual precipitation, and errors in the eco-hydrological parameter Z, are also significant sources of uncertainty [44]. In areas with limited data, the model's accuracy may be limited, and the results may be unreliable [53]. To manage these uncertainties, it is recommended to use multiple models and data sources to validate the results [54]. Incorporating more data sources, such as remote-sensing data, reanalysis, and gridded observations, can improve the accuracy of the model [40,55].

This study aims to assess the effectiveness of the InVEST–AWY model and to estimate the annual average water yield (hereinafter, by "Water yield" we mean "Water discharge") in the Meta River basin (Colombia) from 1983 to 2021 using this model. The study's results provide spatially explicit information on the variability of water yield within the basin. Moreover, it presents a comprehensive assessment of the InVEST–AWY model effectiveness on a large scale in a critical region for future agricultural production in Colombia.

2. Materials and Methods

2.1. Study Area

The Meta River basin was delineated using the ArcSWAT tool version 2012.10.24 for ArcGIS 10.6 (https://swat.tamu.edu/software/arcswat/, accessed on 24 December 2022) with a 30 m resolution Digital Elevation Model (DEM) from the Global Multi-Resolution Topography (GMRT) dataset (https://www.gmrt.org/GMRTMapTool/, accessed on 15 December 2022). The delimitation process resulted in an area of 113,981 km^2. We also evaluated the performance of the InVEST–AWY model in four subbasins where gauging stations were available, in order to identify areas where the model performed best. The Meta River is a major tributary of the Orinoco River, and its basin spans across several departments in Colombia, including Meta, Casanare, Cundinamarca, Boyacá, Arauca, Vichada, and Bogotá (Figure 1).

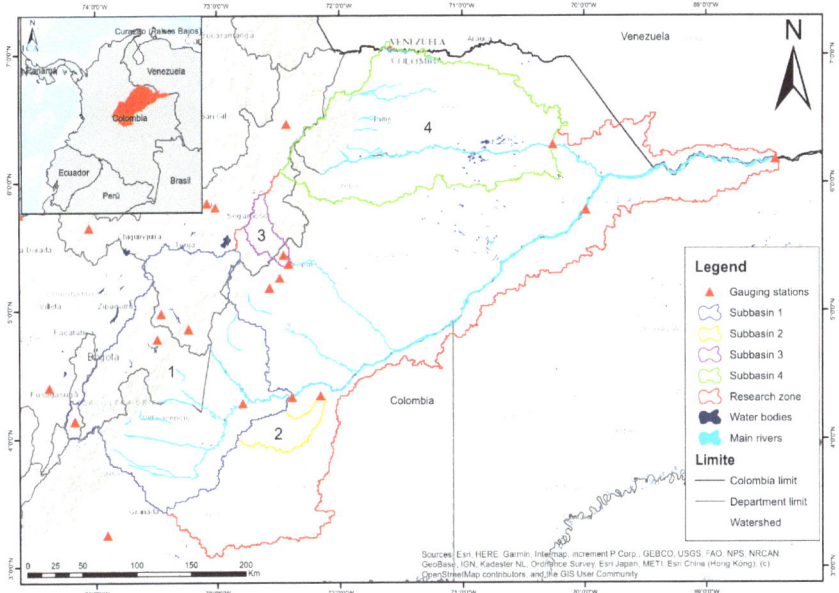

Figure 1. Location of the Meta River basin (Research zone) and its subbasins in Colombia. Subbasin 1: upper Meta River subbasin; Subbasin 2: Yucao River subbasin; Subbasin 3: South Cravo River subbasin; Subbasin 4: upper Casanare River subbasin.

2.2. Materials

2.2.1. Data Requirement

To estimate annual water yield using the InVEST–AWY model, several input variables must be provided, including annual average precipitation, annual average reference evapotranspiration, land use/cover with biophysical table, root restricting layer depth, plant available water content, and watershed and sub-watershed maps.

Once all necessary information has been compiled, it is resampled at a spatial resolution of approximately 1 km and projected onto the World Geodetic System 84 (WGS84) coordinate system to ensure consistency with the LULC (land use/land cover) raster data. Table 1 lists all input variables, including the year, source, tool/equation, and format.

Table 1. Dataset used in the InVEST–AWY modeling.

Data	Period	Source	Tool	Format
Annual average precipitation	1983–2021	Instituto de Hidrología, Meteorología y Estudios Ambientales—IDEAM	RStudio	Raster
Annual average water discharge	1983–2021	Instituto de Hidrología, Meteorología y Estudios Ambientales—IDEAM	-	CSV
Evapotranspiration	1983–2021	Instituto de Hidrología, Meteorología y Estudios Ambientales IDEAM (air temperature)	Hargreaves equation	Raster
Root Restricting Layer Depth	–	[56]	RStudio	Raster
Plant Available Water Content	–	[57]	RStudio	Raster
Land Use/Land Cover	2018	Instituto de Hidrología, Meteorología y Estudios Ambientales—IDEAM	ArcMAP software	Raster
Watersheds DEM	–	GMRTMapTool/ArcSWAT	ArcMAP software	Shapefile
Biophysical Table	–	FAO/IDEAM data	–	CSV
Z Coefficient	–	–	–	Ranges from 1 to 30

2.2.2. Meteorological Data

The meteorological data used in this study, including annual precipitation (Figure 2A), annual average water discharge, and annual mean maximum and minimum air temperature, were obtained from the IDEAM (Instituto de Hidrología, Meteorología y Estudios Ambientales) website [58]. We identified 246 hydrometeorological stations measuring air temperature, precipitation, and water discharge in the upper Meta River subbasin, while only one hydrometeorological station measuring water discharge was found in the Yucao River subbasin, and four hydrometeorological stations measuring precipitation and air temperature were in the South Cravo River subbasin. Finally, we found 20 hydrometeorological stations in the upper Casanare River subbasin. The in-situ gauging station records were available from 1983 onwards. The annual potential evapotranspiration (Figure 2E) was calculated using the Hargreaves equation [59] with air temperature data from in-situ stations and extraterrestrial solar radiation data calculated from [60] using the package environment in R [61]. The resulting data were then spatially interpolated into a resolution of 1 km × 1 km. The following Equation (1) was used to calculate potential evapotranspiration—PET (Eto).

$$Eto = 0.0023 \times Ra \left[\frac{Tmax - Tmin}{2} + 17.8 \right] + (Tmax - Tmin)^{1/2} \qquad (1)$$

where $Tmax$ and $Tmin$ are maximum and minimum air temperatures (°C); Ra is the terrestrial radiation (MJ m^{-2} d^{-1}). The PET, calculated in the upper Meta River, Yucao River, South Cravo River, and upper Casanare River subbasins, ranges from a minimum of

789.5 mm/year in the upper Casanare River subbasin to a maximum of 1834.6 mm/year in the upper Meta River subbasin, with a mean value of 1540.7 mm/year in the latter.

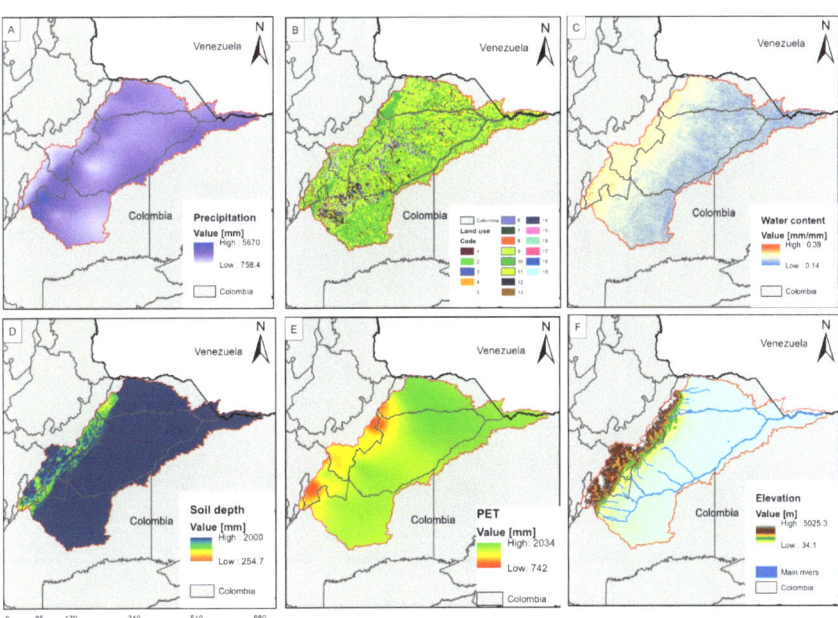

Figure 2. Geospatial data for the InVEST–AWY model: (**A**) Annual precipitation; (**B**) Different LULC types: 1—urban area, 2–8—crops, 9—pastures, 10—forests, 11–13—shrubby area, 14—sands, 15—rocks, 16—bare grounds, 17—snow cover, 18—aquatic vegetation, and 19—water bodies; (**C**) Water content in the soil; (**D**) Soil depth; (**E**) Potential evapotranspiration (PET); (**F**) Digital elevation model (DEM).

2.2.3. Soil Data

The root restricting layer (RRL), as shown in Figure 2D, is the depth of soil where plant roots cannot grow effectively. For this study, a global raster for plant root restricting layer depth was used from [56]. It was found that the upper Meta River, Yucao River, South Cravo River, and upper Casanare River subbasins have different root restricting layer values, ranging from a minimum of 254.7 mm in the upper Meta River subbasin to a maximum of 2000 mm in the Yucao River subbasin, with a mean value of 1815.1 mm in all zones. RRL values can be influenced by factors such as soil compaction, depth to bedrock, and soil structure [62].

Plant available water content (PAWC) is defined as the difference between the fraction of volumetric field capacity and permanent wilting point. In this study, we utilized the global PAWC raster grid from [57]. This dataset provides AWC for seven soil depth intervals (0 to 200 cm depth) and was merged into a single file using the equation recommended by [57]. PAWC values shown in Figure 2C, range from a minimum of 0.1 mm/mm of soil in the upper Casanare River subbasin to a maximum of 0.4 mm/mm of soil in the upper Meta River subbasin, with a mean value of 0.2 mm/mm of soil in all zones.

2.2.4. Land Use/Land Cover Data and *Kc*

In this study, we used a map elaborated by IDEAM, which employs land use/cover data from the period 2014–2018 [63]. We processed this map into a raster file that combines the 36 land-use/land-cover (LULC) classes into 19 land-use types (Figure 2B, Table 2). We also generated a biophysical table in comma-separated values (CSV) format that contains information related to the LULC map. This table consists of five columns: land-use (LU) code, LULC description, Kc, root depth, and LULC vegetation.

Table 2. Crop coefficient (Kc) and land use/land cover (LULC) used in the biophysical table.

LU Code	LULC Description	Kc
1	Urban area	0.1
2	Short duration crops	1.1
3	Cereals	1.2
4	Oilseeds and legumes	1.2
5	Vegetables	0.9
6	Tubers	0.9
7	Permanent crops	1.1
8	Agroforestry crops	1.2
9	Pasture	1.0
10	Forest	1.0
11	Grassland	0.9
12	Shrubland	1.1
13	Secondary vegetation	1.1
14	Sand	0.3
15	Rocks	0.3
16	Bare soils/grounds	0.3
17	Snow cover	0.2
18	Aquatic vegetation	1.0
19	Water surface	1.0

Kc (crop coefficient) values for agricultural land is a dimensionless value used in agriculture to estimate the water needs of crops at different stages of their growth. The FAO (Food and Agriculture Organization of the United Nations) has developed a widely used set of Kc values for various crops, which are based on research carried out in different climatic regions worldwide. The Kc values range from 0 to 1, where 0 represents no water loss, and 1 represents the maximum water loss; these values were extracted from [64]. Land uses different from crops were found in [65] and adapted to our research.

2.2.5. Water Discharge Data

The present study focuses on five hydrometeorological stations (Table 3). The Aceitico gauging station, which is situated in the downstream area of the study basin, represents the final point of the water outflow from the study area. According to the gauge data reported by IDEAM, the maximum annual average water discharge was reported in 2021 with a value of 9288.5 m^3/s. On the other hand, the minimum water discharge was reported in 1992 with a value of 3647.6 m^3/s. The long-term (for 1983–2021) annual average water discharge was calculated as 5256.8 m^3/s. Details of the meteorological stations used in this study are listed in Table 3. To facilitate statistics and to compare water discharges by stations and by the InVEST–AWY model, it was necessary to divide the annual water yield volume (m^3) generated by the InVEST–AWY model by the number of seconds in a standard year (3.156×10^7 s).

Table 3. The gauging stations used in the study (AAWD–annual average water discharge).

Code	Station (River)	Basin Area (km^2)	Automatic	Period	AAWD (m^3/s)
35117010	Humapo (upper Meta River)	26,343	No	1980–2021	1576.3
35127020	Campamento Yucao (Yucao River)	1797	No	1980–2021	88.3
35217010	Puente Yopal (South Cravo River)	1187	Yes	1980–2021	97.2
36027050	Cravo Norte (upper Casanare River)	22,872	No	1994–2021	494.2
35257040	Aceitico (Meta River)	113,981	No	1983–2021	5256.8

2.2.6. Zhang Coefficient

The Zhang coefficient (Z) is a parameter that ranges from 1 to 30 and captures the precipitation pattern and hydrogeological characteristics of the basin. This parameter is not enough to be used as a sensitivity and calibration factor [52]. Ref. [66] carried out a study in Australia and found that Z could be estimated as 0.2 N, where N is the number of rainfall events per year. In this study, we calculated the annual average number of rainfall events ($N > 1$ mm) for the study basin and divided it by 5 to estimate Z. This basin had an annual average of 177 rainy days during the period 1980–2021, and the Z value was assumed to be 30.

2.2.7. The InVEST–AWY Model

The InVEST–AWY model estimates the relative contributions of water from different parts of a landscape, offering insight into how changes in land use/cover patterns affect annual surface water yield and hydropower production [35]. The water yield module in the InVEST–AWY model is built on the annual average precipitation and the Budyko curve [51]. The annual water yield (AWY) for each pixel follows the Equation (2):

$$\text{AWY}(x) = \left(1 - \frac{AET(x)}{P(X)}\right) \times P(x), \quad (2)$$

where $AET(x)$ is annual evapotranspiration for each pixel x, and P is annual precipitation for each pixel x. For land with vegetation or land use/cover types (LULC), the evapotranspiration fraction of the water balance is $\frac{AET(x)}{P(x)}$; it is based on the Budyko curve Expression (3) proposed by [67,68]:

$$\frac{AET(x)}{P(x)} = 1 + \frac{PET(x)}{P(x)} - \left[1 + \left(\frac{AET(x)}{P(x)}\right)^w\right]^{\frac{1}{w}}, \quad (3)$$

where $PET(x)$ is the potential evapotranspiration, which is defined as:

$$PET(x) = Kc(x) \times ET_0(x) \quad (4)$$

where $Kc(x)$ is the yield coefficient per pixel x and ET_0 is the potential evapotranspiration per pixel x. $W(x)$ is a non-physical parameter that characterizes the natural climatic properties of the soil (Equation (5)):

$$W(x) = Z \times \left(\frac{AWC(x)}{P(x)}\right) + 1.25 \quad (5)$$

$AWC(x)$ is the water available to the plant, and Z is the Zhang coefficient, which depends on annual precipitation.

For other land use/cover (LULC) types, such as open water surface, urban areas, and wetlands, actual evaporation (AET) is calculated directly from the reference evaporation $ET_0(x)$ and has an upper limit determined by precipitation (Equation (6)):

$$AET(x) = Min(Kc(lx) \times ET_0(x) \times P(x)), \quad (6)$$

where $ET_0(x)$ is the reference evapotranspiration; $Kc(lx)$ is the evaporation factor for each LULC type. The model generates total and average water yields at the subbasin level.

2.3. Methods

2.3.1. Methodology

The methodology flowchart adapted from [69] and used in this study is illustrated in Figure 3. The first step of this study involved the preparation of various datasets, including precipitation, reference evapotranspiration, plant available water content, root restricting layer, land use/land cover (LULC) with biophysical table, and watershed delimitation maps. These datasets were essential for accurately modeling water yield in the Meta River basin using the InVEST–AWY model.

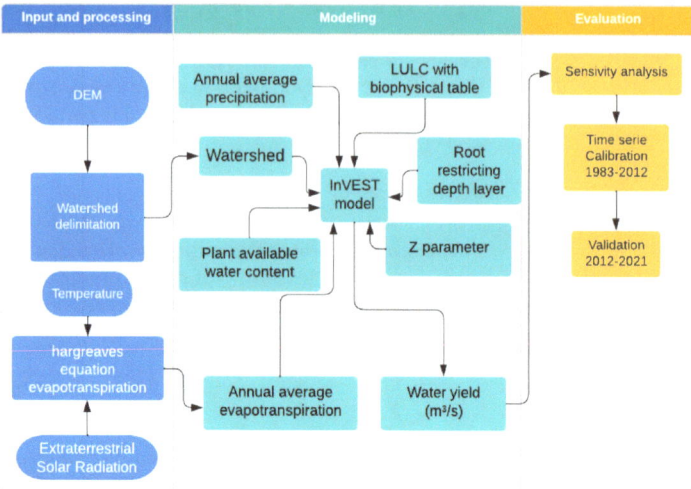

Figure 3. Methodology flowchart for calculation of water yield in the Meta River basin using the InVEST–AWY model.

2.3.2. Sensitivity Analysis

In the sensitivity analysis, a study carried out by [52] demonstrated that the InVEST–AWY model has low sensitivity with respect to the Zhang coefficient. Nonetheless, this study made in different zones in the UK highlighted the importance of selecting appropriate model parameters and input data, especially precipitation, which had a significant impact on water yield. A 10% increase in precipitation resulted in an 11–27% increase in water yield, while in some catchments, a 10% increase in PET resulted in a 14% decrease in water yield. Rooting depth and AWC had little effect on yield, with a 10% increase in either resulting in a yield decrease of 0–3%. K_c sensitivity was found to be like PET sensitivity. In another study by [19], the model was calibrated for five hydrographic subbasins in Ecuador with Z values ≥ 3 and errors of less than 7%. However, the model could not satisfactorily calibrate the remaining four sub-basins, as water production was underestimated by 20% to 50%. In this study, we carried out a sensitivity analysis for the K_C and Zhang coefficients using the 2018 dataset.

Model Sensitivity to Z

To evaluate the sensitivity of the Zhang coefficient, we used a baseline value of $Z = 30$, which is defined as the number of rainfall days in a year divided by 5. As stated earlier, the average number of rainfall days for the study zone is 177. As the Z value ranges from 1 to 30, we decreased this value to 1 to evaluate the change in water yield. Our findings indicate that when $Z = 15$, the water yield increased by 9%, but when $Z = 1$, the water yield increased by 101% (Figure 4).

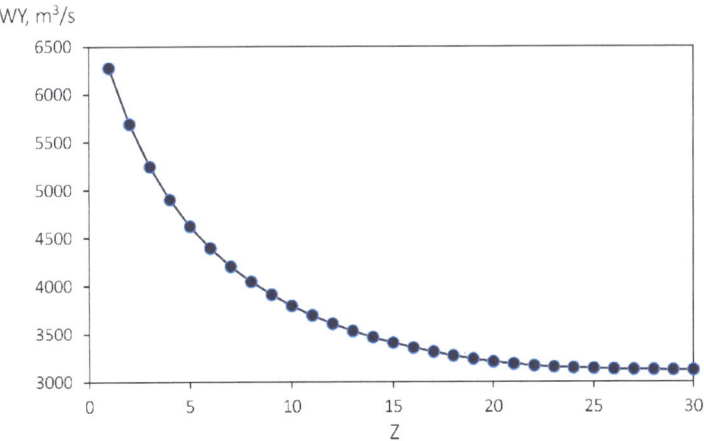

Figure 4. Water yield (WY) variation using different Zhang coefficient (Z).

Model Sensitivity to Kc

To evaluate the sensitivity of water yield to Kc, we varied this value only for the crop covers in the study zone. The FAO has proposed Kc values for crops found in the Meta River basin that vary between 0.4 and 1.2. We used the baseline Kc values shown in Table 2 and subsequently multiplied them by 0.7, 0.8, 1.2, and 1.3 to evaluate the changes in water yield resulting from the variation in Kc values (Table 4).

Table 4. Annual average water yield (AAWY) variation in 2018 using different variation of the Kc coefficient.

Variable	Kc Variation, %				
	−30	−20	0	20	30
AAWY, m³/s	6946.77	6761.73	6273.40	6194.28	6150.58
Change in AWY, %	−10.7	−7.8	0.0	1.3	2.0

The results of the sensitivity analysis showed that a 30% reduction in Kc values in crops would result in a 10.7% decrease in water yield, while increasing Kc values by 30% would only increase water yield by 2%. These findings demonstrate that the Kc value is not a key sensitivity factor for the InVEST–AWY model, unlike Z.

2.3.3. Calibration and Validation

Water yield, the net amount of water produced by a catchment, is a critical factor for sustainable water resource management. It can be estimated by calculating the difference between precipitation and actual evapotranspiration for each LULC type within the catchment [45]. To achieve accurate estimates of water yield, calibration and validation of the model using observed data are essential. A sensitivity analysis is also necessary to determine the variation in the model parameters. Once the optimal parameters have been identified, they can be used for final calibration and validation.

The InVEST–AWY model was calibrated using annual data from 1983 to 2012, which were available at the Aceitico gauging station. The validation period covered the years from 2013 to 2021 (Figure 5). The performance of the model was evaluated by minimizing the average bias and optimizing the coefficient of determination (R^2), and Root Mean Square Error (RMSE).

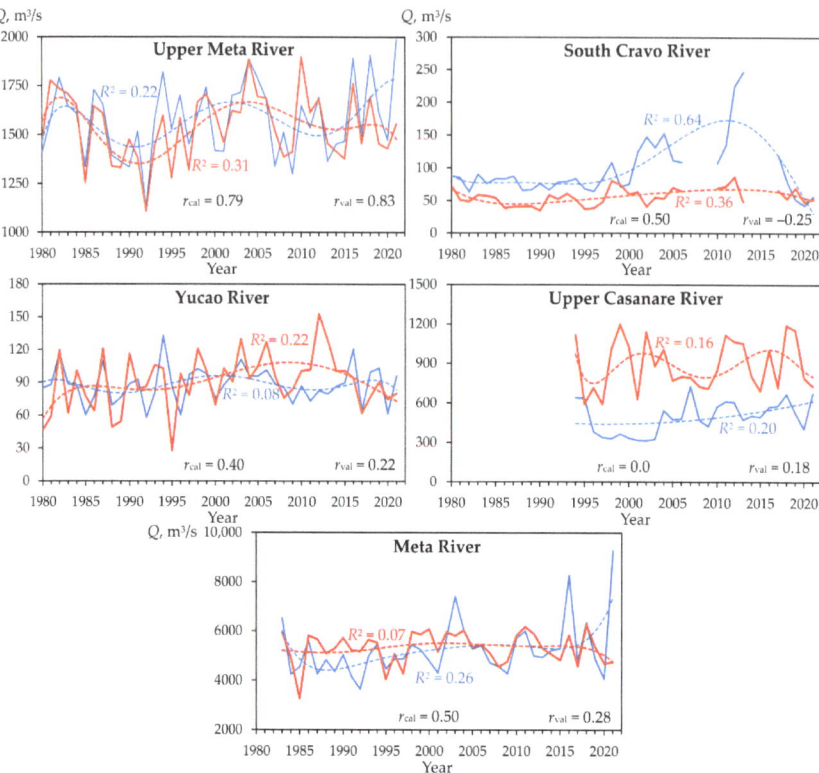

Figure 5. Changes in the observed (solid blue line) and modeled (solid red line) water discharge (Q) of the studied rivers of the Meta River basin for 1980–2021. The dotted line is the sixth-degree polynomial trend of the corresponding (observed or modeled) water discharge. R^2 is the coefficient of approximation of the trend line; r_{cal} and r_{val} are the correlation coefficients for the period of calibration (1983–2012) and validation (2013–2021), respectively.

The calibration process involved the use of the InVEST–AWY model in Python. We employed the Automatic Hyperparameter Optimization (AHO) algorithm to identify the best-calibrated model series generated by the InVEST–AWY model using machine learning [70]. We modeled 100 runs for each year from 1983 to 2012, varying the Kc and Z parameters. Based on the interactions, it was found that the InVEST–AWY model performed best when $Z = 1$ and $Kc = 1.10$.

However, despite finding the best combination of parameters for the Meta River basin, only the upper Meta River subbasin displayed high correlation coefficients during both calibration (0.79) and validation (0.83) phases, indicating that the model captured the observed data well for this zone. Conversely, the Yucao and South Cravo rivers had lower correlation coefficients, 0.4 and −0.25, respectively, indicating that the model may not be well-suited for these zones, particularly during the validation phase. The upper Casanare River showed no correlation during calibration, but an improvement was noted during validation (0.18), which implies that the model may need further refinement for this zone. The Meta River exhibited moderate correlation coefficients during both calibration (0.5) and validation (0.28), suggesting that the model performed reasonably well, but improvements may be needed. Details for each subbasin are listed in Table 5.

Table 5. Metrics for the model performance in the studied subbasin during calibration and validation periods using the InVEST–AWY model.

Basin/Subbasin	NSE	RMSE	r_{cal}	r_{val}	DIF STD
Meta River basin	0.07	1071.61	0.5	0.28	1083.62
Upper Meta River subbasin	0.49	135.37	0.79	0.83	132.81
Yucao River subbasin	0.03	57.49	0.4	0.22	40.61
South Cravo River subbasin	−1.29	24.75	0.5	−0.25	24.92
Upper Casanare River subbasin	−0.49	452.32	0	0.18	261.12

The accurate estimation of water yield is essential for understanding the water balance of a catchment, but the calibration and validation phases may be affected by various factors such as bypassing of gauging stations, catchment transfers, and subsurface runoff [52] found that catchments where a significant proportion of the total water yield leaves via subsurface runoff or other routes were characterized by a significant overestimation of the total yield as gauged from water discharge. In addition, ref. [71] discovered that catchments with a high cover of land-use and land-cover (LULC) classes with a high value of Kc are sensitive to precipitation data, potentially leading to a 150% change in modeled water yield in response to a 30% error.

3. Results, Discussion, and Limitations
3.1. Water Yield Formation

Based on the InVEST–AWY model, we estimated the annual water yield for the Meta River basin from 1983 to 2021. For example, our analysis indicated that the total water yield for the basin in 2018 was 1.98×10^{11} m^3/year (6273.4 m^3/s or 1748.6 mm/year (Figure 6)), which is 1.3% lower than the value reported by IDEAM. The mean precipitation was found to be 2517.3 mm/year; the mean actual evapotranspiration (AET) was 768.7 mm/year.

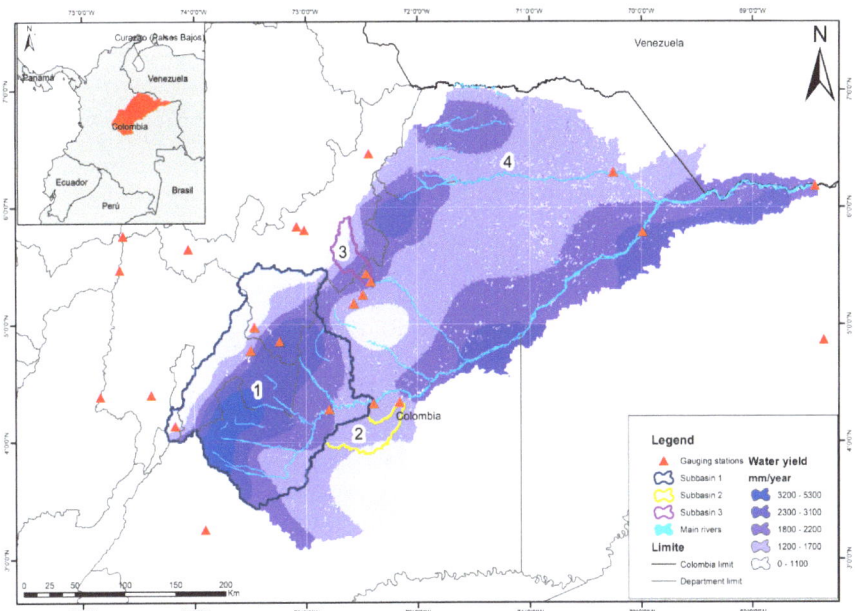

Figure 6. Annual water yield formation in the subbasins of the Meta River basin for 2018. (1) upper Meta River subbasin; (2) Yucao River subbasin; (3) South Cravo River subbasin; (4) upper Casanare River subbasin.

In the upper Meta River subbasin, where the model performed better, we obtained a coefficient of determination (R^2) of 0.55 and Nash–Sutcliffe Efficiency coefficient (NSE) of 0.49 from 1983 to 2021, using the same parameters as the Meta River basin. The results in the upper Meta River subbasin were found to be directly related to the high density of hydrometeorological stations in the area, as the model is highly sensitive to precipitation and evapotranspiration [44,48].

The spatial patterns analysis revealed that the annual water yield exhibited higher values in the northwest of the basin, particularly in the first delimited subbasin, with variations ranging from 1100 to 5300 mm/year. On the other hand, other annual water yield values showed a significant pattern in the southeast of the basin, which represents the lowest part of the study area and where the rivers merge to form the Meta River.

To assess the effectiveness of the model, statistics were computed for five studied zones where the InVEST–AWY model tool was applied. The full climatological dataset from 1983 to 2021 was utilized to evaluate various performance metrics, including Nash–Sutcliffe Efficiency (NSE) coefficient, Root Mean Square Error (RMSE), R-squared (R^2), and standard deviation of the differences (DIF STD) between observed and modeled data. The results of the evaluation are presented in Table 5, which provides a detailed breakdown of the model's performance in each studied zone.

The results of hydrological modeling showed that the Meta River basin had poor performance, with an NSE value of 0.07 and a high RMSE value of 1071.61. The correlation coefficients during calibration (r_{cal}) and validation (r_{val}) were low (0.50 and 0.28, respectively), indicating that the model had low accuracy in predicting the observed annual water discharge. The complexity of the basin's climate and topography, as well as a deficient hydrometeorological monitoring system, could be contributing factors to these results.

The upper Meta River subbasin had the best performance among all subbasins, with an NSE value of 0.49 and a low RMSE value of 135.37. The correlation coefficient values for calibration and validation periods were high (0.79 and 0.83, respectively), indicating that the model had high accuracy in predicting the observed annual water discharge. This could be since the upper Meta River subbasin is the area with the greatest presence of hydrometeorological stations that allows accurate monitoring.

The Yucao River subbasin had moderate performance, with an NSE value of 0.03 and a moderate RMSE value of 57.49. The correlation coefficient during calibration was high (0.40), suggesting that the model had a good ability to capture the variability of the observed annual water discharge. However, the coefficient of determination during validation was low (0.22), indicating that the model had low accuracy in predicting the observed annual water discharge.

The South Cravo River subbasin had the worst performance among all subbasins, with an NSE value of −1.29 and a low RMSE value of 24.75. The correlation coefficients for calibration and validation (r_{cal} and r_{val}) periods were also low (0.50 and −0.25, respectively), indicating that the model had low accuracy in predicting the observed annual water discharge.

The upper Casanare River subbasin had very poor performance, with a negative NSE value of −0.49 and a high RMSE value of 452.32. The correlation coefficients were low for calibration and validation periods (0 and 0.18, respectively), suggesting that the model had low accuracy in predicting the observed annual water discharge. The upper Casanare River subbasin has a heterogeneous land use pattern and complex surface and underground hydraulic dynamics, which could have made it challenging to model the hydrological processes accurately.

3.2. Limitations

3.2.1. Model Limitations

The model relies on yearly averages and disregards temporal (including seasonal) variations in water supply and hydropower production, leading to inadequate estimations of water availability and energy production during extreme events such as droughts or floods. In addition, the model oversimplifies the concept of consumptive demand, which can impact its precision in estimating water availability for various purposes. Consequently, this constraint can have substantial implications in evaluating the effects of LULC changes on water resources [35].

The InVEST–AWY model simplifies the hydrological process by lacking differentiation between surface and subsurface water runoff. Consequently, this oversimplification introduces several uncertainties in the model simulation [50].

The model exhibits low sensitivity to modifications in the Z coefficient, but it is highly sensitive to precipitation. Therefore, it is imperative to evaluate the precision of yearly data [48].

3.2.2. Uncertainties from In-Situ Data

The lack of hydrogeological studies in the Meta River basin poses a limitation in identifying the hydrogeological dynamics that may influence the percentage of groundwater contribution to the primary rivers measured by IDEAM stations. Nonetheless, a study carried out by [9] revealed the existence of groundwater wells with hydraulic transmissivity ranging between 4 to 279 m^2/day in the northeastern region of the study basin, which could mean a varied water dynamics in aquifers.

The study is subject to uncertainties of the model due to the insufficiency of information from the selected stations. One of the five stations used for the study is automated. Moreover, data gaps were observed for several stations within the study area, including the Aceitico gauging station, which lacks annual data from 1980 to 1982 and reported atypical values in 2003, 2016, and 2021. Similarly, for the Cravo Norte gauging station, there was a gap in information from 1980 to 1993; in Puente Yopal, there were also gaps in annual water discharge data for 2007–2009 and 2014–2016. These gaps in information and atypical values could affect the accuracy of the model's calibration and validation, thus limiting its ability to provide precise estimations of water runoff in the study area.

3.2.3. Human Effect on Water Discharge

According to [72], the change in water runoff in the Meta River basin cannot be solely attributed to macroclimatic phenomena or human activities on the local scale. Meanwhile, [18] reported that groundwater extraction provides about 5% of the total demand from various sectors in the region, but the actual value could be higher due to unreported or illegal extractions.

4. Conclusions

While the InVEST–AWY model did not show satisfied results for the Meta River basin as a whole, our study demonstrated that the model could be a valuable tool for identifying subbasins where it could work adequately. This allows for the establishment of selection criteria for areas of interest.

In our study, we identified the upper Meta River subbasin delimited for the Humapo gauging station as having the most climate monitoring stations in the study area. However, due to a lack of hydrogeological studies in the area, it is difficult to establish the proven uncertainty of groundwater contribution to surface runoff measured by IDEAM stations.

Atypical events, such as those reported during 2003, 2016, and 2021, have been observed at the stations that are not related to El Niño and La Niña fluctuations. These reports should be analyzed on a daily scale and related to multiple climatic and anthropogenic variables to better understand their causes.

In future studies, it is important to consider using the InVEST "Annual Water Yield" model in areas with a high density of weather stations. Alternatively, global data such as CHIRPS can be used, with necessary corrections for overestimation or underestimation of precipitation. It is also crucial to validate the calculated evapotranspiration with in-situ data reported by the authorities.

Author Contributions: Conceptualization, J.B.V. and V.V.G.; methodology, J.B.V., V.V.G. and J.M.-D.; analysis, J.B.V. and J.M.-D.; data curation, J.B.V. and J.M.-D.; writing—original draft preparation, J.B.V.; writing—review and editing, J.B.V., A.V.G. and J.T.; visualization, J.B.V., A.V.G. and J.M.-D.; supervision, J.B.V. and J.T. All authors have read and agreed to the published version of the manuscript.

Funding: The work was carried out in accordance with the Strategic Academic Leadership Program "Priority 2030" of the Kazan Federal University of the Government of the Russian Federation.

Data Availability Statement: Data used for this research can be obtained upon request from the authors.

Acknowledgments: We would like to thank Nilton Díaz from the Alliance Bioversity International—CIAT for technical advice on the evaluation of the InVEST–AWY model for annual water discharges in the subbasins of the Meta River basin. We would also like to thank IDEAM for providing timely climate data for the study area.

Conflicts of Interest: The authors declare no conflict of interest.

References

1. Belhassan, K. Water Scarcity Management. In *Water Safety, Security and Sustainability: Threat Detection and Mitigation*; Vaseashta, A., Maftei, C., Eds.; Advanced Sciences and Technologies for Security Applications; Springer International Publishing: Cham, Switzerland, 2021; pp. 443–462. ISBN 978-3-030-76008-3.
2. Boretti, A.; Rosa, L. Reassessing the Projections of the World Water Development Report. *Npj Clean Water* **2019**, *2*, 15. [CrossRef]
3. Cosgrove, W.; Loucks, P. Water Management: Current and Future Challenges and Research Directions. *Water Resour. Res.* **2015**, *51*, 4823–4839. [CrossRef]
4. Milly, P.C.D.; Dunne, K.A.; Vecchia, A.V. Global Pattern of Trends in Streamflow and Water Availability in a Changing Climate. *Nature* **2005**, *438*, 347–350. [CrossRef] [PubMed]
5. Célleri, R.; Feyen, J. The Hydrology of Tropical Andean Ecosystems: Importance, Knowledge Status, and Perspectives. *Mt. Res. Dev.* **2009**, *29*, 350–355. [CrossRef]
6. Acuña, G.J.; Ávila, H.; Canales, F.A. River Model Calibration Based on Design of Experiments Theory. A Case Study: Meta River, Colombia. *Water* **2019**, *11*, 1382. [CrossRef]
7. Ávila, H.; Acuña, G.; Daza, R.; Diaz, K.S. Evaluating the Natural Development of the Meta River for Proposing Hydraulic Works Oriented to River Training for Fluvial Navigation. In Proceedings of the World Environmental and Water Resources Congress 2014, Portland, OR, USA, 1–5 June 2014; pp. 1564–1579. [CrossRef]
8. DNP: BASES DEL PLAN NACIONAL DE DESARROLLO 2018–2022. 2018. Available online: https://colaboracion.dnp.gov.co/CDT/Prensa/BasesPND2018-2022n.pdf (accessed on 18 February 2023).
9. Benavides Guerrero, C.E.; Caro Caro, L.E.; Mariño Martínez, J.E. Determination of the Hydraulic Behavior of Aquifers in Northern Orinoquia, Colombia. *Cienc. E Ing. Neogranadina* **2021**, *31*, 109–126. [CrossRef]
10. Garcia, N. Evaluation of Rainfall Runoff Modelling Using BROOK90 in R in a Case Study of a Catchment Area in Colombia. Master's Thesis, Dresden University of Technology, Dresden, Germany, 2019.
11. Hoyos, N.; Correa-Metrio, A.; Jepsen, S.M.; Wemple, B.; Valencia, S.; Marsik, M.; Doria, R.; Escobar, J.; Restrepo, J.C.; Velez, M.I. Modeling Streamflow Response to Persistent Drought in a Coastal Tropical Mountainous Watershed, Sierra Nevada De Santa Marta, Colombia. *Water* **2019**, *11*, 94. [CrossRef]
12. Moncada, A.M.; Escobar, M.; Betancourth, A.; Vélez Upegui, J.J.; Zambrano, J.; Alzate, L.M. Modelling Water Stress Vulnerability in Small Andean Basins: Case Study of Campoalegre River Basin, Colombia. *Int. J. Water Resour. Dev.* **2021**, *37*, 640–657. [CrossRef]
13. Person, M.; Butler, D.; Gable, C.; Villamil, T.; Wavrek, D.; Schelling, D. Hydrodynamic Stagnation Zones: A New Play Concept for the Llanos Basin, Colombia. *AAPG Bull.* **2012**, *96*, 23–41. [CrossRef]
14. Ramirez Morales, W.D.; Rodriguez, E.A.; Sanchez Lozano, J.L.; Oliveros-Acosta, J.J.; Ardila, F.; Cardona-Almeida, C.; Garay, C.; Bouaziz, L. Hydrologic Modeling of Principal Sub-Basins of the Magdalena-Cauca Large Basin Using Wflow Model. In Proceedings of the 36th International Association for Hydro-Environment Engineering and Research World Congress, The Hague, The Netherlands, 2 July 2015.
15. Restrepo, J.D.; Kjerfve, B.; Hermelin, M.; Restrepo, J.C. Factors Controlling Sediment Yield in a Major South American Drainage Basin: The Magdalena River, Colombia. *J. Hydrol.* **2006**, *316*, 213–232. [CrossRef]
16. Rodríguez, E.; Sánchez, I.; Duque, N.; Arboleda, P.; Vega, C.; Zamora, D.; López, P.; Kaune, A.; Werner, M.; García, C.; et al. Combined Use of Local and Global Hydro Meteorological Data with Hydrological Models for Water Resources Management in the Magdalena—Cauca Macro Basin—Colombia. *Water Resour. Manag.* **2020**, *34*, 2179–2199. [CrossRef]
17. Villamizar, S.R.; Pineda, S.M.; Carrillo, G.A. The Effects of Land Use and Climate Change on the Water Yield of a Watershed in Colombia. *Water* **2019**, *11*, 285. [CrossRef]
18. Pimentel, J.N.; Rogéliz Prada, C.A.; Walschburger, T. Hydrological Modeling for Multifunctional Landscape Planning in the Orinoquia Region of Colombia. *Front. Environ. Sci.* **2021**, *9*, 673215. [CrossRef]
19. Minga-León, S.; Gómez-Albores, M.A.; Bâ, K.M.; Balcázar, L.; Manzano-Solís, L.R.; Cuervo-Robayo, A.P.; Mastachi-Loza, C.A. Estimation of Water Yield in the Hydrographic Basins of Southern Ecuador. *Hydrol. Earth Syst. Sci. Discuss.* **2018**, 1–18. [CrossRef]

20. Kumari, N.; Srivastava, A.; Sahoo, B.; Raghuwanshi, N.S.; Bretreger, D. Identification of Suitable Hydrological Models for Streamflow Assessment in the Kangsabati River Basin, India, by Using Different Model Selection Scores. *Nat. Resour. Res.* **2021**, *30*, 4187–4205. [CrossRef]
21. Shekar, P.R. Rainfall-Runoff Modelling of a River Basin Using HEC HMS: A Review Study. *Int. J. Res. Appl. Sci. Eng. Technol.* **2021**, *9*, 506–508. [CrossRef]
22. Gashaw, T.; Worqlul, A.W.; Dile, Y.T.; Sahle, M.; Adem, A.A.; Bantider, A.; Teixeira, Z.; Alamirew, T.; Meshesha, D.T.; Bayable, G. Evaluating InVEST Model for Simulating Annual and Seasonal Water Yield in Data-Scarce Regions of the Abbay (Upper Blue Nile) Basin: Implications for Water Resource Planners and Managers. *Sustain. Water Resour. Manag.* **2022**, *8*, 170. [CrossRef]
23. Zaccaria, D.; Neale, C.M.U.; Lamaddalena, N. A Methodology for Conducting Diagnostic Analyses and Operational Simulation in Large-Scale Pressurized Irrigation Systems. *SPIE Proc.* **2006**, *63*, 5910. [CrossRef]
24. Chen, Y.; Li, J.; Huang, S.; Dong, Y. Study of Beijiang Catchment Flash-Flood Forecasting Model. *Proc. Int. Assoc. Hydrol. Sci.* **2015**, *368*, 150–155. [CrossRef]
25. Belay, Y.Y.; Gouday, Y.A.; Alemnew, H.N. Comparison of HEC-HMS Hydrologic Model for Estimation of Runoff Computation Techniques as a Design Input: Case of Middle Awash Multi-Purpose Dam, Ethiopia. *Appl. Water Sci.* **2022**, *12*, 237. [CrossRef]
26. Yen, H.; Jeong, J.; Feng, Q.; Deb, D. Assessment of Input Uncertainty in SWAT Using Latent Variables. *Water Resour. Manag.* **2015**, *29*, 1137–1153. [CrossRef]
27. Brulebois, E.; Ubertosi, M.; Castel, T.; Richard, Y.; Sauvage, S.; Sánchez Pérez, J.; Moine, N.; Suchet, P. Robustness and Performance of Semi-Distributed (SWAT) and Global (GR4J) Hydrological Models throughout an Observed Climatic Shift over Contrasted French Watersheds. *Open Water J.* **2018**, *5*, 4.
28. Haris, A.A.; Khan, M.A.; Chhabra, V.; Biswas, S.; Pratap, A. Evaluation of LARS-WG for Generating Long Term Data for Assessment of Climate Change Impact in Bihar. *J. Agrometeorol.* **2010**, *12*, 198–201. [CrossRef]
29. Fu, B.; Merritt, W.S.; Croke, B.F.W.; Weber, T.R.; Jakeman, A.J. A Review of Catchment-Scale Water Quality and Erosion Models and a Synthesis of Future Prospects. *Environ. Model. Softw.* **2019**, *114*, 75–97. [CrossRef]
30. Pandi, D.; Kothandaraman, S.; Kuppusamy, M. Hydrological Models: A Review. *Int. J. Hydrol. Sci. Technol.* **2021**, *12*, 223–242. [CrossRef]
31. Decsi, B.; Ács, T.; Jolánkai, Z.; Kardos, M.K.; Koncsos, L.; Vári, Á.; Kozma, Z. From Simple to Complex—Comparing Four Modelling Tools for Quantifying Hydrologic Ecosystem Services. *Ecol. Indic.* **2022**, *141*, 109143. [CrossRef]
32. Scordo, F.; Lavender, T.M.; Seitz, C.; Perillo, V.L.; Rusak, J.A.; Piccolo, M.C.; Perillo, G.M.E. Modeling Water Yield: Assessing the Role of Site and Region-Specific Attributes in Determining Model Performance of the InVEST Seasonal Water Yield Model. *Water* **2018**, *10*, 1496. [CrossRef]
33. Posner, S.; Verutes, G.; Koh, I.; Denu, D.; Ricketts, T. Global Use of Ecosystem Service Models. *Ecosyst. Serv.* **2016**, *17*, 131–141. [CrossRef]
34. Shrestha, D.L. *Uncertainty Analysis in Rainfall-Runoff Modelling—Application of Machine Learning Techniques: UNESCO-IHE PhD Thesis*; Taylor & Francis: Abingdon, UK, 2009.
35. Natural Capital Project Seasonal Water Yield—InVEST 3.6.0 Documentation. Available online: http://data.naturalcapitalproject.org/nightly-build/invest-users-guide/html/seasonal_water_yield.html (accessed on 4 May 2020).
36. Wei, Y.-M.; Kang, J.-N.; Liu, L.-C.; Li, Q.; Wang, P.-T.; Hou, J.-J.; Liang, Q.-M.; Liao, H.; Huang, S.-F.; Yu, B. A Proposed Global Layout of Carbon Capture and Storage in Line with a 2 °C Climate Target. *Nat. Clim. Chang.* **2021**, *11*, 112–118. [CrossRef]
37. Florian-Vergara, C.; Salas, H.D.; Builes-Jaramillo, A. Analysis of Precipitation and Evaporation in the Colombian Orinoco According to the Regional Climate Models of the CORDEX-CORE Experiment. *TecnoLógicas* **2021**, *24*, 242–261. [CrossRef]
38. Vásquez, E. The Orinoco River: A Review of Hydrobiological Research. *Regul. Rivers Res. Manag.* **1989**, *3*, 381–392. [CrossRef]
39. Gimeno, L.; Gallego, D.; Trigo, R.M.; Ribera, P. Dynamic Identification of Moisture Sources in the Orinoco Basin in Equatorial South America. *Hydrol. Sci. J.* **2008**, *53*, 602–617. [CrossRef]
40. Essou, G.R.C.; Brissette, F.; Lucas-Picher, P. The Use of Reanalyses and Gridded Observations as Weather Input Data for a Hydrological Model: Comparison of Performances of Simulated River Flows Based on the Density of Weather Stations. *J. Hydrometeorol.* **2017**, *18*, 497–513. [CrossRef]
41. Rajib, A.; Merwade, V.; Yu, Z. Rationale and Efficacy of Assimilating Remotely Sensed Potential Evapotranspiration for Reduced Uncertainty of Hydrologic Models. *Water Resour. Res.* **2018**, *54*, 4615–4637. [CrossRef]
42. Krishnan, R. Bayesian Parameter Uncertainty Modeling in a Macroscale Hydrologic Model and Its Impact on Indian River Basin Hydrology under Climate Change. *Water Resour. Res.* **2012**, *48*, 8522. [CrossRef]
43. Trudel, M.; Doucet-Généreux, P.-L.; Leconte, R. Assessing River Low-Flow Uncertainties Related to Hydrological Model Calibration and Structure under Climate Change Conditions. *Climate* **2017**, *5*, 19. [CrossRef]
44. Hamel, P.; Guswa, A.J. Uncertainty Analysis of a Spatially Explicit Annual Water-Balance Model: Case Study of the Cape Fear Basin, North Carolina. *Hydrol. Earth Syst. Sci.* **2015**, *19*, 839–853. [CrossRef]
45. Li, M.; Liang, D.; Xia, J.; Song, J.; Cheng, D.; Wu, J.; Cao, Y.; Sun, H.; Li, Q. Evaluation of Water Conservation Function of Danjiang River Basin in Qinling Mountains, China Based on InVEST Model. *J. Environ. Manag.* **2021**, *286*, 112212. [CrossRef]
46. Li, Z.; Deng, X.; Jin, G.; Mohmmed, A.; Arowolo, A.O. Tradeoffs between Agricultural Production and Ecosystem Services: A Case Study in Zhangye, Northwest China. *Sci. Total Environ.* **2020**, *707*, 136032. [CrossRef]

47. Wang, X.; Liu, G.; Lin, D.; Lin, Y.; Lu, Y.; Xiang, A.; Xiao, S. Water Yield Service Influence by Climate and Land Use Change Based on InVEST Model in the Monsoon Hilly Watershed in South China. *Geomat. Nat. Hazards Risk* **2022**, *13*, 2024–2048. [CrossRef]
48. Yang, D.; Liu, W.; Tang, L.; Chen, L.; Li, X.; Xu, X. Estimation of Water Provision Service for Monsoon Catchments of South China: Applicability of the InVEST Model. *Landsc. Urban Plan.* **2019**, *182*, 133–143. [CrossRef]
49. Yin, G.; Wang, X.; Zhang, X.; Fu, Y.; Hao, F.; Hu, Q. InVEST Model-Based Estimation of Water Yield in North China and Its Sensitivities to Climate Variables. *Water* **2020**, *12*, 1692. [CrossRef]
50. Yu, Y.; Sun, X.; Wang, J.; Zhang, J. Using InVEST to Evaluate Water Yield Services in Shangri-La, Northwestern Yunnan, China. *PeerJ* **2022**, *10*, e12804. [CrossRef]
51. Budyko, M.I. *Climate and Life*; Academic Press: Cambridge, MA, USA, 1974.
52. Redhead, J.W.; Stratford, C.; Sharps, K.; Jones, L.; Ziv, G.; Clarke, D.; Oliver, T.H.; Bullock, J.M. Empirical Validation of the InVEST Water Yield Ecosystem Service Model at a National Scale. *Sci. Total Environ.* **2016**, *569–570*, 1418–1426. [CrossRef] [PubMed]
53. Almeida, B.; Cabral, P. Water Yield Modelling, Sensitivity Analysis and Validation: A Study for Portugal. *ISPRS Int. J. Geo-Inf.* **2021**, *10*, 494. [CrossRef]
54. Dennedy-Frank, P.J.; Muenich, R.L.; Chaubey, I.; Ziv, G. Comparing Two Tools for Ecosystem Service Assessments Regarding Water Resources Decisions. *J. Environ. Manag.* **2016**, *177*, 331–340. [CrossRef] [PubMed]
55. Chacko, S.; Kurian, J.S.; Ravichandran, C.; Vairavel, S.M.; Kumar, K. An Assessment of Water Yield Ecosystem Services in Periyar Tiger Reserve, Southern Western Ghats of India. *Geol. Ecol. Landsc.* **2019**, *5*, 32–39. [CrossRef]
56. Yang, Y.; Donohue, R.J.; McVicar, T.R. Global Estimation of Effective Plant Rooting Depth: Implications for Hydrological Modeling. *Water Resour. Res.* **2016**, *52*, 8260–8276. [CrossRef]
57. Hengl, T.; de Jesus, J.M.; Heuvelink, G.B.M.; Gonzalez, M.R.; Kilibarda, M.; Blagotić, A.; Shangguan, W.; Wright, M.N.; Geng, X.; Bauer-Marschallinger, B.; et al. SoilGrids250m: Global Gridded Soil Information Based on Machine Learning. *PLoS ONE* **2017**, *12*, e0169748. [CrossRef]
58. IDEAM Consulta y Descarga de Datos Hidrometeorológicos. Available online: http://dhime.ideam.gov.co/atencionciudadano/ (accessed on 19 February 2023).
59. Hargreaves, G.H.; Samani, Z.A. Estimating Potential Evapotranspiration. *J. Irrig. Drain. Div.* **1982**, *108*, 225–230. [CrossRef]
60. Laskar, J.; Robutel, P.; Joutel, F.; Gastineau, M.; Correia, A.C.M.; Levrard, B. A Long-Term Numerical Solution for the Insolation Quantities of the Earth. *Astron. Astrophys.* **2004**, *428*, 261–285. [CrossRef]
61. R: Extraterrestrial Solar Radiation. Available online: https://search.r-project.org/CRAN/refmans/envirem/html/ETsolradRasters.html (accessed on 19 February 2023).
62. Peth, S. Soil Compactibility and Compressibility. In *Encyclopedia of Agrophysics*; Gliński, J., Horabik, J., Lipiec, J., Eds.; Encyclopedia of Earth Sciences Series; Springer: Dordrecht, The Netherlands, 2011; pp. 742–745. ISBN 978-90-481-3585-1.
63. IDEAM Mapas de Suelos del Territorio Colombiano a Escala 1:100.000. 2018. Available online: http://www.siac.gov.co/catalogo-de-mapas (accessed on 19 February 2023).
64. Allen, R.; Pereira, L.; Raes, D.; Smith, M. *Evapotranspiración del Cultivo: Guías para la Determinación de los Requerimientos de Agua de los Cultivos*; FAO: Rome, Italy, 2006.
65. IDEAM METODOLOGÍA PARA LA ZONIFICACIÓN DE SUSCEPTIBILIDAD GENERAL DEL TERRENO A LOS MOVIMIENTOS EN MASA. 2012. Available online: https://bit.ly/3mN5DpE (accessed on 19 February 2023).
66. Donohue, R.J.; Roderick, M.L.; McVicar, T.R. Roots, Storms and Soil Pores: Incorporating Key Ecohydrological Processes into Budyko's Hydrological Model. *J. Hydrol.* **2012**, *436–437*, 35–50. [CrossRef]
67. Fu, B.P. On the calculation of the evaporation from land surface. *Chin. J. Atmos. Sci.* **1981**, *5*, 23–31. [CrossRef]
68. Zhang, Y.; Kendy, E.; Qiang, Y.; Changming, L.; Yanjun, S.; Hongyong, S. Effect of Soil Water Deficit on Evapotranspiration, Crop Yield, and Water Use Efficiency in the North China Plain. *Agric. Water Manag.* **2004**, *64*, 107–122. [CrossRef]
69. Bejagam, V.; Keesara, V.R.; Sridhar, V. Impacts of Climate Change on Water Provisional Services in Tungabhadra Basin Using InVEST Model. *River Res. Appl.* **2022**, *38*, 94–106. [CrossRef]
70. Bergstra, J.; Yamins, D.; Cox, D.D. Making a Science of Model Search: Hyperparameter Optimization in Hundreds of Dimensions for Vision Architectures. *arXiv* **2013**, arXiv:1209.5111. Available online: https://arxiv.org/abs/1209.5111 (accessed on 17 February 2023).
71. Pessacg, N.; Flaherty, S.; Brandizi, L.; Solman, S.; Pascual, M. Getting Water Right: A Case Study in Water Yield Modelling Based on Precipitation Data. *Sci. Total Environ.* **2015**, *537*, 225–234. [CrossRef]
72. Arrieta-Castro, M.; Donado-Rodríguez, A.; Acuña, G.J.; Canales, F.A.; Teegavarapu, R.S.V.; Kaźmierczak, B. Analysis of Streamflow Variability and Trends in the Meta River, Colombia. *Water* **2020**, *12*, 1451. [CrossRef]

Disclaimer/Publisher's Note: The statements, opinions and data contained in all publications are solely those of the individual author(s) and contributor(s) and not of MDPI and/or the editor(s). MDPI and/or the editor(s) disclaim responsibility for any injury to people or property resulting from any ideas, methods, instructions or products referred to in the content.

Article

Predictive Modelling of Reference Evapotranspiration Using Machine Learning Models Coupled with Grey Wolf Optimizer

Pangam Heramb [1,2,*], K. V. Ramana Rao [1], A. Subeesh [3] and Ankur Srivastava [4,*]

1. Irrigation and Drainage Engineering Division, ICAR—Central Institute of Agricultural Engineering, Bhopal 462038, India
2. Outreach Program (ICAR-CIAE), ICAR—Indian Agricultural Research Institute, New Delhi 110012, India
3. Agricultural Mechanization Division, ICAR—Central Institute of Agricultural Engineering, Bhopal 462038, India
4. Faculty of Science, University of Technology Sydney, Sydney, NSW 2007, Australia
* Correspondence: herambpangam@gmail.com (P.H.); ankur.srivastava@uts.edu.au (A.S.)

Abstract: Mismanagement of fresh water is a primary concern that negatively impacts agricultural productivity. Judicious use of water in agriculture is possible by estimating the optimal requirement. The present practice of estimating crop water requirements is using reference evapotranspiration (ET_0) values, which is considered a standard method. Hence, predicting ET_0 is vital in allocating and managing available resources. In this study, different machine learning (ML) algorithms, namely random forests (RF), extreme gradient boosting (XGB), and light gradient boosting (LGB), were optimized using the naturally inspired grey wolf optimizer (GWO) viz. GWORF, GWOXGB, and GWOLGB. The daily meteorological data of 10 locations falling under humid and sub-humid regions of India for different cross-validation stages were employed, using eighteen input scenarios. Besides, different empirical models were also compared with the ML models. The hybrid ML models were found superior in accurately predicting at all the stations than the conventional and empirical models. The reduction in the root mean square error (RMSE) from 0.919 to 0.812 mm/day in the humid region and 1.253 mm/day to 1.154 mm/day in the sub-humid region was seen in the least accurate model using the hyperparameter tuning. The RF models have improved their accuracies substantially using the GWO optimizer than LGB and XGB models.

Keywords: evapotranspiration; grey wolf optimizer; machine learning; meta-heuristics; humid; sub-humid; random forests; boosting

Citation: Heramb, P.; Ramana Rao, K.V.; Subeesh, A.; Srivastava, A. Predictive Modelling of Reference Evapotranspiration Using Machine Learning Models Coupled with Grey Wolf Optimizer. *Water* **2023**, *15*, 856. https://doi.org/10.3390/w15050856

Academic Editor: Yongqiang Zhang

Received: 19 January 2023
Revised: 7 February 2023
Accepted: 20 February 2023
Published: 22 February 2023

Copyright: © 2023 by the authors. Licensee MDPI, Basel, Switzerland. This article is an open access article distributed under the terms and conditions of the Creative Commons Attribution (CC BY) license (https:// creativecommons.org/licenses/by/ 4.0/).

1. Introduction

India is projected to be the World's most populous country by 2023, surpassing China, which will have to feed about 1.66 billion people by 2050 [1]. Thus, the pressure on natural resources and food systems to produce more food would become a reality. Effective planning on water resource utilization should be the objective for water resource planners. The per capita availability of water is decreasing day by day due to the increase in population. According to the Ministry of Jal Shakti, Government of India, the average annual per capita water availability was 1816 cubic meters, 1545 cubic meters, and 1487 cubic meters for 2001, 2011, and 2021, respectively. It was estimated to further deteriorate to 1367 cubic meters by 2031.

Efficient water management in agriculture is required in developing nations, which are disadvantaged due to the lack of infrastructure and scientific advancements [2]. The need for crop water requirement-based irrigation practices in these nations is high to improve irrigation efficiency. Various methods and techniques are used to estimate the crop water requirement, of which the reference evapotranspiration (ET_0) is a reliable and standard practice. ET_0 is a parameter that could be employed for all the regions based on the local climatic parameters [3]. The estimation of models is classified as (a) fully physically-based combination models that employ mass and energy conservation principles; (b) semi-physically based models that consider either mass or energy conservation; and (3) black-box models that are empirical in nature [4,5]. Many researchers have formulated empirical and semi-empirical methods to estimate the ET_0, like mass transfer based [6–8], radiation based [9–14], temperature based [15–17], and combination based [18,19]. Some empirical equations might require extensive agro-meteorological data, which are unavailable for every region. Therefore, there is a scope for models with less data requirement [20].

ET_0 is a phenomenon that depends on various meteorological parameters that give rise to a complex non-linear problem. Henceforth, machine learning (ML) models have been extensively used in their estimation which could solve these complex problems [21]. The previous studies available have been discussed below. Various data-driven algorithms like random forests (RF) [22–27], gradient boosting decision tree (GBDT), extreme gradient boosting (XGB) [24,27,28], light gradient boosting (LGB) [27,29–31], etc. have been employed for ET_0 estimation. Most of the research did not confine to a single algorithm. However, a comparison is made either with different machine learning techniques or empirical models. Shiri et al. [22] evaluated 12 different machine learning algorithms like multivariate adaptive regression spline (MARS), boosted regression tree (BT), random forest (RF), model tree (MT), support vector machine (SVM), etc., with other optimizers for stations in Iran using 12-year meteorological data. They have compared two input scenarios, i.e., radiation and temperature based. A study in Brazil [32] used the machine learning models like RF, XGB, artificial neural network (ANN), and convolutional neural network (CNN) models for daily and hourly ET_0 estimates. Zhou et al. [27] have used the agro-meteorological data from twelve stations in China for ET_0 prediction. They have tested the algorithms like extremely randomized trees, RF, and GBDT, and gradient boosting models like XGB, LGB, and gradient boosting with categorical features support (CatBoost), factorization machine-based neural network model (DeepFM), and SVM. They have concluded that the CatBoost and LGB models outperformed the other models, followed by XGB and GBDT.

The evaluation of ET_0 models in New Mexico, United States of America, using extreme learning machine (ELM), genetic programming (GP), RF, and SVM for different climates, was done by [33]. The results of their study indicated that the models performed in the order of SVM > ELM > RF > GP. Another study used 14 stations in different climates, i.e., arid desert, semi-arid steppe, semi-humid cold-temperate, semi-humid warm temperate, humid subtropical, and humid tropical regions in China for ET_0 prediction [30]. They have evaluated multi-layer perceptron (MLP), generalized neural network (GRNN) and adaptive neuro-fuzzy inference system (ANFIS), SVM, kernel-based non-linear extension of arps decline (KNEA), M5 model tree (M5Tree), XGB and MARS models and suggested the use of SVM over other models. Wu et al. [34] compared the basic models like RF, SVM, MLP, and K-Nearest Neighbor (KNN) regression and their stacked and blended ensemble models using data from five stations in China.

The application of different optimizers in conjunction with machine learning and deep learning models has been reported in ET_0 modelling. These research findings have revealed an improvement in accuracy over conventional ML models. Yan et al. [35] evaluated the performance of hybrid XGB coupled with whale optimization algorithm (WOA) for ET_0 modelling at humid and arid stations in China. They concluded that hybrid models had improved the accuracies in both local and external data scenarios. Grey wolf optimizer (GWO) has been employed with ANN by [36] for modelling purposes in Iran. The results were compared with least square support vector regression (LS-SVR) and conventional ANN. They found that the hybrid models were superior in their prediction. Dong et al. [37] attempted to use four types of bio-inspired optimizers with the kernel-based non-linear extension of arps decline (KNEA) model for 51 stations in China. The optimizers they employed were the grasshopper optimization algorithm (GOA), GWO, particle swarm optimization algorithm (PSO), and salp swarm algorithm (SSA). They reported that the GWO-optimized KNEA performed better than other models.

Meta-heuristic optimizers have not been applied widely in Indian conditions, according to previous studies. Additionally, the literature lacked information on how to optimize tree-based ML models. As a result, the goal of this study is to determine if GWO can improve the efficiency of tree-based models. The specific objectives of this study are (1) to estimate the ET_0 using state-of-the-art machine learning models like RF, XGB, and LGB for humid and sub-humid climates of India; (2) to couple these models with a heuristic GWO technique for finding any improvement in the efficiency and (3) to compare various empirical models with the ML models in the study area.

2. Materials and Methods

2.1. Study Area and Data Collection

Indian climatic conditions can be broadly divided into arid, semi-arid, humid, and sub-humid regions. The humid zones over Southeast Asia have a length of growing period (LGP) of more than 270 days and an annual rainfall above 1500 mm, while the sub-humid zones have an LGP of 180 to 270 days and a rainfall amount between 1000 and 1500 mm annually [38]. The percentage of the total geographical area of sub-humid and humid regions in India is about 24% and 17%, respectively. Historically, these regions have recorded high relative humidity and adequate rainfall distribution. However, the change in bio-climates is evident due to the reduction of sub-humid and humid regions' areal extent and subsequent increase in semi-arid and arid regions over India [39]. This poses a challenge to the water availability in these regions, although with ample resources.

The agro-climatic data of sub-humid and humid regions of India were collected from the All India coordinated research project on Agro-meteorology, ICAR, from 2001 to 2020. The locations wherein the data were collected are depicted in Figure 1. The details of the stations are described in Table 1. The elevations of these stations varied from 17 m in Mohanpur to 1800 m in Ranichauri. The daily meteorological data consisting of maximum air temperature (°C), minimum air temperature (°C), mean relative humidity (%), wind speed at 2 m height (m/s), and the number of sunshine hours were collected from the ten locations from both the regions.

Table 1. Details of the locations of the study area.

S. No.	State	Station	Code	AER	Latitude (N)	Longitude (E)	Altitude (m)
1	Assam	Jorhat	JHT	Humid	26°45′	94°12′	116
2	West Bengal	Mohanpur	MHP	Humid	21°50′	87°15′	17
3	Himachal Pradesh	Palampur	PLP	Humid	32°07′	76°32′	1220
4	Kerala	Thrissur	TRS	Humid	10°31′	76°13′	28
5	Uttar Pradesh	Faizabad	FZB	Sub-humid	26°46′	82°08′	97
6	Madhya Pradesh	Jabalpur	JBP	Sub-humid	23°11′	79°59′	412
7	Chattisgarh	Raipur	RPR	Sub-humid	21°15′	81°37′	290
8	Jharkhand	Ranchi	RNI	Sub-humid	23°20′	85°18′	651
9	Uttarakhand	Ranichauri	RCH	Sub-humid	30°19′	78°24′	1800
10	Bihar	Samastipur	SMP	Sub-humid	25°59′	85°40′	51

These meteorological parameters affect the evapotranspiration rate by imparting the energy required for vaporization and the rate of water vapour removal from the evaporating surface. The air temperature surrounding the plant impacts the sensible heat of the air. The humidity data would affect the difference in the vapour power of the air and the evaporating surface. The wind speed affects the vapour removal, thereby affecting the evaporation rate. The sunshine data are utilized to calculate the solar radiation, which mostly affects the vaporization of the water to vapour.

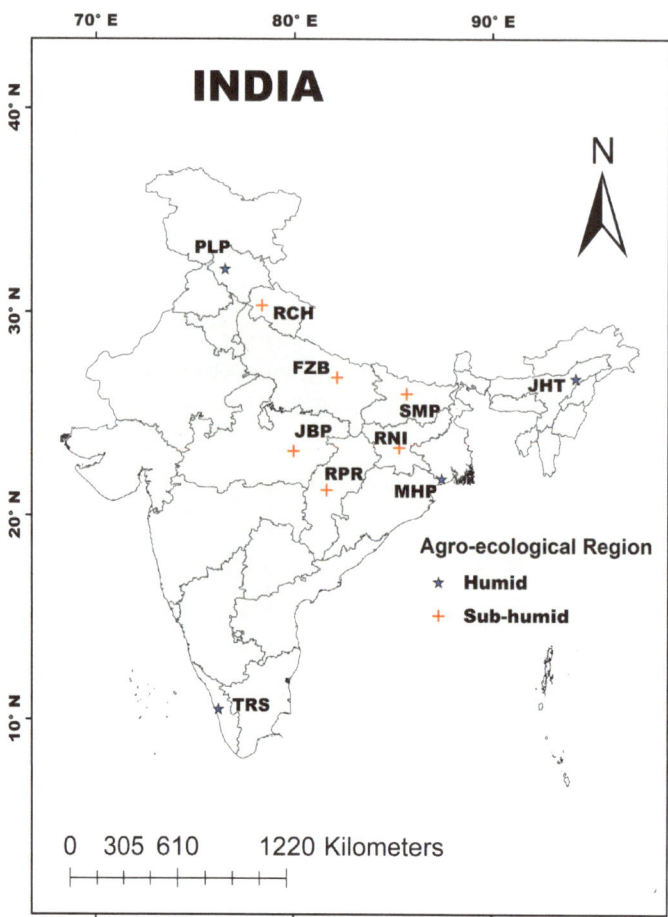

Figure 1. Study area map showing locations in humid and sub-humid regions.

2.2. ET_0 Estimaton Using FAO-56 Penman-Monteith and Empirical Equations

The ASCE Committee on Irrigation and Water requirements analysed different methods in estimating ET_0. They found that the FAO 56 Penman-Monteith can be used in all locations. Hence, the standardised equation of reference evapotranspiration is used as the target variable in the modelling stages. The equation for predicting ET_0 by FAO 56 Penman-Monteith is given below. The machine learning models were compared with different empirical equations. The estimation of ET_0 using different empirical equations using the formulae as described in Table 2.

Table 2. Formulae for FAO 56 Penman-Monteith and empirical equations used.

Method	Symbol and Equations		Reference
	Target for the Models		
FAO-56 Penman-Monteith	$ET_{PM} = \dfrac{0.408\Delta(R_n - G) + \gamma \dfrac{900}{T_{mean}+273} u_2 (e_s - e_a)}{\Delta + \gamma(1 + 0.34\, u_2)}$	(1)	[40]
	Mass Transfer based		
Albrecht (ALB)	$ET_{ALB} = F(e_s - e_a)$, where $F = 0.4$ if $u_2 \geq 1$ m/s and $F = 0.1005 + 0.297\, u_2$, if $u_2 < 1$ m/s	(2)	[6]
Mahringer (MAH)	$ET_{MAH} = 0.15072\sqrt{3.6\, u_2}(e_s - e_a)$, where $(e_s - e_a)$ in hPa	(3)	[7]
Penman (PEN)	$ET_{PEN} = 0.35\left(1 + \dfrac{0.98}{100\, u_2}\right)(e_s - e_a)$, where $(e_s - e_a)$ in mm Hg and u_2 in miles per day	(4)	[8,41]
	Radiation based		
Jensen-Haise (JH)	$ET_{JH} = \left(\dfrac{R_s}{\lambda}\right)(0.025\, T_{mean} + 0.08)$	(5)	[11,42]
Makkink (MAK)	$ET_{MAK} = 0.61\left(\dfrac{\Delta}{\Delta + \gamma}\right)\left(\dfrac{R_s}{\lambda}\right) - 0.12$	(6)	[43]
McGuinness-Bordne (MGB)	$ET_{MGB} = \left(\dfrac{R_a}{\lambda\rho}\right)\left(\dfrac{T_{mean} + 5}{68}\right)$	(7)	[12]
Priestly-Taylor (PT)	$ET_{PT} = 1.26\left(\dfrac{\Delta}{\Delta + \gamma}\right)\left(\dfrac{R_n}{\lambda}\right)$	(8)	[13]
Turc (TUR)	$ET_{TUR} = 0.013\left(\dfrac{T_{mean}}{T_{mean}+15}\right)(23.8846\, R_s + 50)$, for $RH > 50\% = 0.013\left(\dfrac{T_{mean}}{T_{mean}+15}\right)(23.8846\, R_s + 50)\left(1 + \dfrac{50 - RH}{70}\right)$, for $RH < 50\%$	(9)	[14]
	Temperature based		
Hargreaves-Samani (HS)	$ET_{H-S} = 0.0026\sqrt{T_{max} - T_{min}}(T_{mean} + 17.8)(0.408\, R_a)$	(10)	[16]
Hargreaves-Samani 1 (HS1)	$ET_{HS1} = 0.0030\,(T_{max} - T_{min})^{0.4}(T_{mean} + 20)(0.408\, R_a)$	(11)	[17]
Hargreaves-Samani 2 (HS2)	$ET_{HS2} = 0.0025\sqrt{T_{max} - T_{min}}(T_{mean} + 16.8)(0.408\, R_a)$	(12)	[17]
Thorththwaite (Modified) (THO)	$ET_{THO} = 0.533\,\dfrac{N}{12}\left(\dfrac{10\, T_{mean}}{33.617}\right)^{1.033}$	(13)	[44]
	Combination based		
Copais (COP)	$ET_{COP} = 0.057 + 0.277(-0.0033 + 0.00812\, T_{mean} + 0.101\, R_s + 0.00584\, R_s\, T_{mean}) + 0.643\,(0.6416 - 0.00784\, RH + 0.372\, R_s - 0.00364\, RH) + 0.0124\,(0.6416 - 0.00784\, RH + 0.372\, R_s - 0.00364\, RH)(-0.0033 + 0.00812\, T_{mean} + 0.101\, R_s + 0.00584\, R_s\, T_{mean})$	(14)	[18]
Valiantzas 1 (VA1)	$ET_{VA1} = 0.0393\, R_s\sqrt{T_{mean} + 9.5} - 0.19\, R_s^{0.6}\, \varphi^{0.15} + 0.078\,(T_{mean} + 20)\left(1 - \dfrac{RH}{100}\right)$	(15)	[19]
Valiantzas 2 (VA2)	$ET_{VA2} = 0.0393\, R_s\sqrt{T_{mean} + 9.5} - 0.19\, R_s^{0.6}\, \varphi^{0.15} + 0.0061\,(T_{mean} + 20)(1.12\, T_{mean} - T_{min} - 2)^{0.7}$	(16)	[19]

Notes: Units and Description of the parameters unless specified above: ET is the reference evapotranspiration, mm/day; Δ is the slope of the vapour pressure curve, kPa/°C, R_n is the net radiation at the crop surface in MJ/m² day, G is the soil heat flux density in MJ/m² day, γ is the psychrometric constant in kPa/°C, e_s is the saturation vapour pressure, kPa; e_a is the actual vapour pressure, kPa; u_2 is the wind speed at 2 m above the ground surface, m/s; T_{mean} is the mean daily air temperature,°C; R_n is the net solar radiation, MJ/m² day; R_s is the incident shortwave solar radiation flux, MJ/m²/day; R_a is the extra-terrestrial solar radiation, MJ/m² day; T_{max} is the maximum daily air temperature, °C; T_{min} is the minimum daily air temperature, °C; N is the maximum possible duration, hrs; RH is the mean daily relative humidity, %; and φ is latitude, Radians.

2.3. Description of Machine Learning Models and Optimizer

2.3.1. Random Forest (RF)

RF model generates output predictions by combining results from several regression decision trees. RF is capable of capturing complex, non-linear interactions between the features and produces a powerful prediction model. Being an ensemble method, RF trains several decision trees in parallel with bootstrapping followed by aggregation (Figure 2a). The trees in the 'forest' are generated based on a random selection of subset data from the training set, and the bootstrapping ensures that each tree in the forest is unique [45,46]. For the final prediction, the RF regressor aggregates the decision made by individual trees. RF is robust to outliers, produces better generalization, and has easily tunable hyperparameters [47].

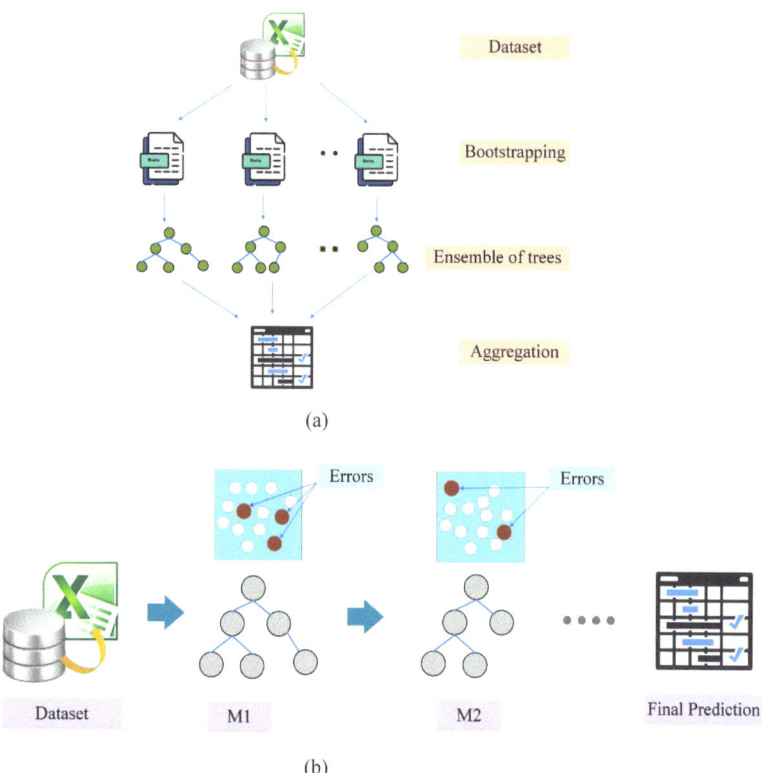

Figure 2. Data flow in (**a**) bagging (RF) and (**b**) boosting (XGB/LGB) models.

2.3.2. Extreme Gradient Boosting Model (XGB)

XGB provides an efficient and scalable implementation of gradients boosting framework [48] suitable for both regression and classification problems. A typical gradient-boosting approach is an ensemble of decision trees that are trained in a sequential manner [49]. In gradient boosting, a better model is built by merging previous models until the best model reduces the cumulative prediction error (Figure 2b). XGB was developed with optimized and supports distributed computing, additionally improving flexibility and portability. XGB leverages parallel computation to build trees across different processing units. The algorithm supports effective pruning of trees for improving the computational speed and sparsity-aware split finding to handle the missing data.

2.3.3. Light Gradient Boosting Model (LGB)

The LGB model is a gradient-boosting framework built on decision trees that boosts the model's effectiveness and consumes less memory. The key characteristic of LGB is that the trees are grown leaf-wise instead of checking all of the previous leaves for each new leaf [50]. LGB uses two novel approaches, viz., Gradient-based One Side Sampling and Exclusive Feature Bundling (EFB), to achieve improved performance. Using the GOSS, the major portion of the data points with small gradients are eliminated from calculating the information gain, achieving significant time saving [51]. Using EFB, the mutually exclusive features are bundled, achieving feature reduction without compromising the model performance. The model works effectively on benchmark datasets with increased training speed compared to the conventional gradient-boosting methods.

2.3.4. Grey Wolf Optimizer (GWO)

GWO is an evolutionary, meta-heuristic algorithm inspired by the structure of the leadership hierarchy and hunting mechanism of grey wolves in nature [52] and has been proven to be a more practical and precise method for optimization problems [53]. It has significant advantages over the other swarm intelligence approaches, such as a reduced number of parameters and no requirement of derivation information during the initial search, etc. [54]. In GWO, a grey wolf herd's members are classified as α, β, δ and ω and depending on the effectiveness, decision-making ability, and way of advancing in the hunting process.

The α wolves are the strongest and most powerful, usually serves as the herd's leader and should be obeyed by the other wolves in the pack. β wolves act as advisors to the alpha group, and δ wolves act in the group as guards, sentinels, and hunters. The ω group of wolves is in the lowest position of decision-making [55] and follows others. The alpha in GWO is believed to be the best answer. In order of priority, the beta, gamma, and omega solutions come next. The wolves in GWO iterations assess the potential for a hunt and adjust their status accordingly (Figure 3).

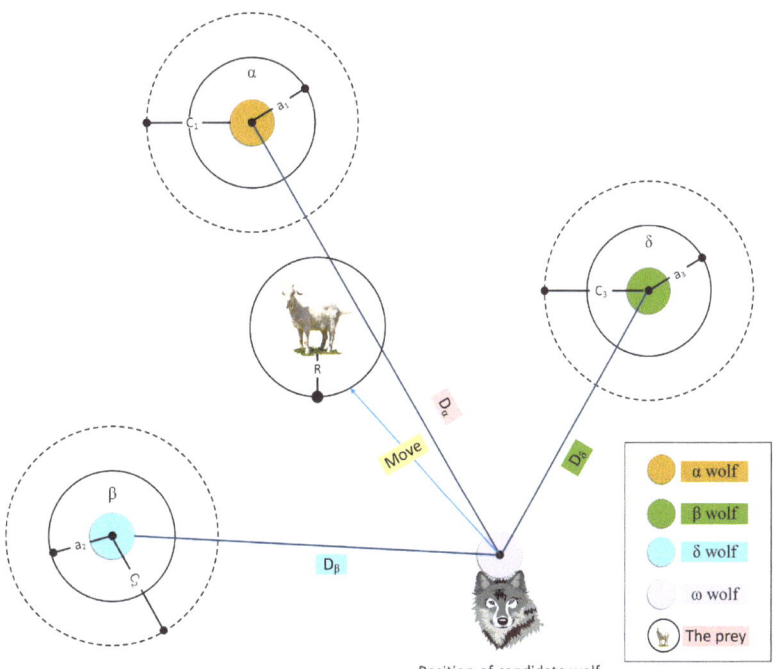

Figure 3. Schematic diagram of GWO optimizers (Source: [56]).

2.4. ET_0 Estimaton Using ML and Hybrid ML

2.4.1. Input Scenarios

The daily meteorological parameters from 2001 to 2020 at all ten stations are used as the inputs for the modelling of daily ET_0. The inputs consisted of maximum air temperature (T_{max}, °C), minimum air temperature (T_{min}, °C), mean relative humidity (RH, %), wind speed at 2 m height (u_2, m/s), number of sunshine hours (n, hours), solar radiation (R_n, MJ/m² day) and extra-terrestrial radiation (R_a, MJ/m² day).

A total of 18 combinations were employed. Table 3 depicts the different combinations used, ranging from two inputs in model index 1 to six inputs in model indices 17 and 18. The target for these models was the daily ET_0 calculated from the FAO-56 Penman-Monteith equation. The statistical indicators of the inputs and output at various stations are presented in Figure S1. The time series graphs of ET_0 from some stations of the study on a daily basis from 2001 to 2020 were shown in Figure S2 (Supplementary Materials).

Table 3. Data input scenarios.

Model Index	Input Combinations	Model Index	Input Combinations
1	T_{max}, T_{min}	10	$T_{max}, T_{min}, RH, R_a$
2	T_{max}, T_{min}, RH	11	$T_{max}, T_{min}, U_2, R_a$
3	T_{max}, T_{min}, U_2	12	T_{max}, T_{min}, n, R_a
4	T_{max}, T_{min}, n	13	$T_{max}, T_{min}, RH, U_2$
5	T_{max}, T_{min}, R_s	14	T_{max}, T_{min}, RH, n
6	T_{max}, T_{min}, R_a	15	T_{max}, T_{min}, U_2, n
7	$T_{max}, T_{min}, RH, R_s$	16	$T_{max}, T_{min}, RH, U_2, n$
8	$T_{max}, T_{min}, U_2, R_s$	17	$T_{max}, T_{min}, RH, U_2, n, R_s$
9	T_{max}, T_{min}, n, R_s	18	$T_{max}, T_{min}, RH, U_2, n, R_a$

2.4.2. Model Development

The data were normalised, which gives scale uniformity, improving the modelling capability. The normalised input data were used for modelling purposes [57]. The equation used for the normalisation of the data is given below:

$$x_{norm} = \frac{x_0 - x_{min}}{x_{max} - x_{min}} \quad (17)$$

where: x_{norm} is the normalised value of the input, x_0 is the actual value of the input that is being normalised, and x_{max} and x_{min} are the maximum and minimum values of all the inputs.

Fivefold cross-validation was employed in each of the ML and hybrid ML models, as shown in Table 4. For example, say in the V1 scenario, 16-year daily data from 2005 to 2020 would be used for the model training, and the rest of the data from 2001 to 2004 would be used for the testing of the model developed. This was done for the rest of the cross-validation stages as well so that the whole of the data set would be tested for accuracy. The employment of cross-validation has been found to reduce the over-fitting of the models [24].

Table 4. Cross-validation stages.

Cross-Validation	Training	Testing
V1	2005–2020	2001–2004
V2	2001–2004 and 2009–2020	2005–2008
V3	2001–2008 and 2013–2020	2009–2012
V4	2001–2012 and 2017–2020	2013–2016
V5	2001–2016	2017–2020

2.4.3. Hyper Parameter Tuning in Hybrid ML

The hybrid ML models were developed by optimization of the hyperparameters of RF, XGB, and LGB models using the GWO algorithm. The default values and the range of hyperparameters used in the study are shown in Table 5. The default values of the hyperparameters were used in the state-of-the-art ML models, whereas the best hyperparameter set in each of the ML models was assessed using the GWO to develop the hybrid models, i.e., GWORF, GWOXGB, and GWOLGB. The fine-tuning of hyperparameters could potentially improve the prediction accuracy of hybrid models [58].

Table 5. Hyperparameter plane for tuning the parameters using GWO.

Model	Parameter	Default Value	Hyperparameter Range for Tuning
RF	n_estimators	100	Range of 10 to 500, increment by 10
	min_samples_leaf	1	Range of 1 to 6, increment by 2
	max_depth	None	Range of 2 to 20, increment by 2 and None
XGB	n_estimators	100	Range of 10 to 500, increment by 10
	learning_rate	0.3	[0.05, 0.1, 0.15, 0.3]
	max_depth	6	Range of 2 to 20, increment by 2 and None
LGB	n_estimators	100	Range of 10 to 500, increment by 10
	learning_rate	0.3	[0.05, 0.1, 0.15, 0.3]
	max_depth	6	Range of 2 to 20, increment by 2 and None

2.5. Model Performance Indicators

The indicators used in the study were root mean square error (RMSE), coefficient of determination (R^2), mean absolute error (MAE) [27], and agreement index (d) [59]. The formulae for these indicators are described in Table 6.

Table 6. Statistical indicators.

Indicator	Code	Formula	
Root mean square error	RMSE	$\sqrt{\frac{\sum_{i=1}^{N}(O_i - P_i)^2}{N}}$	(18)
Coefficient of determination	R^2	$\left(\frac{\sum_{i=1}^{N}\{(O_i - \overline{O}_i)(P_i - \overline{P}_i)\}}{\sqrt{\sum_{i=1}^{N}(O_i - \overline{O}_i)^2 \sum_{i=1}^{N}(P_i - \overline{P}_i)^2}} \right)^2$	(19)
Mean absolute error	MAE	$\frac{\sum_{i=1}^{N}|(P_i - O_i)|}{N}$	(20)
Agreement index	d	$1 - \frac{\sum_{i=1}^{N}(P_i - O_i)^2}{\sum_{i=1}^{N}(|P_i - \overline{O}_i| + |O_i - \overline{O}_i|)^2}$	(21)

Notes: N is the total number of test data, O_i and P_i are the actual ET_0 by FAO 56 Penman-Monteith and predicted values of the models, respectively.

Global Performance Indicator (GPI)

Using different indicators renders a problem in properly selecting or judging the best models. Hence, a summative index that uses the equation called Global Performance Indicator is used in the study [36]. All the above indicators, i.e., RMSE, R^2, MAE, d, were normalized between 0 and 1 using Equation (22), and the value of GPI for a model is found using Equation (23). Higher values of GPI would give the best model compared to other models [60,61].

$$N_j = \frac{S_j - \min(S)}{\max(S) - \min(S)} \quad (22)$$

N_j is the normalized statistical index, S_j is the original statistical index, min(S) is the minimum value in that statistical index, and max(S) is the maximum value in that statistical index.

$$GPI_i = \Sigma_{j=1}^{n}(S_j - S_{ij})\alpha_j \quad (23)$$

GPI_i is the value of the Global Performance Indicator for model i, S_j is the median value of the statistical indicator j, S_{ij} is the value of the statistical indicator j for model i, α_j is a constant with a value of -1 for R^2, d and 1 for MAE, RMSE. The ranking based on the *GPI* value was also done.

3. Results

3.1. Comparison of the Empirical Models in Estimating ET_0

Evaluation of different empirical models was carried out against the FAO-56 Penman-Method as the target for the daily data of 20 years at both humid and sub-humid locations.

The performance indicators of the fifteen models at humid and sub-humid stations were presented in Tables S1 and S2, respectively. The ranking of the various models at humid stations based on the GPI is depicted in Table 7. The comparison at various stations suggests that the radiation-based models were superior at most stations. In contrast, mass-transfer-based models were found to be of low accuracy. It shows that the Turc Model was a promising method compared to other models. It was followed by Makkink, Valiantzas 2, Jensen-Haise. The lowest-performing empirical models in the humid region were McGuinness-Bordne, Mahringer, and Valiantzas 1. The ranking of the various models at sub-humid stations is shown in Table 8. The superior models in sub-humid regions were Turc, Valiantzas 2, Jensen-Haise, and Preistly-Taylor. The worst empirical models at sub-humid stations were Valiantzas 1, Albrecht, Copias, and Mahringer. The results indicated that the empirical model performance varied at different stations. Overall, the Turc model could be used in the study area based on its superior ranking in most stations.

Table 7. Ranking of the best-performing empirical models at humid stations.

	Jorhat		Mohanpur		Palampur		Thrissur	
RANK	MODEL	GPI	MODEL	GPI	MODEL	GPI	MODEL	GPI
1	TUR	1.467	MAK	1.521	TUR	1.423	TUR	1.439
2	PT	1.390	TUR	1.508	VA2	1.292	VA2	1.305
3	MAK	1.276	PT	1.330	JH	0.863	PT	0.818
4	VA2	1.216	VA2	1.027	HS	0.783	MAK	0.769
5	JH	0.550	VA1	0.813	PT	0.721	PEN	0.372
6	VA1	0.484	HS	0.361	HS2	0.663	JH	0.154
7	HS	−0.265	HS2	0.082	MAK	0.613	ALB	0.034
8	ALB	−0.302	HS1	0.052	HS1	0.467	HS	0.028
9	COP	−0.370	THO	0.032	THO	−0.233	MAH	−0.084
10	HS2	−0.488	JH	−0.092	MAH	−0.516	HS2	−0.111
11	HS1	−0.552	COP	−0.812	PEN	−0.517	COP	−0.171
12	THO	−0.579	ALB	−1.033	ALB	−0.586	HS1	−0.351
13	PEN	−0.782	PEN	−1.173	COP	−1.071	VA1	−0.727
14	MAH	−0.807	MAH	−1.687	MGB	−1.323	THO	−0.917
15	MGB	−2.238	MGB	−1.927	VA1	−2.577	MGB	−2.559

Table 8. Ranking of the best-performing empirical models at sub-humid stations.

	Faizabad		Jabalpur		Raipur		Ranchi		Ranichauri		Samastipur	
RANK	MODEL	GPI	MODEL	GPI	MODEL	GPI	MODEL	GPI	MODEL	GPI	MODEL	GPI
1	TUR	1.037	TUR	1.234	TUR	1.117	TUR	1.587	VA2	1.487	TUR	1.037
2	JH	0.882	VA2	1.014	VA2	0.969	PT	1.510	TUR	1.468	JH	0.882
3	VA2	0.840	PT	0.887	HS	0.894	VA2	1.294	MAK	1.258	VA2	0.840
4	HS	0.642	HS	0.686	PT	0.784	MAK	1.122	JH	1.048	HS	0.642
5	HS1	0.520	JH	0.646	HS1	0.722	JH	0.347	PT	0.932	HS1	0.520
6	PT	0.517	HS1	0.487	HS2	0.705	HS	0.311	HS	0.875	PT	0.517
7	HS2	0.500	THO	0.444	JH	0.556	THO	0.262	HS2	0.762	HS2	0.500
8	THO	0.390	HS2	0.440	THO	0.414	HS1	−0.059	HS1	0.544	THO	0.390
9	COP	0.119	MAK	0.377	MAK	0.171	HS2	−0.065	THO	−0.279	COP	0.119
10	PEN	0.050	PEN	−0.150	PEN	−0.131	ALB	−0.643	ALB	−1.032	PEN	0.050
11	MAK	−0.007	COP	−0.554	COP	−0.386	PEN	−0.661	MGB	−1.038	MAK	−0.007
12	MGB	−0.737	MAH	−0.883	MAH	−1.053	MAH	−0.729	MAH	−1.230	MGB	−0.737
13	MAH	−1.148	MGB	−1.016	MGB	−1.106	VA1	−0.744	VA1	−1.552	MAH	−1.148
14	ALB	−1.212	ALB	−1.501	ALB	−1.523	COP	−1.493	COP	−1.567	ALB	−1.212
15	VA1	−2.392	VA1	−2.110	VA1	−2.131	MGB	−2.041	PEN	−1.675	VA1	−2.392

3.2. Comparison of Various Input Combinations in Conventional ML Models

3.2.1. Best-Performing Models in ML

The three conventional models used in the study, i.e., RF, XGB, and LGB, were evaluated with various input combinations. The results in these sections are for the testing data sets in all the cross-validation stages. The statistical indicators at each station using the conventional ML models are given in Tables S3–S12. It was observed that the R^2 value has improved with higher inputs, and LGB models were more accurate than other models. A substantial increase in the accuracy and reduced errors was observed in model indices 8 and 9 across all the stations. The ranking of the eighteen best models (six models in each ML) at humid locations based on the GPI is shown in Table 9. The results indicated that the models that used the most inputs (Index 17 and 18) were superior with higher GPI. The LGB17 and LGB18 performed best in Palampur and Thrissur, whereas the XGB17 was the best at Jorhat and Mohanpur. It was observed that the XGB8 and LGB8, which used wind speed and solar radiation data, performed better in all the stations except Palampur, where the LGB7, RF7, and XGB7 gave accurate estimates. Overall, the performance of RF was found to be inferior to both XGB and LGB. The lowest error (RMSE = 0.096 mm/day) was found using XGB17 at Mohanpur station and, the highest R^2 value (0.994) was observed at Palampur and Thrissur for LGB18 and at Mohanpur for LGB17.

Table 9. Ranking of the best-performing ML models at humid stations.

	Jorhat		Mohanpur		Palampur		Thrissur	
RANK	MODEL	GPI	MODEL	GPI	MODEL	GPI	MODEL	GPI
1	XGB17	1.889	XGB17	1.941	LGB18	1.952	LGB18	1.199
2	XGB18	1.753	LGB17	1.939	LGB17	1.893	LGB17	1.187
3	LGB17	1.717	LGB18	1.721	XGB18	1.777	XGB17	1.159
4	LGB18	1.716	XGB18	1.691	XGB17	1.755	XGB18	1.118
5	RF17	0.795	RF17	1.424	RF18	1.658	RF17	0.911
6	XGB8	0.748	RF18	1.286	RF17	1.501	RF18	0.769
7	LGB8	0.721	LGB8	0.853	LGB7	−0.063	LGB16	0.224
8	RF18	0.582	XGB8	0.702	RF7	−0.146	LGB8	0.130
9	RF8	0.309	RF9	0.607	XGB7	−0.258	XGB16	0.077
10	RF9	0.304	RF8	0.598	LGB16	−0.337	XGB8	0.067
11	LGB12	−0.699	LGB9	−1.208	RF16	−0.527	RF16	−0.008
12	LGB9	−0.726	LGB12	−1.369	XGB16	−0.628	RF8	−0.010
13	RF12	−1.040	RF12	−1.439	LGB8	−1.070	RF9	−0.017
14	XGB9	−1.231	LGB7	−1.546	RF8	−1.191	LGB15	−0.413
15	XGB12	−1.321	XGB9	−1.619	RF9	−1.212	RF15	−0.536
16	LGB7	−1.633	RF7	−1.712	XGB8	−1.373	XGB15	−0.558
17	RF7	−1.806	XGB12	−1.815	LGB12	−1.684	LGB7	−2.499
18	XGB7	−2.079	XGB7	−2.053	XGB12	−2.048	XGB7	−2.801

The eighteen best-ranking models at sub-humid locations are shown in Table 10. It could be seen that the LGB17 and LGB18 were the best performing at all the six stations. The performance of the model indices 8, 9, and 16 was quite promising at all the stations except at Ranichauri, wherein the index 7 models were accurate. It was observed that the addition of solar radiation as an input considerably increased the performance of the models. The models that correlated with the FAO-56 Penman-Monteith are in the order of LGB, XGB, and RF. The LGB18 at Jabalpur station performed well (R^2 = 0.995), whereas the least RMSE (0.094 mm/day) was recorded at Ranichauri for LGB17.

Table 10. Ranking of the best-performing ML models at sub-humid stations.

RANK	Faizabad MODEL	GPI	Jabalpur MODEL	GPI	Raipur MODEL	GPI	Ranchi MODEL	GPI	Ranichauri MODEL	GPI	Samastipur MODEL	GPI
1	LGB17	1.752	LGB18	1.265	LGB18	1.265	LGB17	1.637	LGB17	2.374	LGB17	1.908
2	LGB18	1.682	LGB17	1.222	LGB17	1.248	XGB17	1.593	LGB18	2.303	LGB18	1.821
3	XGB17	1.630	XGB18	1.138	XGB18	1.197	LGB18	1.566	XGB17	2.207	XGB17	1.761
4	XGB18	1.561	XGB17	1.137	XGB17	1.191	XGB18	1.546	XGB18	2.034	XGB18	1.583
5	RF17	1.373	RF17	0.993	RF17	1.036	RF17	1.147	RF18	1.693	RF17	1.397
6	RF18	1.321	RF18	0.965	RF18	0.973	RF18	1.065	RF17	1.531	RF18	1.041
7	LGB16	0.162	LGB16	0.347	LGB16	0.473	LGB8	0.463	LGB7	0.216	LGB8	0.282
8	XGB16	−0.027	XGB16	0.195	XGB16	0.323	RF8	0.321	RF7	−0.005	RF9	0.135
9	LGB8	−0.125	RF16	0.112	RF16	0.247	RF9	0.304	XGB7	−0.071	RF8	0.128
10	RF9	−0.156	LGB8	0.079	LGB8	−0.070	XGB8	0.281	LGB9	−1.159	XGB8	0.037
11	RF8	−0.195	RF8	0.016	RF9	−0.131	LGB16	−0.394	LGB8	−1.164	LGB16	−0.586
12	RF16	−0.289	RF9	0.015	RF8	−0.140	XGB16	−0.601	LGB12	−1.237	RF16	−0.746
13	XGB8	−0.298	XGB8	−0.076	XGB8	−0.193	RF16	−0.749	RF9	−1.358	XGB16	−0.888
14	LGB15	−1.194	LGB15	−0.608	LGB15	−0.607	LGB15	−1.136	RF8	−1.388	LGB7	−1.211
15	XGB15	−1.460	RF15	−0.769	RF15	−0.771	RF15	−1.357	RF12	−1.416	RF7	−1.354
16	RF15	−1.520	XGB15	−0.845	XGB15	−0.851	XGB15	−1.361	XGB9	−1.459	XGB7	−1.502
17	LGB13	−1.970	LGB13	−2.450	LGB13	−2.455	LGB12	−1.962	XGB8	−1.474	LGB15	−1.713
18	XGB13	−2.248	XGB13	−2.735	XGB13	−2.735	XGB12	−2.363	XGB12	−1.626	XGB12	−2.092

3.2.2. Least-Performing Models in ML

The ranking of the low-performing models at humid locations of all the conventional model and their input combinations are shown in Table 11. The results showed that model indices 1, 2, 3, and 6 were the least ranked models. It was obvious that the model that used the least number of inputs (only temperature data) was the worst model in estimating ET_0. The RF models had the lowest GPI values compared to other models' counterparts at most stations, indicating their higher errors. It was observed that the LGB models performed better than other ML models using the same input combinations. The error was found to be highest (RMSE = 0.919 mm/day) at Thrissur using RF1, whereas the least R^2 (0.371) was seen at Jorhat for RF1. The model combination that used extra-terrestrial radiation, i.e., model indices 10 and 11, did not yield accurate results.

Table 11. Ranking of the least-performing ML models at humid stations.

RANK	Jorhat MODEL	GPI	Mohanpur MODEL	GPI	Palampur MODEL	GPI	Thrissur MODEL	GPI
54	RF1	−2.139	RF1	−2.503	RF1	−2.748	RF1	−2.429
53	XGB1	−1.541	XGB1	−1.401	XGB1	−2.185	XGB1	−1.862
52	LGB1	−1.099	RF2	−1.098	LGB1	−1.766	LGB1	−1.542
51	RF3	−0.885	XGB2	−0.907	RF3	−0.781	RF6	−1.450
50	XGB3	−0.743	LGB1	−0.789	XGB3	−0.390	XGB6	−1.296
49	XGB6	−0.458	RF3	−0.404	RF6	−0.249	LGB6	−1.054
48	LGB3	−0.405	LGB2	−0.208	XGB6	−0.071	RF2	−0.006
47	RF6	−0.403	XGB3	−0.142	LGB3	−0.042	XGB2	0.111
46	XGB11	−0.036	RF6	0.032	LGB6	0.410	XGB10	0.332
45	RF11	−0.028	XGB6	0.117	RF4	0.497	LGB2	0.334
44	LGB6	0.029	XGB13	0.513	RF2	0.607	RF10	0.362
43	LGB11	0.198	LGB3	0.533	XGB4	0.704	LGB10	0.569
42	RF2	0.649	RF13	0.728	XGB11	0.733	RF3	1.111
41	XGB2	0.682	LGB6	0.813	XGB2	0.807	XGB3	1.130
40	LGB2	1.076	XGB10	0.884	RF11	0.976	LGB3	1.335
39	XGB10	1.532	RF10	1.141	LGB4	1.110	XGB13	1.372
38	RF10	1.709	LGB13	1.192	LGB11	1.190	RF5	1.413
37	LGB10	1.861	LGB10	1.497	LGB2	1.197	LGB5	1.571

The results at the sub-humid stations were found to be quite similar to that of humid locations (Table 12). The model indices 1, 2, 6, and 3 were ranked the lowest in most stations.

The highest RMSE of 1.253 mm/day was observed at Faizabad station using the RF1 model, whereas the lowest R^2 (0.631) was reported at Samastipur with the same set of ML model.

Table 12. Ranking of the least-performing ML models at sub-humid stations.

	Faizabad		Jabalpur		Raipur		Ranchi		Ranichauri		Samastipur	
RANK	MODEL	GPI	MODEL	GPI	MODEL	GPI	MODEL	GPI	MODEL	GPI	MODEL	GPI
54	RF1	−2.377	RF1	−2.344	RF1	−2.271	RF1	−2.028	RF1	−2.560	RF1	−2.505
53	XGB1	−1.815	XGB1	−1.787	XGB1	−1.686	XGB2	−1.328	XGB1	−1.774	XGB1	−1.999
52	LGB1	−0.991	LGB1	−1.128	LGB1	−0.998	RF2	−1.215	LGB1	−1.307	LGB1	−1.514
51	XGB2	−0.618	XGB2	−1.103	XGB2	−0.758	XGB1	−1.164	RF3	−1.065	RF6	−0.654
50	RF2	−0.471	RF2	−0.919	RF2	−0.629	LGB2	−0.549	XGB3	−1.047	XGB6	−0.624
49	RF6	−0.439	XGB6	−0.504	XGB6	−0.544	LGB1	−0.509	LGB3	−0.596	XGB2	−0.315
48	XGB4	−0.407	LGB2	−0.475	RF6	−0.524	XGB10	−0.480	XGB2	−0.131	RF2	−0.202
47	XGB6	−0.388	RF6	−0.283	LGB2	−0.302	XGB6	−0.419	RF2	−0.075	LGB6	−0.161
46	RF4	−0.171	LGB6	0.106	XGB10	−0.096	RF6	−0.268	LGB2	0.287	XGB3	0.053
45	LGB2	−0.021	XGB10	0.132	LGB6	0.072	RF10	−0.097	XGB6	0.497	LGB2	0.172
44	LGB6	0.068	RF10	0.479	RF10	0.333	LGB10	0.354	RF6	0.560	RF3	0.224
43	LGB4	0.357	LGB10	0.601	XGB4	0.449	LGB6	0.419	XGB13	0.641	LGB3	0.523
42	XGB14	0.792	XGB4	0.842	LGB10	0.615	XGB3	0.629	RF13	0.790	XGB11	0.790
41	RF14	1.069	RF4	0.912	RF4	0.713	RF3	0.677	LGB6	0.843	RF11	1.055
40	XGB10	1.185	LGB4	1.255	LGB4	1.088	XGB13	1.228	LGB3	1.026	XGB10	1.115
39	LGB14	1.263	XGB3	1.277	XGB5	1.178	LGB3	1.306	XGB11	1.104	LGB11	1.232
38	RF5	1.339	RF3	1.285	RF5	1.632	RF13	1.473	RF11	1.366	RF10	1.316
37	LGB10	1.623	LGB14	1.656	LGB14	1.729	LGB13	1.972	LGB11	1.440	LGB10	1.495

3.3. Empirical Models v/s Conventional ML Models

The conventional ML models were compared with the empirical equations that employed a similar combination of inputs for modelling. The results at humid (Table 13) and sub-humid locations (Table 14) depicted that the ML models outperformed the empirical models with high GPI values at all combinations and locations. It could be observed that in indices 13, 5, 6, and 7, the models performed in the order of LGB, RF, and XGB.

Table 13. Comparison of the empirical models with conventional ML models (Humid).

			Jorhat		Mohanpur		Palampur		Thrissur	
Inputs used		RANK	MODEL	GPI	MODEL	GPI	MODEL	GPI	MODEL	GPI
T_{max}, T_{min}, RH, U_2		1	LGB13	1.708	LGB13	1.696	LGB13	1.908	LGB13	1.802
		2	RF13	1.576	RF13	1.639	RF13	1.844	RF13	1.690
		3	XGB13	1.561	XGB13	1.612	XGB13	1.808	XGB13	1.639
		4	ALB	−0.988	ALB	−1.315	MAH	−1.786	PEN	−1.195
		5	PEN	−1.823	PEN	−1.501	PEN	−1.849	ALB	−1.842
		6	MAH	−2.034	MAH	−2.132	ALB	−1.925	MAH	−2.093
T_{max}, T_{min}, R_s		1	LGB5	0.824	LGB5	0.982	LGB5	1.037	LGB5	0.942
		2	RF5	0.792	RF5	0.974	XGB5	0.990	RF5	0.907
		3	XGB5	0.786	XGB5	0.966	RF5	0.975	XGB5	0.902
		4	PT	0.560	MAK	0.501	JH	0.178	PT	0.337
		5	MAK	0.410	PT	0.435	PT	−0.001	MAK	0.293
		6	JH	−0.246	JH	−0.870	MAK	−0.216	JH	−0.323
		7	MGB	−3.126	MGB	−2.988	MGB	−2.963	MGB	−3.058
T_{max}, T_{min}, R_a		1	LGB6	2.110	LGB6	1.864	LGB6	1.306	LGB6	1.678
		2	RF6	1.483	XGB6	1.660	XGB6	1.071	XGB6	1.525
		3	XGB6	1.369	RF6	1.635	RF6	0.984	RF6	1.436
		4	HS	−0.676	HS	−0.685	HS	0.352	HS	−0.212
		5	HS1	−1.245	HS2	−1.400	HS2	−0.163	HS2	−0.746
		6	HS2	−1.328	HS1	−1.416	HS1	−0.856	HS1	−1.398
		7	THO	−1.713	THO	−1.657	THO	−2.694	THO	−2.282
T_{max}, T_{min}, RH, R_s		1	LGB7	1.272	LGB7	1.219	LGB7	1.177	LGB7	1.235
		2	RF7	1.230	RF7	1.206	RF7	1.168	RF7	1.227
		3	XGB7	1.162	XGB7	1.180	XGB7	1.156	XGB7	1.199
		4	TUR	0.731	TUR	0.361	TUR	0.880	TUR	0.854
		5	VA2	0.177	VA2	−0.368	VA2	0.760	VA2	0.638
		6	VA1	−1.113	VA1	−0.455	COP	−1.439	COP	−1.656
		7	COP	−2.728	COP	−2.781	VA1	−2.823	VA1	−2.643

Table 14. Comparison of the empirical models with conventional ML models (Sub-humid).

		Faizabad		Jabalpur		Raipur		Ranchi		Ranichauri		Samastipur	
Inputs used	RANK	MODEL	GPI	MODEL	GPI	MODEL	GPI	MODEL	GPI	MODEL	GPI	MODEL	GPI
T_{max}, T_{min}, RH, U_2	1	LGB13	1.535	LGB13	1.502	LGB13	1.523	LGB13	1.860	LGB13	1.763	LGB13	1.425
	2	RF13	1.517	RF13	1.465	RF13	1.498	RF13	1.746	RF13	1.705	RF13	1.404
	3	XGB13	1.507	XGB13	1.458	XGB13	1.487	XGB13	1.690	XGB13	1.668	XGB13	1.317
	4	PEN	−0.909	PEN	−0.982	PEN	−0.970	PEN	−1.665	ALB	−1.308	PEN	−0.827
	5	MAH	−1.687	MAH	−1.336	MAH	−1.433	ALB	−1.720	MAH	−1.590	MAH	−1.464
	6	ALB	−1.962	ALB	−2.107	ALB	−2.104	MAH	−1.910	PEN	−2.237	ALB	−1.854
T_{max}, T_{min}, R_s	1	LGB5	1.303	LGB5	1.210	LGB5	1.280	LGB5	0.960	LGB5	0.913	LGB5	1.536
	2	RF5	1.211	RF5	1.175	RF5	1.253	RF5	0.924	RF5	0.882	RF5	1.496
	3	XGB5	1.196	XGB5	1.156	XGB5	1.189	XGB5	0.918	XGB5	0.881	XGB5	1.490
	4	JH	0.465	PT	0.064	PT	0.002	PT	0.582	MAK	0.424	JH	−0.090
	5	PT	−0.483	JH	−0.131	JH	−0.141	MAK	0.159	JH	0.058	PT	−0.749
	6	MAK	−1.162	MAK	−0.684	MAK	−0.862	JH	−0.503	PT	−0.071	MAK	−1.365
	7	MGB	−2.530	MGB	−2.790	MGB	−2.720	MGB	−3.040	MGB	−3.087	MGB	−2.318
T_{max}, T_{min}, R_a	1	LGB6	1.866	LGB6	1.741	LGB6	1.716	LGB6	1.517	LGB6	1.138	LGB6	1.917
	2	XGB6	1.615	RF6	1.613	RF6	1.531	RF6	1.280	RF6	0.992	XGB6	1.559
	3	RF6	1.593	XGB6	1.539	XGB6	1.523	XGB6	1.226	XGB6	0.960	RF6	1.535
	4	HS	−0.667	HS	−0.636	HS	−0.367	HS	−0.514	HS	0.522	HS	−0.772
	5	HS1	−1.265	THO	−1.342	HS1	−1.161	THO	−0.632	HS2	0.036	HS1	−1.147
	6	HS2	−1.365	HS1	−1.386	HS2	−1.201	HS1	−1.429	HS1	−0.785	HS2	−1.246
	7	THO	−1.777	HS2	−1.530	THO	−2.040	HS2	−1.448	THO	−2.862	THO	−1.845
T_{max}, T_{min}, RH, R_s	1	LGB7	0.946	LGB7	1.071	RF7	1.063	LGB7	1.156	LGB7	0.979	LGB7	1.141
	2	RF7	0.938	RF7	1.063	LGB7	1.061	RF7	1.132	RF7	0.966	RF7	1.131
	3	XGB7	0.875	XGB7	1.039	XGB7	1.021	XGB7	1.103	XGB7	0.962	XGB7	1.120
	4	TUR	0.477	TUR	0.675	TUR	0.544	TUR	0.724	VA2	0.794	TUR	0.143
	5	VA2	0.275	VA2	0.436	VA2	0.387	VA2	0.441	TUR	0.776	VA2	−0.028
	6	COP	−0.457	COP	−1.354	COP	−1.139	VA1	−1.982	COP	−2.163	COP	−0.648
	7	VA1	−3.054	VA1	−2.929	VA1	−2.937	COP	−2.574	VA1	−2.312	VA1	−2.859

3.4. Comparison of Various Input Combinations in GWO Hybrid ML Models

3.4.1. Best-Performing Models in Hybrid ML

The results of the best hyperparameters in each of the models are attached in Tables S13 to S18. These hyperparameters were used to develop the hybrid ML models at all the stations of humid and sub-humid zones. The statistical indicators at each of the stations using the hybrid ML models are given in Tables S19–S28. The six accurate models in each of the ML models were employed in assessing the best-performing models. The ranking of the best of all the hybrid ML models and their combinations at humid locations based on the GPI is shown in Table 15. The results indicated that the models that used the most inputs (Index 17 and 18) were superior with higher GPI. The GWOXGB17 and GWOXGB18 performed best in all the stations, whereas the GWOLGB18 was the second best at Palampur and Thrissur. It was observed that indices 7, 8, and 9, which solar radiation data performed better in most of the stations. The superiority of RF models in these combinations was observed in all the stations except at Thrissur. The performance of the model GWOXGB18 at Thrissur was the best of the models with an RMSE of 0.073 mm/day and R^2 of 0.997.

Of the 54 hybrid models evaluated, the eighteen best-ranking hybrid ML models at sub-humid locations are shown in Table 16. The performance of the models was in the order of indices: 17, 18, and 16 at the Faizabad, Jabalpur, and Raipur stations. The accuracy of the models with indices 7, 8, and 9 is also high compared to the models that used a higher number of inputs. This could be attributed to the incorporation of solar radiation data. The model indices 15 and 13 also found a place in the best-performing models, with wind speed as a common input. The lowest RMSE (0.083 mm/day) was observed at Ranichauri, which used GWOLGB17, while the R^2 was found to be the highest (0.997) at Jabalpur for both GWOLGB18 and GWOLGB17. The overall performance of the hybrid models is in the order of GWOXGB > GWOLGB > GWORF at most stations.

Table 15. Ranking of the best-performing GWO–ML models at humid stations.

	Jorhat		Mohanpur		Palampur		Thrissur	
RANK	MODEL	GPI	MODEL	GPI	MODEL	GPI	MODEL	GPI
1	GWOXGB17	2.175	GWOXGB17	2.176	GWOXGB18	2.078	GWOXGB18	1.376
2	GWOXGB18	2.134	GWOXGB18	2.072	GWOLGB18	2.078	GWOLGB18	1.360
3	GWOLGB18	1.843	GWOLGB17	2.052	GWOXGB17	2.038	GWOXGB17	1.287
4	GWOLGB17	1.747	GWOLGB18	1.798	GWOLGB17	2.030	GWOLGB17	1.271
5	GWOXGB8	0.854	GWORF17	1.209	GWORF18	1.621	GWORF17	0.820
6	GWORF17	0.530	GWORF18	1.079	GWORF17	1.466	GWORF18	0.687
7	GWOLGB8	0.469	GWOXGB8	0.812	GWOXGB7	−0.197	GWOLGB16	0.220
8	GWORF18	0.313	GWOLGB8	0.731	GWOLGB7	−0.207	GWOXGB16	0.183
9	GWORF8	0.041	GWORF8	0.421	GWORF7	−0.252	GWOLGB8	0.101
10	GWORF9	−0.167	GWORF9	0.357	GWOLGB16	−0.457	GWOXGB8	0.059
11	GWOLGB12	−0.835	GWOLGB9	−1.312	GWOXGB16	−0.468	GWORF16	−0.103
12	GWOLGB9	−0.886	GWOXGB9	−1.368	GWORF16	−0.705	GWORF8	−0.123
13	GWOXGB9	−0.912	GWOLGB12	−1.496	GWOLGB8	−1.258	GWORF9	−0.203
14	GWORF12	−0.971	GWORF12	−1.599	GWORF8	−1.295	GWOXGB15	−0.513
15	GWOXGB12	−0.983	GWOLGB7	−1.673	GWORF9	−1.318	GWOLGB15	−0.538
16	GWOLGB7	−1.765	GWOXGB12	−1.726	GWOXGB8	−1.372	GWORF15	−0.650
17	GWOXGB7	−1.782	GWOXGB7	−1.749	GWOLGB12	−1.861	GWOLGB7	−2.610
18	GWORF7	−1.807	GWORF7	−1.786	GWOXGB12	−1.922	GWOXGB7	−2.624

3.4.2. Least Performing Models in Hybrid ML

The least-performing models of the hybrid ML at humid stations are presented in Table 17. The six least accurate models in each hybrid ML, i.e., GWORF, GWOXGB, and GWOLGB, were used to analyse all the combinations. The models with the lowest GPI values were found in the order of the model indices 1, 3, and 6 in all the hybrid ML at most stations. The models with indices 10 and 11 that used extra-terrestrial radiation as input were also placed in the least-ranking hybrid models at all the stations. There was no specific order found in the accuracy of the various models. The performance ranking of the least accurate hybrid models is given in Table 18. The model GWORF1 at Thrissur station gave the highest RMSE (0.812 mm/day) of all the models, whereas the lowest R^2 (0.478) was observed at Jorhat stations with the same model combination.

The least ranked models in the sub-humid stations were similar to that of the results of humid stations. Models 1, 2, 3, and 6 were the least accurate in most sub-humid locations. Of the four input combination methods, the models with the indices 10, 14, 11, and 13 found a place in the least ranked models. The performance of the different hybrid models did not show any specific trend at this level of comparison in all the stations. The error was observed highest (1.154 mm/day) at Faizabad for both GWOLGB1 and GWOXGB1. The R^2 was found to be the least at Samastipur station, with a value of 0.693. The RF models have got the advantage of improving their efficiency by the hyperparameter tuning by GWO than the XGB and LGB models.

Table 16. Ranking of the best-performing GWO–ML models at sub-humid stations.

RANK	Faizabad MODEL	GPI	Jabalpur MODEL	GPI	Raipur MODEL	GPI	Ranchi MODEL	GPI	Ranichauri MODEL	GPI	Samastipur MODEL	GPI
1	GWOXGB17	1.865	GWOLGB18	1.366	GWOXGB17	1.412	GWOXGB18	1.856	GWOLGB17	2.504	GWOXGB17	1.985
2	GWOXGB18	1.855	GWOXGB18	1.361	GWOXGB18	1.384	GWOXGB17	1.847	GWOXGB17	2.486	GWOLGB17	1.982
3	GWOLGB17	1.826	GWOLGB17	1.360	GWOLGB17	1.332	GWOLGB17	1.747	GWOLGB18	2.476	GWOXGB18	1.883
4	GWOLGB18	1.759	GWOXGB17	1.350	GWOLGB18	1.310	GWOLGB18	1.696	GWOXGB18	2.439	GWOLGB18	1.868
5	GWORF17	1.207	GWORF17	0.900	GWORF17	0.929	GWORF17	0.996	GWORF18	1.547	GWORF17	1.286
6	GWORF18	1.160	GWORF18	0.877	GWORF18	0.866	GWORF18	0.947	GWORF17	1.393	GWORF18	0.985
7	GWOLGB16	0.215	GWOLGB16	0.378	GWOXGB16	0.519	GWOXGB8	0.348	GWOLGB7	0.060	GWOLGB8	0.186
8	GWOXGB16	0.176	GWOXGB16	0.358	GWOLGB16	0.483	GWOLGB8	0.321	GWOXGB7	0.054	GWOXGB8	0.122
9	GWOLGB8	−0.214	GWORF16	0.007	GWORF16	0.149	GWORF8	0.166	GWORF7	−0.176	GWORF8	0.011
10	GWOXGB8	−0.255	GWOXGB8	−0.009	GWOLGB8	−0.113	GWORF9	0.063	GWOLGB8	−1.359	GWORF9	0.004
11	GWORF8	−0.359	GWOLGB8	−0.013	GWOXGB8	−0.142	GWOXGB16	−0.338	GWOXGB8	−1.365	GWOLGB16	−0.653
12	GWORF9	−0.376	GWORF8	−0.092	GWORF8	−0.259	GWOLGB16	−0.423	GWOLGB9	−1.369	GWOXGB16	−0.762
13	GWORF16	−0.447	GWORF9	−0.201	GWORF9	−0.363	GWORF16	−0.904	GWOLGB12	−1.399	GWORF16	−0.894
14	GWOXGB15	−1.269	GWOXGB15	−0.724	GWOXGB15	−0.730	GWOXGB15	−1.253	GWOXGB9	−1.422	GWOXGB7	−1.330
15	GWOLGB15	−1.325	GWOLGB15	−0.764	GWOLGB15	−0.762	GWOLGB15	−1.304	GWOXGB12	−1.455	GWOLGB7	−1.357
16	GWORF15	−1.679	GWORF15	−0.898	GWORF15	−0.903	GWORF15	−1.488	GWORF9	−1.457	GWORF7	−1.475
17	GWOXGB13	−2.011	GWOLGB13	−2.625	GWOXGB13	−2.522	GWOLGB12	−2.131	GWORF12	−1.464	GWOLGB15	−1.837
18	GWOLGB13	−2.128	GWOXGB13	−2.630	GWOLGB13	−2.588	GWOXGB12	−2.144	GWORF8	−1.496	GWOXGB9	−2.001

Table 17. Ranking of the least-performing GWO–ML models at humid stations.

RANK	Jorhat		Mohanpur		Palampur		Thrissur	
	MODEL	GPI	MODEL	GPI	MODEL	GPI	MODEL	GPI
54	GWORF1	−1.832	GWOXGB1	−2.195	GWOXGB1	−2.715	GWOXGB1	−2.220
53	GWOLGB1	−1.798	GWOLGB1	−2.163	GWOLGB1	−2.690	GWORF1	−2.217
52	GWOXGB1	−1.789	GWORF1	−2.158	GWORF1	−2.666	GWOLGB1	−2.183
51	GWOLGB3	−0.965	GWORF2	−1.330	GWOXGB3	−0.542	GWORF6	−1.687
50	GWORF3	−0.944	GWOLGB2	−1.314	GWOLGB3	−0.523	GWOLGB6	−1.648
49	GWOXGB3	−0.802	GWOXGB2	−1.142	GWORF3	−0.513	GWOXGB6	−1.584
48	GWORF6	−0.413	GWORF3	−0.257	GWORF6	−0.002	GWORF2	0.139
47	GWOXGB6	−0.361	GWOXGB3	0.095	GWOXGB6	0.044	GWOLGB2	0.172
46	GWOLGB6	−0.339	GWOLGB3	0.159	GWOLGB6	0.131	GWOXGB2	0.180
45	GWORF11	−0.271	GWORF6	0.487	GWORF4	0.922	GWORF10	0.422
44	GWOLGB11	−0.189	GWOLGB6	0.576	GWOXGB4	0.924	GWOLGB10	0.475
43	GWOXGB11	0.065	GWOXGB6	0.600	GWOXGB11	0.953	GWOXGB10	0.490
42	GWORF2	1.016	GWORF13	0.955	GWOLGB4	0.957	GWORF3	1.447
41	GWOLGB2	1.072	GWOLGB13	1.301	GWORF11	1.066	GWOLGB3	1.495
40	GWOXGB2	1.139	GWOXGB13	1.362	GWOLGB11	1.070	GWOXGB3	1.503
39	GWORF10	2.119	GWORF10	1.560	GWORF2	1.108	GWORF11	1.711
38	GWOLGB10	2.134	GWOLGB10	1.679	GWOXGB2	1.234	GWOXGB13	1.727
37	GWOXGB10	2.157	GWOXGB11	1.786	GWOLGB2	1.241	GWOLGB13	1.777

Table 18. Ranking of the least-performing GWO–ML models at sub-humid stations.

	Faizabad		Jabalpur		Raipur		Ranchi		Ranichauri		Samastipur	
RANK	MODEL	GPI	MODEL	GPI	MODEL	GPI	MODEL	GPI	MODEL	GPI	MODEL	GPI
54	GWOXGB1	−2.067	GWOXGB1	−2.069	GWOXGB1	−2.052	GWOXGB2	−1.696	GWOLGB1	−2.296	GWOLGB1	−2.328
53	GWOLGB1	−2.059	GWORF1	−2.025	GWOLGB1	−2.029	GWOLGB2	−1.618	GWORF1	−2.272	GWORF1	−2.322
52	GWORF1	−1.942	GWOLGB1	−2.018	GWORF1	−1.977	GWORF2	−1.599	GWOXGB1	−2.257	GWOXGB1	−2.276
51	GWORF6	−0.563	GWORF2	−1.151	GWOXGB2	−0.901	GWOXGB1	−1.542	GWORF3	−1.348	GWORF6	−0.666
50	GWOLGB2	−0.460	GWOXGB2	−1.084	GWORF2	−0.900	GWORF1	−1.535	GWOLGB3	−1.296	GWOLGB6	−0.583
49	GWOLGB6	−0.404	GWOLGB2	−1.063	GWOLGB2	−0.853	GWOLGB1	−1.535	GWOXGB3	−1.218	GWOXGB6	−0.552
48	GWOXGB2	−0.402	GWOXGB6	−0.375	GWOLGB6	−0.579	GWORF10	−0.354	GWORF2	0.031	GWOXGB2	−0.230
47	GWOXGB6	−0.373	GWORF6	−0.300	GWOXGB6	−0.548	GWORF6	−0.304	GWOXGB2	0.032	GWORF2	−0.195
46	GWORF2	−0.252	GWOLGB6	−0.273	GWORF6	−0.514	GWOXGB10	−0.148	GWOLGB2	0.046	GWOLGB2	−0.165
45	GWORF4	−0.238	GWOXGB10	0.356	GWOXGB10	0.422	GWOLGB10	−0.106	GWORF6	0.776	GWOXGB3	0.321
44	GWOXGB4	−0.143	GWORF10	0.462	GWORF10	0.429	GWOXGB6	−0.023	GWOLGB6	0.790	GWOLGB3	0.337
43	GWOLGB4	−0.139	GWOLGB10	0.503	GWOLGB10	0.534	GWOLGB6	0.035	GWOXGB6	0.799	GWORF3	0.368
42	GWOXGB14	1.105	GWORF4	1.126	GWORF4	1.036	GWORF3	1.161	GWORF13	0.956	GWORF11	1.073
41	GWOLGB14	1.180	GWOXGB4	1.265	GWOLGB4	1.083	GWOXGB3	1.365	GWOLGB13	1.136	GWOXGB11	1.127
40	GWORF14	1.239	GWOLGB4	1.286	GWOXGB4	1.108	GWOLGB3	1.404	GWOXGB13	1.143	GWOLGB11	1.240
39	GWOXGB10	1.791	GWORF14	1.757	GWOXGB14	1.904	GWORF13	1.959	GWORF11	1.640	GWORF10	1.534
38	GWORF5	1.817	GWOXGB14	1.782	GWORF14	1.915	GWOXGB13	2.237	GWOXGB11	1.645	GWOLGB10	1.651
37	GWOLGB10	1.909	GWOLGB3	1.823	GWOLGB14	1.922	GWOLGB13	2.299	GWOLGB11	1.692	GWOXGB10	1.665

3.5. Best-Performing Models across Conventional and Hybrid MLs

Table 19 depicts the best 36 models out of 108 models that compare all the conventional and hybrid ML at humid locations. The plots showing the RMSE and R^2 at different locations in the humid region are shown in Figures 4 and 5, respectively. The results indicate that the hybrid models outperformed their conventional ML counterparts in most of the combinations. The models that used the six inputs were the superior, followed by the models with indices 7, 8, 9, 16, and 12. The accuracy of the XGB and LGB models was higher than RF models at almost all stations. The use of solar radiation could be attributed to the excellent performance of models 7, 8, and 9 than the other models that have employed more inputs.

Table 19. Ranking of the best-performing models in conventional and hybrid MLs at humid stations.

	Jorhat		Mohanpur		Palampur		Thrissur	
RANK	MODEL	GPI	MODEL	GPI	MODEL	GPI	MODEL	GPI
1	GWOXGB17	2.031	GWOXGB17	2.077	GWOXGB18	1.953	GWOXGB18	1.302
2	GWOXGB18	1.995	GWOXGB18	1.982	GWOLGB18	1.953	GWOLGB18	1.288
3	GWOLGB18	1.740	GWOLGB17	1.964	GWOXGB17	1.916	GWOXGB17	1.222
4	GWOLGB17	1.656	GWOLGB18	1.732	GWOLGB17	1.909	GWOLGB17	1.207
5	XGB17	1.538	XGB17	1.635	LGB18	1.810	LGB18	1.062
6	XGB18	1.419	LGB17	1.633	LGB17	1.754	LGB17	1.051
7	LGB17	1.388	LGB18	1.439	XGB18	1.642	XGB17	1.025
8	LGB18	1.388	XGB18	1.413	XGB17	1.621	XGB18	0.987
9	GWOXGB8	0.869	GWORF17	1.193	GWORF18	1.537	GWORF17	0.799
10	GWORF17	0.589	RF17	1.176	RF18	1.528	RF17	0.793
11	RF17	0.579	GWORF18	1.075	GWORF17	1.395	GWORF18	0.679
12	GWOLGB8	0.533	RF18	1.054	RF17	1.376	RF18	0.661
13	XGB8	0.533	GWOXGB8	0.829	GWOXGB7	−0.110	GWOLGB16	0.252
14	LGB8	0.510	GWOLGB8	0.755	GWOLGB7	−0.119	GWOXGB16	0.220
15	GWORF18	0.399	LGB8	0.673	LGB7	−0.129	LGB16	0.152
16	RF18	0.392	XGB8	0.540	GWORF7	−0.159	GWOLGB8	0.150
17	GWORF8	0.159	GWORF8	0.473	RF7	−0.210	GWOXGB8	0.112
18	RF8	0.148	RF9	0.454	XGB7	−0.318	LGB8	0.063
19	RF9	0.144	RF8	0.445	GWOLGB16	−0.348	XGB16	0.015
20	GWORF9	−0.023	GWORF9	0.414	GWOXGB16	−0.358	XGB8	0.005
21	GWOLGB12	−0.607	GWOLGB9	−1.103	LGB16	−0.393	GWORF16	−0.037
22	GWOLGB9	−0.652	GWOXGB9	−1.154	GWORF16	−0.571	GWORF8	−0.050
23	GWOXGB9	−0.675	LGB9	−1.169	RF16	−0.577	RF16	−0.065
24	GWORF12	−0.726	GWOLGB12	−1.270	XGB16	−0.673	RF8	−0.069
25	GWOXGB12	−0.736	LGB12	−1.313	GWOLGB8	−1.068	RF9	−0.075
26	LGB12	−0.739	GWORF12	−1.363	GWORF8	−1.101	GWORF9	−0.123
27	LGB9	−0.762	RF12	−1.376	LGB8	−1.102	GWOXGB15	−0.407
28	RF12	−1.040	GWOLGB7	−1.433	GWORF9	−1.122	GWOLGB15	−0.430
29	XGB9	−1.208	LGB7	−1.469	GWOXGB8	−1.171	LGB15	−0.445
30	XGB12	−1.288	GWOXGB12	−1.478	RF8	−1.218	GWORF15	−0.529
31	GWOLGB7	−1.422	GWOXGB7	−1.501	RF9	−1.238	RF15	−0.561
32	GWOXGB7	−1.436	GWORF7	−1.535	XGB8	−1.394	XGB15	−0.581
33	GWORF7	−1.458	XGB9	−1.537	GWOLGB12	−1.611	GWOLGB7	−2.275
34	LGB7	−1.564	RF7	−1.617	GWOXGB12	−1.665	GWOXGB7	−2.288
35	RF7	−1.717	XGB12	−1.712	LGB12	−1.694	LGB7	−2.413
36	XGB7	−1.958	XGB7	−1.923	XGB12	−2.047	XGB7	−2.698

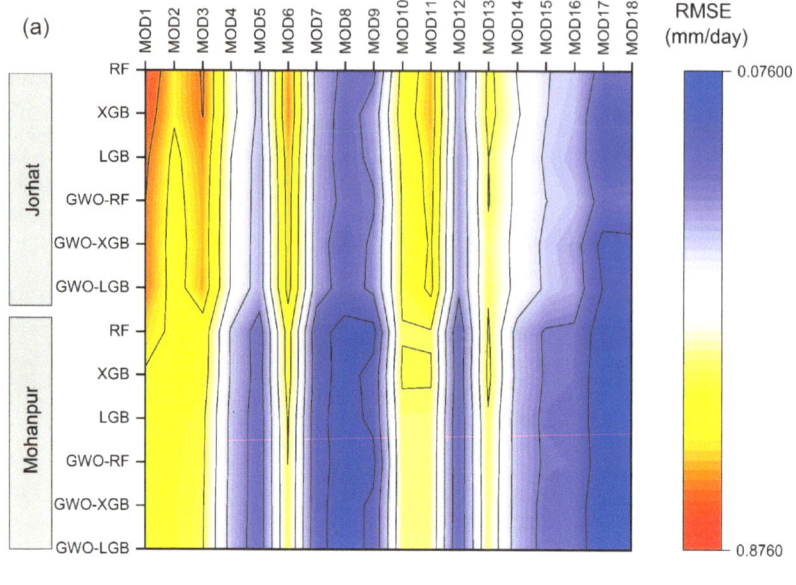
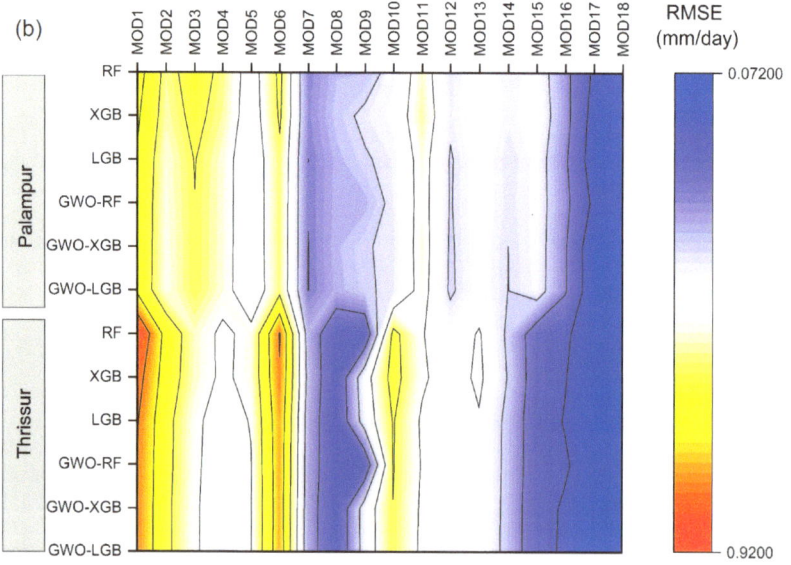

Figure 4. RMSE (mm/day) at humid locations of all ML models at (**a**) Jorhat, and Mohanpur; (**b**) Palampur, and Thrissur.

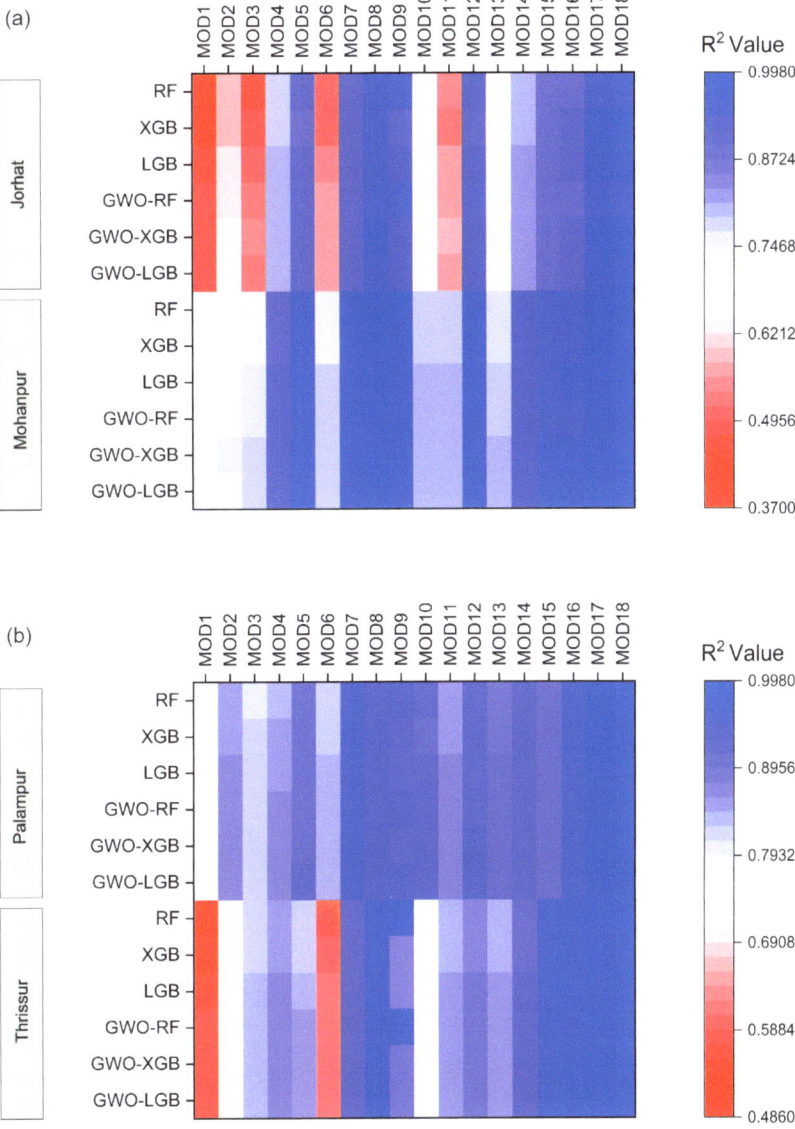

Figure 5. R^2 values at humid locations of all ML models at (**a**) Jorhat, and Mohanpur; (**b**) Palampur, and Thrissur.

The results of the overall best-performing models in conventional and hybrid models at the sub-humid stations are presented in Table 20. The plots showing the RMSE and R^2 at different locations in the humid region are shown in Figures 6 and 7, respectively. The observed results at the sub-humid locations were in good resonance with that of the humid locations. The models with indices 17, 18, and 16 were also predicting with greater accuracy at these locations. The solar radiation data used in models 7, 8, and 9 were also ranked best in comparison. The application of GWO has improved the accuracy of the ML models in all the combinations at all stations. The higher GPI values were observed in LGB and XGB when compared with the RF models using a similar set of inputs.

Table 20. Ranking of the best-performing models in conventional and hybrid MLs at sub-humid stations.

RANK	Faizabad MODEL	GPI	Jabalpur MODEL	GPI	Raipur MODEL	GPI	Ranchi MODEL	GPI	Ranichauri MODEL	GPI	Samastipur MODEL	GPI
1	GWOXGB17	1.810	GWOLGB18	1.315	GWOXGB17	1.368	GWOXGB18	1.739	GWOLGB17	2.383	GWOXGB17	1.944
2	GWOXGB18	1.801	GWOXGB18	1.311	GWOXGB18	1.343	GWOXGB17	1.731	GWOXGB17	2.366	GWOLGB17	1.941
3	GWOLGB17	1.774	GWOLGB17	1.310	GWOLGB17	1.295	GWOLGB17	1.642	GWOLGB18	2.357	GWOXGB18	1.847
4	GWOLGB18	1.711	GWOXGB17	1.301	GWOLGB18	1.273	GWOLGB18	1.595	GWOXGB18	2.323	GWOLGB18	1.834
5	LGB17	1.556	LGB18	1.146	LGB18	1.120	LGB17	1.434	LGB17	2.136	LGB17	1.726
6	LGB18	1.491	LGB17	1.104	LGB17	1.105	XGB17	1.394	LGB18	2.069	LGB18	1.644
7	XGB17	1.443	XGB18	1.025	XGB18	1.056	LGB18	1.369	XGB17	1.980	XGB17	1.588
8	XGB18	1.378	XGB17	1.023	XGB17	1.052	XGB18	1.352	XGB18	1.818	XGB18	1.421
9	RF17	1.203	GWORF17	0.887	GWORF17	0.921	RF17	0.985	GWORF18	1.505	GWORF17	1.284
10	GWORF17	1.199	RF17	0.887	RF17	0.907	GWORF17	0.964	RF18	1.499	RF17	1.245
11	GWORF18	1.155	GWORF18	0.866	GWORF18	0.863	GWORF18	0.921	GWORF17	1.364	GWORF18	1.002
12	RF18	1.155	RF18	0.860	RF18	0.849	RF18	0.910	RF17	1.347	RF18	0.909
13	GWOLGB16	0.278	GWOLGB16	0.406	GWOXGB16	0.540	GWOXGB8	0.382	GWOLGB7	0.144	GWOLGB8	0.247
14	GWOXGB16	0.241	GWOXGB16	0.388	GWOLGB16	0.507	GWOLGB8	0.358	GWOXGB7	0.139	LGB8	0.194
15	LGB16	0.073	LGB16	0.270	LGB16	0.381	LGB8	0.357	LGB7	0.114	GWOXGB8	0.187
16	XGB16	−0.103	XGB16	0.125	XGB16	0.241	RF8	0.226	GWORF7	−0.071	GWORF8	0.083
17	GWOXGB8	−0.119	GWORF16	0.066	GWORF16	0.199	GWORF8	0.219	RF7	−0.094	GWORF9	0.077
18	GWOLGB8	−0.157	GWOXGB8	0.053	RF16	0.169	RF9	0.210	XGB7	−0.156	RF9	0.055
19	LGB8	−0.196	GWOLGB8	0.050	GWOLGB8	−0.042	XGB8	0.189	GWOLGB8	−1.152	RF8	0.048
20	RF9	−0.225	RF16	0.045	GWOXGB8	−0.069	GWORF9	0.127	GWOXGB8	−1.158	XGB8	−0.038
21	GWORF8	−0.253	LGB8	0.014	LGB8	−0.128	GWOXGB16	−0.234	GWOLGB9	−1.161	GWOLGB16	−0.541
22	RF8	−0.262	GWORF8	−0.022	GWORF8	−0.175	GWOLGB16	−0.310	LGB9	−1.178	LGB16	−0.627
23	GWORF9	−0.269	RF8	−0.047	RF9	−0.185	LGB16	−0.432	LGB8	−1.183	GWOXGB16	−0.642
24	RF16	−0.335	RF9	−0.047	RF8	−0.193	XGB16	−0.624	GWOLGB12	−1.189	GWORF16	−0.767
25	XGB8	−0.348	GWORF9	−0.121	XGB8	−0.243	GWORF16	−0.741	GWOXGB9	−1.210	RF16	−0.779
26	GWOXGB15	−0.358	XGB8	−0.135	GWORF9	−0.272	RF16	−0.760	GWOXGB12	−1.240	XGB16	−0.913
27	GWOLGB15	−1.096	GWOXGB15	−0.602	GWOXGB15	−0.612	GWOXGB15	−1.053	GWORF9	−1.242	GWOXGB7	−1.176
28	LGB15	−1.148	GWOLGB15	−0.638	LGB15	−0.631	GWOLGB15	−1.098	GWORF12	−1.248	GWOLGB7	−1.201
29	XGB15	−1.196	LGB15	−0.644	GWOLGB15	−0.642	LGB15	−1.118	LGB12	−1.252	LGB7	−1.219
30	GWORF15	−1.445	GWORF15	−0.760	GWORF15	−0.771	GWORF15	−1.263	GWORF8	−1.277	GWORF7	−1.312
31	RF15	−1.476	RF15	−0.798	RF15	−0.785	RF15	−1.323	RF9	−1.366	RF7	−1.355
32	GWOXGB13	−1.501	XGB15	−0.871	XGB15	−0.860	XGB15	−1.326	RF8	−1.393	XGB7	−1.495
33	GWOLGB13	−1.783	GWOXGB13	−2.335	GWOXGB13	−2.261	GWOLGB12	−1.831	RF12	−1.420	GWOLGB15	−1.653
34	LGB13	−1.891	GWOLGB13	−2.340	GWOLGB13	−2.322	GWOXGB12	−1.843	XGB9	−1.461	LGB15	−1.695
35	XGB13	−1.923	LGB13	−2.411	LGB13	−2.368	LGB12	−1.888	XGB8	−1.475	GWOXGB9	−1.805
36	XGB13	−2.183	XGB13	−2.684	XGB13	−2.632	XGB12	−2.261	XGB12	−1.617	XGB12	−2.054

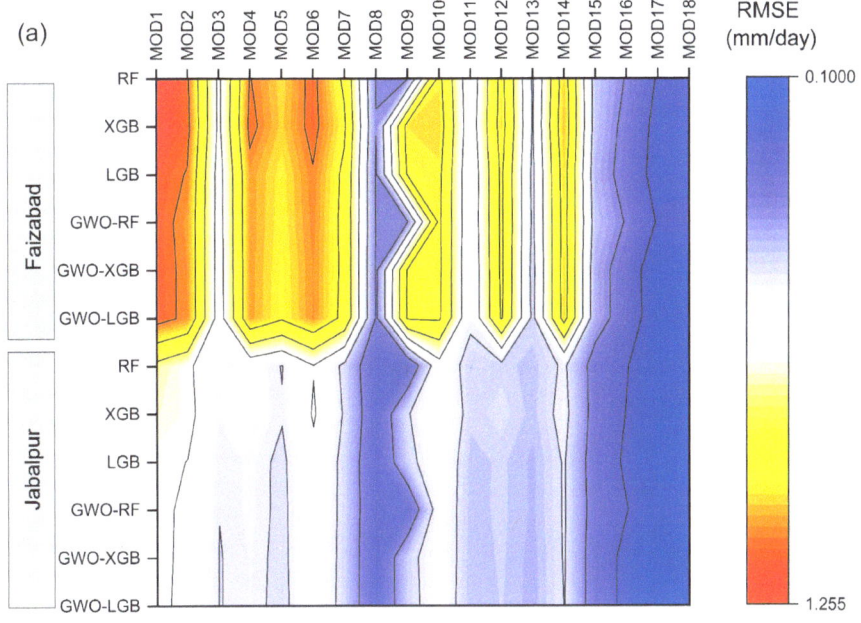

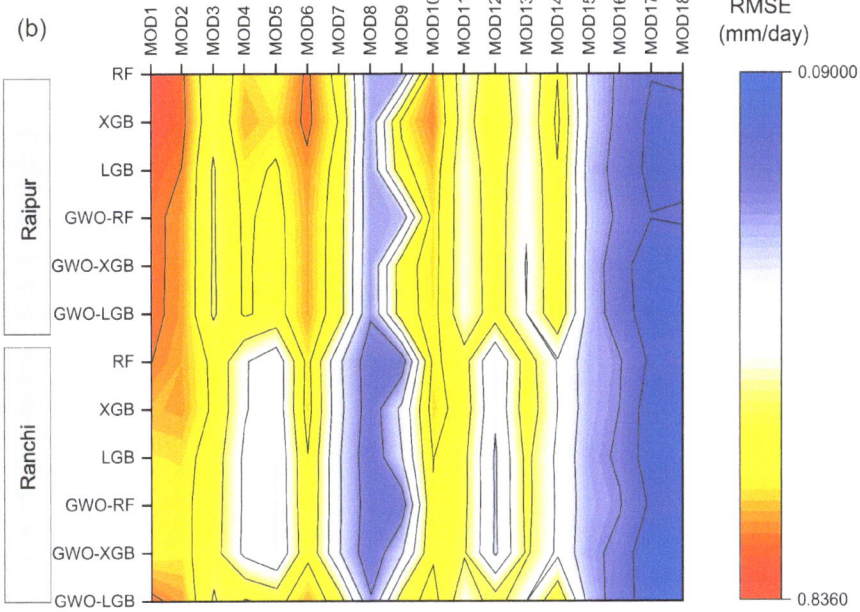

Figure 6. Cont.

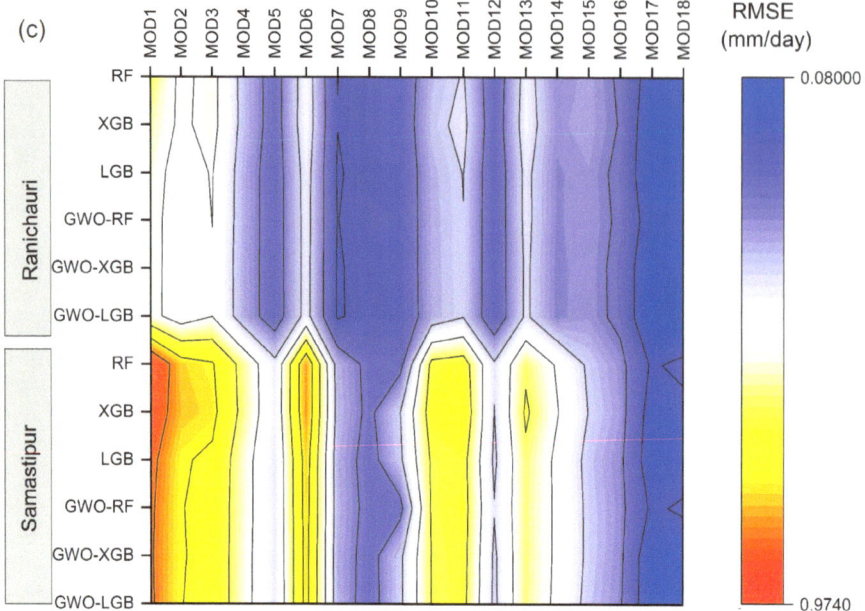

Figure 6. RMSE (mm/day) at sub-humid locations of all ML models at (**a**) Faizabad, and Jabalpur; (**b**) Raipur, and Ranchi; (**c**) Ranichauri, and Samastipur.

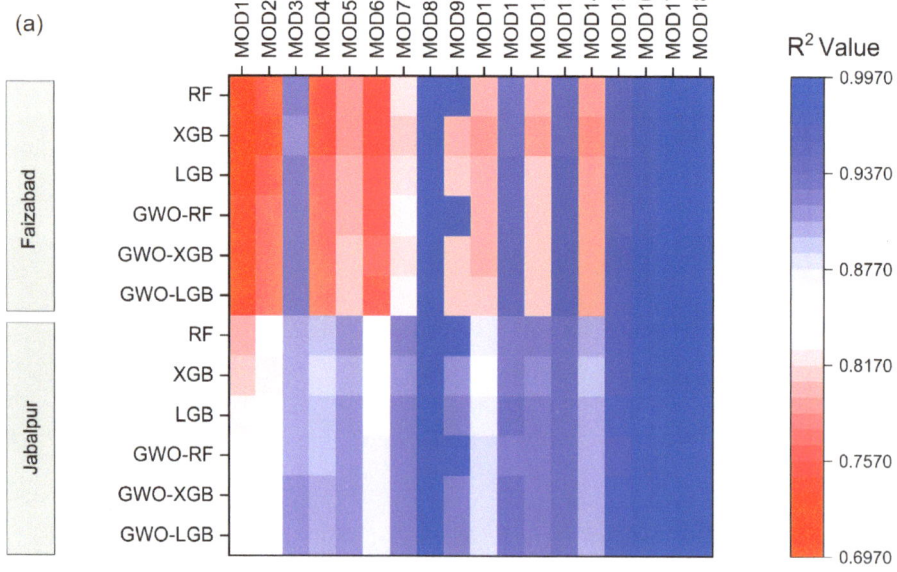

Figure 7. *Cont.*

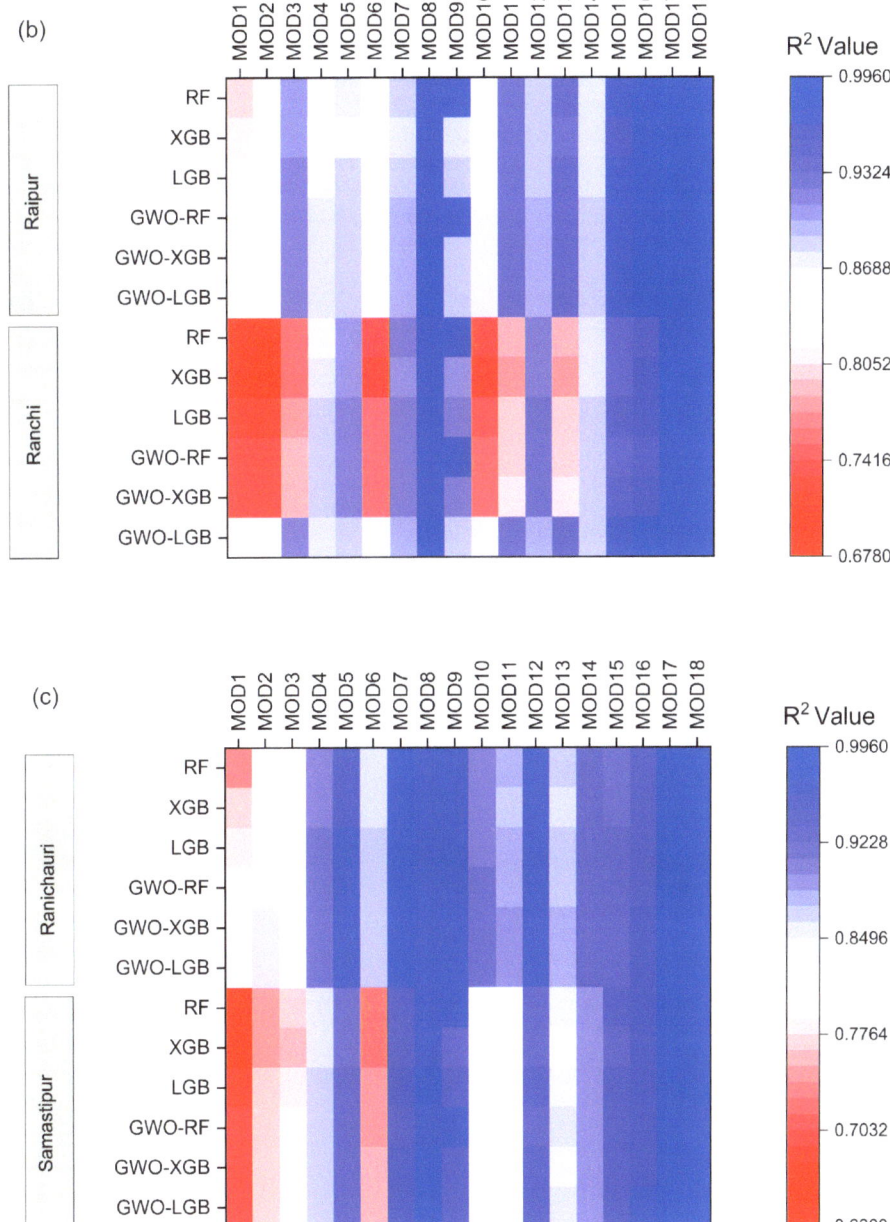

Figure 7. R^2 values at sub-humid locations of all ML models at (**a**) Faizabad, and Jabalpur; (**b**) Raipur, and Ranchi; (**c**) Ranichauri, and Samastipur.

3.6. Least-Performing Models across Conventional and Hybrid MLs

Based on the least GPI values, the six least-performing models from each conventional and hybrid ML model were combined to assess the ranking of all the models. Table 21 illustrates the worst ranking models at the humid stations. It was observed from the results that the models with indices 1, 2, 3, and 6 were found to be the least-ranked models. The conventional ML models were less accurate than their hybrid models. In most instances, the XGB and LGB models were slightly more accurate than the RF models. A similar observation was noted at sub-humid locations, tabulated in Table 22. The combination of inputs that consisted of two and three inputs was the least ranked at almost all the stations. The advantage of using hybrid models could be seen with the higher GPI values of those models than the conventional ML models. The results at sub-humid locations also indicate the inferior accuracy of RF when compared to the boosting models, i.e., LGB and XGB. The addition of extra-terrestrial radiation did not increase the accuracy of the models to a greater extent, which could be observed from the model indices 10 and 11 securing least ranking than other 4-input combination models.

Table 21. Ranking of the least performing models in conventional and hybrid ML at humid stations.

RANK	Jorhat		Mohanpur		Palampur		Thrissur	
	MODEL	GPI	MODEL	GPI	MODEL	GPI	MODEL	GPI
108	RF1	−2.443	RF1	−2.685	RF1	−2.858	RF1	−2.488
107	XGB1	−1.829	XGB1	−1.645	XGB1	−2.313	XGB1	−1.934
106	LGB1	−1.374	RF2	−1.357	LGB1	−1.909	LGB1	−1.620
105	GWORF1	−1.158	XGB2	−1.176	GWOXGB1	−1.811	GWOXGB1	−1.543
104	RF3	−1.150	LGB1	−1.066	GWOLGB1	−1.793	GWORF1	−1.541
103	GWOLGB1	−1.134	GWOXGB1	−0.891	GWORF1	−1.774	RF6	−1.530
102	GWOXGB1	−1.128	GWOLGB1	−0.875	RF3	−0.956	GWOLGB1	−1.515
101	XGB3	−1.001	GWORF1	−0.871	XGB3	−0.578	XGB6	−1.380
100	XGB6	−0.703	RF3	−0.703	RF6	−0.439	LGB6	−1.144
99	LGB3	−0.655	LGB2	−0.517	XGB6	−0.266	GWORF6	−1.143
98	RF6	−0.644	XGB3	−0.455	LGB3	−0.242	GWOLGB6	−1.114
97	GWOLGB3	−0.504	GWORF2	−0.413	GWOXGB3	−0.202	GWOXGB6	−1.066
96	GWORF3	−0.488	GWOLGB2	−0.405	GWOLGB3	−0.188	RF2	−0.120
95	GWOXGB3	−0.379	GWOXGB2	−0.310	GWORF3	−0.180	XGB2	−0.006
94	XGB11	−0.264	RF6	−0.292	LGB6	0.198	XGB10	0.210
93	RF11	−0.259	XGB6	−0.212	GWORF6	0.201	LGB2	0.211
92	LGB6	−0.200	XGB13	0.163	GWOXGB6	0.235	GWORF2	0.221
91	GWORF6	−0.078	GWORF3	0.180	RF4	0.281	RF10	0.239
90	GWOXGB6	−0.040	LGB3	0.182	GWOLGB6	0.299	GWOLGB2	0.246
89	LGB11	−0.025	RF13	0.367	RF2	0.386	GWOXGB2	0.252
88	GWOLGB6	−0.024	GWOXGB3	0.374	XGB4	0.481	GWORF10	0.431
87	GWORF11	0.028	GWOLGB3	0.409	XGB11	0.511	LGB10	0.442
86	GWOLGB11	0.090	LGB6	0.446	XGB2	0.580	GWOLGB10	0.470
85	GWOXGB11	0.284	XGB10	0.513	RF11	0.744	GWOXGB10	0.481
84	RF2	0.450	GWORF6	0.593	LGB4	0.873	RF3	0.971
83	XGB2	0.484	GWOLGB6	0.640	GWORF4	0.882	XGB3	0.989
82	LGB2	0.888	GWOXGB6	0.653	GWOXGB4	0.883	LGB3	1.189
81	GWORF2	1.004	RF10	0.756	GWOXGB11	0.906	GWORF3	1.192
80	GWOLGB2	1.045	LGB13	0.804	GWOLGB4	0.908	XGB13	1.226
79	GWOXGB2	1.097	GWORF13	0.848	LGB11	0.952	GWOLGB3	1.228
78	XGB10	1.359	GWOLGB13	1.038	LGB2	0.957	GWOXGB3	1.234
77	RF10	1.540	GWOXGB13	1.071	GWORF11	0.990	RF5	1.269
76	LGB10	1.695	LGB10	1.092	GWOLGB11	0.993	GWORF11	1.387
75	GWORF10	1.826	GWORF10	1.183	GWORF2	1.019	GWOXGB13	1.398
74	GWOLGB10	1.837	GWOLGB10	1.250	GWOXGB2	1.113	LGB5	1.423
73	GWOXGB10	1.854	GWOXGB11	1.312	GWOLGB2	1.118	GWOLGB13	1.435

Table 22. Ranking of the least-performing models in conventional and hybrid MLs at sub-humid stations.

RANK	Faizabad MODEL	GPI	Jabalpur MODEL	GPI	Raipur MODEL	GPI	Ranchi MODEL	GPI	Ranichauri MODEL	GPI	Samastipur MODEL	GPI
108	RF1	−2.488	RF1	−2.511	RF1	−2.473	RF1	−2.276	RF1	−2.703	RF1	−2.620
107	XGB1	−1.954	XGB1	−1.969	XGB1	−1.909	XGB2	−1.606	XGB1	−1.931	XGB1	−2.127
106	LGB1	−1.173	LGB1	−1.330	LGB1	−1.246	RF2	−1.498	LGB1	−1.471	LGB1	−1.656
105	GWOXGB1	−1.140	XGB2	−1.304	GWOXGB1	−1.036	XGB1	−1.449	GWOLGB1	−1.322	GWOLGB1	−1.492
104	GWOLGB1	−1.135	RF2	−1.126	GWOLGB1	−1.020	LGB2	−0.861	GWORF1	−1.305	GWORF1	−1.487
103	GWORF1	−1.058	GWOXGB1	−1.119	XGB2	−1.013	LGB1	−0.823	GWOXGB1	−1.295	GWOXGB1	−1.454
102	XGB2	−0.819	GWORF1	−1.090	GWORF1	−0.986	XGB10	−0.793	RF3	−1.233	RF6	−0.818
101	RF2	−0.679	GWOLGB1	−1.086	RF2	−0.889	XGB6	−0.735	XGB3	−1.215	XGB6	−0.789
100	RF6	−0.648	XGB6	−0.719	XGB6	−0.806	GWOXGB2	−0.690	LGB3	−0.772	XGB2	−0.488
99	XGB4	−0.618	LGB2	−0.695	RF6	−0.787	GWOLGB2	−0.643	GWORF3	−0.698	RF2	−0.379
98	XGB6	−0.599	GWORF2	−0.520	LGB2	−0.574	GWORF2	−0.631	GWOLGB3	−0.665	LGB6	−0.339
97	RF4	−0.394	RF6	−0.504	XGB10	−0.372	GWOXGB2	−0.597	GWOXGB3	−0.614	GWORF6	−0.293
96	LGB2	−0.253	GWOXGB2	−0.477	GWOXGB2	−0.297	GWOLGB1	−0.593	XGB2	−0.313	GWOLGB6	−0.234
95	LGB6	−0.167	GWOLGB2	−0.463	GWORF2	−0.296	GWORF1	−0.593	RF2	−0.258	GWOXGB6	−0.212
94	GWORF6	−0.139	LGB6	−0.127	GWOLGB2	−0.266	RF6	−0.591	LGB2	0.098	XGB3	−0.131
93	GWOXGB2	−0.075	XGB10	−0.100	LGB6	−0.212	RF10	−0.427	GWOXGB2	0.203	LGB2	−0.016
92	GWOXGB2	−0.036	GWOXGB6	−0.009	GWOLGB6	−0.088	LGB10	0.005	GWORF2	0.203	GWOXGB2	0.015
91	GWOLGB6	−0.034	GWORF6	0.040	GWOXGB6	−0.068	LGB6	0.066	GWOLGB2	0.213	RF3	0.035
90	GWOXGB6	−0.014	GWOLGB6	0.057	GWORF6	−0.044	GWORF10	0.121	XGB6	0.304	GWORF2	0.040
89	GWORF2	0.063	RF10	0.236	RF10	0.040	GWORF6	0.151	RF6	0.366	GWOLGB2	0.062
88	GWORF4	0.074	LGB10	0.354	XGB4	0.152	GWOXGB10	0.246	XGB13	0.445	LGB3	0.326
87	LGB4	0.106	GWOXGB10	0.468	LGB10	0.313	XGB3	0.267	RF13	0.592	GWOXGB3	0.412
86	GWOXGB4	0.137	GWORF10	0.536	RF4	0.405	GWOLGB10	0.271	LGB6	0.645	GWOLGB3	0.423
85	GWOLGB4	0.139	GWOLGB10	0.563	GWOXGB10	0.556	RF3	0.313	GWORF6	0.696	GWORF3	0.446
84	XGB14	0.520	XGB4	0.585	GWORF10	0.559	GWOXGB6	0.321	GWOLGB6	0.706	XGB11	0.586
83	RF14	0.783	RF4	0.652	GWOLGB10	0.626	GWOLGB6	0.356	RF11	0.711	RF11	0.844
82	XGB10	0.893	GWORF4	0.964	LGB4	0.767	XGB13	0.840	GWORF13	0.810	XGB10	0.903
81	LGB14	0.967	LGB4	0.986	XGB5	0.857	LGB3	0.915	LGB13	0.825	GWORF11	0.954
80	GWOXGB14	0.967	XGB3	1.006	GWORF4	0.942	GWORF3	1.036	XGB11	0.902	GWOXGB11	0.993
79	GWOLGB14	1.017	RF3	1.014	GWOLGB4	0.972	RF13	1.075	GWOLGB13	0.927	LGB11	1.016
78	RF5	1.039	GWOXGB4	1.055	GWOXGB4	0.986	GWOXGB3	1.159	GWOXGB13	0.932	GWOLGB11	1.074
77	GWORF14	1.054	GWOLGB4	1.068	RF5	1.293	GWOLGB3	1.183	RF11	1.159	RF10	1.098
76	LGB10	1.309	LGB14	1.377	LGB14	1.387	GWORF13	1.519	LGB11	1.232	LGB10	1.271
75	GWOXGB10	1.420	GWORF14	1.378	GWOXGB14	1.504	LGB13	1.552	GWORF11	1.263	GWORF10	1.287
74	GWORF5	1.439	GWOXGB14	1.394	GWORF14	1.511	GWOXGB13	1.687	GWOXGB11	1.266	GWOLGB10	1.370
73	GWOLGB10	1.497	GWOLGB3	1.417	GWOLGB14	1.514	GWOLGB13	1.724	GWOLGB11	1.297	GWOXGB10	1.380

4. Discussion

Reference evapotranspiration estimation is essential in various applications ranging from agricultural water management, hydrological balancing across basins and water allocation, etc. The study used various empirical, ML and hybrid ML models that were tested across the humid and sub-humid stations across the Indian subcontinent. Among empirical equations, the Turc model was found to be the most reliable method in empirical models used. Similar results were reported in [62,63], wherein the radiation-based Turc model performed better. Many studies have proven that the empirical equations underperformed the ML models, which was also observed in this study. [64] assessed different artificial intelligence models with empirical models like Turc, Ritchie, Thornthwaite, and Valiantzas methods. Their results indicated the supremacy of the ML models in predicting ET_0. The comparison between the conventional ML models based on the performance indicators showed that the XGB and LGB models showed similar accuracies. [30] have also indicated that both of these models exhibited the same model efficacy. The boosting methods were to be a potential tool for humid regions according to [65]. RF models were found to be less accurate than the other boosting models, as reported in [24,29].

The model accuracy increased as increasing the inputs, which was exhibited in most of the studies. The models that used solar radiation have performed reasonably well in both the regions, i.e., humid and sub-humid. [29] also found that the addition of solar radiation improved the accuracy. The models in the sub-humid regions that used wind speed data were found to be of better accuracy. These results were similar that were found in Bangladesh [64]. The best and least performing models' results have been found to vary slightly across the stations. However, the four input combination models, indices 7 and 8, were found to be consistently performing well in both regions. Applying these data-driven models with lower inputs could be promising for developing nations.

The hybrid ML models further enhanced the predictability of the models, which could be possible by proper hyperparameter tuning. This is evident from the observation of the improvement in the GWORF model performance over the conventional RF. RF models showed a greater improvement due to the optimization than the XGB and LGB models. A similar study by [61] reported an improvement in all the combinations of inputs when employing PSO. The hyperparameter values varied considerably in all the combinations and stations. There is no fixed set of hyperparameters for all the ML models and their input combinations that could be suggested for optimal results, as suggested in [36]. Nevertheless, these models have proven to be of good accuracy, and there is a scope for further improvement if different optimizers could be tested across the regions of the World.

5. Conclusions

This study evaluated the ET_0 modelling capabilities of tree-based ML like RF, XGB, and LGB in addition to the GWO-optimized tree-based ML for ten locations in humid and sub-humid regions across India. The daily data from 2001 to 2020 of agro-meteorological parameters like maximum temperature, minimum temperature, wind speed, relative humidity, number of sunshine hours, solar radiation and extra-terrestrial radiation were employed for modelling purposes. The FAO-56 Penman-Monteith was used as the target value. Different input combinations were tested at all the stations using a cross-validation strategy. The comparison of the empirical equations was also made for the ML that used the same input combinations. The ranking of the models based on GPI value for comparison at each level was considered. The conclusions that could be drawn from the study are below.

1. The LGB and XGB models outperformed the RF models, while all the ML models were found to be more accurate than empirical models.
2. Among the empirical methods investigated in the study, the Turc model was determined to have the greatest performance with higher GPI values.
3. Solar radiation was adjudged to be an important parameter that could improve the prediction capability.

4. The GWO hybrid ML models had the highest prediction efficiencies at all the locations, with RF models improving considerably well.
5. The study consolidated the fact that the use of optimizers would substantially reduce the modelling error.
6. Further studies could be done using cross-station data and other optimizers to improve the accuracy.

Supplementary Materials: The following supplementary information can be downloaded at: https://www.mdpi.com/article/10.3390/w15050856/s1, Figure S1. Statistical indicators of inputs and output used in the study; Figure S2. Time series graphs of ET_0 (mm/day) at humid (Jorhat, Thrissur) and sub-humid (Raipur, Samastipur) stations; Table S1. Performance indicators of empirical models at humid stations; Table S2. Performance indicators of empirical models at sub-humid stations; Table S3. Performance indicators of conventional ML models at Jorhat; Table S4. Performance indicators of conventional ML models at Mohanpur; Table S5. Performance indicators of conventional ML models at Palampur; Table S6. Performance indicators of conventional ML models at Thrissur; Table S7. Performance indicators of conventional ML models at Faizabad; Table S8. Performance indicators of conventional ML models at Jabalpur; Table S9. Performance indicators of conventional ML models at Raipur; Table S10. Performance indicators of conventional ML models at Ranchi; Table S11. Performance indicators of conventional ML models at Ranichauri; Table S12. Performance indicators of conventional ML models at Samastipur; Table S13. Best hyper parameters in RF models at humid stations; Table S14. Best hyper parameters in XGB models at humid stations; Table S15. Best hyper parameters in LGB models at humid stations; Table S16. Best hyper parameters in RF models at sub-humid stations; Table S17. Best hyper parameters in XGB models at sub-humid stations; Table S18. Best hyper parameters in LGB models at sub-humid stations; Table S19. Performance indicators of hybrid ML models at Jorhat; Table S20. Performance indicators of hybrid ML models at Mohanpur; Table S21. Performance indicators of hybrid ML models at Palampur; Table S22. Performance indicators of hybrid ML models at Thrissur; Table S23. Performance indicators of hybrid ML models at Faizabad; Table S24. Performance indicators of hybrid ML models at Jabalpur; Table S25. Performance indicators of hybrid ML models at Raipur; Table S26. Performance indicators of hybrid ML models at Ranchi; Table S27. Performance indicators of hybrid ML models at Ranichauri; Table S28. Performance indicators of hybrid ML models at Samastipur.

Author Contributions: Conceptualization, P.H. and K.V.R.R.; methodology, P.H., K.V.R.R. and A.S. (A. Subeesh); software, P.H., A.S. (A. Subeesh) and A.S. (Ankur Srivatsava); formal analysis, P.H. and K.V.R.R.; investigation, P.H. and A.S. (A. Subeesh); writing—original draft preparation, P.H. and K.V.R.R.; writing—review and editing, K.V.R.R., A.S. (A. Subeesh) and A.S. (Ankur Srivatsava); visualization, A.S. (A. Subeesh) and A.S. (Ankur Srivatsava); supervision, K.V.R.R. All authors have read and agreed to the published version of the manuscript.

Funding: This research received no external funding.

Data Availability Statement: The datasets generated and/or analysed during the current study are available from the corresponding author upon reasonable request.

Acknowledgments: The scholarship to the first author through the ICAR JRF/SRF scholarship from Indian Council of Agricultural Research is highly acknowledged. The authors also thank the AICRP on Agro-meteorology, CRIDA, India for providing the data required.

Conflicts of Interest: The authors declare no conflict of interest.

References

1. United Nations Department of Economic and Social Affairs, Population Division. *World Population Prospects 2022: Summary of Results*; UN DESA/POP/2022/TR/NO. 3; United Nations: New York, NY, USA, 2022.
2. Lybbert, T.J.; Sumner, D.A. Agricultural Technologies for Climate Change in Developing Countries: Policy Options for Innovation and Technology Diffusion. *Food Policy* **2012**, *37*, 114–123. [CrossRef]
3. Srilakshmi, M.; Jhajharia, D.; Gupta, S.; Yurembam, G.S.; Patle, G.T. Analysis of Spatio-Temporal Variations and Change Point Detection in Pan Coefficients in the Northeastern Region of India. *Theor. Appl. Climatol.* **2022**, *147*, 1545–1559. [CrossRef]
4. George, B.A.; Reddy, B.; Raghuwanshi, N.; Wallender, W. Decision Support System for Estimating Reference Evapotranspiration. *J. Irrig. Drain. Eng.* **2002**, *128*, 1–10. [CrossRef]

5. Srivastava, A.; Sahoo, B.; Raghuwanshi, N. Evaluation of Variable Infiltration Capacity Model and MODIS-Terra Satellite-Derived Grid-Scale Evapotranspiration Estimates in a River Basin with Tropical Monsoon-Type Climatology. *J. Irrig. Drain Eng.* **2017**, *143*, 04017028. [CrossRef]
6. Albrecht, F. Die Methoden zur Bestimmung der Verdunstung der natürlichen Erdoberfläche. *Arch. Meteorol. Geophys. Bioklimatol. Ser. B* **1950**, *2*, 1–38. [CrossRef]
7. Mahringer, W. Verdunstungsstudien am Neusiedler See. *Arch. Meteorol. Geophys. Bioklimatol. Ser. B* **1970**, *18*, 1–20. [CrossRef]
8. Penman, H.L. Natural Evaporation from Open Water, Bare Soil and Grass. *Proc. R. Soc. Lond. Ser. Math. Phys. Sci.* **1948**, *193*, 120–145.
9. Abtew, W. Evapotranspiration Measurements and Modeling for Three Wetland Systems in South Florida1. *JAWRA J. Am. Water Resour. Assoc.* **1996**, *32*, 465–473. [CrossRef]
10. Hansen, S. Estimation of Potential and Actual Evapotranspiration: Paper Presented at the Nordic Hydrological Conference (Nyborg, Denmark, August—1984). *Hydrol. Res.* **1984**, *15*, 205–212. [CrossRef]
11. Rosenberg, N.J.; Blad, B.L.; Verma, S.B. *Microclimate: The Biological Environment*; John Wiley & Sons: Hoboken, NJ, USA, 1983; ISBN 0-471-06066-6.
12. McGuinness, J.L.; Bordne, E.F. *A Comparison of Lysimeter-Derived Potential Evapotranspiration with Computed Values*; US Department of Agriculture: Washington, DC, USA, 1972.
13. Priestley, C.H.B.; Taylor, R.J. On the Assessment of Surface Heat Flux and Evaporation Using Large-Scale Parameters. *Mon. Weather Rev.* **1972**, *100*, 81–92. [CrossRef]
14. Turc, L. Estimation of Irrigation Water Requirements, Potential Evapotranspiration: A Simple Climatic Formula Evolved up to Date. *Ann. Agron.* **1961**, *12*, 13–49.
15. Hargreaves, G.H. Moisture Availability and Crop Production. *Trans. ASAE* **1975**, *18*, 980–0984. [CrossRef]
16. Hargreaves, G.H.; Samani, Z.A. Reference Crop Evapotranspiration from Temperature. *Appl. Eng. Agric.* **1985**, *1*, 96–99. [CrossRef]
17. Droogers, P.; Allen, R.G. Estimating Reference Evapotranspiration under Inaccurate Data Conditions. *Irrig. Drain. Syst.* **2002**, *16*, 33–45. [CrossRef]
18. Alexandris, S.; Kerkides, P.; Liakatas, A. Daily Reference Evapotranspiration Estimates by the "Copais" Approach. *Agric. Water Manag.* **2006**, *82*, 371–386. [CrossRef]
19. Valiantzas, J.D. Simple ET0 Forms of Penman's Equation without Wind and/or Humidity Data. II: Comparisons with Reduced Set-FAO and Other Methodologies. *J. Irrig. Drain. Eng.* **2013**, *139*, 9–19. [CrossRef]
20. Jing, W.; Yaseen, Z.M.; Shahid, S.; Saggi, M.K.; Tao, H.; Kisi, O.; Salih, S.Q.; Al-Ansari, N.; Chau, K.-W. Implementation of Evolutionary Computing Models for Reference Evapotranspiration Modeling: Short Review, Assessment and Possible Future Research Directions. *Eng. Appl. Comput. Fluid Mech.* **2019**, *13*, 811–823. [CrossRef]
21. Ayodele, T.O. Machine Learning Overview. *New Adv. Mach. Learn.* **2010**, *2*, 9–18.
22. Shiri, J.; Zounemat-Kermani, M.; Kisi, O.; Mohsenzadeh Karimi, S. Comprehensive Assessment of 12 Soft Computing Approaches for Modelling Reference Evapotranspiration in Humid Locations. *Meteorol. Appl.* **2020**, *27*, e1841. [CrossRef]
23. Bellido-Jiménez, J.A.; Estévez, J.; Vanschoren, J.; García-Marín, A.P. AgroML: An Open-Source Repository to Forecast Reference Evapotranspiration in Different Geo-Climatic Conditions Using Machine Learning and Transformer-Based Models. *Agronomy* **2022**, *12*, 656. [CrossRef]
24. Fan, J.; Yue, W.; Wu, L.; Zhang, F.; Cai, H.; Wang, X.; Lu, X.; Xiang, Y. Evaluation of SVM, ELM and Four Tree-Based Ensemble Models for Predicting Daily Reference Evapotranspiration Using Limited Meteorological Data in Different Climates of China. *Agric. For. Meteorol.* **2018**, *263*, 225–241. [CrossRef]
25. Liu, X.; Wu, L.; Zhang, F.; Huang, G.; Yan, F.; Bai, W. Splitting and Length of Years for Improving Tree-Based Models to Predict Reference Crop Evapotranspiration in the Humid Regions of China. *Water* **2021**, *13*, 3478. [CrossRef]
26. Wu, Z.; Cui, N.; Gong, D.; Zhu, F.; Xing, L.; Zhu, B.; Chen, X.; Wen, S.; Liu, Q. Simulation of Daily Maize Evapotranspiration at Different Growth Stages Using Four Machine Learning Models in Semi-Humid Regions of Northwest China. *J. Hydrol.* **2022**, *617*, 128947. [CrossRef]
27. Zhou, Z.; Zhao, L.; Lin, A.; Qin, W.; Lu, Y.; Li, J.; Zhong, Y.; He, L. Exploring the Potential of Deep Factorization Machine and Various Gradient Boosting Models in Modeling Daily Reference Evapotranspiration in China. *Arab. J. Geosci.* **2021**, *13*, 1287. [CrossRef]
28. Wu, L.; Peng, Y.; Fan, J.; Wang, Y. Machine Learning Models for the Estimation of Monthly Mean Daily Reference Evapotranspiration Based on Cross-Station and Synthetic Data. *Hydrol. Res.* **2019**, *50*, 1730–1750. [CrossRef]
29. Fan, J.; Ma, X.; Wu, L.; Zhang, F.; Yu, X.; Zeng, W. Light Gradient Boosting Machine: An Efficient Soft Computing Model for Estimating Daily Reference Evapotranspiration with Local and External Meteorological Data. *Agric. Water Manag.* **2019**, *225*, 105758. [CrossRef]
30. Wu, T.; Zhang, W.; Jiao, X.; Guo, W.; Hamoud, Y.A. Comparison of Five Boosting-Based Models for Estimating Daily Reference Evapotranspiration with Limited Meteorological Variables. *PLoS ONE* **2020**, *15*, e0235324. [CrossRef] [PubMed]
31. Zhang, H.; Meng, F.; Xu, J.; Liu, Z.; Meng, J. Evaluation of Machine Learning Models for Daily Reference Evapotranspiration Modeling Using Limited Meteorological Data in Eastern Inner Mongolia, North China. *Water* **2022**, *14*, 2890. [CrossRef]
32. Ferreira, L.B.; da Cunha, F.F. New Approach to Estimate Daily Reference Evapotranspiration Based on Hourly Temperature and Relative Humidity Using Machine Learning and Deep Learning. *Agric. Water Manag.* **2020**, *234*, 106113. [CrossRef]

33. Mokari, E.; DuBois, D.; Samani, Z.; Mohebzadeh, H.; Djaman, K. Estimation of Daily Reference Evapotranspiration with Limited Climatic Data Using Machine Learning Approaches across Different Climate Zones in New Mexico. *Theor. Appl. Climatol.* **2022**, *147*, 575–587. [CrossRef]
34. Wu, T.; Zhang, W.; Jiao, X.; Guo, W.; Alhaj Hamoud, Y. Evaluation of Stacking and Blending Ensemble Learning Methods for Estimating Daily Reference Evapotranspiration. *Comput. Electron. Agric.* **2021**, *184*, 106039. [CrossRef]
35. Yan, S.; Wu, L.; Fan, J.; Zhang, F.; Zou, Y.; Wu, Y. A Novel Hybrid WOA-XGB Model for Estimating Daily Reference Evapotranspiration Using Local and External Meteorological Data: Applications in Arid and Humid Regions of China. *Agric. Water Manag.* **2021**, *244*, 106594. [CrossRef]
36. Maroufpoor, S.; Bozorg-Haddad, O.; Maroufpoor, E. Reference Evapotranspiration Estimating Based on Optimal Input Combination and Hybrid Artificial Intelligent Model: Hybridization of Artificial Neural Network with Grey Wolf Optimizer Algorithm. *J. Hydrol.* **2020**, *588*, 125060. [CrossRef]
37. Dong, J.; Liu, X.; Huang, G.; Fan, J.; Wu, L.; Wu, J. Comparison of Four Bio-Inspired Algorithms to Optimize KNEA for Predicting Monthly Reference Evapotranspiration in Different Climate Zones of China. *Comput. Electron. Agric.* **2021**, *186*, 106211. [CrossRef]
38. Devendra, C.; Thomas, D. Crop–Animal Systems in Asia: Importance of Livestock and Characterisation of Agro-Ecological Zones. *Agric. Syst.* **2002**, *71*, 5–15. [CrossRef]
39. Mandal, D.; Mandal, C.; Singh, S. Delineating Agro-Ecological Regions. *ICAR-NBSSLUP Technol.* **2016**, 1–8.
40. Allen, R.G.; Pereira, L.S.; Raes, D.; Smith, M. Crop Evapotranspiration-Guidelines for Computing Crop Water Requirements-FAO Irrigation and Drainage Paper 56. *FAO Rome* **1998**, *300*, D05109.
41. Tabari, H.; Grismer, M.E.; Trajkovic, S. Comparative Analysis of 31 Reference Evapotranspiration Methods under Humid Conditions. *Irrig. Sci.* **2013**, *31*, 107–117. [CrossRef]
42. Xystrakis, F.; Matzarakis, A. Evaluation of 13 Empirical Reference Potential Evapotranspiration Equations on the Island of Crete in Southern Greece. *J. Irrig. Drain. Eng.* **2011**, *137*, 211–222. [CrossRef]
43. Rosenberry, D.O.; Stannard, D.I.; Winter, T.C.; Martinez, M.L. Comparison of 13 Equations for Determining Evapotranspiration from a Prairie Wetland, Cottonwood Lake Area, North Dakota, USA. *Wetlands* **2004**, *24*, 483–497. [CrossRef]
44. Bourletsikas, A.; Argyrokastritis, I.; Proutsos, N. Comparative Evaluation of 24 Reference Evapotranspiration Equations Applied on an Evergreen-Broadleaved Forest. *Hydrol. Res.* **2017**, *49*, 1028–1041. [CrossRef]
45. Breiman, L. Random Forests. *Mach. Learn.* **2001**, *45*, 5–32. [CrossRef]
46. Smith, P.F.; Ganesh, S.; Liu, P. A Comparison of Random Forest Regression and Multiple Linear Regression for Prediction in Neuroscience. *J. Neurosci. Methods* **2013**, *220*, 85–91. [CrossRef] [PubMed]
47. Misra, S.; Li, H. Chapter 9—Noninvasive Fracture Characterization Based on the Classification of Sonic Wave Travel Times. In *Machine Learning for Subsurface Characterization*; Misra, S., Li, H., He, J., Eds.; Gulf Professional Publishing: Houston, TX, USA, 2020; pp. 243–287. ISBN 978-0-12-817736-5.
48. Chen, T.; He, T.; Benesty, M.; Khotilovich, V.; Tang, Y.; Cho, H.; Chen, K. Xgboost: Extreme Gradient Boosting. In *R Package*; Version 04-2; R Foundation for Statistical Computing: Vienna, Austria, 2015; Volume 1, pp. 1–4.
49. Friedman, J.H. Greedy Function Approximation: A Gradient Boosting Machine. *Ann. Stat.* **2001**, *29*, 1189–1232. [CrossRef]
50. Al Daoud, E. Comparison between XGBoost, LightGBM and CatBoost Using a Home Credit Dataset. *Int. J. Comput. Inf. Eng.* **2019**, *13*, 6–10.
51. Ke, G.; Meng, Q.; Finley, T.; Wang, T.; Chen, W.; Ma, W.; Ye, Q.; Liu, T.-Y. LightGBM: A Highly Efficient Gradient Boosting Decision Tree. In Proceedings of the Advances in Neural Information Processing Systems, Long Beach, CA, USA, 4–9 December 2017; Curran Associates, Inc.: Red Hook, NY, USA, 2017; Volume 30.
52. Mirjalili, S.; Mirjalili, S.M.; Lewis, A. Grey Wolf Optimizer. *Adv. Eng. Softw.* **2014**, *69*, 46–61. [CrossRef]
53. Sweidan, A.H.; El-Bendary, N.; Hassanien, A.E.; Hegazy, O.M.; Mohamed, A.E. Water Quality Classification Approach Based on Bio-Inspired Gray Wolf Optimization. In Proceedings of the 2015 7th International Conference of Soft Computing and Pattern Recognition (SoCPaR), Fukuoka, Japan, 13–15 November 2015; pp. 1–6.
54. Faris, H.; Aljarah, I.; Al-Betar, M.A.; Mirjalili, S. Grey Wolf Optimizer: A Review of Recent Variants and Applications. *Neural Comput. Appl.* **2018**, *30*, 413–435. [CrossRef]
55. Mohammadi, B.; Guan, Y.; Aghelpour, P.; Emamgholizadeh, S.; Pillco Zolá, R.; Zhang, D. Simulation of Titicaca Lake Water Level Fluctuations Using Hybrid Machine Learning Technique Integrated with Grey Wolf Optimizer Algorithm. *Water* **2020**, *12*, 3015. [CrossRef]
56. Sharma, I.; Kumar, V.; Sharma, S. A Comprehensive Survey on Grey Wolf Optimization. *Recent Adv. Comput. Sci. Commun. Former. Recent Pat. Comput. Sci.* **2022**, *15*, 323–333.
57. Feng, Y.; Cui, N.; Zhao, L.; Hu, X.; Gong, D. Comparison of ELM, GANN, WNN and Empirical Models for Estimating Reference Evapotranspiration in Humid Region of Southwest China. *J. Hydrol.* **2016**, *536*, 376–383. [CrossRef]
58. He, H.; Liu, L.; Zhu, X. Optimization of Extreme Learning Machine Model with Biological Heuristic Algorithms to Estimate Daily Reference Evapotranspiration in Hetao Irrigation District of China. *Eng. Appl. Comput. Fluid Mech.* **2022**, *16*, 1939–1956. [CrossRef]
59. Heramb, P.; Kumar Singh, P.; Ramana Rao, K.V.; Subeesh, A. Modelling Reference Evapotranspiration Using Gene Expression Programming and Artificial Neural Network at Pantnagar, India. *Inf. Process. Agric.* **2022**, *in press*. [CrossRef]

60. Despotovic, M.; Nedic, V.; Despotovic, D.; Cvetanovic, S. Review and Statistical Analysis of Different Global Solar Radiation Sunshine Models. *Renew. Sustain. Energy Rev.* **2015**, *52*, 1869–1880. [CrossRef]
61. Zhu, B.; Feng, Y.; Gong, D.; Jiang, S.; Zhao, L.; Cui, N. Hybrid Particle Swarm Optimization with Extreme Learning Machine for Daily Reference Evapotranspiration Prediction from Limited Climatic Data. *Comput. Electron. Agric.* **2020**, *173*, 105430. [CrossRef]
62. Pandey, P.K.; Dabral, P.P.; Pandey, V. Evaluation of Reference Evapotranspiration Methods for the Northeastern Region of India. *Int. Soil Water Conserv. Res.* **2016**, *4*, 52–63. [CrossRef]
63. Üneş, F.; Kaya, Y.Z.; Mamak, M. Daily Reference Evapotranspiration Prediction Based on Climatic Conditions Applying Different Data Mining Techniques and Empirical Equations. *Theor. Appl. Climatol.* **2020**, *141*, 763–773. [CrossRef]
64. Salam, R.; Islam, A.R.M.T. Potential of RT, Bagging and RS Ensemble Learning Algorithms for Reference Evapotranspiration Prediction Using Climatic Data-Limited Humid Region in Bangladesh. *J. Hydrol.* **2020**, *590*, 125241. [CrossRef]
65. Huang, G.; Wu, L.; Ma, X.; Zhang, W.; Fan, J.; Yu, X.; Zeng, W.; Zhou, H. Evaluation of CatBoost Method for Prediction of Reference Evapotranspiration in Humid Regions. *J. Hydrol.* **2019**, *574*, 1029–1041. [CrossRef]

Disclaimer/Publisher's Note: The statements, opinions and data contained in all publications are solely those of the individual author(s) and contributor(s) and not of MDPI and/or the editor(s). MDPI and/or the editor(s) disclaim responsibility for any injury to people or property resulting from any ideas, methods, instructions or products referred to in the content.

Article

Streamflow and Sediment Yield Analysis of Two Medium-Sized East-Flowing River Basins of India

Nageswara Reddy Nagireddy [1], Venkata Reddy Keesara [1], Venkataramana Sridhar [2,*] and Raghavan Srinivasan [3]

1. Department of Civil Engineering, National Institute of Technology Warangal, Telangana 506004, India
2. Department of Biological Systems Engineering, Virginia Polytechnic Institute and State University, Blacksburg, VA 24061, USA
3. Director of Spatial Sciences Laboratory, Agrilife Research, Texas A&M University, College Station, TX 77843, USA
* Correspondence: vsri@vt.edu

Citation: Nagireddy, N.R.; Keesara, V.R.; Sridhar, V.; Srinivasan, R. Streamflow and Sediment Yield Analysis of Two Medium-Sized East-Flowing River Basins of India. *Water* **2022**, *14*, 2960. https://doi.org/10.3390/w14192960

Academic Editor: Ilyas Masih

Received: 17 July 2022
Accepted: 17 September 2022
Published: 21 September 2022

Publisher's Note: MDPI stays neutral with regard to jurisdictional claims in published maps and institutional affiliations.

Copyright: © 2022 by the authors. Licensee MDPI, Basel, Switzerland. This article is an open access article distributed under the terms and conditions of the Creative Commons Attribution (CC BY) license (https://creativecommons.org/licenses/by/4.0/).

Abstract: With increased demand for water and soil in this Anthropocene era, it is necessary to understand the water balance components and critical source areas of land degradation that lead to soil erosion in agricultural dominant river basins. Two medium-sized east-flowing rivers in India, namely Nagavali and Vamsadhara, play a significant role in supporting water supply and agriculture demands in parts of the Odisha districts of Kalahandi, Koraput and Rayagada, as well as the Andhra Pradesh districts of Srikakulam and Vizianagaram. Floods are more likely in these basins as a result of cyclones and low-pressure depressions in the Bay of Bengal. The water balance components and sediment yield of the Nagavali and Vamsadhara river basins were assessed using a semi-distributed soil and water assessment tool (SWAT) model in this study. The calibrated model performance revealed a high degree of consistency between observed and predicted monthly streamflow and sediment load. The water balance analysis of Nagavali and Vamsadhara river basins showed the evapotranspiration accounted for 63% of the average annual rainfall. SWAT simulated evapotranspiration showed a correlation of 0.78 with FLDAS data. The calibrated SWAT model showed that 26.5% and 49% of watershed area falling under high soil erosion class over Nagavali and Vamsadhara river basins, respectively. These sub watersheds require immediate attention to management practices to improve the soil and water conservation measures.

Keywords: river basin; SWAT; streamflow; sediment yield; critical source area

1. Introduction

Soil erosion is a serious concern for land and water resources because it has a negative impact on soil fertility, agricultural production, and the quality of aquatic environment [1,2]. Soil erosion is caused by the interaction of physical and anthropogenic forces and erosion rates are affected by hydrology, climate, soil conditions, land use land cover changes and their interaction at the sub-watershed scale [3–5]. River basins are confronted with the most serious problems of land degradation and deterioration of water resources as a result of soil erosion [6]. Soil erosion from uplands deposits soil in riverbeds and reservoirs, causing flooding and reservoir capacity loss [7,8]. According to a Central Water Commission (CWC) report, the majority of the reservoirs in India are losing their storage capacity at a rate of 1% per year due to sedimentation [9]. Some tribal-inhabited areas in Andhra Pradesh, Odisha, Madhya Pradesh, Chhattisgarh, and Kerala have faced severe soil erosion as a result of shifting cultivation [10].

The majority of the rainfall in India occurs from June to October, with high intensity and widespread coverage. During these months, some rivers erupt with large floods, causing soil erosion. The eastern coastal belt along the Bay of Bengal (BoB), mainly Tamil Nadu, Andhra Pradesh and Orissa, is flooded by pre- and post-monsoon tropical cyclones that form over the BoB [11,12]. According to Narayana and Babu [7] the average annual soil erosion rate in India is 16.35 t/ha/yr, which exceeds the permissible limit [13]. In India, 147 million ha of land is degraded, with water erosion accounting for 94 million ha [14]. Das [15] found that 12 major Peninsular Indian rivers contribute more than 1% of global river sediment flux.

Various studies were conducted in different regions of India using a modeling approach, field scale, and laboratory studies to have a comprehensive knowledge on soil erosion, sediment yield, and their impact on reservoirs and crop productivity [2,5,16–24]. Using experimental analysis, Vaithiyanathan et al. [16] noticed that the majority of sediment transport, more than 95% of the time, occurs during the monsoon period. Singh et al. [17] prepared a soil erosion rate map for India and they suggested severe soil erosion rates (>20 t/ha/yr) are found at the areas of Peninsular India. Prasannakumar et al. [18] found that the maximum soil loss was associated with a high slope length and steepness (LS) factor from degraded, deciduous forest and grasslands areas. Dutta and Sen [21] concluded that the highest annual sediment yield was associated with agricultural lands. Mahapatra et al. [22] concluded that 48.3% of the Uttarakhand state soil loss exceeds the permissible limit of 11.2 t/ha/yr. Himanshu et al. [20] used the SWAT model to evaluate the best management practices in the Marol watershed, India. In their study, the estimated average annual sediment yield was 12.2 t/ha/yr. Kolli et al. [24] concluded that sandy clay and red soils exported the highest sediment in the Kolleru catchment.

The aforementioned literature suggested that the amount of sediment yield within the basin varies depending on hydrology, climate, topography, land use change, and soil type [5,20,21,23]. Furthermore, soil erosion and sediment yield are not distributed evenly across the basins. As a result, sub-basin scale sediment yield analysis using a physically based distributed hydrological model is required for identifying accurate sediment source areas and controlling sediment yield through soil and water conservation practices. Many physically based hydrological models, such as VIC [25,26], ANSWERS [27], AGNPS [28], WEPP [29] and SWAT [30] have been in use over the past three decades to understand the hydrological processes. Roti et al. [31] reviewed the applicability of physically distributed models and concluded that the SWAT model outperformed AGNPS, ANSWERS and WEPP models [32,33] in both small and large areas [34]. Furthermore, with spatiotemporal variability of the hydrological process, SWAT produces acceptable results all over the world [35–41]. The majority of the recent studies used SWAT in conjunction with a geographical information system (GIS) interface for a variety of purposes, including modeling of runoff, soil moisture, sediment and water balance [19,21,42–44], climate change [45] and identifying critical source areas and evaluation of best management practices (BMPs) for sediments and nutrients [20,33,46] across the world. The aforementioned literature suggests that the SWAT model performance ranged from very good to satisfactory for the streamflow and sediment simulations.

The Nagavali and Vamsadhara river basins in India are vulnerable to frequent floods [11,39,47,48]. These basins are mainly dominated by agricultural activities and forest cover, which provide a livelihood for farmers in the Odisha districts of Kalahandi, Koraput and Rayagada, as well as the Andhra Pradesh districts of Srikakulam and Vizianagaram. The steep slopes towards the NE and NW part of the basins indicates fast runoff which causes soil erosion [12]. These river basins are particularly vulnerable to tropical cyclones caused by low-pressure depressions in the BoB. Cyclones such as the 1996 Andhra Pradesh cyclone, the 1999 Odisha cyclone, and other named cyclones such as Nilam, Laila, Phailin cyclone, Helen, Lehar, Hudhud, and Fani hit the Nagavali and Vamsadhara river basins between 1991 and 2019 [11,49]. Due to these cyclones, floods have occurred, which damaged the property, crops and affected the lives of many people [50]. Water stress in the Nagavali river basin in seasons other than the monsoon season has also been observed [43].

Based on the existing literature, both river basins are frequently flooded, resulting in soil erosion from upland areas and depositing in channels and reservoirs. Every year, the erosion and deposition occur, resulting in a loss of reservoirs storage capacity loss. From 1977 to 2004, the Gotta barrage on the Vamsadhara river basin lost 61.43% of its live storage [9]. Long-term analysis of water balance components is required to reduce water stress over the basins during the dry season [43]. Several studies on soil erosion and sediment yield identified that all sub-basins within the basin have different characteristics and their response to anthropogenic and natural changes also differ [2,21,24]. There is a need for long-term water balance and sediment yield analysis as well as identifying erosion-prone areas for sediment yield and evaluating soil and water conservation practices using a biophysical model. The objective of this study was to implement a semi-distributed hydrological soil and water assessment tool (SWAT) to analyze the water balance components and identify sediment source areas for the Nagavali and Vamsadhara basins.

2. Materials and Methods
2.1. Study Area

The Nagavali and Vamsadhara rivers are two adjacent interstate medium-sized east-flowing river basins in southern Orissa and northern Andhra Pradesh, India (Figure 1), located between the Mahanadi and Godavari river basins.

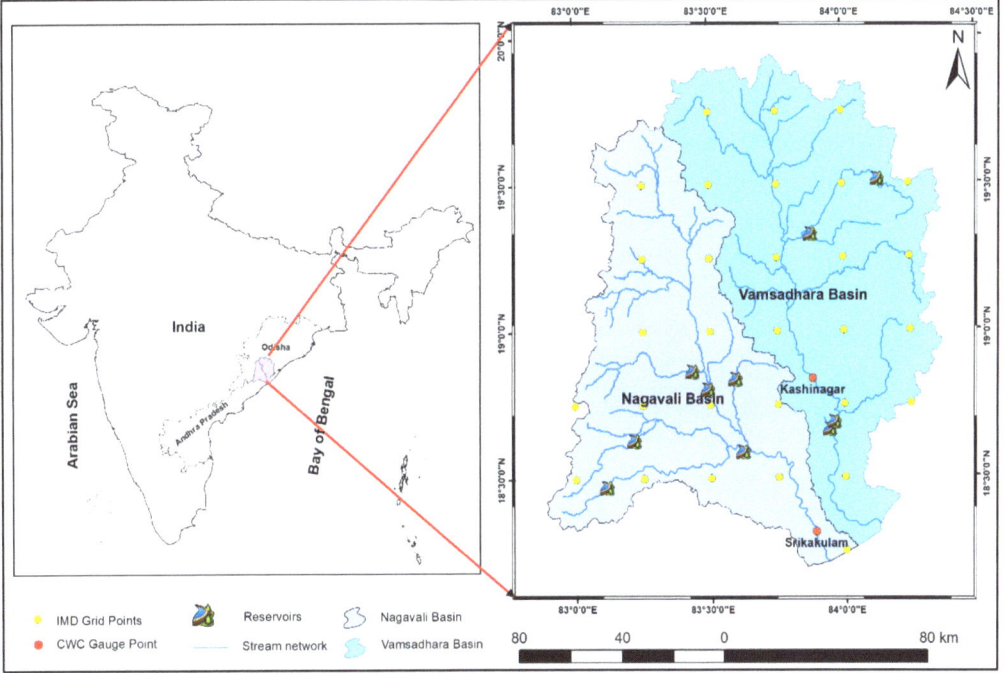

Figure 1. Map of the Nagavali and Vamsadhara river basins.

There are two types of climate in these river basins. The coastal area has a semi-arid climate, while the upper reaches have a dry sub-humid climate. The Nagavali river rises near the village of Lakhbahal in the Odisha. It travels 256 km and has a basin area of 9200 square kilometers before joining the BoB at Kallepalli village near Srikakulam. The major irrigation projects on the Nagavali river basin are Madduvalasa, Thotapalli barrage, and Janjavathi reservoirs, while the minor irrigation projects are Vengalarayasagar, Vottigedda, and Vegavathi (Peddagedda), as shown in Table 1.

Table 1. Details of existing reservoirs in the Nagavali and Vamsadhara river basins.

Reservoir Name	RES_EVOL (10^4 m^3)	RES_ESA (Ha)	RES_PVOL (10^4 m^3)	RES_PSA (Ha)	RES_Operational Year
Madduvalasa reservoir	9551	2673	9358	2405	2002
Thotapalli barrage	8503	1983	7105	1785	1908
Vottigedda reservoir	2713	440	2514	272	1976
Janjavathi reservoir	9628	2680	7855	2450	1978
Vengalarayasagar reservoir	4051	575	3646	518	1998
Vegavathi/Peddagedda reservoir	3038	294	2891	265	2003
Badnalla reservoir	5480	753	4932	678	1997
Harabhangi reservoir	11,116	1107	10,000	1000	1998

Note: RES_EVOL and RES_PVOL are the volumes of water needed to fill the reservoir to the emergency spillway and principal spillway, respectively. RES_ESA and RES_PSA are the reservoir surface areas when the reservoir is filled to the emergency spillway and principal spillway, respectively.

The details of reservoir volumes at emergency spillway and principal spillway, as well as their corresponding surface areas and reservoir operational years are obtained from the respective reservoir authorities and water body information system (WBIS) (https://bhuvan-wbis.nrsc.gov.in/ (accessed on 16 July 2022)) maintained by the National Remote Sensing Centre (NRSC) Hyderabad.

The Vamsadhara river rises near Lanjigarh in Odisha and flows for 254 km before joining the BoB at Kalingapatnam in Andhra Pradesh. It has a basin area of 10,450 square kilometers. The average rainfall amount in the basin is 940.2 mm near the coast, 1551.6 mm in the northeast, and 1250.2 mm in the northwest [12]. The elevation range in the Vamsadhara river basin range from 10 m above MSL in the south near the coast to 1545 m in the northwest (hills near Bissam Cuttack). The Vamsadhara River basin is primarily influenced by cyclones caused by depressions in the BoB. Because of its narrow shape and hilly terrain, the Vamsadhara river basin is prone to flash floods. Table 1 shows the three reservoirs in the Vamsadhara river basin. The reservoirs of Badnalla and Harabhangi are located within the Kashinagar gauge station, while the Gotta barrage is located outside the gauge station.

2.2. Datasets

Below are detailed descriptions of the datasets that were used in this study:

2.2.1. Digital Elevation Model (DEM)

The Vamsadhara and Nagavali river basins are delineated using a 30 m × 30 m grid SRTM DEM obtained from USGS earth explorer (https://earthexplorer.usgs.gov (accessed on 16 July 2022)), as well as slope maps and a stream network. As shown in Figure 2a, the highest elevations in the Vamsadhara and Nagavali river basins are 1634 m and 1505 m, respectively. The drainage basin slope influences the contribution of surface runoff, infiltration, soil moisture, and ground water to the stream. Three slope bands (0–2%, 2–8% and more than 8%) are considered for both river basins.

2.2.2. Land Use Land Cover (LULC)

The LULC data was obtained from NRSC Bhuvan (https://www.nrsc.gov.in/EO_LULC_Portals (accessed on 16 July 2022)) for the year of 2005 on a scale of 1:250 km as shown in Figure 2b. The LULC classification codes for the Nagavali and Vamsadhara river basins have been converted into SWAT land cover codes with 11 classes. Table 2 depicts the land use classification over the Nagavali and Vamsadhara basins. The LULC classification shows the major land use in the Nagavali river basin is agricultural lands (43%) and forest lands (34%) and over the Vamsadhara river basin major land is occupied by forests (52%) and agricultural lands (30%).

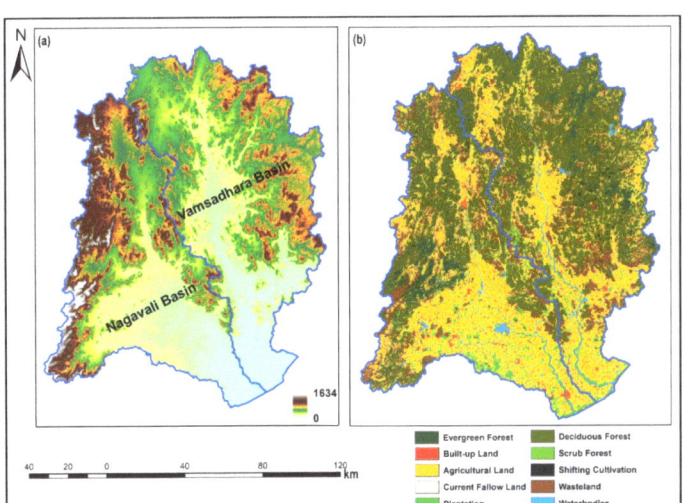

Figure 2. (**a**) DEM (**b**) LULC for the Nagavali and Vamsadhara river basins.

Table 2. Classification of land uses in the Nagavali and Vamsadhara basins.

S. No.	SWAT Code	Class Name	% of Area	
			Nagavali River Basin	Vamsadhara River Basin
1	RICE	Kharif crop	12.3	9.94
2	AGRL	Rabi crop	5.29	2.87
3	ORCD	Plantation	2.94	1.2
4	CRDY	Current fallow	12.21	7.63
5	AGRR	Double or Triple crop	10.22	7.67
6	FRSE	Evergreen forest	3.06	3.09
7	FRSD	Deciduous forest	29.34	46.65
8	RNGB	Degraded or Scrub-forest	1.53	1.44
9	BARR	Wasteland	19.05	17.23
10	WATR	Waterbodies	2.91	1.84
11	URBN	Built-up land	1.14	0.43

2.2.3. Soil Data

The soil map was obtained from the International Soil Reference and Information Centre (ISRIC) (https://www.isric.org (accessed on 16 July 2022)) with 1 km resolution. The soil textures of the basins include loam, sandy loam, sandy clayey loam, clayey loam, and clayey soil. The majority of the upper sub-basins in the Nagavali river basin is covered by sandy clayey soils, while the lower sub-basins is covered by loam soils. Clayey loam soils cover the majority of the Vamsadhara river basin.

2.2.4. Weather Data

Gridded daily rainfall [51] data (0.25° × 0.25°) and 1° × 1° gridded daily maximum and minimum temperature [52] datasets are collected from the Indian Meteorological Department (IMD) Pune (https://www.imdpune.gov.in/Clim_Pred_LRF_New/Grided_Data_Download.html (accessed on 16 July 2022)), India. Srivastava et al. [52] used a modified version of the Shepard's angular distance weighting algorithm for interpolating the station temperature data into 1° latitude × 1° longitude grids. The gridded temperature data was cross validated after development, and errors were estimated and less than 0.5 °C were found. More details about the IMD gridded data are reported in [51,52]. The Nagavali river basin has 12 IMD rainfall grid points and the Vamsadhara river basin has 16 IMD rainfall grid points. Rao et al. [47] compared and found a good correlation of 0.79 between IMD gridded rainfall and gauge rainfall data. Over the Nagavali river basin the annual average rainfall for the period of 1901–2018 is 1230 mm, annual average maximum temperature for the period of 1951–2018 is 32.05 °C and minimum temperature is 21.03 °C. For the Vamsadhara river basin the annual average rainfall is 1260 mm, annual average maximum temperature is 32.21 °C and minimum temperature is 21.27 °C.

2.2.5. Hydrological Data

Streamflow data and sediment data available at Srikakulam gauge station for the Nagavali river basin and Kashinagar gauge station for the Vamsadhara river basin are used in the present study. Streamflow and sediment data was obtained from Central Water Commission (CWC), Mahanadi and eastern rivers organization, Bhubaneshwar, Orissa. The maximum streamflow over the Nagavali river basin is 5624.74 m^3/sec recorded on 4 August 2006 and corresponding sediment load is 3.34 million tons. Over the Vamsadhara river basin the maximum streamflow is 7321.54 m^3/sec recorded on 7 August 2007 and corresponding sediment load is 1.97 million tons. The average annual streamflow is 79.22 m^3/sec and 82.1 m^3/sec, annual average sediment load is 3.69 and 3.72 million ton over the Nagavali and Vamsadhara river basins. Figure 3 shows the inter-annual variability of rainfall and streamflow for the period of 24 years from 1991 to 2014.

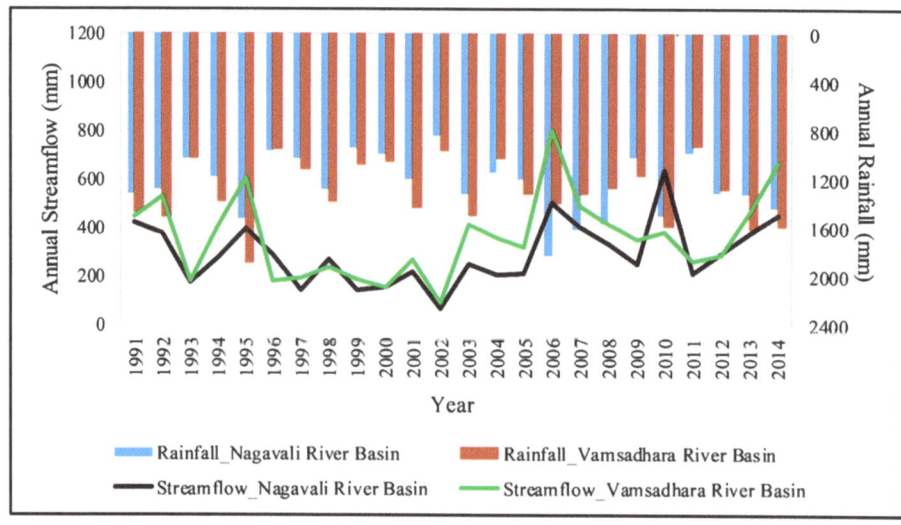

Figure 3. Annual rainfall and streamflow in the Nagavali and Vamsadhara river basins.

From Figure 3, it can be observed that over the Nagavali river basin the highest rainfall observed is 1832 mm in the year 2006, the lowest rainfall observed is 850 mm in 2002, and average rainfall is 1248 mm. Over the Vamsadhara river basin the highest rainfall is 1889 mm in the year 1995, the lowest rainfall is 926 mm in 2011, and average rainfall is 1303 mm. It was observed in both the river basins that 1995 and 2010 are flood years and the immediately following years of 1996 and 2011 are observed as drought years.

2.3. SWAT Model Setup

SWAT is a continuous, semi-distributed hydrologic model, developed by the U.S. Department of Agriculture [35,53–56]. SWAT simulates flow, sediment yield, and agricultural chemical yields from daily time steps to long term simulations.

In SWAT, to predict the sediment yield on a given day modified universal soil loss equation (MUSLE) was used as follows [57]:

$$SY = 11.8 \times (Q_{surf} \times q_{peak} \times A_{hru})^{0.56} \times C \times K \times P \times LS \times CFRG \quad (1)$$

Here, SY is the sediment yield (tons), Q_{surf} is the surface runoff volume (mm/ha), A_{hru} is area of HRU (ha), q_{peak} is peak runoff rate (m^3/s), C is USLE cover and management factor, K is USLE soil erodibility factor, P is USLE support practice factor, LS is USLE topographic factor, $CFRG$ is coarse fragment factor and $Q_{surf} \times q_{peak} \times A_{hru}$ represents the runoff erosive energy variable. SWAT simulates the sediment yield in terms of total sediment loadings and the fraction of silt, clay and sand from sub-watershed.

Initially, to build the SWAT model, SRTM DEM, land use map and soil map were projected into common projection as WGS 1984 UTM 44N. The Nagavali river basin is delineated into 34 sub-basins and 2153 hydrological response units (HRUs) and the Vamsadhara river basin is 30 sub-basins and 2183 HRUs based on homogeneity of soil, land use, slope and 100 ha of threshold area using QSWAT on QGIS interface. The reservoir information, as shown in Table 1, has been updated into the SWAT model database. IMD precipitation, minimum and maximum temperature were given to the model to run simulations.

2.4. Model Performance Evaluation

Initially the SWAT model is calibrated and validated using the daily and monthly streamflow. The SWAT model performance is evaluated using coefficient of determination (R^2), Nash–Sutcliffe efficiency coefficient (NSE) [58] and percent bias (Pbias) [59].

$$NSE = 1 - \frac{\sum_{i=1}^{n}\left(Y_i^{obs} - Y_i^{sim}\right)^2}{\sum_{i=1}^{n}\left(Y_i^{obs} - Y_{mean}^{obs}\right)^2} \quad (2)$$

$$Pbias = \frac{\sum_{i=1}^{n}\left(Y_i^{obs} - Y_i^{sim}\right) \times 100}{\sum_{i=1}^{n}\left(Y_i^{obs}\right)} \quad (3)$$

Here, Y_i^{obs} is the ith observed data, Y_i^{sim} is the ith simulated data, Y_{mean}^{obs} is the mean of observed data.

The optimal value of Pbias is 0, positive value represents the model bias towards underestimation and negative value denotes bias towards overestimation. The model performance was judged as satisfactory if NSE greater than 0.5 and Pbias is less than ±25% for monthly streamflow and less than ±55% for sediment simulations [60].

3. Results and Discussion

This study simulated streamflow and sediment yield, analyzed water balance components and identified critical source areas of erosion in the Vamsadhara and Nagavali river basins. The model was calibrated and validated by SWAT-CUP. The average annual water balance components and sediment yield analyses were performed sub-basin by sub-basin.

3.1. Calibration and Validation Analysis

The SUFI-2 algorithm in the SWAT-CUP [61] was used for model calibration, validation, and sensitivity analysis. The observed streamflow and sediments from Srikakulam and Kashinagar stations were used to calibrate and validate the SWAT model over Nagavali and Vamsadhara river basins (Figure 1). Based on observed streamflow data, the model simulated monthly streamflow for both basins for 29 years, from 1986 to 2014. The first five years of these 29 years were used as a model warm-up period for variable initialization. The following 15 years, from 1991 to 2005, were considered for calibration, and the remaining 9 years, from 2006 to 2014, were considered for validation. Observed sediment concentration data was available for 12 years, from 2002 to 2013 in grams per liter, and is converted to sediment load (tons per month). Data from 2002 to 2010 were used for calibration, and data from 2011 to 2013 were used for validation of sediment yield simulations.

3.1.1. Sensitivity Analysis

The SWAT model is a conceptual, semi-distributed model based on a number of parameters that vary significantly on a spatial and temporal scale. During the calibration period, sensitivity analysis was performed to identify the key parameters. For monthly streamflow simulations, 15 parameters were taken into account. The significance of sensitivity (P) and t-stat values were considered to identify sensitive parameters in Table 3. The parameters were more sensitive as the absolute t-stat values increase. P-values close to 0 indicating that the parameter is significant. The lower p-value and greater absolute t-stat value indicates higher sensitivity.

Table 3. Parameters that are sensitive in the Nagavali and Vamsadhara river basins.

S. No.	Parameter_Name	Nagavali River		Vamsadhara River	
		p-Value	t-Stat	p-Value	t-Stat
1	R__CN2.mgt	0.00	−8.74	0.00	−11.64
2	V__ALPHA_BF.gw	0.00	4.39	0.37	−0.90
3	A__GW_DELAY.gw	0.31	1.03	0.36	0.91
4	A__GWQMN.gw	0.41	0.83	0.00	6.23
5	V__GW_REVAP.gw	0.49	0.69	0.00	3.99
6	A__RCHRG_DP.gw	0.62	0.50	0.87	0.16
7	A__REVAPMN.gw	0.37	−0.90	0.35	−0.93
8	V__ALPHA_BF_D.gw	0.11	−1.61	0.23	−1.21
9	R__SOL_AWC.sol	0.87	0.16	0.01	−2.70
10	V__ESCO.hru	0.41	0.82	0.38	−0.88
11	V__CANMX.hru	0.09	1.69	0.10	1.64
12	V__CH_N2.rte	0.12	−1.55	0.54	−0.62
13	V__CH_K2.rte	0.02	−2.28	0.56	−0.58
14	V__CH_K1.sub	0.01	2.47	0.00	6.17
15	V__CH_N1.sub	0.55	0.59	0.12	1.55

Note: X_Parname.ext "X_" is a code to indicate the type of change to be applied to the parameter. If it is replaced by v_ it means the default parameter is replaced by a calibrated value, a_ means calibrated value added to the default value and r_ means the existing value is multiplied by (1+ calibrated value).

From Table 3, it is evident that CN2, ALPHA_BF, CH_K1, CH_K2, CH_N2, and CANMX are the most sensitive parameters for streamflow over Nagavali river basin and

CN2, GWQMN, CH_K1, GW_REVAP coefficient, SOL_AWC, CH_K2 and CANMX are the most sensitive parameters for streamflow over Vamsadhara river basin. Because CN2 is the most sensitive and directly related to the runoff process in both river basins, changes in CN2 have a direct effect on streamflow and sediment yield. Table 4 represents the calibrated parameters and their fitted values over the Nagavali and Vamsadhara river basins for streamflow simulations, respectively. The parameters were described in detail in [54] and SWAT user manuals.

Table 4. Calibrated parameters and their fitted values for streamflow simulations.

S. No.	Parameter_Name	Min_Value	Max_Value	Fitted Values	
				Nagavali River Basin	Vamsadhara River Basin
1	R__CN2.mgt	−0.1	0.1	−0.088	−0.092
2	V__ALPHA_BF.gw	0	1	0.642	0.093
3	A__GW_DELAY.gw	−30	90	84.300	−11.1
4	A__GWQMN.gw	−1000	1000	5	−345
5	V__GW_REVAP.gw	0.02	0.2	0.053	0.172
6	A__REVAPMN.gw	−750	750	−498.75	123.75
7	V__ALPHA_BF_D.gw	0	1	0.45	0.687
8	A__RCHRG_DP.gw	−0.05	0.05	−0.019	−0.036
9	R__SOL_AWC.sol	−0.1	0.1	0.04	−0.029
10	V__ESCO.hru	0.3	0.6	0.53	0.58
11	V__CANMX.hru	0	20	0.45	9.35
12	V__CH_N2.rte	0.01	0.1	0.033	0.084
13	V__CH_K2.rte	0	100	74.75	24.25
14	V__CH_K1.sub	0	100	73.25	91.75
15	V__CH_N1.sub	0.01	0.3	0.19	0.15

3.1.2. Streamflow Simulation

The statistical results from calibration and validation showed a good agreement between observed and simulated monthly streamflow as presented in Table 5.

Table 5. Calibration and validation statistics.

River Basin	Gauge Station	Calibration				Validation			
		Period	R^2	NSE	Pbias	Period	R^2	NSE	Pbias
		Monthly streamflow simulations							
Nagavali	Srikakulam	1991–2005	0.85	0.84	3.4	2006–2014	0.73	0.71	9.7
Vamsadhara	Kashinagar	1991–2005	0.82	0.8	−6.7	2006–2014	0.74	0.73	10.3
		Monthly sediment simulations							
Nagavali	Srikakulam	2002–2010	0.86	0.85	−13.6	2011–2013	0.76	0.7	−14.3
Vamsadhara	Kashinagar	2002–2010	0.75	0.71	14.8	2011–2013	0.7	0.68	−42.8

The NSE values for the monthly streamflow of the calibration and validation period were 0.84 and 0.71 at Srikakulam station in the Nagavali river basin and 0.8 and 0.73 at Kashinagar station in the Vamsadhara river basin. The percentage bias (Pbias) for the calibration period was 3.4% for the Nagavali basin, indicating that it tends to under-predict, and −6.7% for the Vamsadhara basin, indicating that it tends to over-predict. During validation, Pbias is 9.7% and 10.3% in the Nagavali and Vamsadhara river basins, respectively. The model tends to under-predict for the Nagavali and Vamsadhara river basins during the validation period. The statistics for the SWAT model setup for Vamsadhara and Nagavali river basins are good when compared to standard model statistics [60]. Figures 4 and 5 show the observed versus simulated monthly streamflow at the Srikakulam and Kashinagar gauge stations over the Nagavali and Vamsadhara river basins, respectively.

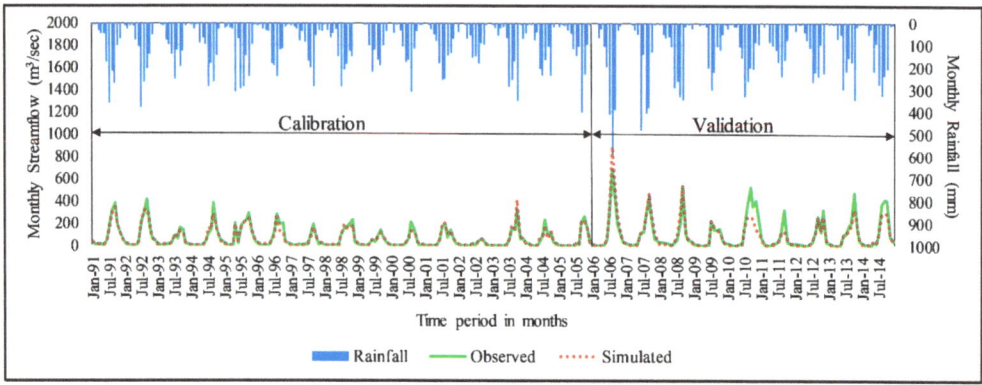

Figure 4. Observed versus simulated monthly streamflow during the calibration and validation period over the Nagavali river basin.

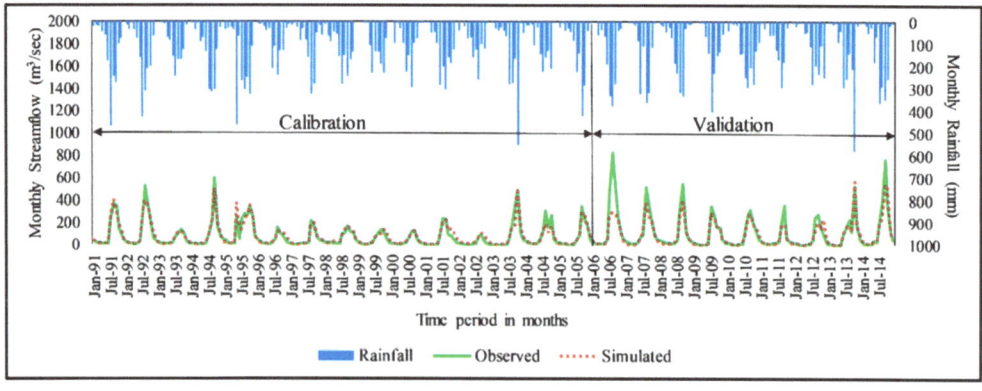

Figure 5. Observed versus simulated monthly streamflow during the calibration and validation period over the Vamsadhara river basin.

From Figures 4 and 5, it is evident that during the calibration and validation period, the time series plot of simulated streamflow reflects the precipitation pattern over the Vamsadhara and Nagavali river basins and matched well with the observed streamflow. In the Vamsadhara and Nagavali river basins, the largest quantity of streamflow occurred from June to October in every year.

3.1.3. Sediment Simulation

Following calibration of streamflow, the calibrated streamflow parameters were updated into the SWAT model, and sediment simulations were carried out. To reduce the high sediment yield from agricultural lands, manual calibration with landscape parameters influencing sediment yield from agricultural lands was performed first, followed by auto calibration [53,54]. Due to watershed uneven slope distribution, the initial LS factor (HRU_SLP and SLSUBBSN) is very high, resulting in an overestimation of sediment yield. Manual calibration was considered only for agricultural HRUs to reduce the sediment load with three landscape parameters [62] including USLE_P, HRU_SLP and SLSUBBSN.

To reduce sediment yield, the LS factors were reduced by replacing HRU_SLP (average slope steepness (m/m)) with 2% for agricultural HRUs and 0.5% for Rice crop HRUs and SLSUBBSN (average slope length (m)) with 75 m. These changes reduced the simulated sediment yield while limiting erosion from agricultural HRUs. The erosion process is influenced by the USLE P (USLE equation support practice) factor, which is reduced from the default value of 1 to 0.5 for agricultural HRUs. Decreasing of USLE_P has a greater impact on sediment yield from agricultural HRUs. After adjusting these three parameters manually, the simulated sediment yield from agricultural HRUs is less than 1 t/ha/yr. Following manual adjustment of these three parameters, auto calibration was performed using the five parameters presented in Table 6.

Table 6. Calibrated parameters and their fitted values for monthly sediment simulation.

S. No.	Parameter_Name	Min_Value	Max_Value	Fitted Values	
				Nagavali River Basin	Vamsadhara River Basin
1	V__CH_COV1.rte	0	0.6	0.23	0.46
2	V__CH_COV2.rte	0	1	0.39	0.17
3	V__SPCON.bsn	0.0001	0.01	0.006	0.0068
4	V__SPEXP.bsn	1	1.5	1.12	1.08
5	R__USLE_K(..).sol	−0.2	0.2	−0.1	−0.09

As indicated in Table 5, the statistical findings between monthly observed and simulated sediment load obtained during calibration and validation revealed a good agreement for the Nagavali river basin and a satisfactory agreement for Vamsadhara river basin. For the calibration and validation periods, the NSE values for monthly sediment at Srikakulam gauge station for the Nagavali river basin were 0.85 and 0.7, respectively, and 0.71 and 0.68 at Kashinagar gauge station for the Vamsadhara river basin, respectively.

The percentage biases (Pbias) for the calibration and validation periods were −13.6% and −14.3% for the Nagavali basin and 14.8% and −42.8% for the Vamsadhara basin. The Pbias values for monthly sediment load show that the model tends to overpredict for the Nagavali river basin and underpredict during calibration, and overpredict during validation for the Vamsadhara river basin. The sediment load in the Nagavali and Vamsadhara river basins were overestimated due to basin barren and scant vegetation over the landscapes, topography and its complexity, and steep slopes, whereas 60% of the basins area was covered by steep slopes that are more than 8 degrees. Figures 6 and 7 show the observed and simulated monthly sediment load over the Nagavali and Vamsadhara river basins during the calibration and validation periods, respectively.

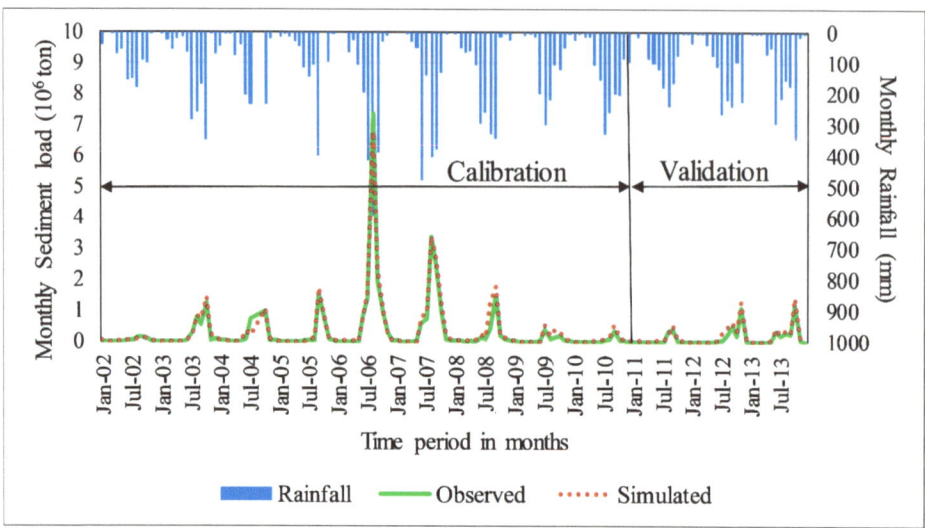

Figure 6. Observed versus simulated monthly sediment load during the calibration and validation period over the Nagavali river basin.

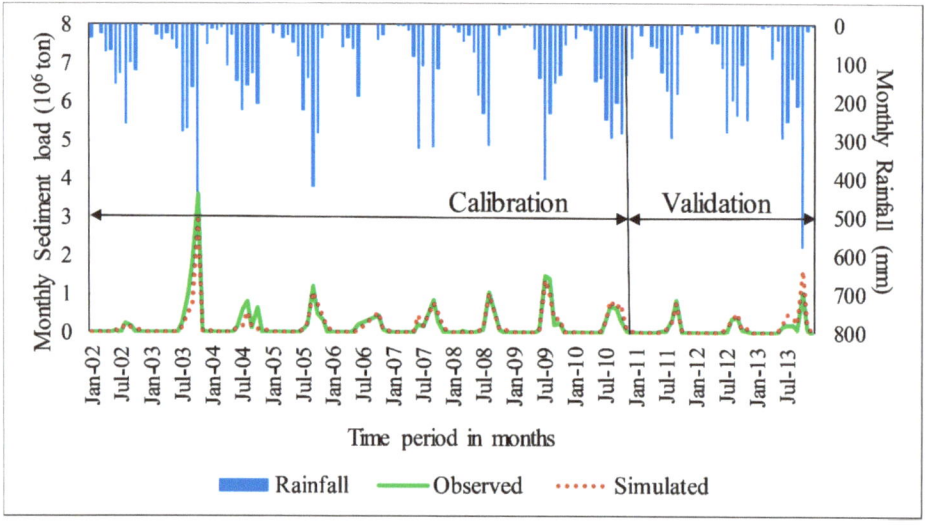

Figure 7. Observed versus simulated monthly sediment load during the calibration and validation period over the Vamsadhara river basin.

3.2. Water Balance of Nagavali and Vamsadhara River Basins

Analyzing and quantifying various elements of hydrological processes occurring within the basin is required for various water management scenarios. Precipitation, surface runoff, water yield, lateral runoff, and evapotranspiration are the primary components of water balance in the basin. The results of the calibrated model were examined in terms of the water balance components on a monthly basis from 1991 to 2014. The annual average rainfall amount in the Nagavali and Vamsadhara river basins is 1259 mm and 1332 mm, respectively. Figure 8a depicts the monthly water balance for the Nagavali and Vamsadhara river basins (b).

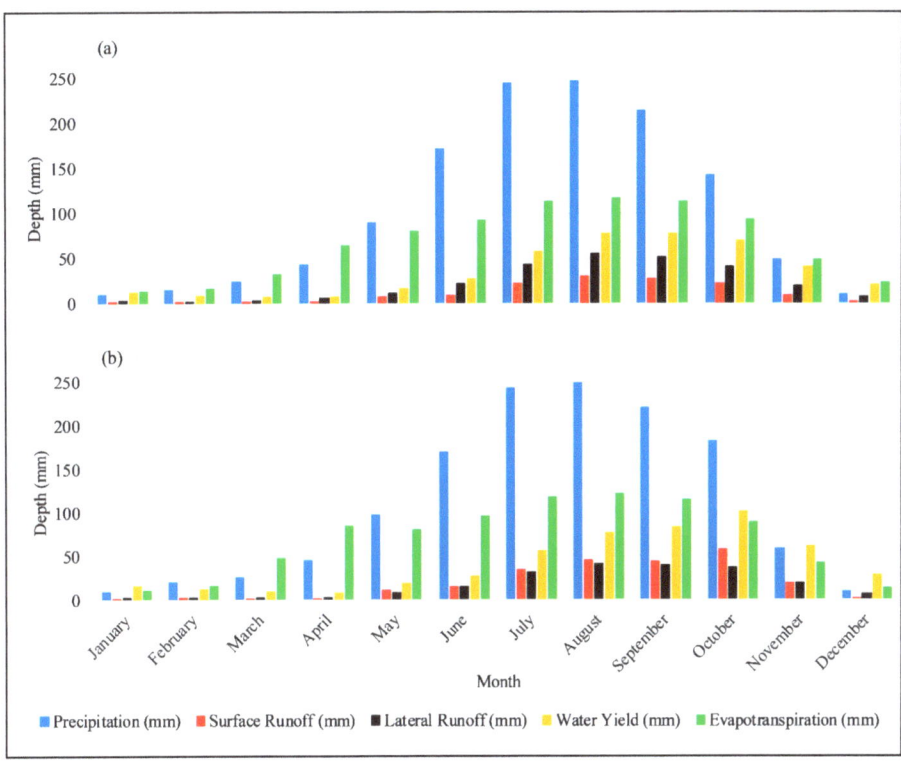

Figure 8. Mean monthly values of water balance components (**a**) Nagavali basin (**b**) Vamsadhara river basin.

During the monsoon season, 80% of the rainfall falls (June to October). Evapotranspiration contributes the most to water loss in both river basins, accounting for 63% of total water loss. The amount of water lost due to evapotranspiration is determined by the soil evaporation compensation factor (ESCO), the ET estimation method, and the leaf area index. Forest land and agriculture land cover the majority of the catchment area over the Nagavali and Vamsadhara river basins. As a result, evapotranspiration has a major impact on both river basin water resources. Because of the amount of plant growth, humidity, and wind velocities are high in these areas during monsoon and post monsoon months, evapotranspiration demands were higher in monsoon and post monsoon months than in pre monsoon months [43]. From Figure 8, in dry months, monthly evapotranspiration is estimated to be greater than total precipitation for both river basins. This is allowed because evapo-transpiration is a continuous process that occurs at varying rates during the day and night, regardless of precipitation, and the water for evapotranspiration comes from near-surface soil moisture. The depth of the plant root, which allows it to gather water via deeper soil layers, affects the rate of evapotranspiration [20]. Furthermore, because the SWAT model is a continuous model that accounts for changes in soil moisture content, it is easier to factor in the soil moisture content from the previous day. As a result, total precipitation in a given month may be less than total evapotranspiration in dry months. From the water balance analysis, there is a need for water-harvesting structures because both basins receive more than 80% of their rainfall during the monsoon season.

3.3. Spatial Distribution of Water Balance Components

The spatial distribution of average annual values of various water balance components was visualized to better understand the hydrological cycle over the Vamsadhara and Nagavali river basins. Figure 9 shows the spatial distribution of average annual precipitation, surface runoff, groundwater flow over the Nagavali river basin.

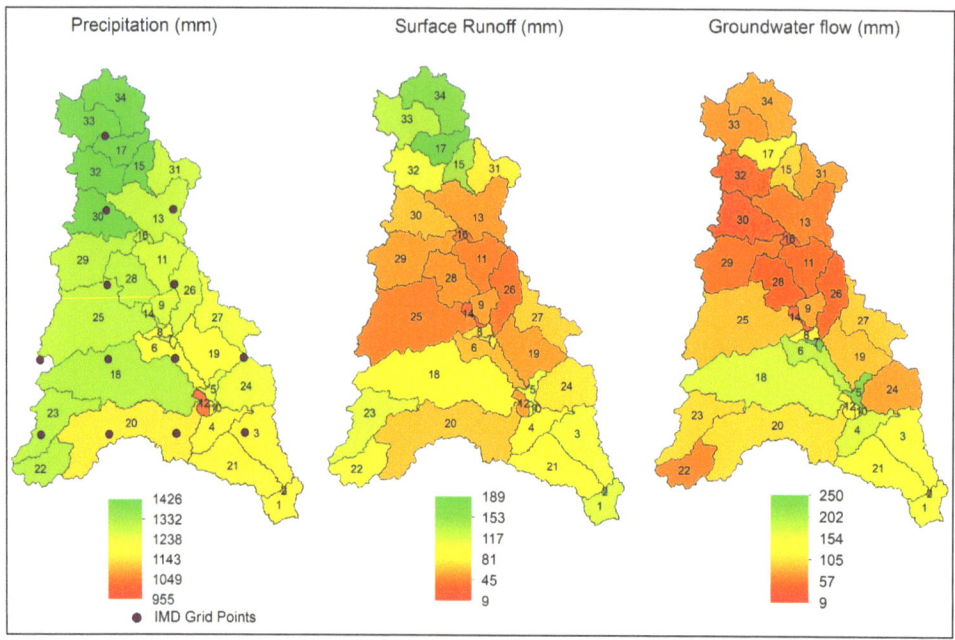

Figure 9. Spatial distribution of average annual precipitation, surface runoff and groundwater flow over the Nagavali river basin for the period of 24 years (1991–2014).

The upper sub-basins received the most precipitation over the Nagavali river basin, while the lower sub-basins received the least. Surface runoff ranges from 9 mm to 189 mm, with sub-basins 1, 2, 15, 17, 33 and 34 producing the most. The groundwater flow ranges from 9 mm to 250 mm, with sub-basins 5 and 7 producing the most groundwater flow. Figure 10 shows the spatial distribution of annual average evapotranspiration and its validation using the Famine Early Warning Systems Network Land Data Assimilation System (FLDAS) [63]. The SWAT model-simulated evapotranspiration varying from 698 mm to 1050 mm. Sub-basins 7, 10 and 12 contribute the most evapotranspiration, while lower sub basins with waterbodies and agricultural lands contribute the least. The FLDAS dataset, on the other hand, ranged from 825 mm to 1131 mm over the Nagavali river basin. The difference in Pbias between the SWAT simulated evapotranspiration and the FLDAS dataset is 15%.

The spatial distribution of average annual precipitation, surface runoff, and groundwater flow over the Vamsadhara river basin is depicted in Figure 11. The highest precipitation over the Vamsadhara river basin was 1410 mm in the upper sub-basins and the lowest was 1192 mm in the lower sub-basins. Surface runoff ranges from 43 mm to 172 mm, with sub-basins 8, 11, 12, 16, 25, and 29 producing the most. Groundwater flow ranges from 59 to 265 mm, with the majority of sub-basins contributing the most groundwater flow. Figure 12 shows the spatial distribution of average annual evapotranspiration and its validation using the FLDAS dataset. The SWAT simulated evapotranspiration varying from 730 mm to 941 mm, with sub-basins 2, 7 and 28 contributing the most. Whereas the FLDAS dataset ranged from 831 mm to 1075 mm over the Vamsadhara river basin. The difference in Pbias between the SWAT simulated evapotranspiration and the FLDAS dataset is 11%.

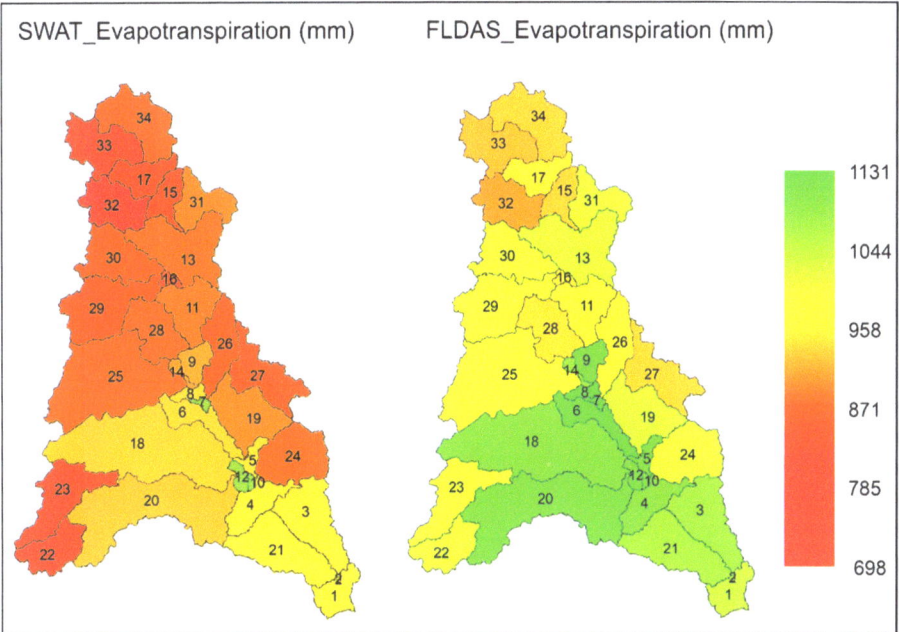

Figure 10. Spatial distribution of average annual evapotranspiration and its validation using FLDAS data over the Nagavali river basin for the period of 24 years (1991–2014).

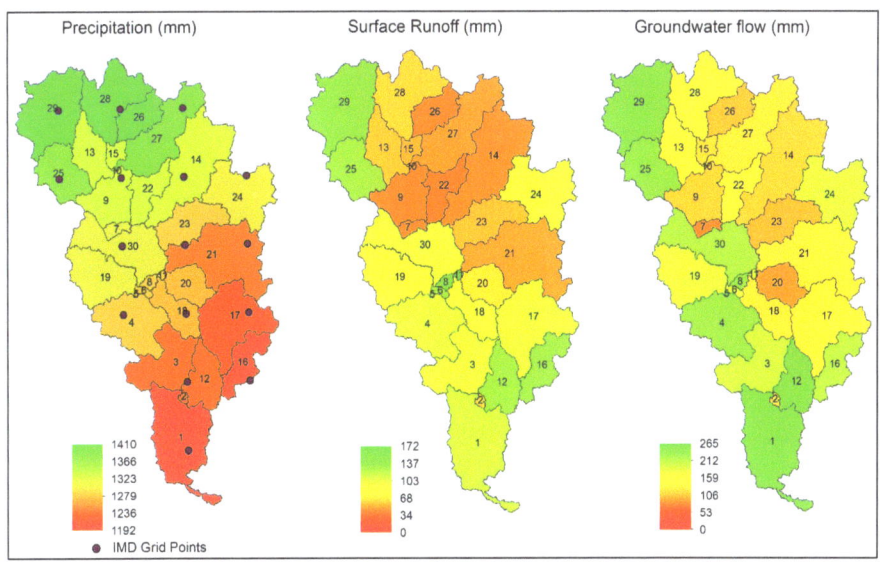

Figure 11. Spatial distribution of average annual precipitation, surface runoff and groundwater flow over the Vamsadhara river basin for the period of 24 years (1991–2014).

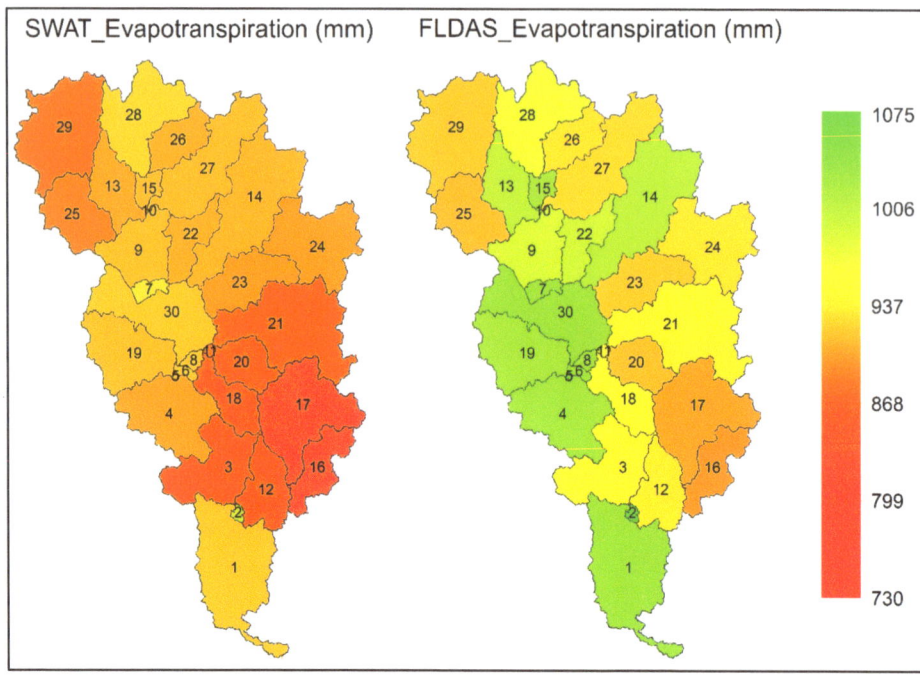

Figure 12. Spatial distribution of average annual evapotranspiration and its validation using FLDAS data over the Vamsadhara river basin for the period of 24 years (1991–2014).

Based on the spatial distribution of average annual hydrological components, it was concluded that the simulated precipitation over the basins for the period of 24 years from 1991 to 2014 showed a decreasing gradient from north to south and follows the altitude gradient over the two basins. Soil type and land use had the greatest influence on groundwater flow. The sub-basins with sandy soil and forest cover contributed the most groundwater flow. Sub-basins with bodies of water and agricultural lands with long-grown plants contribute the most evapotranspiration. The correlation between SWAT simulated evapotranspiration and the FLDAS dataset over the Nagavali and Vamsadhara river basins was 0.78.

3.4. Spatial Variability of Sediment Yield and Identification of Sediment Source Areas

The average trapping efficiency of sediment over the Nagavali and Vamsadhara river basins were identified as 77.65% and 67.59% by reservoirs. Table 7 shows the average annual sediment yield (t/ha/yr) for the two river basins divided into three classes for spatial representation and identification of critical source areas of sediment yield suggested by Singh [64] for Indian conditions [2,65]. The average annual sediment yield from the sub-basin is less than 5 t/ha/yr in the slight erosion class, 5–10 t/ha/yr in the moderate erosion class, and greater than 10 t/ha/yr in the high erosion class. The average annual sediment yield from sub-basins serves as the foundation for identifying critical sediment source areas [2,5,20]. This is useful for sub-watershed agricultural, structural, and watershed management planning.

Table 7. Areas subjected to various levels of soil erosion in the Nagavali and Vamsadhara basins.

S. No.	Sediment Yield (t/ha/yr)	Soil Erosion Class	Nagavali River Basin		Vamsadhara River Basin	
			Percent Area	Sub-Watershed Numbers	Percent Area	Sub-Watershed Numbers
1	0–5	Slight	24	1–7, 10, 12–14, 19, 21	13	5, 10, 21, 22, 26
2	5–10	Moderate	49.5	8, 9, 11, 16, 18, 20, 25, 26, 28–31	38	1, 2, 4, 7–9, 13–15, 27, 30
3	>10	High	26.5	15, 17, 22–24, 27, 32–34	49	3, 6, 11, 12, 16–20, 23–25, 28, 29

3.4.1. Nagavali River Basin

Figure 13a depicts the spatial distribution of average annual simulated sediment yield over the Nagavali river basin for 34 sub-basins.

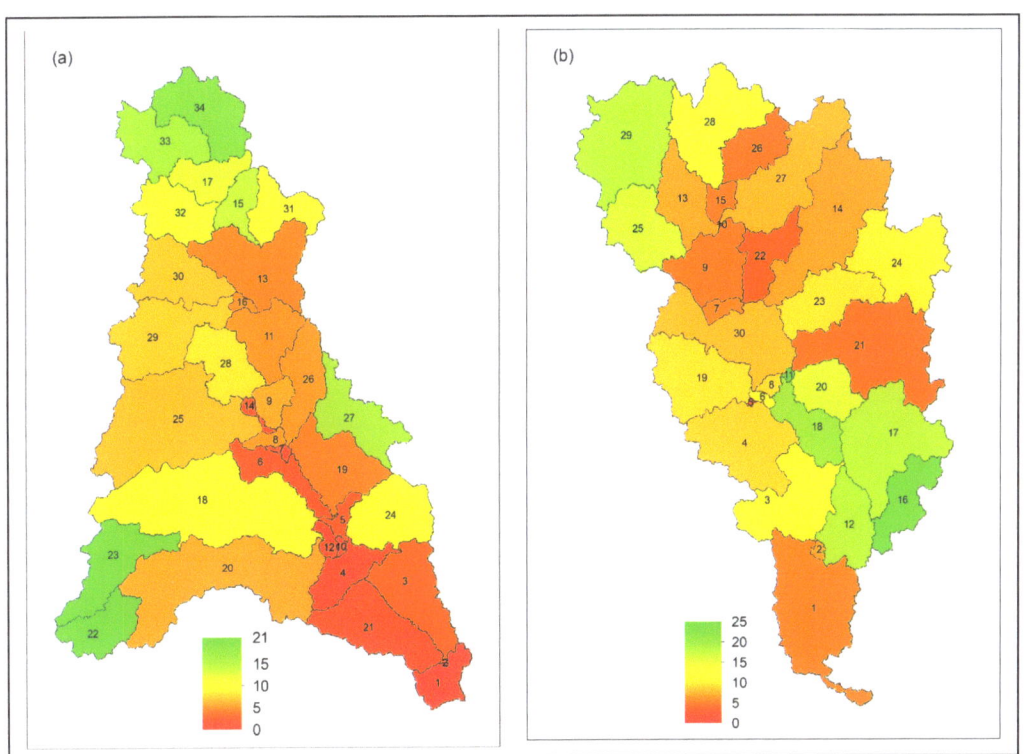

Figure 13. Spatial distribution of average annual sediment yield (t/ha/yr) (a) over the Nagavali river basin (b) over the Vamsadhara river basin for the period of 13 years (2002–2013).

Figure 13a shows that sub-basins 22, 23, and 34 have the highest sediment yield of 20.3 t/ha/yr. These sub-basins are characterized by moderate to steep slopes, and the majority of sub-basin areas are devoid of land use. Table 7 shows that 26.5% of the basin area is subject to high erosion (>10 t/ha/yr), with the corresponding sub-basins being 15, 17, 22–24, 27, 32, 33 and 34. These sub-basins are regarded as critical sediment source areas throughout the Nagavali river basin, and priority is given to them. In total, 49.5%

of basin area is classified as moderate soil erosion (5–10 t/ha/yr) and 24% is classified as slight erosion (5 t/ha/yr). To reduce the severity of soil erosion caused by landscape and reservoir capacity loss, sub-basins with high sediment yields required immediate attention for soil conservation practices. The Nagavali river basin's average annual sediment yield was determined to be 7.18 t/ha/yr. In the Nagavali river basin, sub-basins with lower slopes and dense vegetation contribute a minor sediment yield. It has been observed that the lower portion of the basin produces a minor sediment yield.

3.4.2. Vamsadhara River Basin

Figure 13b depicts the spatial distribution of average annual simulated sediment yield over the Vamsadhara river basin for 30 sub-basins (b). Figure 13b shows that sub-basins 11 and 16 have the highest sediment yield of 24.8 t/ha/yr. These sub-basins, like the Nagavali river basin, have a moderate to steep slope, and the majority of the sub-basin areas are covered in wasteland. Table 7 depicts the Vamsadhara river basin, with 49% of the basin area falling into the high erosion class (> 10 t/ha/yr), and the corresponding sub-basins being 3, 6, 11, 12, 16–20, 23–25, 28, and 29. These sub-basins are regarded as critical sediment source areas throughout the Vamsadhara river basin, and priority is given to them. In total, 38% of basin area is subject to moderate soil erosion (5–10 t/ha/yr) and 13% is subject to slight erosion (5 t/ha/yr). To reduce the severity of soil erosion caused by landscape and reservoir capacity loss, the sub-basins contributing the most sediment yield required immediate attention to management practices. The average annual sediment yield of the Vamsadhara river basin, on the other hand, was found to be 10.7 t/ha/yr.

In both river basins, the majority of the sediment yield was contributed by wastelands with steep slopes (>8°), followed by fallow lands, degraded deciduous forest lands, and agricultural lands. Tribal peoples live along the river and rely on shifting cultivation for a living [12]. It could explain the high sediment yield from deciduous and degraded forest lands and wastelands.

According to average annual sediment yield analysis, the average annual sediment yield of the Nagavali and Vamsadhara river basins was found to be 7.18 and 10.7 t/ha/yr respectively, which is within the permissible limit of 11.2 t/ha/yr [13,22]. The sub-basin average annual sediment yield from the Nagavali and Vamsadhara river basins represents 26.5% and 49% of basin area contributing highest sediment yield, respectively, and the corresponding sub-basins are identified as critical sediment source areas. However, wastelands produced the highest sediment yield, followed by current fallow land, agricultural lands, degraded and deciduous forest lands with steep slopes in both river basins. According to Table 2, wastelands occupy 19.05% and 17.23% of the basin area of the Nagavali and Vamsadhara river basins, respectively. These lands are represented by hilly areas with less vegetation (scrub lands and barren lands), areas with mining activities, and areas where tribal communities previously practiced shifted cultivation.

4. Conclusions

The current study presented a SWAT model-based streamflow and sediment yield analysis of the Nagavali and Vamsadhara river basins, and critical sediment source areas were identified in order to recommend appropriate soil conservation measures at the sub watershed level. Sensitivity analysis reveals that the most sensitive parameters in both river basins are the initial SCS runoff curve number (CN2) and effective hydraulic conductivity in tributary channel alluvium (CH_K1). The obtained statistics over the Nagavali and Vamsadhara river basins range from very good to satisfactory, indicating the SWAT model's acceptance. The calibrated SWAT model simulated the streamflow generally, capturing peak flow events in close correlation with extreme precipitation, the model is influenced by both low and high precipitation events, resulting in under-predicted and over-predicted streamflow. From the water balance analysis evapotranspiration is the dominant process, accounting for 63% of the average annual rainfall over the basins. Evapotranspiration is attributed to plant growth, humidity and wind speed. The calibrated

SWAT model produced an average annual sediment yield of 7.18 t/ha/yr for the entire basin and 10.7 t/ha/yr for the Nagavali and Vamsadhara river basins, which are classified as moderate and high soil erosion class, respectively. From the sub-basin average annual sediment yield analysis, 26.5% and 49% of basin area are classified as high erosion areas, over Nagavali and Vamsadhara river basins and these areas are characterized by steep slope of wasteland, followed by fallow lands, degraded, deciduous forests and agricultural lands and critical sediment source areas. These areas require immediate attention to management practices to improve the soil water conservation measures in the Nagavali and Vamsadhara river basins.

This study contributes to our understanding of water balance analysis, sediment yield analysis and identifying sediment source areas using the SWAT model. Furthermore, this research contributes to an understanding of climate change and the application of best management practices in the Nagavali and Vamsadhara river basins with identified sediment source areas. This study also provides the best calibrated parameters for using the SWAT model for real time flood forecasting. This study is expected to assist the watershed planners and managers in implementing suitable soil and water conservation measures in both watersheds at the sub-basin scale.

Author Contributions: Conceptualization, N.R.N. and V.R.K.; methodology, V.S., V.R.K., N.R.N.; software, R.S., V.R.K.; validation, R.S., V.S. and V.R.K.; formal analysis, N.R.N.; investigation, N.R.N.; resources, V.R.K.; data curation, N.R.N.; writing—original draft preparation, N.R.N.; writing—review and editing, V.S., V.R.K.; visualization, N.R.N.; supervision, V.R.K., V.S., R.S.; project administration, V.R.K.; funding acquisition, V.R.K. All authors have read and agreed to the published version of the manuscript.

Funding: The research described in this paper is carried out with fund by Ministry of Human Resource Development (MHRD), Government of India under Scheme for Promotion of Academic and Research Collaboration (SPARC) through project number P270.

Institutional Review Board Statement: Not applicable.

Informed Consent Statement: Not applicable.

Data Availability Statement: Data available on request from the authors.

Acknowledgments: Authors are thankful to CWC (Central Water Commission Bhubaneswar), Bhuvan-NRSC (National Remote Sensing Centre, Hyderabad) for providing necessary data and information. The corresponding author's (V. Sridhar) effort was funded in part by the Virginia Agricultural Experiment Station (Blacksburg) and through the Hatch Program of the National Institute of Food and Agriculture at the United States Department of Agriculture (Washington, DC) and in part as a Fulbright-Nehru senior scholar funded by the United States India Educational Foundation.

Conflicts of Interest: The authors declare no conflict of interest.

References

1. Liu, Y.; Jiang, H. Sediment Yield Modeling Using SWAT Model: Case of Changjiang River Basin. *IOP Conf. Ser. Earth Environ. Sci.* **2019**, *234*, 012031. [CrossRef]
2. Panda, C.; Das, D.M.; Raul, S.K.; Sahoo, B.C. Sediment yield prediction and prioritization of sub-watersheds in the Upper Subarnarekha basin (India) using SWAT. *Arab. J. Geosci.* **2021**, *14*, 809. [CrossRef]
3. Li, X.H.; Yang, J.; Zhao, C.Y.; Wang, B. Runoff and sediment from orchard terraces in southeastern China. *Land Degrad. Dev.* **2014**, *25*, 184–192. [CrossRef]
4. Beskow, S.; Mello, C.; Norton, L.; Curi, N.; Viola, M.; Avanzi, J. Soil erosion prediction in the Grande River Basin, Brazil using distributed modeling. *Catena* **2009**, *79*, 49–59. [CrossRef]
5. Kumar, S.; Mishra, A. Critical Erosion Area Identification Based on Hydrological Response Unit Level for Effective Sedimentation Control in a River Basin. *Water Resour. Manag.* **2015**, *29*, 1749–1765. [CrossRef]
6. Kabir, A.; Dutta, D.; Hironaka, S. Estimating Sediment Budget at a River Basin Scale Using a Process-Based Distributed Modelling Approach. *Water Resour. Manag.* **2014**, *28*, 4143–4160. [CrossRef]
7. Narayana, D.V.; Babu, R. Estimation of soil erosion in India. *J. Irrig. Drain. Eng.* **1983**, *109*, 419–434. [CrossRef]
8. Xu, K.; Peng, H.Q.; Rifu, D.G.J.; Zhang, R.X.; Xiao, H.; Shi, Q. Sediment Yield Simulation Using SWAT Model for Water Environmental Protection in an Agricultural Watershed. *Appl. Mech. Mater.* **2015**, *713–715*, 1894–1898. [CrossRef]

9. CWC. *Compendium on Sedimentation of Reservoirs in India*; Water Planning and Projects Wing, Environment Management Organisation, Watershed and Reservoir Sedimentation Directorate, Central Water Commission, Govt of India: New Delhi, India, 2020.
10. Saroha, J. Soil Erosion: Causes, Extent, and Management in India. *Int. J. Creat. Res. Thoughts* **2017**, *5*, 1321–1330.
11. Rao, G.V.; Reddy, K.V.; Sridhar, V. Sensitivity of Microphysical Schemes on the Simulation of Post-Monsoon Tropical Cyclones over the North Indian Ocean. *Atmosphere* **2020**, *11*, 1297.
12. Eadara, A.; Kannam, H. Slope studies of Vamsadhara River basin: A Quantitative Approach. *Int. J. Eng. Innov. Technol.* **2013**, *3*, 184–188.
13. Mannering, J.V. Use of soil loss tolerances as a strategy for soil conservation. In Soil Conservation Problems and Prospects, Proceedings of the Conservation 80, the International Conference on Soil Conservation, Bedford, UK, 21–25 July 1980; Wiley: Chichester, UK, 1981; pp. 337–349.
14. Bhattacharyya, R.; Ghosh, B.N.; Mishra, P.K.; Mandal, B.; Rao, C.S.; Sarkar, D.; Das, K.; Anil, K.S.; Lalitha, M.; Hati, K.M.; et al. Soil Degradation in India: Challenges and Potential Solutions. *Sustainability* **2015**, *7*, 3528–3570. [CrossRef]
15. Das, S. Dynamics of streamflow and sediment load in Peninsular Indian rivers (1965–2015). *Sci. Total Environ.* **2021**, *799*, 149372. [CrossRef]
16. Vaithiyanathan, P.; Ramanathan, A.L.; Subramanian, V. Erosion, transport and deposition of sediments by the tropical rivers of India. In *Sediment Budgets*; IAHS Publication: Wallingford, UK, 1988; p. 174.
17. Singh, G.; Babu, R.; Narain, P.; Bhushan, L.S.; Abrol, I.P. Soil erosion rates in India. *J. Soil Water Conserv.* **1992**, *47*, 97–99.
18. Prasannakumar, V.; Vijith, H.; Abinod, S.; Geetha, N. Estimation of soil erosion risk within a small mountainous sub-watershed in Kerala, India, using Revised Universal Soil Loss Equation (RUSLE) and geo-information technology. *Geosci. Front.* **2012**, *3*, 209–215. [CrossRef]
19. Himanshu, S.K.; Pandey, A.; Shrestha, P. Application of SWAT in an Indian river basin for modeling runoff, sediment and water balance. *Environ. Earth Sci.* **2017**, *76*, 3. [CrossRef]
20. Himanshu, S.K.; Pandey, A.; Yadav, B.; Gupta, A. Evaluation of best management practices for sediment and nutrient loss control using SWAT model. *Soil Tillage Res.* **2019**, *192*, 42–58. [CrossRef]
21. Dutta, S.; Sen, D. Application of SWAT model for predicting soil erosion and sediment yield. *Sustain. Water Resour. Manag.* **2018**, *4*, 447–468. [CrossRef]
22. Mahapatra, S.K.; Reddy, G.P.O.; Nagdev, R.; Yadav, R.P.; Singh, S.K.; Sharda, V.N. Assessment of Soil Erosion in the Fragile Himalayan Ecosystem of Uttarakhand, India Using USLE and GIS for Sustainable Productivity. *Curr. Sci.* **2018**, *115*, 108–121. [CrossRef]
23. Saha, A.; Ghosh, P.; Mitra, B. GIS Based Soil Erosion Estimation Using Rusle Model: A Case Study of Upper Kangsabati Watershed, West Bengal, India. *Int. J. Environ. Sci. Nat. Resour.* **2018**, *13*, 119–126. [CrossRef]
24. Kolli, M.K.; Opp, C.; Groll, M. Estimation of soil erosion and sediment yield concentration across the Kolleru Lake catchment using GIS. *Environ. Earth Sci.* **2021**, *80*, 161. [CrossRef]
25. Hoekema, D.J.; Sridhar, V. Relating climatic attributes and water resources allocation: A study using surface water supply and soil moisture indices in the Snake River basin, Idaho. *Water Resour. Res.* **2011**, *47*, W07536. [CrossRef]
26. Sridhar, V.; Jin, X.; Jaksa, W.T.A. Explaining the hydroclimatic variability and change in the Salmon River basin. *Clim. Dyn.* **2012**, *40*, 1921–1937. [CrossRef]
27. Beasley, D.B.; Huggins, L.F.; Monke, E.J. ANSWERS: A Model for Watershed Planning. *Trans. ASAE* **1980**, *23*, 938–944. [CrossRef]
28. Young, R.A.; Onstad, C.A.; Bosch, D.D.; Anderson, W.P. AGNPS: A nonpoint-source pollution model for evaluating agricultural watersheds. *J. Soil Water Conserv.* **1989**, *44*, 168–173.
29. Foster, G.R.; Lane, L.J. *User Requirements: USDA, Water Erosion Prediction Project (WEPP) Draft 6.3. NSERL Report (USA)*; National Soil Erosion Research Laboratory, USDA, Agricultural Research Service: Washington, DC, USA, 1987.
30. Arnold, J.G.; Srinivasan, R.; Muttiah, R.S.; Williams, J.R. Large area hydrologic modeling and assessment part i: Model development. *J. Am. Water Resour. Assoc.* **1998**, *34*, 73–89. [CrossRef]
31. Roti, V.; Kashyap, P.; Kumar, A.; Srivastava, R.; Chandra, H. Runoff and Sediment Yield Estimation by SWAT Model: Review and Outlook. *Int. J. Curr. Microbiol. Appl. Sci.* **2018**, *7*, 879–886. [CrossRef]
32. Matamoros, D.; Guzman, E.; Bonini, J.; Vanrolleghem, P.A. AGNPS and SWAT Model Calibration for Hydrologic Modeling of an Ecuadorian River Basin under Data Scarcity; River Basin Restoration and Management; IWA Publishing: London, UK, 2005; pp. 71–78.
33. Mishra, A.; Kar, S.; Pandey, A.C. Comparison of SWAT with HSPF model in Predicting hydrologic processes of a small Multivegetated watershed. *J. Agric. Eng.* **2008**, *45*, 29–35.
34. Gitau, M.W.; Gburek, W.J.; Bishop, P.L. Use of the SWAT Model to Quantify Water Quality Effects of Agricultural BMPs at the Farm-Scale Level. *Trans. ASABE* **2008**, *51*, 1925–1936. [CrossRef]
35. Gassman, P.W.; Reyes, M.R.; Green, C.H.; Arnold, J.G. The Soil and Water Assessment Tool: Historical Development, Applications, and Future Research Directions. *Trans. ASABE* **2007**, *50*, 1211–1250. [CrossRef]
36. Borah, D.K.; Bera, M. Watershed-scale hydrologic and nonpoint-source pollution models: Review of mathematical bases. *Trans. ASAE* **2003**, *46*, 1553. [CrossRef]
37. Rossi, C.G.; Srinivasan, R.; Jirayoot, K.; Le Duc, T.; Souvannabouth, P.; Binh, N.; Gassman, P.W. Hydrologic evaluation of the Lower Mekong River Basin with the soil and water assessment tool model. *Int. Agric. Eng. J.* **2009**, *18*, 1–13.

38. Sridhar, V.; Kang, H.; Ali, S.A. Human-Induced Alterations to Land Use and Climate and Their Responses for Hydrology and Water Management in the Mekong River Basin. *Water* **2019**, *11*, 1307. [CrossRef]
39. Setti, S.; Maheswaran, R.; Sridhar, V.; Barik, K.; Merz, B.; Agarwal, A. Inter-Comparison of Gauge-Based Gridded Data, Reanalysis and Satellite Precipitation Product with an Emphasis on Hydrological Modeling. *Atmosphere* **2020**, *11*, 1252. [CrossRef]
40. Kang, H.; Sridhar, V.; Mainuddin, M.; Trung, L.D. Future rice farming threatened by drought in the Lower Mekong Basin. *Sci. Rep.* **2021**, *11*, 9383. [CrossRef]
41. Sridhar, V.; Kang, H.; Ali, S.A.; Bola, G.B.; Tshimanga, R.M.; Lakshmi, V. Water Budgets and Droughts under Current and Future Conditions in the Cong River Basin. In *Congo Basin Hydrology, Climate, and Biogeochemistry: A Foundation for the Future*; Wiley: Hoboken, NJ, USA, 2021.
42. Stratton, B.T.; Sridhar, V.; Gribb, M.M.; McNamara, J.P.; Narasimhan, B. Modeling the Spatially Varying Water Balance Processes in a Semiarid Mountainous Watershed of Idaho. *JAWRA J. Am. Water Resour. Assoc.* **2009**, *45*, 1390–1408. [CrossRef]
43. Setti, S.; Rathinasamy, M.; Chandramouli, S. Assessment of water balance for a forest dominated coastal river basin in India using a semi distributed hydrological model. *Model. Earth Syst. Environ.* **2018**, *4*, 127–140. [CrossRef]
44. Loukika, K.N.; Keesara, V.R.; Buri, E.S.; Sridhar, V. Predicting the Effects of Land Use Land Cover and Climate Change on Munneru River Basin Using CA-Markov and Soil and Water Assessment Tool. *Sustainability* **2022**, *14*, 5000. [CrossRef]
45. Reddy, N.N.; Reddy, K.V.; Vani, J.S.L.S.; Daggupati, P.; Srinivasan, R. Climate change impact analysis on watershed using QSWAT. *Spat. Inf. Res.* **2018**, *26*, 253–259. [CrossRef]
46. Niraula, R.; Kalin, L.; Wang, R.; Srivastava, P. Determining Nutrient and Sediment Critical Source Areas with SWAT: Effect of Lumped Calibration. *Trans. ASABE* **2011**, *55*, 137–147. [CrossRef]
47. Rao, G.V.; Reddy, K.V.; Srinivasan, R.; Sridhar, V.; Umamahesh, N.; Pratap, D. Spatio-temporal analysis of rainfall extremes in the flood-prone Nagavali and Vamsadhara Basins in eastern India. *Weather Clim. Extremes* **2020**, *29*, 100265.
48. Iqbal, T.H.P.K.M.; Yarrakula, K. Probabilistic flood inundation mapping for sparsely gauged tropical river. *Arab. J. Geosci.* **2020**, *13*, 940. [CrossRef]
49. Mishra, S.P.; Panigrahi, R. Storm impact on south Odisha coast, India. *Int. J. Adv. Res. Sci. Eng.* **2014**, *3*, 209–225.
50. DECCAN CHRONICLE. 2017. Available online: https://www.deccanchronicle.com/nation/current-affairs/190717/nagavali-vamsadhara-inflows-recede-flash-floods-threat-looms.html (accessed on 16 July 2022).
51. Pai, D.S.; Rajeevan, M.; Sreejith, O.P.; Mukhopadhyay, B.; Satbha, N.S. Development of a new high spatial resolution (0.25 × 0.25) long period (1901–2010) daily gridded rainfall data set over India and its comparison with existing data sets over the region. *Mausam* **2014**, *65*, 1–18. [CrossRef]
52. Srivastava, A.K.; Rajeevan, M.; Kshirsagar, S.R. Development of a high resolution daily gridded temperature data set (1969–2005) for the Indian region. *Atmos. Sci. Lett.* **2009**, *10*, 249–254. [CrossRef]
53. Neitsch, S.L.; Arnold, J.G.; Kiniry, J.R.; Srinivasan, R.; Williams, J.R. *Soil and Water Assessment Tool, Theoretical Documentation: Version 2005*; USDA Agricultural Research Service and Blackland Research Center: Temple, TX, USA, 2005.
54. Arnold, J.G.; Moriasi, D.N.; Gassman, P.W.; Abbaspour, K.C.; White, M.J.; Srinivasan, R.; Santhi, C.; Harmel, R.D.; Van Griensven, A.; VanLiew, M.W.; et al. Swat: Model Use, Calibration, and Validation. *Am. Soc. Agric. Biol. Eng.* **2012**, *55*, 1491–1508.
55. Sehgal, V.; Sridhar, V.; Juran, L.; Ogejo, J.A. Integrating Climate Forecasts with the Soil and Water Assessment Tool (SWAT) for High-Resolution Hydrologic Simulations and Forecasts in the Southeastern U.S. *Sustainability* **2018**, *10*, 3079. [CrossRef]
56. Sehgal, V.; Sridhar, V. Watershed-scale retrospective drought analysis and seasonal forecasting using multi-layer, high-resolution simulated soil moisture for Southeastern U.S. *Weather. Clim. Extrem.* **2018**, *23*, 100191. [CrossRef]
57. Wischmeier, W.H.; Smith, D.D. *Predicting Rainfall-Erosion Losses from Cropland East of the Rocky Mountains: Guide for Selection of Practices for Soil and Water Conservation (No. 282)*; Agricultural Research Service, US Department of Agriculture: Washington, DC, USA, 1965.
58. Nash, J.E.; Sutcliffe, J.V. River flow forecasting through conceptual models part I—A discussion of principles. *J. Hydrol.* **1970**, *10*, 282–290. [CrossRef]
59. Gupta, H.V.; Sorooshian, S.; Yapo, P.O. Status of Automatic Calibration for Hydrologic Models: Comparison with Multilevel Expert Calibration. *J. Hydrol. Eng.* **1999**, *4*, 135–143. [CrossRef]
60. Moriasi, D.N.; Arnold, J.G.; van Liew, M.W.; Bingner, R.L.; Harmel, R.D.; Veith, T.L. Model evaluation guidelines for systematic quantification of accuracy in watershed simulations. *Trans. ASABE* **2007**, *50*, 885–900. [CrossRef]
61. Abbaspour, K.C.; Yang, J.; Maximov, I.; Siber, R.; Bogner, K.; Mieleitner, J.; Zobrist, J.; Srinivasan, R. Modelling hydrology and water quality in the pre-alpine/alpine Thur watershed using SWAT. *J. Hydrol.* **2007**, *333*, 413–430. [CrossRef]
62. Bonumá, N.B.; Rossi, C.G.; Arnold, J.G.; Reichert, J.M.; Minella, J.P.; Allen, P.M.; Volk, M. Simulating Landscape Sediment Transport Capacity by Using a Modified SWAT Model. *J. Environ. Qual.* **2014**, *43*, 55–66. [CrossRef] [PubMed]
63. FLDAS. Available online: https://giovanni.gsfc.nasa.gov/giovanni/ (accessed on 16 July 2022).
64. Singh, V.P. *Computer Models of Watershed Hydrology*; Water Resources Publications: Littleton, CO, USA, 1995.
65. Tripathi, M.; Panda, R.; Raghuwanshi, N. Identification and Prioritisation of Critical Sub-watersheds for Soil Conservation Management using the SWAT Model. *Biosyst. Eng.* **2003**, *85*, 365–379. [CrossRef]

Article

Improving the Prediction of Soil Organic Matter in Arable Land Using Human Activity Factors

Lixin Ning [1,2,3,4], Changxiu Cheng [3,4,*], Xu Lu [1,2], Shi Shen [3,4], Liang Zhang [1,2,*], Shaomin Mu [1,2] and Yunsheng Song [1,2]

[1] College of Information Science and Engineering, Shandong Agricultural University, Taian 271018, China; ninglixin123@163.com (L.N.); lxuu306@sdau.edu.cn (X.L.); msm@sdau.edu.cn (S.M.); sys_sd@126.com (Y.S.)
[2] Agricultural Big Data Research Center, Shandong Agricultural University, Taian 271018, China
[3] Faculty of Geographical Science, Beijing Normal University, Beijing 100875, China; shens@bnu.edu.cn
[4] State Key Laboratory of Earth Surface Processes and Resource Ecology, Beijing Normal University, Beijing 100875, China
* Correspondence: chengcx@bnu.edu.cn (C.C.); zliang@sdau.edu.cn (L.Z.)

Citation: Ning, L.; Cheng, C.; Lu, X.; Shen, S.; Zhang, L.; Mu, S.; Song, Y. Improving the Prediction of Soil Organic Matter in Arable Land Using Human Activity Factors. Water 2022, 14, 1668. https://doi.org/10.3390/w14101668

Academic Editors: Ankur Srivastava and Venkat Sridhar

Received: 13 April 2022
Accepted: 20 May 2022
Published: 23 May 2022

Publisher's Note: MDPI stays neutral with regard to jurisdictional claims in published maps and institutional affiliations.

Copyright: © 2022 by the authors. Licensee MDPI, Basel, Switzerland. This article is an open access article distributed under the terms and conditions of the Creative Commons Attribution (CC BY) license (https:// creativecommons.org/licenses/by/ 4.0/).

Abstract: Detailed spatial distribution of soil organic matter (SOM) in arable land is essential for agricultural management and decision making. Based on digital soil mapping (DSM) theory, much attention has been focused on the selection of environmental covariates. However, the importance of human activity factors in SOM prediction has not received enough attention, especially in arable soil. Moreover, due to the insufficient amount of soil sampling data used to train and validate the DSM model, the prediction results may be questionable, and some even contradictory. This paper explores the effectiveness of the human footprint, amount of fertilizer application, agronomic management level, crop planting type, and irrigation guarantee degree in SOM mapping of arable land in Heilongjiang Province. The results show that the model only including environmental covariates accounts for 41% of the variation in SOM distribution. The model combining the five human activity factors increases the SOM spatial prediction by 39% in terms of R^2 (coefficient of determination), 12% in terms of RMSE (root mean square error), 15% in terms of MAE (mean absolute error), and 11% in terms of LCCC (Lin's concordance correlation coefficient), showing better prediction accuracy and performance. This indicates that human activity factors play a crucial role in determining SOM distribution in arable land. In the SOM prediction, soil moisture is the most important environmental covariate, and the amount of fertilizer application with a relative importance of 11.36% (ranking 3rd) is the most important human activity factor, higher than the annual average precipitation and elevation. From a spatial point of view, the Sanjiang Plain is a difficult area for prediction.

Keywords: soil organic matter prediction; human activity factor; large amount of data; arable land

1. Introduction

Soil organic matter (SOM) is an important soil property [1,2]. Carbon contained in soil is the largest pool in terrestrial ecosystems, containing three times as much carbon as in the atmosphere [3,4], whose small dynamic changes could affect the overall emissions of greenhouse gases [5,6]. Furthermore, SOM, providing nutrients to plants, is a crucial soil property that affects soil quality and soil fertility [7]. SOM of arable land is particularly important because agricultural soil provides most of the food needed for human survival. Unfortunately, due to intensive human activities, the depletion of SOM has been observed in arable land around the world [8–10]. The change will inevitably influence the normal global climate and agricultural production. Thus, adequate information on the spatial distribution of SOM in arable land is essential for quantifying the carbon budget, modeling the ecosystem and climate change, and evaluating soil quality to improve agricultural management and policymaking.

The well-known state factor equation of soil, referred to as CLORPT, was proposed by Jenny to estimate SOM spatial information [11]. Subsequently, McBratney proposed SCORPAN, which considers the soil to be a product of the interaction of environmental covariates [12]. In addition, "Digital Soil Mapping (DSM)" was described. As an inexpensive and efficient method, DSM technologies have received increasing attention. Numerous studies have been conducted to obtain the spatial distribution of soil information over the last few decades, including at the regional scale, national scale, and global scale [13–15].

Based on the DSM theory, much attention has been focused on the selection of covariates for predicting SOM. At early times, most variables used in DSM are natural environmental conditions. With the development of the human cognition level, the importance of anthropogenic factors in soil prediction has been gradually recognized, especially in arable soils with strong human activities. An enhanced conceptual soil equation, STEP-AWBH, has been proposed to add human activity elements as explicit soil forming factors [16]. Recently, many studies have been conducted to investigate the importance of human activities to SOM modeling, which are receiving increasing attention. In Anhui Province (China), Yang built four pools of different variables, containing environmental or agricultural management indicators, to test the effect of agricultural parameters in SOM mapping [6]. In the same area, crop rotation information generated using a Fourier transform was used to explore the effectiveness of such information in SOM prediction based on four pools of variables with different categories [4]. Another study in northeastern China used the same method to quantify the influence of cultivation history with only two prediction models with different variables [7]. Although related studies have been carried out gradually, research on the impact of human activities on SOM is insufficient. Through various productive and living activities, humans have a profound impact on soil formation, especially in arable land with strong human influence. Unfortunately, information or data related to human activities are difficult to acquire compared to environmental conditions. Much of the information can only be acquired through field surveys and personnel interviews, which often consume considerable manpower, resources and time. This further limits related research on the effects of human activities on SOM.

The relationship between soil and environment can only be obtained by collecting many known soil points and their covariates. Because it is difficult to obtain a sufficient amount of SOM sampling data on a wide scale, most DSM studies were based on a certain amount of sampling point data that were collected through specific sampling design, field sampling, and laboratory analysis. Data splitting and cross-validation were used to analyze the accuracy of the DSM [1,4,6,7,17–19]. The amount of soil point data used in DSM studies is obviously different, ranging from dozens [4,6] to thousands [20–22]. Unfortunately, due to the small amount of soil sampling data (compared to the amount of prediction in the study area) used to train the DSM model, many similar studies may draw controversial conclusions [22–26]. The contradictory conclusions may be attributed to the insufficient amount of sampling data. In other words, the sampling density may be too low to capture the actual spatial distribution of SOM [22]. What is worse is that less data were used for model validation, and the accuracy was used to represent the prediction accuracy over the whole area. However, one notable question is how representative the sampled data are and whether the accuracy using sample data can be used to reflect the prediction results of the whole study area. Although this framework has been widely used as a consequence of the time consumption of large-scale soil sampling, the problem associated with the method still requires the attention of researchers. However, this issue can be easily avoided if a large range of soil survey data is available for prediction and accuracy verification.

The Ministry of Natural Resources of the People's Republic of China launched the "the national field-scale evaluation of arable land quality project", which is an important task to realize the trinity protection of the quantity, quality, and ecology of arable land. The project will acquire information on soil properties and soil management, including agronomic management level, irrigation water quality, SOM, etc., in each patch of arable land across the whole nation. To date, soil surveys in some regions have been completed. The project provides sufficient data to solve problems related to DSM, which are mentioned earlier. On the one hand, the large amount of soil survey data can be used to verify the credibility of DSM technologies and theory, which provides a reference for future related DSM research in other specific fields. On the other hand, survey data related to soil management can be employed to explore the impact of human activities on SOM.

In this study, five human activity factors, including the human footprint, amount of fertilizer application, agronomic management level, crop planting type, and irrigation guarantee degree, were used to improve the prediction of SOM of arable land in Heilongjiang Province. To our knowledge, few studies using these variables with sufficient SOM sampling data and field survey data for SOM mapping have been conducted. Little is known about the effectiveness of these factors in SOM mapping. The purpose of this study is: (1) to test the hypothesis that the inclusion of these factors could improve the accuracy of SOM mapping; (2) to identify important environmental and human activity factors on SOM; and (3) to provide credible conclusions for the above research purposes using the soil survey data of entire research areas.

2. Materials and Methods

2.1. Study Area

The research was conducted in Heilongjiang Province, located in northeast China (46°23′~53°24′ N latitude, 121°13′~135°05′ E longitude), covering approximately 4,730,000 km^2 (Figure 1).

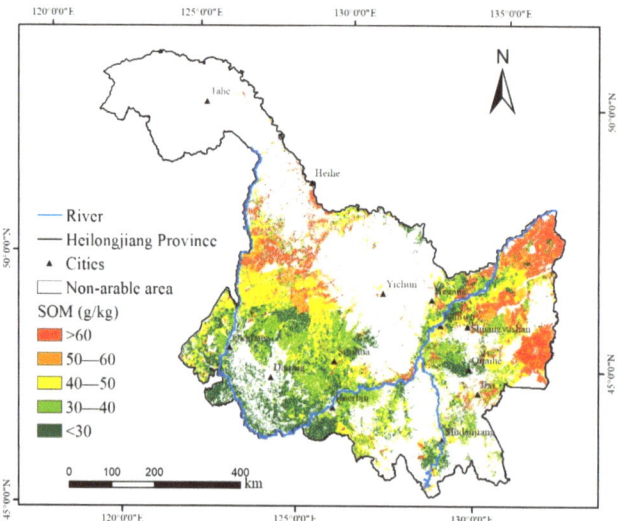

Figure 1. Location of the study area and distribution of observational SOM.

Heilongjiang Province mainly has a continental monsoon climate. In summer, the precipitation is sufficient, and the temperature is high. In winter, the weather is dry and cold for a long time. The annual temperature ranges from −4 to 4 °C. Annual precipitation ranges from 500~600 mm and is mainly concentrated in summer. Mountain areas account for 59% of the province and are concentrated mostly in the northwest, north, and southeast. The Greater Khingan and Lesser Khingan are the two most important mountains in the province. The province has large tracts of land with relatively flat terrain and low elevation, and 80% of the arable land consists of four soil types, Haplic Phaeozem, Haplic Chernozem, Luvic Phaeozem, and Albic Luvisol. The solar resources are relatively abundant, approximately 2300~2800 sunshine hours per year.

The black soil region located in Northeast China is one of the "three major black soil regions" in the world and is mainly concentrated in central and western Heilongjiang Province. The arable land area in the province accounts for 11.75% of the total country's [27], and 83% of the area of the Black Soil region is used as arable land [28]. As a result, Heilongjiang Province is an important commodity grain production base in China, and it became "No.1 Grain Production" in 2016. Total production accounts for 10% of China's total production. Moreover, the province has achieved "12 consecutive increases" in grain production from 2003–2015.

However, the soil resources in the province are facing an over-reclamation problem resulting from the development of the economy and population. Two main factors limiting the utilization of arable land are the thinning of black soil thickness and soil erosion.

2.2. SOM Data

The "Specification of Arable Land Survey, Monitoring and Evaluation" was formulated by the Ministry of Natural Resources of the People's Republic of China to acquire information on soil properties and soil management at each patch of arable land. The SOM data used in this research came from the project that was implemented after 2015.

The project surveyed all arable land in 131 counties in Heilongjiang Province and obtained SOM data for approximately 1.16 million soil patches (Figure 1). Topsoil SOM (g/kg) in each soil patch was determined based on the Method for Determination of Soil Organic Matter in the Agricultural Industry Standard of the People's Republic of China [29] after air-drying, sieving, heating, and titration.

Meanwhile, the project also obtained information on soil management, including the agronomic management level and irrigation water quality.

2.3. Covariates

Fourteen environmental variables for SOM modeling were selected to represent topography, climate, parent materials, vegetation, soil, and others. They are elevation, aspect, slope, landform class, average precipitation, average temperature, lithological unit, average NDVI, sedimentary deposit thickness, average soil moisture, soil type, water table depth, solar radiation, and surface water occurrence (Table 1).

Table 1. Covariates used in the study and their sources.

Forming Factors	Variables	Data Sources	Time Span
Topography	Elevation	GMTED 2010 [30]	-
	Aspect	Processed from Elevation data	-
	Slope	Processed from Elevation data	-
	Landform class	Global Ecological Land Units [31]	2008–2013
Climate	Annual average precipitation	Resource and Environment Data Cloud Platform	2006–2015
	Annual average Temperature	Resource and Environment Data Cloud Platform	2006–2015
Parent material	Lithological unit	Global Ecological Land Units [31]	2008–2013
Vegetation	Annual average NDVI	Resource and Environment Data Cloud Platform	2006–2015
Soil	Sedimentary deposit thickness	ORNL DAAC [32,33]	-
	Average soil moisture	TerraClimate [34]	2009–2017
	Soil type	Resource and Environment Data Cloud Platform	1995
	Water Table Depth	[35]	-
Other	Solar radiation	Global Change Research Data Publishing and Repository [36]	2015
	Surface Water occurrence		1984–2015
Human activities	Human footprint	Socioeconomic Data and Applications Center [37]	2009
	Amount of fertilizer application		-
	Agronomic management level		-
	Crop planting type		-
	Irrigation guarantee degree		-

- means the data will not change for a long time and is a fixed value.

For the topography, a 7.5 arc-second resolution digital elevation model (DEM) was freely downloaded from the U.S. Geological Survey (USGS) [30]. Three terrain variates (elevation, aspect, and slope) were derived from the DEM. The landform classes were derived based on the USGS's Map of Global Ecological Land Units [31]. The sources and resolutions of the data are shown in Table 1 and Figure 2a–d.

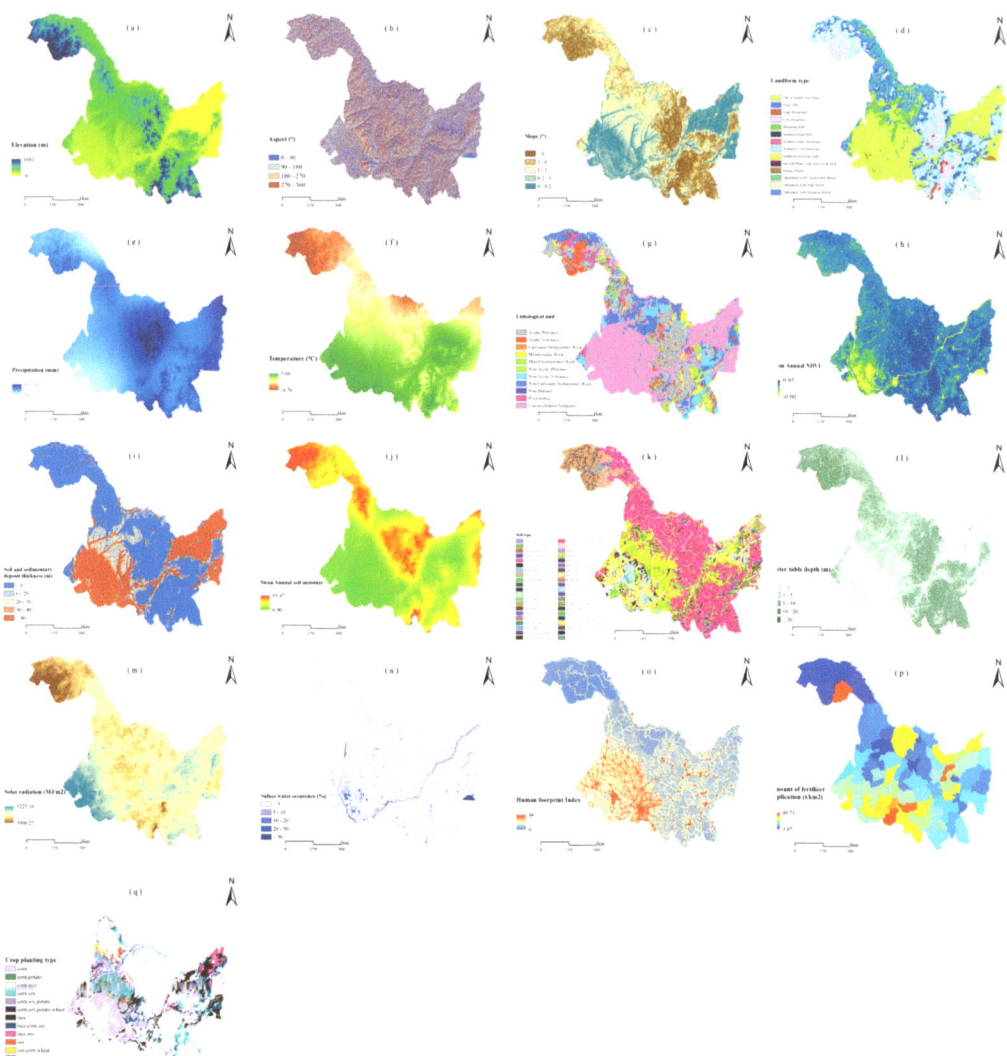

Figure 2. Distribution of covariates used in our study, including environmental covariates and human activities covariates. (**a**): Elevation; (**b**): aspect; (**c**): slope; (**d**): landform class; (**e**): mean annual precipitation; (**f**): mean annual temperature; (**g**): lithological unit; (**h**): mean annual NDVI; (**i**): soil and sedimentary deposit thickness; (**j**): soil moisture; (**k**): soil type; (**l**): water table depth; (**m**): solar radiation; (**n**): surface water occurrence; (**o**): human footprint; (**p**): the amount of fertilizer application; (**q**): agronomic management level.

For climate, two covariates, annual average precipitation and annual average temperature, were selected. Precipitation and temperature data from 2006–2015 were derived from the "Resource and Environment Data Cloud Platform (https://www.resdc.cn/ accessed on 12 April 2022)", which were used to calculate the annual average precipitation and annual average temperature. The source and resolution of the data are shown in Table 1 and Figure 2e,f.

For the parent material, one variate, the lithological unit, was selected. The data were collected from the U.S. Government's open data website. Eleven lithology types exist in the study area, including acidic plutonic, acidic volcanic, carbonate sedimentary rock, metamorphic rock, mixed sedimentary rock, nonacidic plutonic, nonacidic volcanic, noncarbonate sedimentary rock, non-defined, pyroclastic, and unconsolidated sediment [31]. The source and resolution of the data are shown in Table 1 and Figure 2g.

For the vegetation, the annual average NDVI was selected, which exhibits a good correlation with green-leaf density and can be used to estimate aboveground biomass [38]. Mahmoudabadi found that NDVI derived from remote sensing is a very effective parameter for predicting SOC [39,40], although it does not show satisfactory performance compared to other indices, e.g., EVI, at high altitudes [41]. In addition, historical pattern can explain a much larger part of the spatial variability in SOM in comparison to current data [40]. Then, NDVI data of 2007–2016 were obtained from the "Resource and Environment Data Cloud Platform". Then, the annual average NDVI was calculated using these data. The source and resolution of the data are shown in Table 1 and Figure 2h.

For the soil, fore variates, including sedimentary deposit thickness, average soil moisture, soil type, and water table depth, were acquired. Sedimentary deposit thickness was captured from the "Distributed Active Archive Center for Biogeochemical Dynamics" [32,33]. Mean monthly soil moisture data from 2009–2017 were derived from the "Climatology Lab" [34], and the average soil moisture was calculated. Soil type, including 41 types, was obtained from the "Resource and Environment Data Cloud Platform". The water table depth was obtained from the article [35]. The sources and resolutions of the data are shown in Table 1 and Figure 2i–l.

For the others, solar radiation and surface water occurrence were used. Solar radiation was acquired from the "Global Change Research Data Publishing and Repository". The surface water occurrence was derived from the "Global surface Water Explorer"[36]. The sources and resolutions of the data are shown in Table 1 and Figure 2m,n.

For human activity, five factors were used: human footprint, amount of fertilizer application, agronomic management level, crop planting type, and irrigation guarantee degree. Human footprint data were derived from the "Socioeconomic Data and Applications Center (SECAC)" [37]. For the amount of fertilizer application, we reviewed the official statistical yearbooks of cities in 2015 to collect the total amount of fertilizer application and cultivated area in Heilongjiang Province. Then, the total fertilizer application was divided by the cultivated area to obtain the amount of fertilizer application per unit area. The crop planting type in Heilongjiang Province was obtained from the article [42]. In the past decade, the national field-scale evaluation of arable land quality project was implemented to conduct mainland-wide surveys on arable land quality, which invested CNY 0.43 (equivalent to USD 0.067) billion and 1.3 CNY (equivalent to USD 0.2) million by the Ministry of Natural Resources of China [43–45]. The agronomic management level and irrigation guarantee degree were derived from the project, which consists of approximately 1.16 million soil patches over all of Heilongjiang Province. Due to the comprehensive nature, the agronomic management level is mainly graded by local statistical data and the questionnaire. The questionnaire mainly included the selection of good varieties, the planting structure, the popularization of fertilization by soil testing, the cultivation of weeds, water-saving irrigation, and pest control. Level I represents a high level of comprehensive agronomic management. Level III represents a low level of comprehensive agronomic management. The irrigation guarantee degree was obtained by combining field surveys with water map information. Level I indicates that the irrigation requirements for agricultural production are fully met. Level II indicates that the irrigation requirements are met. Level III indicates the general situation, but it is difficult to meet the requirements during a dry year. Level IV indicates no irrigation conditions.

All numeric covariates with a resolution coarser than 250 m were resampled to 250 m using the cubic method. All type covariates with a resolution coarser than 250 m were resampled to 250 m using the nearest method.

2.4. Data Pre-Processing

The original SOM dataset, which is in vector format, was converted into raster format with a resolution of 250 m. The grid dataset was superimposed with 19 covariates, including environmental and human activity covariates after projection transformation and resampling. For type covariates, such as landform class, lithological unit, soil type, agronomic management level, crop planting type, and irrigation guarantee degree, the mean SOM of one type was weighted as the variable value of the type [46].

Collinearity and multicollinearity might exist between series of variables. To avoid this, partial correlation analysis was conducted between different variables to measure the correlation between two variables, removing the effects of other variables [47–49].

The descriptive statistics for SOM and 19 covariates are calculated to show the basic characteristics of the data. Additionally, the box plot method (Tukey's test) was employed to remove outliers of the SOM dataset. Finally, a 2,017,044 grid point dataset with SOM and 19 covariates was derived. A 2-D matrix is created, which is of the size of $n \times c$, where $n = 2{,}017{,}044$ is the number of sampling locations, and $c = 20$ is the SOM value and covariates values.

Then, $n = 100{,}000$ dataset was randomly selected as the training set and performed ten times. All grid points were used as the validation set.

2.5. Modeling and Evaluation

A series of DSM models have been developed to predict SOM spatial distribution, including geostatistical methods, neural networks, and cubists. Random forest (RF) has been widely used in DSM studies. It is an ensemble of regression trees, and each that is built benefits from a random subset of original training data sampling. Only a randomly selected prediction subset is used to generate the best segmentation. RF has a series of advantages compared to other DSM methods, including better error measurement, flexibility with input variable types, and less susceptibility to overfitting [50–52]. In addition, RF has been demonstrated to perform better than other DSM methods in many studies [51,53–56].

To investigate whether adding human activity factors would improve SOM prediction, seven pools of covariates with different categories were derived to investigate whether adding human activity factors would improve SOM spatial prediction (Table 2). Pool 1 only contains the 14 environmental variables, including elevation, aspect, slope, landform class, average precipitation, average temperature, lithological unit, average NDVI, sedimentary deposit thickness, average soil moisture, soil type, water table depth, solar radiation, and surface water occurrence. Pool 2 to Pool 6 were composed of the 14 environmental covariates with the addition of the human footprint, amount of fertilizer application, agronomic management level, crop planting type, and irrigation guarantee degree, respectively. Pool 7 consisted of the 14 environmental covariates and 5 human activity covariates together. For these seven covariate pools, seven prediction models are established, which are Models 1–7.

Table 2. Pools with different covariates. (Environmental covariates consisted of elevation, aspect, slope, landform class, average precipitation, average temperature, lithological unit, average NDVI, sedimentary deposit thickness, average soil moisture, soil type, water table depth, solar radiation, and surface water occurrence).

Pools	Covariates
Pool 1	environmental variates
Pool 2	environmental variates + human footprint
Pool 3	environmental variates + amount of fertilizer application
Pool 4	environmental variates + agronomic management level
Pool 5	environmental variates + crop planting type
Pool 6	environmental variates + irrigation guarantee degree
Pool 7	environmental variates + human footprint, amount of fertilizer application, agronomic management level, crop planting type, irrigation guarantee degree

For evaluation indicators, the mean absolute error (MAE) (Equation (1)), root mean square error (RMSE) (Equation (2)), coefficient of determination (R^2) (Equation (3)), and Lin's concordance correlation coefficient (LCCC) (Equation (4)) were calculated. They are defined as follows:

$$\text{MAE} = \frac{1}{h} \sum_{j=1}^{h} |(P_h - Q_h)| \quad (1)$$

$$\text{RMSE} = \left[\frac{1}{h} \sum_{j=1}^{h} (P_h - Q_h)^2 \right]^{0.5} \quad (2)$$

$$R^2 = 1 - \frac{\sum_{j=1}^{h} (P_h - Q_h)^2}{\sum_{j=1}^{h} (P_h - \overline{Q_h})^2} \quad (3)$$

$$\text{LCCC} = \frac{2 \bullet r \bullet \partial_P \bullet \partial_Q}{\partial_{P^2} + \partial_{Q^2} + (\overline{P} + \overline{Q})^2} \quad (4)$$

where h is the number of predictions, P_h is the observed SOM value at point h, Q_h is the predicted SOM value at point h, $\overline{Q_h}$ is the mean of Q_h, and ∂_P and ∂_Q are variances of P_h and Q_h.

Variable importance was calculated to indicate the predicting power of difference covariates for SOM; it was estimated based on the mean decrease in prediction accuracy of each variable by replacing each covariate in turn by random noise and observing the average increase in the prediction accuracy for all trees [6,19,57–60].

For the RF model, one important parameter, the number of trees, should be set manually before simulation. Here, the GridSearchCV method in the Sklearn package was used to tune the hyperparameters of RF. The tuning result shows that 350 was the best number of trees, which was used in the RF model of the study.

The "RandomForestRegressor" of the sklearn package [61] in Python was used to conduct random forest modeling and calculate variable importance.

3. Results

3.1. Feature Selection

As a result of collinearity examination, Figure 3 shows the partial correlation coefficient between the 19 covariates ranging from −0.48 to 0.56, which are not significant, indicating that there is no collinearity between the covariates. Then, all covariates were used for subsequent modeling and analysis.

3.2. Descriptive Statistics

Table 3 shows the descriptive statistics for SOM and 19 covariates. The SOM content ranged from 2.93 g/kg to 80.13 g/kg, with a mean value of 39.46 g/kg. The SD of SOM was above the mean value, which indicates a high variability in its distribution. The annual average NDVI has the smallest variation, while the aspect and solar radiation have the largest variation.

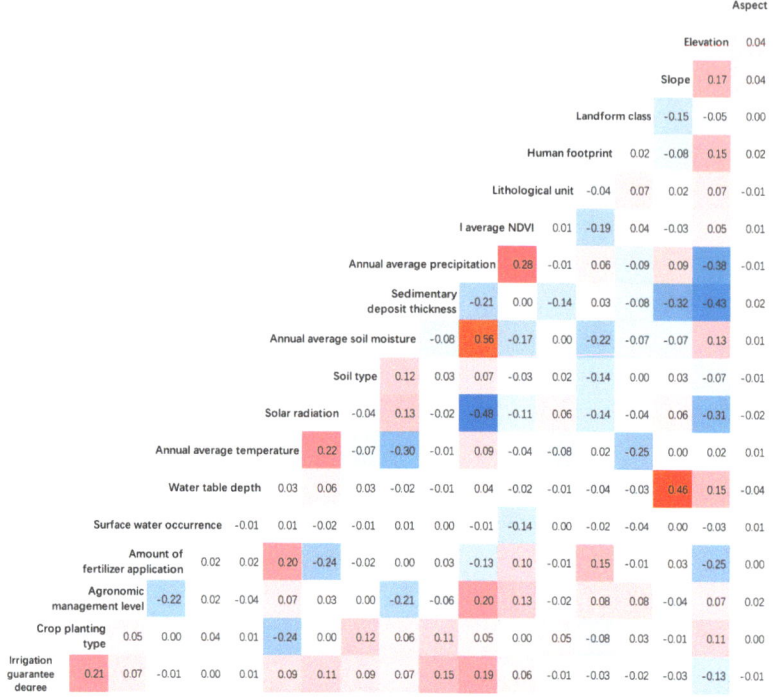

Figure 3. Partial correlation analysis between 19 covariates (the partial correlation coefficients range from −0.48 with blue to 0.56 with red).

Table 3. Summary statistics of SOM and quantitative covariates of all datasets.

Covariates	Max	Mean	Min	SD	Covariates	Max	Mean	Min	SD
SOM (g/kg)	80.13	39.46	2.93	192.75	Annual average soil moisture	56.11	18.39	6.90	59.31
Aspect (°)	359.84	173.08	−1.00	10,414.20	Soil type	111.55	45.63	18.39	205.70
Elevation (m)	799.00	172.88	35.00	7917.64	Solar radiation (MJ/m²)	5151.92	4668.69	4391.01	12,035.60
Slope (°)	25.64	1.01	0.00	2.25	Annual average temperature (°C)	5.60	3.43	−4.87	2.16
Landform class	62.95	46.66	32.91	6.19	Water table depth (m)	159.03	2.01	−16.37	27.53
Human footprint	47.00	12.29	1.00	37.40	Surface Water occurrence	96.42	0.31	0.00	6.55
Lithological unit	53.38	46.66	40.67	5.06	Amount of fertilizer application (t/km²)	37.82	17.50	4.31	51.49
Annual average NDVI	0.95	0.86	0.18	0.00	Agronomic management level	47.28	46.78	45.36	0.71
Annual average precipitation (mm)	690.73	560.67	430.20	1836.79	Crop planting type	80.99	45.92	35.31	116.10
Sedimentary deposit thickness (m)	60.00	32.06	−7.00	399.85	Irrigation guarantee degree	59.98	46.63	39.89	67.59

Max, maximum; Min, Minimum; SD, standard deviation.

As mentioned, ten n = 100,000 samples were randomly selected from all n = 2,017,044 data as the training set. Figure 4 summarizes the comparison of statistical descriptions of SOM between all datasets and ten training sets. This shows that the distribution and concentration of SOM in the ten training sets is consistent with the SOM in the original dataset. The training set selected can well represent the SOM distribution of the entire Heilongjiang Province, which provides an important basis for subsequent analysis.

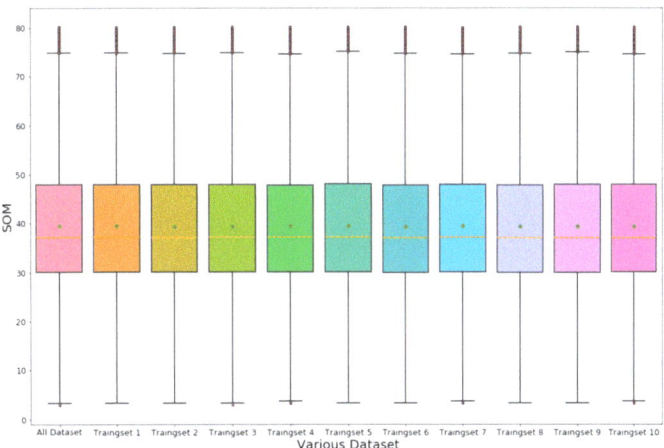

Figure 4. Boxplot of SOM of all datasets and 10 training sets with n = 100,000 samples.

3.3. Covariate Importance

The relative importance of each variable for the seven pools is illustrated in Figure 5. Slight differences are shown among the rankings of the same covariates of the seven pools in the figures. This results from the fact that the relative importance of a given variable in a certain model depends on its correlation with other variables [4,59]. For all covariates, soil moisture, with a relative importance of 26.67%, was the most important factor in the prediction of SOM (Figure 5g). It is followed by the annual average temperature. In general, soil moisture, annual average temperature, annual average precipitation, and elevation are among the most important variables of all seven pools. Each of the four variables in the seven pools has a relative importance higher than 11%, which together accounts for more than 70% of the SOM variation. For human activities, the relative importance of the human footprint ranks 8th in Model 2, with a relative importance of 2.66% (Figure 5b). The amount of fertilizer application ranks 3rd in Model 3, with a relative importance of 12.33% (Figure 5c). The agronomic management level, with a relative importance of 3.10%, ranks 7th in Model 4 (Figure 5d). The crop planting type ranks 8th (2.93%) in Model 5 (Figure 5e). The irrigation guarantee degree ranks 10th (2.00%) in Model 6 (Figure 5f). In Model 7 with all 19 covariates (Figure 5g), the amount of fertilizer application was the 3rd most important variable, with a relative importance 11.36% higher than the annual average precipitation and elevation. The human footprint, agronomic management level, crop planting type, and irrigation guarantee degree rank 9th, 11th, 14th, and 16th, with a relative importance of 1.92%, 1.77%, 1.37%, and 1.15%, respectively. The results indicate the important prediction power of the five human activity factors. Remarkably, fertilizer application is the most important factor for SOM prediction. In contrast, surface water occurrence, lithological unit, and landform class are the last three important variables, and each has a relative importance lower than 1% in Model 7.

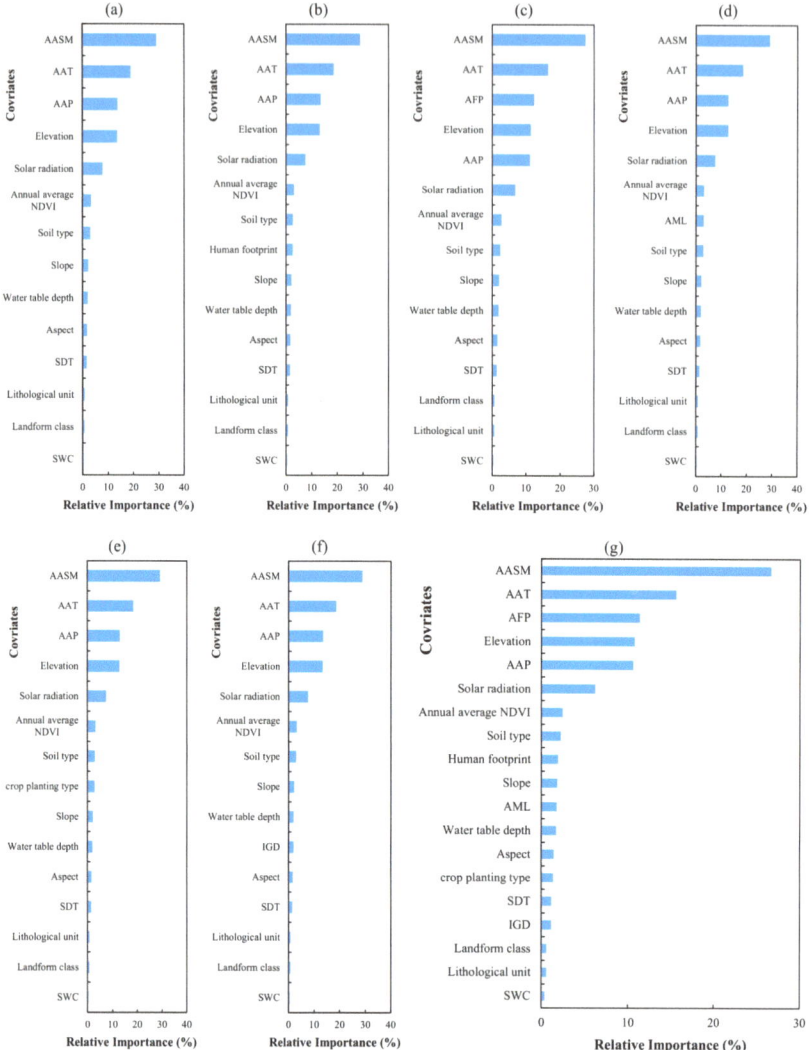

Figure 5. Relative importance of each variable for the seven models calculated by RF (SWC: surface water occurrence; SDT: sedimentary deposit thickness; AAP: annual average precipitation; AAT: annual average temperature; AFP: the amount of fertilizer application; AML: agronomic management level; IGD: irrigation guarantee degree; AASM: annual average soil moisture. (**a**), (**b**), (**c**), (**d**), (**e**), (**f**), (**g**) indicate relative importance of each variable for Model 1, 2, 3, 4, 5, 6, 7, respectively).

3.4. Model Performance and Spatial Difference

The prediction accuracy of SOM with seven combinations of covariates is listed in Table 4. The modeling and validation were performed ten times, and the average value was calculated as the final accuracy value.

Table 4. Prediction performances of SOM for seven models.

No.	Covariates	MAE	RMSE	LCCC	R^2
1	environmental variates	5.87	8.37	0.63	0.41
2	environmental variates + human footprint	5.79	8.27	0.64	0.42
3	environmental variates + amount of fertilizer application	5.29	7.72	0.68	0.53
4	environmental variates + agronomic management level	5.66	8.13	0.65	0.44
5	environmental variates + crop planting type	5.74	8.18	0.65	0.44
6	environmental variates + irrigation guarantee degree	5.73	8.20	0.64	0.43
7	environmental variates + human footprint, amount of fertilizer application, agronomic management level, crop planting type, irrigation guarantee degree	5.02	7.37	0.70	0.57

R^2, coefficient of determination.

The results show that adding the amount of fertilizer application would increase the prediction accuracy by 12% in terms of R^2 compared with when only environmental variables are used. The accuracy is higher than adding the human footprint, agronomic management level, crop planting type, and irrigation guarantee degree only, increasing the prediction accuracy by 1%, 3%, 3%, and 2%, respectively. The MAE and RMSE of the five models show a decreasing trend when only environmental covariates are used. Comparing Model 7 and Model 1, the validation results show that adding the five human activity factors increased the prediction accuracy by 39% in terms of R^2, 12% in terms of RMSE, and 15% in terms of MAE compared to when only environmental covariates were used. Combining the five human activity factors shows more promising prediction power for SOM mapping in arable land. R^2 revealed that the model including the five human activity factors and environmental covariates could explain 57% of the variation in the SOM distribution, whereas including environmental covariates only explained 41% of the variation in the SOM distribution. Additionally, a similar conclusion could be drawn from the higher LCCC of SOM prediction in model 7.

The results prove that the predicted value of Model 7 is closer to the observed value, but the proximity may vary in different SOM intervals. Therefore, this section uses the kernel density method to show the proximity between the predicted and observed values of Model 1 and Model 7. The density distribution of SOM is shown in Figure 6.

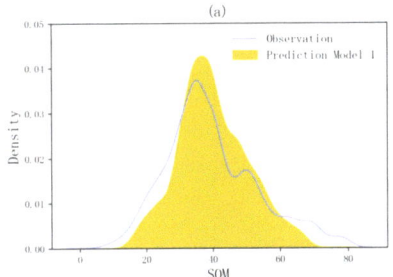
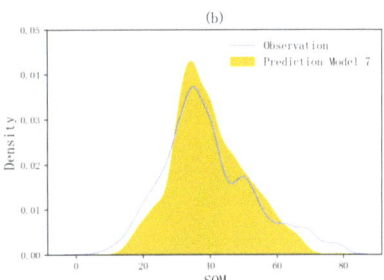

Figure 6. Density distribution of SOM predicted with Model 1 (**a**) and Model 7 (**b**).

A similar conclusion could be drawn from the density distribution. Overall, the prediction of Model 7 is closer to the observed value than Model 1 and better follows the real density distribution. However, the proximity has different performances in different SOM intervals. In the interval of high SOM (>60 g/kg) and low SOM (<30 g/kg), the density distributions of Model 1 and Model 7 were both lower than the observed value, and the difference was more obvious in the former. However, the predictions of the two models have no significant difference and are almost identical. In the middle SOM interval (30 g/kg~60 g/kg), the density distributions of the two models are higher than the observed values. At the same time, there are obvious differences between the two models. In the SOM interval, the density distribution of Model 1 is higher than that of Model 7, and the difference from the observed value is more obvious. Only in a small interval (approximately 30 g/kg and 60 g/kg), the density of Model 7 is higher than that of Model 1. Moreover, one can find that the peak density of the observation is 35 g/kg, and the peak value of Model 1 and Model 7 are 37 g/kg and 35 g/kg, respectively. This suggested that human activity factors have a profound influence on SOM distribution in arable areas, and the prediction is more consistent with the observation.

The addition of human activity factors can improve the proximity between observations and predictions. To show the spatial distribution of the proximity, this section calculates the difference between the observed value and predicted and of Model 1 and Model 7 and spatializes it to characterize the spatial differences.

Figure 7 shows the spatial distribution of the SOM difference between the observations and predictions of Model 1 (Figure 7a) and Model 7 (Figure 7b). Overall, there is an obvious difference between Model 1's result and the real value. The difference in many areas exceeds 10 g/kg, mainly located in the middle of the Songnen Plain and the northeastern part of the Sanjiang Plain, accounting for 16.4% of the total area. There is no obvious difference (−3~3 g/kg) in most areas (approximately 40.0% of the total area), mainly distributed in the Songnen Plain. Compared with Model 1, the difference between the predictions of Model 7 and the observations is obviously reduced. The area with a difference exceeding 10 g/kg only exists sporadically in the northeastern part of the Sanjiang Plain, accounting for 12.6% of the total area, far less than the 16.4% of Model 1. However, the area with no obvious difference (−3~3 g/kg) increased dramatically, accounting for 47.4% of the region. The area has an increase of 18.5% compared with Model 1, and most areas of Songnen Plain belong to this category.

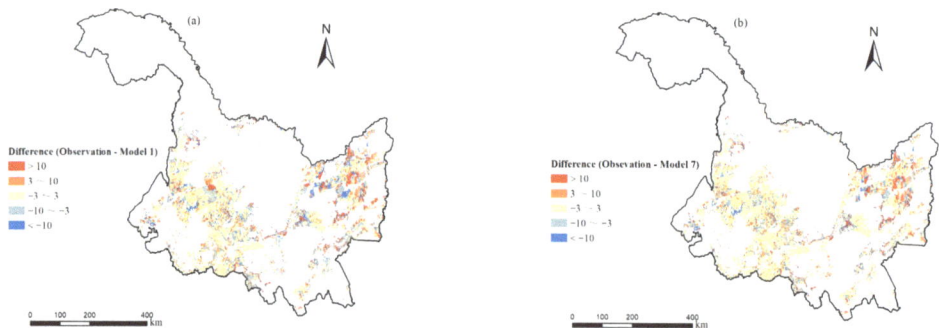

Figure 7. Spatial difference between observation and prediction with Model 1 (**a**) and Model 7 (**b**).

4. Discussion

4.1. Relative Importance of Environmental Covariates

Studies have shown that the importance of explanatory covariates varies with different regions and scales. Generally, due to their high relative importance, topography, climate, and vegetation covariates have been widely used in SOM mapping. A similar conclusion was drawn in this study. The annual average temperature, elevation, annual average precipitation, and annual average NDVI rank 2, 4, 5, and 7, respectively, in Model 7 (Figure 5g).

Topography covariates have been widely employed in SOM prediction [62,63]. Among the series topography covariates, elevation is the most important covariate in this study, followed by slope and aspect. Similarly, previous studies for SOM prediction suggested that elevation is the most effective topographic covariate [19,64]. Mechanistically, topography could control precipitation, temperature, water flow paths, and discharge and significantly influence erosional processes. Therefore, it plays a crucial role for SOM. Sites with high elevations and gentle slopes favor water accumulation, which controls the SOM input. Furthermore, soil erosion and redistribution determined by water flow paths and local microclimate influenced by topography have profound effects on SOM variation in highly variable terrain, as in our study area [7,65]. In addition to our study area, topographic covariates would also significantly affect SOM in northeastern Iran [39], the Mediterranean region [66], Barro Colorado Island [58], eastern China [67], etc.

Climatic influences the spatial variation of SOM [40,65], which is the "C" factor of soil formation. Precipitation and temperature are two key climatic covariates affecting the spatial variation of SOM, and similar results have been reported in similar regions [1,7,68]. In Model 7, AAT was the second most important covariate, whereas AAP ranked fifth (Figure 5g), indicating that temperature played a greater role in SOM prediction than precipitation, which is consistent with previous studies [4,7,19]. Mechanically, the two covariates could affect both C input and SOM decomposition. Precipitation plays a crucial role in net primary productivity and then the input of C into the soil. A higher humidity favors the weathering of parent material and the formation of a soil carbon stabilizing mineral surface [69,70], which reduces the decomposition of SOM [71]. Temperature plays a crucial role in the microbial decomposition rate of SOM by affecting its complex molecular attributes [72–74].

Vegetation is another important covariate that is frequently used to predict SOM [75,76]. Among many vegetation covariates, the annual average NDVI is frequently employed for SOM mapping [6]. In Model 7, the annual average NDVI ranks 7 of all 19 covariates (Figure 5g). Previous studies also reported a very important effect of NDVI on SOM distribution [1,19,77]. As the main source of SOM, it can enrich SOM by adding organic material, conserving soil moisture, and protecting soil erosion [78,79]. Moreover, vegetation will also affect the decomposition of C [65]. In addition to our study area, vegetation has been confirmed to primarily affect SOM in northern America [80], eastern Australia [81], and northwest Iran [13].

Compared to topography, climate, and vegetation covariates, soil moisture is less used in SOM prediction and mapping. In Model 7, annual average soil moisture has the highest relative importance compared to the other 18 covariates, which indicates that soil moisture could significantly affect the spatial variation of SOM and play the most important role in SOM development (Figure 5g). Soil moisture controls net primary productivity; therefore, SOM input plays a crucial role in soil microbial activity and SOM output. High and low soil moisture could reduce the soil aeration rate, substrate mobility/oxygen availability, and microbial activity and therefore favor SOM accumulation [65]. In addition to our study, soil moisture would also significantly affect SOM variation in an alluvial-diluvial plain in northeastern Ningxia Province [82], Flanders (Belgium) [83], Ohio State of the USA [84], and the Santa Fe River watershed in north-central Florida [85].

4.2. Relative Importance of Human Activity Factors

Human activity factors could also affect soil properties to a certain extent, especially in arable land. In the last decade, many studies have been conducted to investigate the importance of human activities to SOM prediction, which are receiving increasing attention [16]. Yang used phenological parameters extracted from NDVI time-series data to improve the prediction of soil organic carbon (SOC) content and found that the spatial SOC is significantly affected by agricultural management in arable land [6]. Crop rotation can also significantly improve the prediction of SOC information in arable land [4]. Cultivation history is another important human activity factor that can influence the spatial distribution of SOM [7]. In this study, five human activity factors are employed to quantify the importance of SOM prediction in arable land in Heilongjiang Province. The results find that the amount of fertilizer application is the most important human activity factor, ranking 3rd in our model, which is higher than elevation, precipitation, NDVI, etc. The human footprint, agronomic management level, crop planting type, and irrigation guarantee degree rank 9th, 11th, 14th, and 16th, respectively.

Actually, the amount of fertilizer application is rarely used in SOM prediction. However, the predictive model is considered to be extended using fertilizer application information to improve performance and accuracy [7]. Based on long-term field experiments, many studies have suggested that nitrogen fertilizer application could lead to significant soil acidification worldwide [86–88]. Mechanistically, the chemical could release hydrogen ions (H^+) through nitrification of NH_4^+ and leaching of NO_3^-. The H^+ and base cations leaching with gully erosion runoff may lead to soil acidification [22,89]. Furthermore, the use of chemical fertilizer could increase crop yields by accelerating SOM accumulation [89] and therefore reduce the use of traditional manure application or straw return in similar areas [90–92]. However, some studies have illustrated that massive fertilizer application could increase crop yield over a short period but could not sustain the level of SOM in the long term [93]. Moreover, unreasonable fertilizer input can lead to a decrease in SOM by accelerating soil carbon decomposition in arable land and therefore cannot guarantee sustainable development in the northeastern black soil region in China [22]. Although different studies have controversial conclusions regarding the effect of fertilizer on SOM, our study suggests that adding the amount of fertilizer application could greatly improve the performance and accuracy of SOM prediction. This finding may result from the high acid buffering capacity of black soil. In highly intensive agriculture, biomass production increased with fertilization, leading to enhanced root growth and exudation of organic molecules, increased microorganism biomass and activity, and higher plant residue accumulation. Thus, fertilization up to a certain level may enhance SOM in soil. Additionally, the cumulative number of fertilizers did not reach the threshold that significantly affected SOM in this region. In addition to our study area, the use of fertilizer would also significantly affect SOM in Mediterranean cropping systems [94], northeast China [90,92], south China [88], and Alabama in southeastern USA [95].

The human footprint, agronomic management level, and crop planting type will affect the spatial variation of SOM to varying degrees. The human footprint is measured using eight variables, including built-up environments, population density, electric power infrastructure, crop lands, pasture lands, roads, railways, and navigable waterways, determining human pressure on the soil. Our finding is consistent with previous research [96]. Dong considered that the distance to the river is the most important variable of SOM prediction in alluvial-diluvial plains in China [82,97]. Yang used phenological parameters extracted from NDVI time-series data to improve the prediction of SOC content, and she found that the spatial variation of SOC is significantly affected by agricultural management in arable land [6]. Crop rotation can also significantly affect the amount and spatial variation of SOC in arable land [4]. The use of the irrigation guarantee degree will increase the accuracy of SOM mapping. It can not only meet crop water requirements but also improve soil quality by leaching salts to deep soil horizons [98]. The study indicated that SOM in arable land decreased with the reduction in the degree of irrigation guarantee (Table 5). The average SOM for different irrigation guarantee degrees ranged from 44.82 g/kg to 35.04 g/kg, and the highest mean value was observed in Level I and the lowest in Level III; however, the mean SOM with no irrigation conditions (Level IV) was higher than that in Level III. This may be a result of the low utilization of arable land with no irrigation conditions.

Table 5. Changes in SOM under different irrigation guarantee degrees.

	Number of Samples	Min (g/kg)	Mean (g/kg)	Max (g/kg)	Variance
Level I	536,753	2.93	44.82	80.12	203.93
Level II	517,441	5.90	39.94	80.13	189.80
Level III	609,342	3.30	35.04	80.12	170.48
Level IV	353,508	9.00	38.26	80.13	139.31

Meanwhile, lots of studies have investigated the influence of other human management on SOM in various regions based on field experiments. In Zhejiang Province (China), Wissing analyzed the management-induced organic carbon accumulation in paddy soils and found that the organic carbon concentrations in paddy soils increased from 18 mg/g to 30 mg/g, resulting from the iron oxides strongly interacting with organic matter and playing an important role in the stabilization of SOM [99]. In the same province, Mi reported the effect of four organic materials mulching on the variance of organic soil and found that cattle manure showed the most profound influence, which, combined with NPK fertilizer, resulted in the highest level of SOM [100]. In contrast to the impact of other indicators, such as spent mushroom compost and rice straw residues.

4.3. Model Performance

As mentioned, DSM is conducted based on the relationship between soil and environment. The relationship can only be acquired by collecting soil sampling data and covariate data. Unfortunately, due to the small amount of soil sampling data (compared to the amount of prediction in the study area) used to train the DSM model, many similar studies may draw controversial conclusions [22–26]. Some studies have found that SOM in the black soil region of northeast China has declined rapidly over the past 30 years due to serious soil erosion [23,24]. Other research similarly found that SOM decomposition has exceeded sequestration as a result of the use of chemical fertilization [25]. However, research [26] has found that the SOM in three counties located in the same region did not show a significant difference between 1980 and 2010. The contradictory conclusions may be attributed to the insufficient amount of sampling data [22]. Another notable question is whether the accuracy using a small part of the soil sampling data can be used to reflect the prediction results of the whole study area. The "Specification of Arable Land Survey, Monitoring and Evaluation" project developed by the Ministry of Natural Resources has obtained information on soil properties and soil management at each patch of arable land in Heilongjiang Province. The large amount of soil survey data provided by the project can be used to solve problems related to DSM, which are mentioned earlier, and provide us with more accurate and credible evaluation results.

Table 4 shows that Model 7 has a lower MAE (5.02) and RMSE (7.37) compared to the MAE (5.87) and RMSE (8.37) in Model 1. Additionally, due to the higher R^2 and LCCC, Model 7 exhibited better performance. R^2 indicates that Model 1 with environmental covariates could explain 41% of the variation in SOM distribution. However, Model 7 with environmental covariates and the five human activity factors could explain 57% of the SOM variation.

Previous studies have predicted SOM spatial distribution, and the R^2 from many studies was smaller than 0.5 [63,101–105] (Table 6). In arable land with relatively flat terrain, many widely used environmental variates, such as vegetables and topography, may be too homogenous to represent SOM variation effectively [106,107]. Similarly, in the flat arable land in Heilongjiang Province, Model 1 with only environmental covariates explains 41% of the variation in SOM distribution, which is lower than 0.5. However, Model 7, containing the five human activity factors, finally obtains a higher explanatory power for SOM. This further illustrates the importance of human activity factors as a predictor for SOM distribution.

For SOM prediction in similar areas, our accuracy result ($R^2 = 0.57$) is lower than those of some other studies. Qi used ten covariates to predict SOC in Liaoning Province with the help of the random forest method, obtaining an accuracy result of $R^2 = 0.58$ [1]. Wang combined the cultivation history and environmental variates to predict the SOC of arable land, obtaining an accuracy result of $R^2 = 0.76$, whereas it was 0.65 when considering only environmental variates [7]. This illustrates that if only a small part of the data is used as the validation set, the evaluation result will be overestimated.

Table 6. Comparison of the results of this study with published achievements.

Areas	R^2 (SOM)	Predictive Models	Reference
Brazil	0.33	RF	[104]
Eastern Himalayas	0.36	RF	[102]
Denmark	0.42	Cubist	[63]
Australia	0.25	SVR	[101]
Jiangsu, China	0.53	RK-REML	[103]
China	0.35	XGBoost	[105]
Liaoning, China	0.63	RF	[1]
Northeastern China	0.76	BRT	[7]

SVR: support vector regression; RK-REML: regression kriging with a mixed linear model fitted by residual maximum likelihood; XGBoost: scalable and efficient tree boosting system, eXtreme gradient boost; BRT: boosted regression trees.

4.4. Limitations and Outlook

In relatively flat arable land, many widely used environmental variates may be too homogenous to represent SOM variation effectively. Some environmental variates, such as topography parameters, are not important in predicting SOM. In contrast, due to the excellent production and living conditions in these areas, strong human activity and urbanization could lead to rapid land use change, which will have a significant impact on SOM variation. However, information about human activities with fine spatiotemporal resolution was not available to us. The data obtained from the city statistical yearbook are too coarse for further research. Obtaining data about human activity with fine spatiotemporal resolution is a great challenge.

Due to the unavailability of human activity information, many studies obtained relative data by field surveys and personnel interviews, which is time-consuming and expensive. Therefore, data sharing is a very important choice to promote scientific research. However, the formulation of related policies is still a major challenge.

5. Conclusions

In the study, five human activity factors, including the amount of fertilizer application, human footprint, agronomic management level, crop planting type, and irrigation guarantee degree, were used to explore their effectiveness in predicting SOM in arable land in Heilongjiang Province, China. As a result of the analysis, answers can be drawn about the initial motivation of the study in the Introduction; (1) The model, by combining the five activity factors, increases the SOM spatial prediction by 39% in terms of R^2, 12% in terms of RMSE, 15% in terms of MAE, and 11% in terms of LCCC, showing better prediction accuracy and performance, whereas only environmental covariates account for 41% of the variation in SOM distribution. (2) In the SOM prediction model, soil moisture was the most important environmental covariate, followed by annual average temperature. The amount of fertilizer application, ranking 3rd, is the most important human activity factor. (3) Sufficient SOM sampling data and field survey data were employed for prediction and accuracy verification, finding that the evaluation result will be overestimated when only a small part of the sampling data is used.

However, the relative importance of environmental conditions and human activity covariates may vary in other regions, which requires more analysis and discussion. During the research process, the data about human activity with fine spatiotemporal resolution are still a great challenge in SOM prediction in arable land.

Author Contributions: Conceptualization, L.N. and C.C.; methodology, S.S.; software, L.Z.; validation, S.M.; writing—original draft preparation, L.N.; writing—review and editing, L.N.; visualization, Y.S.; supervision, C.C. and L.Z.; Software, X.L.; funding acquisition, C.C. All authors have read and agreed to the published version of the manuscript.

Funding: This research was supported by the Strategic Priority Research Program of the Chinese Academy of Sciences, grant number XDA23100303, Shandong Provincial Natural Science Foundation, grant number ZR2020MF146, and Shandong Province Higher Educational Program for Introduction and Cultivation of Young Innovative Talents in 2021.

Data Availability Statement: Not applicable.

Acknowledgments: The authors would like to gratefully thank the Ministry of Natural Resources of China for providing the data.

Conflicts of Interest: The authors declare no conflict of interest.

References

1. Qi, L.; Wang, S.; Zhuang, Q.; Yang, Z.; Bai, S.; Jin, X.; Lei, G. Spatial-temporal changes in soil organic carbon and pH in the Liaoning Province of China: A modeling analysis based on observational data. *Sustainability* **2019**, *11*, 3569. [CrossRef]
2. Dick, W. Organic carbon, nitrogen, and phosphorus concentrations and pH in soil profiles as affected by tillage intensity. *Soil Sci. Soc. Am. J.* **1983**, *47*, 102–107. [CrossRef]
3. Post, W.M.; Kwon, K.C. Soil carbon sequestration and land-use change: Processes and potential. *Glob. Chang. Biol.* **2000**, *6*, 317–327. [CrossRef]
4. Yang, L.; Song, M.; Zhu, A.-X.; Qin, C.; Zhou, C.; Qi, F.; Li, X.; Chen, Z.; Gao, B. Predicting soil organic carbon content in croplands using crop rotation and Fourier transform decomposed variables. *Geoderma* **2019**, *340*, 289–302. [CrossRef]
5. Hoffmann, M.; Pohl, M.; Jurisch, N.; Prescher, A.-K.; Campa, E.M.; Hagemann, U.; Remus, R.; Verch, G.; Sommer, M.; Augustin, J. Maize carbon dynamics are driven by soil erosion state and plant phenology rather than nitrogen fertilization form. *Soil Tillage Res.* **2018**, *175*, 255–266. [CrossRef]
6. Yang, L.; He, X.; Shen, F.; Zhou, C.; Zhu, A.-X.; Gao, B.; Chen, Z.; Li, M. Improving prediction of soil organic carbon content in croplands using phenological parameters extracted from NDVI time series data. *Soil Tillage Res.* **2020**, *196*, 104465. [CrossRef]
7. Wang, Y.; Wang, S.; Adhikari, K.; Wang, Q.; Sui, Y.; Xin, G. Effect of cultivation history on soil organic carbon status of arable land in northeastern China. *Geoderma* **2019**, *342*, 55–64. [CrossRef]
8. Paustian, K.; Andren, O.; Janzen, H.; Lal, R.; Smith, P.; Tian, G.; Tiessen, H.; Van Noordwijk, M.; Woomer, P. Agricultural soils as a sink to mitigate CO_2 emissions. *Soil Use Manag.* **1997**, *13*, 230–244. [CrossRef]
9. Lal, R. Soil carbon sequestration impacts on global climate change and food security. *Science* **2004**, *304*, 1623–1627. [CrossRef]
10. Smith, P. Carbon sequestration in croplands: The potential in Europe and the global context. *Eur. J. Agron.* **2004**, *20*, 229–236. [CrossRef]
11. Hans, J. *Factors of Soil Formation: A System of Quantitative Pedology*; Dover Publication: Mineola, NY, USA, 1941.
12. McBratney, A.B.; Santos, M.M.; Minasny, B. On digital soil mapping. *Geoderma* **2003**, *117*, 3–52. [CrossRef]
13. Hamzehpour, N.; Shafizadeh-Moghadam, H.; Valavi, R. Exploring the driving forces and digital mapping of soil organic carbon using remote sensing and soil texture. *Catena* **2019**, *182*, 104141. [CrossRef]
14. Ramcharan, A.; Hengl, T.; Nauman, T.; Brungard, C.; Waltman, S.; Wills, S.; Thompson, J. Soil property and class maps of the conterminous United States at 100-meter spatial resolution. *Soil Sci. Soc. Am. J.* **2018**, *82*, 186–201. [CrossRef]
15. Hengl, T.; de Jesus, J.M.; Heuvelink, G.B.; Gonzalez, M.R.; Kilibarda, M.; Blagotić, A.; Shangguan, W.; Wright, M.N.; Geng, X.; Bauer-Marschallinger, B. SoilGrids250m: Global gridded soil information based on machine learning. *PLoS ONE* **2017**, *12*, e0169748. [CrossRef]
16. Grunwald, S.; Thompson, J.; Boettinger, J. Digital soil mapping and modeling at continental scales: Finding solutions for global issues. *Soil Sci. Soc. Am. J.* **2011**, *75*, 1201–1213. [CrossRef]
17. Liang, Z.; Chen, S.; Yang, Y.; Zhao, R.; Shi, Z.; Rossel, R.A.V. National digital soil map of organic matter in topsoil and its associated uncertainty in 1980′s China. *Geoderma* **2019**, *335*, 47–56. [CrossRef]
18. Hengl, T.; Leenaars, J.G.; Shepherd, K.D.; Walsh, M.G.; Heuvelink, G.B.; Mamo, T.; Tilahun, H.; Berkhout, E.; Cooper, M.; Fegraus, E. Soil nutrient maps of Sub-Saharan Africa: Assessment of soil nutrient content at 250 m spatial resolution using machine learning. *Nutr. Cycl. Agroecosyst.* **2017**, *109*, 77–102. [CrossRef]
19. Zhou, Y.; Hartemink, A.E.; Shi, Z.; Liang, Z.; Lu, Y. Land use and climate change effects on soil organic carbon in North and Northeast China. *Sci. Total Environ.* **2019**, *647*, 1230–1238. [CrossRef]
20. Wadoux, A.M.-C. Using deep learning for multivariate mapping of soil with quantified uncertainty. *Geoderma* **2019**, *351*, 59–70. [CrossRef]
21. Zhao, R.; Biswas, A.; Zhou, Y.; Zhou, Y.; Shi, Z.; Li, H. Identifying localized and scale-specific multivariate controls of soil organic matter variations using multiple wavelet coherence. *Sci. Total Environ.* **2018**, *643*, 548–558. [CrossRef]
22. Ou, Y.; Rousseau, A.N.; Wang, L.; Yan, B. Spatio-temporal patterns of soil organic carbon and pH in relation to environmental factors—A case study of the Black Soil Region of Northeastern China. *Agric. Ecosyst. Environ.* **2017**, *245*, 22–31. [CrossRef]
23. Zhang, Y.; Wu, Y.; Liu, B.; Zheng, Q.; Yin, J. Characteristics and factors controlling the development of ephemeral gullies in cultivated catchments of black soil region, Northeast China. *Soil Tillage Res.* **2007**, *96*, 28–41. [CrossRef]

24. Wu, Y.; Zheng, Q.; Zhang, Y.; Liu, B.; Cheng, H.; Wang, Y. Development of gullies and sediment production in the black soil region of northeastern China. *Geomorphology* **2008**, *101*, 683–691. [CrossRef]
25. Jiao, X.; Gao, C.; Sui, Y.; Lü, G.; Wei, D. Effects of long-term fertilization on soil carbon and nitrogen in Chinese Mollisols. *Agron. J.* **2014**, *106*, 1018–1024. [CrossRef]
26. Chun-hua, Z.; Zong-ming, W.; Chun-ying, R.; Bai, Z.; Kai-shan, S.; Dian-wei, L. Temporal and spatial variations of soil organic and total nitrogen in the Songnen Plain maize belt. *Geogr. Reserach* **2011**, *30*, 256–268.
27. Zhao, Y.; Jiang, Q.; Wang, Z. The System Evaluation of Grain Production Efficiency and Analysis of Driving Factors in Heilongjiang Province. *Water* **2019**, *11*, 1073. [CrossRef]
28. Xu, S. Temporal and Spatial Characteristics of the Change of Cultivated Land Resources in the Black Soil Region of Heilongjiang Province (China). *Sustainability* **2019**, *11*, 38. [CrossRef]
29. NY/T1121.6-2006; Soil Testing-Part 6: Method for Determination of Soil Organic Matter. Ministry of Agriculture: Beijing, China, 2006.
30. Danielson, J.J.; Gesch, D.B. *Global Multi-Resolution Terrain Elevation Data 2010 (GMTED2010)*; US Department of the Interior, US Geological Survey: Washington, DC, USA, 2011.
31. Sayre, R.; Dangermond, J.; Frye, C.; Vaughan, R.; Aniello, P.; Breyer, S.; Cribbs, D.; Hopkins, D.; Nauman, R.; Derrenbacher, W. *A New Map of Global Ecological Land Units—An Ecophysiographic Stratification Approach*; Association of American Geographers: Washington, DC, USA, 2014.
32. Pelletier, J.D.; Broxton, P.D.; Hazenberg, P.; Zeng, X.; Troch, P.A.; Niu, G.Y.; Williams, Z.; Brunke, M.A.; Gochis, D. A gridded global data set of soil, intact regolith, and sedimentary deposit thicknesses for regional and global land surface modeling. *J. Adv. Model. Earth Syst.* **2016**, *8*, 41–65. [CrossRef]
33. Pelletier, J.; Broxton, P.; Hazenberg, P.; Zeng, X.; Troch, P.; Niu, G.; Williams, Z.; Brunke, M.; Gochis, D. *Global 1-km Gridded Thickness of Soil, Regolith, and Sedimentary Deposit Layers*; ORNL DAAC: Oak Ridge, TN, USA, 2016.
34. Abatzoglou, J.T.; Dobrowski, S.Z.; Parks, S.A.; Hegewisch, K.C. TerraClimate, a high-resolution global dataset of monthly climate and climatic water balance from 1958–2015. *Sci. Data* **2018**, *5*, 170191. [CrossRef]
35. Fan, Y.; Li, H.; Miguez-Macho, G. Global patterns of groundwater table depth. *Science* **2013**, *339*, 940–943. [CrossRef]
36. Pekel, J.-F.; Cottam, A.; Gorelick, N.; Belward, A.S. High-resolution mapping of global surface water and its long-term changes. *Nature* **2016**, *540*, 418–422. [CrossRef] [PubMed]
37. Venter, O.; Sanderson, E.W.; Magrach, A.; Allan, J.R.; Beher, J.; Jones, K.R.; Possingham, H.P.; Laurance, W.F.; Wood, P.; Fekete, B.M. Global terrestrial Human Footprint maps for 1993 and 2009. *Sci. Data* **2016**, *3*, 160067. [CrossRef] [PubMed]
38. Mallick, J.; AlMesfer, M.K.; Singh, V.P.; Falqi, I.I.; Singh, C.K.; Alsubih, M.; Kahla, N.B. Evaluating the NDVI–Rainfall Relationship in Bisha Watershed, Saudi Arabia Using Non-Stationary Modeling Technique. *Atmosphere* **2021**, *12*, 593. [CrossRef]
39. Mahmoudabadi, E.; Karimi, A.; Haghnia, G.H.; Sepehr, A. Digital soil mapping using remote sensing indices, terrain attributes, and vegetation features in the rangelands of northeastern Iran. *Environ. Monit. Assess.* **2017**, *189*, 500. [CrossRef]
40. Lamichhane, S.; Kumar, L.; Wilson, B.J. Digital soil mapping algorithms and covariates for soil organic carbon mapping and their implications: A review. *Geoderma* **2019**, *352*, 395–413. [CrossRef]
41. Kumari, N.; Srivastava, A.; Dumka, U.C.J.C. A long-term spatiotemporal analysis of vegetation greenness over the Himalayan Region using Google Earth Engine. *Climate* **2021**, *9*, 109. [CrossRef]
42. Liu, H.; Yan, Y.; Zhang, X.; Qiu, Z.; Wang, N.; Yu, W. Remote sensing extraction of crop planting structure oriented to agricultural regionalizaiton. *Chin. J. Agric. Resour. Reg. Plan.* **2017**, *38*, 43–54.
43. Yao, X.; Zhu, D.; Ye, S.; Yun, W.; Zhang, N.; Li, L.J.C.; Agriculture, E.i. A field survey system for land consolidation based on 3S and speech recognition technology. *Comput. Electron. Agric.* **2016**, *127*, 659–668. [CrossRef]
44. Ye, S.; Song, C.; Shen, S.; Gao, P.; Cheng, C.; Cheng, F.; Wan, C.; Zhu, D. Spatial pattern of arable land-use intensity in China. *Land Use Policy* **2020**, *99*, 104845. [CrossRef]
45. Wan, C.; Kuzyakov, Y.; Cheng, C.; Ye, S.; Gao, B.; Gao, P.; Ren, S.; Yun, W. A soil sampling design for arable land quality observation by using SPCOSA–CLHS hybrid approach. *Land Degrad. Dev.* **2021**, *32*, 4889–4906. [CrossRef]
46. Liao, Y.; Wang, J.; Meng, B.; Li, X. Integration of GP and GA for mapping population distribution. *Int. J. Geogr. Inf. Sci.* **2010**, *24*, 47–67. [CrossRef]
47. Kenett, D.Y.; Tumminello, M.; Madi, A.; Gur-Gershgoren, G.; Mantegna, R.N.; Ben-Jacob, E. Dominating clasp of the financial sector revealed by partial correlation analysis of the stock market. *PLoS ONE* **2010**, *5*, e15032. [CrossRef]
48. Eichler, M.; Dahlhaus, R.; Sandkühler, J. Partial correlation analysis for the identification of synaptic connections. *Biol. Cybern.* **2003**, *89*, 289–302. [CrossRef]
49. Peng, S.; Piao, S.; Ciais, P.; Myneni, R.B.; Chen, A.; Chevallier, F.; Dolman, A.J.; Janssens, I.A.; Penuelas, J.; Zhang, G. Asymmetric effects of daytime and night-time warming on Northern Hemisphere vegetation. *Nature* **2013**, *501*, 88–92. [CrossRef]
50. Heung, B.; Bulmer, C.E.; Schmidt, M.G. Predictive soil parent material mapping at a regional-scale: A random forest approach. *Geoderma* **2014**, *214*, 141–154. [CrossRef]
51. Zhi, J.; Zhang, G.; Yang, F.; Yang, R.; Liu, F.; Song, X.; Zhao, Y.; Li, D. Predicting mattic epipedons in the northeastern Qinghai-Tibetan Plateau using Random Forest. *Geoderma Reg.* **2017**, *10*, 1–10. [CrossRef]
52. Breiman, L. Random forests. *Mach. Learn.* **2001**, *45*, 5–32. [CrossRef]

53. Forkuor, G.; Hounkpatin, O.K.; Welp, G.; Thiel, M. High resolution mapping of soil properties using remote sensing variables in south-western Burkina Faso: A comparison of machine learning and multiple linear regression models. *PLoS ONE* **2017**, *12*, e0170478. [CrossRef]
54. Akpa, S.I.; Odeh, I.O.; Bishop, T.F.; Hartemink, A.E.; Amapu, I.Y. Total soil organic carbon and carbon sequestration potential in Nigeria. *Geoderma* **2016**, *271*, 202–215. [CrossRef]
55. Deng, X.; Chen, X.; Ma, W.; Ren, Z.; Zhang, M.; Grieneisen, M.L.; Long, W.; Ni, Z.; Zhan, Y.; Lv, X. Baseline map of organic carbon stock in farmland topsoil in East China. *Agric. Ecosyst. Environ.* **2018**, *254*, 213–223. [CrossRef]
56. Jeong, G.; Oeverdieck, H.; Park, S.J.; Huwe, B.; Ließ, M. Spatial soil nutrients prediction using three supervised learning methods for assessment of land potentials in complex terrain. *Catena* **2017**, *154*, 73–84. [CrossRef]
57. Behrens, T.; Schmidt, K.; Ramirez-Lopez, L.; Gallant, J.; Zhu, A.-X.; Scholten, T. Hyper-scale digital soil mapping and soil formation analysis. *Geoderma* **2014**, *213*, 578–588. [CrossRef]
58. Grimm, R.; Behrens, T.; Märker, M.; Elsenbeer, H. Soil organic carbon concentrations and stocks on Barro Colorado Island—Digital soil mapping using Random Forests analysis. *Geoderma* **2008**, *146*, 102–113. [CrossRef]
59. Shi, J.; Yang, L.; Zhu, A.; Qin, C.; Liang, P.; Zeng, C.; Pei, T. Machine-learning variables at different scales vs. Knowledge-based variables for mapping multiple soil properties. *Soil Sci. Soc. Am. J.* **2018**, *82*, 645–656. [CrossRef]
60. Zeng, C.; Yang, L.; Zhu, A.-X.; Rossiter, D.G.; Liu, J.; Liu, J.; Qin, C.; Wang, D. Mapping soil organic matter concentration at different scales using a mixed geographically weighted regression method. *Geoderma* **2016**, *281*, 69–82. [CrossRef]
61. Pedregosa, F.; Varoquaux, G.; Gramfort, A.; Michel, V.; Thirion, B.; Grisel, O.; Blondel, M.; Prettenhofer, P.; Weiss, R.; Dubourg, V. Scikit-learn: Machine learning in Python. *J. Mach. Learn. Res.* **2011**, *12*, 2825–2830.
62. Sumfleth, K.; Duttmann, R. Prediction of soil property distribution in paddy soil landscapes using terrain data and satellite information as indicators. *Ecol. Indic.* **2008**, *8*, 485–501. [CrossRef]
63. Adhikari, K.; Hartemink, A.E.; Minasny, B.; Kheir, R.B.; Greve, M.B.; Greve, M.H. Digital mapping of soil organic carbon contents and stocks in Denmark. *PLoS ONE* **2014**, *9*, e105519. [CrossRef]
64. Yang, R.-M.; Zhang, G.-L.; Liu, F.; Lu, Y.-Y.; Yang, F.; Yang, F.; Yang, M.; Zhao, Y.-G.; Li, D.-C. Comparison of boosted regression tree and random forest models for mapping topsoil organic carbon concentration in an alpine ecosystem. *Ecol. Indic.* **2016**, *60*, 870–878. [CrossRef]
65. Wiesmeier, M.; Urbanski, L.; Hobley, E.; Lang, B.; von Lützow, M.; Marin-Spiotta, E.; van Wesemael, B.; Rabot, E.; Ließ, M.; Garcia-Franco, N. Soil organic carbon storage as a key function of soils—A review of drivers and indicators at various scales. *Geoderma* **2019**, *333*, 149–162. [CrossRef]
66. Schillaci, C.; Acutis, M.; Lombardo, L.; Lipani, A.; Fantappie, M.; Märker, M.; Saia, S. Spatio-temporal topsoil organic carbon mapping of a semi-arid Mediterranean region: The role of land use, soil texture, topographic indices and the influence of remote sensing data to modelling. *Sci. Total Environ.* **2017**, *601*, 821–832. [CrossRef] [PubMed]
67. Ma, Y.; Minasny, B.; Wu, C. Mapping key soil properties to support agricultural production in Eastern China. *Geoderma Reg.* **2017**, *10*, 144–153. [CrossRef]
68. Wang, S.; Zhuang, Q.; Wang, Q.; Jin, X.; Han, C. Mapping stocks of soil organic carbon and soil total nitrogen in Liaoning Province of China. *Geoderma* **2017**, *305*, 250–263. [CrossRef]
69. Chaplot, V.; Bouahom, B.; Valentin, C. Soil organic carbon stocks in Laos: Spatial variations and controlling factors. *Glob. Change Biol.* **2010**, *16*, 1380–1393. [CrossRef]
70. Doetterl, S.; Stevens, A.; Six, J.; Merckx, R.; Van Oost, K.; Pinto, M.C.; Casanova-Katny, A.; Muñoz, C.; Boudin, M.; Venegas, E.Z. Soil carbon storage controlled by interactions between geochemistry and climate. *Nat. Geosci.* **2015**, *8*, 780–783. [CrossRef]
71. Meier, I.C.; Leuschner, C. Variation of soil and biomass carbon pools in beech forests across a precipitation gradient. *Glob. Change Biol.* **2010**, *16*, 1035–1045. [CrossRef]
72. Conant, R.T.; Ryan, M.G.; Ågren, G.I.; Birge, H.E.; Davidson, E.A.; Eliasson, P.E.; Evans, S.E.; Frey, S.D.; Giardina, C.P.; Hopkins, F.M. Temperature and soil organic matter decomposition rates–synthesis of current knowledge and a way forward. *Glob. Chang. Biol.* **2011**, *17*, 3392–3404. [CrossRef]
73. Davidson, E.A.; Janssens, I.A. Temperature sensitivity of soil carbon decomposition and feedbacks to climate change. *Nature* **2006**, *440*, 165–173. [CrossRef]
74. Von Lützow, M.; Kögel-Knabner, I. Temperature sensitivity of soil organic matter decomposition—What do we know? *Biol. Fertil. Soils* **2009**, *46*, 1–15. [CrossRef]
75. Stumpf, F.; Keller, A.; Schmidt, K.; Mayr, A.; Gubler, A.; Schaepman, M. Spatio-temporal land use dynamics and soil organic carbon in Swiss agroecosystems. *Agric. Ecosyst. Environ.* **2018**, *258*, 129–142. [CrossRef]
76. Song, X.-D.; Yang, F.; Ju, B.; Li, D.-C.; Zhao, Y.-G.; Yang, J.-L.; Zhang, G.-L. The influence of the conversion of grassland to cropland on changes in soil organic carbon and total nitrogen stocks in the Songnen Plain of Northeast China. *Catena* **2018**, *171*, 588–601. [CrossRef]
77. Peng, Y.; Xiong, X.; Adhikari, K.; Knadel, M.; Grunwald, S.; Greve, M.H. Modeling soil organic carbon at regional scale by combining multi-spectral images with laboratory spectra. *PLoS ONE* **2015**, *10*, e0142295. [CrossRef]
78. Paul, E.A. The nature and dynamics of soil organic matter: Plant inputs, microbial transformations, and organic matter stabilization. *Soil Biol. Biochem.* **2016**, *98*, 109–126. [CrossRef]
79. Brady, N.C.; Weil, R.R.; Weil, R.R. *The Nature and Properties of Soils*; Prentice Hall: Hoboken, NJ, USA, 2008; Volume 13.

80. Frank, D.A.; Pontes, A.W.; McFarlane, K.J. Controls on soil organic carbon stocks and turnover among North American ecosystems. *Ecosystems* **2012**, *15*, 604–615. [CrossRef]
81. Gray, J.M.; Bishop, T.F.; Wilson, B.R. Factors controlling soil organic carbon stocks with depth in eastern Australia. *Soil Sci. Soc. Am. J.* **2015**, *79*, 1741–1751. [CrossRef]
82. Dong, W.; Wu, T.; Luo, J.; Sun, Y.; Xia, L. Land parcel-based digital soil mapping of soil nutrient properties in an alluvial-diluvia plain agricultural area in China. *Geoderma* **2019**, *340*, 234–248. [CrossRef]
83. Meersmans, J.; De Ridder, F.; Canters, F.; De Baets, S.; Van Molle, M. A multiple regression approach to assess the spatial distribution of Soil Organic Carbon (SOC) at the regional scale (Flanders, Belgium). *Geoderma* **2008**, *143*, 1–13. [CrossRef]
84. Tan, Z.; Lal, R.; Smeck, N.; Calhoun, F. Relationships between surface soil organic carbon pool and site variables. *Geoderma* **2004**, *121*, 187–195. [CrossRef]
85. Vasques, G.; Grunwald, S.; Comerford, N.; Sickman, J. Regional modelling of soil carbon at multiple depths within a subtropical watershed. *Geoderma* **2010**, *156*, 326–336. [CrossRef]
86. Russell, A.E.; Laird, D.; Parkin, T.B.; Mallarino, A.P. Impact of nitrogen fertilization and cropping system on carbon sequestration in Midwestern Mollisols. *Soil Sci. Soc. Am. J.* **2005**, *69*, 413–422. [CrossRef]
87. Vieira, F.; Bayer, C.; Mielniczuk, J.; Zanatta, J.; Bissani, C. Long-term acidification of a Brazilian Acrisol as affected by no till cropping systems and nitrogen fertiliser. *Soil Res.* **2008**, *46*, 17–26. [CrossRef]
88. Zhou, J.; Xia, F.; Liu, X.; He, Y.; Xu, J.; Brookes, P.C. Effects of nitrogen fertilizer on the acidification of two typical acid soils in South China. *J. Soils Sed.* **2014**, *14*, 415–422. [CrossRef]
89. Haynes, R.J.; Naidu, R. Influence of lime, fertilizer and manure applications on soil organic matter content and soil physical conditions: A review. *Nutr. Cycl. Agroecosyst.* **1998**, *51*, 123–137. [CrossRef]
90. Yang, X.; Zhang, X.; Fang, H.; Zhu, P.; Ren, J.; Wang, L. Long-term effects of fertilization on soil organic carbon changes in continuous corn of northeast China: RothC model simulations. *Environ. Manag.* **2003**, *32*, 459–465.
91. Yang, X.; Zhang, X.; Deng, W.; Fang, H. Black soil degradation by rainfall erosion in Jilin, China. *Land Degrad. Dev.* **2003**, *14*, 409–420. [CrossRef]
92. Liu, Z.; Yang, X.; Hubbard, K.G.; Lin, X. Maize potential yields and yield gaps in the changing climate of northeast China. *Glob. Change Biol.* **2012**, *18*, 3441–3454. [CrossRef]
93. Song, C.; Wang, E.; Han, X.; Stirzaker, R. Crop production, soil carbon and nutrient balances as affected by fertilisation in a Mollisol agroecosystem. *Nutr. Cycl. Agroecosyst.* **2011**, *89*, 363–374. [CrossRef]
94. Aguilera, E.; Lassaletta, L.; Gattinger, A.; Gimeno, B.S. Managing soil carbon for climate change mitigation and adaptation in Mediterranean cropping systems: A meta-analysis. *Agric. Ecosyst. Environ.* **2013**, *168*, 25–36. [CrossRef]
95. Sainju, U.M.; Senwo, Z.N.; Nyakatawa, E.Z.; Tazisong, I.A.; Reddy, K.C. Soil carbon and nitrogen sequestration as affected by long-term tillage, cropping systems, and nitrogen fertilizer sources. *Agric. Ecosyst. Environ.* **2008**, *127*, 234–240. [CrossRef]
96. Liu, X.; Herbert, S.; Hashemi, A.; Zhang, X.; Ding, G. Effects of agricultural management on soil organic matter and carbon transformation-a review. *Plant Soil Environ.* **2006**, *52*, 531. [CrossRef]
97. Syswerda, S.; Corbin, A.; Mokma, D.; Kravchenko, A.; Robertson, G. Agricultural management and soil carbon storage in surface vs. deep layers. *Soil Sci. Soc. Am. J.* **2011**, *75*, 92–101. [CrossRef]
98. Yang, J.; Zhang, S.; Li, Y.; Bu, K.; Zhang, Y.; Chang, L.; Zhang, Y. Dynamics of saline-alkali land and its ecological regionalization in western Songnen Plain, China. *Chin. Geogr. Sci.* **2010**, *20*, 159–166. [CrossRef]
99. Wissing, L.; Kölbl, A.; Häusler, W.; Schad, P.; Cao, Z.-H.; Kögel-Knabner, I.J.S.; Research, T. Management-induced organic carbon accumulation in paddy soils: The role of organo-mineral associations. *Soil Tillage Res.* **2013**, *126*, 60–71. [CrossRef]
100. Mi, W.; Wu, L.; Brookes, P.C.; Liu, Y.; Zhang, X.; Yang, X.J.S.; Research, T. Changes in soil organic carbon fractions under integrated management systems in a low-productivity paddy soil given different organic amendments and chemical fertilizers. *Soil Tillage Res.* **2016**, *163*, 64–70. [CrossRef]
101. Somarathna, P.; Malone, B.; Minasny, B. Mapping soil organic carbon content over New South Wales, Australia using local regression kriging. *Geoderma Reg.* **2016**, *7*, 38–48. [CrossRef]
102. Dorji, T.; Odeh, I.O.; Field, D.J.; Baillie, I.C. Digital soil mapping of soil organic carbon stocks under different land use and land cover types in montane ecosystems, Eastern Himalayas. *For. Ecol. Manag.* **2014**, *318*, 91–102. [CrossRef]
103. Zhao, M.-S.; Rossiter, D.G.; Li, D.-C.; Zhao, Y.-G.; Liu, F.; Zhang, G.-L. Mapping soil organic matter in low-relief areas based on land surface diurnal temperature difference and a vegetation index. *Ecol. Indic.* **2014**, *39*, 120–133. [CrossRef]
104. Gomes, L.C.; Faria, R.M.; de Souza, E.; Veloso, G.V.; Schaefer, C.E.G.; Fernandes Filho, E.I. Modelling and mapping soil organic carbon stocks in Brazil. *Geoderma* **2019**, *340*, 337–350. [CrossRef]
105. Liang, Z.; Chen, S.; Yang, Y.; Zhou, Y.; Shi, Z. High-resolution three-dimensional mapping of soil organic carbon in China: Effects of SoilGrids products on national modeling. *Sci. Total Environ.* **2019**, *685*, 480–489. [CrossRef]
106. Zhu, A.; Liu, F.; Li, B.; Pei, T.; Qin, C.; Liu, G.; Wang, Y.; Chen, Y.; Ma, X.; Qi, F. Differentiation of soil conditions over low relief areas using feedback dynamic patterns. *Soil Sci. Soc. Am. J.* **2010**, *74*, 861–869. [CrossRef]
107. Zeng, C.; Zhu, A.-X.; Liu, F.; Yang, L.; Rossiter, D.G.; Liu, J.; Wang, D. The impact of rainfall magnitude on the performance of digital soil mapping over low-relief areas using a land surface dynamic feedback method. *Ecol. Indic.* **2017**, *72*, 297–309. [CrossRef]

Article

Optimal Operation of Nashe Hydropower Reservoir under Land Use Land Cover Change in Blue Nile River Basin

Megersa Kebede Leta [1,2,*], Tamene Adugna Demissie [2] and Jens Tränckner [1]

1. Faculty of Agriculture and Environmental Sciences, University of Rostock, Satower Str. 48, 18051 Rostock, Germany; jens.traenckner@uni-rostock.de
2. Faculty of Civil and Environmental Engineering, Jimma Institute of Technology, Jimma University, Jimma 378, Ethiopia; tamene.adugna@ju.edu.et

* Correspondence: megersa.kebede@uni-rostock.de

Citation: Leta, M.K.; Demissie, T.A.; Tränckner, J. Optimal Operation of Nashe Hydropower Reservoir under Land Use Land Cover Change in Blue Nile River Basin. *Water* **2022**, *14*, 1606. https://doi.org/10.3390/w14101606

Academic Editors: Ankur Srivastava and Venkat Sridhar

Received: 9 April 2022
Accepted: 16 May 2022
Published: 17 May 2022

Publisher's Note: MDPI stays neutral with regard to jurisdictional claims in published maps and institutional affiliations.

Copyright: © 2022 by the authors. Licensee MDPI, Basel, Switzerland. This article is an open access article distributed under the terms and conditions of the Creative Commons Attribution (CC BY) license (https://creativecommons.org/licenses/by/4.0/).

Abstract: Changes in LULC (land use land cover), which significantly influence the spatial and temporal distribution of hydrological processes and water resources in general, have a substantial impact on hydropower generation. The utilization of an optimization approach in order to analyze the operation of reservoirs is an important concern in the planning and management of water resources. The SWAT (Soil and Water Assessment Tool) and the HEC-ResPRM (Hydrologic Engineering Center reservoir evaluation system Prescriptive Reservoir Model) were combined to model and optimize the Nashe hydropower reservoir operation in the Blue Nile River Basin (BNRB). The stream flow into the reservoir was determined using the SWAT model, considering the current and future impacts of LULC changes. The HEC-ResPRM model has been utilized in order to generate the optimal hydropower reservoir operation by using the results of the SWAT calibrated and validated stream flow as input data. This study proposes a method for integrating the HEC-ResPRM and SWAT models to examine the effects of historical and future land use land cover change on the watershed's hydrological processes and reservoir operation. Therefore, the study aimed to investigate the current and future optimal reservoir operation scenarios for water resources management concerning hydropower generation under the effect of LULC changes. The results reveal that both the 2035 and 2050 LULC change scenarios show the increased operation of hydropower reservoirs with increasing reservoir inflows, releases, storage, and reservoir elevation in the future. The effects of LULC change on the study area's hydrological components reveal an increase in surface runoff until 2035, and its decrease from 2035 to 2050. The average annual reservoir storage and elevation in the 2050 LULC scenario increased by 7.25% and 2.27%, respectively, when compared to the current optimized scenario. Therefore, changes in LULC have a significant effect on hydropower development by changing the total annual and monthly reservoir inflow volumes and their seasonal distribution. Reservoir operating rule curves have been commonly implemented in the operation of hydropower reservoirs, since they help operators to make essential, optimal decisions with available stream flow. Moreover, the generated future reservoir rule curves can be utilized as a reference for the long-term prediction of hydropower generation capacity, and assist concerned authorities in the successful operation of the reservoir under the impact of LULC changes.

Keywords: HEC-ResPRM; hydropower; LULC change; optimization; reservoir operation; storage

1. Introduction

Reservoirs are the most critical infrastructure components for integrating management and development of water resources through impounding water and controlling stream flow [1,2]. The management of water resources has become a primary issue in today's fast-developing world, and the global economy's development is hampered by the continuous increase in water demand and the limited supply of water resources [3]. The most common reservoir purposes that regulate water resources through changing natural stream flow include flood control, hydropower production, irrigation, water supply, recreation, navigation, and fisheries [4–7]. Due to a lack of optimal operation policies, the majority of reservoirs are unable to serve their intended purposes, even though they are designed to serve a variety of purposes [8]. Furthermore, reservoir development aims to alleviate regional problems of water scarcity via re-distribution of water resources with temporal variability and spatial heterogeneity [9].

The operation of a reservoir is very challenging for water resource planners and managers; it involves numerous, intricately linked variables, such as storage, power production, hydrological, environmental, institutional, political, as well as the uncertainty of reservoir inflow and stochastic fluctuation of water demands [10–13]. Historical and future LULC changes will alter the pattern, intensity, and frequency of rainfall events, influencing regional and global stream flows and water resource reliability, which may cause significant challenges for reservoir management [14–17]. Therefore, changes in LULC have a significant impact on the distribution and timing of water changes, which affect a variety of water resource operations and managements, including the operation rule curves in addition to the capacity of basins to generate hydropower [14,18,19].

Land Change Modeler (LCM) has been using to predict future LULC, and estimate historical and future LULC changes. As a result, in each given watershed, estimating and predicting stream flow and hydropower generation in the face of changing LULC is crucial for effective water management and decision-making. Consequently, the effects of LULC changes on hydrological processes must be considered in the management and planning of water resources so that measures can be made to adapt future LULC scenarios [20,21]. Various hydrological simulation models are currently being used to simulate and predict the effects of LULC change on hydrological processes, such as the following: Hydrologic Simulation Program-FORTRAN (HSPF), MIKE-system Hydrologic European (MIKE-SHE), Soil and Water Integrated Model (SWIM), Distributed Hydrology Soil Vegetation Model (DHSVM), Soil and Water Assessment Tool (SWAT), Dynamic Watershed Simulation Model (DWSM), and Hydrologic Engineering Center Hydrologic Modeling System (HEC–HMS) [14,15,22,23]. For any hydrological response evaluation and stream flow predictions, it is essential to select the proper model.

The significant factors considered in selecting the appropriate model to achieve the objectives of the study are the following: the ability to simulate hydrological components, efficiency, long-term temporal scaling, flexibility, continuous-time modeling, ease of utility, performance demonstrated through numerous validation studies using readily available data, model complexity, ability to simulate for small to large scale watersheds, freely available, and widely used modeling for assessing the impacts of LULC changes on water resources [23–26]. Based on the criteria outlined here and after a thorough literature review, the SWAT model was selected for analyzing and predicting the stream flow. The hydrological SWAT model is widely used to model and analyze the stream flow simulations that were affected by the uncertainties of LULC changes into the reservoir [24,27–29]. Similarly, various model reviews found that the SWAT can model the desired hydrological processes in more detail than many other watershed models, and can better replicate stream flow than other hydrological models [22].

In reservoir system analysis, the basic modeling approaches utilized to provide quantitative information that can improve operational water management are descriptive simulation, prescriptive optimization, and hybrid models [30]. Optimization algorithms have been used to solve water resource management problems, and to find the best rule curves, optimize the storage and release by minimizing total penalty functions at designated locations throughout the water resource network [31,32]. The descriptive simulation models describe reservoir system performance under a given set of control actions [30,33]. Simulation models simulate decisions of reservoir operations in predefined logical rules, resulting in good reservoir operation but with an inability to optimize the solution [34]. Therefore, recently, a combination of optimization and simulation models (hybrid models) has been applied to reservoir operation in order to address these problems [35,36].

According to Fayaed et al. [12], a review of optimization and simulation models used in resolving essential concerns in reservoir systems emphasized that reservoir optimization is the most crucial element. Reservoir operation rule curves are the utmost popular tool used to determine the rate of water release and storage, by considering the interests of the reservoir stakeholders, inflows, stored water volume, release capacity, current reservoir level, water demands, and downstream constraints [20]. Therefore, developing a rule curve is one type of proper management system frequently used for reservoir operation [37]. In order to achieve the best potential system performance in reservoir operation, decisions on releases and storage must be made over, time while taking into account the variations [7,35,38].

A combination of simulation and optimization models, the Hydrologic Engineering Centre Reservoir Evaluation System Perspective Reservoir Model (HEC-ResPRM) of the US Army Corps of Engineers, was utilized in this study for reservoir optimization. The HEC-ResPRM prescriptive reservoir model is a network flow, monthly based optimization model that determines the optimal releases and storage for multi-reservoir systems over time by minimizing the total penalties in the system [39,40]. In this study, the HEC-ResPRM model was selected above the other optimization models, since it integrates simulation and optimization modeling, and overcomes the limitations of traditional optimization techniques. According to Faber and Harou [41], the HEC-ResPRM was applied to optimize multi-objective reservoir systems in the Mississippi Headwaters. Prasanchum and Kangrang [16] investigated the effect of land use change in the future using the Soil and Water Assessment Tool (SWAT) hydrologic model to assess the future inflow, and the GA optimization algorithm, as one of the popular algorithms due to its random search capability and near-global optimal values, to optimize the reservoir operation rules.

There are a few studies in East Africa that look at the impact of land use land cover change on hydropower production [42]. However, the studies conducted are primarily focused on the effects of the LULC change on past and predicted hydropower generation. The findings suggest that yearly hydropower generation capacity will increase significantly [42,43]. In developing countries, rapid economic development can result in LULC changes within a watershed reservoir [44]. Ethiopia, like many other developing countries, has been grappling with fundamental environmental problems such as LULC change, soil erosion, and water resource degradation, and these are very serious in the highland parts of the country [14]. The main source of renewable energy in developing countries, particularly in sub-Saharan countries, is affected by LULC changes and their associated impacts. Hydropower is the most widely used renewable energy source in many African power systems [45]. The African population and energy demands are increasing rapidly; the hydropower plants and their share of electricity production are developing gradually. Ethiopia has a potential energy source in the country, with plenty of water and a suitable topographical aspect for the establishment of hydropower projects.

The Blue Nile River Basin is one of Ethiopia's twelve major river basins. The Nashe watershed is a tributary of the Blue Nile River Basin and the upper watershed of the Grand Ethiopian Renaissance Dam (GERD), Africa's largest dam, which is located near the border with Sudan. It began operation since February 2022. The goal of the Ethiopian government with the construction of the GERD is to increase the power generation capacity of the country without affecting its downstream users. Similarly, the GERD was expected to help with meeting the increasing domestic electricity demand, exporting electricity to neighboring countries for regional integration, in addition to economic benefits and fisheries growth.

The Blue Nile River Basin is politically significant, since it is a transboundary basin shared by Ethiopia, Sudan, and Egypt. The Blue Nile River Basin is one of the international river basins with the potential for water conflicts between riparian countries [46]. In order to address the growing demand for energy and economic growth, each of the basin countries is developing water resource projects unilaterally [47,48]. McCartney and Menker Girma [49] argue that unilateral management restricts the potential benefits from transboundary water resources, which can be expanded beyond shared water system management. Consequently, one feature of the conflicts in the Blue Nile River Basin is that downstream countries have a high dependency on the water generated from upstream countries.

The effects of the GERD on downstream users have been investigated in different studies. For example, Arjoon et al. [50] developed a hydro-economic model based on the Stochastic Dual Dynamic Programming (SDDP) model in order to examine the positive and negative effects of the GERD on Sudan and Egypt. The findings revealed that the GERD would provide significant irrigation and hydropower benefits for Egypt, Sudan, and Ethiopia under cooperative management. Similarly, according to the findings, the GERD would also have a key role in decreasing hydrological uncertainty during low flow periods. However, according to research by Jeuland et al. [48], non-cooperative management reduces Egypt's total flow compared to cooperative management. Furthermore, the study by Mulat and Moges [51] estimates a 12% and 7% decline in electricity generation from the High Aswan Dam (HAD) during filling and after the GERD is operational, respectively.

A high level of cooperation, especially during reservoir filling, may help Sudan and Egypt minimize negative consequences. In general, a basin-wide cooperative agreement can help to manage the risks to downstream users. The Blue Nile River Basin has a tremendous hydropower production potential that can be fully realized through cooperative water resource development and management. Effective management strategies are becoming more critical as Ethiopia's River Basins become increasingly stressed. Therefore, it is crucial to assess the reservoir operation of the Nashe hydropower reservoir based on historical and predicted LULC changes.

The performance of the HEC-ResPRM in combination with the SWAT model for the LULC pattern was not assessed previously over this watershed study nor in Ethiopia, as far as the authors are aware. Similarly, no study has been conducted on this watershed in order to determine the extent of historical and future land use land cover change effects on the watershed's hydrological processes and reservoir operation. In fact, one of the previous studies investigated the performance of optimization algorithms (HEC-ResPRM) on the Tekeze Reservoir in the Eastern Nile, taking into consideration climate change scenarios [39,40]. Thus, this research presents a novel method for combining the HEC-ResPRM model with the SWAT model in order to assess the effects of historical and future land use land cover change on the watershed's hydrological processes and reservoir operation. As a result, a hybrid methodology is provided in this study as a simulation-optimization framework to investigate the Nashe reservoir operation under various LULC change scenarios.

Therefore, this study was carried out to investigate the impact of individual LULC changes on reservoir operation, as LULC changes in the study watershed are now increasing at an astonishing rate [52]. Furthermore, assessing the perspectives of individual land use land cover changes in hydrological components is critical for long-term water and land resource management. The aims of the study are as follows: (1) to assess the impact of historical and future LULC change on reservoir inflow using Soil and Water Assessment Tool (SWAT); (2) to assess the hydropower generation of Nashe reservoir operation considering the LULC change; and (3), to develop new reservoir operation guide curves for the Nashe hydropower reservoir system in order to increase yearly energy production under the LULC change, using the optimization-simulation model.

2. Materials and Methods

2.1. Description of the Study Watershed

The Nashe River originates from a long and wide river valley in the high mountainous area of Ethiopia. The land relief is up-down, with a low ridge separating the Nashe River from the adjacent river basins. The Nashe dam site is located in the central Ethiopian highlands, about 300 km northwest of the capital of Ethiopia, Addis Ababa, on the Nashe River (Figure 1). The Nashe River basin is located on the plateau, with an average altitude of 2200 m. The watershed plateau is characterized by a hilly topography interspersed with high mountain ranges, volcanic cones, and deep gorges. The Nashe River has a sharp drop of about 600 m at the Nashe cliff, forming a fall and torrents. The river basin has a sub-tropical climate with distinct dry and wet seasons. The Nashe hydropower plant, which has a reservoir located on the left side bank of the Blue Nile River Basin, is the principal tributary, and is mainly utilized for electricity generation for the country. The Nashe dam was developed by building a homogeneous earth-fill dam across the Nashe River, with a height of 38 m, crest length of 1000 m, and a crest elevation of 2235 m. The total water storage capacity of the reservoir is 448 million cubic meters (MCM), of which 85 MCM is dead storage and 363 MCM is live storage.

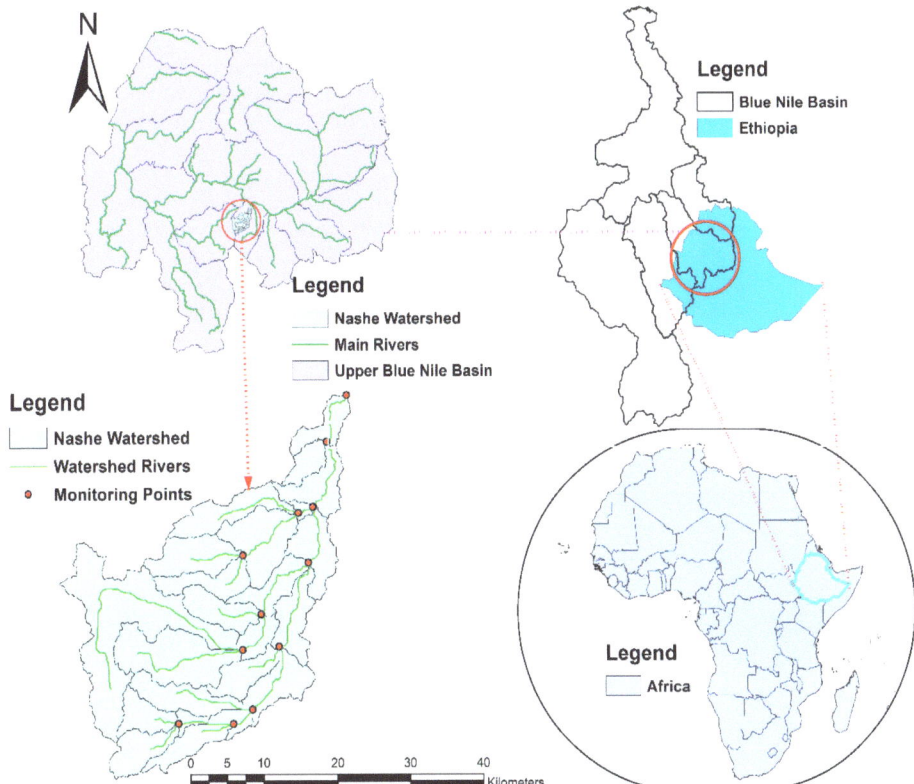

Figure 1. Map of the study area.

The watershed is geographically found between 9°35′ to 9°52′ N latitudes and 37°00′ to 37°20′ E longitudes. The purpose of the Nashe reservoir is primarily for hydropower production, with a total installed capacity of 97 MW in two 48.5 MW Pelton turbines installed at an elevation of 1614 masl (meters above sea level) at the surface powerhouse. The project is aimed to irrigate 6000 ha of land area downstream of the watershed for sugar cane cultivation. The annual mean temperature and rainfall of the watershed are 22 °C and range from 1200 mm to 1600 mm, respectively. Agricultural land and Haplic Alisols are the dominant LULC and soil types of the watershed, respectively.

2.2. Input Data Sets

2.2.1. Hydrological and Meteorological Data

In order to achieve the research goal, it is critical to have relevant and appropriate data before the simulation and optimization of any model [53]. The historical, current, and future hydrological data corresponding to LULC change scenarios have been investigated. The observed stream flow data of the watershed was used for comparison with the simulation results. The SWAT2012 hydrological model was used to examine the historical and future stream flow of the watershed, considering LULC changes. The necessary input data used for the SWAT model to simulate the stream flow of the watershed were DEM (Digital Elevation Model), weather data (rainfall, temperature, wind speed, relative humidity, and solar radiation), land use land cover data, soil data, and observed stream flow data.

The results of these hydrological simulations are instead used as input into an optimization model that determines the optimal reservoir operations given a time series of reservoir inflows. The reservoir's stream flow prediction has been carried out by changing LULC maps, while the remaining model parameters from the calibrated model and other SWAT inputs remain constant. The observed historical stream flow data, soil, and DEM of the Nashe watershed were collected from the Ministry of Water, Irrigation, and Energy, Ethiopia. The weather data was obtained from the Meteorological Service Agency, Ethiopia.

2.2.2. Reservoir Data

The following data is typically required when using the HEC-ResPRM model to perform the reservoir operation: elevation-area-storage curve, historical reservoir storage and water surface level, reservoir outlet capacities, outflow-energy generation relationship, power production, background map of the watershed, and flow time series. The calibrated and validated SWAT model was used to estimate reservoir inflow data for the Nashe watershed [24]. The background map is helpful for setting up the model and visualizing its spatial layout, whereas the physical data is utilized to develop model constraints and allow the model to calculate penalties.

Therefore, the inflow data were first configured in the HEC-DSS (Hydrologic Engineering Center- Data Storage System) for efficient storage and retrieval of scientific input and output time series data. The historical flow time series data was collected from the Ministry of Water, Irrigation, and Energy of Ethiopia. The background map of the study area was extracted by importing the geo-referenced GIS data map of the watershed area using ArcGIS. The other required reservoir data were collected from the Ethiopian Electric Power Corporation.

2.3. Land Use Land Cover Change Scenarios

Changes in land use land cover affect a catchment's hydrological cycle through altering rainfall, evaporation, and runoff. The impact of LUCC on surface runoff has been related to land use types. The LULC types are one of the SWAT model's input parameters. One of the most important factors influencing surface runoff generation is LULC change within a watershed [24,29,54]. In order to investigate the spatiotemporal dynamics of LULC and to predict future LULC change in the Nashe watershed, an integrated method that includes remote sensing, GIS, and a Multi-Layer Perceptron Neural Network-based Cellular Automata-Markov Chain model was employed by Leta et al. [14]. The historical LULC maps developed from Landsat images for the years 1990, 2005, and 2019 (Figure 2) were utilized as the base map and imported into the TerrSet model's Land Change Modeler (LCM) interface to develop the future LULC maps and change scenarios for the years 2035 and 2050 [14] (Figure 3).

The potential LULC change in the watershed was examined using the LCM TerrSet software [14,55]. According to Leta et al. [14], the accuracy of the classified map was compared to ground truth data, and the model was validated for the predicted LULC by simulating the recent LULC map of 2019. The percentage changes of the historical and future LULC change were conducted by [14] and adopted in this study. Based on available land use maps, LCM is extensively used to simulate the projection of LULC changes between two periods. The comprehensive framework of the study is depicted in Figure 4.

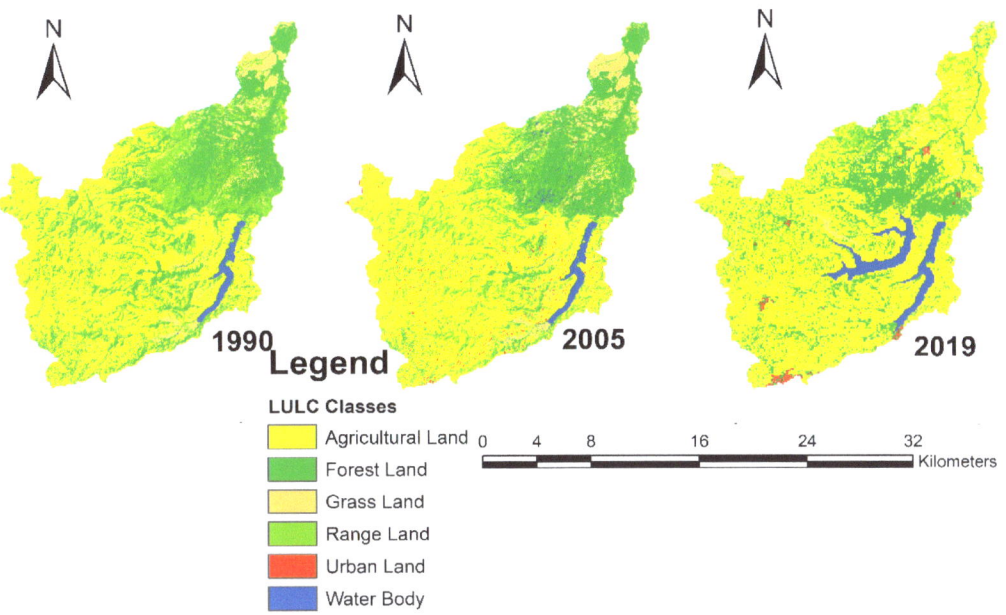

Figure 2. Current and historical land use land cover of the Nashe watershed.

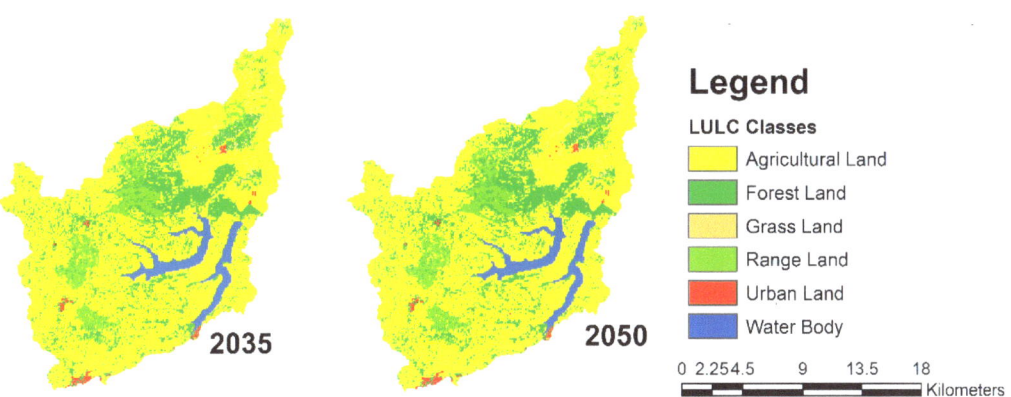

Figure 3. Predicted land use land cover of the Nashe watershed.

The LULC results between 1990 and 2050 revealed a significant change. From 2035 to 2050, agricultural lands, urban areas, and water bodies were predicted to increase continuously. However, compared to the result of the previous change, the rate of agricultural land expansion is lower. This might be due to the limited area of land available for the agricultural land expansion. Furthermore, the distances from urban areas and water bodies could also be another possible reason.

The LULC types of the study watershed include agricultural land, forest land, grass land, range land, water body, and urban areas. Essentially, transition potential maps were developed and processed, after which the data were linked from the current time LULC map to the predicted time. The SWAT model was used to examine the existing and future stream flow of the reservoir using current and future LULC maps as inputs.

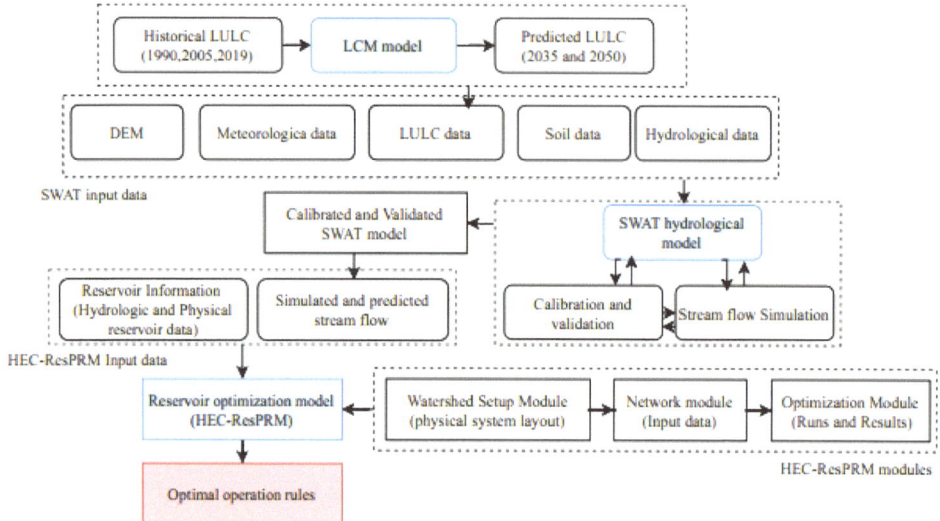

Figure 4. Framework of simulation-optimization model for reservoir operation.

2.4. Model Development

2.4.1. SWAT Hydrological Model

The Soil and Water Assessment Tool is a hydrological model that has been used for investigation of hydrological processes, reservoir operation, assessing the impact of LULC change, climate change on water resources, and for evaluating the effects of land management practices at the level of a watershed that operates over a daily period of time [24,54,56,57]. Precipitation, evapotranspiration, surface runoff, peak runoff, percolation, lateral flows, transmission losses, and ground water flows are the primary components required in the surface and ground water hydrology assessed by the SWAT. In order to simulate the future inflow projections and analyze the LULC change impact on the stream flow utilized as an input for reservoir operation, this study applied the SWAT hydrological model.

It is crucial to consider the impact of different parameters on how much the model simulates the hydrological processes in a watershed. The method of identifying the most substantial parameters for the model is by using sensitivity analysis. The sensitive parameters should be identified in order to improve the hydrological model's calibration. The most sensitive parameters identified by Leta et al. [24] were adopted in this study. The SWAT splits the watershed into hydrologic response units (HRUs) based on topography, each of which has homogeneous land use, soil properties, slope, and estimates the relative effects of soil and LULC changes within each hydrologic response unit (HRU) [24,54].

The flow in each HRU is further simulated according to the hydrologic cycle equation Equation (1). The watershed of the Nashe has been divided into 23 sub-basins and 321 hydrological response units. The sensitivity analysis, model calibration, and validation were conducted to adjust and confirm the parameters in order to optimize the agreement between the observed and simulated stream flow of the Nashe watershed. In order to assess the goodness of the SWAT hydrological model in the Nashe watershed, the coefficients of determination (R^2), Nash–Sutcliffe efficiency (NSE), and percent bias (PBIAS) were implemented. Detailed information about model input, sensitivity analysis, calibration, validation, and model performance assessment has been given by Leta et al. [24].

$$SWt = SWo + \sum_{i=1}^{n}(Rday - QSurf - Ea - Wseep - Qgw) \qquad (1)$$

where SWt: final soil water content (mm H$_2$O); SWo: initial water content (mm H$_2$O); Rday: precipitation on day i (mm H$_2$O); Qsurf: surface runoff on day i (mm H$_2$O); Ea: evapotranspiration on day i (mm H$_2$O); Wseep: water entering the vadose zone from the soil profile on day i (mm H$_2$O); Qgw: return flow on day i (mm H$_2$O); and t: time (days).

2.4.2. HEC-ResPRM Model Description and Setup

The HEC-ResPRM, a hybrid reservoir system optimization operation developed by Hydrologic US Army Corps of Engineering Centers, has been implemented to support planners, operators, and managers with reservoir operation planning and decision making. The reservoir system is modeled as a network of nodes and arcs by the network flow programming algorithm developed in HEC-ResPRM. The HEC-ResPRM modeling platform was developed to facilitate the joint development and use of simulation and optimization models in reservoir system planning and management, by coupling the HEC-PRM (Hydrologic Engineering Center-Prescriptive Reservoir Model) in graphical user interfaces (GUIs) shared with HEC-Res (common interface to both HEC-ResSIM and HEC-ResPRM) [58].

The HEC-ResPRM model stores and retrieves input and output time series data using HEC-DSS. The system is characterized as a network of nodes (reservoirs and junctions) and conveyance links with gain/loss coefficients. The optimization problem represented by a network flow system implemented in the HEC-ResPRM model with costs associated with the flow can be described as follows:

$$\text{Minimize} : \sum_{k}^{n} C_k Q_k \tag{2}$$

$$\text{Subject to} : \sum Q_k - \sum a_k Q_k = 0 \text{ (For all nodes)} \tag{3}$$

$$L_k \leq Q_k \leq U_k \text{ (For all arcs)} \tag{4}$$

where n is the total number of network arcs; C_k is unit cost, weighting factor for flow along arc k; Q_k is flow along arc k; a_k is multiplier (gain) for arc k; L_k is lower bound on flow along the arc k; and U_k is upper bound on flow along the arc k.

The arcs represent the outflow and inflow links in the reservoir system, whereas the node represents a river and reservoir, or channel junctions in this case. Equation (2) depicts the objective function of the flow network optimization model, which minimizes the cost of the flow network. Equation (3) represents model constraints and the continuity equation at each node of the flow network. Equation (4) represents the model constraint, and the maximum and minimum flow constraints at each arc.

The reservoir simulation model is based on the water balance for tracking the movement of water through a reservoir-stream system [59], which fluctuates from time to time. The HEC-ResPRM model allows modelers to create penalty functions that reflect system objectives by relating storage or flow with cost or benefit that derive the solution to the optimization problem. Penalty functions combine a penalty (cost) or reward (negative penalty) with the designated levels of storage or flow. The penalty functions characterize the relative economic, social, environmental, and political penalties linked to the failure to achieve operational goals (storage, pool level, and power production). As a result of unavailable cost data, making penalty functions that reflect costs is a complex economic activity in this study. Therefore, the two categories of penalty functions expressed in the Nashe watershed are storage and flow.

In this study, the constraint values for reservoirs are the lower and upper bounds of reservoir storage. Penalty functions for hydropower releases and storage were established when the inflow time series was specified and reservoir constraints were added. Consequently, as long as the volume of the reservoirs is between the MFL (maximum flood level) and the MOL (minimum operating level), the cost of storage will be zero; if these values are exceeded or not reached, then penalties are applied in the Nashe watershed. The penalties applied in this study were done by changing the shape or magnitude of penalty curves, and by changing the initial and ending reservoir storage volumes.

2.5. Reservoir Optimization Operation

An effective reservoir operation requires policies that optimize releases from the reservoir or storage volume in order to achieve the desired objectives, such as maximizing power generation or minimizing operation costs. The reservoir's water yield is determined by the stream flow flowing into the reservoir in each time period, since the model's principle is predicated on water balance [59]. Mostly, throughout the process of water balance determination, the storage capacity must be determined first, then the water release can be computed using the standard operating rule curves. The rule curves consist of lower and upper limits to guide the release to different water demand target levels.

The power generation requirement can be expressed in various hydropower rules as a relationship between storage and seasons; it can also be directly expressed as an external time series in some circumstances. If the available water is greater than the upper rule curve level, water is discharged from the reservoir into the downstream river; if it is below the lower rule curve, a reduction in supply is required to maintain the water level at the conservation zone. The management of the reservoir for maximum efficiency using basic tools to release water following reservoir rule curves for which LULC change relationships has been studied [60], including improved reservoir rule curves that are appropriate for the dynamics of the hydrological environment in the future [61].

Therefore, the available water in the reservoir should be managed between the upper and lower rule curve levels. The Nashe hydropower reservoir has three major water management zones, which are the inactive (dead storage) zone, the conservation zone, and the flood control zone. In this study, the two boundary rule curves (upper and lower) are used to define the operational zones of the Nashe reservoir that yield greater energy generation. Basically, three types of rule curves, the lower rule curve, upper rule curve, and operating rule curve, were developed and used in operating a reservoir. The operation of the Nashe hydropower reservoir was investigated in this study under three LULC scenarios (2019, 2035, and 2050). Optimization was attempted using alternative options for the three scenarios in order to establish the dynamic features of the reservoir and to determine the optimal solution that could generate maximum energy.

3. Results and Discussion

3.1. Reservoir Inflow under Land Use Land Cover Change

Land use land cover change has an impact on stream flow, which is a critical hydrological response used in water resource management planning and environmental assessments [62]. The influences of LULC change on annual, seasonal, and monthly stream flow were investigated with regard to the baseline period of 1990, and to 2005 for the current (2019) and future (2035 and 2050) LULC changes. Multiple land use transitions in the watershed were projected using the Land Change Modeler integrated TerrSet model [14]. The stream flow corresponding to the individual LULC variations was simulated using the SWAT hydrological model. The SWAT model was calibrated and validated from 1987 to 1999, and from 2000 to 2008, respectively, on a monthly basis.

The model result shows a strong correlation between the simulated and observed stream flows for the calibration and validation periods, as depicted in Figure 5. A detailed investigation of SWAT model performance utilizing graphical and statistical evaluation was presented by [24]. The study conducted by Leta et al. [24] on the hydrological responses of the watershed to historical and future LULC changes of the Nashe watershed, proved the efficacy of the SWAT model to simulate stream flow under varying time periods of LULC changes. The calibrated and validated SWAT model was simulated using inputs of the soil data, DEM, weather data, and projected LULC data, in order to simulate future reservoir inflow. As a result, the future reservoir inflow variation as a function of LULC change was projected using the calibrated SWAT model.

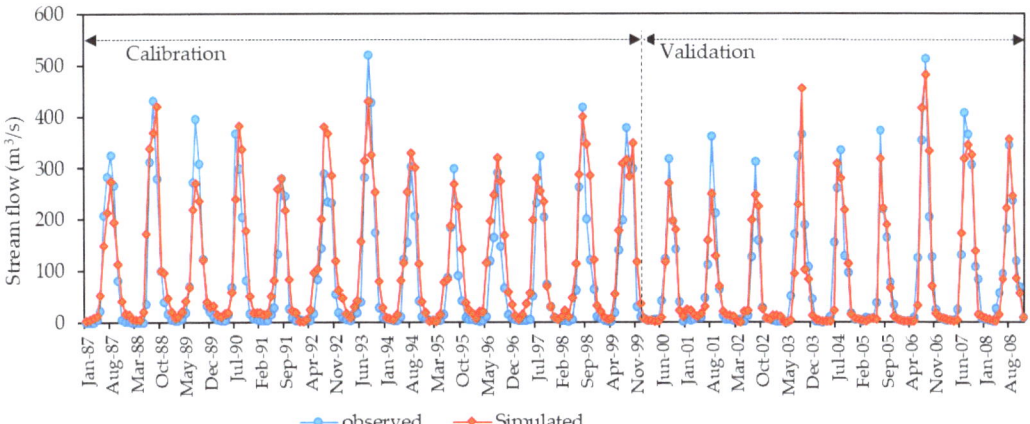

Figure 5. Observed and simulated average monthly stream flow of the Nashe watershed.

The average annual changes of stream flow show 1.15%, 1.36%, and 1.62% in 2019, 2035, and 2050, respectively, with respect to the historical (2005) simulated stream flow. Consequently, the results indicate that the average annual future stream flow into the reservoir shows an increasing trend for all time periods. The trend of increment and decline depend upon the rate of LULC changes. Mostly, the stream flow slightly decreased in the short rainy season, and showed an increasing trend for the other seasons in the watershed. In particular, during the high rainfall season between June and September, the stream flow accounts for more than 70% of the total, whereas it is below 10% in the short rainfall season.

Figure 6 depicts the average monthly percentage change of current and predicted hydropower reservoir inflow patterns under LULC change impacts. The results are in agreement with the results of the study conducted by Sajikumar and Remya [63] on the impact of land use land cover change on inflow characteristics. The average monthly stream flow change shows a maximum increase of 2.43% in 2050, and a maximum decrease of 1.74% in 2019. The trend of monthly stream flow shows that, individually, there was an increasing trend from August to February, and a decreasing tendency from March to July.

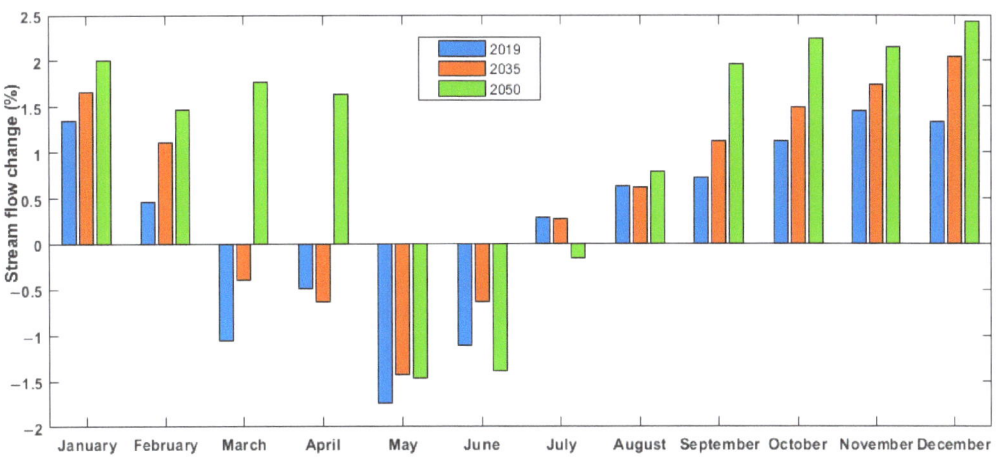

Figure 6. Average monthly stream flow change under land use land cover scenarios.

3.2. Reservoir Operation

In this study, the operation of the hydropower reservoir of the Nashe was performed under current and future trends. The foremost purpose of the Nashe hydropower reservoir construction on the Nashe River was to generate hydropower energy, which will help to substantially meet the energy requirements of the country. Furthermore, the dam produces a managed flow throughout the year, in contrast to the fluctuating seasonal flows that existed prior to dam construction. This has resulted in significant potential for downstream irrigation operations, which would improve the performance of downstream activities that were not investigated in this study as a result of unavailable diversion structure data. Operational decisions have to be made in order to reasonably balance the effects on the storage capacity and water releases between reservoirs and users throughout the time periods that further affect power generation.

The HEC-ResPRM optimization operation model used the SWAT model's simulated stream flow to determine the storage, elevation (pool level), and hydropower generation of the reservoir system. The optimization model was employed under current conditions (2012–2019) after the Nashe hydropower reservoir was constructed to assess the performance of the reservoir operating model in the future. The comparison between the current optimized and actual values of the Nashe hydropower reservoir operation is presented with respect to the dynamics of current flows, elevation, storage, and power production. According to the results, the optimized hydropower reservoir operation (storage and pool level) values exhibited an increase when compared to the current actual reservoir operation status (Figures 7 and 8).

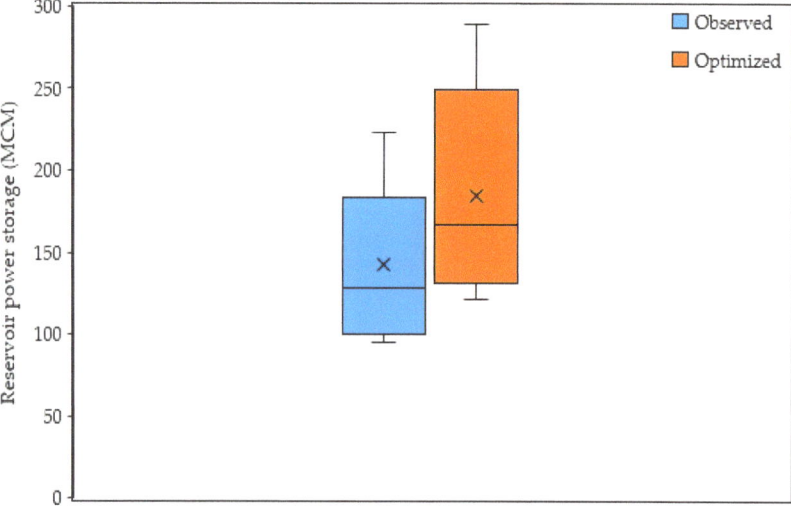

Figure 7. Average monthly current observed and optimized power storage of the Nashe reservoir.

The aim of performance measures is to provide a mechanism to compare the effectiveness of the reservoir system in accomplishing specific objectives quantitatively for different operating plans. In addition to the current reservoir operation, optimization strategies for the sole purpose of hydropower generation are frequently used in the area of water resources management [18]. The average annual optimized reservoir power storage and reservoir pool level increased by 10.58 MCM and 3.12 m, respectively. Figure 9 shows the associated optimal hydropower generation compared to the actual hydropower output. As can be seen, optimized operation performs better. Since the total volume passing the turbines is generally the same in both operation scenarios, the add-on for power supply is mainly generated by an increased storage level, and with that, an increased water head.

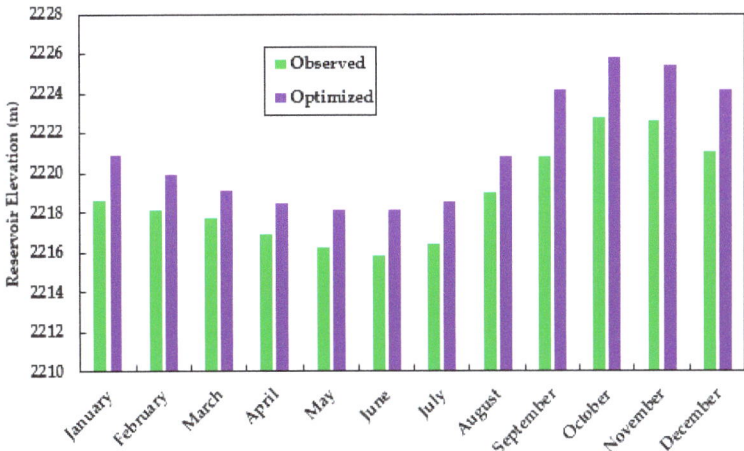

Figure 8. Average monthly current observed and optimized elevation of the Nashe reservoir.

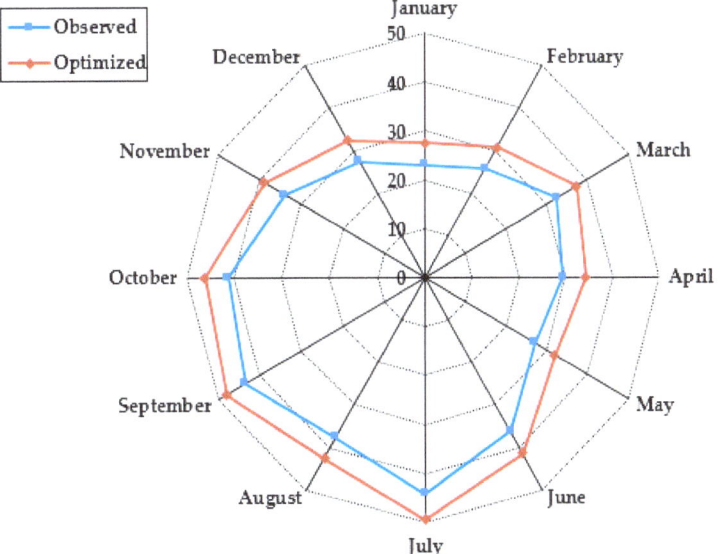

Figure 9. Average monthly current observed and optimized power generated of the Nashe reservoir.

3.3. Hydropower Generation under Land Use Land Cover Changes

3.3.1. Reservoir Inflow and Outflow

The average simulated total inflows to the study hydropower reservoir show an increasing trend, as per the inflow prediction model under all LULC change scenarios. Inflows are also a limiting factor for mean hydropower. Releases (outflows) are used for the watershed optimization model to determine reservoir storage, water levels, and power generation. Similarly, the releases from the reservoir are utilized to assess the objective function for reservoir optimization, and depend on the water availability in the reservoir, prevailing users, and projected reservoir inflow. The surplus water release and water shortage, as well as the average annual shortage, were determined using the released water from the reservoir.

The optimization model was applied for the Nashe hydropower reservoir in order to generate the monthly optimal releases to meet the target demand of the watershed under LULC scenarios for the time periods of 2019, 2035, and 2050. In order to avoid the significant penalties associated with high releases, the model optimizes hydropower release using pre-release before high inflows. The HEC-ResPRM has knowledge of all inflows throughout the network. Thus, the reservoir release decisions are based on specified storage zones defined by elevation, and on a set of rules that specify the aims and constraints governing releases when the storage level falls within each zone. Therefore, the increased inflow in the development scenarios resulted in an accordingly adapted water release.

Correspondingly, the increased reservoir inflow also increases the reservoir outflow in all future periods, producing more energy from hydropower. According to Kangrang et al. [28], excess water release while increasing stream flow to produce more energy was demonstrated on active future rule curves for multipurpose reservoir operation under the effect of land use changes. As depicted in Figure 10, the results of optimal reservoir operation, including inflows and reservoir release, were compared to those of the current period. The volume of reservoir inflow begins to increase in May, and reaches its maximum in July, but afterward begins to decrease significantly from October, following the decline of rainfall. In addition to variations in mean monthly inflows and outflows, seasonal and annual distributions of inflows and outflows have also been investigated.

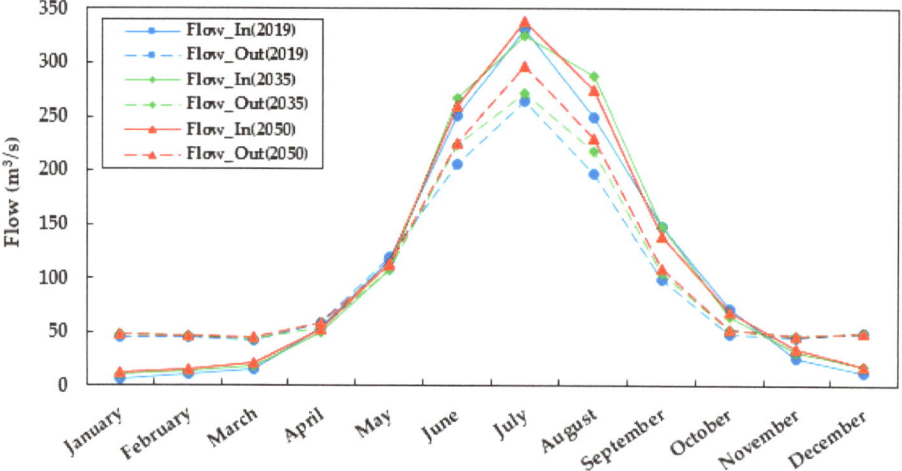

Figure 10. Average monthly reservoir inflow and optimized outflow under LULC changes.

The increased outflow in the Nashe watershed will increase the inflow to the Grand Ethiopian Renaissance Dam. Thus, the downstream users also benefited from the increased stream flow in the future. Zhang et al. [64] found similar results following analysis of the inter-annual and decades scale stream flow variations of the GERD. Reservoir development, according to [9], intends to relieve regional water scarcity problems through the redistribution of water resources with temporal variability and spatial heterogeneity. Besides greater net benefits with increasing storage in Ethiopia, floods and droughts will be reduced, and the hydrological uncertainties will be nullified, particularly during low flow periods.

During the season of rain, the water volume flowing into the reservoir is typically at its maximum, making it difficult to control the excessive outflow. Similarly, as depicted in Figure 10, average outflow values were also highest during the wet season, mostly in June, July, August, while decreasing in the other seasons. The high runoff season of the study area begins mostly in June and ends in September. From November to April, it is the only base flow that flows into the reservoir. Similarly, during this time period, the outflow exceeds the inflow. From the results, it was observed that the average maximum monthly reservoir inflow ranges between 320 m^3/s and 350 m^3/s in 2019, 2035, and 2050.

The average monthly optimal reservoir inflow and releases (outflow) in the 2050 LULC change scenario are greater than the other scenarios in all time periods. Generally, plentiful rainfall in the wet season increased both the Nashe reservoir inflow and outflow. During the short rainy season, the difference between the inflows and outflows was minimal, especially in April and May. According to Guo et al. [15], future land use land cover changes will almost definitely continue to alter stream flow patterns, posing considerable reservoir management challenges.

3.3.2. Reservoir Storage and Elevation

The desired storage, which was determined by applying the HEC-ResPRM model for hydropower generation, is a variable in the reservoir operation optimization model. The storage capacity of a reservoir varies, depending on inflow and outflow variations. However, the increment of reservoir inflow is the main factor for increasing reservoir storage. Therefore, the specified reservoir storage for the various operating strategies was achieved using the three time period (2019, 2035, and 2050) optimization scenarios. The reservoir optimization model results revealed a significant increase in predicted mean annual hydropower reservoir storage under the 2035 and 2050 LULC change scenarios of the Nashe watershed. Reservoir storage varies with inflow and outflow. The maximum average monthly optimum reservoir storage shows 289 million cubic meter (Mm^3) in 2019, 307 Mm^3 in 2035, and 313 Mm^3 in 2050 (Figure 11).

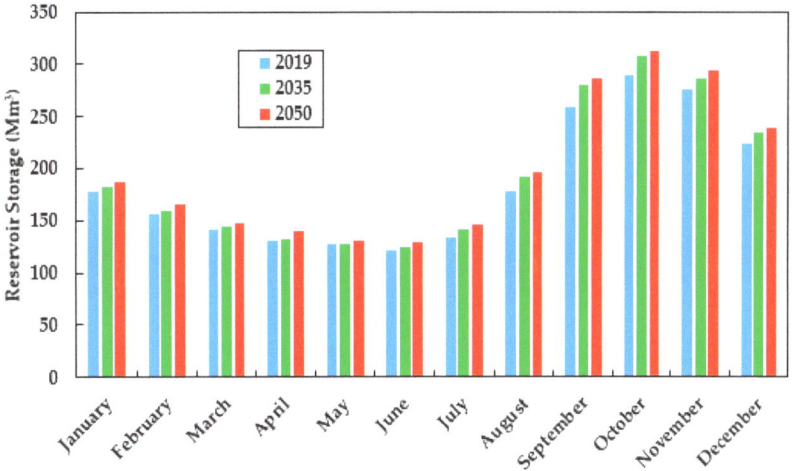

Figure 11. Average monthly current optimized and future reservoir storage of Nashe reservoir.

The optimum reservoir storage occurred between September to December, with peak storage in October. The optimized future storage volumes for the reservoir within scenarios are greater than the current actual and optimized reservoir operations. However, most of the average storage volumes are close to the optimized current reservoir storage operation, especially during dry and short rainy seasons. Likewise, the storage volumes for the 2035 LULC scenario's maximum volume are more comparable to the 2050 future scenario operation. According to [65,66] investigations, the optimum reservoir storage obtained by using the optimization algorithm for the reservoir should be better than the currently used operational storage for optimizing annual hydropower production. Figure 11 illustrates the average monthly reservoir storage results derived by the HEC-ResPRM optimization model for operations in 2019, 2035, and 2050.

In order to generate more head and hence more energy, the first scenario requires greater amounts of water storage within the reservoir relative to the second scenario. Furthermore, the findings depicted that the reservoir storage declined from the middle of February, and reached a minimum storage level in June. During this month, it helps to release more water volume in order to prepare for the next main rainy season. However, the simulation process determines the reservoir at each time step and the resulting downstream flows by considering the reservoir storage balance equation while keeping the system in balance. In conclusion, based on the results of the optimization model approach, power storage generation could be optimized, and should not result in significant water shortages in most of the years (Figures 11 and 12).

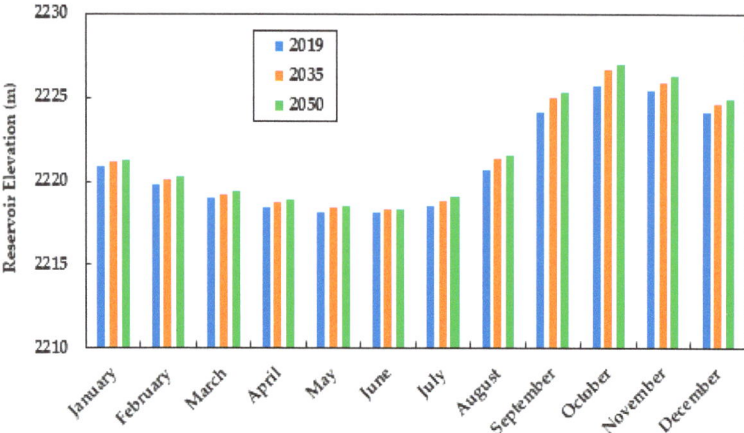

Figure 12. Average monthly current optimized and future reservoir elevation of the Nashe reservoir.

Nevertheless, it is recommended to further decrease the spill of water during the wet season to avoid shortages of water in the following year. Therefore, the results show that the maximum reservoir storage in scenarios is more than the historical projected operations. This finding is in agreement with Lu et al. [1], Azizipour et al. [4], and He et al. [67] in their indications for the optimal levels of release and optimal volumes of storage in different parts of the world. The impacts of the change in LULC on the Nashe hydropower reservoir operation through the use of optimization models reveal a positive impact on the reservoir storage and its pool level. The major features of the reservoir pool define the volume of storage and the surface area at each level.

The Nashe hydropower reservoir pool level contains the relationship of the elevation-storage-area curve. The average monthly maximum and minimum reservoir levels for the future vary between 2226.76 m and 2227.01 m, and 2218.34 m and 2218.40 m, respectively, for the 2035 and 2050 LULC change scenarios, respectively. The results of reservoir elevation between operations in 2019, 2035, and 2050 were compared and are illustrated in Figure 12. From the results, it was observed that the optimized pool level is greater than the current optimal reservoir levels of the Nashe hydropower reservoir. This significant elevation difference will allow more water to be stored during the rainy season for energy production during the dry season.

Similar to reservoir storage, the reservoir pool level remains at a high level every year from September to December. However, the reservoir reaches a maximum level in October, near the end of the rainy season. In general, the findings show that the reservoir system has appropriate storage distributions and water allocations for the entire period. Hydropower generation is a priority when available water is above average and increased hydropower generation is required [6]. The reservoir authority and policymakers could use the various possible operational storage and elevation rules to assist them in developing efficient and long-term guidelines for several competing issues.

3.3.3. Reservoir Power Generation

The change in the hydropower generation caused by the LULC changes in the future scenarios (2035 and 2050) was explored by utilizing the current LULC scenario (2019) as a point of comparison. The optimization operation model employed the future stream flow data simulated by the SWAT hydrological model, and observed power production as input to develop the Nashe reservoir future power generation. The average annual power generation from the Nashe reservoir under different LULC time period scenarios (currently optimized and future), including the actual operation of the reservoir, is depicted in Figure 13. Therefore, Figure 13 shows that 2050 reservoir operation leads to improved power generation compared to the observed, optimized, 2019, and 2035 scenarios.

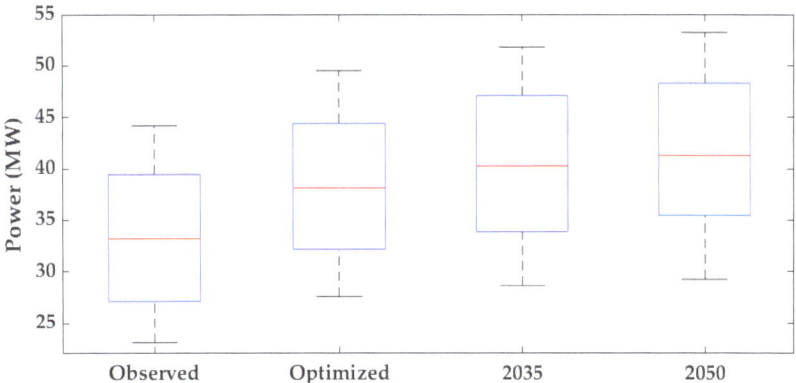

Figure 13. Boxplots of monthly hydropower generation of the Nashe watershed under different scenarios.

These findings propose that the outcomes of the future scenario optimization model are the most promising for increasing energy development. However, the fluctuations in power generation over time suggest that LULC changes have an impact on reservoir performance for energy production. Furthermore, the average annual energy production utilizing the HEC-ResPRM model for the 2035 and 2050 time periods is higher than that for the current actual and optimized energy generation of the reservoir. In comparison to the reservoir's optimal operation in 2019; the average hydropower generation increased by 4.83%, and 8.32% for 2035 and 2050, respectively. As a result, when compared to earlier periods, this indicates a gradually increasing trend. Generally, there are no significant variations between the scenarios in terms of hydropower potential generation.

The results of the hydropower generation are consistent with the results of the stream flow simulation. The trend of average annual stream flow and hydropower generation show an increment in each of the future LULC time period scenarios due to the close relationship between hydropower generation and stream flow. Optimal hydropower occurs mostly during the rainy season under all scenarios, as a result of the increased inflow and water release. Between October and April, reservoir inflow decreases, resulting in a significant reduction in hydropower generation. In contrast, the increment of inflow from May to September contributes to a high pre-water level.

In all scenarios, the months of October to January, considered as dry months for the watershed, are projected to have a considerable increase in hydropower generation. Additionally, the peak value of hydropower generation is detected mostly in the wet season, especially in July, with minimum power generation happening in January. Similarly, the reason for a significant increment in inflow during the rainy period is that it encourages water impoundment, resulting in higher power output. Consequently, when the reservoir accumulates a high amount of water during the wet season, a high water level can be reached in the dry season, providing a larger water head for hydropower generation.

Generally, reservoir management is expected to be affected by changes in the spatial and temporal availability of water at reservoir locations [68].

3.4. Optimal Operating Rule Curves

The operating rules for the reservoir system under this investigation were derived from the time series for reservoir storage and pool level generated by the optimization model during the entire period. It is necessary to obtain an appropriate guideline for effective reservoir storage and release balance, taking into consideration the project's objectives for reservoir operation. Rule curves could be expressed in a number of ways, including water surface elevation or storage volume with respect to time of the year. The HEC-ResPRM optimization model was utilized to operate the current and future reservoir rule curves of the Nashe hydropower reservoir. Reservoir operation rule curves are the most frequent techniques used to determine the pace at which water is released and stored depending on currently existing information, such as the current status of storage volume and forecasted inflow [20]. The optimization results for the storage volume (Figure 14a) and pool level (Figure 14b) indicate that the 2035 and 2050 future scenarios rule curves are slightly higher than the current curves.

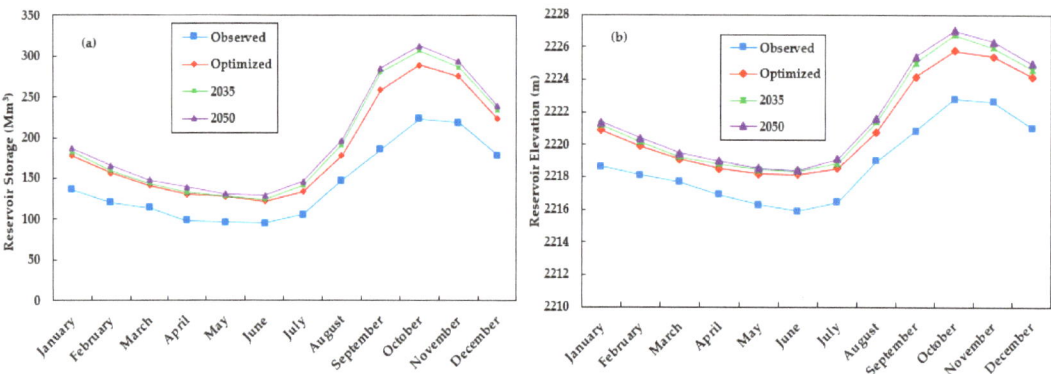

Figure 14. Nashe reservoir mean monthly power storage (**a**) and pool level (**b**) rule curves for current and future time periods.

Figure 14 shows the optimal rule curves for the 2035 and 2050 scenarios in comparison to the existing rule curves. The rule curve features are based on the quantity of the inflow, which is ascribed to rainfall patterns and reservoir operation in proportion to monthly energy requirements. The power rule curves of the future scenarios also follow similar tendencies, but are higher compared to current optimized and efficient rule curves, with uneven power distribution from month to month. The 2050 LULC scenario rule curve shows the highest average power storage, reservoir level, power production, and total energy. According to [65,66], the optimal operating rules for reservoirs should be better than the current random operational rules using an optimization algorithm for annual hydropower production.

The reservoir operation focuses on the upper rule curves throughout the rainy season, since the volume of water flowing into the reservoir is very high, and is necessary to control the excess release reservoir operation focuses on the lower rule curves in the event of lower-than-average rainfall, resulting in low flow. The reservoir always wants to release more water than that entering the pool when the reservoir's pool elevation is above the guide curve in flood control, and releases less water than that entering the pool when below the guide curve in conservation. In addition, the reservoir will be able to withstand the excessive volume of water that might finally lead to a flood, since it has more space to reserve excess amounts of water without an overflow situation.

Therefore, rule curves are crucial in order to control the effects of flash floods through dams. As a result, these curves can be suggested to be guidelines for reservoir operation, ensuring that all water demands are satisfied on a monthly basis. In general, all demands are satisfied as long as the reservoir's current water levels and storage fall between the upper and lower rule curves. The water level in the Nashe reservoir is generally in the conservation zone, which is a safe zone for power generation, and reduces risks to dam safety and other structures. Therefore, the curves show the desired storage levels in the reservoir during the operation of reservoirs to satisfy the demands of hydropower production, environmental release, and flood protection.

The model's optimized rule curve indicates that the reservoir's maximum water level is about 2227.01 masl (Figure 14b), while the full reservoir level is 2230 masl. The study by Prasanchum and Kangrang [16] proved that the new rule curves can be helpful when connected to the simulation model, and this could prevent water shortages in the future. Generally, in the Nashe watershed, decisions based on reservoir operating rule curves are critical to achieving seasonally and annually balanced water release, as well as protecting reservoir downstream areas from flooding.

4. Conclusions

In this study, the LULC changes from the Land Change Modeler, which represent the current and future prediction scenarios, were assessed in order to determine the base and future inflows into the Nashe hydropower reservoir. As a result, the calibrated and validated SWAT model was utilized to generate LULC change-driven stream flow, which was then used as an input for modeling optimal reservoir operation. The reservoir optimization model has been utilized to develop optimal hydropower reservoir operation policies (storage and releases) for the Nashe hydropower reservoir, using a combination of the SWAT and the HEC-ResPRM optimization algorithm; this was implemented in order to meet the target storage and maximize reservoir capacity to generate hydropower under current and future LULC conditions. The following conclusions were reached as a result of the study's key contributions:

- The estimated optimal reservoir operations for all scenarios have distinct values but follow similar tendencies. This indicates that the seasonal hydropower generation is affected by stream flow, and that the future inflow from the reservoir area is substantially more susceptible to future LULC changes. The optimal rule curves that were developed perform significantly better under future inflow scenarios compared to current rule curves, which allow the reservoir to be more effective and appropriate in terms of water release and storage for future scenarios to generate more energy.
- The optimal solution could maintain a higher level of water in the reservoir, and the optimized policy may increase hydropower generation during the wet season, while also increasing the possibility of water accessibility during the following dry season.
- The possibility of improved water resource utilization in the future, particularly with vigorous operating rules that consider optimization and uncertainty, can be utilized as a guide for the future operation of hydropower planning. The development of appropriate reservoir operating rules is critical for planning and management, particularly from the perspective of LULC change.
- The findings are intended to provide information to policymakers, water resource managers, and other interested stakeholders so that future development in the Nashe watershed of the Blue Nile River Basin can be more effective.
- Furthermore, the findings suggest that the methodology utilized in this research can be used to evaluate and optimize current systems, as well as emphasize the importance of using predicted land use land cover change as an assessment tool for reservoir management in the future.
- Generally, changes in LULC have an impact on the quantity of water available for energy generation in hydropower reservoirs. Land use land cover changes can cause soil deterioration (silting), which can affect both the watershed and the reservoir

- level as a result of sediment transport, and thus exacerbate the negative effects of climate change.
- As a result, it is essential to perform studies that take into account a variety of variables in order to produce accurate scenarios for the future availability of water resources for hydropower generation, and to define regulations for flexible reservoir operation.

Author Contributions: Conceptualization, M.K.L., T.A.D. and J.T.; development of the work methodology, M.K.L.; software, M.K.L.; validation, M.K.L., T.A.D. and J.T.; formal analysis, M.K.L.; investigation, M.K.L.; data curation, M.K.L.; writing original draft preparation, M.K.L.; writing review and editing, M.K.L., T.A.D. and J.T.; visualization, M.K.L.; supervision of the manuscript T.A.D. and J.T. All authors have read and agreed to the published version of the manuscript.

Funding: This research was part of the DAAD-EECBP Home Grown PhD Scholarship Program under (EECBP Homegrown PhD Program-2019).

Institutional Review Board Statement: Not applicable.

Informed Consent Statement: Not applicable.

Data Availability Statement: The authors can provide the data used in this study upon reasonable request.

Acknowledgments: The first author is grateful for the German Academic Exchange Service (DAAD) for providing a scholarship during the study. The authors would like to express their gratitude to the University of Rostock for financing the publication under the Open Access Publication funding program.

Conflicts of Interest: The authors declare no conflict of interest.

References

1. Lu, B.; Li, K.; Zhang, H.; Wang, W.; Gu, H. Study on the optimal hydropower generation of Zhelin reservoir. *J. Hydro-Environ. Res.* **2013**, *7*, 270–278. [CrossRef]
2. Yazdi, J.; Moridi, A. Interactive Reservoir-Watershed Modeling Framework for Integrated Water Quality Management. *Water Resour. Manag.* **2017**, *31*, 2105–2125. [CrossRef]
3. Xu, M.; Li, C.; Wang, X.; Cai, Y.; Yue, W. Optimal water utilization and allocation in industrial sectors based on water footprint accounting in Dalian City, China. *J. Clean. Prod.* **2018**, *176*, 1283–1291. [CrossRef]
4. Azizipour, M.; Ghalenoei, V.; Afshar, M.H.; Solis, S.S. Optimal Operation of Hydropower Reservoir Systems Using Weed Optimization Algorithm. *Water Resour. Manag.* **2016**, *30*, 3995–4009. [CrossRef]
5. Birhanu, K.; Alamirew, T.; Dinka, M.O.; Ayalew, S.; Aklog, D. Optimizing Reservoir Operation Policy Using Chance Constraint Nonlinear Programming for Koga Irrigation Dam, Ethiopia. *Water Resour. Manag.* **2014**, *28*, 4957–4970. [CrossRef]
6. Yang, T.; Gao, X.; Sellars, S.L.; Sorooshian, S. Improving the multi-objective evolutionary optimization algorithm for hydropower reservoir operations in the California Oroville-Thermalito complex. *Environ. Model Softw.* **2015**, *69*, 262–279. [CrossRef]
7. Chou, F.N.-F.; Wu, C.-W. Stage-wise optimizing operating rules for flood control in a multi-purpose reservoir. *J. Hydrol.* **2015**, *521*, 245–260. [CrossRef]
8. Daniel, A. Water Use and Operation Analysis of Water Resource Systems in Omo Gibe River Basin. Master's Thesis, Addis Ababa University, Addis Ababa, Ethiopia, May 2011.
9. Soleimani, S.; Bozorg-Haddad, O.; Loáiciga, H.A. Reservoir Operation Rules with Uncertainties in Reservoir Inflow and Agricultural Demand Derived with Stochastic Dynamic Programming. *J. Irrig. Drain. Eng.* **2016**, *142*, 04016046. [CrossRef]
10. Feng, M.; Liu, P.; Guo, S.; Gui, Z.; Zhang, X.; Zhang, W.; Xiong, L. Identifying changing patterns of reservoir operating rules under various inflow alteration scenarios. *Adv. Water Resour.* **2017**, *104*, 23–36. [CrossRef]
11. Sangiorgio, M.; Guariso, G. NN-Based Implicit Stochastic Optimization of Multi-Reservoir Systems Management. *Water* **2018**, *10*, 303. [CrossRef]
12. Fayaed, S.S.; El-Shafie, A.; Jaafar, O. Reservoir-system simulation and optimization techniques. *Stoch. Hydrol. Hydraul.* **2013**, *27*, 1751–1772. [CrossRef]
13. Zhou, J.; Jia, B.; Chen, X.; Qin, H.; He, Z.; Liu, G. Identifying Efficient Operating Rules for Hydropower Reservoirs Using System Dynamics Approach—A Case Study of Three Gorges Reservoir, China. *Water* **2019**, *11*, 2448. [CrossRef]
14. Leta, M.; Demissie, T.; Tränckner, J. Modeling and Prediction of Land Use Land Cover Change Dynamics Based on Land Change Modeler (LCM) in Nashe Watershed, Upper Blue Nile Basin, Ethiopia. *Sustainability* **2021**, *13*, 3740. [CrossRef]
15. Guo, Y.; Fang, G.; Xu, Y.-P.; Tian, X.; Xie, J. Responses of hydropower generation and sustainability to changes in reservoir policy, climate and land use under uncertainty: A case study of Xinanjiang Reservoir in China. *J. Clean. Prod.* **2020**, *281*, 124609. [CrossRef]
16. Prasanchum, H.; Kangrang, A. Optimal reservoir rule curves under climatic and land use changes for Lampao Dam using Genetic Algorithm. *KSCE J. Civ. Eng.* **2017**, *22*, 351–364. [CrossRef]

17. Asadieh, B.; Afshar, A. Optimization of Water-Supply and Hydropower Reservoir Operation Using the Charged System Search Algorithm. *Hydrology* **2019**, *6*, 5. [CrossRef]
18. Fan, J.-L.; Hu, J.-W.; Zhang, X.; Kong, L.-S.; Li, F.; Mi, Z. Impacts of climate change on hydropower generation in China. *Math. Comput. Simul.* **2018**, *167*, 4–18. [CrossRef]
19. Paliwal, V.; Ghare, A.D.; Mirajkar, A.B.; Bokde, N.D.; Lorenzo, A.E.F. Computer Modeling for the Operation Optimization of Mula Reservoir, Upper Godavari Basin, India, Using the Jaya Algorithm. *Sustainability* **2019**, *12*, 84. [CrossRef]
20. Zhang, J.; Liu, P.; Wang, H.; Lei, X.; Zhou, Y. A Bayesian model averaging method for the derivation of reservoir operating rules. *J. Hydrol.* **2015**, *528*, 276–285. [CrossRef]
21. Zuo, D.; Xu, Z.; Yao, W.; Jin, S.; Xiao, P.; Ran, D. Assessing the effects of changes in land use and climate on runoff and sediment yields from a watershed in the Loess Plateau of China. *Sci. Total Environ.* **2016**, *544*, 238–250. [CrossRef]
22. Waseem, M.; Kachholz, F.; Tränckner, J. Suitability of common models to estimate hydrology and diffuse water pollution in North-eastern German lowland catchments with intensive agricultural land use. *Front. Agric. Sci. Eng.* **2018**, *5*, 420–431. [CrossRef]
23. Kumari, N.; Srivastava, A.; Sahoo, B.; Raghuwanshi, N.S.; Bretreger, D. Identification of Suitable Hydrological Models for Streamflow Assessment in the Kangsabati River Basin, India, by Using Different Model Selection Scores. *Nonrenew. Resour.* **2021**, *30*, 4187–4205. [CrossRef]
24. Leta, M.K.; Demissie, T.A.; Tränckner, J. Hydrological Responses of Watershed to Historical and Future Land Use Land Cover Change Dynamics of Nashe Watershed, Ethiopia. *Water* **2021**, *13*, 2372. [CrossRef]
25. Zhang, L.; Meng, X.; Wang, H.; Yang, M. Simulated Runoff and Sediment Yield Responses to Land-Use Change Using the SWAT Model in Northeast China. *Water* **2019**, *11*, 915. [CrossRef]
26. Anand, J.; Gosain, A.K.; Khosa, R. Optimisation of Multipurpose Reservoir Operation by Coupling Soil and Water Assessment Tool (SWAT) and Genetic Algorithm for Optimal Operating Policy (Case Study: Ganga River Basin). *Sustainability* **2018**, *10*, 1660. [CrossRef]
27. Megersa, K.; Ankit, C.; Tamene, A. Stream Flow and Land Use Land Cover Change in Finchaa Hydropower, Blue Nile Basin, Ethiopia. *Int. J. Civil. Struct. Environ. Infrastruct. Eng. Res. Dev.* **2017**, *7*, 1–12. [CrossRef]
28. Kangrang, A.; Prasanchum, H.; Hormwichian, R. Active future rule curves for multi-purpose reservoir operation on the impact of climate and land use changes. *J. Hydro-Environ. Res.* **2019**, *24*, 1–13. [CrossRef]
29. Lin, B.; Chen, X.; Yao, H.; Chen, Y.; Liu, M.; Gao, L.; James, A. Analyses of landuse change impacts on catchment runoff using different time indicators based on SWAT model. *Ecol. Indic.* **2015**, *58*, 55–63. [CrossRef]
30. Labadie, J.W. Optimal Operation of Multireservoir Systems: State-of-the-Art Review. *J. Water Resour. Plan. Manag.* **2004**, *130*, 93–111. [CrossRef]
31. Rozos, E. An assessment of the operational freeware management tools for multi-reservoir systems. *Water Supply* **2018**, *19*, 995–1007. [CrossRef]
32. Choi, Y.; Lee, E.; Ji, J.; Ahn, J.; Kim, T.; Yi, J. Development and Evaluation of the Hydropower Reservoir Rule Curve for a Sustainable Water Supply. *Sustainability* **2020**, *12*, 9641. [CrossRef]
33. Ozkaya, A.; Zerberg, Y. Water storage change assessment in the Seyhan Reservoir (Turkey) using HEC-ResSim model. *Arab. J. Geosci.* **2021**, *14*, 1–12. [CrossRef]
34. Zeng, X.; Hu, T.; Guo, X.; Li, X. Water Transfer Triggering Mechanism for Multi-Reservoir Operation in Inter-Basin Water Transfer-Supply Project. *Water Resour. Manag.* **2014**, *28*, 1293–1308. [CrossRef]
35. Chou, F.N.-F.; Linh, N.T.T.; Wu, C.-W. Optimizing the Management Strategies of a Multi-Purpose Multi-Reservoir System in Vietnam. *Water* **2020**, *12*, 938. [CrossRef]
36. Ehteram, M.; Koting, S.B.; Afan, H.A.; Mohd, N.S.; Malek, M.A.; Ahmed, A.N.; El-Shafie, A.H.; Onn, C.C.; Lai, S.H.; El-Shafie, A. New Evolutionary Algorithm for Optimizing Hydropower Generation Considering Multireservoir Systems. *Appl. Sci.* **2019**, *9*, 2280. [CrossRef]
37. Nourani, V.; Rouzegari, N.; Molajou, A.; Hosseini, B.A. An integrated simulation-optimization framework to optimize the reservoir operation adapted to climate change scenarios. *J. Hydrol.* **2020**, *587*, 125018. [CrossRef]
38. Nandalal, K.D.W.; Bogardi, J.J. Dynamic programming based operation of reservoirs: Applicability and limits. *Dyn. Program Based Oper. Reserv. Appl. Limits* **2013**, *31*, 1–130.
39. Ashrafi, S.; Ashrafi, S.; Moazami, S. Developing Self-adaptive Melody Search Algorithm for Optimal Operation of Multi-reservoir Systems. *J. Hydraul. Struct.* **2017**, *3*, 35–48.
40. Abera, F.F.; Asfaw, D.H.; Engida, A.N.; Melesse, A.M. Optimal Operation of Hydropower Reservoirs under Climate Change: The Case of Tekeze Reservoir, Eastern Nile. *Water* **2018**, *10*, 273. [CrossRef]
41. Faber, B.A.; Harou, J.J. Multi-objective optimization of reservoir systems using HEC-ResPRM. Restoring Our Nat Habitat. In Proceedings of the 2007 World Environmental and Water Resources Congress, Tampa, FL, USA, 15–19 May 2007; pp. 1–14.
42. Khare, D.; Patra, D.; Mondal, A.; Kundu, S. Impact of landuse/land cover change on run-off in the catchment of a hydro power project. *Appl. Water Sci.* **2015**, *7*, 787–800. [CrossRef]
43. Bahati, H.K.; Ogenrwoth, A.; Sempewo, J.I. Quantifying the potential impacts of land-use and climate change on hydropower reliability of Muzizi hydropower plant, Uganda. *J. Water Clim. Chang.* **2021**, *12*, 2526–2554. [CrossRef]
44. Nguyen, A.; Cochrane, T.; Pahlow, M. A Framework to Assess the Reliability of a Multipurpose Reservoir under Uncertainty in Land Use. *Water* **2021**, *13*, 287. [CrossRef]

45. Falchetta, G.; Kasamba, C.; Parkinson, S.C. Monitoring hydropower reliability in Malawi with satellite data and machine learning. *Environ. Res. Lett.* **2019**, *15*, 014011. [CrossRef]
46. Samaan, M.M. *The Win-Win-Win Scenario in the Blue Nile's Hydropolitical Game: Application on the Grand Ethiopian Renaissance Dam*; GESIS-Leibniz-Institut für Sozialwissenschaften: Mannheim, Germany, 2014.
47. Goor, Q.; Halleux, C.; Mohamed, Y.; Tilmant, A. Optimal operation of a multipurpose multireservoir system in the Eastern Nile River Basin. *Hydrol. Earth Syst. Sci.* **2010**, *14*, 1895–1908. [CrossRef]
48. Jeuland, M.; Wu, X.; Whittington, D. Infrastructure development and the economics of cooperation in the Eastern Nile. *Water Int.* **2017**, *42*, 121–141. [CrossRef]
49. McCartney, M.P.; Girma, M.M. Evaluating the downstream implications of planned water resource development in the Ethiopian portion of the Blue Nile River. *Water Int.* **2012**, *37*, 362–379. [CrossRef]
50. Arjoon, D.; Mohamed, Y.; Goor, Q.; Tilmant, A. Hydro-economic risk assessment in the eastern Nile River basin. *Water Resour. Econ.* **2014**, *8*, 16–31. [CrossRef]
51. Mulat, A.G.; Moges, S.A. Assessment of the Impact of the Grand Ethiopian Renaissance Dam on the Performance of the High Aswan Dam. *J. Water Resour. Prot.* **2014**, *6*, 583–598. [CrossRef]
52. Yesuph, A.Y.; Dagnew, A.B. Land use/cover spatiotemporal dynamics, driving forces and implications at the Beshillo catchment of the Blue Nile Basin, North Eastern Highlands of Ethiopia. *Environ. Syst. Res.* **2019**, *8*, 21. [CrossRef]
53. Fang, H.; Bin, H.T.S.; Zeng, X.; Wu, F.Y. Simulation-optimization model of reservoir operation based on target storage curves. *Water Sci. Eng.* **2014**, *7*, 433–445.
54. Megersa, K.L.; Tamene, A.D.; Sifan, A.K. Impacts of Land Use Land Cover Change on Sediment Yield and Stream Flow. *Int. J. Sci. Technol.* **2017**, *6*, 763–781.
55. Ansari, A.; Golabi, M.H. Prediction of spatial land use changes based on LCM in a GIS environment for Desert Wetlands—A case study: Meighan Wetland, Iran. *Int. Soil Water Conserv. Res.* **2018**, *7*, 64–70. [CrossRef]
56. Buakhao, W.; Kangrang, A. DEM Resolution Impact on the Estimation of the Physical Characteristics of Watersheds by Using SWAT. *Adv. Civ. Eng.* **2016**, *2016*, 8180158. [CrossRef]
57. Liu, Y.; Wang, W.; Hu, Y.; Cui, W. Improving the Distributed Hydrological Model Performance in Upper Huai River Basin: Using Streamflow Observations to Update the Basin States via the Ensemble Kalman Filter. *Adv. Meteorol.* **2016**, *2016*, 1–14. [CrossRef]
58. USACE. *HEC-ResPRM Prescriptive Reservoir Model-Quick Start Guide*; U.S. Army Corps of Engineers, Institute for Water Resources, Hydrologic Engineering Center: Davis, CA, USA, 2011.
59. Zhao, T.; Zhao, J. Optimizing Operation of Water Supply Reservoir: The Role of Constraints. *Math. Probl. Eng.* **2014**, *2014*, 853186. [CrossRef]
60. Jothityangkoon, C.; Hirunteeyakul, C.; Boonrawd, K.; Sivapalan, M. Assessing the impact of climate and land use changes on extreme floods in a large tropical catchment. *J. Hydrol.* **2013**, *490*, 88–105. [CrossRef]
61. Zhou, Y.; Guo, S. Incorporating ecological requirement into multipurpose reservoir operating rule curves for adaptation to climate change. *J. Hydrol.* **2013**, *498*, 153–164. [CrossRef]
62. Srivastava, A.; Kumari, N.; Maza, M. Hydrological Response to Agricultural Land Use Heterogeneity Using Variable Infiltration Capacity Model. *Water Resour. Manag.* **2020**, *34*, 3779–3794. [CrossRef]
63. Sajikumar, N.; Remya, R. Impact of land cover and land use change on runoff characteristics. *J. Environ. Manag.* **2015**, *161*, 460–468. [CrossRef]
64. Zhang, Y.; Erkyihum, S.T.; Block, P. Filling the GERD: Evaluating hydroclimatic variability and impoundment strategies for Blue Nile riparian countries. *Water Int.* **2016**, *41*, 593–610. [CrossRef]
65. Wu, Y.; Chen, J. Estimating irrigation water demand using an improved method and optimizing reservoir operation for water supply and hydropower generation: A case study of the Xinfengjiang reservoir in southern China. *Agric. Water Manag.* **2013**, *116*, 110–121. [CrossRef]
66. Loucks, D.P.; van Eelco, B. Water resource systems planning and analysis-An Introduction to Methods, Models, and Applications. *Adv. Water Resour.* **2016**, *4*, 146.
67. He, Y.; Xu, Q.; Yang, S.; Liao, L. Reservoir flood control operation based on chaotic particle swarm optimization algorithm. *Appl. Math. Model.* **2014**, *38*, 4480–4492. [CrossRef]
68. Gu, W.; Shao, D.; Tan, X.; Shu, C.; Wu, Z. Simulation and Optimization of Multi-Reservoir Operation in Inter-Basin Water Transfer System. *Water Resour. Manag.* **2017**, *31*, 3401–3412. [CrossRef]

Article

Modeling Average Grain Velocity for Rectangular Channel Using Soft Computing Techniques

Anuradha Kumari [1], Akhilesh Kumar [1], Manish Kumar [1,2,*] and Alban Kuriqi [3,*]

[1] Department of SWCE, G. B. Pant University of Agriculture and Technology, Pantnagar 263145, India; ct49481d@gbpuat.ac.in (A.K.); tswak1@gbpuat.ac.in (A.K.)
[2] College of Agricultural Engineering and Technology, Dr. Rajendra Prasad Central Agricultural University, Pusa 848125, India
[3] CERIS, Instituto Superior Técnico, Universidade de Lisboa, 1049-001 Lisboa, Portugal
* Correspondence: manishgbpuat@yahoo.com (M.K.); alban.kuriqi@tecnico.ulisboa.pt (A.K.)

Abstract: This study was undertaken with the primary objective of modeling grain velocity based on experimental data obtained under the controlled conditions of a laboratory using a rectangular hydraulic tilting channel. Soft computing approaches, i.e., support vector machine (SVM), artificial neural network (ANN), and multiple linear regression (MLR), were applied to simulate grain velocity using four input variables; shear velocity, exposed area to base area ratio (EATBAR), relative depth, and sediment particle weight. Quantitative performance evaluation of predicted values was performed with the help of three different standard statistical indices, such as the root mean square error (RMSE), Pearson's correlation coefficient (PCC), and Wilmot index (WI). The results during the testing phase revealed that the SVM model has RMSE (m/s), PCC, and WI values obtained as 0.1195, 0.8877, and 0.7243, respectively, providing more accurate predictions than the MLR and ANN models during the testing phase.

Keywords: grain velocity; sediment transportation; shear velocity; ANN; SVM

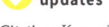

Citation: Kumari, A.; Kumar, A.; Kumar, M.; Kuriqi, A. Modeling Average Grain Velocity for Rectangular Channel Using Soft Computing Techniques. *Water* 2022, 14, 1325. https://doi.org/10.3390/w14091325

Academic Editor: Giuseppe Pezzinga

Received: 14 March 2022
Accepted: 17 April 2022
Published: 19 April 2022

Publisher's Note: MDPI stays neutral with regard to jurisdictional claims in published maps and institutional affiliations.

Copyright: © 2022 by the authors. Licensee MDPI, Basel, Switzerland. This article is an open access article distributed under the terms and conditions of the Creative Commons Attribution (CC BY) license (https://creativecommons.org/licenses/by/4.0/).

1. Introduction

In rivers, sediment grain velocity measurement is generally required to assess sediment load, river geometry, flood control, and long-term morphology evolution. A large number of variables govern the sediment movement process. Thus, its physical measurements under actual field conditions become difficult. Alternatively, experiments are conducted under controlled laboratory conditions to observe the sediment particle movement phenomenon and record data to develop mathematical models for sediment grain velocity. Consequently, experiments were conducted in this study considering a single grain moving near the channel bed due to sliding. These experiments indicated that sediment transport is an incredibly complicated mechanism. It may not be possible to describe it using simple deterministic models. The predictive precision is always doubtful, with predictive errors in several realistic cases being unacceptably high, as is investigated and reported [1–4]. Therefore, to model sediment grain velocity, the application of new modeling approaches such as machine learning (ML) soft computing techniques have arisen to establish models that rely on experience and data [5,6]. This has opened up new modeling possibilities, mainly when the information available is insufficient to devise a relevant mathematical structure, or there is too little data to calibrate an acceptable model.

Novak and Nalluri [7] examined the incipient motion in fixed, flat, rough beds with roughness elements smaller than the particle size for single and clustered particles. Van Rijn [2] and Karimaee Tabarestani and Zarrati [8] have carried out such regression experiments ostensibly involving the fluid viscous effects on the bedload grain flow in the bed. Papanicolaou et al. [9] estimated the bedload using the idea of particle velocity. Julien and Bounvilay [10] investigated the effect of particles of different sizes with different densities on reach-average bedload particle velocity for smooth and rough surfaces. The impact of the roughness of the bed on the bedload sediment grain velocity was reported by Cheng and Emadzadeh [11]. Frey [12] worked on the fluid velocity of particles and examined the concentration-depth profiles for bedload transport on a high slope at the particle scale. All this research focused on the effects on sediment motion considering the characteristics of channel bed and sediment particles properties.

Further, machine learning (ML) is often considered a replacement or augmentation to the more conventional physical process simulation approach in nearly all research branches. ML uses modeling approaches and techniques such as ANN, SVM, fuzzy logic, decision-tree processes, and improved computing techniques [13–17]. In recent times, several research departments have been influenced by the artificial neural networks (ANN) approach. The ANN method is quickly gaining traction as a useful tool for delivering effective details on the usage in design and management operations for hydraulic, hydrological, and environment fields [18–22]. ML has been efficient for application in the hydrological processes field, e.g., water system management, water quality evaluations, stage-discharge relations, and meteorological data estimations. These implementations, however, demonstrate that ML does not produce new process information. Instead, it uses existing process knowledge to pick the input and output variables, accompanied by sophisticated regression techniques, to the best match for the calculated results. Bhattacharya et al. [23] evaluated sediment transport modeling using ML models such as ANN and model trees. These models used calculated data to model the bedload estimate and total load transport. ANN and regression models to estimate the incipient flow velocity at sediment deposition in the rectangular channel were developed by Sheikh Khozani et al. [24]. Combining the available data from each cross-section created a generalized regression model. Based on the performance assessment, they found ANN models superior to regression models. Mehr and Safari [25] applied soft computing techniques to obtain correct sewer designs via particle Froude number estimates in sewer pipes, including multi genetic programming, gene expression, and multilayer perceptron. Montes et al. [26] have predicted bedload sediment transportation in sewage pipes of noncoherent material using polynomial regression, which describes multiple objective genetic algorithms. In forecasting incipient sediment movement in sewers using artificial neural networks, Wan Mohtar et al. [27] found the impact of bed deposits. Thus, many researchers have shown that the ML approach establishes relationships and is applicable for estimating sediment grain particle motion using various channel and particle characteristics.

In comparison, the support vector machine (SVM) is very recent. It has shown substantial success in studying the classification and regression process [28–31]. One of the early attempts was made by Einstein [32], who suggested that the average bedload velocity was commensurate with the grain's shear velocity. Fernandez Luque and Van Beek [33], Abbott et al. [34], and Bridge and Dominic [35] have separately formulated their formula since the measured velocity of grain tends to be linear to dependence on the shear velocity of the sheet. After reviewing the available literature, it was found that significantly little work has been reported to predict grain velocity using soft computing techniques considering EATBAR, relative depth, weight, and shear velocity as input variables. Due to larger particles, sediment movement in steeply sloping gravel-bottomed streams occurs mainly by surface creep in mountainous areas. The flow of sediment particles is influenced by many factors, including discharge, channel bottom slope, specific weight, and the shape and size of the sediment particle. Natural streams contain sediment particles of irregular shape, not spherical or cubical shape. The ratio of exposed area to the base area of flow (EATBAR) and relative depth, i.e., the ratio of flow and particle height, will play an essential role in their movement. These parameters change with a change in the sediment particle's orientation (i.e., placement position) over the channel bed and slope, eventually deciding their movement rate. This study has been carried out with the main objectives being the (a) investigation of the grain velocity for different weights of sediment particles by conducting laboratory experiments on the different slopes under varying discharges in a rectangular channel, (b) modeling of the grain velocity with selected input variables using different data-driven techniques, and (c) to assess the effectiveness of the developed models. The objectives are novel, and the research has not been carried out earlier. The paper is organized as follows: Section 2 includes explanations of the data-driven models as well as a brief overview of the experimental setup, data observations, and methodology adopted for the study; the main findings and outcomes are discussed in Section 3; last, concluding reflections are addressed in Section 4.

2. Materials and Methods

2.1. Experimental Setup and Data Observation

The experiments were carried out in a rectangular channel with a length of 7 m, a width of 0.30 m, and a depth of 0.60 m using three different sediment particles with $(2 \times 2 \times 3)$ cm, $(2 \times 2 \times 4)$ cm, and $(3 \times 3 \times 4)$ cm. Figure 1 shows the experimental setup, with its different components used for conducting experiments. The particles were cast with cement mortar to model sediment grains of different sizes. The water was delivered by a centrifugal pump downstream of the flume and received from a water storage tank. Regulatory valves were placed on the flume's water supply line-controlled discharge. A water flow meter was used to monitor the flow discharge. Flow depth was measured using a sophisticated point gauge mounted on the trolley for movement throughout the length of the flume. The flume channel was adjusted to the required bed slope with the help of the hydraulic screw jack provided in the mechanism.

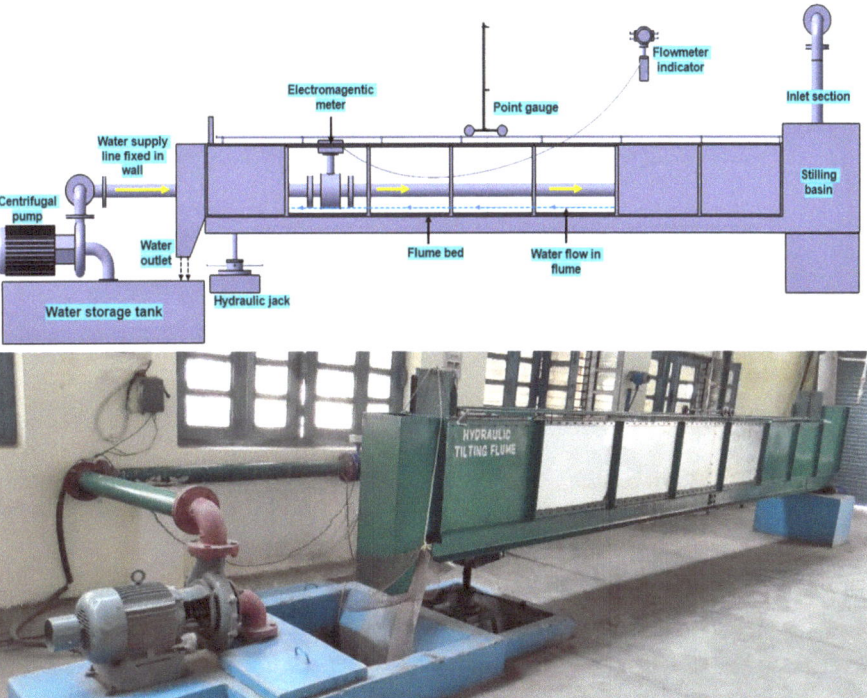

Figure 1. Experimental setup of the hydraulic flume; schematic presentation (**top part**) and lab view (**lower part**).

A total of 108 experiments were conducted to determine grain velocity for three particle sizes, six discharges, and six-channel bed slopes. Experiments used six different discharges consisting of (12.8, 17.6, 23.2, 25.9, 29.6, and 33.6) L/s/m, while the channel bed slope changed from 1% to 4%. To achieve a fully developed flow, a grain particle of a specific size was put in a suitable position on the bed at 3.5 m from the flume's upstream end. Attention was paid to avoiding turbulence and ensuring a steady flow along the channel's length. A fixed span of 2.7 m length in the flume was considered for the particle's movement. For every combination of experimental variables, flow depth, discharge, grain velocity, and the time took was recorded. Three times were, three replications performed to ensure precision in the observations.

2.1.1. Methodology

The present study focuses on establishing mathematical models using data-driven techniques to estimate single grain velocity based on the data generated using laboratory experiments. As discussed above, the experimental work was carried out in a rectangular hydraulic flume. Experimentally investigating single grain velocity in a rectangular channel flume was estimated and compared with different data-driven techniques, namely, support vector machine (SVM), artificial neural network (ANN), and multilinear regression (MLR) models. The developed models were evaluated using different performance indicators such as Pearson correlation coefficient (PCC), root mean square error (RMSE), Wilmot index, line diagram, scatter diagram, and Taylor diagram. Figure 2 describes the methodology used to estimate a single grain velocity in the study.

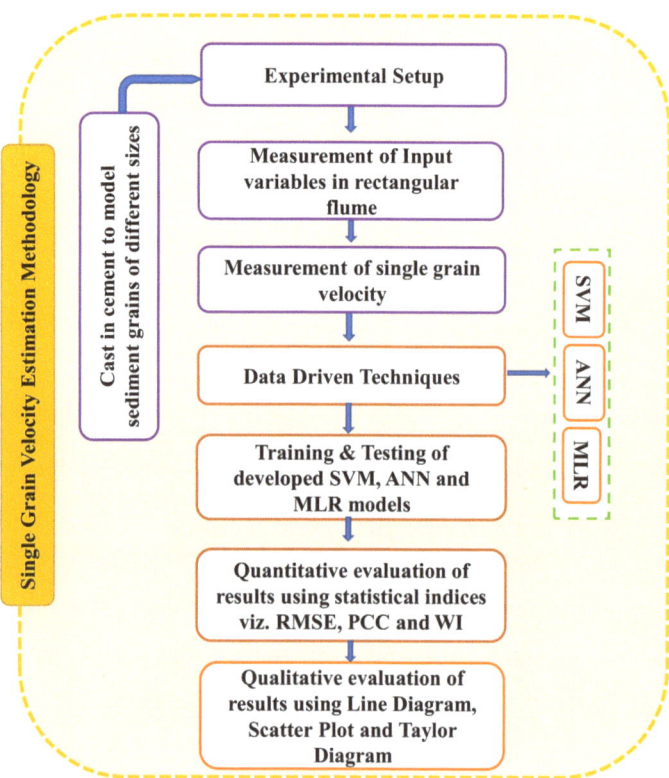

Figure 2. Flow diagram for single grain velocity estimation.

2.1.2. Input Parameters

EATBAR (λ) is the ratio of the exposed area (A_e) to the base area (A_b) of the particle, which changes with the change in the discharge and slope of the channel for the same particle and is calculated as

$$\text{EATBAR } (\lambda) = \frac{A_e}{A_b} \quad (1)$$

The shear velocity (U*) is evaluated by the following formula:

$$U* = \sqrt{gRS} \quad (2)$$

R represents the hydraulic radius in a section. S is the channel bed slope in fraction, and g is the gravitational acceleration.

Relative depth (y/d) is the ratio of flow depth to thickness (d).

The weight (W) is one of the fundamental parameters in sediment transport, which affects the particle's movement. Due to varying submergence, the particle's submerged weight also varies, altering the entire force dynamics for sediment transport.

2.2. Multiple Linear Regression—MLR

MLR stands for regression analysis, which involves more than one independent variable. The benefit of MLR is that it is straightforward, demonstrating how dependent and independent variables are related. The general form of the MLR model is:

$$V_p = -3.284 + 1.935\lambda - 0.008\,W + 25.953\,U* + 0.503\,(y/d) \quad (3)$$

where Vp denotes the grain velocity (m/s), λ is EATBAR, W is the weight of the sediment particle, g, U* denotes the shear velocity (m/s), and y/d are the relative depth. These values are derived using the least square approach and reflect localized behavior, e.g., Kisi and Çobaner [36].

2.3. Artificial Neural Network—ANN

ANN is based on the training knowledge of the biological nervous system. It consists of several processing elements related to varying weights. The network consists of many layers of parallel processing elements called neurons. The most commonly used among ANN paradigms, the multilayer backpropagation network (MLP), was considered for this study. The MLP has a three-layered construction, namely, (a) an input layer, (b) a hidden layer, and (c) an output layer [37]. The input layer accepts data, handles it by the hidden layer, and shows the model's results in the output layer. The input layer signals are dispersed to every hidden layer node depending on connection weights assigned between input (i.e., first layer) and hidden (i.e., middle) layers. These interconnection weights have been determined for respective inputs. In this present study, a hyperbolic tangent activation function (ranging from -1 to $+1$) was used as architecture for data normalization. Epoch = 1000 and threshold value = 0.001 were used to train the models based on trial-and-error methods. Each neuron in the middle and output layers receives the weighted sum of the previous layer's output as input. The net output (NET_h) for layer j is given as:

$$NET_h = \sum_{n=1}^{N} \left(W_{ih} O_{pi} + b_h \right) \quad (4)$$

where b_h represents the neuron threshold value for h, O_{pi} is the i-th output of the previous layer, and W_{ih} is the weight between the layers i and h. The Levenberg-Marquardt (LM) training algorithm was considered to adjust the weights for the current study.

2.4. Support Vector Machine-SVM

SVM is a concept that was proposed by Vapnik [28]. The SVM technique finds a hyperplane between the input spaces. It disintegrates a given dataset and allows as much distance as close to both sides of the hyperplane to determine the points at which estimated errors are equal to and more significant than the so-called SVM tube scale. SVM techniques facilitate the development of a non-linear boundary by mapping the original input space to a higher-dimensional space. This dimensional space is called feature space. A kernel function characterizes this feature space mapping from a given input space. A penalty factor C is added for error classification to optimize this model. The cumulative penalty can be achieved by applying the penalties for each misclassification. As a result, the technique identifies a hyperplane that minimizes the margin and the total penalty. For optimization of the model, the combined penalty function is used as an objective function of the model. It has good generalization performance and is applicable in an approximation of both linear and non-linear datasets.

Considering a training dataset, T, represented as

$$T = (x_1, y_1), (x_2, y_2), \ldots, (x_m, y_m) \quad (5)$$

where $x \ X \subset \mathbb{R}^n$ represents the training inputs, and $y \ Y \subset \mathbb{R}^n$ represents the training outputs. that a nonlinear function $f(x)$ which is non-linear, is given by:

$$f(x) = w^T \Phi(x_i) + b \quad (6)$$

where w represents the weight vector, b represents the bias, and $\Phi(x_i)$ denotes the high-dimensional feature space. Furthermore, data set T and, Equation (6) is transformed into Equation (7) as a constrained complex optimization problem stated as

Minimize: $\frac{1}{2} w^T w$

$$\text{subject to}: \left\{ y_i - \left(w^T \Phi(x_i) + b \right) \leq \varepsilon y_i - \left(w^T \Phi(x_i) + b \right) \geq \varepsilon \right. \quad (7)$$

where $\varepsilon \ (\geq 0)$ represents the maximum acceptable deviation.

Furthermore, the derived Equation for SVM is given in [15,38,39].

The final expansion of support vector regression is given by;

$$f(x) = \sum_{i=1}^{m} \left(\alpha_i^+ - \alpha_i^- \right) K(x_i, x_j) + b \quad (8)$$

where, α_i^+, α_i^- are Lagrangian multipliers, and the term $K(x_i, x_j)$ is the kernel function. The kernel function allows for non-linear approximations. The kernel function used in the study was the linear kernel. The simplest type of kernel function is given as [40]:

$$K(x_i, x_j) = (x_i, x_j) \quad (9)$$

The three key parameters (kernel, C, γ, and ε) on which the performance of SVM techniques depends (Figure 3).

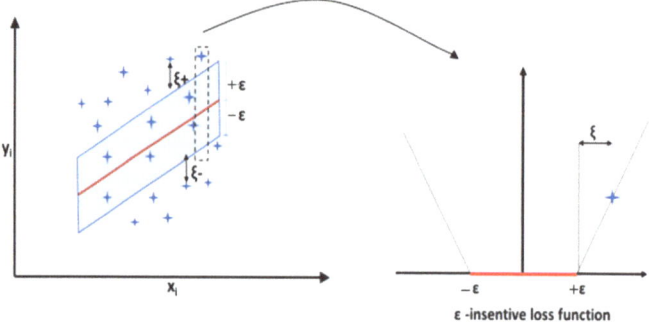

Figure 3. Soft margin loss setting for a linear SVM and ε-insentive loss function adapted after Lin et al. [41].

However, the C and ε values influence the complexity of the final model for every specific kernel type. The parameters ε are responsible for regulating the number of support vectors. The values support vectors intuitively, when ε values are larger, lesser support vectors exit and thus lead to lower regression estimates. On the other side, the C value is essential in optimization. It represents the trade-off between the model's sophistication and the degree of deviation. As a result, a higher C value reduces model complexity [42].

2.5. Performance Evaluation

Three performance criteria were used to evaluate the goodness of fit of the models in the present study. These are the root mean square error (RMSE), the Pearson correlation coefficient (PCC), and the Wilmot index (WI). The usage of RMSE, PCC, and WI offers a sufficient evaluation of each model's performance. It compares the precision of the various trial and modeling methodologies employed in this work, further discussed by Ghorbani, Khatibi, Goel, FazeliFard and Azani [29], Kumar, Pandey, Sharma and Flügel [30], and Kumar et al., 2020.

$$\text{RMSE} = \sqrt{\frac{\sum_{i=1}^{N}\left(V_{\text{Pobs},i} - V_{\text{Ppre},i}\right)^2}{N}} \quad (0 \text{ to } \infty) \tag{10}$$

$$\text{PCC} = \frac{\sum_{i=1}^{N}\left(V_{\text{Pobs},i} - \overline{V}_{\text{Pobs},i}\right)\left(V_{\text{Ppre},i} - \overline{V}_{\text{Ppre},i}\right)}{\sqrt{\sum_{i=1}^{N}\left(V_{\text{Pobs},i} - \overline{V}_{\text{Pobs},i}\right)^2 \sum_{i=1}^{N}\left(V_{\text{Ppre},i} - \overline{V}_{\text{Ppre},i}\right)^2}} \quad (-1 \text{ to } 1) \tag{11}$$

$$\text{WI} = 1 - \frac{\sum_{i=1}^{N}\left(V_{\text{Pobs},i} - V_{\text{Ppre},i}\right)^2}{\sum_{i=1}^{N}\left(|V_{\text{Ppre},i} - \overline{V}_{\text{Pobs},i}| + |\overline{V}_{\text{Pobs},i} - \overline{V}_{\text{Pobs},i}|\right)^2} \quad (0 < \text{WI} \leq 1) \tag{12}$$

where, $V_{\text{Pobs},i}$ and $V_{\text{Ppre},i}$ are observed and predicted grain velocity of i-th observation, whereas, $\overline{V}_{\text{Pobs},i}$ and $\overline{V}_{\text{Ppre},i}$ are the average of the i-th observation, and N is the total number of observations.

3. Results and Discussion

As per the objectives of this study, the grain velocity was analyzed for several combinations of particle size, selected discharges, and channel slopes. To achieve these objectives, experiments were conducted on a hydraulic tilting flume in the laboratory. Three sizes of particles such as (2 × 2 × 3) cm, (2 × 2 × 4) cm, and (3 × 3 × 4) cm were used in this study. Six discharges of (12.8, 17.6, 23.2, 25.9, 29.6, and 33.6) L/s/m and bed slopes of 1, 1.5, 2, 2.5, 3 and 4% were considered for experimentation. The grain velocity with a particular orientation increased with channel slope and discharge but decreased with sediment particle weight. After critically analyzing the experimental results, four input parameters, shear velocity, EATBAR, relative depth, and particle weight, were selected as important variables to model grain velocity. Figure 4 and Table 1 show the details of the observations from the experimentation. The shear velocity increased with discharge and channel slope for particular particle sizes. The shear velocity ranged from 0.0529 m/s to 0.1030 m/s. It was also observed that the EATBAR and relative depth values changed under three conditions first when there was a change in discharge, but the slope and particle size remained fixed; second, with a change in slope, but the other two variables remained fixed, and the third, when discharge and slope were fixed. However, the size of the sediment particle was changed. The EATBAR and relative depth values ranged from 0.57–1.00 and 0.25–2.35, respectively. When the sediment particle was fully submerged, i.e., particle height was less than the depth of flow of the particle. The exposed area and the base area remained the same. The value of EATBAR became 1.00, which was the maximum in this study. As depth flow decreased due to increased channel slope or decrease in discharge, the EATBAR value deviated from 1.0 due to a change in the exposed area.

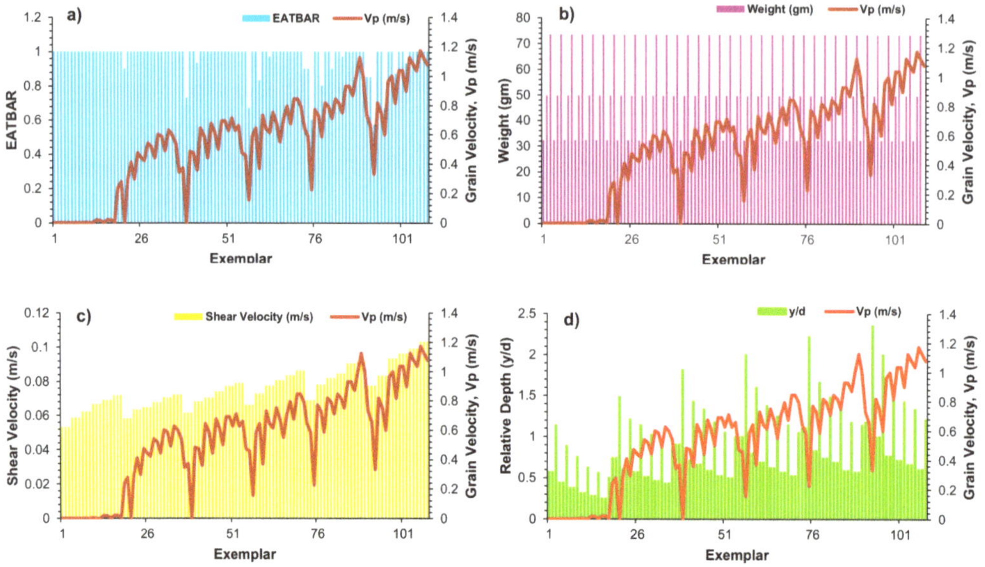

Figure 4. Plots of the dependent variable V_p (m/s) and input variable: (**a**) EATBAR, (**b**) weight (gm), (**c**) shear velocity (m/s), (**d**) relative depth.

Table 1. Statistical analysis of dependent (V_p) and independent variables (λ, W, U*, and y/d).

Variables	Mean	Median	Minimum	Maximum	Std. Dev.	C.V.	Skewness
All Data							
λ	0.9707	1.000	0.5700	1.000	0.0823	0.0848	−3.283
W	51.733	49.60	32.200	73.40	16.966	0.32795	0.1874
U*	0.0754	0.0731	0.0529	0.1030	0.0120	0.1598	0.4072
y/d	0.8573	0.7142	0.2500	2.352	0.4281	0.4994	1.220
V_p	0.5473	0.600	0.0	1.174	0.3352	0.6124	−0.2776
Training Data							
λ	0.9793	1.0	0.6	1.0	0.0706	0.0721	−3.964
W	51.476	49.6	32.2	73.4	17.035	0.3309	0.2091
U*	0.0696	0.0688	0.0529	0.0862	0.008	0.1150	0.0828
y/d	0.7894	0.6667	0.25	2.222	0.4031	0.5106	1.295
V_p	0.4070	0.474	0.0	0.8440	0.2793	0.6863	−0.3741
Testing Data							
λ	0.9503	1.0	0.57	1.0	0.1035	0.1089	−2.368
W	52.344	49.6	32.2	73.4	17.05	0.3258	0.1369
U*	0.0892	0.0903	0.0774	0.103	0.0081	0.0914	0.1011
y/d	1.0185	0.8012	0.5714	2.352	0.4489	0.4407	1.1701
V_p	0.8806	0.8855	0.333	1.174	0.1901	0.2159	−0.6570

(Where λ = EATBAR, W = particle weight, U* = shear velocity, y/d = relative depth, V_p = grain velocity).

In contrast, the base area remained the same. The grain velocity was maximum at 1.174 m/s for lighter weight particles of 32.2 gm, at 0.103 m/s shear velocity, 0.606 relative depth, and 1.0 EATBAR, at 4% channel bed slope and 33.6 L/s/m discharge, respectively. At the 1% slope of the channel bed, no movement in particles was observed in the discharge range of 12.8 L/s/m to 23.2 L/s/m. The movement in particles with a weight of 32.2 gm could be observed at a discharge of 25.9 L/s/m with 0.0033 m/s grain velocity.

3.1. Statistical Parameters

The statistical analysis of different independent variables, that is, EATBAR (λ), weight (gm), U* (m/s), y/d, and dependent variable V_p of all data, training, and testing sets included various statistical parameters such as mean, median, minimum and maximum value, standard deviation, CV and skewness. These statistical parameters showed data heterogeneity over the whole time series. Cross-validating is essential for the same statistical population if the data is divided into training and test subsets. Due to the high skewness, the model's efficiency was adversely affected. The standard deviation values suggest that the values are farther from zero, indicating that the data heterogeneity is more significant. The mean value variance is greater (Table 1).

3.2. Trial Selection

MLR, ANN, and SVM were analyzed in two phases to select the best model: the training and testing phases. The performance was evaluated based on the lower value of RMSE (0: +: satisfactory: unsatisfactory), the higher value of PCC, and WI (close to +1) for selections of the best model. Several trials were performed on a single output in the best model selection process for ANN and SVM. The best trials of the developed models during the training and testing phases are presented in Table 2. Trial-3 of both ANN and SVM, respectively, given in Table 2, were more promising than the other trials for the combination.

Table 2. During the training and testing phase, performance evaluations of MLR, ANN, and SVM models.

Model	Training			Testing		
	RMSE (m/s)	PCC	WI	RMSE (m/s)	PCC	WI
MLR	0.1340	0.8756	0.7532	0.1459	0.8375	0.6789
ANN						
Trial-1	0.1266	0.8911	0.8106	0.3109	0.1509	0.3420
Trial-2	0.0873	0.9502	0.8756	0.2154	0.3636	0.4579
Trial-3	0.0689	0.9692	0.8799	0.1721	0.5176	0.5012
Trial-4	0.0663	0.9728	0.8999	0.2302	0.1945	0.3666
Trial-5	0.0699	0.9678	0.8916	0.1906	0.4365	0.4751
Trial-6	0.0759	0.9625	0.9439	0.1821	0.4900	0.5058
SVM						
Trial-1	0.1423	0.8595	0.7475	0.1208	0.8852	0.7231
Trial-2	0.1381	0.8675	0.7531	0.1341	0.8688	0.7022
Trial-3	0.1431	0.8577	0.7479	0.1195	0.8877	0.7243
Trial-4	0.1408	0.8622	0.7513	0.1247	0.8795	0.7150

3.3. Quantitative Performance Evaluation

After considering the three techniques for best tests (Table 2), the values of the RMSE, PCC, and WI values of the MLR techniques for the training phase were obtained as 0.1340, 0.8756, and 0.7532; respectively, while for the testing phase, these values were 0.1459, 0.8375, and 0.6789. In the ANN-based model, the value of RMSE was obtained in the range of 0.0663 to 0.1266, and PCC was obtained in the range of 0.8911 to 0.9728. In contrast, WI was obtained in the range of 0.8106 to 0.8999 during the training phase. During the testing phase in the RMSE ANN model, the value was obtained in the range of 0.1721 to 0.3109, and PCC was observed to be in the range of 0.1509 to 0.5176. In contrast, WI was observed in the range of 0.3420 to 0.5012. The results of the ANN model did not improve when the number of layers in the hidden layer was increased to two (Trial 5) and three (Trial 6). The performance indices in SVM techniques were as RMSE ranged from 0.1381 to 0.1431,

PCC ranged from 0.8577 to 0.8675, and WI ranged from 0.7475 to 0.7531 training phase. In contrast, in the testing phase of the SVM techniques, the value of RMSE was obtained in the range of 0.1195 to 0.1341, PCC was in the range of 0.8688 to 0.8877, and WI was observed in the range of 0.7022 to 0.7243. The architecture used for all developed ANN and SVM models is shown in Table 3.

Table 3. The architecture used for the development of ANN and SVM models.

Model/Trial		Architecture
ANN		
	Trial-1	4-1-1
	Trial-2	4-4-1
	Trial-3	4-5-1
	Trial-4	4-7-1
	Trial-5	4-5-5-1
	Trial-6	4-4-4-4-1
SVM		
	Trial-1	$C = 10, \gamma = 0.25, \varepsilon = 0.01$
	Trial-2	$C = 10, \gamma = 0.25, \varepsilon = 0.1$
	Trial-3	$C = 10, \gamma = 0.45, \varepsilon = 0.01$
	Trial-4	$C = 10, \gamma = 0.45, \varepsilon = 0.05$

Based on the values of the performance indices during the testing phase of the models developed using three different techniques, the values of RMSE were obtained as SVM (0.1195) > MLR (0.1459) > ANN (0.1721). The values of PCC were obtained as SVM (0.8877) > MLR (0.8375) > ANN (0.5176) of the values was obtained as SVM (0.7243) > MLR (0.6789) > ANN (0.5012). Thus, the overall comparison of performance indicators for these models revealed that the model's performance based on the SVM technique was the best. In contrast, the model's performance developed using ANN was the worst. To assess the dissimilarity among the results obtained from various models, a t-test was performed, which provided the p-value of these three models ($P = 1.11 \times 10^{-6}$ for ANN, $P = 6.34 \times 10^{-5}$ for MLR, and $P = 9.4 \times 10^{-5}$ for SVM), which is less than 0.05 and suggested that there is a significant difference between observed and predicted mean values of grain velocity in all three models. The observed mean values of grain velocity were 0.8806 m/s. They predicted that the mean grain velocity was 0.7565 m/s, 0.970815 m/s, and 0.9529 m/s for the ANN, MLR, and SVM models. Thus, the mean absolute difference between observed and predicted grain velocities was 0.1240 for ANN, 0.09019 for MLR, and 0.07236 for SVM. Therefore, it is confirmed that the SVM-based model predicted close to the corresponding observed values than MLR and ANN-based models. The Friedman test also verified a significant ($p < 0.05$) difference between observed and predicted grain velocity in MLR, ANN, and SVM models.

3.4. Qualitative Performance Evaluation

To assess the qualitative performance of these models, the observed data was plotted with the model estimated data of the model, as shown in Figure 5. These plots revealed that the developed models slightly over-predicted higher grain velocity in MLR and SVM-based models. In contrast, the grain velocity was underpredicted in the entire range in the ANN-based model variation. The values of the coefficient of determination (R^2) were highest (0.8608) for the SVM model, and the lowest value (0.6729) was obtained for the ANN-based model. The value of (R^2) was 0.7967 in the case of the MLR-based model.

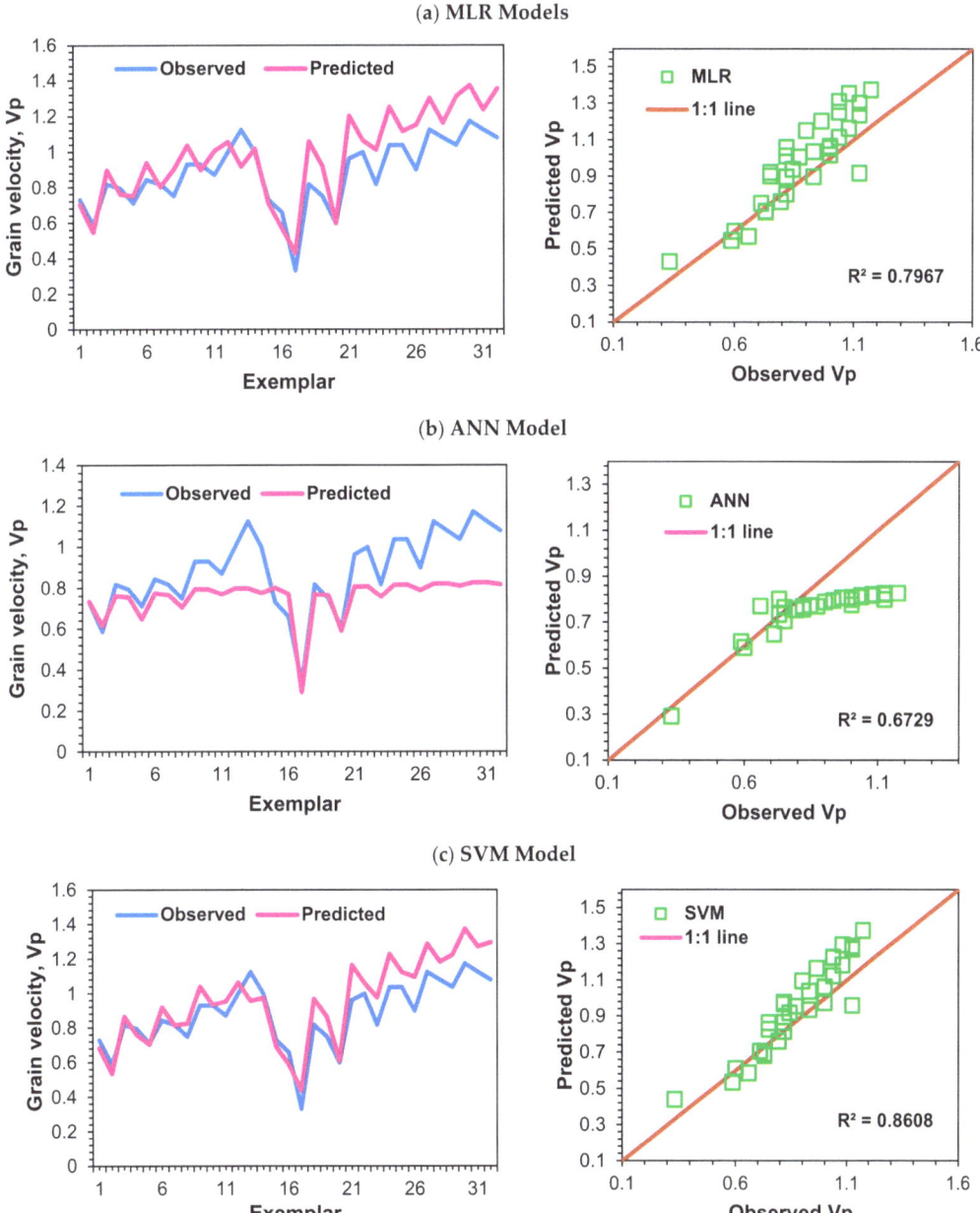

Figure 5. Observed versus predicted grain velocity by the (**a**) MLR, (**b**) ANN, and (**c**) SVM models during the testing phase.

Taylor diagrams (Figure 6) indicated that although the model correlation was satisfactory, it was highest in the case of SVM and lowest in the case of ANN. As another comprehensive graphical presentation, a Taylor diagram compared the observed and predictive values using three statistical parameters: the CC, the root mean square difference

(RMSD), and the standard deviation. The best model is the one that has less distance to the observed point [30,43].

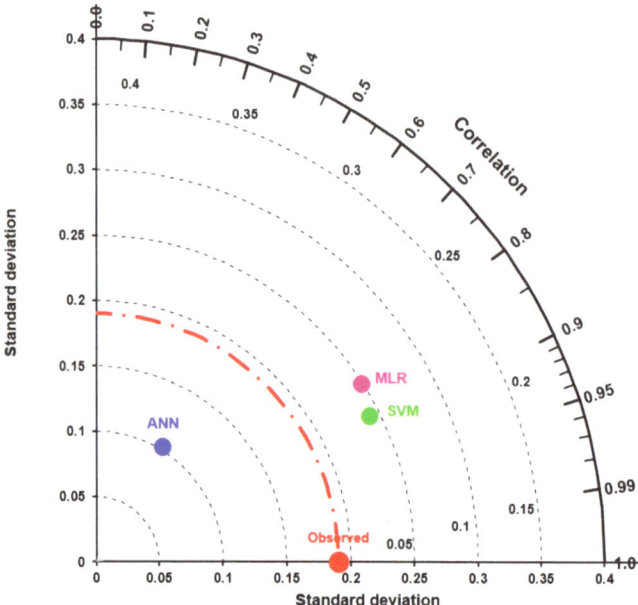

Figure 6. Taylor diagram of MLR, ANN, and SVM corresponding to observed grain velocity (V_p).

From Taylor diagrams (Figure 6), the order of correlation value from best to worst was the same as explained earlier, i.e., SVM (0.9277) > MLR (0.8926) > ANN (0.8203). The standard deviation value for the observed data was obtained as 0.1901. The MLR, ANN, and SVM model predicted values; the standard deviation was 0.2487, 0.1025, and 0.2419, respectively. Therefore, the deviation between observed and model-predicted values was lowest (0.0518) for the SVM technique, followed by MLR- (0.0586) and ANN- (0.0876) based models. Thus, from a qualitative evaluation of observed data and predicted data using different techniques, it was found that the SVM technique performed better, followed by the MLR and then ANN techniques. Based on this analysis, it thus could be inferred in terms of the input parameters such as EATBAR, weight, shear velocity, and relative depth; the model developed using the support vector machine technique was superior for predicting single grain velocity compared to the models developed using ANN and MLR techniques.

Further, the MLR-based model better predicted the performance of single grain velocity than the model developed using the ANN technique. Previous studies on the simulation of experimental data have been made in Kumari [44], which integrates the soft computing techniques with experimental results to estimate post-fire bond behavior. The bond strength and bond-slip behavior have been estimated using gene expression programming (GEP) and the ANN. The ANN has a significant positive association with experimental results and makes more precise predictions than the investigated codes. Further, Sheikh Khozani, Safari, Danandeh Mehr and Wan Mohtar [24] developed incipient sediment motion models with ensemble genetic programming in rectangular form. The new models incorporate dimensionless input factors such as relative particle size, relative deposited bed thickness, channel friction factor, and channel bed slope to evaluate the particle Froude number in rectangular channels. It was revealed that the combined use of fluid, flow, sediment and channel characteristics was superior in estimating incipient motion. Earlier, Wan Mohtar, Afan, El-Shafie, Bong, and Ab. Ghani [27] estimated incipient sediment motion by the effects of bed deposits in sewers using ANN. For predicting the motion of sediment, feed-forward neural network (FFNN) and radial basis function (RBF) were two algorithms of ANN employed to predict the critical velocity over varying sediment thickness, median grain size, and water depth. Thus, soft computing techniques have been an effective tool for simulating experimental data.

4. Conclusions

The experimental results showed that the grain velocity increased with an increase in channel slope and discharge but decreased with sediment particle weight. The models developed to simulate the output parameter, grain velocity in input parameters such as the exposed area to base area ratio, relative depth, shear velocity, and particle weight using SVM, ANN, and MLR techniques were developed to predict grain velocity. However, based on the prediction performance in terms of statistical indices, namely, RMSE, PCC, and WI, the SVM technique-based model with RMSE = 0.1195, PCC = 0.8877. WI = 0.7243 was found to be the best. The lowest prediction performance was obtained for the ANN technique's model. Similar findings were obtained with the scatter plot and Taylor diagram.

Author Contributions: A.K. (Anuradha Kumari), A.K. (Akhilesh Kumar) and M.K.: conceptualization, methodology, investigation, formal analysis, data curation, visualization, original draft writing, review and editing. A.K. (Alban Kuriqi): conceptualization, writing—review and editing, resources, supervision. All authors have read and agreed to the published version of the manuscript.

Funding: This research received no external funding.

Data Availability Statement: Upon request to the first Author.

Acknowledgments: The authors is thankful for continuous support from the Department of SWCE, G. B. P. U. A. & T., Pantnagar in conducting the experimental work. Anuradha Kumari has also thankful to ICAR (JRF) for providing scholarships during the research period. Anuradha Kumari is highly thankful to her mother, Smt. Nilam Kumari and her elder brother Gulshan Kumar for providing her with the opportunity to pursue higher study. Alban Kuriqi acknowledges the Portuguese Foundation for Science and Technology (FCT) support through PTDC/CTA-OHR/30561/2017 (WinTherface).

Conflicts of Interest: The authors declare no conflict of interest.

Abbreviations and Nomenclature

SVM—support vector machine, ANN—artificial neural network, MLR—multiple linear regression, PCC—Pearson correlation coefficient, RMSE—root mean square error, WI—Wilmott index, EATBAR (λ)—exposed area (Ae) to base area (Ab), U*—shear velocity, g—acceleration due to gravity, R—hydraulic radius, S—slope of the channel bed, y—depth of flow, d—particle thickness, W—particle weight, Vp—grain velocity, C—penalty factor, ε—insensitive loss function.

References

1. Chien, N.; Wan, Z. *Mechanics of Sediment Transport*; American Society of Civil Engineers (ASCE): Reston, VA, USA, 1999.
2. Van Rijn, L.C. Sediment Transport, Part I: Bed Load Transport. *J. Hydraul. Eng.* **1984**, *110*, 1431–1456. [CrossRef]
3. Van Rijn, L.C. Sediment Transport, Part II: Suspended Load Transport. *J. Hydraul. Eng.* **1984**, *110*, 1613–1641. [CrossRef]
4. Gomez, B.; Church, M. An assessment of bed load sediment transport formulae for gravel bed rivers. *Water Resour. Res.* **1989**, *25*, 1161–1186. [CrossRef]
5. Zhang, X.-D. Machine Learning. In *A Matrix Algebra Approach to Artificial Intelligence*; Zhang, X.-D., Ed.; Springer Singapore: Singapore, 2020; pp. 223–440.
6. Safari, M.J.S.; Arashloo, S.R. Kernel ridge regression model for sediment transport in open channel flow. *Neural Comput. Appl.* **2021**, *33*, 11255–11271. [CrossRef]
7. Novak, P.; Nalluri, C. Incipient Motion of Sediment Particles Over Fixed Beds. *J. Hydraul. Res.* **1984**, *22*, 181–197. [CrossRef]
8. Tabarestani, M.K.; Zarrati, A.R. Sediment transport during flood event: A review. *Int. J. Environ. Sci. Technol.* **2015**, *12*, 775–788. [CrossRef]

9. Papanicolaou, A.N.; Knapp, D.; Strom, K. Bedload Predictions by Using the Concept of Particle Velocity: Applications. In *Hydraulic Measurements and Experimental Methods 2002*; American Society of Civil Engineers: Reston, VA, USA, 2002; pp. 1–10. Available online: https://www.researchgate.net/publication/299813875_Bedload_Predictions_by_Using_the_Concept_of_Particle_Velocity_Applications (accessed on 12 March 2022).
10. Julien, P.Y.; Bounvilay, B. Velocity of Rolling Bed Load Particles. *J. Hydraul. Eng.* **2013**, *139*, 177–186. [CrossRef]
11. Cheng, N.-S.; Emadzadeh, A. Average Velocity of Solitary Coarse Grain in Flows over Smooth and Rough Beds. *J. Hydraul. Eng.* **2014**, *140*, 04014015. [CrossRef]
12. Frey, P. Particle velocity and concentration profiles in bedload experiments on a steep slope. *Earth Surf. Process. Landf.* **2014**, *39*, 646–655. [CrossRef]
13. Nourani, V.; Hosseini Baghanam, A.; Adamowski, J.; Kisi, O. Applications of hybrid wavelet–Artificial Intelligence models in hydrology: A review. *J. Hydrol.* **2014**, *514*, 358–377. [CrossRef]
14. Demirci, M.; Baltaci, A. Prediction of suspended sediment in river using fuzzy logic and multilinear regression approaches. *Neural Comput. Appl.* **2013**, *23*, 145–151. [CrossRef]
15. Misra, D.; Oommen, T.; Agarwal, A.; Mishra, S.K.; Thompson, A.M. Application and analysis of support vector machine based simulation for runoff and sediment yield. *Biosyst. Eng.* **2009**, *103*, 527–535. [CrossRef]
16. Kakaei Lafdani, E.; Moghaddam Nia, A.; Ahmadi, A. Daily suspended sediment load prediction using artificial neural networks and support vector machines. *J. Hydrol.* **2013**, *478*, 50–62. [CrossRef]
17. Meshram, S.G.; Singh, V.P.; Kisi, O.; Karimi, V.; Meshram, C. Application of Artificial Neural Networks, Support Vector Machine and Multiple Model-ANN to Sediment Yield Prediction. *Water Resour. Manag.* **2020**, *34*, 4561–4575. [CrossRef]
18. Jain, S.K.; Chalisgaonkar, D. Setting Up Stage-Discharge Relations Using ANN. *J. Hydrol. Eng.* **2000**, *5*, 428–433. [CrossRef]
19. Garbrecht, J.D. Comparison of Three Alternative ANN Designs for Monthly Rainfall-Runoff Simulation. *J. Hydrol. Eng.* **2006**, *11*, 502–505. [CrossRef]
20. Mukerji, A.; Chatterjee, C.; Raghuwanshi, N.S. Flood Forecasting Using ANN, Neuro-Fuzzy, and Neuro-GA Models. *J. Hydrol. Eng.* **2009**, *14*, 647–652. [CrossRef]
21. Rajaee, T.; Nourani, V.; Zounemat-Kermani, M.; Kisi, O. River Suspended Sediment Load Prediction: Application of ANN and Wavelet Conjunction Model. *J. Hydrol. Eng.* **2011**, *16*, 613–627. [CrossRef]
22. Ab Ghani, A.; Azamathulla, H.M. Development of GEP-based functional relationship for sediment transport in tropical rivers. *Neural Comput. Appl.* **2014**, *24*, 271–276. [CrossRef]
23. Bhattacharya, B.; Price, R.K.; Solomatine, D.P. Machine Learning Approach to Modeling Sediment Transport. *J. Hydraul. Eng.* **2007**, *133*, 440–450. [CrossRef]
24. Sheikh Khozani, Z.; Safari, M.J.S.; Danandeh Mehr, A.; Wan Mohtar, W.H.M. An ensemble genetic programming approach to develop incipient sediment motion models in rectangular channels. *J. Hydrol.* **2020**, *584*, 124753. [CrossRef]
25. Mehr, A.D.; Safari, M.J.S. Application of Soft Computing Techniques for Particle Froude Number Estimation in Sewer Pipes. *J. Pipeline Syst. Eng. Pract.* **2020**, *11*, 04020002. [CrossRef]
26. Montes, C.; Berardi, L.; Kapelan, Z.; Saldarriaga, J. Predicting bedload sediment transport of non-cohesive material in sewer pipes using evolutionary polynomial regression–multi-objective genetic algorithm strategy. *Urban Water J.* **2020**, *17*, 154–162. [CrossRef]
27. Wan Mohtar, W.H.M.; Afan, H.; El-Shafie, A.; Bong, C.H.J.; Ab Ghani, A. Influence of bed deposit in the prediction of incipient sediment motion in sewers using artificial neural networks. *Urban Water J.* **2018**, *15*, 296–302. [CrossRef]
28. Vapnik, V.N. An overview of statistical learning theory. *IEEE Trans. Neural Netw.* **1999**, *10*, 988–999. [CrossRef]
29. Ghorbani, M.A.; Khatibi, R.; Goel, A.; FazeliFard, M.H.; Azani, A. Modeling river discharge time series using support vector machine and artificial neural networks. *Environ. Earth Sci.* **2016**, *75*, 685. [CrossRef]
30. Kumar, D.; Pandey, A.; Sharma, N.; Flügel, W.-A. Daily suspended sediment simulation using machine learning approach. *Catena* **2016**, *138*, 77–90. [CrossRef]
31. Rahgoshay, M.; Feiznia, S.; Arian, M.; Hashemi, S.A.A. Modeling daily suspended sediment load using improved support vector machine model and genetic algorithm. *Environ. Sci. Pollut. Res.* **2018**, *25*, 35693–35706. [CrossRef] [PubMed]
32. Einstein, H.A. *The Bed-Load Function for Sediment Transportation in Open Channel Flows*; US Government Printing Office: Washington, DC, USA, 1950; p. 71.
33. Fernandez Luque, R.; Van Beek, R. Erosion And Transport Of Bed-Load Sediment. *J. Hydraul. Res.* **1976**, *14*, 127–144. [CrossRef]
34. Abbott, J.E.; Francis, J.R.D.; Owen, P.R. Saltation and suspension trajectories of solid grains in a water stream. *Philos. Trans. R. Soc. Lond. Ser. A Math. Phys. Sci.* **1977**, *284*, 225–254. [CrossRef]
35. Bridge, J.S.; Dominic, D.F. Bed Load Grain Velocities and Sediment Transport Rates. *Water Resour. Res.* **1984**, *20*, 476–490. [CrossRef]
36. Kisi, Ö.; Çobaner, M. Modeling River Stage-Discharge Relationships Using Different Neural Network Computing Techniques. *Clean Soil Air Water* **2009**, *37*, 160–169. [CrossRef]
37. Rajaee, T.; Mirbagheri, S.A.; Zounemat-Kermani, M.; Nourani, V. Daily suspended sediment concentration simulation using ANN and neuro-fuzzy models. *Sci. Total Environ.* **2009**, *407*, 4916–4927. [CrossRef]
38. Hipni, A.; El-shafie, A.; Najah, A.; Karim, O.A.; Hussain, A.; Mukhlisin, M. Daily Forecasting of Dam Water Levels: Comparing a Support Vector Machine (SVM) Model With Adaptive Neuro Fuzzy Inference System (ANFIS). *Water Resour. Manag.* **2013**, *27*, 3803–3823. [CrossRef]

39. Gholami, R.; Fakhari, N. Chapter 27-Support Vector Machine: Principles, Parameters, and Applications. In *Handbook of Neural Computation*; Samui, P., Sekhar, S., Balas, V.E., Eds.; Academic Press: Cambridge, MA, USA, 2017; pp. 515–535.
40. Han, D.; Chan, L.; Zhu, N. Flood forecasting using support vector machines. *J. Hydroinformatics* **2007**, *9*, 267–276. [CrossRef]
41. Lin, J.-Y.; Cheng, C.-T.; Chau, K.-W. Using support vector machines for long-term discharge prediction. *Hydrol. Sci. J.* **2006**, *51*, 599–612. [CrossRef]
42. Cherkassky, V.; Ma, Y. Practical selection of SVM parameters and noise estimation for SVM regression. *Neural Netw.* **2004**, *17*, 113–126. [CrossRef]
43. Sharafati, A.; Haghbin, M.; Haji Seyed Asadollah, S.B.; Tiwari, N.K.; Al-Ansari, N.; Yaseen, Z.M. Scouring Depth Assessment Downstream of Weirs Using Hybrid Intelligence Models. *Appl. Sci.* **2020**, *10*, 3714. [CrossRef]
44. Kumari, A. Effect of Sediment Particle Orientation on its Movement under Varying Channel Slope and Discharge Conditions. Master's Thesis, GB Pant University of Agriculture and Technology, Pantnagar, India, 2017.

MDPI AG
Grosspeteranlage 5
4052 Basel
Switzerland
Tel.: +41 61 683 77 34

Water Editorial Office
E-mail: water@mdpi.com
www.mdpi.com/journal/water

Disclaimer/Publisher's Note: The title and front matter of this reprint are at the discretion of the Guest Editors. The publisher is not responsible for their content or any associated concerns. The statements, opinions and data contained in all individual articles are solely those of the individual Editors and contributors and not of MDPI. MDPI disclaims responsibility for any injury to people or property resulting from any ideas, methods, instructions or products referred to in the content.

www.ingramcontent.com/pod-product-compliance
Lightning Source LLC
LaVergne TN
LVHW072317090526
838202LV00019B/2301